MOBY-DICK AS DOUBLOON

Essays and Extracts

(1851–1970)

NORTON CRITICAL EDITIONS

AUSTEN *Pride and Prejudice* edited by Donald Gray

BRONTË, CHARLOTTE *Jane Eyre* edited by Richard J. Dunn

BRONTË, EMILY *Wuthering Heights* edited by William M. Sale, Jr.

CLEMENS *Adventures of Huckleberry Finn* edited by Sculley Bradley, Richmond Croom Beatty, and E. Hudson Long

CONRAD *Heart of Darkness* edited by Robert Kimbrough

CONRAD *Lord Jim* edited by Thomas Moser

CRANE *The Red Badge of Courage* edited by Sculley Bradley, Richmond Croom Beatty, and E. Hudson Long

Darwin edited by Philip Appleman

DICKENS *Hard Times* edited by George Ford and Sylvère Monod

John Donne's Poetry selected and edited by A. L. Clements

DOSTOEVSKY *Crime and Punishment* (the Coulson translation) edited by George Gibian

DREISER *Sister Carrie* edited by Donald Pizer

FLAUBERT *Madame Bovary* edited with a substantially new translation by Paul de Man

HARDY *The Return of the Native* edited by James Gindin

HARDY *Tess of the D'Urbervilles* edited by Scott Elledge

HAWTHORNE *The House of the Seven Gables* edited by Seymour L. Gross

HAWTHORNE *The Scarlet Letter* edited by Sculley Bradley, Richmond Croom Beatty, and E. Hudson Long

IBSEN *The Wild Duck* translated and edited by Dounia B. Christiani

JAMES *The Ambassadors* edited by S. P. Rosenbaum

JAMES *The Turn of the Screw* edited by Robert Kimbrough

MELVILLE *The Confidence-Man* edited by Hershel Parker

MELVILLE *Moby-Dick* edited by Harrison Hayford and Hershel Parker

NEWMAN *Apologia Pro Vita Sua* edited by David J. De Laura

SHAKESPEARE *Hamlet* edited by Cyrus Hoy

SHAKESPEARE *Henry IV, Part I,* Revised edited by James L. Sanderson

Bernard Shaw's Plays edited by Warren Sylvester Smith

Edmund Spenser's Poetry selected and edited by Hugh Maclean

SOPHOCLES *Oedipus Tyrannus* translated and edited by Luci Berkowitz and Theodore F. Brunner

STENDHAL *Red and Black* translated and edited by Robert M. Adams

SWIFT *Gulliver's Travels,* Revised edited by Robert A. Greenberg

Tennyson's Poetry selected and edited by Robert W. Hill, Jr.

THOREAU *Walden and Civil Disobedience* edited by Owen Thomas

TOLSTOY *Anna Karenina* (the Maude translation) edited by George Gibian

TOLSTOY *War and Peace* (the Maude translation) edited by George Gibian

TURGENEV *Fathers and Sons* edited with a substantially new translation by Ralph E. Matlaw

VOLTAIRE *Candide* translated and edited by Robert M. Adams

A *Norton Critical Edition of Modern Drama* edited by Anthony Caputi

MOBY-DICK AS DOUBLOON

ESSAYS AND EXTRACTS (1851–1970)

"I look, you look, he looks; we look, ye look, they look." Ch. 99, "The Doubloon."

Edited by

HERSHEL PARKER, comp.
UNIVERSITY OF SOUTHERN CALIFORNIA

HARRISON HAYFORD
NORTHWESTERN UNIVERSITY

W · W · NORTON & COMPANY · INC · *New York*

Library of Congress Catalog Card No. 77–95518

SBN 393 9883 4

Printed in the United States of America

2 3 4 5 6 7 8 9 0

Contents

Burial, Disinterment, and Revival, 1853–1925

Foreword

This collection of reviews, essays, and extracts contains most of the best and some of the worst that has been written about *Moby-Dick*. It displays the range of approaches, interpretations and judgments of the first century-and-a-quarter of *Moby-Dick* criticism; it points up some of the persisting critical questions; and it documents the consolidated critical gains. Since the chief purpose of *MOBY-DICK as Doubloon* is to make it conveniently possible for readers to follow for themselves the most significant part of the scattered and voluminous critical record (almost none of it ever anthologized before) we do not wish to summarize that record here.

Our problems and principles of selection do require some comment. The first section contains seventy reviews of *The Whale* (as the expurgated and truncated English edition was called) and *Moby-Dick*—all that scholars like Meade Minnegerode, O. W. Riegel, Willard Thorp, Jay Leyda, John H. Birss, and Hugh W. Hetherington have discovered since the 1920's, and several that we and our associates have discovered during the preparation of *MOBY-DICK as Doubloon*. We include them all partly because everything written about the book in 1851–1852, when reviews were affecting Melville's audiences and probably Melville himself, is inherently more interesting than everything written in, say, 1951–1952. A more important reason is that the basic evidence for study of the critical reception of *Moby-Dick* (it could be argued that there were in fact two critical receptions, one of *The Whale* and one of *Moby-Dick*) has never before been available to any scholar at any one time. Research on the subject was mostly done when scholars had to work from painfully-taken and often incomplete and inaccurate notes rather than from photocopies of full reviews. Even if an investigator mentioned all the significant sections of a review, he frequently overlooked its relation to an earlier or later one. Even the "standard" study by Hetherington (1961) omits several important reviews, misdates several others, mistakes derivative reviews for original ones, and makes errors of varying seriousness in almost all quotations from the reviews. Therefore we print all the reviews that we know of, and for the completeness of the record we list in a headnote several items that we exclude because they are extracts from *Moby-Dick* or reprintings of other reviews. We have not abbreviated the reviews, except to shorten long quotations from *Moby-Dick* (there we have supplied chapter numbers and page-and-line references to the Norton Critical Edition of *Moby-Dick*, since what and how much a reviewer quotes may be as revealing as what he says). We are convinced that this large collection of reviews will create new respect for the reviewers and new interest in their critical assumptions and practices, and that it will stimulate new scrutiny of the critical reception of other nineteenth-century works, both British and American.

In the second section are assembled almost all the significant comments on *Moby-Dick* between 1853 and 1925 (an arbitrary date chosen here to mark the end of the initial excitement of the Melville revival, which gathered momentum in 1919, Melville's centennial). Many of the comments from before Melville's death in 1891, and even into the twentieth century, are random, brief, perfunctory, and second-hand; the only full essay on *Moby-Dick* published between 1853 and 1920 was Archibald MacMechan's, in 1899. Yet these comments show that in every decade, except possibly the 1860's and 1870's, *Moby-Dick* had adherents who proclaimed its virtues in print and wondered publicly at its being so little known, as well as admirers who recommended it privately to certain choice friends. While the appreciative essays of the Melville revival contained deep if scattered insights and confirmed an astonishing revaluation of the book and of Melville's work as a whole, they contained almost no sustained examinations of the characters, themes, or structure of *Moby-Dick*. Reflecting the isolation of many of the critics from each other—especially before the revival—the comments from 1853 to 1925 form a less coherent unit than either the first reviews or the later criticism; but the random and isolated quotations convey the state of the reputation of *Moby-Dick* better than any smooth retrospective essay could do.

In the period covered by the third section (1926–1970) so much has been written about *Moby-Dick* that no collection is likely to include quite all of the studies that have seemed major. In selecting the longer essays we have included most landmarks of *Moby-Dick* criticism and represented most major critics, although sometimes briefly, and once or twice not by their best-known analyses. We have tried also to choose essays which both encompass the insights of the chief critical approaches and mark the accumulation of understanding; a few times these aims were best accomplished by choosing essays from younger scholars who could see the various "landmarks" of modern criticism in clear perspective. One or two fine studies have been largely superseded by work that they themselves helped to stimulate: the insights of Lewis Mumford's long chapter in *Herman Melville* (1929), for instance, are blended with new perceptions in essays like Newton Arvin's (1950), and Mumford is represented here by a passage from *The Golden Day* (1926). No essay has been excluded merely because it has often been reprinted, but that consideration influenced our decision to excerpt R. P. Blackmur's essay (1938) and to represent Dr. Henry A. Murray by an early comment (and an essay by one of his students) rather than by his best-known "In Nomine Diaboli." The "extracts" in this section (as well as the previous one) do not necessarily give the gist of the authors' main arguments; indeed, one of them is an incidental expatiatory footnote. They serve much the same function as the "Extracts" in *Moby-Dick* in being "solely valuable or entertaining, as affording a glancing bird's eye view of what has been promiscuously said, thought, fancied, and sung of Leviathan, by many nations and generations, including our own." Yet this glancing bird's eye view illustrates the range of critical interests and approaches, displays the aperçus and vagaries of individual critics, and substantiates or refutes parts of the longer essays. Ishmael's own warning applies to both the essays and the extracts: "you must not, in every case at least, take the higgledy-piggledy whale statements, however authentic . . . for veritable gospel cetology."

MOBY-DICK as Doubloon has been designed as both an independent anthology and a companion volume to the Norton Critical Edition of *Moby-Dick*. Because that edition contains extensive sections of "Reviews and Letters by Melville," "Analogues and Sources," and "Biography," we have felt free to make the present book what we specified that the Norton Critical Edition was not: "a historical overview of critical opinion" and "a conspectus of conflicting interpretations." Yet the Norton *Moby-Dick* contains a hundred-page section of "Criticism" and we have made the present selection with the knowledge that Carl Van Doren (a major American inspirer of the revival), Stanley Geist, William Ellery Sedgwick, Charles Olson, Howard P. Vincent, Leon Howard, Walter E. Bezanson, Charles Feidelson, Edward Rosenberry, and others were represented in the earlier book. Occasionally the same critic appears in both books, but very rarely has any overlapping seemed required. We have had less steadily in view the other collections of *Moby-Dick* criticism. We drew upon *MOBY-DICK Centennial Essays* (1953) for the short selection by Henry Nash Smith. The generous treatment of the so-called gams in *Discussions of MOBY DICK* (1960) encouraged us not to exhaustively review critical opinion on that topic. The short *Melville: A Collection of Critical Essays* (1962) did not affect our choices, since it consists of often-reprinted essays and sections from readily available books. *The Recognition of Herman Melville* (1967) was planned so as to avoid substantial overlapping with either the Norton Critical Edition of *Moby-Dick* or *MOBY-DICK as Doubloon.* It contains five reviews of *Moby-Dick,* several nineteenth- and early twentieth-century comments not included here, and essays on *Moby-Dick* by Willard Thorp, Leon Howard, F. O. Matthiessen, Millicent Bell, and others. *The Charles E. Merrill Studies in MOBY-DICK* (1969) was completed after our selections were made. (In the Bibliography we itemize the sections on *Moby-Dick* in all these collections.) Despite our attempts to avoid duplication of essays, our final choices were always made on the basis of what was significant and representative in the history of *Moby-Dick* criticism, not on the basis of what was or was not readily accessible elsewhere.

A few comments on form are also necessary. The reviews in the first section are all listed by the name of the newspaper or magazine where they appeared, and ordinarily we do not indicate that some reviews appeared under headings like "Herman Melville's Whale" or "Literature." The reviews were anonymous (one English review was signed with initials), and except when authorship has been very plausibly argued we do not give conjectural ascriptions. We retain citations like "Moby-Dick; or, The Whale. By Herman Melville, author of 'Typee,' 'Omoo,' &c. I vol, 12 mo, 635 pages. Harper and Brothers." and instructions like "The volume may be found at Fetridge & Co's." only when they are printed as part of the text of the review. At the risk of seeming over-obvious to some users of this book, we indicate where magazines and newspapers were published. For our extracts from long essays we supply titles in square brackets and cite the original title in the first footnote. All items are printed essentially as they occur in the sources cited, but a few times in recent extracts we had to omit, renumber, or slightly recast some footnotes. In recent selections, roman chapter numbers have been changed to arabic and page citations have been changed from other editions to the Norton Critical Edition. We have not tried to transmit peculiarities of typographical detail like opening display capitals or to perpetuate mere typographical errors. There is some historical point in retaining what appear to be the critics' own errors; misspellings of names from *Moby-Dick,* for instance, indicate something about the extent to which critics and compositors had become familiar with the book. Misspellings and other errors, however, are not ordinarily pointed out (either by *sic* or otherwise) and neither are the various instances of plagiarism and more routine borrowings which a reader may ferret out in these pages. In general, English reviewers quoted rather accurately from the Bentley edition and American reviewers quoted rather accurately from the Harper edition, but casual departures from the texts are not indicated. Occasionally the reviewers (mainly British) or later critics allude to a passage that appears in a different form in the

Norton Critical Edition of *Moby-Dick;* at such times the reader should consult "The Text: History, Variants, and Emendations" in that edition. A few authors of recent essays have taken this opportunity to correct slight errors in their quotations from *Moby-Dick.* Unless otherwise specified, all square brackets in the texts of any of the reviews, essays, or extracts enclose our own editorial interpolations, and all sets of three asterisks indicate our omissions; all ellipsis dots (no matter how many) are in the originals. The title *Moby-Dick* appears variously here, as it does in our sources, both with and without hyphen, quotation marks, and italics; and the name of the White Whale appears sometimes with but usually without a hyphen. In the Bibliography, we have evaded the problem by using the abbreviation *MD* for the title. Without pretending to have settled the problem, we use in our other references the hyphenated form for the title, following the first American edition, and the unhyphenated form for the name of the White Whale.

In *Moby-Dick* the doubloon preserves "its Quito glow" though placed "amongst a ruthless crew" and interpreted subjectively by Ahab, Starbuck, and others. By the title *MOBY-DICK as Doubloon,* we acknowledge the tormenting fascination that *Moby-Dick* has exercised upon its readers and stress that the book, like the coin, has remained finally inviolable.

HERSHEL PARKER
UNIVERSITY OF SOUTHERN CALIFORNIA

HARRISON HAYFORD
NORTHWESTERN UNIVERSITY

1970

Acknowledgments

In assembling photocopies of the reviews in this book we were aided by many people. Hetherington (1961) was drawn upon for an initial finding-list. The advertisement in the London *Morning Post* was discovered by Mrs. David Bennett while she was obtaining for us a copy of the *Post*'s review of *The Whale*. Mrs. Bennett went on to locate one of the two unknown reviews quoted in the advertisement, the extraordinary one in the London *Morning Advertiser;* the other was in the mysterious London "Evening paper." Mrs. Bennett was our luckiest and most ingenious benefactress, but other friends and associates, including Richard Ellmann, Virginia Heiserman, Richard Colles Johnson, Amy Puett, Ross Steinhauer, and Sandra J. Winney, helped us obtain copies of some of the scarcer reviews. We are obligated to the many librarians who managed to find safe techniques for copying from fragile magazines and newspapers. We are greatly beholden to two members of the Norton staff: Miss Emily Garlin, whose copy-editing of the manuscript brought order out of chaos, and Mrs. Carol Paradis, without whose work in the obtaining of permissions and other administrative details the book would have remained nothing but a nice thought. Mary Meyerhoff generously helped with the proofreading.

Reviews of *The Whale* and *Moby-Dick*

1851–1852

This section contains all the reviews of *The Whale* and *Moby-Dick* yet discovered, including a few found during the preparation of *MOBY-DICK as Doubloon*. It does not include mere notices of publication, like the announcement in the New York *International Magazine* (November 1, 1851) that "Mr. MELVILLE's new novel, *The Whale*, will be published in a few days, simultaneously, by the Harpers and by Bentley of London." It does not include the following, which are merely extracts from *Moby-Dick* and reprintings of reviews or extracts:

1. The pre-publication printing of Ch. 54 ("The Town-Ho's Story") in the October, 1851, *Harper's New Monthly Magazine*.
2. The reprinting of Ch. 54 in the Baltimore *Weekly Sun* (November 8) reported in Leyda (1951).
3. The reprinting of Ch. 54 in the Cincinnati *Daily Gazette* (November 29 and December 6).
4. The extract from Ch. 61 ("Stubb Kills a Whale") in the Hartford, Connecticut, *Daily Courant* (November 29), since both the introductory sentence and the quotation from *Moby-Dick* are derived from the New Haven *Journal and Courier* (November 22) or possibly from some other undiscovered source. There is only one insignificant change in the introductory sentence ("this exciting event" instead of "the exciting event") but although the *Journal and Courier* had spelled Stubb's name Stub the *Courant* spells it correctly.
5. The same introductory sentence and extract from Ch. 61 in the New Bedford *Daily Evening Standard* (December 1). Trivial variations show that the *Standard* copied from the *Journal and Courier* or some undiscovered source, but not from the *Courant*.
6. The same basic introductory sentence and extract from Ch. 61 in the North Adams, Massachusetts, *Greylock Sentinel* (December 13). The *Greylock Sentinel* presumably copied from the *Courant;* it did not copy from the *Journal and Courier* or the *Daily Evening Standard*.
7. The reprinting of both parts of the *Literary World* review as one essay in the December *Holden's Dollar Magazine*, which like the *Literary World* was edited by Evert A. and George L. Duyckinck.
8. The reprinting of the *Courier and New-York Enquirer* review in the Boston *Littell's Living Age* (January 17, 1852).

We do include in this section a few reviews which derive from earlier ones (either admittedly, like the Boston *Post* review, or not, like the New York *Morning Express* review) and we print the only advertisement known to contain quotations from reviews. Our object in allowing these small repetitions of material is to show the range of publicity given the book.

Morning Herald†

Herman Melville is on the right track now. His "Omoo," "Typee," and "White-jacket," gave evidence of great and peculiar

† London *Morning Herald*, October 20, 1851.

powers; but the audacity of youthful genius impelled him to throw off these performances with "a too much vigour," as Dryden has it, which sometimes goes near to defeat its own end. But in "The Whale," his new work, just published, we see a concentration of the whole powers of *the man*. Resolutely discarding all that does not bear directly on the matter in hand, he has succeeded in painting such a picture—now lurid, now a blaze with splendour—of sea life, in its most arduous and exciting form, as for vigour, originality, and interest, has never been surpassed.

Morning Advertiser†

To convey an adequate idea of a book of such various merits as that which the author of "Typee" and "Omoo" has here placed before the reading public, is impossible in the scope of a review. High philosophy, liberal feeling, abstruse metaphysics popularly phrased, soaring speculation, a style as many-coloured as the theme, yet always good, and often admirable; fertile fancy, ingenious construction, playful learning, and an unusual power of enchaining the interest, and rising to the verge of the sublime, without overpassing that narrow boundary which plunges the ambitious penman into the ridiculous: all these are possessed by Herman Melville, and exemplified in these volumes.

In the first chapter, bearing the title of "Loomings," we are introduced to the author, who on its threshold desires us to call him Ishmael. The very name being significant of a propensity to wander, we are prepared for an adventurer's acquaintance.

We have said that the writer is philosophically playful, and we will back his opening chapter, descriptive of New York, with its disquisitions on men's motives, the sea, nay water in the abstract as well as the concrete, against the same amount of prose in any book of fiction for the last dozen years, with a couple of exceptions, which we shall keep to ourselves. He tells us that a ship, when "the soul's November" comes upon him, is what a charged pistol is to a hypochondriac; and thence he plunges into a dissertation on the sea, its uses, glories, and beauties, enough to tempt a hydrophobic patient to a voyage, or at least a cold bath. He resolves to go a whaling voyage. Ishmael sets forth from "Old Manhatto" for New Bedford, and puts up at the "Spouter Inn." This whalers' hostelrie and its inmates are pencilled with the mastery and minuteness of Washington Irving. The strange bedfellow of Ishmael, Queequeg, a South Sea cannibal, who deals in embalmed men's heads, goes to bed with his tomahawk, pipe [tomahawk-pipe?], and razor-like harpoon, and is a skilful "harpooneer," figures prominently in the after

† London *Morning Advertiser*, October 24, 1851.

portion of the story. The cannibal turns out to be a good, a generous, and a feeling fellow, and Ishmael consoles himself with the reflection "that it is better to sleep with a sober cannibal than a drunken Christian." And the oddly-assorted couple become sworn friends.

"In New Bedford, fathers give whales for dowers to their daughters, and portion off their nieces with a few porpoises a-piece. You must go to New Bedford to see a brilliant wedding, for, they say, they have reservoirs of oil in every house, and every night recklessly burn their lengths in spermaceti candles." After a sketch of this queer whaling town, "where they tell us the young girls breathe such musk, their sailor sweethearts smell them miles off shore, as though they were drawing near the odorous Moluccas instead of these Puritanic sands," he exhibits his faculty of passing

"From gay to grave, from lively to severe,"

by taking us into the whaler's chapel.

Then describing the "silent islands of men and women, who sat steadfastly eyeing certain small marble tablets set on the walls," to the memory of whalemen lost in the far-off seas, he proceeds:—"Here were assembled the victims of unceasing grief; here you might mark those, in whose unhealing hearts the sight of those bleak tablets sympathetically caused the old wounds to bleed afresh."

"Oh, ye, whose dead lie buried beneath the green grass; who, standing among flowers, can say—'here, *here*, even in this sweet spot lies my beloved;' ye know not the desolation that broods in bosoms like these. What bitter blanks in those black-bordered marbles which cover no ashes! What despair is those immovable inscriptions! What deadly voids, and unbidden infidelities, in the lines which seem to gnaw on all faith, and refuse resurrections to those beings who have so placelessly perished that we cannot imagine them a grave. As well might those tablets stand in the cave of Elephanta as here.

"In what census are these dead of mankind included? why are they alone proofs of the universal proverb, that they tell no tales? . . . But Faith, like a jackal, feeds among the tombs, and even from these dead doubts she gathers her most vital hope.

"It needs scarcely be told with what feelings, on the eve of a Nantucket voyage, I regarded those marble tablets, and by the murky light of that darkened doleful day, read the fate of the whalemen who had gone before me. Yes, Ishmael, the same fate may be thine. . . . Yet somehow I grew merry. What then? Methinks we have hugely mistaken this matter of life and death. Methinks, that what they call my shadow here on earth is my true substance. Methinks that, in looking at things spiritual, we are too much like oysters observing the sun through the water, and thinking that thick water the thinnest and purest of air. Methinks my body is but the lees of my better being. In fact, take my body who will—take it, I say, it is not myself. Therefore, three cheers for Nantucket, and come a stove boat and a stove body when they will; but to stave my soul—who can do this?"

Many a bold fellow may have thought thus before our author, but which of them could thus analyze his thoughts, or thus express the ideas which in ordinary men refuse to shape themselves in words?

We remember reading in the life of Whitefield, a story of his power over the passions of uncultivated hearers. The anecdote runs that he was preaching to a congregation of seamen on the perils of sin and of the judgment-day, when he so worked upon them by his vivid description of the perils of a storm, that, maddened with the reality of the sinking ship thus word-painted before them, the entire auditory jumped up, and in reply to his question:—"Oh my brethren, what will you do then?" shouted out, "Take to the long-boat!" The unsophisticated reply was well used by the preacher. Let those who would read such a sermon as that which we have lost of Whitefield's, turn to the 9th chapter of this book, and he may realise the idea by a perusal of the discourse of Father Mapple.

The odd pair, our hero and Queequeg, reach Nantucket in due time, when we get the biography of Queequeg. He is the son of a savage king, and, impelled by curiosity, has shipped himself on board a whaler. His skill as a "harpooneer" has made him valuable, and the roving life of a whaleman at present suits him.

There is a kernel of philosophy in the quiet little anecdote of Queequeg, who, unaware of the application of a wheelbarrow, to the great derision of the Sag Harbour people, fixes his luggage thereon, and placing it on his back, carries the whole load by means of the handles; and "didn't the people laugh?" Queequeg retorts by telling a story of "a grand sea captain," who visited Kokovoko, his native isle. He was invited to a grand ceremonial, where a bowl, according to the country's custom, was introduced, into which the High Priest dips his finger as an act of consecration, ere any partake thereof. The sea captain, taking the holy cup for a sort of large finger-glass, followed the example by washing his hands in the beverage. "Now," said Queequeg, "what you tink now? did *our* people laugh?" The savages were the best-mannered here. What follows reminds us of Charles Lamb.

"A good laugh is a mighty good thing, and rather too scarce a good thing, the more's the pity. So, if any man, in his own proper person, afford stuff for a good joke to anybody, let him not be backward, but let him cheerfully allow himself to spend and be spent in that way. And the man that has anything bountifully laughable about him, be sure that there is more in that man than you perhaps think for."

Our hero and his companion enter on board a whaler, "The Pequod," whose owners, Captains Bildad and Peleg, are such samples of Nantucketers, as must interest every student of the social varieties of man. Quakers by descent, Nantucket having been originally settled by that sect, they retain many of the peculiarities of the Friends, modified most anomalously by things and pursuits altogether incongruous—some of these Quakers being the most sanguinary and resolute of whale-hunters. In truth, fighting Quakers, swearing Quakers, and drinking Quakers, are no rarity in Nantucket.

The portraits of these men, which you can see must have been taken from the life, and that they are the types of a class, are exquisitely finished. The signing ship's articles, by our hero and Queequeg, with the latter's fast, or ramadan, and the reasoning thereon, to which that ceremony gives rise, will well repay perusal. Captain Ahab, who is the hero of the whaling voyage, the commander of the Pequod, and thereafter the soul of the romance, is now introduced.

We will not weaken the effect which must be produced upon every one fortunate enough to obtain this work, by such brief extracts as we could here give: suffice it to say, that the fierce monomaniac, Ahab, has long pursued in the vast southern ocean a white whale, of unparalleled ferocity, size, and cunning. Not only has this monster of the deep baffled him, but in his last voyage has added to the destruction of his boats and stores a fearful mutilation; no less than the tearing off with its fearful jaws of the old whaler-captain's leg. The deficient limb is characteristically supplied by a supplemental piece of fish ivory, whereon the fierce old whale-hunter supports himself, steadied, when on deck, by a couple of socket-holes made in the ship's floor on each side of the vessel, at convenient holding-distance from the shrouds of the mizenmast. As a sample of Herman Melville's learning, we may refer to the chapter headed "Cetology," in the second volume; and that we have not overrated his dramatic ability for producing a prose poem, read the chapter on the "whiteness of the whale," and the scene where Ahab nails the doubloon to the mast, as an earnest of the reward he will give to the seaman, who just "sights" "Moby Dick," the white whale, the object of his burning and unappeasable revenge. Then come whale adventures wild as dreams, and powerful in their cumulated horrors. Now we have a Carlylism of phrase, then a quaintness reminding us of Sir Thomas Brown, and anon a heap of curious out-of-the-way learning after the fashion of the Burton who "anatomised" "melancholy." Mingled with all this are bustle, adventure, battle and the breeze. In brief the interest never palls, although we are free to confess that in the latter scenes of Ahab's fierce madness we were fain to exclaim, "Somewhat too much of this!" Finally, we have a series of fierce combats with "the white whale," ending, on the third day's chase, with the death of Ahab, and a mysterious Parsee "harpooneer," in the boats. Thereafter the white whale, "Moby Dick," attacks the fated ship, staves her, the catastrophe is complete, and thus sinks the Pequod into the wild waste of waters. "Now small fowls fly screaming over the yet yawning gulf, a sullen white surf beat against its steep sides, then all collapsed, and the great shroud of the sea rolled on as it rolled five thousand years ago."

As a sample of pleasantry, take the author's view of his task:—

"By good right the whale should only be treated of in imperial folio. Fain are we to stagger to this emprise under the weightiest words of the dictionary. And here be it said, that whenever it has been convenient to consult one in the course of these dissertations, we have invariably used a huge quarto of Johnson, purchased for this especial purpose; because that famous lexicographer's uncommon personal bulk more fitted him to compile a lexicon to be used by a whale author."

In another place this is a small part of his defence of the pursuit of leviathan:—

"But though the world scouts at us whalehunters, yet does it unwittingly pay us the profoundest homage, yea, an all-abounding adoration. For almost all the tapers, lamps, and candles that burn in the high places of the globe, burn, as before so many shrines, to our glory.

"Why did the Dutch in De Witt's time have admirals of their whaling fleets? Why did Louis XVI. of France, at his own personal expense, fit out whaling ships from Dunkirk, and politely invite from Nantwich a score or two of whaling families to that town? Why did Britain, between the years 1750 and 1788, pay to her whalesmen in bounties upwards of 1,000,000*l.*? And how comes it, that we whalemen of America, now outnumber all the rest of the banded whalemen of the world; sail a navy of upwards of 700 vessels, manned by 18,000 men, yearly consuming 4,000,000 dollars; the ships' worth, at the time of sailing, 20,000,000 dollars; and every year importing into our harbours a well-reaped harvest of 7,000,000 dollars? How comes all this, if there be not something puissant in whaling?

"But this is not the half: look again." . . . .

Did space permit us we might be tempted to the injustice of giving more of the defence; as it is, we can only again refer the reader to the volumes, than which three more honourable to American literature, albeit issued in London, have not yet reflected credit on the country of Washington Irving, Fenimore Cooper, Dana, Sigourney, Bryant, Longfellow, and Prescott.

Athenaeum†

This is an ill-compounded mixture of romance and matter-of-fact. The idea of a connected and collected story has obviously visited and abandoned its writer again and again in the course of composition. The style of his tale is in places disfigured by mad (rather than bad) English; and its catastrophe is hastily, weakly, and obscurely managed. The second title—'Moby Dick'—is the name given to a particular sperm whale, or white sea monster, more malignant and diabolical even than the sperm whale in general is known to be. This ocean fiend is invested with especial horrors for our ship's crew;—because, once upon a time, a conflict with him cost their Captain a limb. Captain Ahab had an ivory leg made,—took an oath of retribution,—grew crazy,—lashed himself up into a purpose of cruising in quest of his adversary,—and bound all who sailed with him to stand by him in his wrath. With this cheerful Captain, on such a wise and Christian voyage of discovery, went to sea Ishmael, the imaginary writer of this narrative.

Frantic though such an invention seems to be, it might possibly have been accepted as the motive and purpose of an *extravaganza* had its author been consistent with himself. Nay, in such a terrible cause—when Krakens and Typhoons and the wonders of Mid-Ocean, &c. &c. were the topics and toys to be arranged and manoeuvred—we might have stretched a point in admission of electrical verbs and adjectives as hoarse as the hurricane. There is a time for everything in imaginative literature;—and, according to its order, a place—for rant as well as for reserve; but the rant must be good, honest, shameless rant, without flaw or misgiving. The voice of "the storm wind Euroclydon" must not be interrupted by the facts of Scoresby and the figures of Cocker. Ravings and scraps of useful knowledge flung together salad-wise make a dish in which there may be much surprise, but in which there is little savour. The real secret of this patchiness in the present case is disclosed in Mr. Melville's appendix; which contains such an assortment of curious quotations as Southey might have wrought up into a whale-chapter for 'The Doctor,'—suggesting the idea that a substantial work on the subject may have been originally contemplated. Either Mr.

† London *Athenaeum*, October 25, 1851.

Melville's purpose must have changed, or his power must have fallen short. The result is, at all events, a most provoking book,—neither so utterly extravagant as to be entirely comfortable, nor so instructively complete as to take place among documents on the subject of the Great Fish, his capabilities, his home and his capture. Our author must be henceforth numbered in the company of the incorrigibles who occasionally tantalize us with indications of genius, while they constantly summon us to endure monstrosities, carelessnesses, and other such harassing manifestations of bad taste as daring or disordered ingenuity can devise.

The opening of this wild book contains some graphic descriptions of a dreariness such as we do not remember to have met with before in marine literature. Sick of shore, Ishmael, the narrator, resolves to go to sea in a whaler; and on his way to Nantucket with that object, he is detained at New Bedford. The following passage will give gentlemen who live at home—as the song says—a new idea of taking their ease in their inn.—

> "Having a night, a day * * * capering about most obstreporously [*sic*]." [17.24–23.26, with several short omissions and no indication of paragraphs or the break between ch. 2 and ch 3.]

The dark-complexioned harpooner turned out to be a cannibal, one Queequeg,—as sweet-tempered a savage as if he had been a prize vegetarian. It seemed odd enough to find Miss Martineau in her 'Eastern Travel' professing that "she had never rested till she had mastered the religious idea involved in cannibalism,"—but Mr. Melville's impersonation of the virtues and humanities which are to light up and relieve his terrible story is yet odder as a selection. The Battas, who, as Sir Stamford Raffles assures us, eat their progenitors when the latter are sixty years old, are henceforth not beyond the reach of *réhabilitation*:—nay, those most dismal of Gnomes, the aborigines who devour clay, may now expect their laureate and their apologist. To such lengths will a craving for effect carry a sane man!

We have little more to say in reprobation or in recommendation of this absurd book,—having detailed its leading incident. Mr. Melville has been on former occasions characterized by us as one who thoroughly understands the tone of sea superstition. There is a wild humorous poetry in some of his terrors which distinguishes him from the vulgar herd of fustian-weavers. For instance, his interchapter on 'The Whiteness of the Whale' is full of ghostly suggestions for which a Maturin or a Monk Lewis would have been thankful. Mr. Melville has to thank himself only if his horrors and his heroics are flung aside by the general reader, as so much trash belonging to the worst school of Bedlam literature,—since he seems not so much unable to learn as disdainful of learning the craft of an artist.

John Bull†

Of all the extraordinary books from the pen of Herman Melville this is out and out the most extraordinary. Who would have looked for philosophy in whales, or for poetry in blubber. Yet few books which professedly deal in metaphysics, or claim the parentage of the muses, contain as much true philosophy and as much genuine poetry as the tale of the *Pequod's* whaling expedition. Hardly has the ship set sail from Nantucket than it is, with its strangely assorted crew on board, isolated from the rest of creation; wholly engulphed, as it were, in the world of whales, a world peculiar to itself, and, as the reader of these volumes will find, as brimful of matters of deepest interest as any other sublunary world. In that wonderful world the most extravagant specimens of the genus *homo*, the offspring of Herman Melville's wild and grotesque fancy, are pursuing their career of adventure and of danger with an energy not unlike that of the whale himself; their chieftain, Captain Ahab, being a perfect match in every way for his foe-whale Moby Dick.

To give anything like an outline of the narrative woven together from materials seemingly so uncouth, with a power of thought and force of diction suited to the huge dimensions of its subject, is wholly impossible. Those who seek acquaintance with "the whale" must needs embark on board the venturesome craft, and bear company to her commander with the ivory leg and the heart of steel. They must be prepared, however, to hear much on board that singularly-tenanted ship which grates upon civilized ears; some heathenish, and worse than heathenish talk is calculated to give even more serious offence. This feature of Herman Melville's new work we cannot but deeply regret. It is due to him to say that he has steered clear of much that was objectionable in some of his former tales; and it is all the greater pity, that he should have defaced his pages by occasional thrusts against revealed religion which add nothing to the interest of his story, and cannot but shock readers accustomed to a reverent treatment of whatever is associated with sacred subjects.

All that is idiomatically American in the tone of his sentiments, and in the slang which runs through his discourse, we are most willing to forgive him. These things belong to the individuality of the author and the book. The perfect Yankee, surrounded as he is, in reality no less than in Mr. Melville's fiction, with savage and demi-savage life, is a picture which, like everything that is true to nature, possesses a charm of its own, though it may not fall within the ordinary canons of beauty. The exhibition of it is both a novelty, and a study; and the artist is entitled to his meed of praise;

† London *John Bull*, October 25, 1851.

even though his subject should in itself be of a somewhat repulsive character. And in the present case that praise is the more abundantly due, because the artist has succeeded in investing objects apparently the most unattractive with an absorbing fascination. The flashes of truth, too, which sparkle on the surface of the foaming sea of thought through which the author pulls his readers in the wake of the whale-ship,—the profound reflections uttered by the actors in the wild watery chase in their own quaint forms of thought and speech,—and the graphic representations of human nature in the startling disguises under which it appears on the deck of the *Pequod*,—all these things combine to raise *The Whale* far beyond the level of an ordinary work of fiction. It is not a mere tale of adventures, but a whole philosophy of life, that it unfolds.

We are unwilling to part with a book so intensely interesting without placing before our readers at least a leaf or two from the sketch-book of "Ishmael," the spinner of this wonderful whale yarn. One of the finest scenes of the tale is that in which the half-crazy Captain, intent on the pursuit of Moby Dick, threatens to shoot the chief mate for attempting by his advice to interfere with his authority.

> Starbuck found Ahab * * * up Burtons, and break out in the mainhold." [Ch. 109, 393.5–394.30.]

As a sample of the manner in which the author extracts lessons of life from the carcass of a dead whale, we give the following passage:—

> A word or two more * * * how few vast as the whale! [Ch. 68, 260.43–261.35.]

We shall conclude our extracts with the following apostrophe, addressed by the whaling Captain to the head of a captured whale lashed to his ship's side:—

> "Speak, thou vast and venerable head," * * * outstretched, longing arms!" [Ch. 70, 264.4–264.23.]

Spectator†

This sea novel is a singular medley of naval observation, magazine article writing, satiric reflection upon the conventionalisms of civilized life, and rhapsody run mad. So far as the nautical parts are appropriate and unmixed, the portraiture is truthful and interesting. Some of the satire, especially in the early parts, is biting and

† London *Spectator*, October 25, 1851.

reckless. The chapter-spinning is various in character; now powerful from the vigorous and fertile fancy of the author, now little more than empty though sounding phrases. The rhapsody belongs to wordmongering where ideas are the staple; where it takes the shape of narrative or dramatic fiction, it is phantasmal—an attempted description of what is impossible in nature and without probability in art; it repels the reader instead of attracting him.

The elements of the story are a South Sea whaling voyage, narrated by Ishmael, one of the crew of the ship Pequod, from Nantucket. Its "probable" portions consist of the usual sea matter in that branch of the industrial marine; embracing the preparations for departure, the voyage, the chase and capture of whale, with the economy of cutting up, &c., and the peculiar discipline of the service. This matter is expanded by a variety of digressions on the nature and characteristics of the sperm whale, the history of the fishery, and similar things, in which a little knowledge is made the excuse for a vast many words. The voyage is introduced by several chapters in which life in American seaports is rather broadly depicted.

The "marvellous" injures the book by disjointing the narrative, as well as by its inherent want of interest, at least as managed by Mr. Melville. In the superstition of some whalers, (grounded upon the malicious foresight which occasionally characterizes the attacks of the sperm fish upon the boats sent to capture it,) there is a *white* whale which possesses supernatural power. To capture or even to hurt it is beyond the art of man; the skill of the whaler is useless; the harpoon does not wound it; it exhibits a contemptuous strategy in its attacks upon the boats of its pursuers; and happy is the vessel where only loss of limb, or of a single life, attends its chase. Ahab, the master of the Pequod—a mariner of long experience, stern resolve, and indomitable courage, the high hero of romance, in short, transferred to a whale-ship—has lost his leg in a contest with the white whale. Instead of daunting Ahab, the loss exasperates him; and by long brooding over it his reason becomes shaken. In this condition he undertakes the voyage; making the chase of his fishy antagonist the sole object of his thoughts, and, so far as he can without exciting overt insubordination among his officers, the object of his proceedings.

Such a groundwork is hardly natural enough for a regular-built novel, though it might form a tale, if properly managed. But Mr. Melville's mysteries provoke wonder at the author rather than terror at the creation; the soliloquies and dialogues of Ahab, in which the author attempts delineating the wild imaginings of monomania, and exhibiting some profoundly speculative views of things in general, induce weariness or skipping; while the whole scheme mars, as we have said, the nautical continuity of story—greatly assisted by various chapters of a bookmaking kind.

Perhaps the earliest chapters are the best, although they contain little adventure. Their topics are fresher to English readers than the whale-chase, and they have more direct satire. One of the leading personages in the voyage is Queequeg, a South Sea Islander, that Ishmael falls in with at New Bedford, and with whom he forms a bosom friendship.

> "Queequeg was a native of Kokovoko * * * I'll die a Pagan." [Ch. 12, 56.13–57.19.]

The strongest point of the book is its "characters." Ahab, indeed, is a melodramatic exaggeration, and Ishmael is little more than a mouthpiece; but the harpooners, the mates, and several of the seamen, are truthful portraitures of the sailor as modified by the whaling service. The persons ashore are equally good, though they are soon lost sight of. The two Quaker owners are the author's means for a hit at the religious hypocrisies. Captain Bildad, an old sea-dog, has got rid of everything pertaining to the meeting-house save an occasional "thou" and "thee." Captain Peleg, in American phrase "professes religion." The following extract exhibits the two men when Ishmael is shipped.

> "I began to think it was high time * * * down to the fiery pit, Captain Peleg.' " [Ch. 16, 73.24–75.17.]

It is a canon with some critics that nothing should be introduced into a novel which it is physically impossible for the writer to have known: thus, he must not describe the conversation of miners in a pit if they *all* perish. Mr. Melville hardly steers clear of this rule, and he continually violates another, by beginning in the autobiographical form and changing ad libitum into the narrative. His castastrophe overrides all rule: not only is Ahab, with his boat's-crew, destroyed in his last desperate attack upon the white whale, but the Pequod herself sinks with all on board into the depths of the illimitable ocean. Such is the go-ahead method.

Household Narrative†

Beside these graver publications there has been a great gathering of voyages and travels.[1] The Rev. Henry Cheever, an American,

† London *Household Narrative of Current Events (Monthly Supplement to "Household Words," Conducted by Charles Dickens)*, September 28–October 28, 1851.

1. In this survey recent books are divided into four categories: "works of pretension" like Carlyle's *Life of John Sterling*; books of voyages and travels (in which category *The Whale* is reviewed); "books of general interest" like *Memorials of Chantrey the Sculptor*; and novels like Mrs. Trollope's *Mrs. Matthews, or Family Mysteries* [*Editors' note*].

gives us *Life in the Sandwich Islands:* a countryman of his, Mr. Herman Melville, relates more of the ocean experiences of his Typees and Omoos in a motley book called *The Whale*; another countryman, the Rev. Mr. Cotton, tells us all the incidents of a cruise with an American frigate to California, in a dirty little volume, entitled *Deck and Port;* and Mr. Pridham excites his readers by announcing *Kossuth and the Magyar Land* as the title of a book which contains not very much of either. * * *

London *Atlas*†

In all Mr. Melville's previous works, full of original genius as they are, there was to be found lurking a certain besetting sin of extravagance. Sometimes we saw merely the tendency—at others, we traced a startling development of the tendency unchecked. We might get over a volume smoothly enough, delighted with the fancy, profoundly impressed with the descriptive powers, not a little pleased with a quaint and original vein of philosophy of the author, when suddenly the sluice would be lifted, the torrent would burst forth, and for a score of chapters, perhaps for the remainder of the book, we would wade wearily through a waste of satirical or quasi-philosophical rhapsody, vainly longing and vainly looking for an island of firm treadable common sense, on which to clamber out of the slough, it might be of clever, but after all, of vain and unprofitable words. The book before us offers no exception to the general rule which more or less applies to all Mr. Melville's fictions. In some respects we hold it to be his greatest effort. In none of his previous works are finer or more highly soaring imaginative powers put forth. In none of them are so many profound, and fertile, and thoroughly original veins of philosophic speculation, or rather perhaps philosophic fancy, struck. In none of them, too, is there a greater affluence of curious, quaint, and out of the way learning brought to bear upon the subject in hand. In none of them are the descriptions of seafaring and whaling matters so wonderfully graphic, and in none of them is there to be found a more thorough command over the strength and the beauties of our language. Extravagance is the bane of the book, and the stumbling block of the author. He allows his fancy not only to run riot, but absolutely to run amuck, in which poor defenceless Common Sense is hustled and belaboured in a manner melancholy to contemplate. Mr. Melville is endowed with a fatal facility for the writing of rhapsodies. Once embarked on a flourishing topic, he knows not when or how to stop. He flies over the pages as Mynheer Von Clam flew over

† London *Atlas*, November 1, 1851 (First Notice).

Holland on his steam leg, perfectly powerless to control the impulse which has run away with him, and leaving the dismayed and confounded reader panting far behind. We open one of the volumes at random, and we find the mate of a whale ship soliloquising over a Spanish doubloon as follows:—

THE DOUBLOON.

"There now's the old Mogul," * * * So, so; he's beginning.["] [Ch. 99, 360.19–361.31.]

And this unbridled extravagance in writing, this listless and profitless dreaming, and maundering with the pen in the hand, is as it were supported and backed by the wildness of conception and semi-supernatural tone of the whole story. The author tells it *in propria persona.* He is a fore-mast man on board a South Sea whaler, the Old Peequod, of New Bedford. Ere he embarks, he seems to have left this mortal world, and lived in wild limbo of signs and portents. First he falls in with a strange, wild, savage harpooneer, a tatooed cannibal from a South Sea island, called Queequeg[,] between whom and Melville a strange and mystic sympathy springs up. In Queequeg he recognises the sublimity of the animal man, and the grandeur of the savage hero. The scenes in which the harpooneer and Melville pay adoration to Yojo, the god of the former, a deformed little graven image, and those in which Queequeg keeps his Ramadan, sitting fasting for six and thirty hours, with his wooden god upon his head, are strange specimens of powerfully imaginative writing. So again is the interview between Melville and the two retired whaling captains, the owners of the Peequod, one of them a generous old sailor, the other a griping old screw; but both pervaded with a certain species of quaint mystery, breaking out in strange hints and prophecies and allusions to the captain who is to sail the ship,—Captain Ahab, a morbidly strange conception of character, on which the notion of the book chiefly turns. Melville and the savage harpooneer do not embark without multitudinous warnings as to the "grand ungodly godlike man, Captain Ahab." A strange beggarly-looking personage, who calls himself Elijah, and utters whole sybilline leaves, full of mysterious hints about the terrible captain, haunts the newly-engaged sailors, appears suddenly to them round corners, whispers ghostly words in their ears, mopes and momes, and says "morning to ye, morning," when they would question him, and flits away, and is seen no more. Melville, however, screws up his courage, pronounces this gentleman a humbug, and they sail.

Once afloat, we soon find out what Captain Ahab is. In the first place, "he looked like a man cut away from the stake when the fire has overrunningly wasted all the limbs without consuming them, or taking away one particle from their compacted, aged robustness." Furthermore, Ahab is one-legged, his missing limb being supplied by a leg fashioned from the bone of the jaw of the sperm whale, and a strange livid scar, said to run from his forehead all down his body, marks him like Cain. This personage is a sort of unearthly monomaniac. For years and years he has been chacing one particular whale—a white, albino whale, a huge livid unnatural monster, awful in his cunning, his strength, and his ferocity. This whale is called Moby Dick. All the South Sea whale-men know him. He has smashed boats by dozens, drowned men by scores. His name is a word of fear upon the ocean. He swims round and round the world stuck full of harpoons, and minds them no more than pins. He is, in fact, the very Old Bogey of Cetology, and he is the particular Old Bogey of Captain Ahab. Among all the whalers, Ahab has devoted himself to the destruction of Moby Dick. A dozen of times has he given him battle; as often has Moby Dick been the conqueror, and in the last struggle, in a gale off Cape Horn, the whale has smashed his assailant's leg into a jelly. This injury results in delirium, which drives Ahab fairly out of his senses. Thenceforth, to slay Moby Dick is his mission in the world. All his being, all his energies, all his soul, are, as it were, melted and fused into one undying mass of intensest hate for Moby Dick. To kill Moby Dick and then die is all he wants—vengeance, vengeance on Moby Dick, is burning the very life out of him; give him that vengeance, and even, as some spirit whose task is accomplished vanishes from the night, so Captain Ahab will become void and silent, and be heard of no more.

It will be acknowledged that there are fine poetic elements in this conception. Wild and extravagant as it is, Captain Ahab would strongly move us, were it not that the intensity of the conception is continually impaired by the constant rigmarole rhapsodies placed in the monomaniac's mouth. A little of this sort of thing would be well in character, and might be made very effective; but pages and chapters of it become simply tedious. A model speech of Captain Ahab's, however, the reader shall have. He has nailed a golden doubloon to the mast, to be the property of the man who first descries the white whale, and then calls on all the crew to swear a solemn oath that they will never desert him in the hunt:—

THE BAPTISM OF THE HARPOONS.

"Drink and pass!" * * * when, waving his free hand to them, they all dispersed; and Ahab retired within his cabin. [Ch. 36, 145.24–146.37.]

And so the Peequod turns her bows to that part of the Indian Ocean where the ancient Captain, well versed in the mysterious peregrinations of whales—knowing the ocean currents with which they float—and the season when and the place where their food principally abounds—expects to find Moby Dick. Melville's sketches of his shipmates are amongst the poorest things he has done. We recognize no flesh and blood aboard the Peequod. The sailors might have voyaged with the "Ancient Mariner," or have been borne on the hooks of the "Flying Dutchman." The three mates are mere phantoms—stupid, characterless phantoms, too. The black cook is a caricature. Pip, the negro boy, is a clumsy monstrosity. Queequeg and his fellow-harpooneers, both savages, one of them a Red Indian from the lakes, the other a coal-black man from Africa, are the happiest, because the most fanciful of the minor sketches. Nor is the forecastle more happily painted. Most of the conversation allotted to the seamen is in the wild, rhapsodic vein to which we have alluded—destitute either of sense, appropriateness, or character, and, as a specimen of which, we would refer to the nightwatch colloquy in Chapter 39 of Vol. I. [Ch. 40, since Ch. 25, "Postscript," was omitted in *The Whale*.]

Meantime, while the Peequod is cruising hither and thither in pursuit of sperm whales in general and the white whale in particular, Herman Melville also cruises backwards and forwards in all manner of philosophic, philologic, physiologic, zoologic, and metaphysic reveries as regards whales and whaling. Over all these the sin of rhapsody more or less extends; but, granting this fault, the portion of the book in question is full of strange and novel beauties. Herman Melville plunges, as it were, among the whales as if he loved them, and accounted them the grandest and most glorious of the creatures of the globe. Upon the whale, its mysteries, and its terrors, he dwells as if the subject had enchantment for him. If Captain Ahab was bewitched by Moby Dick, Mr. Melville is not the less spell-bound by Leviathan in general. He pours into multitudinous chapters a mass of knowledge touching the whale—its habits and its history—its haunts in the sea, and its peregrinations from ocean to ocean—the minutest details of its feeding, or sporting, or swimming, strangely mixed with ingenious and daring speculation on the more mysterious habits and peculiarities of the great brute—the whole written in a tone of exaltation and poetic sentiment which has a strange effect upon the reader's mind in refining and elevating the subject of discourse, and at last making him look upon the whale as a sort of awful and unsoluble mystery—the most strange and the most terrible of the wonders of the great deep. That Herman Melville knows more about whales than any man from Jonah downwards, we do really believe. He has studied their written history like a bookworm, and he must have passed years and years in hunting them, always closely observing their habits, always fixing on them an eye which, if we be not mistaken, nothing could escape—an eye which would see strange things where less favoured organs found but barrenness, and always, too, as may be well believed, picking up and profiting by the practical experience of older, if not wiser, mariners. The sum, then, of Mr. Melville's experience induces him to reject as a bit of finical refining, the common dictum that a whale is not a fish. Animals, he says, which live in the sea, not being amphibious, are fish, and it is mere scientific cant to prate about warm blood and the characteristics of the mammalia. A whale, says Mr. Melville, is "a spouting fish with a horizontal tail," and as even humble porpoises spout in a small way, and carry horizontal tails, Mr. Melville does not scruple to say that they are little whales. All creatures of the species he divides into three families, classing them ingeniously enough by the technical terms applied to the size and shape of books. Thus we have the *folio* whale, comprising all the big fellows, such as the Greenland whale, the sperm, the fin-back, the hump-backed, the razor-back, and the sulphur bottom whales. Next we have the *octavo* whale, typified by the grampus, the narwhal, and such middling-sized monsters. And, thirdly, we come to the *duodecimo* whale, of which, as we have said, the porpoise tribe is the most common representative. The whale which people in general know most of, and that which they generally refer to when they use the word—the Greenland whale—Mr. Melville treats with summary contempt as an interloper and an impostor, in so far as he wears the crown of the kingdom of the whales. The sperm whale, the oil of which is infinitely more valuable, and which is generally larger, swifter, more ferocious, and more cunning, he considers to be the true monarch of the ocean. The descriptions of this creature are wonderfully minute. Inside and outside Mr. Melville surveys him inch by inch, leaving not a muscle of his flesh or a barnacle on his sides unvisited —these minute details being constantly enlivened and elevated by the peculiarly exalted and enthusiastic tone of the writer, by the strong flash of what we cannot but call a certain poetic light, even although it play upon oil casks and blubber, with which he constantly invests even the meanest subject which he takes in hand. We have already referred to the curious hints given of the peregrinations of the whales, and of the skill with which an old hunter will follow the fish from bank to bank and zone to zone of the Indian Ocean and the Southern Sea. In connexion with this part of the subject Mr. Melville gives a number of curious details and speculations, coming to the conclusion that could the sperm whale be well watched and closely observed all over the world, his movements would be found to be as regular and guided by as unswerving a law as those of the herring or the swallow. While on this subject, we may add that the identification within a very short period, by two ships, of a whale—first, in the North Atlantic, and afterwards in the North Pacific Ocean—seems to prove to Mr. Melville's mind that the secret of the north-west passage, so long a problem to man, has never been a problem to the whale. Of the individual whales noted, and which have received names from mariners, Mr. Melville mentions several, and thus apostrophises four of the most famous:—

> But not only did each of these famous whales enjoy great individual celebrity * * * or Sylla to the classic scholar. [Ch. 45, 177.3–177.19.]

Illustrated News†

The excitement of the Exhibition over, the disturbed publishing trade is beginning to resume its activity, and a fair outburst of works of all classes is announced. Railway books hold a conspicuous place in the list—the growing habit of wiling away the hours upon the rail by reading being apparently likely to exercise as much, and I hope a more, salutary effect upon popular literature than even circulating libraries. The peculiarity of railway books is that they must be pithy, short, and cheap; and, if I am not much mistaken, they will speedily give the spun-out thirty-shilling three-volume novels a blow which will greatly accelerate the downward progress which has been observable for some time in the class of books in question. Among the works of travel announced, Hungarian adventures take the lead; and all opinions about the late revolution and its champions will, no doubt, find their advocates. As to the works of fancy, two, in two very different departments, seem to be attracting most attention—one a controversial and pro-Catholic novel called "Cecile," and understood to be the production of the Count de Jarnac, under the *nom-de-guerre* of Sir Charles Rockingham; and the other Herman Melville's last and best and most wildly imaginative story, "The Whale." The controversial novel is remarkable for fairness, good temper, and good humour—most rare qualities in books of the kind; and the personages are so conceived as to be types of the principal different parties and classes into which the late Aggression agitation split up the community. Mr. Melville's romance will worthily support his reputation for singularly vivid and reckless imaginative power—great aptitude for quaint and original philosophical speculation, degenerating, however, too often into rhapsody and purposeless extravagance—an almost unparalleled power over the capabilities of the language.

Thus, everybody says a whale is not a fish. "Pooh, pooh!" replies

† *Illustrated London News,* November 1, 1851.

Herman Melville, "don't talk such fiddle faddle to me; an animal who is not amphibious, and who lives totally in the sea, is, if the common sense of language is to be preserved, a fish, and nothing but a fish, his lungs and warm blood to the contrary, notwithstanding." Here, indeed, is Melville's definition of a whale—"A spouting fish with a horizontal tail." Now, porpoises spout, or at all events have a spout-hole, and perpendicular tails. Mr. Melville is no whit daunted. "Good," he replies, "and porpoises are nothing but small whales."

A.B.R.

London *Atlas*†

We must now hasten after the Peequod, only pausing for a moment to note that in this encyclopædia of information, rhapsody, and speculation about the whale, Mr. Melville carefully examines all great pictures and representations of whaling, unmercifully cuts up Cuvier, and, more or less, all the scientific naturalists, who, he declares, know nothing about the matter; pronounces the plates of whales in most natural history books to be unutterable humbugs; dives deep into the theologic and mythologic history of the whale; and is especially great upon Jonah, continually alternating with the strangest coolness from the grandest to the smallest themes, leaping from the world before the flood, with its megatheria and mastadons, to a discussion upon the merits, in a culinary point of view of whales' steaks, and oscillating from rhapsodically expressed tirades upon the doctrine of metempsychosis to a closely argued demonstration that the skin of a whale is its blubber. Meantime the Peequod is rapidly filling her empty barrels with sperm oil; while, to the unspeakable wonder of the crew, the first time that the look-out man from the hull of the main-royal mast sings out, "There she blows," a tawny Indian boat's crew—"tiger-yellow" Manilla men—who had never before been heard of in the ship, suddenly spring, no one knows from where, like theatrical demons, up trap-doors, and leap into Ahab's boat. This mystic crew seem the coadjutors of Captain Ahab in his crusade against Moby Dick, and the steersman is a semi-supernatural sage, who ultimately, when the excitement is properly wound up, in mysterious and doubtful terms, prophecies his own fate and that of his master. The ordinary whaling adventures, before Mr. Moby Dick is descried, are told with rare and impassioned power. The "first lowering," *i.e.* of the boats in pursuit, is thwarted by the sudden outburst of a southern squall. The scene is magnificently told. The four boats are in pursuit of a shoal or "school" of whales:—

† London *Atlas*, November 8, 1851 (Second Notice).

AFTER THE WHALE.

Meanwhile, all the boats tore on * * * and the whale, merely grazed by the iron, escaped. [Ch. 48, 193.5–194.25.]

Now and then whalers are met with, and the crews "gam," that is, go and visit each other and give mutual dinners. On these occasions wild whaling legends are told; one of them being to the effect that the white whale, or Moby Dick, is no less a personage than the incarnation of the God of the Shakers! Strange details are also given of "brit" and "squid," the food of the Greenland and sperm whale. The former is a yellow slimy weed, covering the sea to the horizon, so that the ship seemed to be sailing through boundless fields of ripe and golden wheat. In this ocean pasture is descried a shoal of whales, and painted, as it were, with one dash of the brush, in this magnificently picturesque sentence:—

As morning mowers, who side by side slowly and seethingly advance their scythes through the long wet grass of marshy meads, even so these monsters swam, making a strange, grassy, cutting sound; and leaving behind them endless swaths of blue upon the yellow sea.

The "squid" is a species of polypus animal, which, when it rises from the depths of the sea, is said to forebode death to the man who sees it. "A vast pulpy mass, furlongs in length and breadth, of a glancing cream-colour, it lay floating in the water, innumerable long arms radiating from its centre, and curling and twisting like a nest of anacondas. . . . . No perceptible face or front did it have—no conceivable token of either sensation or instinct; but undulated there on the billows—an unearthly, formless, chance-like apparition of life."

At length another shoal of sperm whales is discovered, and thus is the capture of the first described:—

THE DEATH OF THE WHALE.

"Start her, start her, my men! * * * His heart had burst! [Ch. 61, 243.4–245.17.]

After the death of this the first whale, copious and interesting details are given of the equipments of the whale boats; of the gear used, in all its minutiæ, and of the entire processes gone through in attaching the dead monster to the ship, in cutting off his blubber and hoisting it into the hold, in bucketting up the true sperm from the cavity in his head, and in "trying out" or expressing the other oil from the masses of fishy lard piled in the blubber-room. We heartily wish that we had room for copious extracts of these details, but we must refer the reader to the book itself, where he will find a picture of life on board a South-Sea whaleman, with the *rationale* of all the operations in relation to the prey, living and dead, painted in colours which will not soon be forgotten. We, however, must hurry past. As Captain Ahab nears the seas wherein he expects to find Moby Dick, his monomania rises into frenzy. A number of beautifully told episodes are introduced, apropos of the different whalers of many nations, whom he hails for news of his huge enemy. One has seen him and allowed him to pass undisturbed. One has fairly fled from him. The captain of another, the Samuel Enderby, of London, holds up his whalebone arm. He has been maimed by the monster. A third ship exhibits her stoven boats, smashed by a blow of his flukes. A fourth has maimed corpses lying on the gratings by the gangway, ready for burial, the victims of the same all-potent conqueror. Ahab becomes furious in his mania, and not being able to ascend the shrouds, has himself hoisted to the heel of the royal mast, where he clings from dawn to dark, gazing after Moby Dick. At length the white whale is espied, and by the captain himself, and away go the four boats in hot and eager chase. For an account of the long struggle which ensues we must refer to the book. For three days is it kept up, boat after boat falling victims to the crush of Moby Dick's jaws, or the blow of his tail—Captain Ahab uselessly planting harpoon after harpoon in the blubber of the monster, which seems immortal and invincible. On the second day, while pulling hard in the wake of the whale, the "tiger-yellow" Indian, the steersman of the captain's boat, is suddenly seized with the spirit of prophecy, and predicts that Ahab will die but one day after himself; that he will die by hemp, and that before he dies he will see two hearses—one of them made of American wood. This strange jumble of prediction soothes Ahab, who does not deem the apparition of hearses in the middle of the Pacific Ocean a very likely one. It is hardly made, however, when a new "iron" is fixed in the white whale, and Fedallah is carried overboard, entangled in the line, which is speedily exhausted by the deep sounding of the monster, and obliged to be cut. With difficulty regaining the ship, Ahab passes the night in delirious raving. The next morning he is after Moby Dick again; and as the whale rises, rushing from a thousand-fathom dive, he sees borne upon his back, entangled in the twisted line, the stark-staring corpse of Fedallah. "Aha!" says Ahab—a light breaking in upon him—"the First Hearse." The second is soon provided. Leaving the boat, the vast whale rushes headlong at the ship. A yell of unutterable despair bursts from Ahab. He feels in his soul that Moby Dick, predestined to conquer, is about to fulfil his destiny. But Herman Melville must speak for himself:—

THE TRIUMPH OF MOBY DICK.

From the ship's bows, nearly all the seamen now being inactive * * * as it rolled five thousand years ago. [Ch. 135, 468.2–469.32.]

The last word quoted is the last in the book,[2] and as we close it we feel as if waking from what was partly a gorgeous vision, partly a night-mare dream, but both vision and dream intense, overmastering in their power the spell of a magician who works wildly, recklessly, but with a skill and a potency which few, we should think, will be disposed either to deny or resist.

Britannia†

The Whale is a most extraordinary work. There is so much eccentricity in its style and in its construction, in the original conception and in the gradual development of its strange and improbable story, that we are at a loss to determine in what category of works of amusement to place it. It is certainly neither a novel nor a romance, although it is made to drag its weary length through three closely printed volumes, and is published by Bentley, who, *par excellence*, is the publisher of the novels of the fashionable world, for who ever heard of novel or romance without a heroine or a single love scene? The plot of the narrative is scarcely worthy of the name, as it hangs entirely on the inveterate pursuit by a monomaniac old Captain after a certain humpbacked whale, who in some previous voyage had bitten off one of his legs, and whose destruction he had bound himself and his crew by terrible oaths to accomplish, in revenge for the injury he had himself sustained. The tragical catastrophe, which innumerable signs, omens, and superstitious warnings are constantly predicting to the infatuated commander, is the wreck of the ship, and the loss of the whole crew in the frantic attack that is made upon the invincible white whale.

The story has merit, but it is a merit *sui generis*, and does not consist in the work either when viewed as a whole or with reference to the arrangement of its separate parts. The plot is meagre beyond comparison, as the whole of the incident might very conveniently have been comprised in half of one of these three interminable volumes. Nevertheless, in his descriptions of character, in his analysis of the motives of actions, and in the novelty of the details of a whaling expedition, the author has evinced not only a considerable knowledge of the human heart, combined with a thorough acquaintance with the subject he is handling, but a rare versatility of tal-

2. That is, in the English edition, which omitted the "Epilogue"; but this chapter was followed in the English edition by an "Appendix" containing the "Etymology" and "Extracts" [*Editors' Note*].

† London *Britannia*, November 8, 1851.

ent. The crew of the Pequod, the inharmonious name given to the whaler, is composed of mariners of all countries and all colours, from the civilised British sailor to the savage and cannibal harpooner of the South Sea Islands. In describing the idiosyncracies of all these different castes of men our author has evinced acuteness of observation and powers of discrimination, which would alone render his work a valuable addition to the literature of the day. The monomaniac Captain Ahab, whose whole soul, to the exclusion of every other idea, is bent upon the destruction of "Moby Dick," the nickname of the whale who robbed him of his leg, is a most eccentric conception, and is well contrasted with the character of his common-place mates, Starbuck, Stubbs, and Flask. Queequeg, the cannibal harpooner, notwithstanding his man-eating propensities, is made a most interesting hero amongst whale-slayers, and in the curious details of this heathen's worship of his idol, "Yojo," our author has shown that he has a fund of humour at command. Tashtego, the unmixed Indian, and Daggoo, the coal-black negro slave, are excellent types of their class, and by no means common-place characters. These original sketches constitute as we have said the principal merit of the work, but in the latter half of the third volume, the action of the story, which had halted considerably through the preceding chapters, assumes all at once an exciting interest, which is as gratifying as it is unexpected. The three days' chase of the destructive white whale, whose attempted capture had lured so many mariners to their destruction, are most graphically described. The following account of the approach of the boats on the first day, when after months of pursuit the watch on the forecastle had at last descried the dreaded antagonist, is characteristic of the author's style:—

> Soon all the boats but Starbuck's were dropped * * * and at intervals one of the cloud of soft-toed fowls hovering, and to and fro skimming like a canopy over the fish, silently perched and rocked on this pole, the long tail-feathers streaming like pennons. [Ch. 133, 447.6–447.31.]

The concluding paragraph of the last chapter, in which the white whale, after spurning the small fry of boats from which harpoons are darted into it on all sides, shoots itself against the advancing prows of the vessel which it staves in, is at once so grand, so awful, and so harrowing, that we quote the paragraph:—

> The harpoon was darted; the stricken whale flew forward * * * then all collapsed, and the great shroud of the sea rolled on as it rolled five thousand years ago. [Ch. 135, 468.37–469.32.]

The first and second volumes are spun out with long descriptions of the various cetacious tribes, which do now, and have at different periods of time inhabited the ocean. The information these chapters convey may be important to naturalists or whalers, but will have little interest for the general reader. Bating a few Americanisms, which sometimes mar the perspicuity and the purity of the style, the language of the work is appropriate and impressive; and the stirring scenes with which the author concludes are abundant evidencc of thc power he possesses of making his narrative intensely interesting.

Examiner†

The approach of winter shows itself at the circulating libraries. A "Cynthia of the minute" is not more difficult to catch than the last novel, so well kept up is the race for the perishable charm of novelty. "Each minute teems a new one." * * *

From such scenes of ordinary life the transition to Mr Herman Melville's *Whale* (4) is extremely violent.[3] We cannot say that we recognise in this writer any advance on the admirable qualities displayed in his earlier books—we do not see that he even greatly cares to put forth the strength of which he has shown himself undoubtedly possessed. If there is not carelessness in the book now under notice, there is at least so much wilfulness, that our enjoyment is small even of what we must admit to be undeniably and remarkably clever in it. It professes to be the narrative of a South-Sea whaling voyage performed in a Nantucket ship with one of the queerest of crews and the most unearthly of captains. But all the regular rules of narrative or story are spurned and set at defiance. For a great part of the book it is Ahab the captain monologuizing in a wild mad way; then it is the seaman Ishmael; and then Mr Melville himself. But the hero of the book we should perhaps most accurately indicate in none of these, but rather in a particular whale, a supernatural *white* indomitable whale, a quite unequalled monster of ferocity and cunning, who swims about the limitless seas a perfect pincushion of harpoons, whom Captain Ahab has been hunting for years, with whom he has often engaged in desperate battle, on whom he has again and again inflicted thrice-mortal

† London *Examiner*, November 8, 1851.

3. The "(4)" means that *The Whale* is the fourth novel being reviewed. The previous three, all three-deckers like *The Whale*, were *Florence Sackville; or, Self-Dependence*, by Mrs. Burbury; *Mrs. Mathews; or, Family Mysteries*, by Mrs. Trollope; and *The Livingstones: A Story of Real Life*, published anonymously. The phrase "scenes from ordinary life" may apply to all three, but it more likely applies mainly to *The Livingstones*, of which the reviewer had just said: "it has a real interest, and notwithstanding somewhat too much of melodrama and red fire in the incidental villainy portrayed, has a sober truthful purpose in its main design which impresses us favourably" [*Editors' note*].

injuries, taking nothing for his pains but a smashed leg; and to the destruction of which mysterious creature, 'yclept Moby Dick, the captain has devoted what remains of his life and limbs, after replacing his shattered member by part of the jaw-bone of a less potent scion of the cetacious family than Moby Dick. The catastrophe is a final encounter with Dick, in which the ship, and the ship's boat, and Ahab, and his crew, are all plunged headlong into Davy's locker; "and" (says Mr Melville, who has kindly taken up the narrative which must otherwise have gone to the bottom with Ishmael and everybody else concerned) "the great shroud of the sea rolled on as it rolled five thousand years ago." Certainly, since Tom Thumb, there has been no such tragedy. The only survivor is Moby Dick, very properly perhaps the sole survivor in a book which presents not a particle of interest connected with humanity to compare with that which it yields in regard of cetology. It excellently vindicates its title in this respect. It contains more about the whale, its habits, manners, morals, oil, blubber, feeding, swimming, mode of chasing, capturing, harpooning, cutting up, and all the distinctions which exist between the shabby Greenlander and the magnificent Sperm, than we should have supposed possible to be poured out from "one small head." Freely and fully is the book to be commended, therefore, to all who are curious in such matters. But Mr Melville is a man of too real an imagination, and a writer with too singular a mastery over language and its resources, to have satisfied our expectations by such an extravaganza as this.

Leader†

Want of originality has long been the just and standing reproach to American literature; the best of its writers were but second-hand Englishmen. Of late some have given evidence of originality; not *absolute* originality, but such genuine outcoming of the American intellect as can be safely called national. Edgar Poe, Nathaniel Hawthorne, Herman Melville are assuredly no British offshoots; nor is Emerson—the *German* American that he is! The observer of this commencement of an American literature, properly so called, will notice as significant that these writers have a wild and mystic love of the supersensual, peculiarly their own. To move a horror skilfully, with something of the earnest faith in the Unseen, and with weird imagery to shape these Phantasms so vividly that the most incredulous mind is hushed, absorbed—to do this no European pen has apparently any longer the power—to do this American literature is without a rival. What *romance* writer can be named with

† London *Leader*, November 8, 1851.

Hawthorne? Who knows the terrors of the seas like Herman Melville?

The Whale—Melville's last book—is a strange, wild, weird book, full of poetry and full of interest. To use a hackneyed phrase, it is indeed "refreshing" to quit the old, wornout pathways of romance, and feel the sea breezes playing through our hair, the salt spray dashing on our brows, as we do here. One tires terribly of ballrooms, dinners, and the incidents of town life! One never tires of Nature. And there is Nature here, though the daring imagery often grows riotously extravagant.

Then the ghostly terrors which Herman Melville so skilfully evokes, have a strange fascination. In vain Reason rebels. Imagination is absolute. Ordinary superstitions related by vulgar pens have lost their power over all but the credulous; but Imagination has a credulity of its own respondent to power. So it is with Melville's superstitions: we believe in them imaginatively. And here we will take the occasion to introduce the reader to a splendid passage from our greatest prose writer, descriptive of the superstitious nature of sailors—(you divine that we are to quote from De Quincey). He says they are all superstitious. "Partly, I suppose, from *looking out so much upon the wilderness of waves empty of human life*; for mighty solitudes are generally fear-haunted and fear-peopled; such, for instance, as the solitudes of forests where, in the absence of human forms and ordinary human sounds, are discerned forms more dusky and vague not referred by the eye to any known type, and sounds imperfectly intelligible. Now, the sea is often peopled amidst its ravings with what seem innumerable human voices, 'ancestral voices prophesying war'; often times laughter mixes from a distance (seeming to come also from distant times as well as distant places) with the uproar of waters; and, doubtless, shapes of fear or shapes of beauty not less awful are at times seen upon the waves by the diseased eye of the sailor. Finally, the interruption habitually of all ordinary avenues to information about the fate of their dearest relatives; the consequent agitation which must often possess those who are reëntering upon home waters; and the sudden burst, upon stepping ashore, of *heart-shaking news in long-accumulated arrears*—these are circumstances which dispose the mind to look out *for relief towards signs and omens as one way of breaking the shock by dim anticipations*."

This passage is a fit prelude to the thrilling pages of Melville's *Whale*. The book is not a romance, nor a treatise on Cetology. It is something of both: a strange, wild work with the tangled overgrowth and luxuriant vegetation of American forests, not the trim orderliness of an English park. Criticism may pick many holes in this work; but no criticism will thwart its fascination. As we mean you to read it and relish it, we shall give no hint of the story: an extract or so by way of whet to the appetite is all you must expect. Here is a picture of

AHAB WITH THE IVORY LEG.

"So powerfully did the whole grim aspect of Ahab affect me * * * would have soon flowered out in a smile." [Ch. 28, 110.31–111.36.]

There is a chapter on the "Whiteness of the Whale" which should be read at midnight, alone, with nothing heard but the sounds of the wind moaning without, and the embers falling into the grate within. From it we quote this on—

THE ALBATROSS A BIRD OF TERROR.

"I remember the first albatross I ever saw * * * but never with such emotions as when I beheld the Antarctic fowl." [Ch. 42, 165.25–165.75.]

Here you have a glimpse into—

THE MERCILESS SEA.

"But, though to landsmen in general, the native inhabitants of the seas have ever been regarded with emotions unspeakably unsocial and repelling * * * Push not off from that isle—thou canst never return!" [Ch. 58, 235.3–236.9.]

Let us first tell you that the sharks are in fierce shoals tearing away at the flesh of a dead whale fastened to the ship, and you will then listen with pleasure to—

THE NIGGER'S SERMON TO SHARKS.

" 'Fellow-critters: I'se ordered here to say dat you must stop dat dam noise dare * * * fill your dam' bellies till dey bust—and den die.' " [Ch. 64, 251.4–252.8.]

Although this is not a set treatise on Whales, it contains a large amount of information on the subject, and the materials for a treatise evidently were collected. We have no room for a tithe of the curious things he tells us; but we must give a passage from his chapter on the "Monstrous Pictures of Whales." He expresses the most emphatic disapprobation of almost all the portraits that have been published of his favourite fish. Nay, even these given by such eminent naturalists as Lacépède and F. Cuvier, are pronounced monstrous absurdities. He adds, however:—

"But these manifold mistakes in depicting the whale are not so very surprising after all * * * you had best not be too fastidious in your curiosity touching this Leviathan." [Ch. 55, 227.33–228.41.]

Evening Journal†

We have enjoyed ourselves so richly in following Melville's heroes in "Typee," "Omoo," &c., that we look forward with pleasure to the hours of leisure that will allow us to look through "Moby-Dick." We are sure there is amusement in it; for it opens promisingly. For sale by E. H. Pease & Co.

Daily Evening Transcript‡

We very cordially welcome Mr Melville back to the field, where he has won so many laurels. He will be at home among the whalers, and his book will be eagerly sought for by those, who remember the first two nautical romances from his pen. This volume is inscribed to Nathaniel Hawthorne, in token of "admiration for his genius." Ticknor & Co have the work.

Argus §

After bestowing as much time as we can afford upon this somewhat bulky duodecimo, we have come to the following conclusions respecting it: First, that it is the production of a man of genius, and abounds in bright, witty and attractive things; secondly, that it tells us many things about the whale that are true and many that are not, and that the line between the credible and the apocryphal is not always very distinct; and last and worst, that there is an air of irreverence pervading many parts of it, which will greatly impair its interest with many who will nevertheless admire its bold and graphic sketches.

*Morning Post***

There is much that is incredible and a little that is incomprehensible in this latest effort of Mr. Melville's wayward and romantic pen; but despite its occasional extravagancies, it is a book of extraordinary merit, and one which will do great things for the literary reputation of its author. "Take it fore and aft," as the sailors say, it is a work of great power and beauty, and our remembrance cannot fellow it with any other modern work of a similar class, equally clever and equally entertaining. Judgment is occasionally shocked by the improbable character of the incidents narrat-

† Albany, New York, *Evening Journal*, November 12, 1851.
‡ Boston *Daily Evening Transcript*, November 12, 1851.
§ Albany, New York, *Argus*, November 14, 1851.
** London *Morning Post*, November 14, 1851.

ed—and even reason is not always treated with that punctilious deference she has a right to expect—but imagination is banquetted on celestial fare, and delight, top-gallant delight, is the sensation with which the reader is most frequently familiar. There is a wild and wonderful fascination in the story against which no man may hope to secure himself into whose intellectual composition the faculty called fancy has in any degree entered. So surprising are many of the adventures recorded—so singular and unearthly are many of the scenes depicted, that there are occasions when the reader is disposed to believe that the whole book is one vast practical joke. We are half inclined to believe that the author is humbugging us, and with that suspicion comes its invariable accompaniment, a sense of offended dignity; but the spell of genius is upon us, and we are powerless to resist. The author's radiant imagination enthrals us in a delicious bondage, and the tide of his animal spirits sweeps all doubts and misgivings triumphantly before it. We bolt down all events, however unlikely—all achievements, however impossible—all hard things, visible and invisible, never mind how knobby, as an ostrich of potent digestion gobbles down bullets and gun-flints.

The author takes us a-whaling with him, and the fierce uniqueness of that wild Scandinavian vocation inspires an emotion of fireside interest and awe which is delightfully exciting. He has a clever knack of identifying his own cause with ours, and of making his readers parties to his own proceedings. He takes us by the hand with an air of affectionate patronage, and we surrender ourselves without a murmur to the guidance of a companion so fearless, chivalrous, and romantic. His manner is so winning, and his language so persuasive, that there is no resisting him. We go aboard the whaler at Old Nantucket on a shivering winter's night. "Ship and boat diverged; the cold damp night wind blew between; a screaming gull flew overhead; the two hulls wildly rolled; we gave three hearty cheers, and blindly plunged like fate into the lone Atlantic." From that moment we are by his side everywhere. His descriptive powers are so vivid and appealing that we share with him the perils he so graphically pictures, and merge our own identity in his. We keep the night watches with him in savage and solitary seas—we feel the Pequod thrusting her vindictive bows into the cold malicious waves—we stand with him on the mast-head, and sway and swing with him over the writhing waters—we hear the pumps clanking—the blocks creaking—the sails flapping against the masts—the Cape winds whistling through the cordage—the billows roaring like an army of wolves around his devoted craft. We watch the seas leap madly over her bows, and recognise in the dismal scream of the inscrutable sea-raven which hovers in her wake the appropriate music for such a scene. As the gull (no inapt emblem, the matter-of-fact philosopher will say, of him who allows another man's imagination so to influence his own)—folds up her wings at night, lies down upon the surface of the water, and is wildly rocked through the hills and hollows of the waves—so does the mind of the sympathetic reader yield an unconscious allegiance to the resistless sway of this powerful writer. We share his romantic loneliness, bivouac with him in the wilderness of waters, participate in his wild achievements, and combine the delicious excitement of a peril-fraught life with that sense of personal security which, however ignoble, is eminently comfortable.

Of the utility of this work, as a contribution to natural history, we shall not presume to speak. Whether the writer is a good authority on the subject of whales—whether his classification of them is such as would be likely to find favour with Linnæus—whether his statements respecting their properties and propensities are strictly (or at all) consistent with the fact—these are questions on which, not being versed in cetology, we do not feel ourselves qualified to pronounce an opinion. The work comes before us simply in its literary aspect, and regarding it in that point of view, we cheerfully acknowledge its claim to cordial commendation. It is brimful of interest. The adventures, whether genuine or apocryphal, are so deliciously exciting—the descriptions are so graphic and pictorial—and the dialogue, like *Touchstone's* conversation, is "so swift and sententious," that we cannot hesitate to accord to Mr. Melville the praise of having produced one of the cleverest, wittiest, and most amusing of modern books.

That there are many things in this work which appear to us extravagant and unlikely, we have already stated. From that opinion we are not disposed to recede, but it is right that we should qualify the censure by the admission that we, who have never gone sailor to a whale-ship, may be no very competent judges of what things are of probable and what of improbable occurrence in the pursuit of whales under difficulties. The captain of the ship in which our author sailed—or professes to have sailed—is an old man—one Ahab—who, having had his right leg bitten off by a sperm whale, conceives feelings of the deadliest and most inexpiable animosity against the offending animal, and devotes his life to the vindictive purpose of hunting the identical fish that mutilated him through all the waters of the globe. To us who have less to do with harpoons than pens it seems as though the man who would undertake such a pursuit would be engaged in a search about as hopeful as that of the Brahmin in the Eastern tale, whose wife sent him all over the world on a fool's errand to look for the fifth volume of the Hindoo Scriptures, there never having been but four. But the point is too abstruse for us, and we leave it to the decision of that select few to whom the whale is a "familiar creature." We will not longer detail the reader from the gratification of perusing some passages from Mr. Melville's most entertaining pages:—[4]

"What wonder, then, that these Nantucketers * * * while under his very pillow rush herds of walruses and whales." [Ch. 14, 62.26–63.21.]

* * * * *

"I freely assert, that the cosmopolite philosopher cannot, for his life point out one single peaceful influence * * * Ah, the world! Oh, the world!" [Ch. 24, 99.25–100.12.]

* * * * *

"The three masts are kept manned from sunrise to sunset * * * and no more can you make a convenient closet of your watchcoat." [Ch. 35, 136.32–137.34.]

* * * * *

" 'Look at that chap now,' philosophically drawled Stubb * * * The ship had given us up, but was still cruising, if haply it might light upon some token of our perishing—an oar or a lance pole." [Ch. 48, 192.33–195.24.]

Advertisement from the *Morning Post*†

"The Whale," says the Athenaeum, "contains graphic descriptions such as we do not remember to have met with before in marine literature."

"The Whale is intensely interesting. It is not a mere tale of adventures, but a whole philosophy of life that it unfolds." John Bull.

"The Whale is a singular novel. The satire is biting and reckless." Spectator.

"The Whale displays an unusual power of enchaining the interest." Morning Advertiser.

"The Whale is the raciest thing of the kind that was ever produced." Evening paper.

"The Whale is a most extraordinary work." Britannia.

Morning Courier‡

No American writer is more sure, at every re-appearance, of a more cheerful welcome than the author of Typee. His purity and freshness of style and exquisite tact in imparting vividness and

4. The rows of asterisks between quotations are in the original [*Editors' note*].

† London *Morning Post*, November 14, 1851.

‡ *Morning Courier and New-York Enquirer*, November 14, 1851.

life-likeness to his sketches long since gained him hosts of admirers on both sides of the water. This book has all the attractiveness of any of its predecessors; in truth, it possesses more of a witching interest, since the author's fancy has taken in it a wilder play than ever before. It is ostensibly taken up with whales and whalers, but a vast variety of characters and subjects figure in it, all set off with an artistic effect that irresistibly captivates the attention. The author writes with the gusto of true genius, and it must be a torpid spirit indeed that is not enlivened with the raciness of his humor and the redolence of his imagination.[5]

Daily Evening Traveller†

We have here a new book, from one of the most sprightly and entertaining writers of our day. It appears to be a sort of hermaphrodite craft—half fact and half fiction. It professes to be a narration of the incidents of a whaling voyage out of Nantucket. But there is so much of caricature and exaggeration mixed with what may be facts, that it is not easy to discriminate. Many of Mr. Melville's descriptions are extremely graphic, lifelike and entertaining. He certainly holds the pen of a ready writer; but he indulges frequently in profaneness, and occasionally in indelicacies, which materially detract from the merits of the book, which exhibits much tact, talent and genius. The volume may be found at Fetridge & Co's.

Daily Courant‡

Melville's stories are decidedly interesting and graphic, and, as he writes, he improves in the minor details of incident, management, and style. There is always one singular character about them—you don't know whether they are truth or fiction. There is the same want of unity of subject—of a regular beginning and end—of the form and shape and outline of a well built novel—which we find in real life. But there is a little too much romance and adventure, of "imminent perils" and hair-breadth escapes, to be any thing but fiction. The present story is the most interesting and the best told of any of the group. There is in it the same happy carelessness of style and the same abandonment to all the easy slipshod luxuries of story

5. Hugh W. Hetherington (1961) says that this review was "boldly flaunted before the world, for it was—a thing almost unheard of those days on either side of the Atlantic—actually signed, and not just with initials, but aggressively, 'J. Watson Webb.' " In the New York Public Library file of the paper, the review is not signed at all, so it seems doubtful that it was signed in other copies [*Editors' note*].

† Boston *Daily Evening Traveller*, November 15, 1851.

‡ Hartford, Connecticut, *Daily Courant*, November 15, 1851.

telling. It is well worth reading as a book of amusement, and well worth a place on the book shelf from the beautiful style of its publication.

Daily Register†

"Moby Dick; or the Whale."—By Herman Melville, author of "Typee," "Omoo," and other popular and singularly interesting narratives. The Harpers have just issued this last work of Melville's, in a neat volume, which will undoubtedly have a great run. For sale at Downes.—Also the 15th number of "*London Labor and London Poor.*"

Literary World‡

Every reader throughout the United States has probably perused in the newspapers the account of a recent incident in the whale fishery which would stagger the mind by its extent of the marvellous, were it not paralleled by a well known case—that of the Essex of Nantucket, still authenticated by living witnesses. It appears from a narrative published in the *Panama Herald* (an American newspaper in that region, itself one of the wonders of the age!), taken down from the lips of the captain of the vessel, John S. Deblois, that the ship Ann Alexander, of New Bedford, having left that port in June of last year with the usual vicissitudes of Cape Horn service, losing a New Hampshire man overboard in a storm at that point, had entered upon her Pacific hunting-grounds, and in the recent month of August was coursing within a few degrees of the Equator—a well known haunt of the whale. On the 20th of that month, nine in the morning, fish were discovered; two boats were lowered in pursuit, and by mid-day a particular sperm whale was struck and fast to the line. The first mate commanded the boat, thus far successful, and the Captain himself the other. After running some time, in the words of the narrative, the whale turned upon the boat to which he was attached, and rushing at it with tremendous violence, lifted open its enormous jaws, and taking the boat in, actually crushed it to fragments as small as a common-sized chair. Captain Deblois struck for the spot, and rescued the nine members of the boat's crew—a feat, we presume, which could only be accomplished among men hardy, resolute, and full of vitality as whalemen, strung [stung?] at the moment by excitement to almost superhuman energy and superiority to the elements. The Captain, with his double boat's crew, proceeded to the ship, some six miles off.

† New Haven, Connecticut, *Daily Register*, November 15, 1851.

‡ New York *Literary World*, November 15, 1851 (First Notice).

There the waist-boat was fitted out, the men divided, and both parties went again in pursuit of the whale, the mate again taking the lead. The whale perceived the coming renewal of the attack, made for the boat, crushed it with his jaw, the men again throwing themselves into the deep. The Captain once more rescuing them, was himself pursued by the whale, which passed the boat with distended jaw; but they reached the ship in safety. A boat was sent for the oars of the broken vessels floating on the water, which were secured. Sail was set on the ship, and it was determined to proceed after the whale. He was overtaken, and a lance thrown into his head! The ship passed on, when it was immediately discovered that the whale was in pursuit. The ship manoeuvred out of his way. *After he had fairly passed they kept off to overtake and attack him again*. The whale settled down deep below the surface. It was then near sundown. Capt. Deblois, continues the account, was at this time standing on the knight-heads on the larboard bow, with shaft in hand, ready to strike the monster a deadly blow should he appear, the ship moving about five knots, when looking over the side of the ship he discerned the whale rushing towards her at the rate of fifteen knots. In an instant the monster struck the ship with tremendous violence, shaking her from stem to stern. She quivered under the violence of the shock as if she had struck upon a rock. Captain Deblois descending to the forecastle, discovered that *the whale had struck the ship about two feet from the keel, abreast the foremast, knocking a great hole entirely through her bottom*. The ship was sinking rapidly. All hands were ordered into the boats, the captain leaving the deck last, throwing himself into the sea, and swimming to his comrades. That night was passed in the boats, with but twelve quarts of water saved, and no provisions for twenty-two men. In the morning the ship still lay on her beam-ends. Not a man would board her to cut away the masts, right the vessel, and procure provisions—fearing her sinking instantly—except the captain, who undertook the work with a single hatchet, and succeeded in getting the ship nearly on her keel. Nothing could be procured by cutting through the decks but some vinegar and a small quantity of wet bread, with which they abandoned the dangerous vessel. At the close of the next day they hailed the ship Nantucket of Nantucket, and were welcomed by its Captain, Gibbs, with the utmost hospitality. They were landed at Paita, where an authenticated protest of this extraordinary series of occurrences was made before the United States Consul.

By a singular coincidence this extreme adventure is, even to very many of the details, the catastrophe of Mr. Melville's new book, which is a natural-historical, philosophical, romantic account of the person, habits, manners, ideas of the great sperm whale; of his haunts and of his belongings; of his associations with the world of the deep, and of the not less remarkable individuals and combinations of individuals who hunt him on the oceans. Nothing like it has ever before been written of the whale; for no man who has at once seen so much of the actual conflict, and weighed so carefully all that has been recorded on the subject, with equal powers of perception and reflection, has attempted to write at all on it—the labors of Scoresby covering a different and inferior branch of the history. To the popular mind this book of Herman Melville, touching the Leviathan of the deep, is as much of a discovery in Natural History as was the revelation of America by Christopher Columbus in geography. Let any one read this book with the attention which it deserves, and then converse with the best informed of his friends and acquaintances who have not seen it, and he will notice the extent and variety of treatment; while scientific men must admit the original observation and speculation.

Such an infuriated, resolute sperm whale as pursued and destroyed the Ann Alexander is the hero, Moby Dick, of Mr. Melville's book. The vengeance with which he is hunted, which with Capt. Deblois was the incident of a single, though most memorable day, is the leading passion and idea of Captain Ahab of the Pequod for years, and throughout the seas of the world. Incidentally with this melo-dramatic action and spiritual development of the character of Ahab, is included a full, minute, thorough investigation, and description of the whale and its fishery. Such is a short-hand account of this bulky and multifarious volume.

It opens, after a dedication to Nathaniel Hawthorne, with a preliminary flourish in the style of Carlyle and the "Doctor" of etymology, followed by a hundred or so of extracts of "Old Burton," passages of a quaint and pithy character from Job and King Alfred to Miriam Coffin; in lieu of the old style of Scott, Cooper, and others, of distributing such flourishes about the heads of chapters. Here they are all in a lump, like the grace over the Franklin barrel of pork, and may be taken as a kind of bitters, a whet and fillip to the imagination, exciting it to the curious, ludicrous, sublime traits and contemplations which are to follow.

It is some time after opening with Chapter I. before we get fairly afloat, but the time is very satisfactorily occupied with some very strange, romantic, and, withal, highly humorous adventures at New Bedford and Nantucket. A scene at the Spouter Inn, of the former town, a night in bed with a Pacific Islander, and a mid-ocean adventure subsequently with a Frenchman over some dead whales in the Pacific, treat the reader to a laugh worthy of Smollet. We might perhaps as well introduce this at once. The Pequod, the ship in which the reader embarks from Nantucket, one day meets a French whaler under peculiar circumstances, in a calm, with two carcases of whales secured to her, which the unadventurous crew had picked up, dead waifs of previous conflicts on the ocean. The Mate, Stubb, had boarded this vessel seeking information for Capt. Ahab, of Moby Dick, and returns to circumvent the ambergris, a product found in the diseased animal.

THE ROSE-BUD.

"By this time the faint air had become a complete calm * * * entreaties and indignations at times." [Ch. 91, 338.9–340.2.]

And this is the rest of the joke—

"Marking all this, Stubb * * * for it's so calm they won't drift.' " [Ch. 91, 340.3–341.20]

Something more earnest is this, one of several

DEATH SCENES OF THE WHALE.

"But the monster's run was a brief one * * * the last long dying spout of the whale." [Ch. 81, 299.19–302.4.]

This is no everyday writing, and in Herman Melville's best manner.

Of some other characteristics of the book we must say something in our next number.[6]

New York *Atlas*†

MOBY DICK; or, THE WHALE.—This is the title of the last work from the pen of Herman Melville, whose fame as the author of "Typher," "Omoo" and other works, has extended wherever British and American literature is known. It is published in the best style of Harper & Brothers, and will command the attention of the lovers of romance throughout the country. The name of the author will ensure it an immense sale.

Daily Palladium‡

Herman Melville has long ago made his name current among men of taste and letters. His "Typee," "Omoo," and "White Jacket," have all afforded pleasure to thousands of readers, and his

6. Melville's friends Evert A. and George L. Duyckinck were owner-editors of the *Literary World*, and one or both of them almost surely wrote this review. Presumably the author was Evert A. Duyckinck, who was closer than his brother to Melville and more interested in Melville's literary reputation. The December, 1851, *Holden's Dollar Magazine*, which the Duyckinck brothers also edited, contained a full reprint of both the first and second notice from the *Literary World*, run together as one essay [*Editors' note*].

† New York *Atlas*, November 16, 1851.

‡ New Haven, Connecticut, *Daily Palladium*, November 17, 1851.

lively, roving story of Moby-Dick, we presume will be as popular as any other work that bears his name. It has numerous thrilling sketches of sea life, whale captures, shark massacres, &c.—but in some of the colloquies between old weatherbeaten Jacks, there is a little more irreverence and profane jesting than was needful to publish, however true to life the conversation may be. The work possesses all the interest of the most exciting fiction, while, at the same time, it conveys much valuable information in regard to things pertaining to natural history, commerce, life on ship board, &c. Published by Harper & Brothers. For sale by Durric & Peck.

Morning Express†

Another book by the author of "Typee." What writer is more welcome? We have had a touch of his qualities on the sea, and some squintings at his whaling experiences, before, and are prepared to find in his new book a great deal of amusement and instruction, combined with his usual felicity. One who has read "Moby-dick" tells us that it "has all the attractiveness of any of its predecessors; in truth it possesses more of a witching nature, since the author has taken in it a wilder play than ever before. It is ostensibly taken up with whales and whalers, but a vast variety of characters and subjects figure in it, all set off with an artistic effect that irresistibly captivates the attention. The author writes with the gusto of true genius, and it must be a torpid spirit indeed that is not enlivened with the raciness of his humor and the redolence of his imagination."

Republican‡

"Moby Dick" is the name of a fabulous white whale of the Northern regions of the Pacific, and in this, his last book Mr Melville has woven around this cumbrous bulk of romance, a large and interesting web of narrative, information, and sketches of character and scenery, in a quaint though interesting style, and with an easy, rollicking freedom of language and structure, characteristic of himself. What the author does not know about the sea, is not worth knowing, and there is not an experience of sea life, but he has the happy power of surrounding with romance. This book, and all hitherto written by the author, are as much superior to the sea books of Marryatt, as are the latter to those of the blanket weeklies. But there is one painful thought connected with the tale. There is no Fayaway in it. Alas! fickle and forgetful Melville, that thou

† New York *Morning Express*, November 17, 1851.

‡ Springfield, Massachusetts, *Republican*, November 17, 1851.

should'st ever forget the gentle native who gave herself to thee in her far-off, savage home, and take to wantoning with "the monsters of the bubbling deep!"

Daily Mercury†

This is a bulky, queer looking volume, in some respects "very like a whale" even in outward appearance. We have had before volume upon volume of narratives of whaling voyages, and adventures with the leviathans of the deep, but never before a work combining so much of natural history of Moby-Dick, nor in so attractive guise as the volume before us. After some introductory chapters of luminous etymological illustrations, etc., we find our author quitting the good city of old Manhatto, "for Cape Horn and the Pacific," and in due time arriving in New Bedford on a Saturday night in December, on his way to Nantucket—having made up his mind to sail in no other than a Nantucket craft; for though New Bedford, as he says, has of late been gradually monopolizing the business of whaling, and though in this matter poor old Nantucket is yet much behind her, yet Nantucket was her great original—the place where the first dead American whale was stranded. His adventures in New Bedford are extended through several pages, and are followed by others of greater importance. Although as a whole the book is made to serve as a "tub for the whale," the characters and subjects which figure in it are set off with artistic effect, and with irresistible attraction to the reader. We have marked several passages for extracts. The book may be found at C. & A. Taber's.

Daily Bee‡

MOBY DICK: OR THE WHALE. This is the title of HERMAN MELVILLE's new work, just published by the HARPERS, and said to be the best written and most entertaining book put forth by that popular and clever author.

Our readers cannot fail to remember the recent destruction of the ship Ann Alexander, of New Bedford, in the Pacific hunting grounds, by an enormous and infuriated sperm whale. After crushing two of the ship's boats with his ponderous jaw, the captain and crew narrowly escaping death in each instance, the adventurous whalers at last succeeded in plunging a lance into the monster's head. This maddened him, and in a few minutes afterwards he succeeded in striking the ship such a tremendous blow that he *knocked a great hole in the bottom of it!* and the vessel immedi-

† New Bedford, Massachusetts, *Daily Mercury*, November 18, 1851.

‡ Boston *Daily Bee*, November 19, 1851.

ately sunk! The captain and crew escaped in boats, and were afterwards picked up. There is but one known parallel to this almost incredible story.—The last number of the *Literary World*, in introducing some extracts from MR. MELVILLE's new work, makes the following comments:—

> By a singular coincidence this extreme adventure is, even to very many of the details, the catastrophe of Mr. Melville's new book * * * curious, ludicrous, sublime traits and contemplations which are to follow.[7]

Daily Gazette†

This new novel by the author of "Typee," "Omoo," etc., is pronounced the best written and most entertaining of his works. This is certainly strong praise, for few authors have succeeded in getting up stories of deeper interest, narrated in more attractive style.—The hero of this story is a Whale, to which the one that sunk the Ann Alexander was a calf. It will be seen that the subject is one affording the finest field for the rich imaginative powers and sea-faring experience of the author.

Palladium‡

There is life, elasticity, and freedom from restraint, in Mr Melville's manner as a writer; and originality and freshness in his matter. He has no mannerism which holds him down as an imitator of other men; but with tarpaulin and roundjacket he plunges into the wide world of adventure, and jots down whatever there comes within the scope of his vision. "Moby-Dick" is full of spirit and energy, and will match his previous works in the race for popularity. For sale at Mr Grout's.

Daily Atlas §

This is a large, thick volume, well printed, and written in the author's well-known style and spirit. We cannot claim to be admirers of Mr. Melville's productions, but to those who are—and their name is Legion—we can commend this volume, as fully equal in interest to any of its predecessors.

7. Here the *Bee* quotes from the *Literary World* the extract from Ch. 81 (the first paragraph in the issue of the 19th, the rest on the 20th), introducing it with the following comment and title, both of which demonstrate the extent of the writer's indebtedness to the *Literary World*: "We make the following extract. It is in Melville's best style, and is no ordinary every-day writing: DEATH SCENES OF THE WHALE." [*Editors' note.*]

† Utica, New York, *Daily Gazette*, November 19, 1851.

‡ Worcester, Massachusetts, *Palladium*, November 19, 1851.

§ Boston *Daily Atlas*, November 20, 1851.

Post†

We have read nearly one half of this book, and are satisfied that the London Athenaeum is right in calling it "an ill-compounded mixture of romance and matter-of-fact." It is a crazy sort of affair, stuffed with conceits and oddities of all kinds, put in artificially, deliberately and affectedly, by the side of strong, terse and brilliant passages of incident and description. The Athenaeum's notice throughout seems to us a fair one, and we copy the greater portion for the sake of economy and good taste:—[8]

> "The style of his tale is in places disfigured by mad (rather than bad) English * * * Our author must be henceforth numbered in the company of the incorrigibles who occasionally tantalize us with indications of genius, while they constantly summon us to endure monstrosities, carelessnesses, and other such harrassing manifestations of bad taste as daring or disordered ingenuity can devise."

After giving an interesting and powerfully written extract, the Athenaeum resumes:—

> "The dark-complexioned harpooner turned out to be a cannibal, one Queequeg * * * Mr Melville has to thank himself only if his horrors and his heroics are flung aside by the general reader, as so much trash belonging to the worst school of Bedlam literature,—since he seems not so much unable to learn as disdainful of learning the craft of an artist."

The production under notice is now issued by the Harpers in a handsome bound volume for *one dollar and fifty cents*—no mean sum, in these days. It seems to us that our publishers have gone from one extreme to the other, and that instead of publishing good books in too cheap a form, they are issuing poor books, in far too costly apparel. "The Whale" is not worth the money asked for it, either as a literary work or as a mass of printed paper. Few people would read it more than once, and yet it is issued at the usual cost of a standard volume. Published at *twenty five cents*, it might do to buy, but at any higher price, we think it a poor speculation.

Daily Mercury‡

Mr. Melville in his '*Moby-Dick, or the Whale,*' just published, gives the following vivid sketch of the chase and capture of the Sperm Whale:—

† Boston *Post,* November 20, 1851.
8. For the full quotations see the *Athenaeum* review, above [*Editors'* *note*].

‡ New Bedford *Daily Mercury,* November 20, 1851.

'Start her, start her, my men! * * * eyeing the vast corpse he had made. [Ch. 61, 243.4–245.22, without the footnotes.]

In the lively description of Mr. Melville, even the implements of 'Whaling gear' acquire a degree of interest which is almost irresistible:—

'The whale line is only two-thirds of an inch in thickness. * * * Yet habit—strange thing! what cannot habit accomplish?' [Ch. 60, 238.36–240.27.]

Christian Intelligencer†

The author of this volume is one that has often amused his many readers. Although he has a most prolific pen, he always writes like one who has complete command of it, and knows right well what he ought to say, and *how* to say it. His "Omoo" has had many admirers; and we venture to predict for this an equal, if not a greater number. His descriptions of land scenery are always exquisite; and taking the volume before us as a sample, we know of none who can excel him in his delineations of the sea, and the wonders that pass before the eyes of those who traffic thereon. Marryatt has written without stint or measure, and with many has long been a favorite; but we never thought he was capable of making such a correct use of English undefiled as Mr. Melville, or even could paint so beautifully.

Evangelist‡

Mr. Melville grows wilder and more untameable with every adventure. In Typee and Omoo, he began with the semblance of life and reality, though it was often but the faintest kind of semblance. As he advanced, he threw off the pretense of probability, and wandered from the verisimilitude of fiction into the mist and vagueness of poetry and fantasy, and now in this last venture, has reached the very limbo of eccentricity. From first to last, oddity is the governing characteristic. The extraordinary descriptive powers which Typee disclosed, are here in full strength. More graphic and terrible portraitures of hair-breadth 'scapes we never read. The delineation of character, too, is exquisitely humorous, sharp, individual and never-to-be forgotten. The description of Father Mapple's sermon is a powerful piece of sailor-oratory; and passages of great eloquence, and artistic beauty and force, are to be found everywhere. It will add to Mr. Melville's repute as a writer, undoubtedly, and furnishes, incidentally, a most striking picture of sea life and adventures.

† New York *Christian Intelligencer*, November 20, 1851.

‡ New York *Evangelist*, November 20, 1851.

Observer†

The Whale, by Herman Melville, is a beautiful book, just out of the press of the Harpers, a complete exhibition of the art and mystery of whaleology, with graphic pictures of the life and times of whalemen, in which the peculiar tact of Melville appears on every page.

Journal and Courier‡

We have read many accounts of the chase and capture of the sperm whale, but none so absorbingly interesting, or which have presented so vivid a picture of the exciting event, as the following:—

"Start her, start her, my men! * * * eyeing the vast corpse he had made. [Ch. 61, 243.4–245.22, without the footnotes.]

Albion§

This mere announcement of the book's and the author's name will prepare you in a measure for what follows; for you know just as well as we do that Herman Melville is a practical and practised sea-novelist, and that what comes from his pen will be worth the reading. And so indeed is "Moby-Dick," and not lacking much of being a great work. How it falls short of this, we shall presently endeavour to show. Let us in the first place briefly describe it.

It treats then mainly of whales, whaling, whalers, and whaling-men—incidentally it touches on mythology, sharks, religion, South Sea islanders, philosophy, cannibalism and curiosity shops. The writer uses the first person in narrating his tale, without however any attempt at making himself its hero. He was (or says he was, which is the same thing) but a seaman on board the vessel whose voyage he relates, and a consequent eye-witness of the strange characters on board her. Foremost amongst these is the Captain, in the conception of whose part lies the most original thought of the whole book, stamping it decidedly as the production of a man of genius. This Captain, a Nantucketer, Ahab by name, has lost a leg; it was snapped off by Moby-Dick, in the course of a boat adventure with an individual sperm-whale of the most dangerous kind, whose peculiar appearance, and repeated escapes from harpooneers,

† New York *Observer*, November 20, 1851. *Moby-Dick* had been announced in New York as *The Whale* before its publication, a fact which presumably accounts for the title given in this review.

‡ New Haven, Connecticut, *Journal and Courier*, November 22, 1851.

§ New York *Albion*, November 22, 1851.

together with the amount of destruction done by him, had earned him a nick-name and made him a terror in the trade. The bodily and mental anguish endured by Capt. Ahab had, ere the commencement of our tale, converted him into a monomaniac, whose sole and absorbing object in life was revenge on Moby-Dick. The *Pequod* of Nantucket is outfitted under his command for a new voyage, the officers and crew shipping, as usual, in quest of oil and gain therefrom, whilst their commander is bent on circumnavigating the globe, in hopes of satiating his thirst for vengeance. At times the subordinates murmur at his palpable neglect of their interests; but his undaunted courage and authoritative air, and their own superstitious fears of him, prevail over every other consideration.

> "Aye, Starbuck; aye, my hearties all round; it was Moby Dick that dismasted me; Moby Dick that brought me to this dead stump I stand on now. Aye, aye," he shouted with a terrific, loud animal sob, like that of a heart-stricken moose; "Aye, aye! it was that accursed white whale that razeed me; made a poor pegging lubber of me for ever and a day!" Then tossing both arms, with measureless imprecations he shouted out: "Aye, aye! and I'll chase him round Good Hope, and round the Horn, and round the Norway Maelstrom, and round perdition's flames before I give him up. And this is what ye have shipped for, men! to chase that white whale on both sides of land, and over all sides of earth, till he spouts black blood and rolls fin out. What say ye, men, will ye splice hands on it, now? I think ye do look brave."
>
> "Aye, aye!" shouted the harpooneers and seamen, running closer to the excited old man: "A sharp eye for the White Whale; a sharp lance for Moby Dick!"
>
> "God bless ye," he seemed to half sob and half shout. "God bless ye, men. Steward! go draw the great measure of grog."

The idea of even a nautical Don Quixote chasing a particular fish from ocean to ocean, running down the line of the Equator, or rushing from Torrid to Temperate zones—this may seem intolerably absurd. But the author clearly shows the *possibility* of such a search being successful, which is more than sufficient motive.

> Now, to any one not fully acquainted with the ways of the leviathians, it might seem an absurdly hopeless task thus to seek out one solitary creature in the unhooped oceans of this planet. But not so did it to Ahab, who knew the sets of all tides and currents; and thereby calculating the drifting of the sperm whale's food; and, also, calling to mind the regular, ascertained seasons for hunting him in particular latitudes; could arrive at reasonable surmises, almost approaching to certainties, concerning the timeliest day to be upon this or that ground in search of his prey. . . . And hence not only at substantiated times, upon well known

> separate feeding grounds, could Ahab hope to encounter his prey; but in crossing the widest expanses of water between those grounds he could, by his art, so place and time himself on his way, as even then not to be wholly without prospect of a meeting.

A variety of interesting details proves the personal identity of whales; and the author, not without reason, thus apostrophises a set of Cetacean braves.

> But not only did each of these famous whales enjoy great individual celebrity—nay, you may call it an ocean-wide renown; not only was he famous in life and now is immortal in forecastle stories after death, but he was admitted into all the rights, privileges, and distinctions of a name; had as much a name indeed as Cambyses or Caesar. Was it not so, O Timor Tom! thou famed leviathan, scarred like an iceberg, who so long did'st lurk in the Oriental straits of that name, whose spout was oft seen from the palmy beach of Ombay? Was it not so, O New Zealand Jack! thou terror of all cruisers that crossed their wakes in the vicinity of the Tattoo Land? Was it not so, O Morquan! King of Japan, whose lofty jet they say at times assumed the semblance of a snow-white cross against the sky? Was it not so, O Don Miguel! thou Chilian whale, marked like an old tortoise with mystic hieroglyphics upon the back? In plain prose, here are four whales as well known to the students of Cetacean History as Marius or Sylla to the classic scholar.

A deadly strife, then, between Capt. Ahab and Moby-Dick, is the vein of romance woven through the varied wanderings of the good ship *Pequod* and her crew, and to which the reader is brought back from matter-of-fact details of the fishery, from abstruse and sceptical and comical speculations on men and things, from hand-breadth escapes, and from thrilling adventures. The book opens with the writer's personal search for a berth on ship-board, at New Bedford and Nantucket, and closes with the total loss of the *Pequod* in the Pacific, the fated vessel being deliberately run into by Moby-Dick, just as the *Ann Alexander* was lately sunk in the same seas by a malicious sperm whale, as mentioned in our columns a few weeks since. It is a singular coincidence that Mr. Melville should have wound up with this catastrophe, and that its truthfulness should have met such sad and immediate confirmation. Be it further noted that "Moby-Dick" was published in London, before the fate of the *Ann Alexander* could have been known there.

Not only is there an immense amount of reliable information here before us; the *dramatis personæ*, mates, harpooneers, carpenters, and cooks, are all vivid sketches done in the author's best style. What they do, and how they look, is brought to one's perception with wondrous elaborateness of detail; and yet this minuteness does not spoil the broad outline of each. It is only when Mr. Melville puts words into the mouths of these living and moving beings, that his cunning fails him, and the illusion passes away. From the Captain to the Cabin-boy, not a soul amongst them talks pure seaman's lingo; and as this is a grave charge, we feel bound to substantiate it—not by an ill-natured selection of isolated bits, but by such samples as may be considered an average. We pass by Capt. Ahab for a few moments, and take his mates. Starbuck is the Chief; Ahab had nailed a sixteen-dollar gold doubloon to the main-mast as a prize for the first man that sighted Moby-Dick.

> "No fairy fingers can have pressed the gold, but devil's claws must have left their moulding there since yesterday," murmured Starbuck to himself, leaning against the bulwarks. "The old man seems to read Belshazzar's awful writing. I have never marked the coin inspectingly. He goes below; let me read."

The soliloquy of Stubb, the second Mate—a bold, jolly tar as ever flung harpoon—at the moment when Moby-Dick rushes headlong on the *Pequod,* is ludicrous in the extreme.

> "Stand not by me, but stand under me, whoever you are that will now help Stubb; for Stubb, too, sticks here. I grin at thee, thou grinning whale! Who ever helped Stubb, or kept Stubb awake, but Stubb's own unwinking eye? And now poor Stubb goes to bed upon a mattress that is all too soft; would it were stuffed with brushwood! I grin at thee, thou grinning whale! Look ye, sun, moon, and stars! I call ye assassins of as good a fellow as ever spouted up his ghost. For all that, I would yet ring glasses with ye, would ye but hand the cup! Oh, oh! oh, oh! thou grinning whale, but there'll be plenty of gulping soon! Why fly ye not, O Ahab! For me, off shoes and jackets to it; let Stubb die in his drawers! A most mouldy and over salted death, though; —cherries! cherries! cherries! Oh, Flask, for one red cherry ere we die!"

Flask, the third mate, happily for us says little; but the Carpenter thus mutters to himself over a new bone leg, that he is making for Capt. Ahab.

> Oh! I don't wonder he looked so scornful at me! I'm a sort of strange-thoughted sometimes, they say; but that's only haphazard like. Then, a short, little old body like me, should never undertake to wade out into deep waters with tall, heron-built captains; the water chucks you under the chin pretty quick, and there's a great cry for life-boats. And here's the heron's leg! long and slim, sure enough! Now, for most folks one pair of legs lasts a lifetime, and that must be because they use them mercifully, as a tender-hearted old lady uses her roly-poly old coach horses. But

> Ahab; oh he's a hard driver. Look, driven one leg to death, and spavined the other for life, and now wears out bone legs by the cord. Halloa, there, you Smut! bear a hand there with those screws, and let's finish it before the resurrection fellow comes a-calling with his horn for all legs, true or false, as brewery-men go round collecting old beer barrels, to fill 'em up again.

But there is no pleasure in making these extracts; still less would there be in quoting anything of the stuff and nonsense spouted forth by the crazy Captain; for so indeed must nine-tenths of his dialogue be considered, even though one bears in mind that it has been compounded in a maniac's brain from the queer mixture of New England conventicle phraseology with the devilish profanity too common on board South-Sea Whalers. The rarely-imagined character has been grievously spoiled, nay altogether ruined, by a vile overdaubing with a coat of book-learning and mysticism; there is no method in his madness; and we must needs pronounce the chief feature of the volume a perfect failure, and the work itself inartistic. There is nevertheless in it, as we have already hinted, abundant choice reading for these who can skip a page now and then, judiciously; and perhaps, when one's mind is made up to disregard the continuous interest, the separate portions may be better relished. We offer a sample or two of the best. There is for instance both truth and satire in the following peep into a particular mood of mind.

> There are certain queer times and occasions in this strange mixed affair we call life when a man takes this whole universe for a vast practical joke, though the wit thereof he but dimly discerns, and more than suspects that the joke is at nobody's expense but his own. However, nothing dispirits, and nothing seems worth while disputing. He bolts down all events, all creeds, and beliefs, and persuasions, all hard things visible and invisible, never mind how knobby; as an ostrich of potent digestion gobbles down bullets and gun flints. And as for small difficulties and worryings, prospects of sudden disaster, peril of life and limb; all these, and death itself, seem to him only sly, good-natured hits, and jolly punches in the side bestowed by the unseen and unaccountable old joker. That odd sort of wayward mood I am speaking of, comes over a man only in some time of extreme tribulation; it comes in the very midst of his earnestness, so that what just before might have seemed to him a thing most momentous, now seems but a part of the general joke. There is nothing like the perils of whaling to breed this free and easy sort of genial, desperado philosophy; and with it I now regarded the whole voyage of the *Pequod,* and the great White Whale its object.

It is to be hoped that this sketch of one of the owners of the *Pequod* was not drawn from the life at Nantucket.

> Now Bildad, I am sorry to say, had the reputation of being an incorrigible old hunks, and in his sea-going days a bitter, hard task-master. They told me in Nantucket, though it certainly seems a curious story, that when he sailed the old Categut whaleman, his crew, upon arriving home, were mostly all carried ashore to the hospital, sore exhausted and worn out. For a pious man, especially for a Quaker, he was certainly rather hard-hearted, to say the least. He never used to swear, though, at his men, they said; but somehow he got an inordinate quantity of cruel, unmitigated hard work out of them. When Bildad was a chief-mate, to have his drab-coloured eye intently looking at you, made you feel completely nervous, till you could clutch something—a hammer or a marling-spike, and go to work like mad, at something or other, never mind what. Indolence and idleness perished from before him. His own person was the exact embodiment of his utilitarian character. On his long, gaunt body, he carried no spare flesh, no superfluous beard, his chin having a soft, economical nap to it, like the worn nap of his broad-brimmed hat.

We conclude with part of a clever chapter on the honour and glory of whaling.

> There are some enterprises * * * why not the prophet? [Ch. 82, 304.14–306.13].

Mr. Melville has crowded together in a few prefatory pages a large collection of brief and pithy extracts from authors innumerable, such as one might expect as headings for chapters. We do not like the innovation. It is having oil, mustard, vinegar, and pepper served up as a dish, in place of being scientifically administered sauce-wise.

Daily Tribune†

Everybody has heard of the tradition which is said to prevail among the old salts of Nantucket and New-Bedford, of a ferocious monster of a whale, who is proof against all the arts of harpoonery, and who occasionally amuses himself with swallowing down a boat's crew without winking. The present volume is a "Whaliad," or the Epic of that veritable old leviathan, who "esteemeth iron as straw, and laughs at the spear, the dart, and the habergeon," no one being able to "fill his skin with a barbed iron, or his head with fish-hooks." Mr. Melville gives us not only the romance of his history, but a great mass of instruction on the character and habits of

† New York *Daily Tribune*, November 22, 1851.

his whole race, with complete details of the wily stratagems of their pursuers.

The interest of the work pivots on a certain Captain Ahab, whose enmity to Moby-Dick, the name of the whale-demon, has been aggravated to monomania. In one rencounter with this terror of the seas, he suffers a signal defeat; loses a leg in the contest; gets a fire in his brain; returns home a man with one idea; feels that he has a mission; that he is predestined to defy his enemy to mortal strife; devotes himself to the fulfillment of his destiny; with the persistence and cunning of insanity gets possession of another vessel; ships a weird, supernatural crew of which Ishmael, the narrator of the story, is a prominent member; and after a "wild huntsman's chase" through unknown seas, is the only one who remains to tell the destruction of the ship and the doomed Captain Ahab by the victorious, indomitable Moby-Dick.

The narrative is constructed in Herman Melville's best manner. It combines the various features which form the chief attractions of his style, and is commendably free from the faults which we have before had occasion to specify in this powerful writer. The intensity of the plot is happily relieved by minute descriptions of the most homely processes of the whale fishery. We have occasional touches of the subtle mysticism, which is carried to such an inconvenient excess in Mardi, but it is here mixed up with so many tangible and odorous realities, that we always safely alight from the excursion through mid-air upon the solid deck of the whaler. We are recalled to this world by the fumes of "oil and blubber," and are made to think more of the contents of barrels than of allegories. The work is also full of episodes, descriptive of strange and original phases of character. One of them is given in the commencement of the volume, showing how "misery makes a man acquainted with strange bed-fellows." We must pass over this in which the writer relates his first introduction to Queequeg, a South Sea cannibal, who was his chum at a sailor boarding house in New-Bedford and afterward his bosom friend and most devoted confederate. We will make a room for the characteristic chapter, which describes the ripening of their acquaintance into the honeymoon of friendship:

> Returning to the Spouter-Inn * * * and all the world. [Ch. 10, 51.24–54.26.]

But we must go out to sea with Ishmael, if we would witness his most remarkable exploits. We are now, then, in the midst of things, and with good luck, may soon get a sight of Moby-Dick. Meantime, we may beguile our impatience with the description of a rope on which Melville gives us a touch of his quaint moralizings.

With reference to the whaling scene shortly to be described * * * and not a harpoon, by your side. [Ch. 60, 238.15–241.18.]

We are now ready to kill our first whale. Here is the transaction in full:

KILLING A WHALE.

If to Starbuck the apparition of the Squid * * * thoughtfully eyeing the vast corpse he had made. [Ch. 61, 241.21–245.22.]

At last, Moby-Dick, the object of such long vigilant, and infuriate search, is discovered. We can only give the report of

THE CHASE—FIRST DAY.

That night, in the mid-watch * * * as desolate sounds from out ravines. [Ch. 133, 445.31–451.2.]

Here we will retire from the chase, which lasts three days, not having a fancy to be in at the death. We part with the adventurous philosophical Ishmael, truly thankful that the whale did not get his head, for which we are indebted for this wildly imaginative and truly thrilling story. We think it the best production which has yet come from that seething brain, and in spite of its lawless flights, which put all regular criticism at defiance, it gives us a higher opinion of the author's originality and power than even the favorite and fragrant first-fruits of his genius, the never-to-be-forgotten Typee.

Literary World†

A difficulty in the estimate of this, in common with one or two other of Mr. Melville's books, occurs from the double character under which they present themselves. In one light they are romantic fictions, in another statements of absolute fact. When to this is added that the romance is made a vehicle of opinion and satire through a more or less opaque allegorical veil, as particularly in the latter half of Mardi, and to some extent in this present volume, the critical difficulty is considerably thickened. It becomes quite impossible to submit such books to a distinct classification as fact, fiction, or essay. Something of a parallel may be found in Jean Paul's German tales, with an admixture of Southey's Doctor. Under these combined influences of personal observation, actual fidelity to local truthfulness in description, a taste for reading and sentiment, a fondness for fanciful analogies, near and remote, a rash daring in speculation, reckless at times of taste and propriety, again refined and eloquent, this volume of Moby Dick may be pronounced a most remarkable sea-dish—an intellectual chowder of romance, phi-

† New York *Literary World,* November 22, 1851 (Second Notice).

losophy, natural history, fine writing, good feeling, bad sayings—but over which, in spite of all uncertainties, and in spite of the author himself, predominates his keen perceptive faculties, exhibited in vivid narration.

There are evidently two if not three books in Moby Dick rolled into one. Book No. I. we could describe as a thorough exhaustive account admirably given of the great Sperm Whale. The information is minute, brilliantly illustrated, as it should be—the whale himself so generously illuminating the midnight page on which his memoirs are written—has its level passages, its humorous touches, its quaint suggestion, its incident usually picturesque and occasionably sublime. All this is given in the most delightful manner in "The Whale." Book No. 2 is the romance of Captain Ahab, Queequeg, Tashtego, Pip & Co., who are more or less spiritual personages talking and acting differently from the general business run of the conversation on the decks of whalers. They are for the most part very serious people, and seem to be concerned a great deal about the problem of the universe. They are striking characters withal, of the romantic spiritual cast of the German drama; realities of some kinds at bottom, but veiled in all sorts of poetical incidents and expressions. As a bit of German melodrama, with Captain Ahab for the Faust of the quarter-deck, and Queequeg with the crew, for Walpurgis night revellers in the forecastle, it has its strong points, though here the limits as to space and treatment of the stage would improve it. Moby Dick in this view becomes a sort of fishy moralist, a leviathan metaphysician, a folio Ductor Dubitantium, in fact, in the fresh water illustration of Mrs. Malaprop, "an allegory on the banks of the Nile." After pursuing him in this melancholic company over a few hundred squares of latitude and longitude, we begin to have some faint idea of the association of whaling and lamentation, and why blubber is popularly synonymous with tears.

The intense Captain Ahab is too long drawn out; something more of *him* might, we think, be left to the reader's imagination. The value of this kind of writing can only be through the personal consciousness of the reader, what he brings to the book; and all this is sufficiently evoked by a dramatic trait or suggestion. If we had as much of Hamlet or Macbeth as Mr. Melville gives us of Ahab, we should be tired even of their sublime company. Yet Captain Ahab is a striking conception, firmly planted on the wild deck of the Pequod—a dark disturbed soul arraying itself with every ingenuity of material resources for a conflict at once natural and supernatural in his eye, with the most dangerous extant physical monster of the earth, embodying, in strongly drawn lines of mental association, the vaster moral evil of the world. The pursuit of the White Whale thus interweaves with the literal perils of the fishery—a problem of fate and destiny—to the tragic solution of which Ahab hurries on, amidst the wild stage scenery of the ocean. To this end the motley crew, the air, the sky, the sea, its inhabitants are idealized throughout. It is a noble and praiseworthy conception; and though our sympathies may not always accord with the train of thought, we would caution the reader against a light or hasty condemnation of this part of the work.

Book III., appropriating perhaps a fourth of the volume, is a vein of moralizing, half essay, half rhapsody, in which much refinement and subtlety, and no little poetical feeling, are mingled with quaint conceit and extravagant daring speculation. This is to be taken as in some sense dramatic; the narrator throughout among the personages of the Pequod being one Ishmael, whose wit may be allowed to be against everything on land, as his hand is against everything at sea. This piratical running down of creeds and opinions, the conceited indifferentism of Emerson, or the run-a-muck style of Carlyle is, we will not say dangerous in such cases, for there are various forces at work to meet more powerful onslaught, but it is out of place and uncomfortable. We do not like to see what, under any view, must be to the world the most sacred associations of life violated and defaced.

We call for fair play in this matter. Here is Ishmael, telling the story of this volume, going down on his knees with a cannibal to a piece of wood, in the second story fire-place of a New-Bedford tavern, in the spirit of amiable and transcendent charity, which may be all very well in its way; but why dislodge from heaven, with contumely, "long-pampered Gabriel, Michael and Raphael." Surely Ishmael, who is a scholar, might have spoken respectfully of the Archangel Gabriel, out of consideration, if not for the Bible (which might be asking too much of the school), at least for one John Milton, who wrote Paradise Lost.

Nor is it fair to inveigh against the terrors of priestcraft, which, skilful though it may be in making up its woes, at least seeks to provide a remedy for the evils of the world, and attribute the existence of conscience to "hereditary dyspepsias, nurtured by Ramadans"—and at the same time go about petrifying us with imaginary horrors, and all sorts of gloomy suggestions, all the world through. It is a curious fact that there are no more bilious people in the world, more completely filled with megrims and head shakings, than some of these very people who are constantly inveighing against the religious melancholy of priestcraft.

So much for the consistency of Ishmael who, if it is the author's object to exhibit the painful contradictions of this self-dependent, self-torturing agency of a mind driven hither and thither as a flame in a whirlwind, is, in a degree, a successful embodiment of opinions, without securing from us, however, much admiration for the result.

With this we make an end of what we have been reluctantly compelled to object to this volume. With far greater pleasure, we acknowledge the acuteness of observation, the freshness of perception, with which the author brings home to us from the deep, "things unattempted yet in prose or rhyme," the weird influences of his ocean scenes, the salient imagination which connects them with the past and distant, the world of books and the life of experience—certain prevalent traits of manly sentiment. These are strong powers with which Mr. Melville wrestles in this book. It would be a great glory to subdue them to the highest uses of fiction. It is still a great honor, among the crowd of successful mediocrities which throng our publishers' counters, and know nothing of divine impulses, to be in the company of these nobler spirits on any terms.

Saturday Courier†

Who is Herman Melville? There, dear reader, you puzzle us. We only know just what you and all other general readers know, that he is one of the most spirited, vigorous, good-natured writers in existence; as sparkling and racy as old wine and sweet as nuts, with a constant flow of animating description and thrilling incident, picked up all along shore, or in the polished drawing-room—on land or upon the far-off ocean. His home has been so much upon the mountain deep, that he has become wedded to the wide waters, and yet lives and moves upon the solid earth with all the ease and polish of a finished gentleman.

There, reader, is about all we know of this unique character, and, for further particulars, you are referred to Stokes' supply of "*that* whale."[9] If there is not enough "blubber" there to satisfy every "land lubber," we shall be exceedingly mistaken, and that, too, notwithstanding the blunt phraseology which we sometimes meet in Melville. For real, easy, pleasant, social enjoyment, this is decidedly the richest book out; and though the "long yarn" runs out to 635 pages, not a reader will lay down the book without wishing that "Moby Dick" had driven the whale a thousand leagues further, spouting and spinning his yarn as he went. No one can tire of this volume; and notwithstanding the many astounding "whale" stories, and miscellaneous wonders with which it abounds, the

† Philadelphia *American Saturday Courier*, November 22, 1851.

9. "Stokes' supply" is a reference to the Stokes Brothers bookstore in Philadelphia, where copies of *Moby-Dick* were on sale [*Editors' note*].

reader may be the better prepared to credit all after reading the whale shipwreck in last week's Courier.[10]

Commercial Advertiser†

The reputation attained by Mr. Melville's previous publications will secure extensive circulation for this book, but the greatest diversity of opinion will be entertained as to its merits. There are few readers who will not be at first repulsed by its eccentricity. Such a salmagundi of fact, fiction and philosophy, composed in a style which combines the peculiarities of Carlyle, Marryatt and Lamb, was never seen before. Moby Dick is an old white whale, of extraordinary magnitude and malignity, and he escapes with impunity from so many attacks, that the superstitious whalemen believe him to be a sort of supernatural creature. Capt. Ahab, in one of these attacks, is struck by the monster's tail, and loses a leg. Thus maimed, he devotes his life to revenge, and pursues Moby Dick through divers seas, making frequent assaults upon him, but always without success. In the last encounter, the infuriated whale rushes headlong against the Pequod, the ship in which Capt. Ahab sails, and all the crew perish, except one Ishmael, who survives to tell the story. The science of cetology is pleasantly interwoven with this legend. We regret to see that Mr. Melville is guilty of sneering at the truths of revealed religion. On page 58, he makes his hero, "a good Christian—born and bred in the bosom of the infallible Presbyterian church," unite with a Polynesian in worshipping and offering incense to an idol, and in this connexion virtually questions the authenticity of the first commandment.

Weekly News‡

This is a wild, weird book, full of strange power and irresistible fascination for those who love to read of the wonders of the deep. The poetry of the great South Seas, the rude lawless adventure of the rough mariners who for years of continuous voyaging peril themselves on its waters; the excitement and the danger of the fishery for the sperm whale, the fiercest and hugest monster "of all who swim the ocean stream," combine to make these pages attractive and interesting to many different classes of readers. Artists and sportsmen, the lovers of scenery, and the lovers of excitement, will alike find in them ample material of gratification. The blemish of

10. The reference is to the account of the sinking of the *Ann Alexander* in the *Courier* for November 15, 1851 [*Editors' note*].

† New York *Commercial Advertiser*, November 28, 1851.

‡ London *Weekly News and Chronicle*, November 29, 1851.

the book is its occasional extravagance and exaggeration—faults which mar the effect they were intended to heighten, and here and there, as in the character of Captain Ahab, make a melodramatic caricature of what, with a little more simplicity, might have been a striking and original picure.

The story of the book is brief; the supposed voyager having been long desirous of seeing somewhat of the whale fishery, takes ship at Nantucket, United States, on board the "Pequod" of that port, commanded by Captain Ahab—a veteran whaler, who, having lost a leg on his last voyage, in an encounter with a vast sperm whale—the terror of the Pacific—called by the sailors "Moby Dick,"—sails on his present cruise with the fixed intention of never returning till he shall have slaked his vengeance in the blood of his monstrous enemy. The whole narrative consists of the search through the vast Pacific, for this fierce and formidable antagonist, of his final discovery, of the life-and-death contest which ensues between the enraged Leviathan and the fated crew of the "Pequod." The catastrophe with which the book terminates, viz., the sinking of the ship in mid ocean from the effects of a direct charge by "Moby Dick" on her quarters, is not to be set down amongst the extravagancies of Herman Melville. It is on credible record, that in the year 1820 precisely such a casualty befel the ship "Essex;" and, even as we write, our eye rests on an extract from the *New Bedford Mercury*, given in the *Times* of Friday, the 21st ult., containing a circumstantial account of the destruction by a sperm whale of the ship "Ann Alexander," Captain J. Deblois, of New Bedford, United States. In this case the whale had previously destroyed the boats, and the chase was being continued in the ship, against which the monster rushed at the rate of about fifteen knots an hour, and, striking her about two feet from the keel, abreast the foremast, knocked a great hole entirely through her bottom, from the effects of which she foundered in less than ten minutes.

This may serve to show that the peril of the sperm whale fishery is by no means imaginary: in these volumes the excitement felt about the mysterious monster "Moby Dick"—the great White Whale—the terror of all whalers—is singularly increased by every kind of dramatic artifice. Every one of the crew on board the "Pequod" has some tale about him—every solitary whale-ship which the "Pequod" encounters in her long years of wandering over the great world of waters, has some tidings to give of the destructive prowess of the monster; so that, to all who can enter into the spirit of the book, the eagerness of expectation becomes at last most pleasurably painful. Another point which shows the power of the writer, is the utter "whalishness" (we must coin the word) of everything that meets you in his volumes, from the first page to the last. You feel yourself at once in a new and strange element. The snugly-curtained room and the cheery fire-side are forgotten as you read: the hand of a master carries you far away into wild scenes and the companionship of wilder men, you are sailing under the moonshine over the broad Pacific, watching from the mast head if haply you may discern some stray whale-spout jetting up amid the interminable waste of waters, or it may be the great White Whale himself, gliding phantom like through the solitudes of the midnight ocean.

But it is time to let Ishmael, the whaler, speak for himself. This is his description of the "Spouter Inn," at New Bedford, where he put up before sailing on his four years' cruise:—

> "Entering that gable-ended Spouter-Inn, you found yourself in a wide, low, straggling entry, with old-fashioned wainscots, reminding one of the bulwarks of some condemned old craft * * * Within are shabby shelves, ranged round with old decanters, bottles, flasks; and in those jaws of swift destruction, bustles a little withered old man, who, for their money, dearly sells the sailors deliriums and death." [Ch. 3, 20.6–21.37.]

Once abroad, upon the great Pacific, Ishmael, like the rest of the crew, has to take his turn at the mast-head, which he thus moralises:—

> "The three masts are kept manned from sun-rise to sun set; the seamen taking their regular turns, as at the helm, and relieving each other every two hours. * * * You cannot put a shelf or chest of drawers in your body, and no more can you make a convenient closet of your watch-coat." [Ch. 35, 136.32–137.34.]

Our readers doubtless would like to learn something of the great White Whale himself. Here are some dim intimations of him:—

> "I, Ishmael, was one of that crew; my shouts had gone up with the rest: my oath had been welded with theirs; and stronger I shouted, and more did I hammer and clinch my oath, because of the dread in my soul. * * * So that in many cases such a panic did he finally strike, that few who by those rumours, at least, had heard of the White Whale, few of those hunters were willing to encounter the perils of his jaw." [Ch. 41, 155.9–156.44.]

Here we must pause. The extracts we have given will serve to show the quality of this book—which is, to our minds, by far the most powerful and original contribution that Herman Melville has yet made to the Romance of Travel. And be it remembered that, though abounding in the wild and imaginative, the book is, by no means, deficient in accurate information. The chapter on Cetology contains an admirable analysis of the different varieties of the whale tribe, while the various processes of capturing the fish and extracting the oil are described with the minute and graphic vividness which no mere literary ability could have accomplished, and which evidently betoken the close observation of an attentive and gifted eye-witness. To the artist, the naturalist and the general reader these volumes may be confidently recommended as among the freshest and most vigorous that the present publishing season has produced.

Evening Post†

[Mr. Herman Melville, in his new sea-story, describes a marvellous chase by a whaling monomaniac after the "Moby Dick," the fabulous leviathan of the sailors, during which he probably let us into the realities of actual whaling as minutely and faithfully as any sea-author has ever done. We shall give a couple of passages, hoping that they will put the reader on the look-out for the book itself.]

> If to Starbuck the apparition of the Squid * * * stood thoughtfully eyeing the vast corpse he had made. [Ch. 61, 241.21–245.22, without the footnotes.]

Home Journal‡

If we mistake not, the author of "Typee" and "White Jacket," conscious of the vivid expectation excited in the reading public by his previous books, resolved to combine in the present all his popular characteristics, and so fully justify his fame. Accordingly he has chosen a subject which affords the greatest scope for adventure and the most striking phases of sea-life, and at the same time, by its relation to commerce and natural history, is associated with the most matter-of-fact interests. He has treated of the Whale under three points of view—as the nucleus of maritime adventure, as a subject of scientific curiosity, and as a kind of hero of romance. The result is a very racy, spirited, curious and entertaining book, which affords quite an amount of information, while it enlists the curiosity, excites the sympathies, and often charms the fancy.

† New York *Evening Post*, November 29, 1851. The review was headed "WHALE KILLING. / From 'Moby Dick.'" The square brackets in the first paragraph are in the *Evening Post*.

‡ New York *Home Journal for the Cultivation of the Memorable, the Progressive, and the Beautiful*, November 29, 1851.

Eclectic†

Mr. Melville's new work, Moby Dick, published by the HARPERS, also gets a severe handling in the *Athenæum*—not with its accustomed candor, as it seems to us. Faulty as the book may be, it bears the marks of such unquestionable genius, and displays graphic powers of so rare an order, that it cannot fail to add to the popular author's reputation.

Harper's‡

A new work by HERMAN MELVILLE, entitled *Moby Dick; or, The Whale*, has just been issued by Harper and Brothers, which, in point of richness and variety of incident, originality of conception, and splendor of description, surpasses any of the former productions of this highly successful author. *Moby Dick* is the name of an old White Whale; half fish and half devil; the terror of the Nantucket cruisers; the scourge of distant oceans; leading an invulnerable, charmed life; the subject of many grim and ghostly traditions. This huge sea monster has a conflict with one Captain Ahab; the veteran Nantucket salt comes off second best; not only loses a leg in the affray, but receives a twist in the brain; becomes the victim of a deep, cunning monomania; believes himself predestined to take a bloody revenge on his fearful enemy; pursues him with fierce demoniac energy of purpose; and at last perishes in the dreadful fight, just as he deems that he has reached the goal of his frantic passion. On this slight framework, the author has contrasted a romance, a tragedy, and a natural history, not without numerous gratuitous suggestions on psychology, ethics, and theology. Beneath the whole story, the subtle, imaginative reader may perhaps find a pregnant allegory, intended to illustrate the mystery of human life. Certain it is that the rapid, pointed hints which are often thrown out, with the keenness and velocity of a harpoon, penetrate deep into the heart of things, showing that the genius of the author for moral analysis is scarcely surpassed by his wizard power of description.

In the course of the narrative the habits of the whale are fully and ably described. Frequent graphic and instructive sketches of the fishery, of sea-life in a whaling vessel, and of the manners and customs of strange nations are interspersed with excellent artistic effect among the thrilling scenes of the story. The various processes

† New York *Eclectic Magazine*, December, 1851.

‡ New York *Harper's New Monthly Magazine*, December, 1851.

of procuring oil are explained with the minute, painstaking fidelity of a statistical record, contrasting strangely with the weird, phantom-like character of the plot, and of some of the leading personages, who present a no less unearthly appearance than the witches in Macbeth. These sudden and decided transitions form a striking feature of the volume. Difficult of management, in the highest degree, they are wrought with consummate skill. To a less gifted author, they would inevitably have proved fatal. He has not only deftly avoided their dangers, but made them an element of great power. They constantly pique the attention of the reader, keeping curiosity alive, and presenting the combined charm of surprise and alternation.

The introductory chapters of the volume, containing sketches of life in the great marts of Whalingdom, New Bedford and Nantucket, are pervaded with a fine vein of comic humor, and reveal a succession of portraitures, in which the lineaments of nature shine forth, through a good deal of perverse, intentional exaggeration. To many readers, these will prove the most interesting portions of the work. Nothing can be better than the description of the owners of the vessel, Captain Peleg and Captain Bildad, whose acquaintance we make before the commencement of the voyage. The character of Captain Ahab also opens upon us with wonderful power. He exercises a wild, bewildering fascination by his dark and mysterious nature, which is not at all diminished when we obtain a clearer insight into his strange history. Indeed, all the members of the ship's company, the three mates, Starbuck, Stubbs, and Flash, the wild, savage Gayheader, the case-hardened old blacksmith, to say nothing of the pearl of a New Zealand harpooner, the bosom friend of the narrator—all stand before us in the strongest individual relief, presenting a unique picture gallery, which every artist must despair of rivaling.

The plot becomes more intense and tragic, as it approaches toward the denouement. The malicious old Moby Dick, after long cruisings in pursuit of him, is at length discovered. He comes up to the battle, like an army with banners. He seems inspired with the same fierce, inveterate cunning with which Captain Ahab has followed the traces of his mortal foe. The fight is described in letters of blood. It is easy to foresee which will be the victor in such a contest. We need not say that the ill-omened ship is broken in fragments by the wrath of the weltering fiend. Captain Ahab becomes the prey of his intended victim. The crew perish. One alone escapes to tell the tale. Moby Dick disappears unscathed, and for aught we know, is the same "delicate monster," whose power in destroying another ship is just announced from Panama.

North American†

Melville's new work, "The Whale, or Moby Dick," is pronounced by the Athenaeum an absurd book. Its catastrophe, it says, is hastily, weakly, and obscurely managed, and the style in places disfigured by mad (rather than bad) English.

International‡

The new nautical story by the always successful author of *Typee*, has for its name-giving subject a monster first introduced to the world of print by Mr. J. N. Reynolds, ten or fifteen years ago, in a paper for the *Knickerbocker*, entitled *Mocha Dick*. We received a copy when it was too late to review it ourselves for this number of the *International*, and therefore make use of a notice of it which we find in the London *Spectator*.[11]

> "This sea novel is a singular medley of naval observation, magazine article writing, satiric reflection upon the conventionalisms of civilized life, and rhapsody run mad * * *"

Daily Advertiser§

Fresh and buoyant as ever, our old friend dashes out in another realm of sea-life, and with "a long pull, and a strong pull," rows us away from brick wall and homely thoughts into the ocean of fancy. But the scenes into which we are taken are not all imaginative. The web upon which the work is constructed is undoubtedly a creation of the brain, but the scenes therein are the daily occurrences in the life of the adventurous whaler. And this is evidently the object of the writer—to plainly portray the daily adventures and dangers of the hardy sailor in quest of the great leviathan. In the course of the volume, we have a description of the varieties of the whale; their various characteristics and values; the numerous difficulties attendant upon their capture and the statistics of the vessels and men engaged in this branch of the marine; the capital invested therein, and the returns made upon it. Insomuch the work is of practical value. We doubt if ever the whale has been so scientifically described by any preceding writer, and his account is worthy to be, and probably will be, incorporated into all future natural histories. It is astonishing that among all the myriads that have frequently

† New York *North American Miscellany*, December, 1851.
‡ New York *International Magazine of Literature, Art, and Science*, December 1, 1851.

11. For the *Spectator* review, which the *International Magazine* reprinted in full, see above [*Editors' note*].
§ Newark *Daily Advertiser*, December 5, 1851.

seen these monsters of the deep, none, till now, have been able to describe them intelligibly, not to say correctly. A semi-marvelous narrative or tale is the link which connects the various chapters and retains the interest of the reader until the very last page.

Notwithstanding the numerous works which Melville has written, and upon similar subjects too, it is very noticeable how little he repeats himself. Even Cooper in successive tales continued many of his characters, but here we have constant novelty drawn by an apparently inexhaustible pen. Every character seems pictured by a daguerreotype, so natural are the features, and so clear the outlines.

With each succeeding book too, there is an improvement in the artistic character of the work; in some respects this is not a gain to the general reader, not that there is a want of freshness, but we think the metaphysical discussions, half earnest and half banter, might well be omitted. This fault may be glaring in Mardi, though but little observable in this, which we think will increase the popularity of the author.

Literary Gazette†

Thrice unlucky Herman Melville! Three goodly volumes has he written, with the main purpose of honouring the Cachalot, and disparaging the *Mysticete*, and his publisher has sent them into the world in brilliant covers of blue and white, with three Greenland whales stamped in gold on their binding. How they spout! Three unmistakeable Mysticeti, sloping heads, and jaws fringed with long combs of baleen. Shade of extinguished spermaceti, how thy light has been put out by the bookbinders!

This is an odd book, professing to be a novel; wantonly eccentric; outrageously bombastic; in places charmingly and vividly descriptive. The author has read up laboriously to make a show of cetalogical learning. He has turned over the articles Whale, Porpoise, Cachalot, Spermaceti, Baleen, and their relatives, in every Encyclopædia within his reach. Thence he has resorted to the original authorities—a difficult and tedious task, as every one who has sought out the sources of statements set forth without reference in Cyclopædias knows too well. For our own part, we believe that there must have been some old original Cyclopædia, long since lost or destroyed, out of which all the others have been compiled. For when one is compared with another, it becomes too plain that one or other is a barefaced pillage and extract from a secondhand source. Herman Melville is wise in this sort of wisdom. He uses it as stuffing to fill out his skeleton story. Bad stuffing it makes, serving only to try the patience of his readers, and to tempt them to

† London *Literary Gazette and Journal of Science and Art*, December 6, 1851.

wish both him and his whales at the bottom of an unfathomable sea. If a man will light his lamp with whale oil, when gas and camphine are at hand, he must be content with a dull illumination.

The story of this novel scarcely deserves the name. The supposed author, a young sailor, resolves to join the whalers. He falls in with a strange bedfellow at starting, a picturesque savage, one Queequeg, a New Zealand prince, who has abdicated his dignities in order to see the world, and who moves through nautical society with a harpoon in his hand and a wooden god in his pocket. Mr. Melville cannot do without savages, so he makes half of his *dramatis personæ* wild Indians, Malays, and other untamed humanities. Queequeg and the writer become sworn friends. They join a whale-ship, commanded by a strange old one-legged Captain Ahab, who cherishes a mysterious purpose—no less than the intention of pursuing to death a ferocious white spermaceti whale, who has knocked no end of ships to pieces, and chewed off any number of legs, arms, and heads of whale-fishers. Ahab peregrinates the ocean in search of his enemy, for it was Moby Dick—that is the name of the whale—who abbreviated the Captain's lower extremities. What the author's original intention in spinning his preposterous yarn was, it is impossible to guess; evidently, when we compare the first and third volumes, it was never carried out. He seems to have despaired of exciting interest about a leviathan hero and a crazy whale-skipper, and when he found his manuscript sufficient for the filling up of three octavos, resolved to put a stop to whale, captain, crew, and savages by a *coup de main*. Accordingly, he sends them down to the depths of ocean all in a heap, using his milk-white spermaceti as the instrument of ruthless destruction. How the imaginary writer, who appears to have been drowned with the rest, communicated his notes for publication to Mr. Bentley is not explained. The whole affair would make an admirable subject for an Easter entertainment at Astley's.[12]

Having said so much that may be interpreted as censure, it is right that we should add a word of praise where deserved. There are sketches of scenes at sea, of whaling adventures, storms, and ship-life, equal to any we have ever met with. A single extract will serve as an illustration. It is a description of an attack upon a whale during a squall, and the fearful consequences of the rash exploit:—

> "Our sail was now set * * * The ship had given us up, but was still cruising, if haply it might light upon some token of our perishing,—an oar or a lance pole." [Ch. 48, 193.39–195.24.]

12. Astley's Royal Amphitheatre, in London. Melville's brother Gansevoort saw a typical entertainment there in 1846—"a grand oriental melodrama, in which two elephants figured conspicuously, also gymnastics—& some capital feats of riding in the arena" [*Editors' note*].

Mr. Herman Melville has earned a deservedly high reputation for his performances in descriptive fiction. He has gathered his own materials, and travelled along fresh and untrodden literary paths, exhibiting powers of no common order, and great originality. The more careful, therefore, should he be to maintain the fame he so rapidly acquired, and not waste his strength on such purposeless and unequal doings as these rambling volumes about spermaceti whales.

Spirit of the Times†

Our friend Melville's books begin to accumulate. His literary family increases rapidly. He had already a happy and smiling progeny around him, but lo! at the appointed time another child of his brain, with the accustomed signs of the family, claims our attention and regard. We bid the book a hearty welcome. We assure the "happy father" that his "labors of love" are no "love's labor lost."

We confess an admiration for Mr. Melville's books, which, perhaps, spoils us for mere criticism. There are few writers, living or dead, who describe the sea and its adjuncts with such true art, such graphic power, and with such powerfully resulting interest. "Typee," "Omoo," "Redburn," "Mardi," and "White Jacket," are equal to anything in the language. They are things of their own. They are results of the youthful experience on the ocean of a man who is at once philosopher, painter, and poet. This is not, perhaps, a very unusual mental combination, but it is not usual to find such a combination "before the mast." So far Mr. Melville's early experiences, though perhaps none of the pleasantest to himself, are infinitely valuable to the world. We say *valuable* with a full knowledge of the terms used; and, not to enter into details, which will be fresh in the memory of most of Mr. Melville's readers, it is sufficient to say that the humanities of the world have been quickened by his works. Who can forget the missionary *expose*—the practical good sense which pleads for "Poor Jack," or the unsparing but just severity of his delineations of naval abuses, and that crowning disgrace to our navy—flogging? Taken as matters of art these books are amongst the largest and the freshest contributions of original thought and observation which have been presented in many years. Take the majority of modern writers, and it will be admitted that however much they may elaborate and rearrange the stock of ideas pre-existant, there is little added to the "common fund." Philosophers bark at each other—poets sing stereotyped phrases—John Miltons re-appear in innumerable "Pollock's Courses

† New York *Spirit of the Times*, December 6, 1851.

of Time"—novelists and romances [romancers?] stick to the same overdone incidents, careless of the memories of defunct Scotts and Radcliffs, and it is only now and then when genius, by some lucky chance of youth, ploughs deeper into the soil of humanity and nature, that fresher experiences—perhaps at the cost of much individual pain and sorrow—are obtained; and the results are books, such as those of Herman Melville and Charles Dickens. Books which are living pictures, at once of the practical truth, and the ideal amendment: books which mark epochs in literature and art.

It is, however, not with Mr. Melville generally as a writer that we have now to deal, but with "Moby Dick, or the Whale," in particular; and at first let us not forget to say that in "taking titles" no man is more felicitous than our author. Sufficiently dreamy to excite one's curiosity, sufficiently explicit to indicate some main and peculiar feature. "Moby Dick" is perhaps a creation of the brain—"The Whale" a result of experience; and the whole title a fine polished result of both. A title may be a truth or a lie. It may be clap-trap, or true art. A bad book may have a good title, but you will seldom find a good book with an inappropriate name.

"Moby Dick, or the Whale," is all whale. Leviathan is here in full amplitude. Not one of your museum affairs, but the real, living whale, a bona-fide, warm-blooded creature, ransacking the waters from pole to pole. His enormous bulk, his terribly destructive energies, his habits, his food, are all before us. Nay, even his lighter moods are exhibited. We are permitted to see the whale as a lover, a husband, and the head of a family. So to speak, we are made guests at his fire-side; we set our mental legs beneath his mahogany, and become members of his interesting social circle. No book in the world brings together so much whale. We have his history, natural and social, living and dead. But Leviathan's natural history, though undoubtedly valuable to science, is but a part of the book. It is in the personal adventures of his captors, their toils, and, alas! not unfrequently their wounds and martyrdom, that our highest interest is excited. This mingling of human adventure with new, startling, and striking objects and pursuits, constitute one of the chief charms of Mr. Melville's books. His present work is a drama of intense interest. A whale, "Moby Dick"—a dim, gigantic, unconquerable, but terribly destructive being, is one of the persons of the drama. We admit a disposition to be critical on this character. We had doubts as to his admissibility as an actor into dramatic action, and so it would seem had our author, but his chapter, "The Affidavit," disarms us; all improbability or incongruity disappears, and "Moby Dick" becomes a living fact, simply doubtful at first, because he was so new an idea, one of those beings whose whole life, like the Palladius or the Sea-serpent, is a romance, and whose memoirs unvarnished are of themselves a fortune to the first analist or his publisher.

"Moby Dick, or the Whale," is a "many-sided" book. Mingled with much curious information respecting whales and whaling there is a fine vein of sermonizing, a good deal of keen satire, much humor, and that too of the finest order, and a story of peculiar interest. As a romance its characters are so new and unusual that we doubt not it will excite the ire of critics. It is not tame enough to pass this ordeal safely. Think of a monomaniac whaling captain, who, mutilated on a former voyage by a particular whale, well known for its peculiar bulk, shape, and color—seeks, at the risk of his life and the lives of his crew, to capture and slay this terror of the seas! It is on this idea that the romance hinges. The usual staple of novelists is entirely wanting. We have neither flinty-hearted fathers, designing villains, dark caverns, men in armor, nor anxious lovers. There is not in the book any individual, who, at a certain hour, "*might have been seen*" ascending hills or descending valleys, as is usual. The thing is entirely new, fresh, often startling, and highly dramatic, and with those even, who, oblivious of other fine matters, scattered with profusest hand, read for the sake of the story, must be exceedingly successful.

Our space will not permit us at present to justify our opinions by long quotations; but, at the risk of doing Mr. Melville injustice by curtailment, let us turn to the chapter headed "The Pequod meets the Rose Bud," pp. 447, in which a whaling scene is described with infinite humor. The "Pequod"—our author's ship—was sailing slowly "over a sleepy, vapory, mid-day sea," when "the many noses on her deck proved more vigilant discoverers than the three pair of eyes aloft."[13] * * *

Did our limits permit we would gladly extract the fine little episode, contained in the chapter called "The Castaway," as a favorable specimen of Mr. Melville's graphic powers of description. But we must conclude by strongly recommending "Moby Dick, or the Whale," to all who can appreciate a work of exceeding power, beauty, and genius.

Daily Evening Standard†

HEAR THE "BLUBBER!"—Herman Melville, in his new book on the Whale, *pays* out the following *lines* about the ladies of New Bedford and Salem:

13. Omitted here is a long account of Ch. 91, 337.4–342.16, partly in the form of summaries, but mainly in extended quotations [*Editors' note*].

† New Bedford *Daily Evening Standard*, December 11, 1851.

"The Women of New Bedford bloom like their own red roses. But roses bloom only in summer, whereas the fine carnation of their cheeks is perennial as sunlight in the seventh heavens. Elsewhere match that bloom of theirs, ye cannot, save in Salem, where they tell me the young girls breathe such musk, their sailor sweethearts smell them off shore, as though they were drawing nigh the odorous Moluccas instead of the Puritanic sands."

This is a very handsome compliment to our New Bedford girls, and we presume it is just, but we are sorry Herman "piles on the agony" to so great an extent, as it may make the dear creatures proud. It is very desirable that a woman be pretty, but it is not always well for her to know it.

Christian Freeman†

This is a large book, of more than 600 pages, and takes a wide and diversified scope of descriptive, sketching, anecdote, &c., directly and indirectly connected with the whaling and other seafaring locations and business.

National Intelligencer‡

* * * The professional criticism of the present day has run into channels somewhat remote from that which was once considered its legitimate province. It concerns itself not only with the application of critical rules to the judgment of literary productions, in which alone criticism may be said technically to consist, but has gradually developed itself into essay writing, so that our critical reviews, quarterlies, and similar periodical literature have become serial publications of essays on all literary and scientific subjects, the name and work of some author being taken as a mere caption to the articles, and having no more to do with the subsequent matter than the texts of certain clergymen have with their sermons: thus, instead of a critical analysis of Mr. Tennyson's "Princess," we have an elaborate disquisition on poetry in its nature and essence; instead of a critical examination of Mr. Macaulay's History of England, we are treated to recondite disquisitions on the Philosophy of History, until the periodical review has become a pamphlet of essays or a fragment of the encyclopædia. If we were disposed on the present occasion to follow the example thus set us by our betters, we should forthwith proceed, taking "Moby Dick, or the Whale," as our text, to indite a discourse on cetology. Such, however, is not

† Boston *Christian Freeman and Family Visitor*, December 12, 1851.

‡ Washington *National Intelligencer*, December 16, 1851.

our intention. Nor do we propose, like a veritable devil's advocate, [14] to haul Mr. Herman Melville over the coals for any offences committed against the code of Aristotle and Aristarchus: we have nothing to allege against his admission among the few writers of the present day who give evidence of some originality; but, while disposed to concede to Mr. Melville a palm of high praise for his literary excellencies, we must enter our decided protest against the querulous and cavilling innuendoes which he so much loves to discharge, like barbed and poisoned arrows, against objects that should be shielded from his irreverent wit. On this point we hope it is unnecessary to enlarge in terms of reprehension, further than to say that there are many passages in his last work, as indeed in most that Mr. Melville has written, which "dying he would wish to blot." Neither good taste nor good morals can approve the "forecastle scene," with its maudlin and ribald orgies, as contained in the 40th chapter of "Moby Dick." It has all that is disgusting in Goethe's "Witches' Kitchen," without its genius.

Very few readers of the lighter literature of the day have forgotten, we presume, the impression produced upon their minds of Mr. Melville's earlier publications—Typee and Omoo. They opened to all the circulating library readers an entirely new world. His "Peep at Polynesian Life," during a four months' residence in a valley of the Marquesas, as unfolded in Typee, with his rovings in the "Little Jule" and his rambles through Tahiti, as detailed in Omoo, abound with incidents of stirring adventure and "moving accidents by flood and field," replete with all the charms of novelty and dramatic vividness. He first introduced us to cannibal banquets, feasts of raw fish and *poee-poee*; he first made us acquainted with the sunny glades and tropical fruits of the Typee valley, with its golden lizards among the spear-grass and many colored birds among the trees; with its groves of cocoa-nut, its tattooed savages, and temples of light bamboo. Borne along by the current of his limpid style, we sweep past bluff and grove, wooded glen and valley, and dark ravines lighted up far within by wild waterfalls, while here and there in the distance are seen the white huts of the natives, nestling like birdsnests in clefts gushing with verdure, while off the coral reefs of each sea-girt island the carved canoes of tattooed chieftans dance on the blue waters. Who has forgotten the maiden Fayaway and the faithful Kory-Kory, or the generous Marheyo[,] or the Doctor Long Ghost, that figure in his narratives? So new and interesting were his sketches of life in the South Sea islands that few were able to persuade themselves that his story of adventure was

14. This article opens with a long and charming essay on the critic's role as Devil's Advocate. Since that essay is not properly a review of *Moby-Dick*, we omit the first column and an eighth of the second—nearly half of the entire article [*Editors' note*].

not authentic. We have not time at present to renew the inquiry into their authenticity, though we incline to suspect they were about as true as the sketches of adventures detailed by De Foe in his Robinson Crusoe. The points of resemblance between the inimitable novel of De Foe and the production of Mr. Melville are neither few nor difficult to be traced. In the conduct of his narrative the former displays more of naturalness and *vraisemblance;* the latter more of fancy and invention; and while we rather suspect that Robinson's man Friday will always remain more of a favorite than Kory-Kory among all readers "in their teens," persons of maturer judgment and more cultivated taste will prefer the mingled *bonhommie,* quiet humor, and unstrained pathos which underlie and pervade the graphic narratives of Mr. Melville. Still we are far from considering Mr. Melville a greater artist than Daniel De Foe in the general design of his romantic pictures; for is it not a greater proof of skill in the use of language to be able so to paint the scenes in a narration as to make us forget the narrator in the interests of his subjects? In this, as we think, consists the charm of Robinson Crusoe—a book which every boy reads and no man forgets; the perfect naturalness of the narrative, and the transparent diction in which it is told, have never been equalled by any subsequent writer, nor is it likely that they will be in an age fond of point and pungency.

Mr. Melville is not without a rival in this species of romance-writing, founded on personal adventure in foreign and unknown lands. Dr. Mayo, the author of "Kaloolah" and other works, has opened to us a phantasmagorical view of life in Northern Africa similar to the "peep" which Mr. Melville has given us of the South Sea Islands through his kaleidoscope. Each author has familiarized himself with the localities in which his dramatic exhibition of men and things is enacted, and each have doubtless claimed for themselves a goodly share of that invention which produced the Travels of Gulliver and the unheard-of adventures and exploits of the Baron Munchausen. Framazugda, as painted by Dr. Mayo, is the Eutopia of Negrodom, just as the Typee valley has been called the Eutopia of the Pacific Islands, and Kaloolah is the "counterfeit presentment" of Fayaway.

Moby-Dick, or the Whale, is the narrative of a whaling voyage; and, while we must beg permission to doubt its authenticity in all respects, we are free to confess that it presents a most striking and truthful portraiture of the whale and his perilous capture. We do not imagine that Mr. Melville claims for this his latest production the same historical credence which he asserted was due to "Typee" and "Omoo;" and we do not know how we can better express our conception of his general drift and style in the work under consideration than by entitling it a prose Epic on Whaling. In whatever light it may be viewed, no one can deny it to be the production of a man of genius. The descriptive powers of Mr. Melville are unrivalled, whether the scenes he paints reveal "old ocean into tempest toss'd," or are laid among the bright hillsides of some Pacific island, so warm and undulating that the printed page on which they are so graphically depicted seems almost to palpitate beneath the sun. Language in the hands of this master becomes like a magician's wand, evoking at will "thick-coming fancies," and peopling the "chambers of imagery" with hideous shapes of terror or winning forms of beauty and loveliness. Mr. Melville has a strange power to reach the sinuosities of a thought, if we may so express ourselves; he touches with his lead and line depths of pathos that few can fathom, and by a single word can set a whole chime of sweet or wild emotions into a pealing concert. His delineation of character is actually Shakespearean—a quality which is even more prominently evinced in "Moby Dick" than in any of his antecedent efforts. Mr. Melville especially delights to limn the full-length portrait of a savage, and if he is a cannibal it is all the better; he seems fully convinced that the highest type of man is to be found in the forests or among the anthropophagi of the Fejee Islands. Brighter geniuses than even his have disported on this same fancy; for such was the youthful dream of Burke, and such was the crazy vision of Jean Jacques Rosseau.

The humor of Mr. Melville is of that subdued yet unquenchable nature which spreads such a charm over the pages of Sterne. As illustrative of this quality in his style, we must refer our readers to the irresistibly comic passages scattered at irregular intervals through "Moby Dick;" and occasionally we find in this singular production the traces of that "wild imagining" which throws such a weird-like charm about the Ancient Mariner of Coleridge; and many of the scenes and objects in "Moby Dick" were suggested, we doubt not, by this ghastly rhyme. The argument of what we choose to consider as a sort of prose epic on whales, whalers, and whaling may be briefly stated as follows:

Ishmael, the pseudonymous appellative assumed by Mr. Melville in his present publication, becoming disgusted with the "tame and docile earth," resolves to get to sea in all possible haste, and for this purpose welcomes the whaling voyage as being best adapted to open to his gaze the flood-gates of the oceanic wonder world; the wild conceits that swayed him were two—floating pictures in his soul of whales gliding through the waters in endless processions, and "midst them all one grand hooded phantom, like a snow hill in the air." This "grand hooded phantom," thus preternaturally impressed on his mental retina, proves to be *Moby Dick*, a great white whale, who had long been the terror his "whaling grounds," noted for his invincible ferocity and for a peculiar snow-white wrinkled forehead, and a high pyramidical white hump on his back. It is not, however, his prodigious magnitude, nor his strange white hue, nor his deformed visage that so much invested the monster with unnatural terror, as the unexampled and intelligent malignity which he had repeatedly evinced when attacked by different whalers, so that no turbaned Turk; no hired Venetian or Malay, could smite his foes with more seeming malice. Ishmael embarks on board the whaling vessel "Pequod," whose captain, Ahab, had been previously bereft of a leg in an encounter with the terrible "Moby Dick;" a spirit of moody vindictiveness enters his soul, and he determines to be avenged upon the fell monster that had, with such intelligent and prepense maliciousness, rendered him a cripple for life; the white whale swam before him as the incarnation of all those wicked agencies which some deep men, according to Mr. Melville, feel eating in them, till they are left living on with half a heart and half a lung; in other words, Capt. Ahab became a monomaniac, with the chase and capture of Moby-Dick for his single idea; so that all his powers were thus concentrated and intensified with a thousand-fold more potency than he could have brought to bear on one reasonable object. The "Pequod" encounters Moby Dick, and in the deadly struggle which ensues the whole crew perish save the fortunate Ishmael. On such a slender thread hangs the whole of this ingenious romance, which for variety of incident and vigor of style can scarcely be exceeded.

Morning Chronicle†

When the author of "Omoo and Typee" appeared, we were happy to hail a new and bright star in the firmament of letters. There was vast promise in these finely imagined fictions. Sea stories had been gradually waning in attraction. A vast number of respectable sailors, who never ought to have had their hands blacked in any fluid save tar, were discolouring them in ink. Cooper was not much imitated, but Marryat had a shoal of clumsy followers, who believed that the public liked to read of the most ordinary naval manœuvers told in technical language, and who imagined and let loose upon the world a swarm of *soi-disant* naval characters, who were either weak and conventional, or wildly extravagant and clumsily caricatured. Herman Melville was a man of different mettle: originality—thorough originality—was stamped upon every line he wrote. There never was a fresher author. He took up a new subject,

† London *Morning Chronicle*, December 20, 1851.

and treated it in a new fashion. Round his readers he flung a new atmosphere, and round his fictions a new light. Herman Melville, in fact, gave the world a new sensation: springing triumphantly away from the old scenes of naval romances, abjuring the West Indies, and the English Channel, and the North Sea; recognising as classic ground neither the Common Hard nor Portsmouth Point—treating us to no exciting frigate battles—absolutely repudiating all notion of daring cuttings out of French luggers moored under batteries of tremendous power—never chasing slavers, and never being chased by pirates—inventing no mysterious corsairs, and launching no renowned privateers, Herman Melville flung himself entirely into a new naval hemisphere. The Pacific, with its eternally sunny skies and tranquil seas—the great ocean of the world—with its mysterious inhabitants—its whales, to which the whales of Greenland are babies, and its ships—worn, battered, warped, and faded ships, cruising for months and months, and years and years in that great illimitable flood—its glorious isles, too—ocean Edens—the very gardens of the south, coral girt and palm crowned, set in sparkling surf, smiled over by everlasting summer skies, and fanned by never-dying summer breezes—the birth-place of a happy, mirthful, Epicurean race, living in the balmy air and the tepid seas—pure and beautiful in their wildness, loving and kind, simple and truthful—such was the semi-fairy world into the gorgeous midst of which Herman Melville, like a potent and beneficent magician, hurled his readers. The power and the skill of the new literary enchanter were at once admitted. With a bursting imagination, and an intellect working with muscles which seemed not likely soon to tire, Herman Melville bid high for a high place among the spirits of the age. There never was an author more instinct with the flush of power and the pride of mental wealth. He dashed at his pages and overflowed them with the rushing fulness of his mind. A perception of the picturesque and of the beautiful—equally powerful and equally intense—an imagination of singular force, and capable of calling up the wildest, most vivid, and most gorgeous conceptions, and a genuine, hearty, warm, and genial earnestness—in all he imagined, and in all he wrote—marked Herman Melville, not for a man of talent and a clever writer, but for a genius. And his style was just as thoroughly characteristic. Its strength, its living energy, its abounding vitality, were all his own. He seemed to write like a giant refreshed. He bounded on and on, as if irresistibly impelled by the blast of his own inspiration, and the general happiness of phrase, and the occasional flash of thought rendered in the most deliciously perfect words, were subsidiary proofs of the genuineness of the new powers which addressed the world.

But still, even in the best parts of the best books of the American sailor, there lurked an ominous presence which we hoped would disappear, but which, as we feared, has increased and multiplied. We could not shut our eyes to the fact that constantly before us we saw, like a plague spot, the tendency to rhapsody—the constant leaning towards wild and aimless extravagance, which has since, in so melancholy a degree, overflown, and, so to speak, drowned the human interest—the very possibility of human interest—in so great a portion of Herman Melville's works. First, indeed, there was but a little cloud the size of a man's hand. Unhappily it has overspread the horizon, and the reader stumbles and wanders disconsolately in its gloom. It was in "Mardi" that the storm of extravagance burst fairly forth. The first volume was charming. What could be more poetic, yet life-like, than the picture of the sea-worn whaler, with her crew yearning again for a sight of a clod of dry green land—what finer than the canoe voyage—what more strangely thrilling, yet truth-like, than the falling in with the island schooner, with her grass ropes and cotton sails, drifting with two savages along the sea? So far Melville had held his fine imagination in curb. It had worked legitimately, and worked right well. It had proceeded by the eternal rules of art and the unchanging principles of the truthful and the symmetrical. But with the second volume the curb of judgment is removed. Common sense, which Herman Melville can depose or keep enthroned at will, was driven out by one *coup d'état*, and the two last volumes are melancholy rhodomontade—half raving, half babble—animated only by the outlines of a dull cold allegory, which flits before the reader like a phantom with a veiled face, and a form which is but the foldings of vapour wreaths. You yearn for the world again—for sea and sky and timber—for human flesh, white or brown—for the solid wood of the ship and the coarse canvass of the sail—as did the whaler's crew for land and grass. What are these impalpable shadows to you? What care you for these misty phantoms of an indefinite cloud-land? You want reality—you want truth—you want *vraisemblance*. Close the book—there are none in the last two volumes of "Mardi."

Next, if we remember rightly, came a three-volume series of sketches called "White Jacket." They depicted life on board an American frigate in the Pacific—the severe, and in many points brutal, discipline of a Transatlantic ship of war, elaborated with such daguerreotype exactitude and finish, so swarming with the finest and minutest details, and so studded with little points never to be imagined, that you are irresistibly impelled to the conclusion that, from the first word to the last, every syllable is literal, downright truth. Here Herman Melville rushes into the other extreme from "Mardi." In one he painted visions, in the other he engraves still life. The first is all broad, vague dashes—the second all carefully finished lines. You look at one book, as it were, through a hazy telescope with many coloured glasses—at the other, through a carefully cleaned microscope, which shows you every infinitesimal blister of the tar in the ship's seams—every fibre in a topsail haulyard, and every hair in a topman's whisker. And yet, every now and then, even in the midst of all this Dutch painting, comes a dash at the old fashion of raving. Every now and then a startling chapter lugs you from the forecastle, or the cock-pit, or the cable-tiers, or the very run, up into the highest, bluest Empyrean—you are snatched up from bilge-water to the nectar of the Gods—you are hurried from the consideration of maggots in biscuits, to that of the world beyond the stars or the world before the flood: in one chapter there is a horrifying account of the amputation of a man's leg—in the next you are told how the great mountain peaks of the Andes raised all their organ notes to peal forth hallelujahs on the morning when the world was born.

One other work by Herman Melville divides his wildly extravagant "Mardi" from the little less extravagant fiction before us. It is called, if we remember right, "My First Voyage," and is the literally and strongly told experiences of a sailor boy on his first trip from New York to Liverpool. The work smacks strongly of reality, but it is written in a lower, less buoyant, and less confident key than the earlier fictions. It seemed to us, also, as we read it, that some, at all events, of the virtue of the author had departed, and that he knew it. He walked feebly and groped. The inward sunshine was wanting, and the strong throb of the vigorous brain was neither so full nor so steady as before.

Here, however—in "The Whale"—comes Herman Melville, in all his pristine powers—in all his abounding vigour—in the full swing of his mental energy, with his imagination invoking as strange and wild and original themes as ever, with his fancy arraying them in the old bright and vivid hues, with that store of quaint and out-of-the-way information—we would rather call it reading than learning—which he ever and anon scatters around, in, frequently, unreasonable profusion, with the old mingled opulence and happiness of phrase, and alas! too, with the old extravagance, running a perfect muck throughout the three volumes, raving and rhapsodising in chapter after chapter—unchecked, as it would appear, by the very slightest remembrance of judgment or common sense, and occasionally soaring into such absolute clouds of phantasmal unreason, that we seriously and sorrowfully ask ourselves whether this can be anything other than sheer moonstruck lunacy.

Let us put it to our readers, for example, what they think of the following as the speech of a whaling captain to his crew:—

CAPTAIN AHAB.

"'Drink and pass!' he cried * * * God hunt us all, if we do not hunt Moby Dick to his death!' ["] [Ch. 36, 145.24–146.32.]

But it may be replied that Captain Ahab is represented as being a monomaniac. So be it: but the crew are not, and what is to be thought of such a conversation as the following amongst the hands of a whaler:—

FORECASTLE TALK.

"MATE'S VOICE FROM THE QUARTERDECK.

"Eight bells there forward * * * Thou showest thy black brow, Seeva!" [Ch. 40, 150.1–152.10.]

And so on indefinitely.

But it is high time to inform our readers what they may expect to find in "The Whale." The author tells the story, as usual *in propria persona*. He determines to sail from the harbour of New Bedford on board a whaler, for a four years' cruise in the Pacific. In a sailors' tavern, roughly and powerfully drawn, he is put to sleep with a South Sea Island harpooner, a tatooed cannibal, and a Pagan who worships a wretched little black graven image called Gogo, and in whom Herman recognises a noble and heroic soul—insomuch, indeed, that with certain philosophic mental reservations—he does not scruple to go on his knees to Gogo, set upright in the empty grate as a shrine, and join the orisons of his South Sea acquaintance. As soon as this personage appears, the story assumes that nightmare unreality, and becomes overshadowed by that uncertain looming of imaginative recklessness, which is only here and there dispersed by the intensely-written whaling adventures, and the minute truth of the descriptions not only of the whales themselves, but of the utensils used for capturing them, and the process of cutting up the monsters and extracting the oil. Queequeg, the harpooneer, and Herman Melville embark on board the Pequod, an ancient whaler—a sort of mystic prophet of evil—a strange sepulchral voiced phantom-like man having several times warned them against the voyage in vain. All this, and in fact the entire book, except the portions we have mentioned, reads like a ghost story done with rare imaginative power and noble might of expression. The captain of the Pequod—Captain Ahab—is a mystery of mysterics. He looms out of a halo of terrors—scents prophecies, omens, and auguries. He is an ancient mariner—an ancient whaler—and there seems on him a doom and a curse. His destiny is linked to the destiny of a certain whale—a strange horrible whale—perfectly white—an albino whale, a monster famous since the South Sea fisheries began for his ferocity, his cunning, and his strength. This white whale's name is "Moby Dick." He is held to be hundreds, if not thousands, of years old. He has ploughed the oceans before a sail was set above them. He may have been, for all Captain Ahab knows, the very whale who swallowed Jonah. Well, this whale has Captain Ahab pursued voyage after voyage. This whale he has chased, we know not how many times round the earth; to kill this whale he has devoted all his means, all his energies, all his thoughts in this world, and, so far as we can make out, is supposed to have bartered all his prospects in the next. Often has he encountered it, but Moby Dick bears a charmed life. There are scores and scores of rusted harpoons wedged deeply in his blubber. He trails miles of line behind him, until the hemp rots off and sinks in the brine. He has smashed boats by scores—drowned men by dozens. Every South Sea man knows the "white whale," and, taught by dread experience, gives him a wide berth. The sailors tell dreadful tales of him in the sleepy mid-watch. He is, in fact, a sort of ocean fiend—a tremendous *bogey* of the sea—an apparition which no one seeks but Captain Ahab, whose destiny is bound up in the doomed pursuit. So, then, the Pequod turns her battered bows to the Indian Ocean, and Captain Ahab commences his final hunt of Moby Dick.

The personages introduced as the author's shipmates are even more phantom-like, un-human, and vaguely uninteresting than the Captain. There are three mates—Starbuck, Stubb, and Flash—mere talking shadows—and rare rhapsodies of nonsense they sometimes talk. Queequeg, the Pagan harpooner, is the only flesh and blood like portraiture, and he is little save an animal. A cook and a carpenter, and a half-witted negro called Pip, are absolutely shadows. The voyage out to the whaling grounds is told with all those extraordinary plunges into all manner of historical, allegorical, and metaphysical disquisitions and rhapsodies which distinguish the author; but, mixed up with these, there are very many chapters devoted to the natural history of the whale, containing, in our view, some of the most delightful pages in the book. Herman Melville, we believe, knows more about whales than any man alive, or who ever lived. He seems to have read every page upon the subject of cetology ever written. Theoretic naturalists and practical harpooneers, he has them all at his finger ends, publishing, indeed, as if to show his lore, in an Appendix an extraordinary collection of sentences touching whales, from texts in Genesis down to songs sung by Nantucket harpooneers. Mr. Melville treats our old friend the Greenland, or, as he calls it, the "right whale," with considerable contempt. He is neither fierce nor cunning, and his oil is coarse and of little value. The Sperm whale of the South Sea is declared to be the rightful monarch of the ocean, and the only creature worthy of the deadly iron flung by the brawny arm of a true Nantucketer. The whole tribe of whales, Herman Melville divides into three classes; taking his illustrative titles from the technical language of the book trade, and dividing the blubbery monsters of the deep into folio whales, of which the sperm whale is a type; octavo whales, typified by the grampus and the norwhal; and duodecimo whales, typified by the propoise. Flinging overboard—not, however, by any means after stating satisfactory reasons why—the commonly received hypothesis that a whale is not a fish, as a mere empty and useless mystification—Melville defines a whale to be "any spouting fish with a perpendicular tail," and under that definition he ranges numerous tribes of animals, such as the porpoise, which are not above four feet long. So much for the scientific divisions of whales. Their appearance, their habits, their manner of swimming, diving, breathing, spouting, and so forth, are described in wonderful detail, and with a vivid picturesqueness and freshness of language which brings the mighty animals at once before us. Let anybody who wants to understand the full difference between drawing at once from nature and merely copying from books, contrast one of Herman Melville's descriptions with a page from, say, Goldsmith's "Animated Nature," or any book of the same class. How utterly uneffective and unsatisfactory the cold prosy general truths about the animal described, compared with the bright variety of confident detail into which Melville enters, familiar as he seems with every motion, gesture, and peculiarity of Leviathan, as we are with the dogs and cats of our own fire-side.

Arrived first in the Indian Ocean, the whale hunt begins. We have already quoted the scene in which Captain Ahab makes the crew decide to follow Moby Dick to the death; but the captain is not quite mad enough not to "lower" in pursuit of the other whales which chance to come first in the way. Only the first time the boats are in the water after the cheering cry of "there she spouts," Captain Ahab's boat appears manned by a crew of "Zigo Yellow" and turbanned Manilla men, or Chinese, who then, for the first time, make their appearance, leaping up at the summons from some unknown recess of the ship in which they had hitherto been buried. The steersman of this strange company is a semi-supernatural personage, who prophesies in a mystic way his own death, and then Captain Ahab's, in the last encounter with Moby Dick, and the whole band are looked upon by the whalers as something half demoniac. Turning, however, from the jumble of mysticism and rhapsody with which all that appertains to Captain Ahab is enveloped, we prefer setting before our readers a few extracts from certainly the most vivid accounts of whaling ever written. A magnificent sperm whale is descried, and the boat starts furiously in chace:—

THE KILLING OF THE WHALE.

" 'Start her, start her, my men * * * His heart had burst!" [Ch. 61, 243.4–245.17.]

Wandering here and there, up and down through the trackless wastes of the southern seas, the Pequod pursues her trade of sperm-whale killing; Captain Ahab of course keeping a bright look-out for Moby Dick. Mingling with rhapsodic outbursts about all imaginable subjects, we have masses of vivid detail about whale fishing; dissertations of remarkable interest, on the ocean wanderings of the great leviathans, dependent upon the set of the currents and the drift of their food—"brit," a slimy, yellow, vegetable substance, through which the ship sails for leagues, as through meadows of golden grain, and "squid," a white pulpy mass seemingly of the polypus order—"furlongs and furlongs in length, of a glancing cream colour—innumerable long arms radiating from its surface, and curling and twisting like a nest of anacondas, as if blindly to clutch at any object within reach. No perceptible face or front did it have—no conceivable token of either sensation or instinct, but undulated there on the billows, an unearthly, formless, chancelike apparition of life." This substance, or animal, is imagined by whalemen to be the largest living thing in the ocean, and to furnish its sole food to the sperm whale; and Herman Melville hazards the conjecture that "squid" is no more or less than the kraken of good old Bishop Pontoppidan. The substance is so seldom seen on the surface, that its appearance is reckoned ominous. "The great live squid," says one of the mates, "which few whale ships ever beheld and returned to their ports to tell of it." Then we have pleasant details of "gamming," that is of the visits paid by one whale crew to another on the ocean, wild legends told by dark midwatches of battles with whales, and desperate mutinies thousands of miles from land. Then the author will suddenly start into a consideration of the "honour and glory of whale fishing"—next, perhaps, into a wild and whirling rhapsody on the origin of whales—on the huge monsters of the sea contemporary with the mastodons and the megatheria of the pre-adamite world—anon he will discourse greatly and learnedly upon the anatomy of the whale—next, perhaps, he will take to discussing all known pictures of the whale, or to smashing all theories of stay-at-home cetologists.

After a chapter on the excellence of whale steaks, and the perfect possibility of enjoying a blubber supper, we may look out for one chapter of critical inquiry into the history of Jonah, followed, perhaps, by a sort of prose pœan upon the delights of squeezing half congealed sperm oil with the bare hands. To form anything like an idea of this strange conglomeration of fine description, reckless fancy, rhapsodic mistiness, and minute and careful Dutch painting, the book itself must be referred to. We can only give a faint and outlined idea of its strange contents. After passing through the Straits of Sunda, an immense herd or school of whales is descried. The boat in which Herman Melville pulls an oar is forced by the frantic motions of the bewildered creatures into the centre of the squadron—the grand armada the author calls it—in which are swimming the females and young ones of the herd. The following is a magnificent piece of painting:—

THE BABY WHALE.

"Now, inclusive of the occasional wide intervals * * * deep down and deep inland there I still bathe me in eternal mildness of joy." [Ch. 87, 324.41–326.18.]

We could fill a whole page with extracts, but we forbear. We have already given one of the harpooning scenes, and we will add to it a very minute and curious account of the management of the whale line, showing how it so often sweeps an unwary or an unlucky man overboard:—

THE WHALE LINE.

"The whale line is only two-thirds of an inch in thickness * * * where the all-seeming sun himself could never pierce you out." [Ch. 60, 238.36–241.2.]

At length, deep in the third volume, Moby Dick is descried. Ship after ship had been met with, and battered boats, and maimed and drowned men have told of her [their?] conflicts with the fearful whale. Captain Ahab's delirium waxes to its full fury. The enemy of his life, and the destroyer of his reason, Moby Dick, is before him. For three days he chases the fated whale. Twice is his boat smashed, and he himself rescued by a miracle. His crew would fain flee from the monster; but it is not to be. Captain Ahab fascinates them. They all obey him, as enchanted men a charm. His Manilla men pull him like fiends, and work his will as imps obey a conjuror. On the second day, Fedallah prophesies that Captain Ahab will be killed by hemp, after he has seen two hearses—one of them made of American wood. This extraordinary prediction is thus fulfilled—Fedallah, carried over by a hitch of the line, is lost. The next day his body is seen borne by Moby Dick upon his back, enveloped in twisted whale lines. This is hearse the first. Then comes the last attack. Moby Dick, wounded by the harpoon of Captain Ahab, suddenly rushes, not at the boat, but at the ship, and smiting it with his vast forehead, crushes in its bows. The sinking Pequod is hearse the second, and, of course, made of American wood. As Ahab sees his foundering ship, and knows that the white whale has conquered, he bursts out into one of his delirious rhapsodies, and with this, and the magnificent piece of writing describing the disappearance of the whale-ship, we close our notice of this strange and unaccountable book:—

THE LAST OF AHAB.

" 'I turn my body from the sun * * * and the great shroud of the sea rolled on as it rolled five thousand years ago." [Ch. 135, 468.21–469.32.]

New Quarterly Review†

It will be fresh in the memory of our readers that an account lately appeared in the morning papers of the demolition of sundry boats and the destruction of a goodly vessel (the Ann Alexander, of New Bedford), in consequence of the terrific and successive onslaughts upon them of an indomitable South Sea whale.

Punch poetically and pathetically narrated the details of the sad disaster. The *Illustrated News* graphically represented the scene of fearful demolition, and all London for four-and-twenty hours was aghast at the frightful catastrophe.

The fearful event only occurred on the 20th of last August (in lat. 5 deg. 50 min. S., long. 102 deg. W.), and yet already has Mr. Bentley, with the assistance of that prolific writer Mr. Herman Melville, presented the public with a three-volume novel, of which the above incident forms the entire plot! Many, doubtless, will cavil at the application of the term "novel" to such a production as this, seeing that no tale of love is interwoven with the strange ana of which it is compounded. Still we cannot trouble ourselves to devise for it a happier term.

The characters are rough and ungentle in the extreme, and consist almost entirely of the crew of a Yankee whaler the Pequod, and her skipper one Captain Ahab—a strange incomprehensible being he is. Nearly the whole of his life has been passed upon the ocean, and chiefly on the whaling grounds of the South Pacific. On one occasion in his youth he had the misfortune, in a conflict with a monster of the deep, to lose one of his nether limbs. "It was," to

† London *New Quarterly Review*, First Quarter, 1852.

use our author's own terms, "devoured, chewed up, crunched, by the monstrousest parmacetty that ever chipped a boat." Enraged at this misadventure, he vows eternal vengeance against the redoubtable whale who caused it. The whale, it seems, is one of notoriously bad character, about the worst in fact of any known in the Antarctic regions; the havoc he has occasioned among ships, boats, and their crews, are fearful to peruse—all stand in awe of Moby Dick (the sobriquet he has received), but Captain Ahab, who, during a long series of years, has been animated by one hope only—that of vengeance and the destruction of his foe. At the commencement of his last voyage he impresses this strongly upon his men:—

MOBY DICK.

"Aye, aye! it was that accursed white whale that razeed me; made a poor pegging lubber of me for ever and a day!" Then tossing both arms, with measureless imprecations he shouted out: "Aye, aye! and I'll chase him round Good Hope, and round the Horn, and round the Norway Maelstrom, and round perdition's flames, before I give him up. And this is what ye have shipped for, men! to chase that white whale on both sides of land, and over all sides of earth, till he spouts black blood and rolls fin out. What say ye, men, will ye splice hands on it, now? I think ye do look brave."

"Aye, aye!" shouted the harpooners and seamen, running closer to the excited old man: "A sharp eye for the White Whale; a sharp lance for Moby Dick!"

After a long voyage, during which we have sundry digressions concerning the nature, attributes, and physical properties of whales, interspersed with wild rhapsodies from the crack-brained captain, and dissertations upon a variety of topics, Moby Dick is descried in all his glory basking in the morning sun. A three days' chase ensues. A mortal encounter takes place. All the boats are crunched by the monster's jaws—men are slain; the whale has for a moment retired pierced with harpoons and lances, and interlaced with an inextricable network of tangled lines:—

THE FINAL CATASTROPHE

From the ship's bows, nearly all the seamen now hung inactive * * * then all collapsed, and the great shroud of the sea rolled on as it rolled five thousand years ago. [Ch. 135, 468.2.–469.32.]

Such is the melancholy termination of Captain Ahab and of Mr. Herman Melville's whaling narrative. As there was no survivor of the catastrophe, how became the author or Mr. Bentley possessed of all these minute and painful details? We shall not be surprised to find the whole shortly reproduced as an Adelphi melodrama, with Paul Bedford nightly impersonating Moby Dick.

Southern Quarterly Review†

In all those portions of this volume which relate directly to the whale, his appearance in the oceans which he inhabits; his habits, powers and peculiarities; his pursuit and capture; the interest of the reader will be kept alive, and his attention fully rewarded. We should judge, from what is before us, that Mr. Melville has as much personal knowledge of the whale as any man living, and is better able, than any man living, to display this knowledge in print. In all the scenes where the whale is the performer or the sufferer, the delineation and action are highly vivid and exciting. In all other respects, the book is sad stuff, dull and dreary, or ridiculous. Mr. Melville's Quakers are the wretchedest dolts and drivellers, and his Mad Captain, who pursues his personal revenges against the fish who has taken off his leg, at the expense of ship, crew and owners, is a monstrous bore, whom Mr. Melville has no way helped, by enveloping him in a sort of mystery. His ravings, and the ravings of some of the tributary characters, and the ravings of Mr. Melville himself, meant for eloquent declamation, are such as would justify a writ *de lunatico* against all the parties.

Bentley's‡

In the earlier portion of his yet brief career, there was much questioning whether Herman Melville was a man of genius or not. There was something so new in the author's style, and in the sentiments it clothed, that sundry decision-loving critics hesitated not to pronounce him a charlatan, whilst the more cautious or sager veterans shook their heads with a world of meaning in the motion, or demurely suspended their opinion. It is ever thus when a man of original genius appears before the public. As it was with Byron, so was it with Kean. Accordingly, "Let us wait and see what Herman Melville will do next," remarked some, and others authoritatively cried out, "There is nothing more to be expected from him: his bolt is shot."

But his bolt was not shot, neither had he but one bolt, or if so, he knew how to recover it again. His genius is not the sole arrow of a foolish archer; it is more like the Australian boomerang, which, with whatever force it may be thrown, comes back to the hand of its possessor.

We always had faith in the genius of Herman Melville, or rather, we had eyes to see it. Who could not perceive the fine

† Charleston, South Carolina, *Southern Quarterly Review*, January, 1852.

‡ London *Bentley's Miscellany*, January, 1852.

things (and how thickly studded they were!) in Omoo and Typhee, and Mardi—who except those mightily critical connoisseurs who, detecting faults at a glance, proposed to discover beauties by shutting one eye, that they might direct a keener glance with the other, and by a mistake—arising haply from over-eagerness—closed both.

The foregoing remarks have been suggested by a perusal of Melville's last work, "The Whale," which is certainly one of the most remarkable books that has appeared for many years past. It is, however, a performance of which no brief, and at the same time intelligible, description can be rendered. Who, in a few sentences can supply such a summary of the mental and physical qualities of Captain Ahab, as shall distinctly present to the mind's eye of the reader that extraordinary character? The one over-mastering passion of the man—his furious hatred of the white whale, Moby Dick,—through what scenes of grandeur and of beauty that monomania impels him; to what encounters it leads—what catastrophe it precipitates; who is to tell in a score or two of lines? There are descriptions in this book of almost unrivalled force, coloured and warmed as they are, by the light and heat of a most poetical imagination, and many passages might be cited of vigorous thought, of earnest and tender sentiment, and of glowing fancy, which would at once suffice to show—contest or dispute about the matter being out of the question—that Herman Melville is a man of the truest and most original genius.

Harper's†

Herman Melville's last work, *Moby Dick*, or *The Whale*, has excited a general interest among the critical journals of London. The bold and impulsive style of some portions of the book, seems to shock John Bull's fastidious sense of propriety. One of the most discriminating reviewals we have seen is from the *London Atlas*: "In some respects we hold it to be his (Mr. Melville's) greatest effort. In none of his previous works are finer or more highly-soaring imaginative powers put forth. In none of them are so many profound and fertile and thoroughly original veins of philosophic speculation, or rather, perhaps, philosophic fancy struck. . . . . . Upon the whale, its mysteries, and its terrors, he revels as if the subject had enchantment for him. He pours into multitudinous chapters a mass of knowledge touching the whale—its habits and its history—the minutest details of its feeding or sporting, or swimming, strangely mixed with ingenious and daring speculations on the mysterious habits and peculiarities of the great brute—the

† New York *Harper's New Monthly Magazine*, January, 1852.

whole written in a tone of exaltation and poetic sentiment, which has a strange effect upon the reader's mind, in refining and elevating the subject of discourse, and, at last, making him look upon the whale as a sort of awful and unsoluble mystery—the most strange and the most terrible of the wonders of the deep. That Herman Melville knows more about whales than any man from Jonah down, we do really believe."

Hunt's†

Those who expect to find an agreeable and entertaining volume in this will not be disappointed. In some parts it may be rather diffuse, but as a whole it will be read with gratification. The Whale forms the subject of it; in connection with it is introduced character and scenes of that peculiar kind which impart so much life and spirit to this author's works.

Knickerbocker‡

Some years ago there appeared in the KNICKERBOCKER a long and wonderful story, '*Mocha-Dick, of the Pacific*,' a mountainous old whale, that used to loom up like an island in the midst of the sea, and when approached, was observed to be trailing the lines of countless harpoons, which streamed like horrid hair, green with sea-slime and knotted with barnacles, from his sides. Under the title of '*Moby-Dick*' Mr. MELVILLE has taken up this whale, and made him the subject of one of his characteristic and striking romances. His ocean-pictures are exceedingly graphic. Indeed, his descriptions of taking the whale are a succession of moving pictures; the detail bringing out every point of light and shadow with wonderful effect.

Methodist Quarterly Review§

"*Moby-Dick; or the Whale*," (New-York: Harper & Brothers, 1851; 12mo., pp. 634), is the latest effusion of HERMAN MELVILLE's versatile genius. It is a wonderful mixture of fact and fancy—of information about the whale and its habits, and of the wildest whimsies of a seething brain. The book displays the same power of dashing description, of vivid picture-painting, which characterizes all the other works of this writer. We are bound to say, however, that the book contains a number of flings at religion, and

† New York *Hunt's Merchants' Magazine and Commercial Review*, January, 1852.

‡ New York *Knickerbocker Magazine*, January, 1852.

§ New York *Methodist Quarterly Review*, January, 1852.

even of vulgar immoralities that render it unfit for general circulation. We regret that Mr. Melville should allow himself to sink so low.

United States Magazine†

Mr. Melville is evidently trying to ascertain how far the public will consent to be imposed upon. He is gauging, at once, our gullibility and our patience. Having written one or two passable extravagancies, he has considered himself privileged to produce as many more as he pleases, increasingly exaggerated and increasingly dull. The field from which his first crops of literature were produced, has become greatly impoverished, and no amount of forcing seems likely to restore it to its pristine vigor. In bombast, in caricature, in rhetorical artifice—generally as clumsy as it is ineffectual—and in low attempts at humor, each one of his volumes has been an advance upon its predecessors, while, in all those qualities which make books readable, it has shown a decided retrogression from former efforts. Mr. Melville never writes naturally. His sentiment is forced, his wit is forced, and his enthusiasm is forced. And in his attempts to display to the utmost extent his powers of "fine writing," he has succeeded, we think, beyond his most sanguine expectations.

The truth is, Mr. Melville has survived his reputation. If he had been contented with writing one or two books, he might have been famous, but his vanity has destroyed all his chances of immortality, or even of a good name with his own generation. For, in sober truth, Mr. Melville's vanity is immeasurable. He will either be first among the book-making tribe, or he will be nowhere. He will centre all attention upon himself, or he will abandon the field of literature at once. From this morbid self-esteem, coupled with a most unbounded love of notoriety, spring all Mr. Melville's efforts, all his rhetorical contortions, all his declamatory abuse of society, all his inflated sentiment, and all his insinuating licentiousness.

"Typee" was undoubtedly a very proper book for the parlor, and we have seen it in company with "Omoo," lying upon tables from which Byron was strictly prohibited, although we were unable to fathom those niceties of logic by which one was patronized, and the other proscribed. But these were Mr. Melville's triumphs. "Redburn" was a stupid failure, "Mardi" was hopelessly dull, "White Jacket" was worse than either; and, in fact, it was such a very bad book, that, until the appearance of "Moby Dick," we had set it down as the very ultimatum of weakness to which its author could attain. It seems, however, that we were mistaken.

† New York *United States Magazine and Democratic Review*, January, 1852.

We have no intention of quoting any passages just now from "Moby Dick." The London journals, we understand, "have bestowed upon the work many flattering notices," and we should be loth to combat such high authority. But if there are any of our readers who wish to find examples of bad rhetoric, involved syntax, stilted sentiment and incoherent English, we will take the liberty of recommending to them this precious volume of Mr. Melville's.

Peterson's†

Those who have read "Typee," and "Mardi," and can imagine a book compounded of the two, will have as correct an idea of this work as it is possible for a critic to give. Regarded in one light it is a skilfully told narrative of sea-adventures: viewed in another it is a philosophical romance. We confess that we like it best in its former aspect. Had the story been compressed one-half, and all the transcendental chapters omitted, it would have been decidedly the best sea-novel in the English language. No man can serve two masters, even in fiction; and Mr. Melville, by attempting it, has spoilt his book. Still the demerit of "Moby-Dick" is only comparative. It is not an indifferent work, but a very superior one, after all. In describing the chase and capture of a whale, or any other stirring incident of Ocean life, the author displays even more than his usual powers. The concluding chapters of the volume, representing the attempt to destroy the great white whale, from whom the book is named, are really beyond rivalry. It is somewhat remarkable that the catastrophe of the novel, a ship run down by a whale, has been verified, within a few months, in the Pacific, and that the intelligence of so extraordinary a feat reached the United States the very week the work went to press. In conclusion, we would add, that nowhere can so authentic an account of the habits of the whale be found, as in this volume.

To-day‡

We have always hailed with joy the announcement of a new book by Mr. Melville whenever it has occurred since the time when we read his first book "Typee," upon its appearance. But the expectations of pleasure excited by the memory of that book have always been disappointed as we have read those which have followed from the same pen. In fact the merit of Mr. Melville's books has decreased almost in the order of their publication; "Omoo," and "Mardi," were certainly each inferior to its predecessor; and "Redburn" and "White-Jacket" in comparison with "Typee" hardly

† Philadelphia *Peterson's Magazine,* January, 1852.

‡ *To-day: A Boston Literary Journal,* January 10, 1852.

deserve to be mentioned. Perhaps the cause of our repeated disappointment has been that we over-rated "Typee." Our interest in that remarkable book, its exciting incidents and beautiful descriptions was increased by its faithfulness even in slight particulars to what we knew was true with regard to the island where its scene was laid. Or perhaps the extraordinary success of that book caused the author to feel too secure in his laurels and to neglect too much his subsequent literary labors.

The book before us is a new disappointment. It is a curious mixture of fact and fancy; of statistical and historical statements about the whale and the whale fishery, and a fictitious narrative of the adventures of a young man of unsettled habits and roving disposition, who embarks in a whale ship from Nantucket. Over this mixture is thrown a veil of a sort of dreamy philosophy and indistinct speculation just sufficient to obscure the value of the facts stated, and which in our opinion does not improve the quality of the tale.

The hero is named Ishmael, and as he tells his story in the first person it has the charming accessory of apparent reality which characterizes this sort of writing, and which cannot but make the reader feel that his author has experienced what he writes about. Moby Dick is the name of a whale. The closest companion of Ishmael in his voyage, is a half-civilized New Zealand cannibal named Queepeg. Some of the descriptions of their adventures are narrated inimitably and are almost sufficient to excuse any faults in other parts of the book. Yet the humor of those parts where sacred things are made light of—as for instance, the scene in which the hero joins his pagan friend in worshipping an idol and defends his course by half a page of wretched sophistry, is revolting to good taste, and may still, we fear, be dangerous to many of those persons who will be likely to read the book.

The parts of the book which come under its second title, "The Whale," would be of much value if their connexion with other parts of so totally different a character did not cast a shade of uncertainty over their accuracy.—The history of the Whale Fishery, is very remarkable and is particularly interesting to Americans. Belonging entirely to modern times, it has increased in this country from the 304 vessels of 27,840 tons, employing 4059 seamen, which there were in Massachusetts alone, between 1771 and 1775, (according to Mr. Jefferson's report to Congress) to 650 vessels, of 200,000 tons, employing 17,500 seamen, in 1844; the vessels costing at the time of sailing *twenty millions* of dollars, consuming annually $3,845,500, and importing in the same time $7,000,000 worth of oil and whalebone. These last statistics we gather from a report made by Mr. Grinnell, of Massachusetts, to Congress in 1844. We have seen no later authentic statistics, which are so full, although Mr. Melville gives a sort of summary of these same numbers apparently without date or authority, on page 120, as representing the present state of things. It is this loose way of stating matters as facts that we object to. Nevertheless there is doubtless much of value in the account of the Whale in this book; and the form in which it is given, mixed with the events of the story, may perhaps attract more readers than a professed matter-of-fact history.

The book appears to us rather drawn out, and could easily afford considerable paring down. This is particularly prominent when we observe its bulky and uncouth size; 635 pages making an ugly volume. It was not our intention however, on the whole, to speak disparagingly of it. Its defects strike us as glaring only when we compare them with its beauties, and with the original work of the same author. There are enough fine and valuable passages in it to amply repay its perusal.

Dublin University Magazine†

From such scenes and such personages,[15] the transition to the book we now proceed to notice is rather violent than otherwise; but we enter into a more healthy region, and we trust the reaction will not be too much for the nature of our readers; on the contrary, we hope and trust it may be of use to them. We are now, it will be observed, upon the high seas in a whaling vessel, bound from Nantucket, whither we cannot even guess. In truth, it is many a long day since it has been our fate to peruse a more extraordinary book than Mr. Melville's. The title is a strange one, but the work is as strange as the title. All the rules which have been hitherto understood to regulate the composition of works of fiction are despised and set at naught. Of narrative, properly so called, there is little or none; of love, or sentiment, or tenderness of any sort, there is not a particle whatever; and yet, with all these glaring defects, it would be in vain to deny that the work has interest. The opening is sufficiently surprising to startle the reader into going a little farther, if only for the purpose of seeing what can possibly come next. A man, who must be a gentleman and a person of education, or he never could have described the scenes as he does—for the book is in an autobiographical form—having a headache, and being otherwise "poorly" and indisposed in his general health, resolves, "ut mos est," we mean as his habit was, whenever he felt himself out of order, to take a voyage in a whaling vessel, and, throwing physic to the dogs, trust to the bracing sea-air for the recovery of his

† *Dublin University Magazine*, February, 1852.

15. The reference is to the previous book in this series of reviews ("A Budget of Novels")—Mrs. Trollope's *Mrs. Mathews; or, Family Mysteries*, which the reviewer thought salacious and contrived [*Editors' note*].

health. Well, he arrives at some town the name of which we forget, but a place frequented by whalers, and where he is likely to hear of a vessel which will suit his purpose. He puts up at a little inn, is informed by the landlord that the house is so full he can only offer him half of a bed, the residue of which is in the occupation of a gentleman who is a "harpooner." The guest, after a little demurring, accedes to the quaint proposition. He retires to his allotted chamber, tucks himself comfortably in among the blankets, falls asleep, is wakened shortly after midnight by an appalling noise, starts up, and finds himself in bed with—what, dear reader, do you think?—why, neither more nor less than a cannibal! This scene is so naïve, so extraordinary, and told withal in a style so graphic and full of humour, that we shall give it in Mr. Melville's own words:—

> "I lay perfectly still, and resolved not to say a word until spoken to. * * * I sung out—I could not help it now; and giving a sudden grunt of astonishment, he began feeling me." [Ch. 3, 28.28–31.7, condensed, mainly by the omission of 30.4–30.39.]

The hero of the story, if we can call the author the hero, and this strange savage, become excellent friends, and having in due time embarked on board the Pequod of Nantucket, sail forth upon their eventful cruize, in search, as it would subsequently appear, of a tremendous white-sperm whale, the terror of the seas, whose name is Moby Dick. In a previous encounter with this awful monster of the great deep, the captain of the Pequod had lost his leg; he had had it replaced, not by a wooden one, as is usual in such cases, but by a limb of veritable ivory, made out of the jaw bone of an interesting member of the same cetacious family whereof Moby Dick the indomitable appeared to be the head. This huge whale had been seen at various times in various seas, disporting himself after the fashion of his kind, but stuck all over with the harpoons of his varied assailants, as a pincushion might be full of pins. To the destruction of this leviathan the future life of the disabled captain of the Pequod is resolutely devoted. He pursues his enemy with a species of savage pertinacity which can scarcely be described. We will venture to assert that the immortal Nelson never hunted down a French frigate, in the heyday of his nautical reputation, with more determined energy than Ahab, commander of the Pequod, sailed after the white whale. He caught him at last, it is true, but if he did he caught a Tartar. There were, as well as we recollect, three distinct fights, in each of which the whale routed his assailant, and in the last, after capsizing the boats despatched in pursuit of him, ran a muck, Tartar fashion, right to the persecuting whaler, and seizing the vessel in his mouth, as a schoolboy of tender years would a cherry, smashed her to pieces with a single bite, and so down went the Pequod with all hands on board, her flags flying to the last. In this way terminates a story, which, to say the least of it, is somewhat singular. There is one point we can scarcely fail to notice, which seems, somehow, to have escaped the notice of the author. It is simply this: he sailed, as we have already intimated, in the ill-fated Pequod; he was present at those scenes which he so vividly described, or else he could not have described them at all; he must also necessarily have been present, too, at the final catastrophe, or how could he have known anything about it?—and if he was present when the whale smashed the ship to pieces, capsized the boats, and drowned every mother's son among the crew, how does it happen that the author is alive to tell the story? Eh! Mr. Melville, answer that question, if you please, Sir. We believe you to be an American, we have always heard so at least; were it not so, we should certainly have taken you for a countryman of our own. But badinage apart, this book, strange as it is, contains some scenes of stirring interest; and scattered through its motley pages the reader will find more curious and varied information about the whale, its habits, manners, morals, oil, blubber, feeding, swimming, mode of chasing, and harpooning, and cutting up, than in any other treatise, probably, extant. One extract from a battle scene, before we pass on to "pastures new:"—

> "Like noiseless nautilus shells their light prows sped through the sea; but only slowly they neared the foe. * * * And as he thus vainly strove, the jaw slipped from him, the frail gunwale collapsed and snapped, as both jaws, like an enormous shears, sliding further aft, bit the craft completely in twain, and locked themselves fast again in the sea midway between the two floating wrecks, and there floated aside, the broken ends drooping, the crew at the stern-wreck clinging to the gunwale, and striving to hold fast by the oars to lash them across." [Ch. 133, 447.10–449.30, slightly condensed.]

De Bow's Southern and Western Review†

This is another of the attractive series of sea stories, by Mr. Melville, which embraces, "Typee," "Omoo," "Redburn," "Mardi," &c. The English critics are extravagant in their praises of them. Blackwood declares that, after reading these, all other sea stories must appear flat and unprofitable. The Times thinks they will ever have greedy devourers. Douglas Jerrold finds in them much of the charm which has made Robinson Crusoe immortal—life-like description, &c. Speaking of Mardi, the Literary World, New-York,

† New Orleans *De Bow's Southern and Western Review,* February, 1851.

says, "There is a world of poetical, thoughtful, ingenious, moral writing in it, exhibiting the most various reflection and reading.["][16] It is impossible not to be hurried away delightfully with the author from chapter to chapter of his most attractive books. New-York: Harper & Brothers. New-Orleans: J. C. Morgan.

Godey's†

This is what is called a compact volume of upwards of six hundred pages, all about "the whale," whalers, and whaling, being itself a perfect literary whale, and worthy of the pen of Herman Melville, whose reputation as an original writer has been established the world over.

Graham's‡

This volume sparkles with the raciest qualities of the author's voluble and brilliant mind, and whatever may be its reception among old salts, it will be sure of success with the reading public generally. It has passages of description and narration equal to the best that Melville has written, and its rhetoric revels and riots in scenes of nautical adventure with more than usual glee and gusto. The style is dashing, headlong, strewn with queer and quaint ingenuities moistened with humor, and is a capital specimen of deliberate and felicitous recklessness, in which a seeming helter-skelter movement is guided by real judgment. The whole work beams with the analogies of a bright and teeming fancy—a faculty that Melville possesses in such degree that it sometimes betrays his rhetoric into fantastic excesses, and gives a sort of unreality to his most vivid descriptions. The joyous vigor and elasticity of his style, however, compensate for all faults, and even his tasteless passages bear the impress of conscious and unwearied power. His late books are not only original in the usual sense, but evince originality of nature, and convey the impression of a new individuality, somewhat composite, it is true, but still giving to the jaded reader of every-day publications that pleasant shock of surprise which comes from a mental contact with a character at once novel and vigorous.

Harper's §

A late number of the *London Leader* in a review of HERMAN MELVILLE's *Moby Dick, or the Whale,* says, "Want of originality has long been the just and standing reproach to American litera-

16. The reviewer picked up his critical quotations from the ads for *Omoo* and *Mardi* bound in the back of the Harper edition of *Moby-Dick*.

† Philadelphia *Godey's Magazine and Lady's Book*, February, 1852.

‡ Philadelphia *Graham's Magazine*, February, 1852.

§ New York *Harper's New Monthly Magazine*, April, 1852.

ture; the best of its writers were but second-hand Englishmen. Of late some have given evidence of originality; not *absolute* originality, but such genuine outcoming of the American intellect as can be safely called national. Edgar Poe, Nathaniel Hawthorne, and Herman Melville are assuredly no British offshoots; nor is Emerson—the *German* American that he is! The observer of this commencement of an American literature, properly so called, will notice as significant that these writers have a wild and mystic love of the super-sensual, peculiarly their own. To move a horror skillfully, with something of the earnest faith in the Unseen, and with weird imagery to shape these phantasms so vividly that the most incredulous mind is hushed, absorbed—to do this no European pen has apparently any longer the power—to do this American literature is without a rival. What *romance* writer can be named with HAWTHORNE? Who knows the horrors of the seas like HERMAN MELVILLE?"

Burial, Disinterment, and Revival

1853–1925

E.-D. FORGUES

La Chasse à la Baleine†

* * * Est-ce un roman, est-ce un livre positif, plein de souvenirs et de réalité, que nous avons tenté de résumer en quelques pages? D'autres que nous décideront cette question. L'auteur, M. Herman Melville, est un des conteurs les plus populaires aux États-Unis. En Angleterre même, quelques-uns de ses livres ont obtenu depuis quelques années une certaine vogue; les premiers surtout (*Typee* et *Omoo*), peintures animés des moeurs insulaires polynésiennes, venant à paraître au moment où les luttes de la Grande-Bretagne et de la France, relativement au protectorat des îles Marquises, préoccupaient l'attention publique, participèrent de la popularité acquise alors aux déportemens du missionnaire Pritchard et de la grande reine Pomaré.

Une fois en possesion d'une renommée qui lui donnait libre carrière, M. Herman Melville en a profité pour étendre le champ de ses conquêtes littéraires, et, comme tant d'autres, revendiquer les bénéfices en même temps que les dangers d'une individualité et d'une originalité plus complètement accusées. Nous ne l'en blâmerions point, il s'en faut, si, dans l'essor trop peu modéré qu'il a pris ainsi, il ne nous semblait s'être aventuré un peu plus loin que de raison. Sa verve incontestable, la valeur pittoresque de son style, l'imprévu de ses conceptions, gagneraient, selon nous, à être maintenus sous le contrôle d'un bon sens plus rigoureux, d'un goût plus épuré; puis, comme Nathaniel Hawthorne, auquel est dédié l'ouvrage que nous venons d'analyser, M. Herman Melville s'est imbu, peut-être plus qu'il ne faudrait, de la prestigieuse philosophie dont Emerson est l'apôtre inspiré. Cette philosophie, nous la goûtons et nous l'adoptons très-volontiers dans ses origines comme dans ses conclusions, mais avec cette réserve cependant, qu'elle ne vienne pas, se mêlant aux réalités de l'ordre le plus positif,—par exemple à des récits de pêche,—introduire des créations purement allégoriques (fantastiques si l'on veut) au milieu de créatures en chair et en os que le voisinage de ces fantômes finit par dénaturer étrangement.

Nous pensons aussi que M. Herman Melville eût gagné à ne point user autant de ces excentricités purement extérieures qui consistent dans une grande prodigalité de titres bizarres, de digressions inattendues de bibliographie à contre-temps, d'érudition superflue. Il avait assez de talent naturel, d'esprit *argent comptant*, d'inven-

† From E.-D. Forgues, "La Chasse à la Baleine," the Paris *Revue des Deux Mondes*, Vol. 1 (Feb., 1853), 491–515; the quotation is from 514–15.

tion réelle pour dédaigner ces semblans dont on a trop abusé à notre époque. Cependant, avec ces réserves, nous n'hésitons pas à reconnaitre que l'auteur de *Redburn, Mardi, White-Jacket* et de *the Whale* s'est placé à un rang distingué parmi les romanciers américains qui continuent de nos jours, Brockden Brown, Washington Irwing et Fenimore Cooper.

FITZ-JAMES O'BRIEN

[Interregnum of Nonsense]†

Mr. Melville does not improve with time. His later books are a decided falling off, and his last scarcely deserves naming; this however we scarce believe to be an indication of exhaustion. Keats says beautifully in his preface to Endymion, that "The imagination of a boy is healthy, and the mature imagination of a man is healthy, but there is a space of life between, in which the soul is in a ferment, the character undecided, the way of life uncertain, the ambition thick-sighted."

Just at present we believe the author of Pierre to be in this state of ferment. Typee, his first book, was healthy; Omoo nearly so; after that came Mardi, with its excusable wildness; then came Moby Dick, and Pierre with its inexcusable insanity. We trust that these rhapsodies will end the interregnum of nonsense to which Keats refers, as forming a portion of every man's life; and that Mr. Melville will write less at random and more at leisure, than of late.

"SIR NATHANIEL"

[Maniacal Style and Furibund Story]‡

For so successful a trader in "marine stories" as Mr. Melville, "The Whale" seemed a speculation every way big with promise. From such a master of his harpoon might have been expected a prodigious hit. There was about blubber and spermaceti something unctuously suggestive, with him for whaleman. And his three volumes entitled "The Whale" undoubtedly contain much vigorous description, much wild power, many striking details. But the effect

† From Fitz-James O'Brien, "Our Young Authors—Melville," *Putnam's Monthly*, Vol. 1 (Feb., 1853), 155–64; the quotation is from 163.

‡ From "Sir Nathaniel," "American Authorship, No. IV.—Herman Melville," London *New Monthly Magazine*, Vol. 98 (July, 1853), 300–308; the quotation is from 307–8.

is distressingly marred throughout by an extravagant treatment of the subject. The style is maniacal—mad as a March hare—mowing, gibbering, screaming, like an incurable Bedlamite, reckless of keeper or strait-waistcoat. Now it vaults on stilts, and performs *Bombastes Furioso* with contortions of figure, and straining strides, and swashbuckler fustian, far beyond *Pistol* in that Ancient's happiest mood. Now it is seized with spasms, acute and convulsive enough to excite bewilderment in all beholders. When he pleases, Mr. Melville can be so lucid, straightforward, hearty, and unaffected, and displays so unmistakable a shrewdness, and satirical sense of the ridiculous, that it is hard to suppose that *he* can have indited the rhodomontade to which we allude. Surely the man is a Doppelganger—a dual number incarnate (singular though he be, in and out of all conscience):—surely he is two single gentlemen rolled into one, but retaining their respective idiosyncrasies—the one sensible, sagacious, observant, graphic, and producing admirable matter—the other maundering, drivelling, subject to paroxysms, cramps, and total collapse, and penning exceeding many pages of unaccountable "bosh." So that in tackling every new chapter, one is disposed to question it beforehand, "Under which king, Bezonian?"—the sane or the insane; the constitutional and legitimate, or the absolute and usurping? Writing of Leviathan, he exclaims, "Unconsciously my chirography expands into placard capitals. Give me a condor's quill! Give me Vesuvius' crater for an inkstand! Friends, hold my arms!" Oh that his friends had obeyed that summons! They might have saved society from a huge dose of hyperbolical slang, maudlin sentimentalism, and tragi-comic bubble and squeak.

His Yankeeisms are plentiful as blackberries. "I am tormented," quoth he, "with an everlasting itch for things remote." Remote, too frequently, from good taste, good manners, and good sense. We need not pause at such expressions as "looking a sort of diabolically funny;"—"beefsteaks done rare;"—"a speechlessly quick chaotic bundling of a man into eternity;"—"bidding adieu to circumspect life, to exist only in a delirious throb." But why wax fast and furious in a thousand such paragraphs as these:—"In landlessness alone resides the highest truth, indefinite as the Almighty. . . . Take heart, take heart, O Bulkington! Bear thee grimly, demi-god! Up from the spray of thy ocean-perishing—straight up, leaps thy apotheosis!"—"Thou [*scil.* Spirit of Equality][1] great God! who didst not refuse to the swart convict, Bunyan, the pale, poetic pearl; Thou who didst clothe with doubly hammered leaves of finest gold the stumped and paupered arm of old Cervantes; Thou who didst pick up Andrew Jackson from the pebbles; who didst hurl him upon

1. The square brackets in this paragraph are in the original [*Editors' note*].

a war-horse; who didst thunder him higher than a throne!"—"If such a furious trope may stand, his [Capt. Ahab's] special lunacy stormed his general sanity, and carried it, and turned all its concentrated cannon upon its own mad mark . . . . then it was, that his torn body and gashed soul bled into one another; and so interfusing made him mad."—"And the miser-merman, Wisdom, revealed [to a diving negro] his hoarded heaps; and among the joyous, heartless, ever-juvenile eternities, Pip saw the multitudinous, God-omnipresent, coral insects, that out of the firmament of waters heaved the colossal orbs. He saw God's foot upon the treadle of the loom, and spoke it; and therefore his shipmates called him mad."

The story itself is a strange, wild, furibund thing—about Captain Ahab's vow of revenge against one Moby Dick. And who is Moby Dick? A fellow of a whale, who has made free with the captain's leg; so that the captain now stumps on ivory, and goes circumnavigating the globe in quest of the old offender, and raves by the hour in a lingo borrowed from Rabelais, Carlyle, Emerson, newspapers transcendental and transatlantic, and the magnificent proems of our Christmas pantomimes. Captain Ahab is introduced with prodigious efforts at preparation; and there is really no lack of rude power and character about his presentment—spoiled, however, by the Cambyses' vein in which he dissipates his vigour. His portrait is striking—looking "like a man cut away from the stake, when the fire has overrunningly wasted all the limbs without consuming them, or taking away one particle from their compacted aged robustness"—a man with a brow gaunt and ribbed, like the black sand beach after some stormy tide has been gnawing it, without being able to drag the firm thing from its place. Ever since his fell encounter with Moby Dick, this impassioned veteran has cherished a wild vindictiveness against the whale, frantically identifying with him not only all his bodily woes, but all his feelings of exasperation—so that the White Whale swims before him "as the monomaniac incarnation of all those malicious agencies which some deep men feel eating in them, till they are left living on with half a heart and half a lung." The amiable cannibal Queequeg occasions some stirring and some humorous scenes, and is probably the most reasonable and cultivated creature of the ship's company. Starbuck and Stubb are both tiresome, in different ways. The book is rich with facts connected with the natural history of the whale, and the whole art and process of whaling; and with spirited descriptions of that process, which betray an intense straining at effect. The climax of the three days' chase after Moby Dick is highly wrought and sternly exciting—but the catastrophe, in its whirl of waters and fancies, resembles one of Turner's later nebulous transgressions in gamboge.

ANONYMOUS

[The Wildness of Melville's Stories]†

The reader who is wearied by sentimental fiction, may find relief in turning to the tales of adventure by Dr MAYO, Lieutenant WISE, and HERMANN MELVILLE. To write a grave critique on these books, would be ridiculous; and to make any protest against the extravagances of the writer last named, would be useless; for it would never be read by those who find delight in the pages of *Mardi*, *Kaloolah*, and similar tales. It must not be supposed that we deny the peculiar merits of these romances: we intend only to shew the impossibility of giving any critical account of them. They must be received as reports of the fluent, careless, and often brilliant talk of imaginative travellers, or dreamers of travel, who have written without any care for rules of art, or fear of critics. The passion for reading of the class to which we refer, is a curious feature in recent years. It prevails in England and Germany as in America. As practical life becomes tame and monotonous, the youthful imagination goes back to barbarism and the wildness of nature, to find excitement. Tales of adventure by land and sea, in the forests, or on the prairies of the far west, or highly coloured pictures of sensuous and luxurious life in the islands of the South Seas—these supply the intellectual refreshment of numerous young readers, and lure away their minds from the study of realities. The wildness of Melville's stories—*Typee*, *Omoo*, *Mardi*, and others—seems to be infectious; for in a review of *Mardi*, we find a *critic* writing in the following style:—'Reading this wild book, we can imagine *ourselves* mounted upon some Tartar steed, golden caparisons clank around our person, ostrich plumes of driven whiteness hang over our brow, and cloud our vision with dancing snow. . . . . Away, away, along the sandy plain!' &c. This is perhaps our most concise mode of indicating the rhapsodical style of the book itself. *Typee*, the first of Melville's books, tells the story of two sailors who escaped from their ship and landed on an island of the Pacific, where they were received by the Typee natives, with whom they lived luxuriously, feasting on sucking-pigs and breadfruit, and enjoying all the licence of a primitive state of society. *Mardi* intermingles with its voluptuous scenery a dreamy philosophy of which we can give no clear account.

† From *Hand-Book of American Literature: Historical, Biographical and Critical,* attributed to Margaret E. Forster (Philadelphia, 1855 [?]), p. 189.

EVERT A. DUYCKINCK AND GEORGE L. DUYCKINCK

[Metaphysical Energy *vs.* Physical Sublime]†

In 1851 *Moby-Dick, or the Whale,* appeared, the most dramatic and imaginative of Melville's books. In the character of Captain Ahab and his contest with the whale, he has opposed the metaphysical energy of despair to the physical sublime of the ocean. In this encounter the whale becomes a representative of moral evil in the world. In the purely descriptive passages, the details of the fishery, and the natural history of the animal, are narrated with constant brilliancy of illustration from the fertile mind of the author.

ANONYMOUS

[Undeniable Merits and Inconceivable Extravagancies]‡

The last work we have to notice is a large one, entitled "The Whale," and it is quite as eccentric and monstrously extravagant in many of its incidents as even "Mardi;" but it is, nevertheless, a very valuable book, on account of the unparalleled mass of information it contains on the subject of the history and capture of the great and terrible cachalot, or sperm-whale. Melville describes himself as having made more than one cruise in a South-sea-whaler; and supposing this to have been the fact, he must nevertheless have laboriously consulted all the books treating in the remotest degree on the habits, natural history, and mode of capturing this animal, which he could obtain, for such an amazing mass of accurate and curious information on the subject of the sperm-whale as is comprised in his three volumes could be found in no other single work—or perhaps in no half-dozen works—in existence. We say this with the greater confidence, because we have written on the sperm-whale ourselves, and have consequently had occasion to consult the best works in which it is described. Yet the great and undeniable merits

† From Evert A. Duyckinck and George L. Duyckinck, *Cyclopaedia of American Literature* (New York: Charles Scribner, 1855), II, 673.

‡ From "A Trio of American Sailor-Authors," *Dublin University Magazine,* Vol. 47 (January, 1856) 47–54; the quotation is from 53, 54. The other two sailor-authors are Cooper and Dana.

of Melville's book are obscured and almost neutralised by the astounding quantity of wild, mad passages and entire chapters with which it is interlarded. Those who have not read the work cannot have any conception of the reckless, inconceivable extravagancies to which we allude. Nevertheless, the work is throughout splendidly written, in a literary sense; and some of the early chapters contain what we know to be most truthful and superlatively-excellent sketches of out-of-the-way life and characters in connexion with the American whaling trade. * * *

Perhaps we have so far indicated our opinion of the merits and demerits of Herman Melville in the course of the foregoing remarks, that it is hardly necessary to state it in a more general way. Yet, in conclusion, we may sum up our estimate of this singular author in a few short sentences. He is a man of genius—and we intend this word to be understood in its fullest literal sense—one of rare qualifications too; and we do not think there is any living author who rivals him in his peculiar powers of describing scenes at sea and sea-life in a manner at once poetical, forcible, accurate, and, above all, original. But it is his *style* that is original rather than his *matter*. He has read prodigiously on all nautical subjects—naval history, narratives of voyages and shipwrecks, fictions, &c.—and he never scruples to deftly avail himself of these stores of information. He undoubtedly is an original thinker, and boldly and unreservedly expresses his opinions, often in a way that irresistibly startles and enchains the interest of the reader. He possesses amazing powers of expression—he can be terse, copious, eloquent, brilliant, imaginative, poetical, satirical, pathetic, at will. He is never stupid, never dull; but, alas! he is often mystical and unintelligible—*not* from any inability to express himself, for his writing is pure, manly English, and a child can always understand what he *says*, but the ablest critic cannot always tell what he really *means*; for he at times seems to construct beautiful and melodious sentences only to conceal his thoughts, and irritates his warmest admirers by his provoking, deliberate, wilful indulgence in wild and half-insane conceits and rhapsodies. These observations apply mainly to his latter works, "Mardi" and "The Whale," both of which he seems to have composed in an opium dream; for in no other manner can we understand how they could have been written.

Such is Herman Melville! a man of whom America has reason to be proud, with all his faults; and if he does not eventually rank as one of her greatest giants in literature, it will be owing not to any lack of innate genius, but solely to his own incorrigible perversion of his rare and lofty gifts.

ANONYMOUS

[Who is this Madman?]†

Who is this rough "sailor before the mast," in jacket and tarpaulin, with rolling gait and tarry aspect, who intrudes so unceremoniously upon the grave and black-coated fraternity of American Authors, and boldly elbows his way to a front seat among the best of them? Who is this new Rasselas, who runs away from a happier valley than the Prince of Abysinia ever saw, to beguile civilized ears with glowing pictures of life among the gentle savages of Typee? Who is this pleasant, witty, dashing companion, who in "Omoo," "White Jacket," and "Redburn" has given us some of the most brilliant and high-colored, though not always reliable, salt-water books ever published? Who is this madman, who in "Moby Dick, or the Whale," has mingled the coolest and calmest matter-of-fact with the wildest midsummer lunacy—who in one chapter scientifically cuts up Leviathan, and stows away his oil with an eye to dollars, and in the next, out-Carlyles Carlyle in some wild rhapsody, some insane Babel-talk, in which nothing can be clearly made out save that there has been a woeful waste of learning and genius in its concoction. Who is this imitator of the worst French school, who in "Pierre" has poured out a flood of lurid nonsense which, it is to be hoped, no one save the devoted proof-reader has ever had the patience to wade through? Who is this philosophical poet, who in "Mardi" has so beautifully depicted a romantic Utopia, with Polynesia for the background, and filled so many ardent minds with unquenchable longings—

—"thus to wander far away
On from island unto island. At the gateways of the day—
Larger constellations burning, mellow moons and happy skies,
Breadths of tropic shade and palms in cluster—knots of Paradise—
Drops the heavy blossomed bower, hangs the heavy-fruited tree;
Summer isles of Eden, lying in dark purple spheres of sea.

* * *

These books [*Typee, Omoo, Mardi, Redburn, White-Jacket, Moby-Dick, Pierre, Israel Potter, The Piazza Tales*] are certainly among the most remarkable productions of our literature. The author wields a wondrous and witching pen, and once under their influence, the reader cannot easily shake off his spells. There is a

† From the New York *Christian Intelligencer* (January 22, 1857). Robert G. Newman generously sent us a reprint of this article in the Ilion, New York, *Independent*, April 16, 1857, from which we traced the original article.

perennial vigor and vitality in his writings. They fascinate, startle, astound. He is so wealthy in imagination, and so profuse in the expenditure of his treasures, that in reading him one is apt to labor under what our Gallic neighbors call an "embarrassment of riches." He is a bundle of incongruities. Sometimes he will coil up delicate little bits of beauty in out-of-the-way places, where they are scarcely appreciable by any but a spirit of sympathetic criticism, and anon, he will shock both the æsthetic and moral sense by some broad, coarse, glaring *ad captandum* effect. Sometimes he is fresh, wholesome, and natural—at others, he is morbid, fantastic, spectral. But whatever else he may be, he is never weak—he never fails to leave an impression of power. His genius is original, and creative; he has struck out a new path for himself; he is always thoroughly in earnest, and here lies the real secret of his popularity.

FITZ-JAMES O'BRIEN

[Nature *vs.* Obstinate Cultivation]†

Mr. Melville is not a *dilettante* in metaphysics. If he is fantastically philosophical in his language, it is because he wants to say something subtle and penetrating which he has discerned, or *thinks he has* discerned, and takes this to be the most effective way of saying it. And this is just the issue we have to make with him. We made it when we read "Mardi;" we have been obliged to make it, again and again, in reading his subsequent books. What, for instance, did Mr. Melville mean when he wrote "Moby Dick?" We have a right to know; for he carried us floundering on with him after his great white whale, through all manner of scenes, and all kinds of company—now perfectly exhausted with fatigue and deafened with many words whereof we understood no syllable, and then suddenly refreshed with a brisk sea breeze and a touch of nature kindling as the dawn. There was so much truth in the book that we knew the author must have meant to give us more, and we were excessively vexed with him for darkening his counsel by words which we could not but esteem to be words without knowledge. Is it not a hard case, O sympathizing reader? Here is a man of distinct and unquestionable genius; a man who means righteously and thinks sensibly; a man whose aims do honor to himself and to his country; a man who wishes to understand life himself, and to help

† From Fitz-James O'Brien, "Our Authors and Authorship: Melville and Curtis," *Putnam's Monthly*, Vol. 9 (April, 1857), 384–93; the quotation is from 389–90.

other people to understand it; a man, too, who has proved not once only but fifty, yea, a hundred times, that he can write good English—good, strong, sweet, clear English—a man who has music in his soul, and can ring fair chimes upon the silver bells of style—and this man will persist in distorting the images of his mind, and in deodorizing the flowers of his fancy; a man born to create, who resolves to anatomize; a man born to see, who insists upon speculating.

The sum and substance of our fault-finding with Herman Melville is this. He has indulged himself in a trick of metaphysical and morbid meditations until he has almost perverted his fine mind from its healthy productive tendencies. A singularly truthful person—as all his sympathies show him to be—he has succeeded in vitiating both his thought and his style into an appearance of the wildest affectation and untruth. His life, we should judge, has been excessively introverted. Much as he has seen of the world, and keen as his appreciation is of all that is true and suggestive in external life, he has turned away habitually, of late years, at least, to look in upon his own imaginations, and to cultivate his speculative faculties in a strange, loose way. We do not know a more curious and instructive spectacle than some of his books afford, of the conflict between resolute nature and stubborn cultivation.

Nature says to Herman Melville, "You shall tell the world what you have seen and see, in a warm, quick, nervous style, and bring the realities of life and man before your readers in such a way that they shall know your mind without calling on you to speak it. You shall be as true as Teniers or Defoe, without the coarseness of the Fleming or the bluntness of the Englishman."

Obstinate cultivation rejoins: "No! you shall dissect and divide; you shall cauterize and confound; you shall amaze and electrify; you shall be as grotesquely terrible as Callot, as subtly profound as Balzac, as formidably satirical as Rabelais."

Sometimes, nature, for a while, carries her point and then what charming pages we have; what pictures, rather than pages, pregnant with truth and wise with beauty! Sometimes obstinate cultivation has it all her way, and then what a maze we get into; what a whirl of fantastic names—of unintelligible quotations—of alarming mysteries! Skeletons grin at us; waves wash over us; monsters glower at us, until, in our bewilderment and despair, we are ready to take the place of that Casabianca of the Pacific, Tashtego, who goes down in the story of "Moby Dick," nailing the red flag of Ahab to the mast of the sinking Pequod, and, with the flag, the wing of an unhappy falcon which swoops down at a fatal moment for itself upon the fluttering ensign.

HENRY T. TUCKERMAN

[The Rare Fault of Redundant Power]†

Not far from his [Oliver Wendell Holmes's] old residence lives Herman Melville, author of "Typee," "Omoo," "Moby Dick," and other adventurous narratives, which have more of the genuine Robinson Crusoe spell about them than any American writings. The first and second were entirely new subjects, treated with a mingled simplicity and spirit that at once made the author's name a household and a shipboard word; the last, for curious and eloquent descriptions and details about the whale and whale fishing, rivals Michelet's brilliant and copious brochures on the sea, woman, and other generic themes; but Melville is more scientific as to his facts, and more inventive as to his fiction. "Moby Dick," indeed, has the rare fault of redundant power; the story is wild and wonderful enough without being interwoven with such a thorough, scientific, and economical treatise on the whale; it is a fine contribution to natural history and to political economy, united to an original and powerful romance of the sea. Melville has written other and more casual things, indicative of great versatility; witness his "Life of Israel Potter," and his remarkable sketch of a Wall Street scrivener in "Putnam's Monthly." Impaired health induced him to retire to this beautiful region, and in the care of his fruits and flowers, and the repose of domestic life, he seems to have forsworn the ambition of authorship, but we trust only for a time.

JOHN H. DILLINGHAM

[Natural History Flawed by Metaphysics]‡

This was followed in 1851, by Moby Dick, or the Whale; the details of the fishery and the natural history of the animal are well told, but the metaphysical portions of the narrative destroy its interest. He also published Pierre, or the Ambiguities; The Piazza Tales; The Confidence Man, his Masquerade; and a number of magazine articles in Putnam's and Harper's magazines.

† From Henry T. Tuckerman, "Authors in Berkshire," Philadelphia *American Literary Gazette and Publishers' Circular*, Vol. 2 (Nov. 16, 1863), 38–40; the quotation is from p. 40.

‡ From Rufus Wilmot Griswold, *The Prose Writers of America*, revised and enlarged by John H. Dillingham (Philadelphia: Porter & Coates, 1870), p. 666.

Herman Melville is an original thinker, and boldly and unreservedly expresses his opinions, often in a way that irresistibly startles and enchains the interest of the reader. He possesses amazing powers of expression: he can be terse, copious, eloquent, brilliant, imaginative, poetical, satirical, pathetic, at will. He is never stupid, never dull; but, alas! he is often mystical and unintelligible,—not from any inability to express himself, for his writing is pure, manly English, and a child can always understand what he says,—but the ablest critic cannot always tell what he really means; solely from his incorrigible perversion of his rare and lofty gifts.

W. CLARK RUSSELL

[Melville: The Poet of the Deep]†

Cooper pleases and has pleased, and is to this day read and admired by thousands; but speaking from a sailor's point of view, I really have no words to express the delight with which I quit his novels for the narratives of his countrymen, Dana and Herman Melville.

Whoever has read the writings of Melville must I think feel disposed to consider "Moby Dick" as his finest work. It is indeed all about the sea, whilst "Typee" and "Omoo," are chiefly famous for their lovely descriptions of the South Sea Islands, and of the wild and curious inhabitants of those coral strands; but though the action of the story is altogether on shipboard, the narrative is not in the least degree nautical in the sense that Cooper's and Marryat's novels are. The thread that strings a wonderful set of fancies and incidents together, is that of a whaler, whose master, Captain Ahab, having lost his leg by the teeth of a monstrous white whale, to which the name of Moby Dick has been given, vows to sail in pursuit of his enemy. The narrator embarks in the ship that is called the *Pequod*, which he describes as having an "old-fashioned, claw-footed look about her."

> "She was apparelled like any barbaric Ethiopic Emperor, his neck heavy with pendants of polished ivory. She was a thing of trophies. A cannibal of a craft, tricking herself forth in the

† From W. Clark Russell, "Sea Stories," London *Contemporary Review*, Vol. 46, (September, 1884), 343–63; the quotation is from 356–57. Russell begins by lamenting the "depression of the marine novel to the level of the intelligence of boys," and observes that the sea has been so debased in fiction written by landsmen that "it does not and never yet has appealed to us as the land has been made to appeal by the exquisite perceptions of such poets as Milton and Wordsworth and Keats." Then Russell says: "Who are the poets of the deep? Their names may be counted upon the fingers of one hand: they are Herman Melville, and I rank him first; Michael Scott; Dana, the author of "Two Years before the Mast," and Captain Cupples, the author of "The Green Hand" (344) [*Editors' note*].

chased bones of her enemies. All round her unpanelled, open bulwarks were garnished like one continuous jaw, with the long sharp teeth of the sperm-whale, inserted there for pins to fasten her old hempen thews and tendons to. Those thews ran not through base blocks of land wood, but deftly travelled over sheaves of ivory. Scorning a turnstile wheel at her reverend helm she sported there a tiller; and that tiller was in one mass, curiously carved from the long narrow jaw of her hereditary foe. The helmsman, who steered by that tiller in a tempest, felt like the Tartar when he holds back his fiery steed by clutching its jaw. A noble craft, but somehow a most melancholy! All noble things are touched with that."

Melville takes this vessel, fills her full of strange men, and starts her on her insane quest, that he may have the ocean under and around him to muse upon, as though he were in a spacious burial-ground, with the alternations of sunlight and moonlight and deep starless darkness to set his thoughts to. "Moby Dick" is not a sea-story—one could not read it as such—it is a medley of noble impassioned thoughts born of the deep, pervaded by a grotesque human interest, owing to the contrast it suggests between the rough realities of the cabin and the forecastle, and the phantasms of men conversing in rich poetry, and strangely moving and acting in that dim weather-worn Nantucket whaler. There is a chapter where the sailors are represented as gathered together on the forecastle; and what is made to pass among them, and the sayings which are put into their mouths, might truly be thought to have come down to us from some giant mind of the Shakespearean era. As we read, we do not need to be told that seamen don't talk as those men do; probabilities are not thought of in this story. It is like a drawing by William Blake, if you please; or, better yet, it is of the "Ancient Mariner" pattern, madly fantastic in places, full of extraordinary thoughts, yet gloriously coherent—the work of a hand which, if the desire for such a thing had ever been, would have given a sailor's distinctness to the portrait of the solemn and strange Miltonic fancy of a ship built in the eclipse and rigged with curses dark. In "Typee," and "Omoo," and "Redburn," he takes other ground, and writes—always with the finest fancy—in a straight-headed way.

ANONYMOUS

[The Classic Story of Whaling Adventure]†

It is an old remark that the matter of a good book is more important than its style, but Captain Newell would have done well

† From an anonymous review of C. M. Newell's *The Voyage of the Fleetwing*, New York *Nation*, Vol. 46 (April 19, 1888), 330.

to remember that without an effective style the best matter is thrown away. Here is abundant material—the adventures of an old-fashioned whaling cruise; but the author has told his story in a manner which does it great injustice. Similar scenes are described with wonderful power and felicity in Herman Melville's 'Moby Dick,' the classic story of whaling adventure; and it is with work like this that Captain Newell's present story (as well as an earlier one covering similar ground, and called 'Pehe Nui') must challenge comparison. As a story of exciting adventure based upon large experience of whaling life, Captain Newell's 'Fleetwing' has great reality; but its effect is sadly marred, not to say destroyed, by faults of obscurity or excess in the telling. Least of all can a story-teller afford to dispense with the literary element in his work.

JULIAN HAWTHORNE

Man-Books†

Novelists pay altogether too little attention to the wants of the male portion of their audience. We are told that women—and unmarried women at that—do three-fourths of the novel-reading in the world; and that, consequently, novels must be so fashioned as to please and attract the feminine mind, and especially the junior feminine. We must have love, and beauty, and heroic self-sacrifice, and gruesome tragedy and pathos. There must be gushing descriptions of scenery, and, as a late reviewer in the *Critic* insists, it must symbolize the moods and even the characters of the *dramatis personae*. Men novelists accordingly exhaust their resources in furnishing this sort of stuff; and women novelists easily outdo them both in numbers and in sentimentality; though of them all, only one living woman writer ever produces anything worth a sane man's attention; and that one—Mrs. Elizabeth Stoddard—writes as men ought to write, if they have brains and courage enough. * * *

The last man-novel written in this country, with the exception of Mrs. Stoddard's, was published full thirty years ago. It was called "Kaloolah; or, the Adventures of Jonathan Romer," and its author was Dr. W. S. Mayo. That book was Man from title-page to colophon: it was of man, for man, by a man. It is true that "Kaloolah" herself is a woman, and a very lovely one. But she occupies her proper place in the story: she is what a woman ought to be; she

† From Julian Hawthorne, "Man-Books," *America: A Journal of To-day*, Vol. 1 (Sept. 27, 1888), 11–12.

does not loaf and invite her soul all over the book; on the contrary, the book is the more masculine because she is in it. This admirable work was republished lately; but it was got up in Christmas-book form, and we gave it to our boys, and never thought to look into it ourselves. Perhaps even the boys themselves failed to appreciate it. It seems to me that the American boy of to-day is a good deal like a girl in trousers.

Herman Melville, in his "Typee" and "Omoo," and in his "Moby Dick" and "White-Jacket," wrote books that were certainly not meant for women; but they were not exactly man-books, either, if we except "Moby Dick"; they were books of adventure—boy's books; and, therefore, admirable though they were, and unequaled since, they did not quite fill the bill. "Moby Dick" was published, I think, in 1854. That exhausts our native list, back as far as Franklin. As for England, she has, in this century (for we will not go back to Daniel Defoe, Henry Fielding, Tobias Smollett, *et id genus nobile*)—she has, I say, George Borrow—honored name!—the author of "Lavengro," "Rommany Rye," "Gypsies in Spain"; a man as original as a new planet, and a man's man exclusively. Murray, the London publisher, has lately brought out a complete edition of his works; and if that were the only thing the house of Murray had ever done, it would entitle it to our enduring gratitude. There is meat for men in "Lavengro," and plenty of it: the roast beef and strong ale of England. I wish we were nourished on it. And Borrow, original though he is, does not stand alone; beside him, less known and less productive, but solid as granite and good as gold, stands Trelawny, the great Trelawny, the friend of Byron and Shelley, their biographer, and a better man than either. Trelawny wrote an autobiographical romance called "The Adventures of a Younger Son;" it was published by Henry Colburn and Richard Bentley, in London, in 1831; and I am not aware that it has been republished since then. No man can read that book without feeling himself more a man; even our beloved Jonathan Romer must be content to occupy a second place in comparison with it: it is so true, so strong, so simple, so rank with man nature. After reading it, you understand better the "Memoirs of Byron, Shelley, and the author," and perceive why those famous poets so quickly and completely attached themselves to him. Talk about Rider Haggard's battles! Read the battles that Trelawny fought in "A Younger Son."

As for Mr. Haggard and Mr. Stevenson, who deserve all honor for not writing for women, they still cannot rank with the man I have mentioned; they are tellers of adventure: and though a man's book may be full of adventure, it is not the adventures that give it its essential quality. But is the secret lost? Will no man arise and prophesy for his sex? I believe that the great American novelist, when he comes, will give us a man-book; and I trust I may be alive to read it.

CHARLES F. RICHARDSON

[Brisk and Stirring Tales]†

At this period English and American literature (of course including poetry and prose fiction) were beginning to feel the scientific and economic influence of the age,—an age which on its superficial side was searching for facts rather than dreams or fancies. Periodical literature, too, was multiplying a miscellaneous but in its way somewhat definite sort of information, and was thereby responding to a public curiosity, and creating it as well. Reflective or imaginative sentimentalism was presently to yield, in part, to the widespread wish for some new thing. The clever pseudo-scientific tales of Poe made answer to this wish, yet without sacrifice of integrity of literary merit; and were followed by a long line of American, English, and French imitations. Another response was made by Herman Melville in his brisk and stirring tales of the sea or sketches of travel, in which fact and fancy were mingled by the nervously impatient author, in the proportion desired by his immediate public. Melville's own adventures had been those of a modern Captain John Smith in the Pacific islands and waters; so that the *pars magna fui* of his lively books gave them the needed fillip of personality, and duly magnified their elements of wonder. That brilliant power of delineation which, in Melville's conversation, so charmed his warm friends the Hawthornes, is apparently not heightened in his books, but would seem to be rather diminished by the exigencies of writing. But the personal narrative or fiction of "Typee," "Omoo," and "Moby Dick," with their adventurous rapidity of description of Pacific seas, ships, savages and whales, represented the restless facility which has always been an American trait, and which occasionally develops into some enduring literary success.

Dr. W. S. Mayo, like Melville, had endured many vicissitudes of travel and adventure, and in his African romance "Kaloolah, or Journeyings to the Djébel Kumri, an Autobiography of Jonathan Romer," he drew upon his experiences abroad and at home, reverting to his school-days in northern New York, and to his father's marine exploits. That "Kaloolah" has barely outlived Melville's

† From Charles F. Richardson, *American Literature, 1607–1885* (New York: G. P. Putnam's Sons, 1889), II, 403–5.

sprightly but now forgotten improvisations in literature is due to the combination, in its pictures of a far-away world, of the improbably romantic and the obviously satirical. Melville made some essays in the same direction, but failed completely for lack of a firm thought and a steady hand.

H. S. SALT

[Harmonious Blending of Fact and Metaphysics]†

Moby Dick; or, The White Whale (1851) is perhaps more successful as a whole than *Mardi,* since its very extravagances, great as they are, work in more harmoniously with the outline of the plot. Ishmael, the narrator, having embarked on board a whaling-vessel with a savage harpooner named Queequeg, whose character is admirably drawn, gradually discovers that they are committed to an extraordinary voyage of vengeance. It seems that, in a former expedition, Captain Ahab, their commander, a mysterious personage, who 'looked like a man cut away from the stake when the fire has overrunningly wasted all the limbs without consuming them,' had lost one of his legs, which had been 'reaped away' by Moby Dick, a famous white sperm-whale of unequalled strength and malignity. Frenzied by his loss, he was now devoting the rest of his life to the single object of destroying Moby Dick, who 'swam before him as the monomaniac incarnation of all those malicious agencies which some deep men feel eating in them.' The book is a curious compound of real information about whales in general and fantastic references to this sperm-whale in particular, that 'portentous and mysterious monster,' which is studied (as the bird is studied by Michelet) in a metaphysical and ideal aspect—'a mass of tremendous life, all obedient to one volition, as the smallest insect.' Wild as the story is, there is a certain dramatic vigour in the 'quenchless feud' between Ahab and Moby Dick which at once arrests the reader's attention, and this interest is well maintained to the close, the final hunting-scene being a perfect nightmare of protracted sensational description.

Moby Dick was published when Melville was still a young man of thirty-three. Before he was forty he produced several other volumes, none of which were calculated to add in any degree to his fame, one of them, entitled *Pierre; or, The Ambiguities,* being perhaps the *ne plus ultra* in the way of metaphysical absurdity.

† From H. S. Salt, "Herman Melville," *Scottish Art Review,* Vol. 2 (Nov., 1889), 186–90; the quotation is from 188–89.

'Physic of metaphysic begs defence,
and metaphysic calls for aid on sense.'

It may seem strange that so vigorous a genius, from which stronger and stronger work might reasonably have been expected, should have reached its limit at so early a date; but it must be remembered that the six really notable books of which I have made mention were produced within a period of less than six years. Whether the transcendental obscurities in which he latterly ran riot were the cause or the consequence of the failure of his artistic powers is a point which it would be difficult to determine with precision. His contemporary critics were inclined, not unnaturally, to regard his mysticism as a kind of *malice prepense*, and inveighed mournfully against the perversity of 'a man born to create, who resolves to anatomise, a man born to see, who insists upon speculating,' and warned him, after the publication of *Pierre*, that his fame was on the edge of a precipice, and that if he were wise he would thenceforth cease to affect the style of Sir Thomas Browne, and study that of Addison. Yet how successfully he could at times reproduce the quaint conceits of the earlier writer may be seen from the following passage of *Mardi*:—

'And truly, since death is the last enemy of all, valiant souls will taunt him while they may. Yet, rather, should the wise regard him as the inflexible friend, who, even against our own wills, from life's evils triumphantly relieves us. * * *

'Tis no great valour to perish sword in hand and bravado on lip cased all in panoply complete. For even the alligator dies in his mail, and the sword-fish never surrenders. To expire, mild-eyed, in one's bed, transcends the death of Epaminondas.'

The chief characteristic of Herman Melville's writings is this attempted union of the practical with the ideal. Commencing with a basis of solid fact, he loves to build up a fantastic structure, which is finally lost in the cloudland of metaphysical speculation. He is at his best, as in *Typee*, when the mystic element is kept in check, and made subservient to the clear development of the story; or when, as in certain passages of *Mardi* and *Moby Dick*, the two qualities are for the time harmoniously blended. His strong attraction to the sea and to ships, which has already been alluded to as dating from his earliest boyhood, was closely connected with this ideality of temperament; for the sea, he tells us, was to him 'the image of the ungraspable phantom of life,' while a ship was 'no piece of mechanism merely, but a creature of thoughts and fancies, instinct with life, standing at whose vibrating helm you feel her beating pulse.' 'I have loved ships,' he adds, 'as I have loved men.'

ANONYMOUS

[A Queer Yarn]†

I see that he [Melville] is dead after a life of mingled storm and almost sluggish calm. Do boys between the ages of 10 and 70 read his books now? I fear not, for some of them are out of print; and yet I was mightily pleased at finding the copy of "Moby Dick"—and what a queer yarn it is—thumbed beyond repair, and with broken back, the testimony of the appreciation of frequenters of the Public Library. What a grand fellow that harpoon man was—I have forgotten his name—who, when he was in the New Bedford Inn, began dressing by putting on his stove-pipe hat. * * *

To me Herman, the spinner of yarns, was more real than Herman the quiet man who found a port in the New York Custom House. His stories were not ruined by allusions to science; his sailors were either naturally simple or crazed by strange sights at sea; they were not akin to the creations of the ingenious Verne, and the books in which they figured taught no useful lesson for the benefit of the priggish boys. I wish there were more stories like them. And I wish Melville had explained before his death the reasons of the fierce and long-established hatred between the White Whale and Captain Ahab.

RICHARD HENRY STODDARD

[A Wealth of Untrained Imagination]‡

There was a wealth of imagination in the mind of Mr. Melville, but it was an untrained imagination, and a world of the stuff out of which poetry is made, but no poetry, which is creation and not chaos. He saw like a poet, felt like a poet, thought like a poet, but he never attained any proficiency in verse, which was not among his natural gifts. His vocabulary was large, fluent, eloquent, but it was excessive, inaccurate and unliterary. He wrote too easily, and at too great length, his pen sometimes running away with him, and from his readers. There were strange, dark, mysterious elements in his nature, as there were in Hawthorne's, but he never learned to

† From "Here in Boston," the Boston *Post* (October 2, 1891).

‡ From Richard Henry Stoddard, obituary of Melville, New York *Critic,* Vol. 16 (n.s.) (Nov. 14, 1891), 272, as quoted from the New York *Mail and Express.*

control them, as Hawthorne did from the beginning, and never turned their possibilities into actualities.

HENRY S. SALT

[The Crown and Glory of the Later Phase]†

As "Typee" is the best production of the earlier and simpler phase of Melville's authorship, so undoubtedly is "The Whale" (or "Moby Dick," as it is sometimes styled) the crown and glory of the later phase; less shapely and artistic than "Typee," it far surpasses it in immensity of scope and triumphant energy of execution.[1] It is in "The Whale" that we see Melville casting to the winds all conventional restrictions, and rioting in the prodigality of his imaginative vigour. It is in "The Whale" that we find the fullest recognition of that magical influence of the sea—the "image of the ungraspable phantom of life"—which from first to last was the most vital inspiration of his restless and indomitable genius. ("The ocean," he finely wrote in a later volume, "brims with natural griefs and tragedies; and into that watery immensity of terror man's private grief is lost like a drop.") Ostensibly nothing more than a wild story of a strange voyage of vengeance, a "quenchless feud" between a fierce old sea-captain and a particular white sperm-whale of renowned strength and audacity, the book, which abounds with real facts concerning the details of the whale-fishery, has a mystic esoteric significance which lifts it into a wholly different category. In the character of Captain Ahab, who "looked like a man cut away from the stake when the fire has overrunningly wasted all the limbs without consuming them," we see a lurid personification of the self-destructive spirit of Hatred and Revenge, while Moby Dick, the white whale, "swam before him as the monomaniac incarnation of all those malicious agencies which some deep men feel eating in them." To quote detached passages from a work of such ambitious conception and colossal proportions would be worse than useless; I must therefore content myself with saying that "The Whale," faulty as it is in many respects, owing to the turgid mannerisms of Melville's transcendental mood, is nevertheless the supreme production of a master mind—let no one presume to pass judgment on

† From Henry S. Salt, " 'Marquesan Melville,' " London *Gentleman's Magazine*, Vol. 272 (March, 1892), 248–57; the quotation is from 252–54, 256–57.

1. *The Whale* was dedicated to Hawthorne, and is referred to in his "Wonder-Book." "On the hither side of Pittsfield sits Herman Melville, shaping out the gigantic conception of his 'White Whale,' while the gigantic shadow of Greylock looms upon him from his study window."

American literature unless he has read, and re-read, and wonderingly pondered, the three mighty volumes of "The Whale."

The increasing transcendentalism of Melville's later thought was accompanied and reflected by a corresponding complexity of language, the limpid simplicity so remarkable in "Typee," and "Omoo," and "White Jacket" being now succeeded by a habit of gorgeous and fantastic word-painting, which, though brilliantly effective at its best, degenerated, at its worst, into mere bombast and rhetoric, a process which had already been discernible in the concluding portions of "Mardi," while in "Pierre" (or "The Ambiguities," as it was appropriately designated) it reached the fatal climax of its development. * * *

His love of literature was fully sustained to the end. I have before me a most interesting batch of letters, dated between 1884 and 1888, addressed by him to Mr. James Billson, of Leicester, and mostly dealing with the poems of James Thompson ("B. V."), of which he was a great admirer. Some of these comments and appreciations are in Melville's best style. " 'Sunday up the River,' " he writes, "contrasting with the 'City of Dreadful Night,' is like a Cuban humming-bird, beautiful in faery tints, flying against the tropic thundercloud. Your friend was a sterling poet, if ever one sang. As to pessimism, although neither pessimist nor optimist myself, nevertheless I relish it in the verse, if for nothing else than as a counterpoise to the exorbitant hopefulness, juvenile and shallow, that makes such a muster in these days—at least in some quarters."

"Exorbitant hopefulness" could indeed have been hardly otherwise than distasteful to one who, like his own "John Marr" (a retired sailor whose fate it was to live on a "frontier-prairie," among an unresponsive inland people who cared nothing for the sea), had so long experienced the solitude of disappointed genius. But it is impossible to believe that this undeserved neglect can be permanent. The opinion of those competent judges who are students of Melville's works is so clear and emphatic in his favour,[2] that it is not too much to say that to read his books is generally to appreciate them; nor is it only those who have what is called an "educated taste" who are thus impressed, for I have been told of instances in which English working-men became his hearty admirers. It is satisfactory to know that a new edition of his best books is forthcoming, both in America and England, and that the public will thus have an opportunity, I will not say of repairing a wrong done to a distinguished writer, for, as I have already shown, the decay of his fame was partly due to circumstances of his own making, but at

2. I may instance Mr. William Morris, Mr. Theodore Watts, Mr. R. L. Stevenson, Mr. Robert Buchanan, and Mr. W. Clark Russell.

least of rehabilitating and confirming its earlier and truer judgment. Herman Melville will then resume his honourable place in American literature (for, to end as I began, I hold that the existence of an American literature is a fact and not a supposition), as the prose-poet of the Pacific—

> the sea-compelling man,
> Before whose wand Leviathan
> Rose hoary-white upon the deep,
> With awful sounds that stirred its sleep;
> Melville, whose magic drew Typee,
> Radiant as Venus, from the sea.[3]

ARTHUR STEDMAN

[The Highest Domain of Romance]†

With "Moby Dick; or, the Whale" (1851), Melville reached the topmost notch of his fame. The book represents, to a certain extent, the conflict between the author's earlier and later methods of composition, but the "gigantic conception" of the "White Whale," as Hawthorne expressed it, permeates the whole work, and lifts it bodily into the highest domain of romance. "Moby Dick" contains an immense amount of information concerning the habits of the whale and the methods of its capture, but this is characteristically introduced in a way not to interfere with the narrative. The chapter entitled "Stubb Kills a Whale" ranks with the choicest examples of descriptive literature.

"Moby Dick" appeared; and Melville enjoyed to the full the enhanced reputation it brought him. He did not, however, take warning from "Mardi," but allowed himself to plunge more deeply into the sea of philosophy and fantasy.

DONALD G. MITCHELL

[The Metaphysic Subtleties of Moby Dick]‡

Herman Melville was a not-far-off neighbor [of Hawthorne, G. P. R. James, Fanny Kemble Butler, and J. T. Headley], whose *Typee* and *Omoo* had delighted Hawthorne as well as a world of

3. Robert Buchanan's *Socrates in Camden.*

† From Arthur Stedman, "Introduction," in *Typee* (New York: American Publishers Corporation, 1892), p. xxxiii.

‡ From Donald G. Mitchell, *American Lands and Letters* (New York: Charles Scribner's Sons, 1899), II, 235.

readers; and who at this epoch of his life—distrained of earlier simplicities—was torturing himself with the metaphysic subtleties of *Moby Dick* and whipping all the depths of his thought into turbulent and misty spray.

ANONYMOUS

[Unrivalled Tale of the Demon White Cachalot]†

A careful perusal of this work has led us to the conclusion that it is intended to be taken as a narrative of adventures "written round" the subject of whaling, and merely founded on facts. So far as the story goes Mr. Bullen does not appear to have been the first mate of the Cachalot, whatever position he may have filled in any other craft; in fact, it is only after the tragical death of the fourth mate, a gigantic negro, that he rises to even that rank. He tells us in the preface that this is believed to be the first attempt to write an account of the cruise of a South Sea whaler from the seaman's stand-point, and we will therefore enlighten him by stating that nearly half a century ago Herman Melville, who was every inch a sailor, produced a work which not only remains unrivalled for accuracy as regards the details of sperm whaling, but is also of enthralling interest on account of the (fictional) tragedy with which it ends. Under the title of 'The Whale,' this was published by Messrs. Bentley in 1851, the American editions usually bearing the prefix 'Moby Dick.' That was the name of the demon white cachalot with which Ahab Peleg of the ivory leg went forth in the Pequod to join battle; and we are sure that no one who had commenced the drama of "the three days' pursuit" ever laid down the volume until the final catastrophe was reached. The work is, however, too little known on this side of the Atlantic.

ARCHIBALD MacMECHAN

"The Best Sea Story Ever Written"‡

Anyone who undertakes to reverse some judgment in history or criticism, or to set the public right regarding some neglected man or

† From an anonymous review of Frank T. Bullen's *The Cruise of the "Cachalot" round the World after Sperm Whales*, London *Athenaeum*, 3718 (Jan. 28, 1899), 107.

‡ From Archibald MacMechan, " 'The Best Sea Story Ever Written,' " *Queen's Quarterly*, Vol. 7 (Oct., 1899), 120–30; the quotation is from 120–21, 124–26, 127, 130.

work, becomes at once an object of suspicion. Nine times out of ten he is called a literary snob for his pains, or a prig who presumes to teach his betters, or a "phrase-monger," or a "young Osric," or something equally soul-subduing. Besides, the burden of proof lies heavy upon him. He preaches to a sleeping congregation. The good public has returned its verdict upon the case, and is slow to review the evidence in favour of the accused, or, having done so, to confess itself in the wrong. Still, difficult as the work of rehabilitation always is, there are cheering instances of its complete success; notably, the rescue of the Elizabethan dramatists by Lamb and Hazlitt and Leigh Hunt. Nor in such a matter is the will always free. As Heine says, ideas take possession of us and force us into the arena, there to fight for them. There is also the possibility of triumph to steel the raw recruit against all dangers. Though the world at large may not care, the judicious few may be glad of new light, and may feel satisfaction in seeing even tardy justice meted out to real merit. In my poor opinion much less than justice has been done to an American writer, whose achievement is so considerable that it is hard to account for the neglect into which he has fallen.

This writer is Herman Melville, who died in New York in the autumn of 1891 * * *

For a tale of such length, *Moby Dick* is undoubtedly well constructed. Possibly the "Town-Ho's Story," interesting as it is, somewhat checks the progress of the plot; but by the time the reader reaches this point, he is infected with the leisurely, trade-wind, whaling atmosphere, and has no desire to proceed faster than at the "Pequod's" own cruising rate. Possibly the book might be shortened by excision, but when one looks over the chapters it is hard to decide which to sacrifice. The interest begins with the quaint words of the opening sentence: "Call me Ishmael"; and never slackens for at least a hundred pages. Ishmael's reasons for going to sea, his sudden friendship with Queequeg, the Fijian harpooneer, Father Mapple's sermon on Jonah, in the seamen's bethel, Queequeg's rescue of the country bumpkin on the way to Nantucket, Queequeg's Ramadan, the description of the ship "Pequod" and her two owners, Elijah's warning, getting under way and dropping the pilot, make up an introduction of great variety and picturesqueness. The second part deals with all the particulars of the various operations in whaling from manning the mast-heads and lowering the boats to trying out the blubber and cleaning up the ship, when all the oil is barrelled. In this part Ahab, who has been invisible in the retirement of his cabin, comes on deck and in various scenes different sides of his vehement, iron-willed, yet pathetic nature, are made intelligible. Here also is much learning to be found, and here, if anywhere, the story dawdles. The last part deals with the fatal three days' chase, the death of Ahab, and the escape of the White Whale.

One striking peculiarity of the book is its Americanism—a word which needs definition. The theme and style are peculiar to this country. Nowhere but in America could such a theme have been treated in such a style. Whaling is peculiarly an American industry; and of all whale-men, the Nantucketers were the keenest, the most daring, and the most successful. Now, though there are still whalers to be found in the New Bedford slips, and interesting as it is to clamber about them and hear the unconscious confirmation of all Melville's details from the lips of some old harpooneer or boat-header, the industry is almost extinct. The discovery of petroleum did for it. Perhaps Melville went to sea for no other purpose than to construct the monument of whaling in this unique book. Not in his subject alone, but in his style is Melville distinctly American. It is large in idea, expansive; it has an Elizabethan force and freshness and swing, and is, perhaps, more rich in figures than any style but Emerson's. It has the picturesqueness of the new world, and, above all, a free-flowing humour, which is the distinct *cachet* of American literature. No one would contend that it is a perfect style; some mannerisms become tedious, like the constant moral turn, and the curiously coined adverbs placed before the verb. Occasionally there is more than a hint of bombast, as indeed might be expected; but, upon the whole, it is an extraordinary style, rich, clear, vivid, original. It shows reading and is full of thought and allusion; but its chief charm is its freedom from all scholastic rules and conventions. Melville is a Walt Whitman of prose.

Like Browning he has a dialect of his own. The poet of *The Ring and the Book* translates the different emotions and thoughts and possible words of pope, jurist, murderer, victim, into one level uniform Browningese; reduces them to a common denominator, in a way of speaking, and Melville gives us not the actual words of American whalemen, but what they would say under the imagined conditions, translated into one consistent, though various Melvillesque manner of speech. The life he deals with belongs already to the legendary past, and he has us completely at his mercy. He is completely successful in creating his "atmosphere." Granted the conditions, the men and their words, emotions and actions, are all consistent. One powerful scene takes place on the quarter-deck of the "Pequod" one evening, when, all hands mustered aft, the Captain Ahab tells of the White Whale, and offers a doubloon to the first man who "raises" him * * *

Where every page, almost every paragraph, has its quaint or telling phrase, or thought, or suggested picture, it is hard to make a selection; and even the choicest morsels give you no idea of the richness of the feast. Melville's humour has been mentioned; it is a constant quantity. Perhaps the statement of his determination after the adventure of the first lowering is as good an example as any * * *

This book is at once the epic and the encyclopaedia of whaling. It is a monument to the honour of an extinct race of daring seamen; but it is a monument overgrown with the lichen of neglect. Those who will care to scrape away the moss may be few, but they will have their reward. To the class of gentleman-adventurer, to those who love both books and free life under the wide and open sky, it must always appeal. Melville takes rank with Borrow, and Jefferies, and Thoreau, and Sir Richard Burton; and his place in this brotherhood of notables is not the lowest. Those who feel the salt in their blood that draws them time and again out of the city to the wharves and the ships, almost without their knowledge or their will; those who feel the irresistible lure of the spring, away from the cramped and noisy town, up the long road to the peaceful companionship of the awaking earth and the untainted sky; all those—and they are many—will find in Melville's great book an ever fresh and constant charm.

ANONYMOUS

[The Dramatic Force of Melville]†

Mr. Bullen has much more than a small capacity; but we want to point out clearly that the principal value of his work is his career. He must not be classed with such a fine imaginative artist as Mr. Conrad, whose *Nigger of the "Narcissus"* is beyond him altogether. Mr. Bullen, in his *Log of a Sea Waif*, does, indeed, play with part of Mr. Conrad's theme—the terrors of a gale which, it would seem, is to be appeased and pacified only by a human sacrifice; but he does it simply as a sincere reporter. Mr. Conrad's inner fire is a thing apart. Nor is Mr. Bullen another Michael Scott—he lacks that robust temperament: nor another Marryat—he has not the humour; nor another Melville—he is without the dramatic force. But he supplements them all by virtue of lacking these qualities and because, in their place, he possesses a power of careful, patient description, a gift of close observation, an eye for natural beauty, a reverence for human goodness, a tenacious memory, and, above all, the desire to be truthful. A man who has seen men and

† From an anonymous review of Frank T. Bullen's *Log of a Sea Waif*, London *Academy*, Vol. 57 (December 9, 1899), 691.

things and desires to pass on his impressions uninjured will command attention.

ALPHONSO G. NEWCOMER

[The Series of Partly Fanciful Tales]†

To New York belonged several writers of tales of adventure whose scenes were laid on shipboard or in remote quarters of the earth. One of these was Dr. Mayo, the author of *Kaloolah* (1849), an extravagant story of Yankee exploration in the wilds of Africa. Another, and more important, was Herman Melville, who in his youth embarked upon a whaling vessel bound for the Pacific and spent several years, a portion of the time in captivity, among the South Sea Islands. The series of partly fanciful tales founded upon his experiences—*Typee* (1846), *Omoo* (1847), *Moby Dick, or the White Whale* (1851), etc.,—had a wide circulation, and an occasional admirer can still be found who will pronounce them superior to Cooper's. They differ from Cooper's tales of the sea in that they portray, not the life of the merchant or the naval officer, but the life of the common sailor who ships "before the mast."

Superior, however, to all these tales in quality, and scarcely inferior in romantic interest, is the wholly truthful narrative of *Two Years Before the Mast*.

ANONYMOUS

[An Informative Whaling Romance]‡

October 18. 31s. 6d. By HERMANN MELVILLE, of Pittsfield, Berkshire County, Massachusetts.

A romance of life on a Nantucket Whaler in the South Seas, with much information vividly conveyed at first hand regarding the Sperm Whale fishery. [Chap. XXXI., Vol I. (Cetology), mentions a number of works on Whales, and especially commends F. D. Bennett's *Whaling Voyage round the Globe*, issued from New

† From Alphonso G. Newcomer, *American Literature* (Chicago: Scott, Foresman, 1901), p. 128.

‡ From the *List of the Principal Publications Issued from New Burlington Street During the Year 1851* (London: Richard Bentley and Son, 1902), privately printed "for official use only." This entry is under the date of English publication, October 18, 1851. [George] Louis Becke had written an introduction to the Putnam's English edition of *Moby-Dick*, 1901.

Burlington Street in 1840. Chaps. XIII.-XV., Vol. II., criticise the Whale as represented pictorially.] The Appendices contain a list of the word "whale" in various languages, from Hebrew to Erromangoan, and a collection of references to the same from Genesis to Darwin.

The title of the American Edition, published in the same year, was "Moby Dick; or, The Whale." ["Moby Dick" was a solitary white whale of mysterious size and power (a variant probably on the great sea serpent), in encountering which the *Pequod* and her captain are finally lost.]

Modern reprints in one volume appeared elsewhere in 1893, 1900, and 1901 (under the American title, and with a brief epilogue). The Rev. Henry T. Cheever also wrote a work on the Whale (issued elsewhere), while in recent years Mr. Frank T. Bullen, in his "*Cruise of the Cachalot,*" covers, though in a somewhat different manner, much of the same ground. (Mr. Bullen eulogizes Bennett's work, but is silent regarding Melville's contribution to the subject.)

> "The one man who knew his subject and knew how to write about it, though much of his brilliancy of description is too often marred and obscured by a headlong and purposeless dash away from his main theme into the vague realms of weird and fantastic metaphysical imagination."—LOUIS BECKE.

Melville embarked in January, 1841, on a whaling vessel for the Pacific, but absconded on arriving at the Marquesas Islands in the following year. After adventures, which formed the basis of "Typee," he obtained further material for the present work in a Sydney whaler that rescued him.

For a biographical note and references to Melville's other works see September 29, 1849, and January 23, 1850. His *Typee; or, Marquesas Islands,* and *Omoo; or South Sea Islands,* were published by Murray in 1846 and 1847 respectively.

CHARLES F. RICHARDSON

[Stirring Records of Adventure]†

His writings are numerous, and of varying merit; his verse, patriotic and other, is quite forgotten; and his works of fiction and

† From Charles F. Richardson, "Herman Melville," *Encyclopaedia Britannica,* 10th ed. (New York: The Encyclopædia Britannica Company, 1902), VI, 631.

of travel are of irregular execution. Nevertheless, few authors have been enabled so freely to introduce romantic personal experiences into their books: in his first work, *Typee: A Peep at Polynesian Life, or Four Months' Residence in a Valley of the Marquesas* (1846), he described his escape from the cannibals; while in *Omoo, a Narrative of Adventures in the South Seas* (1847), *White Jacket, or The World in a Man-of-War* (1850), and especially *Moby Dick, or The Whale* (1851), he portrayed seafaring life and character with vigour and originality, and from a personal knowledge equal to that of Cooper, Marryat, or Clark Russell. The experiences of sailor-life in forecastle or on deck, in storm and in sunshine, in pursuit of the whale or in danger of capture by savages, as narrated by Melville in his chief works, have never ceased to interest a limited yet loyal public of readers in America and England. But these stirring records of adventure were accompanied by other tales so turgid, eccentric, opinionative, and loosely written as to seem the work of another author. Melville was the product of a period in American literature when the fiction written by writers below Irving, Poe, and Hawthorne was measured by humble artistic standards.

MARIE CLOTHILDE BALFOUR

[The "Masterpiece of His Later Period"]†

In "The Whale" we already find a change from the simple and charming style of its predecessors, and a tendency to the transcendental. This book has been called the "masterpiece of his later period," and certainly contains much that is very fine; but in the midst of brilliant character sketches, and an almost turbulent wealth of langauge and incident, the easy pen riots occasionally into mere wordiness, and the story recedes into the mists of symbolism. At the same time, the book is full of information about the whale-fishing that is not only true in every detail, but would be difficult to find elsewhere so concisely, so clearly, and so effectively put together. "Mardi," again, was published in 1849, only two years later than "Omoo;" here and there it contains pages that are worthy of "Typee," but at the last it travels wearily away into bombast and a verbosity that I have no heart to describe.

† From Marie Clothilde Balfour, "Appendix," in *Omoo* (London: John Lane, 1904), pp. 448–49.

W. CLARK RUSSELL

[Melville's Finest Performance]†

"Moby Dick; or, The Whale," is generally and with justice regarded as Melville's finest performance. It is, indeed, taken on the whole, a very noble piece. Some of the conversations among the sailors remind one for their strength, sweetness and courage of such passages in Dekker, Webster, Massinger, Fletcher, and other old dramatists as Charles Lamb loved to select. The opening chapters of this book are extraordinarily impressive. He gives us a picture of New Bedford by night. His sketch of the Spouter Inn, its hoarse, salt landlord, its delicious clam chowder, the frightful Mowrèe harpooner whose bed the hero has to share, enchant the imagination and chisel the memory with the delights and impressions produced by a masterpiece in Dutch painting.

Yet it is easy to understand why "Moby Dick" should never reach the popularity of "Typee" or "Omoo." In parts it is too obscure. The reader, moreover, is harassed by the frequent interpolation of a transcendental mysticism which often ill-fits the mouths of the rough tarpaulins who are made to deliver their minds of the sublimated fancies which appear to oppress them even more than the brine-hardened food they consume.

JOSEPH CONRAD

[A Rather Strained Rhapsody]‡

15 January, 1907
Riche Hotel,
Montpellier.

DEAR SIR,

Your letter reached me today only. The heading of this letter explains the delay.

I am greatly flattered by your proposal; but the writing of my own stuff is a matter of so much toil and difficulty that I am only

† From W. Clark Russell, "Introduction," in *Typee* (London; John Lane, 1904), pp. vii–viii.

‡ In *American Literature*, Vol. 29 (Jan., 1958) 463–64, Frank MacShane explains in his article "Conrad on Melville": "In 1907, while Joseph Conrad was staying, at the suggestion of Ford Madox Ford, in the south of France, he received a letter from Mr. (later Sir) Humphrey Milford, sometime Publisher to the University of Oxford, which contained, as is evident from Conrad's reply, a request for a preface to an edition of Herman Melville's *Moby-Dick* which the Oxford Press intended to publish." The letter is in the possession of Messrs. B. H. Blackwell of Oxford. Permission to publish the letter has been graciously granted by the Conrad Estate and J. M. Dent & Sons Ltd.

too glad to leave other people's books alone. Years ago I looked into *Typee* and *Omoo*, but as I didn't find there what I am looking for when I open a book I did go no further. Lately I had in my hand *Moby Dick*. It struck me as a rather strained rhapsody with whaling for a subject and not a single sincere line in the 3 vols of it.

On the other hand W. H. Hudson was enthusiastic about that very book and generally the whole of Melville's work. Couldn't he write the preface you need?

Pardon this suggestion. It got under the pen and I let it be.

Believe me dear Sir,

very sincerely yours,
JOSEPH CONRAD

ERNEST RHYS

[A Transcendentalist in Oilskin]†

[A]n intellectual change had passed over Melville between the writing of "Typee" and "Omoo" and the writing of "Moby Dick." He was not only a writer of sea-tales but a transcendentalist in oil-skin, who found a vaster ocean than the Pacific in his own mind, and symbolised in the whale the colossal image of the forces of nature that produce and that overpower man. * * *

"Moby Dick" was the last book in which the balance between transcendentalism and reality in Melville was maintained with any effective control of his art as a romancer. Some of his books, such as "Pierre; or, The Ambiguities," an ominous sub-title, 1852, and "The Confidence Man," are all but unreadable.

C. S. NORTHRUP

[Melville's Uneven Masterpiece]‡

A follower of Cooper—though at some distance in point of quality—in writing stories of the sea, was Herman Melville (1819–91). * * * Melville's masterpiece was "Moby Dick, or The Whale" (1851); though an uneven work of excessive length, written partly in a strained, Carlylesque style, it nevertheless fills the reader with

† From Ernest Rhys, "Editor's Note" to *Moby Dick; or the White Whale* (London: J. M. Dent, 1907), pp. vii–viii. Reprinted by permission of J. M. Dent and E. P. Dutton & Co., Inc., publishers of Everyman's Library Edition.

‡ From C. S. Northrup, "Herman Melville," *A Manual of American Literature*, ed. Theodore Stanton (New York: G. P. Putnam's Sons, 1909), pp. 164–65. Reprinted by permission of the publishers.

the fascination of the sea. The fierce contest of Captain Ahab with the great whale, which "becomes a representative of moral evil in the world," is not unworthy of the pen of a greater writer. Melville never afterward came up to the standard of this work, though he wrote several other stories and novels, among them "Pierre, or The Ambiguities" (1852), "Israel Potter" (1855), narrating the adventures of a Revolutionary soldier, and praised by Hawthorne for its portraits of Paul Jones and Benjamin Franklin, "The Piazza Tales" (1856), and "The Confidence Man" (1857).

JOHN MASEFIELD

[A Noble and Beautiful Book]†

"You produced a great prose writer," he [Masefield] said, "in Herman Melville, who wrote about the sea. A noble and beautiful book is his 'Moby Dick.' Then the 'Cowboy Songs,' which have been sent to me lately, struck me as having precisely the same qualities of picturesqueness and directness."

JOHN MACY

[A Madly Eloquent Romance of the Sea]‡

The stories of Poe, Hawthorne, Howells, James, Aldrich, Bret Harte, are admirable in manner, but they are thin in substance, not of large vitality. On the other hand, some of the stronger American fictions fail in workmanship; for example, "Uncle Tom's Cabin," which is still vivid and moving long after its tractarian interest has faded; the novels of Frank Norris, a man of great vision and high purpose, who attempted to put national economics into something like an epic of daily bread; and Herman Melville's "Moby Dick," a madly eloquent romance of the sea.

WILLIAM B. CAIRNS

[Full of Excitement, Wholesome, Well Told]§

Among New York storytellers was Herman Melville, who went to sea before he was twenty, and a little later sailed on a

† From John Cournos, "A Visit to John Masefield," New York *Independent*, Vol. 73 (Sept. 5, 1912), 537.

‡ From John Macy, *The Spirit of American Literature* (New York: Modern Library, 1913), p. 16.

§ From William B. Cairns, *American Literature for Secondary Schools* (New York: Macmillan, 1914), p. 226. Reprinted by permission of The Estate of William B. Cairns.

whaler for the South Pacific Ocean, and had many exciting experiences on ship and on land before his return. Three of his books, *Typee, Omoo,* and *White Jacket,* tell of occurrences on this trip. He also wrote novels of adventure, the best being *Moby Dick or the White Whale.* Both the autobiographical books and the novels are full of excitement, are wholesome, and well told.

D. H. LAWRENCE

[A Very Odd, Interesting Book]†

I am reading *Moby Dick.* It is a very odd, interesting book: to me interesting, the others can't bear it. I read the *History of the East*—it is a very bad little book. But something in me lights up and understands these old, dead peoples, and I love it: Babylon, Nineveh, Ashurbanipal, how one somehow suddenly understands it.

D. H. LAWRENCE

[The Oldness of Classic American Literature]‡

Have you still got humming birds, as in Crèvecoeur? I like Crèvecoeur's 'Letters of an American Farmer,' *so* much. And how splendid Herman Melville's 'Moby Dick' is, & Dana's 'Two Years before the Mast.' But your classic American literature, I find to my surprise, is *older* than our English. The tree did not become new, which was transplanted. It only ran more swiftly into age, impersonal, nonhuman almost. But how good these books are! Is the *English* tree in America almost dead? By the literature, I think it is.

† From *The Letters of D. H. Lawrence,* ed. Aldous Huxley (New York: The Viking Press, 1936), p. 322. D. H. Lawrence to Lady Ottoline Morrell, from Porthcothan, St. Merryn, N. Cornwall, February 7, 1916. Reprinted by permission of The Viking Press, Inc., and Laurence Pollinger, Ltd. Richard Aldingham in *D. H. Lawrence: Portrait of a Genius But . . .* (New York, 1950), p. 205, says the copy of *Moby-Dick* which Lawrence was reading belonged to the novelist J. D. Beresford, in whose cottage the Lawrences were staying. In his famous essay in *Studies in Classic American Literature* Lawrence used the expurgated English text [Editors' note].

‡ From S. Foster Damon, *Amy Lowell: A Chronicle* (Boston: Houghton Mifflin Company, 1935). Copyright © 1963 by S. Foster Damon. Reprinted by permission of Houghton Mifflin Company. D. H. Lawrence to Amy Lowell, from Higher Tregerthen, Zennor, St. Ives, Cornwall, August 23, 1916.

F. C. OWLETT

[The Finest Sea Book Ever Written in English]†

Coming at last to treat of "Moby Dick," one feels the utter futility of any attempt to convey a just idea of that marvellous tale. "In that wild, beautiful romance"—the words are Mr. Masefield's—"Herman Melville seems to have spoken the very secret of the sea, and to have drawn into his tale all the magic, all the sadness, all the wild joy of many waters. It stands quite alone; quite unlike any other book known to me. It strikes a note which no other sea writer has ever struck." Here is a book about which Criticism is wonderfully agreed. Whatever the faults of it, there is only one opinion—as far as I have been able to discover there has never been more than one opinion touching its greatness. Writing people who have read it and have written around it—however diverse the judgments they may have pronounced on other books, and whatever the critical doctrines they may severally swear to—unite in acclaiming "Moby Dick" as the finest sea book ever written in English. That a finer will ever be written is simply not to be conceived. The crown of this king of the sea writers is secure as Shakespeare's own.

RAYMOND M. WEAVER

[An Amazing Masterpiece]‡

Born in hell-fire, and baptized in an unspeakable name, "Moby-Dick, or the Whale" (1851), reads like a great opium dream. The organizing theme of the book is the hunting of Moby-Dick, the abhorred white whale, by the monomaniac Captain Ahab. To Ahab, this ancient and vindictive monster is the incarnation of all the vast moral evil of the world; he piles on the whale's white hump the sum of all the rage and hate of mankind from the days of Eden down. There are in "Moby-Dick" long digressions, natural, historical, and philosophical on the person, habits, manners, and ideas of whales; there are long dialogues and soliloquies, such as were never spoken by mortal man in his waking senses, conversations that for sweetness, strength, and courage remind one of passages from Dekker, Webster, Massinger, Fletcher, and the other

† From F. C. Owlett, "Herman Melville (1819–1891): A Centenary Tribute," London *Bookman*, Vol. 56 (Aug., 1919), 164–67; the quotation is from 166.

‡ From Raymond M. Weaver, "The Centennial of Herman Melville," New York *Nation*, Vol. 109 (Aug. 2, 1919), 145–146; the quotation is from 146.

old dramatists loved by Charles Lamb; perhaps a fifth of the book is made up of Melville's independent moralizings, half essay, half rhapsody; withal, the book contains some of the most finished comedy in the language. If one logically analyzes "Moby-Dick," he will be disgusted, just as Dr. Johnson, who had no analysis but the logical, was disgusted with "Lycidas." And so with Melville's novel. If one will forget logic and common sense, and "abandon himself"—as Dr. Johnson would contemptuously have said—to this work of Melville's, he will acknowledge the presence of an amazing masterpiece. But neither "Lycidas" nor "Moby-Dick" should be read by philistines or pragmatists. * * *

"Like a frigate," Melville once wrote of himself, "I am full with a thousand souls; and as on, on, on, I scud before the wind, many mariners rush up from the orlop below, like miners from caves; running shouting across my decks; opposite braces are pulled and boisterous speaking trumpets are heard, and contending orders, to save the good ship from the shoals. In my tropical calms, when my ship lies tranced on Eternity's main, the many, many souls in me speak one at a time, then all with one voice, rising and falling and swaying in golden calls and responses." Because of this multiplicity of personality, Melville eludes summary classification. In his composite achievement he is severally a gentle Smollett, a glorified Whitman, an athletic Coleridge, a dandified Rabelais, a cynical Meredith, a doubting Sir Thomas Browne. Essentially was he a mystic, a treasure-seeker, a mystery-monger, a delver after hidden things spiritual and material. The world to him was a darkly figured hieroglyph; and if he ever deciphered the cabalistic sign, the meaning he found was too terrible, or else too wonderful, to tell. Whenever he sat down to write, at his elbow stood ever the chosen emissary of Satan, the Comic Spirit—a demoniac familiar that saved him in many a trying pass. The versatility and power of his genius was extraordinary. If he does not eventually rank as a writer of overshadowing accomplishment, it will be owing not to any lack of genius, but to the perversity of his rare and lofty gifts.

FRANK JEWETT MATHER, JR.

[Melville's Masterpiece]†

In 1849, about two years before "Moby Dick," appeared that strangest of allegories, "Mardi, and a Voyage Thither." The two

† From Frank Jewett Mather, Jr., "Herman Melville," New York *Review*, Vol. 1 (Aug. 9, 1919), 276–78 and (Aug. 16, 1919), 298–301; the quotation is from 298–99.

works are companion pieces: "Mardi" is a survey of the universe in the guise of an imaginary voyage of discovery, "Moby Dick" is a real voyage skilfully used to illustrate the cosmos; "Mardi" is a celestial adventure, "Moby Dick" an infernal. "Mardi" is highly general—the quest of a mysterious damsel, Zillah, a sort of Beatrice, a type of divine wisdom; "Moby Dick" is specific, the insanely vengeful pursuit of the dreaded white whale. The people of "Mardi" are all abstractions, those of "Moby Dick" among the most vivid known to fiction. "Mardi" was far the most ambitious effort of Melville's, and it failed. Personally I like to read in it; for its idealism tinged with a sane Rabelaisianism, for its wit and rare pictorial quality, for the strange songs of Yoomy, which, undetachable, are both quaintly effective in their context, and often foreshadow oddly our modern free verse. It is often plethoric and overwritten, it drops out of the Polynesian form in which it is conceived, and becomes too overt preaching and satire. It justifies the Bacchic philosopher Babbalanja's aphorism—"Genius is full of trash"; but it is also full of wisdom and fine thinking. It represents an intellectual effort that would supply a small library, and I suppose it is fated to remain unread. Perhaps its trouble is its inconclusiveness. Again Babbalanja is enlightening:

> Ah! my lord, think not that in aught I've said this night, I would assert any wisdom of my own. I but fight against the armed and crested lies of Mardi, that like a host, assail me. I am stuck full of darts; but tearing them from out me, gasping, I discharge them whence they came.

The very seriousness of "Mardi" tells against it. One feels something, a breaking heart under the literary horseplay. Thus it can not hold its own either with such neatly fashioned ideal republics as Edward Bellamy's "Looking Backward," nor with the Horatian elegance of Samuel Butler's "Erewhon," nor of course with the grim impassivity of "Gulliver's Travels." The occasional delver in "Mardi," however, will pluck out of it all sorts of surprises from foreshadowings of the superman to an anticipation of Samuel Butler's vitalism.

"Moby Dick" has the tremendous advantage of its concreteness. Captain Ahab's mad quest of the white whale imposes itself as real, and progressively enlists and appalls the imagination. Out of the mere stray episodes and minor characters of "Moby Dick" a literary reputation might be made. The retired Nantucket captains, Bildad and Peleg, might have stepped out of Smollett. Father Mapple's sermon on the Book of Jonah is in itself a masterpiece, and I know few sea tales which can hold their own with the blood feud of Mate Radney and sailor Steelkilt. The style still has the freshness and delicate power of "Typee," but is subtler. Take the very modern quality of a passage which a Loti might envy:

> It was while gliding through these latter waters that one serene and moonlight night, when all the waves rolled by like scrolls of silver; and by their soft, suffusing seethings, made what seemed a silvery silence, not a solitude; on such a silent night a silvery jet was seen far in advance of the white bubbles at the bow. Lit up by the moon, it looked celestial; seemed some plumed and glittering god uprising from the sea.

There is also a harsher note befitting the theme. The tang of it is in the passage with which this essay opened.[1] The tragic and almost incredible motive of the quest of the demon whale gains credibility from the solid basis of fact, as mad captain Ahab himself is based, so to speak, on his ivory leg. The insane adventure itself grows real through the actuality of its participants: Was there ever such a trio as the savage harpooners? Their very names, Feddallah, Tashetego, Queequeg, are a guarantee of good faith. A reader instinctively hurrahs at the deeds of such mates as Starbuck and Stubbs while with them he cowers under the fateful eye of Captain Ahab. Throughout the book are shudders, sympathies, and laughs.

But "Moby Dick" is more than what it undisputedly is, the greatest whaling novel. It is an extraordinary work in morals and general comment. In the discursive tradition of Fielding and the anatomist of melancholy, Melville finds a suggestion or a symbol in each event and fearlessly pursues the line of association. As he and Queequeg plait a mat on the same warp, the differing woofs and resulting surfaces become a symbol for man's free will asserting itself against the background of fate. Such reflections are in a grave, slow-moving style in which Burton has counted for much and Carlyle for something. It is the interplay of fact and application that makes the unique character of the book. As for the Christian fathers the visible word was merely a similitude or foreshadowing of the eternal world, so for Melville the voyage of the Pequod betokens our moral life in the largest sense. An example may best show the qualities and defects of the method. "Ishmael" (Herman Melville) is at the wheel at night gazing at the witches' kitchen of "trying out" the blubber. The glare sends him into a momentary doze and a strange thing happens:

> Starting from a brief standing sleep, I was horribly conscious of something fatally wrong. * * *
>
> Look not too long in the face of the fire, O man! Never dream with thy hand on the tiller! Turn not thy back to the compass; accept the first hint of the hitching tiller, believe not the artificial

1. Ch. 48, 191.46–192.7; 193.14–32 [*Editors' note*].

fire when its redness makes all things look ghastly. Tomorrow, in the natural sun, the skies will be bright; those who glared like devils in the forking flames will show in far other, at least gentler relief; the glorious, golden, glad sun, the only true lamp—all others but liars.

Upon the reader's slant towards this sort of parable will very much depend his estimate of "Moby Dick." Are we dealing with trimmings or essentials?—that is the critical question. Cut out the preachments, and you will have a great novel, some readers say. Yes, but not a great Melville novel. The preachments are of the essence. The effect of the book rests on the blend of fact, fancy, and profound reflection, upon a brilliant intermingling of sheer artistry and moralizing at large. It is Kipling before the letter [latter?] crossed with Sir Thomas Browne, it comprises all the powers and tastes of Herman Melville, is his greatest and most necessary work. So while no one is obliged to like "Moby Dick"—there are those who would hold against Dante his moralizing and against Rabelais his broad humor—let such as do love this rich and towering fabrique adore it whole-heartedly—from stem to stern, athwart ships and from maintruck to keelson.

In a sense "Moby Dick" exhausted Melville's vein. At thirty-two he had put into a single volume all that he had been in action, all that he was to be in thought. The rest is aftermath, yet it, too, is considerable.

VIOLA MEYNELL

[The Rarest Quality of Imagination]†

Within limits most people could say what special form of writing they prefer. Even the most just literary judgment may be subject to preferences for one kind of greatness over another kind. If the great book which is the subject of this article has in some way just missed people's preferences, that and nothing else may account for the neglect of it. It is possible that many of those even who are alert for treasure have an unconscious preference for finding it elsewhere than in a story about a whale-hunt. This much-ignored book is *Moby Dick*, written in 1851 by Herman Melville, and it is the story of the hunting of whales in general and of a white whale in particular.

Though it tells with scientific accuracy of every part of the whale

† From Viola Meynell, "Herman Melville," *Dublin Review*, Vol. 166 (Jan.-March, 1920), 96–105; the quotation is from 96–97. Reprinted by permission. Miss Meynell was a friend of D. H. Lawrence, but there seems to be no evidence as to whether or not he introduced her to *Moby-Dick*. Her edition of *Moby-Dick* for Oxford University Press in the same year as this essay helped to precipitate the Melville revival.

and every detail of its capture, it is a work of wonderful and wild imagination. His whale is real, like Blake's tiger, but in thinking of it he occasionally loses hold of reality as we know it—as Blake's imagination also flies loose from his sinewy tiger to infinity. Herman Melville has that rarest quality, rare even in genius, of wildness, imagination escaping out of bounds. But the whale is the cause—this natural object, and its order, and the truth that we know of it, and its laws, are the occasion of his wildness. There may be people who do not love such an occasion for imagination. There are all those, one must always remember, who like to find imagination, for instance, in fairies, fantasies, trees with living limbs, imps, gnomes, etc. If they can enter by that easy open door, how should they expect that a whale, its measurements, its blubber, its oil, its lashless eyes, its riddled brow, and harpoons and ropes and buckets are the way to imagination? Preferences will range people into two groups in this regard. One group requires that imagination shall begin in facts, and in its wildest flights shall still owe an acknowledgment to fact, and requires, too, to believe that Truth is at the other unseen end of that imagining. The other group distrusts reality or the natural object even for a start, and would not wait to measure a whale, but hastens after a fairy whom fancy can make as large or as small as it likes. Or, since terms of fact, such as colour, must be used in description, then mere profusion is supposed to lend fancy. The fairy's robe may be of many colours, there is no reason why one should be excluded. Is that profusion imagination?—or will imagination not rather spring from some great restriction, such as the whiteness of this whale—whiteness "which strikes more of panic to the soul than that redness which affrights in blood?" Fairies have no starting-place in valuable reality, and, what is worse, no ultimate reality to arrive at. Fairies begin and end in themselves. The very freedom allowed to fancy in that world of fairy (or faerie as believers like it written) is somehow fatal to its interest; it has the deadly freedom of being utterly outside truth.

But it is of facts and figures that the imagination in *Moby Dick* is made.

D. H. LAWRENCE

[The Final Hunting of Sexual Consciousness]†

Herman Melville's biggest book is *Moby Dick,* or *The White Whale*. It is the story of the last hunt. The last hunt, the last conquest—what is it?

† From D. H. Lawrence, *The Symbolic Meaning: The Uncollected Versions of* "Studies in Classic American Literature," ed. Armin Arnold (New York: The Viking Press, Inc. and Fontwell, England: Centaur Press, 1962), 235–50; the quotation is from 235 38. Copyright 1923, renewed 1951 by

American art symbolises the destruction, decomposition, mechanizing of the fallen degrees of consciousness. Franklin and Crèvecoeur show the mechanizing of the shallowest instincts and passions, appetites; Cooper and Melville the deeper worship-through-contumely of the fallen sexual or sacral consciousness; Poe the direct decomposition of this consciousness; and Dana and Melville the final hunting of the same consciousness into the very Matter, the very watery material, last home of its existence, and its extinction there. Remains the entry into the last state, and into fulness, freedom.

St. John said, "there shall be no more sea." That was esoteric. Exoterically, Dana and Melville say the same. The Sea, the great Waters, is the material home of the deep sacral-sexual consciousness. To the very depths of this home Melville pursues the native consciousness in himself, and destroys it here. When he has really destroyed this sacral-sexual consciousness, destroyed or over-thrown it, then John's prophecy will be fulfilled. There will be no more sea.

Moby Dick is the story of this last symbolic hunt. Moby Dick is a great white whale, the Leviathan of the waters. He is old, hoary, monstrous and snow-white; unspeakably terrible in his wrath; having been repeatedly attacked, he swims now alone in the great, pathless seas.

He is the last warm-blooded tenant of the waters, the greatest and last. He is the deep, free sacral consciousness in man. He must be subdued.

In himself he is warm-blooded, even lovable. But he must be conquered. Curious are his counterparts in the world. The whole of the South Pacific seems to worship, in hate, the shark or the crocodile, the great cold-blooded tenants, lords of the water, fiendish and destructive lords. Curious how shark and crocodile patterns, with grinning teeth, dominate aboriginal decoration-designs in those regions. The same crocodile worship is found in Africa, very widespread. In China, however, the dragon, the Leviathan is the dragon of the sun: as the Mantis, surely another dragon of the sun, dominates the Bushmen. Is not this the inordinately ancient relic of the pre-Flood worship, a relic from that era when the upper conscious-

---

 According to Arnold, this version was completed at latest by June, 1920, and unsuccessfully offered to some American periodicals during the next year; it seems likely that it was finished on September 30, 1919, when Lawrence wrote the American publisher B. W. Huebsch that he had "finished the *Classic American* essays," and mentioned the possibility that the *Atlantic Monthly* might publish "the Dana and Herman Melville essays." This letter is in *The Collected Letters of D. H. Lawrence*, I, ed. Harry T. Moore (New York, 1962), 595–96. [*Editors' note.*]

ness was the anathema, and the glory and the triumph was all in the sensual understanding, incomprehensible to us now?

Melville writes in the peculiar, lurid, glamorous style which is natural to the great Americans. It gives us at first a sense of spuriousness. To some it merely seems wordy and meaningless, unreal. It comes, I think, from the violence native to the American Continent, where force is more powerful than consciousness, and so is never gracefully expressed. The life-force itself is so strong that it tends to come forth lurid and clumsy, obscure also. It causes also a savage desire to go to extremes, to hasten to extremes, whether of idealism or of violent action.

So, in beginning *Moby Dick,* we must be prepared for the curious lurid style, almost spurious, almost journalism, and yet *not* spurious: on the verge of falsity, still real. The book starts off with a semi-metaphysical effusion about water, and about the author's attraction to this element; it goes on with some clumsy humorisms, till it arrives in the sea-town of New Bedford. Then actual experience begins. It is curiously like cold material record, touched-up into journalese: neither veritable nor created. One cannot help feeling that the author is pretentious, and an amateur, wordy and shoddy. Yet something glimmers through all this: a glimmer of genuine reality. Not a reality of real, open-air experience. Yet it is a reality of what takes place in the dark cellars of a man's soul, what the psychoanalysts call the unconscious. There is the old double set of values: the ostensible Melville, a sort of Emersonian transcendentalist, and the underneath Melville, a sort of strange underworld, under-sea Yankee creature looking with curious, lurid vision on the upper world. It is the incongruous mixture of ideal heaven and the uncouth incoherence of a self-conscious adolescent. The reality comes from the adolescent, the uncouth, unformed creature, not from the idealist.

It is no use pretending that Melville writes like a straightforward, whole human being. He is hardly a human being at all. He gives events in the light of their extreme reality: mechanical, material, a semi-incoherent dream-rendering. What the futurists have tried hard to do, Dana and Melville have pretty well succeeded in doing for them. These two are masters of the sheer movement of substance in its own paths, free from all human postulation or control. The result is nearly like artifice, a sort of rank journalism. But we must restrain a too hasty judgment. The author is never quite himself. He is always at the mercy of the rank, self-conscious idealism which still rules white America, he always has to handle artificial values.

Melville tries to square himself with the intellectual world by dragging in deliberate transcendentalism, deliberate symbols and "deeper meanings." All this is insufferably clumsy and in clownish bad taste: self-conscious and amateurish to a degree, the worst side of American behavior. When however he forgets all audience, and renders us his sheer apprehension of the world, he is wonderful, his book commands a stillness in the soul, an awe.

Let us repeat that it is in rendering the sheer naked slidings of the elements, and the curious mechanical cause-and-effect of materials [sic] events, that he is a master. For near as he is to sheer materialism, the central creative spark is still unquenched, the integral soul is present, if alone. His mind lags far, far behind his physical comprehension. His mind is cumbered up with the hopeless aggregation of fixed ideas, which spin on together like little wheels. But his bodily knowledge moves naked, a living quick among the stark elements. In sheer physical, vibrational sensitiveness, like a marvellous wireless-station, he registers the effects of the outer world. And he records also, almost beyond pain or pleasure, the extreme transitions of the isolated, far-driven soul, the soul which is now alone, without human connection.

E. L. GRANT WATSON

[The Highest Plane of Spiritual Daring]†

An imaginative writer can never be more pertinent nor convincing than when writing his autobiography. If he will but tell the story of himself, it is the best he can give. We well know the charm of the simple narration of events, events which find their significance in their simplicity (as in the works of Jefferies or Hudson), lightening with a mild lucidness the occasions of everyday life. This is the imagination of nature in a tranquil mood, and the beauty that is there revealed is of a harmony between man's spirit and the spirit of all that is unknowable. But there are degrees of intensity for the creative passion, and there are those who beat with fierce hands upon the walls of the unknowable. There are men touched so deeply by the vivid consciousness of living that they need to create beyond-worlds for their imagination, wherein, by means of symbols, they indicate the history of their perceptions. Shakespeare created his enchanted island, peopling it with men and spirits, each but a part and symbol of his own experience. Ibsen, in his last play, *When We Dead Awaken*, has told in direct and simple speech the story of his soul. He tells of his failure as a great artist, his bitter repentance, and his resurrection. In this play the chief actors are but symbols, and the world in which they move is no

† From E. L. Grant Watson, "Moby Dick," *London Mercury*, Vol. 3 (Dec., 1920), 180–86; the quotation is from 180–81, 185–86.

"real" world. It is an imaginary creation of the artist; the air breathed is so thinly diffused that each word and idea uttered takes a mystical significance, so that we draw back appalled at the abysses over which human actions are suspended.

Melville also his his story to tell, and he also has his transcendental values; but this story is not told so simply as is Ibsen's. In *Moby Dick or the White Whale*, which is Melville's greatest and best-known work, there is a richness of material that might well puzzle the casual reader. He plunges, in the first pages, into schoolboy adventures with cannibal chiefs, to be followed quickly by rhetoric, by sermons, the magic of embarkation, the magic of voyages, of the sea and of ships. There is natural history, text-books on cetology, wayside philosophisings, realistic descriptions of whale hunts, pictures of the sea and of the sea's dread and beauty such as no other man has penned, and, winding through the whole, giving cohesion and intensity, is the story of the author's own fiercely vivid life-consciousness, which, like the vindictive *Pequod*, journeys upon the most adventurous of all quests, drawn always onward by the beauty and terror of that symbol of madness, the white whale. This inner history is well hidden amongst high adventures. The lives of real men whom Melville has known and loved enfold it. It is tossed with the *Pequod* round all the seas of the ocean, yet once fairly sighted, the story of the soul's daring and of the soul's dread is never lost, but holds the reader in a grip of awful anticipation, till at the end he is left aghast at the courage of one who dares with unflinching perception follow into the heart of its uttermost ocean that quality which, in our cowardice, we call madness.

The separate elements of personality, their divisions and their affinities are well known to Melville; he analyses with a marvellous lucidness the stages of his own peculiar mentality. The *Pequod*, with her monomaniac captain and all her crew, is representative of his own genius, and in this particular sense that each character is deliberately symbolic of a complete and separate element. Yet all are equally involved in the case, their fates are not to be separated. The interplay and struggle between them are but portrayals of the vehement impulsion and repercussion of a richly-endowed spirit that draws inevitably, and yet of its own volition, towards the limit of human sanity. Moby Dick is the symbol of the nameless thing that they pursue; he is the sensuous symbol of nature's beauty and terror:

> A gentle joyousness, a mighty mildness of repose in swiftness invested the white whale. . . . No wonder there had been some among the hunters who, namelessly transported and allured by all this serenity, had ventured to assail it; but had fatally found that quietude but the vesture of tornadoes. Yet calm, enticing calm, oh, whale! thou glidest on, to all who for the first time eye

> thee, no matter how many in that same way thou may'st have bejuggled and destroyed before. And thus through the serene tranquillities of the tropical sea, among waves whose hand-clappings were suspended by exceeding rapture, Moby Dick moved on, still withholding from sight the full terrors of his submerged trunk, entirely hiding the wretched hideousness of his jaw.

In this story the white whale is the symbol or mask of that outer mystery, which, like a magnet, for ever attracts, and in the end overwhelms the imagination. Ahab, the monomaniac captain of the *Pequod*, that godlike, godless old man, is its counterpart. He is the incarnation of the active and courageous madness that lies brooding and fierce, ever ready to spring to command, within the man of genius. He is the atheistical captain of the tormented soul. * * *

At last Moby Dick is sighted. Ahab himself is the first to descry the white hump, for, like that dark impulse that overpowers the lemmings and compels them to cast themselves into a destroying sea, so has Ahab's insanity responded to the more transcendental, more far-reaching potency of Moby Dick. The white whale is the magnet that has drawn the *Pequod* round all the seas of the world. He embodies the stark forces of Nature; he is the symbol of imaginative life, of life which surpasses itself and continues beyond into realms where few men dare follow; and his strange whiteness is both the sign and veil of his mystery.

To this quality of whiteness Melville devotes a long chapter. It has for him an *unearthly* significance, combining the grandeur of snow-capped mountains, the treachery of rock-broken waters and the dread of phantoms. The absence of all colour which is the concrete of all colours leads beyond the bounds of personality and reason. He struggles to explain this mystical, well-nigh ineffable quality. "But," he cries, "how can I hope to explain myself here? And yet in some dim random way explain myself I must, else all these chapters might be naught." And explain himself he does, in so far that as we read we feel that it is the whiteness of Moby Dick that bestows upon him so surpassing a beauty, so malevolent a cunning. The white whale's whiteness is the whiteness of insanity; "the concrete of all colours, yet the absence of all colour." Only Godlike, godless Ahab would have courage to pursue and meet in deadly strife so terrible a monster. Ahab's is the history of a man who sees the world as the creation of a suffering and malignant Deity, a Deity whose highest thought is inferior to his own high courage. This demon who is his god and his apotheosis he will meet with contempt, exultation, and the rapture of conflict.

In the last chapters this passionate meeting is described. Three days of chase and conflict lead to the inevitable end; but never is Ahab's courage broken. Though boats are smashed beneath him, though the prophecies of Fedallah are one by one fulfilled with such contrary cunning as only a malign fate could contrive, though sharks nibble at the oars, and though his bone leg is severed a second time he follows with unquenchable fury. He is the needle drawn by the magnet. His madness is of such quality that the white whale and all that is there symbolised needs *must* render its consummation or its extinction.

Melville finishes his book upon a note of such seeming extravagance that to any but a symbolical interpretation it would appear bombastic. If, however, the undercurrents of his thought are perceived, the concluding incidents are of the inevitable structure of the tragedy. And this use of symbols does not only concern the main characters, but can be traced into the smallest details.

As the writer upon the sea, Melville's power of description is unsurpassed. It would be easy to multiply the quotation of passages of nobility and beauty. Again and again the reader pauses in a kind of spell-bound intoxication before the grandeur of his vision. Where, indeed, could be found an equal to his description of the sea the morning after the storm? And yet this extreme richness of the work tends towards its misinterpretation. That its high quality as a piece of psychological synthesis has been so much neglected is due to this very richness of material. A casual reader might often skip the more transcendental passages, and classify it as a mere book of adventure. It is indeed a book of adventure, but upon the highest plane of spiritual daring. A profound wisdom is here joined with a suffering and a courage which gropes beyond the limits of sanity. "There is a wisdom that is woe, and there is a woe that is madness." Both the wisdom and the woe are here mingled in this history of a soul's adventure.

AUGUSTINE BIRRELL

[The Great White Whale: A Rhapsody]†

Where the sea beasts ranged all round
Feed in the ooze of their pasture ground,
Where the sea-snakes coil and twine,
Dry their mail and bask in the brine;
Where GREAT WHALES come sailing by,
Sail and sail with unshut eye
Round the world for ever and aye.

MATTHEW ARNOLD.

And amongst these great whales, first, foremost and immortal, is Moby Dick, the Great White Whale.

† Augustine Birrell, "The Great White Whale: A Rhapsody," London *Athenaeum*, No. 4735 (Jan. 28, 1921), 99–100. Reprinted by permission of the *New Statesman*, London.

It is seventy years, just the measure of my own lifetime, since the white head and hump of Moby Dick suddenly loomed out of the blue water not very far to leeward. "There she blows, there she blows, a hump like a snow-hill. It is Moby Dick."

Earlier in the same year "The Whale" had been published in New York, and at once, as indeed might have been expected, aroused the enthusiasm of Nathaniel Hawthorne, but, though "Moby Dick" has been reprinted in England three or four times since 1851, none of these reprints has attracted sufficient attention.

Books have their fates no less than their authors, and it must not for one moment he supposed that this masterpiece of eloquence, character and adventure, despite a small circulation, hard to explain even in the year of "Uncle Tom's Cabin," fell flat. It did nothing of the kind, for from the very first it numbered good intellects among the "grown-ups," and excited the same enchanted admiration among a limited number of fortunate children as then did and do now the books of that kindred spirit, though of the Earth and not the Sea, George Borrow.

Among those lucky youngsters, the godchildren of Apollo, were included some subsequently celebrated writers who, having been allowed to feed their infant genius on the quintessential oils and the delectable blubber of this incomparable Beast, have risen into fame and attained a circulation quite beyond the dreams of the New Yorker who, born in 1819, of (so Miss Meynell tells us) mixed Dutch and English stock, went to sea as a cabin-boy on a vessel trading to Liverpool, and wrote "Moby Dick" in his thirty-second year. The sea remained Melville's element through a life which ended in 1891. The ocean he loved best was the Pacific, which "rolls the midmost waters of the world."

But though there is no need to commiserate Herman Melville on his limited "sales," it was none the less a hideous deprivation to a man of my age never to have encountered in the days of his youth, amid his various book-adventures, the Great White Whale, the ship "Pequod," the monomaniacal and crippled Captain Ahab for ever pursuing Moby Dick round the world, the tattooed lovable cannibal Queequeg with his pocket idol, the mysterious stranger Fedallah, the unaccountable Elijah, Starbruck, Stubbs and Flask, and the rest of the crew of the doomed whaler.

How this came about I cannot guess, for the house was otherwise well-stored with masterpieces, but so it was; nor was it until I was some years older than Melville when he wrote "Moby Dick" that I first heard his name. I owed my introduction to "Omoo," "Typee" and "The Whale" to that exquisite judge of a good book, Sir Alfred Lyall, who was shocked at my ignorance, and most emphatically urged me to read "Omoo" and "Typee"; but, as ill luck would have it, he did not specially dwell upon "The Whale." To hear was, in those days, to obey, and a second-hand bookseller almost at once supplied me with these three books. Even then I was not out of the Wood of Ignorance, for though I was greatly taken with "Omoo" and "Typee" I was not so bewitched by them as to begin at once upon the three volumes of "The Whale"—which I allowed to remain for a whole decade unread. One happy day I took them down, and then and then only did Moby Dick swim into my ken. Oh, woeful waste! Is there, I wonder (looking all round me), another such book lying neglected in this very room? And yet now, when full of my wrongs, I have discovered that all this time I had intimate friends, and even relatives, not much addicted to holding their peace, who knew all about Ahab and Bildad and Peleg and Moby Dick, and yet never gave me a hint of their existence. What on earth were they talking about all these years! I cannot remember. Now that "Moby Dick" is in the "World's Classics," and can be had for half-a-crown of all booksellers, the excuses of Ignorance or Concealment can no longer be urged on anyone's behalf in the High Court of Taste.

The two striking features of this book, after allowing for the fact that it is a work of genius and therefore *sui generis,* are, as it appears to me, its most amazing eloquence, and its mingling of an ever-present romanticism of style with an almost savage reality of narrative.

Eloquence is no common quality in English books, for to be really eloquent in cold print requires great courage, almost impudence, mixed with an extreme sensitiveness of nature; and sensitive men are apt to be timid with their pens and to hesitate long before beginning a sentence with the particle O! "I think it may be observed," says Dr. Johnson, in his "Life of Pope," "that the particle O at the beginning of a sentence always offends." Like most of the sayings that issued from the Johnsonian Mint, this dread *dictum* has a ring of truth about it, but it will not bear close examination. In the June number of the *Gentleman's Magazine* for 1787 a learned critic, signing himself J. A., had no difficulty in supplying the cultivated readers of that admirable periodical with a number of famous passages both of prose and poetry, culled from Hebrew, Latin and English authors of the greatest celebrity, all beginning with this bold particle. (See Walker's "Selection from the *Gentleman's Magazine,*" vol. ii. p. 341.)

I own to thinking but little of any author, be he poet or proseman, who dares not occasionally run the risk (and it is a risk) of beginning a sentence with an O! George Borrow never hesitated, and though Herman Melville is not so prodigal, he provides his readers with some splendid examples of this audacity; nor can I think that any reader of "The Whale" will deny the claim of its author to be one of the most eloquent of our English writers. To give curtailed examples, torn from the context of a book, the absorbing interest of which is all hung upon one peg—the pursuit of Moby Dick by the monomaniacal captain whose leg had been devoured by the sea-monster—would be a blunder, so I pass on to the second feature.

That most distinguished writer known to us all as R. L. S., who, in his bundle of good humours, had one especially delightful shaft which he often employed to make fun of himself, invented a new word whereby to describe his method of "dressing up" a romance. He called it *tushery*. Now there is no "tushery" in "The Whale." It is romantic from end to end, and eloquent throughout, but it is also grim and real. As an acute feminine critic once said to me about Melville's style in "The Whale," "it bruises you all over." You not only share the feelings, but all the hardships of the crew of the "Pequod," and your bones ache accordingly.

To give quotations, as I have already said, would be ridiculous, but to those who fight shy of a book they know nothing about, "The Town-Ho's story" (as told at the Golden Inn, Lima), or the chapter entitled "The Whiteness of the Whale," may safely be recommended to timid beginners.

It will be curious to observe whether a generation of readers brought up on another kind of fare will repair the injustice done by their grandparents in 1851.

Here and there a page or even a chapter of "The Whale" may be skipped with comparative impunity, but nobody but a sea-gudgeon can ever be sent to sleep between its pages. "And whereas all the other things, whether beast or vessel, that enter into the dreadful gulf of the whale's mouth, are immediately lost and swallowed up, the sea-gudgeon retires into it in great security *and there sleeps*" (Montaigne in his "Apology for Raimond de Sebonne").

We're not as "gudgeons" are;
Smith, take a fresh cigar!
Jones, the Tobacco-jar!
Here's to thee, "Melville"!

FRANK SWINNERTON

[It Is Not Everybody's Book]†

Another great discovery of the London critics is Herman Melville, of whose works there is to be a collected edition. Years ago I

† From Frank Swinnerton, "The Londoner," New York *Bookman*, Vol. 53 (May, 1921), 239.

read "Typee", "Omoo", and "Moby Dick", and then came to the conclusion that the later books of Melville were unreadable. "Omoo" and "Typee" have long been popular works. "Moby Dick" has for some time been included in the excellent "Everyman's Library". But only lately have the quidnuncs discovered the latter book, of which a new edition has just appeared in "The World Classics" with an introduction by Viola Meynell. This edition has called forth just such another chorus of praise from the critics as has the Keats centenary. "Moby Dick" has been formally "found" and placed as one of the masterpieces of all time. It can never again be wholly forgotten; but I wonder how long it will be before it is half forgotten. Not long, I fear. For one thing, it is not everybody's book. It is too fervid, as the author's later works are superabundantly too fervid. It is magnificent, full of color, a glorious example of what can be done with words urged to their task by a willing spirit. I do not question the virtue of Melville. But I find it hard to believe that his recent discoverers have done more than scratch the soil above the treasure of "Moby Dick"; and when once another old book has been rediscovered their enthusiasm will flow easily into the new channels with hardly a trace of memory to savor the fresh allegiance. Let us hope I am wrong. I have noticed, however, other discoveries and their precarious hold upon the attention of booklovers. The complete edition will doubtless do much to establish Melville as a permanent figure. Will not somebody discover the best of Marryat's work? It would be a kindly task, and one most grateful to those who are forever losing patience with what is current and representative of our own time. The time is with us and it is easier to retrieve a classic than to make a new one, particularly if the author be alive.

OLIVER WENDELL HOLMES, JR.

[It Seemed to Me a Great Book]†

Did I mention *Moby Dick*, by Herman Melville? I remember him in my youth. It seemed to me a great book—as ten years later may some of George Borrow's things, possibly influenced by him—but I should think a much greater man. It shook me up a good deal. It is wonderful already that a book published in 1851 doesn't seem thin, now. Hawthorne did when last I read *The Scarlet Letter*. Not so *Moby Dick*.

† From *Holmes-Pollock Letters*, ed. Mark DeWolfe Howe (Cambridge, Mass.: Harvard University Press, 1941), II, 68. Oliver Wendell Holmes, Jr., to Sir Frederick Pollock, from Washington, D.C., May 18, 1921. Reprinted by permission of the publisher.

H. M. TOMLINSON

[The Odd Priorities of American Professors: Time for Wordsworth but not Melville]†

The popular fiction which an English critic has called "wild treacle" is not all the American printed matter which reaches this side, though it is all, perhaps, that our reading public ever hears about. As a world of books, America lived before, and continued after, "David Harum." It is not easy to shake in friendship that hand across the sea which lately has disfigured our hoardings and bookstalls with Tarzan, no doubt the worst thing that ever came from America in bulk. But, having stated that not inconsiderable grievance, I must confess that the American public appears much more alert to the importance of books than would be guessed from the the popular stuff which forms one of its principal exports to this country.

The American public spares a greater share of its interest in general gossip to the news about literature than does the British. A number of New York dailies issue weekly literary supplements, and any one of these supplements contains more reviews of books and more articles with a literary content than all the morning and evening journals of London publish in a month. The scant attention and the still more meagre knowledge shown by some important London newspapers for any art except that of the picture-palace are scandalous, and give their prints the monotonous character of an appeal to the mentally defective; and it is worth noting that it is in just these papers, too, that the demand for ruthless economy in popular education is most cacophonous.

It is probable that Oxford would say that America's gusto for books is that of the young and thirsty fellow who would take dillwater with as hearty an appreciation as good wine. Very likely. Yet it is good to be young, and with an appetite so robust that it is more eager to get something than something in particular. The thought of the devotion which most of the American seats of learning give to "studies" in literature, for example, judging by some exceptionally weighty evidence which comes to THE NATION AND THE ATHENÆUM for review, fills a critic on this side with awe. I

† H. M. Tomlinson, "The World of Books," London *Athenaeum*, Vol. 29 (June 4, 1921), 363. Reprinted by permission of the *New Statesman*, London.

think it was Wisconsin which took Wordsworth, and made of that simple-hearted poet a learned book of about seven pounds avoirdupois, which I tried in vain to get any lover of letters here to examine critically. Each critic to whom I offered it gave it one startled glance, and at once changed the subject. The research work and these analyses and statistics certainly show an ardor to which even a lover of fine literature cannot always rise, and it would be very unwise to discourage it. On the contrary, while thanking America for its devotion to our classics, may a Britisher suggest to any American who has the leisure and the will for a little research work that what whole crowds of us over here would be delighted to get would be a monograph, as weighty and as crowded with detail as he likes, of Herman Melville?

A recent issue of the New York "Freeman" had some notes on the author of "Moby Dick," which did little more than excite one's appetite. It is clear that it is time this task was undertaken by an American who is properly aware that his country has produced a work which is not only unique of its kind, and a great achievement, but is the expression of an imagination that rises to the highest, and so is amongst the world's great works of art. There is something unusually fascinating in the case of Melville. We must learn more about that man. We know hardly anything at all at present. Let Wordsworth wait. How was it that the author who did two merely lively and observant books of travel, and a story, "White Jacket," which does not call for any special attention, on one occasion soared clear into the empyrean, and maintained himself among the stars through all one long book?

The American critics who find time for prolonged inquiries, published later in ponderous and even unreadable volumes, on English authors who are classical, but frequently dim to general readers in a well-earned obscurity, and who yet neglect the strange case of Melville, astonish me. There must be people living who have seen Melville, and have talked to him—the man who, it is reported, once remarked, "All fame is patronage; let me be infamous"; and, "I shall go down to them (posterity) in all likelihood. 'Typee' will be given to them with their gingerbread." Now is the very time to tackle that book about him. If this task is neglected a little longer, so that some priceless recollections of Melville, now available, are lost, and documents and other evidence of the man, which now exist, are buried still deeper beneath the litter of the years, then the book about him will be but tentative, and will leave the mystery darker than ever. And what a jolly task the writing of that biography would be! If only one lived near Nantucket.

VAN WYCK BROOKS

[The Melville Boom: Only a Question of Time]†

For some time now vague rumours have been going about of the presence of a great lost author in the cloudy depths—or the beclouded shallows, if you will—of our American literary history. The name of Herman Melville, an obscure clerk in the New York custom-house, dead these thirty years, the centenary of whose birth passed, two summers ago, unnoticed, is to-day in every one's mouth. Melville is emerging, portentous as his own White Whale: next month is to witness the publication of the first book that has been written about his life. "Though I wrote the Gospels in this century," he himself remarked to his friend Hawthorne, "I should die in the gutter." Melville did not die: for forty years after his great work was done he lived, unseen, forgotten, in the city where he was born. He did not even die in the historical manuals: the rising generation was assured, on the contrary, that his talent was quite as great as that of a dozen seventh-rate poets and romancers who had been his contemporaries. That his talent was a sovereign talent, or had at least its sovereign moments (let us insist only on the moments), his fellow-countrymen had not observed: it was only in England that he had been justly appreciated. For how many years I do not know, but certainly for many, it has been a common experience for American travellers in England to be asked why it is that no one has written a biography of Herman Melville. Well, it was only a question of time: sooner or later the darkness that surrounds this extraordinary man was certain to yield before our indefatigable national appetite for investigation and research. Next year Melville will have been forgotten again. The "hatred of literature," as Flaubert called it, which prevents our literary authorities from recognizing a genius prevents them also from retaining the memory of one. But for the next six months there is to be a Melville boom. Ishmael is to emerge at last: he is to have his little hour. And there will be a few hundred or a few dozen readers, moreover, who, discovering him for the first time in this limelight, will seize upon his gift as a permanent possession.

A complete edition of Melville's works is said to be in preparation, to follow the appearance of Professor Weaver's biography. The publishers of "Everyman's Library," meanwhile, have just issued reprints of their editions of "Omoo," "Typee" and "Moby

† From Van Wyck Brooks, "A Reviewer's Notebook," New York *Freeman*, Vol. 4 (October 26, 1921), 166–167. Reprinted by permission of E. P. Dutton & Co., Inc.

Dick." The first two of these books have already had their hour of late, thanks to the vogue of the South Seas. It is in "Moby Dick," however, that Melville rises to his real height and reveals himself not as a chronicler but as a creator. All these books were written before he was thirty-two. Thereafter the transcendental mystic got the best of the "man of this world": in "Moby Dick" itself there are strange lapses into the inexpressible that show us how insecure the artistic element was in its control over the various parts of Melville's mind. Melville seems to have been constitutionally unable to keep his eye on his subject, he was devoid of the sentiment of form: an artist of miraculous power in the minting of a phrase, a paragraph, a sudden, sharp, momentary episode, he wanders, when it comes to a large composition, like a garrulous old man who can not recall, at the conclusion of a discourse, the idea with which he began. This weakness was the ultimate undoing of him as a writer. It is sufficiently pronounced in his one masterpiece.

To those, indeed, for whom literature is a question of the theme, of the intention, no book could be more exasperating than "Moby Dick." The great characters, that of the narrator, that of the cannibal Queequeg, vanish in the midst of it as if one had not been led to suppose that they, with Captain Ahab, were the chief strands in the rope of the tale. Captain Ahab himself, who emerges at the end so superbly, disappears for hundreds of pages in the middle. The author forgets his story, he loses himself in the details of cetology, he tells us about ambergris and about the erroneous and the "less erroneous" pictures of whales by Hogarth, by Guido, by Dürer; he has a chapter on the tails of whales, another on the spouting of whales, another on "Jonah Historically Regarded"; he speculates, he mythologizes, he indulges, like some incorrigible old Burton, every quaint conceit, every whim of the bookworm in the dressing-gown. Does one regret it? I am speaking of the opportunity he appears to miss by such a procedure. If Coleridge had permitted the ancient mariner to tell his story in his own language, we should have had no doubt a thousand pages of entrancing talk. Something was gained, however, by Coleridge's taking the words out of his mariner's mouth and shaping them with the last severity. Melville has an ancient mariner, too, that strange Elijah who plucks Ishmael's sleeve on the wharf at Nantucket and warns him against putting to sea in the "Pequod." What a place "Moby Dick" would have had among the great stories of the world if its author, having seized upon that thread, had held it firmly in his hand and followed it, with a single eye!

If Melville had been capable of this, moreover, he might have given us many another great book. As well ask a George Borrow to write like a Prosper Mérimée! Melville is an American Borrow, a

Borrow of the sea: to say that is to surrender all one's regets and simply yield to the delight of the anomalous. "He lived in the world," our author says of Captain Ahab, "as the last of the grizzly bears lived in settled Missouri." Melville was himself a sort of unique anachronism. One can easily discern here and there in his writings the traces of his age. There is the touch of mystical democratism which he shares with Whitman; there is the occasional note of "Sartor Resartus" in his ecstatic soliloquizings. For the style, for the method of "Moby Dick," one has to go back, on the other hand, to the seventeenth century. "Out of the trunk the branches grow; out of them the twigs. So, in productive subjects, grow the chapters." True enough, if the subject happens to be the Anatomy of Melancholy or the Religio Medici. When Melville begins to discuss the theme of standing mastheads do not expect him to stop until he has told you that the earliest successful standers-of-mastheads were the Egyptians, inasmuch as the great stone mast of the builders of Babel went down with the first gale, that Simeon Stylites was dauntless in this pursuit and that something is to be claimed even for Napoleon, who has held his place for some years on the top of a column; do not, when the chapter happens to be concerned with the "honour and glory of whaling," look for the last word till our author has explained how Perseus was the first whaleman and how Hercules and St. George have the right to be enrolled in this guild, not to mention Jonah and Vishnu. If Melville's learned loquacity takes one back three hundred years, so does his use of language. He can carry an apostrophe to the length of a page, and his words have the strong natural flavour of Shakespeare's prose, or of Southdown mutton. No seasoning there! It would be difficult to find in any other American book pages to compare with his in this power of retaining the primitive juices of the English tongue. And I am not speaking of the temperament of the man, which is that of an Elizabethan voyager, "boldly dipping," to quote a phrase of his own, "into the Potluck of both worlds."

To return, however, to "Moby Dick." If Melville constantly loses the thread of his tale, he more than makes up for this by the intensity with which he returns to it. He has a ravenous eye, he clings to the visible fact as a pouncing hawk clings to its prey. What has ever been more fiercely seen than such episodes, for example, as that of the great squid, or Captain Ahab's watch, or the appalling chase of the White Whale? Melville somewhere expresses the fear that his book will be taken for a "hideous and intolerable allegory." An allegory it is, and he is in general at no pains to conceal the fact: this white-headed whale with his wrinkled brow, his crooked jaw and his high, snowy hump, personifies, our author frankly tells us, "the heartless voids and immensities of the universe," and again "all that most maddens and torments, all that stirs up the lees of things, all truth with malice in it, all that cracks the sinews and cakes the brain, all the subtle demonisms of life and thought." He is fate, this Moby Dick, and the terrible old Captain Ahab is the tragic will of man which defies it and tracks it down, only to be overwhelmed and to perish by it. But no allegory could less confuse the reader's imagination, seized as it can not fail to be by the personal tragedy of the terrible old man himself, a truly Shakespearean figure. I have spoken of the opportunity which Melville appears to miss by wandering from his main theme. The marvel of the book is that he leaves one, after all, so much at the mercy of the single impression he has done his best to destroy.

An American Borrow, a Borrow of the sea: let us return to this. Let us remark in conclusion, however, that Melville was indeed the "word-master" that Borrow professed to be and was not. Who excels him in the gift of the phrase? Recall, for example, how Queequeg darts from the side of the ship "with a long living arc of a leap." In the ability to flash a sudden picture upon the retina? Who can forget that moment in the " 'Town-Ho's' Story" when the White Whale emerges from the sea and the dogged crew eye askance "the appalling beauty of the vast milky mass, that lit up by a horizontal spangling sun, shifted and glistened like a living opal in the blue morning sea"? Who can forget the last appearance of the whale, emerging on the third day of the chase to give battle to the doomed "Pequod" and all its men?

> Suddenly the waters around them slowly swelled in broad circles; then quickly upheaved, as if sideways sliding from a submerged berg of ice, swiftly rising to the surface. A low rumbling sound was heard, a subterranean hum; and then all held their breaths, as, bedraggled with trailing ropes, and harpoons, and lances, a vast form shot lengthwise, but obliquely, from the sea. Shrouded in a thin drooping veil of mist, it hovered for a moment in the rainbowed air; and then fell swamping back into the deep. Crushed thirty feet upwards, the waters flashed for an instant like heaps of fountains, then brokenly sank in a shower of flakes, leaving the circling surface creamed like new milk round the marble trunk of the whale.

To these blinding moments some will prefer such scenes as the old black cook's sermon to the sharks or Queequeg the cannibal's prostration before his idol in the chamber of the New Bedford inn. But Melville is himself, like the White Whale, emerging again. He does not need to be pointed out.

H. M. TOMLINSON

[A Supreme Test of a Reader]†

We come to "Moby Dick." When one enters that book one is instantly aware of an overshadowing presence. From the opening passage there is no doubt about it. Nor is it now a fitful presence. It meets us at that entrance which is quite rightly entitled "Loomings." We go at once into a world where all is familiar—streets, ships, men, sea, and sky—but where all has been enchanted. Another spirit is there, creative, dominant, which knows us, but is itself unknown. What has happened it is impossible to say. We hear Melville's voice. It is easily recognizable. His words are familiar and the rhythm of their ordering. But they are somehow changed. They have been transmuted. They shine with an unearthly light. Their music can be even terrifying, like nameless sounds heard at night in the wilderness.

These, of course, are generalities. But who has resolved poetry into its elements? We know it only from the thrill it gives, neither of joy nor of fear, but something of each, when we encounter it. "Moby Dick" is a supreme test. If it captures you, then you are unafraid of great art. You may dwell in safety with fiends or angels and rest poised with a quiet mind between the stars and the bottomless pit.

CARL VAN VECHTEN

[The Greatest American Book]‡

As for "Moby Dick," so much has been written about this great book (perhaps not enough, but enough for the present) that it seems unnecessary to pause very long even here. I may say, however, that I have scant patience with those who consider "Moby Dick" only a sea story. One man, indeed, a well-known critic of literature, recently told me that he had not read the book because he did not care for tales of adventure! Equally pertinently, he might have said that he could not read "Hamlet" because he did not care for plays about Danes. "Moby Dick" *is* a tale of adventure in the sense that "Hamlet" is, in the sense that Dante's "Divine Comedy" is. It is the narrative of man's great struggle against the

† From H. M. Tomlinson, "A Clue to 'Moby Dick,'" New York *Literary Review*, Vol. 2 (Nov. 5, 1921), 142.

‡ From Carl Van Vechten, "The Later Work of Herman Melville," New Orleans *Double Dealer*, Vol. 3 (Jan., 1922), 15–16.

natural and supernatural and man's final defeat. It is surely Melville's greatest book, surely the greatest book that has yet been written in America, surely one of the great books of the world.

T. E. LAWRENCE

[A Shelf of "Titanic" Books]†

Confession is in the air. Do you remember my telling you once that I collected a shelf of 'Titanic' books (those distinguished by greatness of spirit, 'sublimity' as Longinus would call it): and that they were *The Karamazovs, Zarathustra,* and *Moby Dick*. Well, my ambition was to make an English fourth. You will observe that modesty comes out more in the performance than in the aim!

ANONYMOUS

The Vogue of Herman Melville‡

Three years ago perhaps six literary critics in a national congress of their kind might have been able to name the author of "Piazza Tales," "Mardi," and "The Confidence Man," though that is doubtful; it is fairly certain, however, that not more than two of the six could have said that they had read those books. This reviewer, so long ago, would have had to admit his ignorance to be complete. Even the British Museum, at that time, did not possess a copy of "Piazza Tales," and no doubt even a good second-hand bookseller would have let a copy of it go for a shilling or two. We heard last week that £30 was being asked in London for a first edition of it; not an unreasonable price either, for, though incorrectly described as the only example of its kind in the country, we know of the existence of but two other copies.

The demand here and in America for the very rare first editions of Melville's books—the fire many years ago at Harpers of New York destroyed a large stock of his early editions—arises from a simple cause. A recent cheap edition of "Moby Dick" has resulted

† From *The Letters of T. E. Lawrence*, ed. David Garnett (New York: Doubleday & Company, Inc., and London: Jonathan Cape Ltd., 1938), p. 360. Copyright 1938, 1939 by Doubleday & Company, Inc. Reprinted by permission of the publishers and The Trustees of the Letters of T. E. Lawrence. T. E. Lawrence to Edward Garnett, from London, August 26, 1922.

‡ "The Vogue of Herman Melville," *The Nation & The Athenaeum* (London), Vol. 31 (September 31, 1922), 857–58. Reprinted by permission of the *New Statesman*, London. A review of *Typee* and *Omoo*, the first volumes of the Constable edition of Melville.

in a common confession that the book is a masterpiece, and in a general curiosity about its author. That book, indeed, appears to have been a wonder treasured as a sort of secret for years by some select readers who had chanced upon it. They said little about it. We gather that they had been in the habit of hinting the book to friends they could trust, so that "Moby Dick" became a sort of cunning test by which genuineness of another man's response to literature could be proved. If he was not startled by "Moby Dick," then his opinion on literature was of little account. It should be observed, however, that the victim was never told this, because this test was made by those who seemed scared by the intensity of their own feelings aroused by the strange, subliminal potency of the monster called the White Whale. And they observed, too, that "Moby Dick" was not a book whose merits, so remarkable to them, had been noted by the authorized surveyors of literature. They were confident in their opinion, but they were in the position of the amateur astronomer who feels sure that, with a home-made telescope, he has discovered a star of the first magnitude, yet hardly cares to announce it because Greenwich is strangely silent about this obvious celestial wonder.

To-day, Herman Melville is admitted to be one of the best things America has done. So whole-hearted, indeed, has been the admiration of English critics for "Moby Dick" that the more intellectual of the American critics have, quite naturally, retorted that the White Whale is not such a fine whale after all. It might have been bigger, or different. It is not the kind of whale to which a modern American man of letters would have given birth. Which, we will admit, is probable; yet, nevertheless, the significance of "Moby Dick" is so portentous that a deep curiosity concerning its author and his other works is natural. Owing to Messrs. Constable's enterprise, Melville's other books, which not only were out of print but were almost forgotten, will now be accessible—at least, to those with the requisite guineas for a praiseworthy investment.

To those who know only "Omoo" and "Typee"—the initial volumes of this standard edition—and "Moby Dick," Melville's other books may prove not only puzzling, but disappointing. Some of his novels and narratives are but pedestrian, others are flamboyant and wild, and there are others so congested and tough that it is only the drive of one's desire to find a clue to the mind of so extraordinary a man which gets one through them. An interest which will carry a reader through even an attractive writer's worst work is rare. Darwin, too, was an extraordinary man, but a reading of the "Origin of Species" does not awaken a passion to learn all that is to be known about him. Nor is the desire to read all that Melville wrote merely a hopeful expectation of finding another book like

"Moby Dick." One knows at once, or ought to know, that that book is unique.

What makes it so remarkable a book is not easy to define. It is certain, however, that its writer was as different from the majority of his species as a man is from a sheep. Melville gives hints, in his masterpiece, that his mind at times moved to a plane where he saw things in a way we will call phantasmal, because our intelligence cannot do it. What he knew cannot be related to anything we know, and some of us, therefore, are likely to explain it as a vagary of dementia. But that will not do. The exquisite poise, so perilously maintained throughout "Moby Dick," mocks us out of that explanation. There are moments in great music when the listener can believe he has heard echoes out of deeps he cannot know. There are such thrills in great poetry, as those hints and warnings which transcend the drama of "Macbeth." It is this fearful apprehension, the suspicion that there was a sound from beyond our horizon, which moves us at times in reading "Moby Dick." An ardent curiosity concerning all that its author has written is, therefore, natural.

ARTHUR HOBSON QUINN

[Melville's Besetting Weakness]†

One has to wade through much that is forbidding—the introductory chapters and the tiresome lectures on the structure and classification of whales illustrate again Melville's besetting weaknesses, his lack of humor, and his inability to distinguish fact from fiction. But when the great chase nears its end and the White Whale turns on its pursuers and rends them, there is painted for us an unforgettable scene, in which the fury of man goes down, defeated, by the fury of the great beast, driven to bay in its own selected battle-ground.

H. M. TOMLINSON

[Melville's Emergence from Limbo]‡

With "The Confidence Man" and "Israel Potter," Messrs. Constable have completed in twelve volumes the first Standard Edition

† From Arthur Hobson Quinn, review of Raymond Weaver's biography of Melville, *Yale Review*, Vol. 12 (Oct., 1922), 205–9; the quotation is from 208.

‡ H. M. Tomlinson, "The World of Books," London *Athenaeum*, Vol. 33 (April 7, 1923), 17. Reprinted by permission of the *New Statesman*, London.

of Herman Melville's prose works. Melville died in 1891; but, until a year or two ago, except that many of us had gone to "Omoo" and "Typee" because we had been told it was those books which sent Stevenson to the South Seas, and that one or two friends of ours, otherwise dependable, passed into incoherent rapture whenever they mentioned another of Melville's books, Melville was merged in that great company of writers which lives, but only in Limbo. The pious, who would have us believe that what is righteous cannot perish, have an easy case to maintain, because if what was good has perished unheard of, then how can we know of it? Yet Melville could have been acclaimed at any moment. There were "Tristram Shandy" and "Pickwick Papers" to show what was the line in the royal descent. Much that Melville had written was to be bought, including that one book which is as remarkable a prose narrative as there is in English, and is itself sufficient to justify the independence of the American Republic. We flew no signal bunting, however, till recently, and that celebration came, not by premeditation and appointment, but by chance. For it is little more than two years since the Oxford University Press, in the "World's Classics," published "Moby Dick," with a preface by Viola Meynell giving the White Whale just measure. That little edition dates the accession of Herman Melville.

As a consequence of the publication of that edition, he has been lifted out of the estimable company of oddities whose literary works we will not willingly let die but seldom read, into the company of the great. For "Moby Dick," as my readers may remind me they are weary of hearing—though never again on this page will I whisper it—is an immense experience in one's reading life. Incoherent rapture is its first fruits. If it electrifies us, then we are still young. If it does not, then either we have lignified, or we have reached Nirvana and so are beyond even those regions surmised on the outer bounds of Moby's vagaries. There is no intermediate state. It must be either one or the other.

When I began to read it, I did not believe it. That first chapter was too good to be true. Books beginning at that elevation cannot be maintained there except by magicians; and how often do we meet writers of that kind? Moreover, I had come to it late, for I had ridiculed at least one rare and exciting rumor about it. And the editor of this journal, when he heard my own exclamations about the Whale—she blows, she blows!—(and from Adelphi Terrace, too) replied quietly that, in a general way, and when his well-being was not in forfeit, he was prepared to accept a fair proportion of whatever I might say without niggling verification. But this was too much. There were no whales about. My mind was disturbed. What! Believe that not only had I seen a whale, but that it had swallowed me? Would I ask him next to agree that he had a Jonah in the office? He then ran his pen over a whetstone absently, and addressed himself to the last peculiarity of our great political Jonah and teller of wonder-tales. But when I went from him I left Moby with him. Later I peeped in. He had passed hence. He was not writing politics; transfigured and tense, he was hunting a monster amid the shadows of the profounds that are quite beyond soundings. He was making the noises of wonder, awe, and delight. I knew perfectly well, all the time, I had seen a whale. Now the editor saw it. What does Charing Cross matter? The monster had breached over the railway bridge.

VAN WYCK BROOKS

[A Third Look at Melville]†

So much has been written lately about "Moby-Dick" that I hesitate to bring the subject up again; but the beautifully clear and spacious pages of the new collected edition of Melville to which I referred last week have beguiled me into reading the book a third time, and I am wondering if all its felicities have dawned even yet on people's minds. It seems to me now less chaotic, better shaped, than it seemed at first: nothing has surprised me more than to discover how conscious Melville was of what he was doing. I had taken too seriously the statement with which he opens Chapter 82: "There are some enterprises in which a careful disorderliness is the true method"—or rather, I had not placed enough weight on this word "careful." It seemed to me intolerable that he had not removed the chapters on whales in general, on whaling, whales' heads, pitchpoling, ambergris, the try-works, etc., and published them separately: they were glorious, but I could not believe that they had been deliberately introduced to retard the action. It struck me that the action should have been retarded as it were within the story. I do not feel this now. The book is an epic, and an epic requires ballast. Think of the catalogue of ships in Homer, the mass of purely historical information in the "Æneid," the long descriptions in "Paradise Lost": how immensely these elements add to the density and the volume of the total impression, and how they serve to throw into relief the gestures and activities of the characters! This freight of inanimate or partially inanimate material gives "Moby-Dick" its bottom, its body, in the vintner's phrase;

† From Van Wyck Brooks, "A Reviewer's Notebook," New York *Freeman*, Vol. 7 (May 16, 1923), 238–39.

and I am convinced that Melville knew exactly what he was about.

It is only when we have grasped the nature of the book that we begin to perceive how cunning is its craftsmanship throughout. Of the larger lines I shall speak presently; but glance for a moment at the single episode of Father Mapple's sermon in the Whaleman's Chapel. Why is it that, once read, this episode seems to have built itself permanently into the tissues of our imagination? It is because of the skill with which Melville has excluded from our minds every irrelevant detail. He wishes, first, to establish the nautical character of the preacher, so he has him stoop down, after he has climbed into the pulpit, and drag up the ladder step by step, till the whole is deposited within. This may have been taken from reality, for Father Mapple is known to have been drawn from Father Taylor, Emerson's friend, the apostle to the sailors in Boston. But Melville's skill here consists in not remarking that Father Mapple might have been boarding a ship: the image already conveys this connotation—Melville uses it to heighten our sense of the preacher's momentary "withdrawal from all outward worldly ties and connexions." This nautical character, moreover, is preserved by every detail of the sketch. When Father Mapple kneels and prays, his prayer is so deeply devout that he seems to be "kneeling and praying at the bottom of the sea." When he rises, he begins to speak "in prolonged solemn tones, like the continual tolling of a bell in a ship that is foundering at sea in a fog." This impression, once established, is maintained by the imagery of the sermon; but, to pass to another point, why do we remember the sermon so vividly? Partly because of the storm that is beating outside the chapel. We are never allowed to forget this storm. It shrieks and drives about us as we enter the chapel, it pelts the door from without, it howls between the hymn and the sermon, it appears to "add new power to the preacher, who, when describing Jonah's sea-storm, seemed tossed by a storm himself." The effect of all this is to redouble the solemn intimacy of the scene. The chapel is cut off from the world like the cabin of a ship; our minds are focused with an almost painful intensity upon the visible and audible facts that immediately surround us.

I have dwelt on this episode because it shows with what deliberate art Melville has ensnared his readers. To turn now to the work as a whole: how carefully, with what prevision, he has built up the general scheme: the pitch of the book, the "mystery" of the White Whale, the character of Captain Ahab. First of all, the pitch with what a mighty rhythm the "Pequod" starts on its voyage:

> Ship and boat diverged; the cold, damp night breeze blew between; a screaming gull flew overhead; the two hulls wildly

rolled; we gave three heavy-hearted cheers, and blindly plunged like fate into the lone Atlantic.

There we have the note of the saga; and this is consistently sustained by a dozen different means. Take the portraits of the three mates, Starbuck, Stubb and Flask, "momentous men" all; and the three fantastic harpooneers, the cannibal Queequeg, Tashtego, the Gay Head Indian, and Daggoo, the gigantic Negro. By a process of simplification that heightens their effect without removing it from reality, Melville invests these characters with a semblance as of Homer's minor heroes:

> Daggoo retained all his barbaric virtues, and erect as a giraffe, moved about the decks in all the pomp of six feet five in his socks. There was a corporeal humility in looking up at him; and a white man standing before him seemed a white flag come to beg truce of a fortress.

> [Tashtego.] To look at the tawny brawn of his lithe snaky limbs, you would almost have credited the superstitions of some of the earlier Puritans, and half believed this wild Indian to be a son of the Prince of the Powers of the Air.

This method of characterization, indeed, prevails throughout the book. Take the captain of the "Jeroboam," for instance:

> A long-skirted, cabalistically cut coat of a faded walnut tinge enveloped him; the overlapping sleeves of which were rolled up on his wrists. A deep, settled, fanatic delirium was in his eyes.

We are living from beginning to end in a world by one degree larger than life. The constant mythological allusions, the sweep of the style, the bold splendour of the similes support this impression, till at last the battles with the whales begin and we feel beneath the book the very pulse of the ocean itself. "Give me a condor's wing!" Melville exclaims in the excitement of his inspiration. "Give me Vesuvius's crater for an inkstand!" And then he adds, proudly conscious of his achievement: "Such, and so magnifying, is the virtue of a large and liberal theme! We expand to its bulk. To produce a mighty book, you must choose a mighty theme."

No less extraordinary is the development of the legend of "Moby-Dick," of the sense of impending fatality. Towards the end it may be thought that Melville strains a point or two in order to produced this latter effect. I am thinking especially of the chapter in which the sea-hawk darts away with Ahab's hat; but the chapters on the "candles" and the needle are open to the same objection. There is an electrical storm and the corposants appear on the yard-arms; and soon afterwards it is found that the compasses have been turned. All these phenomena are natural, but they are certainly exceptional; and, occurring so close together, they seem to me to overshoot their mark, which is, of course, to inform the reader that the calamitous whale is approaching. Machinery of this kind is much more in place in works like "The Ancient Mariner" that frankly embody supernatural elements. But consider, at the outset of the book, the apparition of Elijah. Consider that astonishing chapter on the whiteness of the whale. Consider the reports of Moby-Dick that come to us, one after another, from the sailors, from wandering sea-captains encountered during the voyage, from the mad Gabriel of the "Jeroboam," from the captain of the "Samuel Enderby" whose arm the monster has torn away as he tore away Ahab's leg. The fabulous whale torments our imagination till we, like Gabriel, think of him as "no less a being than the Shaker God incarnated"; and all this, be it noted, without a word of direct description on Melville's part. Until he reveals himself just before the chase, we see Moby-Dick solely through the consequences of his actions and the eyes of superstitious men.

I should like to linger over another aspect of the fabulous element of the book—fabulous but entirely consonant with reality. I mean the theme of the "five dusky phantoms" who appear midway in the story, suddenly surrounding Ahab and as if "fresh formed out of air." We get our first hint of their existence in the dark words of Elijah, when Ishmael and Queequeg encounter him near the wharf in the grey dawn:

> But he stole up to us again, and suddenly clapping his hand on my shoulder, said, 'Did ye see anything looking like men going toward that ship a while ago?'
>
> Struck by this plain matter-of-fact question, I answered, saying 'Yes, I thought I did see four or five men; but it was too dim to be sure.'
>
> 'Very dim, very dim,' said Elijah. 'Morning to ye.'
>
> Once more we quitted him; but once more he came softly after us; and touching my shoulder again, said, 'See if you can find 'em now, will ye?'
>
> 'Find who?'
>
> 'Morning to ye! Morning to ye!' he rejoined, again moving off.

Later, on the voyage, Stubb remarks that Captain Ahab is always disappearing at night: "Who's made appointments with him in the hold? Ain't that queer, now?" These vaguely defined Orientals are satisfactorily accounted for as the story moves on; but they remain dim, and their presence and their dimness and the pale, opalescent light that emanates from them spread I can hardly say what magic through the book. It is to be observed, moreover, that all this fantasy in "Moby-Dick" has behind it everywhere a substantial fabric of fact: that is why we never feel that we are reading a romantic novel, why, even at the most extravagant moments, we accept every detail as veracious. There were actually to be seen, in the Nantucket of the 'forties, such figures as Queequeg and Fedallah, just as there were old "fighting Quakers, Quakers with a vengeance," lords of whales like Bildad and Peleg, with their "thousand bold dashes of character, not unworthy a Scandinavian sea-king, or a poetical pagan Roman." We can trace the whole story, trunk, branches and twigs, back to the scene out of which it springs, and which we feel between the lines, just as we can trace the Arabian genie back to Aladdin's lamp; and this, by enabling us to compare the fact with the treatment, inevitably and immensely heightens the effect of the latter.

Of Captain Ahab I should never stop talking if I once began. But here again, to recur to the aspect of the book upon which I have been dwelling, how admirable is Melville's power of construction. "Ahab's soul's a centipede that moves upon a hundred legs." So he himself asseverates, in the midst of the chase; and this character of a "mighty pageant creature, formed for noble tragedies" is developed and sustained with uncanny adroitness. First we are presented with the other captains who give us the scale of the Nantucket whale-masters in general. Then we see him through a cloud of strange rumours, and not till the ship is well at sea does he appear at all. Suddenly he emerges; he stands on the quarter deck, and Melville describes him minutely in a magnificent passage. Then he vanishes again, to remain omnipresent but only intermittently visible, the soul, the brain, the will of the ship, and in the end the embodiment of a bedevilled humanity. We are never permitted to become familiar with him: he is never mentioned, he never appears, indeed, save to the accompaniment of some superb phrase, some new majestic image. He is a "grand, ungodly, godlike man," a "good man—not a pious good man, like Bildad, but a swearing good man"; he is a "khan of the plank, a king of the sea, and a great lord of leviathans"; he "lives in the world as the last of the grizzly bears lived in settled Missouri." It can fairly be said that by the time the chase begins, Ahab is as mighty and terrible a figure in our minds as Moby-Dick himself. The two fabulous characters have grown, by similar means, side by side.

Much more might be said of the form of the book—of the shredded Shakespearean drama, for example, the scraps and fragments of which, among other diverse elements, have been pressed into the moving mass of the narrative. But I can not attempt to develop these points. "The great task of an artist," said Taine, "is to find subjects which suit his talent." Melville had this good fortune once and once only; but his masterpiece is worth more than libraries of lesser books. "Moby-Dick" is our sole American epic, no less an epic for being written in prose; and has it been observed that it revives in a sense the theme of the most ancient epic of the English-speaking peoples? Grendel in "Beowulf" might almost be described as the prototype of the White Whale. Was not Grendel also the symbol of "all that most maddens and torments, all that stirs up the lees of things, all truth with malice in it, all that cracks the sinews and cakes the brain, all the subtle demonisms of life and thought, all evil—visibly personified"?

J. W. N. SULLIVAN

[Melville's Lonely Journey]†

Herman Melville is one of those writers who make it clear beyond all controversy that much of the apparatus of literary criticism which has been elaborated up to our time is fit only to deal with unessentials. In the greatest work of Herman Melville we are in the presence of a kind of literature where the "scientific" analysis of Taine would be solemn buffoonery, and where the delicate sensibility of Pater would be irrelevant. The principles for the formation of a proper literary taste, the principles so carefully expounded in old lectures on rhetoric, with their subdivisions of "character-drawing," "description," "style," and so on, tell us, when applied to Melville, nothing of the slightest consequence. "Who touches this book," said Whitman of his own, "touches a man." It is to that kind of literature that Melville's best work belongs. We are not in the presence of what is usually called a work of art, something that can be separated off from its author in the same way, although not to the same degree, as a scientific theory can be separated off from its originator. "Moby Dick" is not, as it has been so often called, the greatest of sea stories; it is not a vast, elaborate account of the hunting of a mighty and mysterious whale. It is an account of the mighty, mysterious, and troubled soul of Herman Melville.

It is possible that "Moby Dick" is a great work of art. Those wonderful descriptions of New Bedford, the Spouter Inn, Father Mapple's sermon, fair and foul weather at sea, the technique of whale hunting, probably satisfy all the canons. And possibly there are some to whom Ahab, Starbuck and the rest of them are credible and satisfying sea heroes. But as the great whale grows more

† J. W. N. Sullivan, "Herman Melville," London *Times Literary Supplement*, No. 1123 (July 26, 1923), 493–94. Reproduced from *The Times Literary Supplement* by permission. This review-essay was occasioned by the publication of the Constable and Cape editions of Melville. [*Editors' note.*]

imminent even the most resolutely realistic reader must have strange qualms. Is this a ship, are these men, and is the great whale really a whale. Can anything which happens on a real sea evoke this dark, profound passion; make natural the terrible tension of this hardly controlled prose; justify these sudden soundings to depths of which we were unconscious? We realize that the great ocean itself and the leviathans that inhabit it are scarcely big enough to shadow forth the real deeps and the real monsters with which Melville is concerned. And the story, which perhaps seemed so clear, becomes a veil. Melville, we realize, is dealing with things that even great writers rarely touch; he is trying to say things which are not fully to be said. But it is only in so far as we have understood the inexpressible that we have read Melville.

There has been, we must suppose, a growth of consciousness in man. The journey from the sub-microscopic organism or the amoeba, or whatever began it all, has been a very long one. And who can say what kinds of awareness, what other sorts of consciousness, were not implicit in those beginnings? Who can say what price we have paid for being what we are? Many men must be suspicious at times that these clear, adequate minds of ours extend very little beyond their usefulness, that they are, essentially, reasonably successful devices of accommodation. A premium has been put upon a part of us; a certain kind of environment has made incessant demands upon us. But we have grown to this, and it may be that we shall grow beyond it. It is unreasonable to suppose that the whole of us is exhausted by what we have now to be. And it seems, now and then, that a man appears in whom our fast-slumbering faculties have been stirred to a little life. He has a little escaped from the bond of circumstance; he can see, very dimly, shapes lurking in our featureless blackness. He sees our world differently; the happenings of life are differently pregnant for him. If he be a writer, this vision will give a curious quality to his writing: he will be trying to say something language was not invented to say, and it will only be in so far as our world affords symbols for what he has to say that he will be able to communicate with us. Even so, he may wait a long time for an audience.

The recent emergence of a large public for Melville's work, as testified by these collected editions, is one of the most interesting indications of the change which is taking place in the general mind. Melville's complete lack of popularity in his own time was due to the great dissimilarity between his personal vision and the general *Weltanschauung*. The world of the Victorians was hardly a mysterious world. Their material world was a perfectly clear-cut and comprehensible affair, and everything that was not material was merely moral. Every aspect of their world, as it seems to us now, was most strangely finite and most strangely clear; their most comprehensive schemes left out so much. Perhaps it was only in that age that the biological theory of evolution could have been welcomed as a world philosophy; when it was objected to, it was objected to as "degrading." Important people felt their dignity to be outraged, but the entire irrelevance of the theory to the central mystery of man himself seems hardly to have been remarked either by the antagonists or the supporters of the theory. The severer science of that time, splendid as it was, was equally naïve. "Matter," it was accepted everywhere, was the sort of stuff that made up the stone Dr. Johnson kicked—and obviously there was no mystery about that. To the kind of awareness possessed by Herman Melville it must have seemed that his contemporaries understood hardly anything. Even to us there is often something invisibly superficial about their outlook. They were islanders who lived unconscious of the sea. No murmur from far-off regions could reach their ears. The rumblings of "Moby Dick" were quite inaudible to them, and even that most mystical of composers, Beethoven himself, became somebody remarkable for the elevation of his style and the nobility of his sentiments. This is not to say that there were no exceptions. But to the general consciousness of that age Melville probably had less to say than he would have had in almost any other age, and certainly much less than he has to say to us. And it may be mentioned, incidentally, that the complete lack of comprehension he encountered was hardly a good thing for Melville. A kind of recklessness in fantasy, the growing lack of a sense of proportion, observable in Melville's later work, sprang, we think, from the complete lack of public understanding of his essential purpose. He became more and more content to make less and less effort to communicate to others the profundities of his inner life. It is not without significance that whereas "Moby Dick" is dedicated to Nathaniel Hawthorne, "Pierre" is dedicated to no human being, but to Greylock, the mountain near which Melville lived. And it is in "Pierre" that Melville shows a more bitter scorn for his contemporaries than it is good for a man, so little shallow, to have.

> So beforehand he felt the unrevealable sting of receiving either plaudits or censures, equally unsought for, and equally loathed ere given. So beforehand he felt the pyramidical scorn of the genuine loftiness for the whole infinite company of infinitesimal critics. His was the scorn which thinks it not worth the while to be scornful. Those he most scorned never knew it.

But worse things come of this lonely and implacable voyaging than loss of contact with one's fellows. As Melville says later, "But man does not give himself up thus, a doorless and shutterless house for the four loosened winds of heaven to howl through, without still additional dilapidations."

As we say, we think there has been a change in the general mind. It would seem that there is a *Zeitgeist* swaying peoples as a whole; it seems that man's consciousness develops, or at least acquires a new direction. Things which were dark become clear; there is a perpetual shifting up and down of great ones on their thrones; the region of the possible becomes enlarged, and more and more adventurous spirits are driven to peep over the edge of the world. In our own time we think that science has been the chief agent in liberating men from the clear but too finite world of the Victorians. There is a great difference between the random collocations of atoms which were supposed to produce us and the modern universe whose matter, space, and time, it appears, are largely creations of our own. Such ideas do not nestle isolated in the mind. They subtly modify the whole of a man's outlook; they make a sensitive surface where there was nothing but a blind integument; they create dim centres of vision for what was before total darkness. It is characteristic of our time that there is a sense of unprecedented possibilities; the firm lines of our accustomed world are growing indistinct. In science and philosophy, chiefly, we feel that the soul of man has started on new adventures. We get glimpses of greater and perhaps more lonely seas than man has ever adventured on before. And although the general consciousness may have no more than the dimmest apprehension of what is being attempted, it is aware that something is afoot. It stirs, a little blindly, but not much more blindly than the most far-sighted man amongst us. These troubled waters may presage some great tidal movement, but no man can yet say what the direction will be. And we are now sufficiently tremulous, sufficiently sensitive, for that strange class of writers to which Melville belongs to be, not perhaps intelligible, but certainly not meaningless. We are aware of possibilities; man is once more a mystery to us, and a greater mystery than ever before. We feel that Melville's oceans and leviathans are credible symbols. That man hunts through a great deep who looks into himself.

It is in "Moby Dick" that Melville first became unintelligible to his age and valuable for ours. In his earlier writings the Melville who revealed himself in "Moby Dick" seems to be almost wholly absent. This cannot have been more than very slightly due to circumspection, to the reluctance of a young author to attempt a theme beyond his powers; we must suppose that a rapid, almost sudden, change occurred in Melville shortly before he undertook "Moby Dick." There is a letter to Hawthorne which bears out this surmise. We cannot, of course, know in any intimate way what happened, but such sudden liberations of a man's powers are by no means unprecedented. Thus Einstein has testified to the extraordinarily sudden release of his energies—"like a storm breaking loose"—which occurred in the year he composed his first paper on relativity. Until "Moby Dick" is reached, Melville is not, truth to tell, a very interesting writer. His South Sea stories and accounts of voyages have often extraordinary felicities of expression, but, unless we embark on a minute detective hunt, there is little of great interest in the mind revealed to us. As being what they profess to be, these earlier stories doubtless have merits, but they are not very pertinent to the real problem presented by Melville. Perhaps a partial exception should be made in the case of one of the worst constructed and most inchoate books that can ever have been written—"Mardi." In this extraordinary work the fantastic reflections, the laboured and wearisome satires, the clumsy humour, and the curiously naïve and extreme romanticism are the incoherent and, as it were, scattered manifestations of a mind which is merely flying loose. Perhaps no one could have said that there was real promise in "Mardi," and yet perhaps most people could find promise in it after knowing what Melville went on to do. It is interesting as showing how great was Melville's need of discipline. For him to gain true austerity and depth it was necessary for him to confine himself, as it were, within the limits of an iron scheme, to think out a coherent group of symbols within which he could give some sort of definite body and shape to his perceptions. This is magnificently realized in "Moby Dick," whose mechanism is by far the most comprehensive and flexible that Melville ever invented. In "Pierre" he may be concerned with something even profounder, but the mechanism is comparatively puerile. Even in "Moby Dick" Melville has his resting places. There are whole chapters where the hunt is abandoned, and Melville will discourse on species of whales or on methods of extracting spermaceti with a practical and sometimes incongruous realism. Melville was never fully in control of his own vision; he was always more dominated than dominating.

At the time of writing "Moby Dick" the problem that was always to haunt Melville was, as it were, fairly straightforward. The great white whale may be said to symbolize what some old theologians have called the evil principle of the universe. It is something which can be ignored; men need not encounter it. But there is an experience which comes to some men, and which Melville more than once likened to setting out alone on an uncharted sea, when this principle of evil, this sinister underside of things, becomes their dominating problem. One is irresistibly reminded of Dostoevsky's Polar expeditions, and his broodings over the problem of whether all things are lawful. To Melville the matter is, in a way, more simple. He does not doubt, at the time of writing "Moby Dick," the existence of the white whale; there is evil and there is good. It is clear to Melville that the spirit of man is at enmity with the whale. The horror of the thing to Melville is that he sees the whale will be victorious. Opposed to the whale is the giant heroism and resolution of Ahab, but in the person of Ahab Melville introduces another aspect of the general problem. Ahab is at the very pinnacle of human self-assertion against the vast and mystically apprehended forces which are at enmity with all human ideals. He is one of the few who have the courage and the insight necessary to be a champion of mankind. He is one whose unshakable strength of purpose fits him to be a hunter of the whale. It is a lonely, sad eminence, and it has its own danger. It brings with it a terrible pride. Again and again Melville stresses this Lucifer-like pride until we realize, in some subtle way, that it is Ahab's pride, as much as the awful power of the whale, which foredooms him to destruction. It would seem that Melville is here describing something which is profoundly true. Dostoevsky's hero, Stavrogin, who is also one of those who assert the human will against whatever else there may be, is also like Lucifer in his pride, and his pride contributes to his final destruction. So that the old religious warning against the danger of taking glory to oneself may contain a profound human experience. Melville's problem becomes less clear-cut in "Pierre," but already in "Moby Dick" there are foreshadowings of Melville's later perception of the confusing beauty of evil—a beauty which can lead one to doubt whether there is any real distinction between evil and good, and which led Melville to give "Pierre" the second title, "The Ambiguities." Melville's description of the whale, just before the final battle is joined, hints at this perplexing fascination:—

> A gentle joyousness—mighty mildness of repose in swiftness—invested the gliding whale. Not the white bull Jupiter swimming away with ravished Europa clinging to his graceful horns; his lovely, leering eyes sideways intent upon the maid; with smooth bewitching fleetness, rippling straight for the nuptial bower in Crete; not Jove, not that great majesty Supreme! did surpass the glorified White Whale as he so divinely swam. On each soft side—coincident with the parted swell, that but once leaving him, then flowed so wide away—on each bright side, the whale shed off enticings.

But although in "Moby Dick" the real voyage is a spiritual voyage, it is apparent that Melville is still interested in the objective world. To regard "Moby Dick" merely as a sea story is to misunderstand it, but it is true that it is incidentally incomparably the finest sea story in the language. Melville has a passion for the actual sea; the impulse that sent him voyaging as a young man has not yet completely ebbed. The infinite vagaries of the sea, every stick and board in a ship, are still dear to the still youthful Melville, the born sea-rover. No one else can communicate so overwhelming an impression of the boundlessness and profundity of the sea; no one else has floated so gently and tenderly in its azure calms. And this may explain his strange lingerings over what seems unessential to his main purpose. He catalogues with infinite zest all the species of whale. Every operation of a whale ship, from the fierce technique of the actual hunt to the messy labour of storing the blubber, is described by a loving hand. Almost reluctantly, it seems at times, he brings his stormy Ahab on the deck. But he had to obey his demon. There was that in him which looked into greater deeps than those of the ocean, and which knew vaster monsters than the whale. By the time Melville came to write "Pierre" he seems wholly concerned with the inner life. The disparity between the symbolism of this story and the meaning that Melville forces his symbols to carry is so great as to be occasionally ludicrous and even repulsive. An ardent young man who wishes to spare his father's name the stigma of having had an illegitimate daughter; the extravagant device, therefore, of pretending to marry his unacknowledged sister, rejecting the girl he had promised to marry and breaking his mother's heart—none of this produces the slightest illusion of reality. The book has been dismissed as unintelligible, as the work of a man too abnormal to be called sane. But it is sane enough. It is profound. But Melville, either perfunctorily or through that curious lack of a sense of proportion which he exhibits in all his writings, has tried to embody his thoughts in a vehicle which cannot contain them. Isabel, the unacknowledged sister, is Melville's last and subtlest presentment of the white whale. But Isabel, beautiful and mysterious, is as attractive as any angel of light. And perhaps the deepest point at which Melville had arrived is his conviction that it was the very nobility of Pierre, his faultless and unswerving grasp of the good, which led him to abandon Lucy and marry Isabel. Isabel is no siren; if she be the principle of evil, then evil is not to be distinguished from good. Is there good and evil? Melville seems to ask. Are we aware of anything but ambiguities? Isabel herself, so far as any human insight can pierce, is wholly good. In cleaving to her Pierre unfalteringly obeyed the god within him. And his end is the hopeless, pointless, irremediable destruction of himself and those he loves. The world is a lie, through and through a lie, is Melville's final conclusion. In this world it is hopeless to distinguish good from evil, or even to know whether there is any distinction. There is nothing but ambiguities. There is despair in this book and much bitter wisdom. Melville's lonely journey has taken him into a deeper and deeper night. There is no room here for heroic purpose or unyielding pride. For there is no foe, except in the sense that the whole context of things is at enmity with the soul of man, poisoning his virtue and giving heavenly radiance to his vice, entangling him in ambiguities, leaving him with nothing indubitable, no loyalties and no aspirations. It is a comfortless last word, but we must take Melville as we find him. He is one of the men who have adventured far; perhaps one has to go farther yet to find light. We are convinced that Melville's knowledge was no empty fantasy. He has a high place amongst those who adventure even if we believe, as we prefer to believe, that there are others who have adventured farther and passed through Melville's night.

MORLEY ROBERTS

[Melville's Magnificent Achievement]†

In another place, when noting some of Hudson's favourite haunts, "some woods of Westermain" or an ancient city, I shall have to speak of his powers of historic vision which were allied to this mystic animism, and therefore shall not dilate upon it here. But I cannot leave this favourite book of mine [Hudson's *Idle Days in Patagonia*] without noting that it was to Hudson that I owed my first knowledge of Herman Melville and his magnificent achievement, *Moby Dick*. Often Hudson and I wondered how it was that the Americans still looked forward to some great American book when all they had to do was to cast their eyes backward and find it. Some day they will turn upon their path and see that in the cloud and mist which covered their passage they have missed one of their two great monuments of literature. It is obvious, of course, that *Moby Dick* is not flawless. There are pages of it in that fatal style which is not prose and yet has not the majesty of poetry, but when we contemplate it as a whole it has a strange unequalled power, an insight into character hardly to be surpassed by its grasp of great natural phenomena, and with all its terror there is also laughter. It is said to be a book of the whale. It is also a book of the ship and of the sea and of man, and Hudson knew it and learnt from it and spread its name.

† From Morley Roberts, *W. H. Hudson: A Portrait,* (New York: E. P. Dutton and Company, 1924), p. 131. Reprinted by permission of E. P. Dutton & Co., Inc., A. P. Watt & Son, and the Estate of Morley Roberts.

Modern Criticism: The Quest for Veritable Gospel Cetology 1926–1970

LEWIS MUMFORD

[The Fable and the Myth of the White Whale]†

The absolute condition of present things was what Melville sought to track down in the fable and the myth of the White Whale. One may read Moby Dick as a story of the sea, and be irritated by the lengthy description of whales and whaling; one may read it as a treatise on the whaling industry, and be irritated by the irrelevant heroic figure of Ahab, or the innocent sinister beauty of Queequeeg; and since it is also this, one may read it as an epic of the human spirit, and discover an equivalent of its symbolism in one's own consciousness. For me, the Whale is Nature, the Nature man warily hunts and subdues, the Nature he captures, tethers to his ship, cuts apart, scientifically analyzes, melts down, uses for light and nourishment, sells in the market, the Nature that serves man's purposes so long as he uses his wits and can ride on top. But with all this easy adventuring, there is another and deadlier Nature—the White Whale—a Nature that threatens man and calls forth all his heroic powers, and in the end defeats him with a final lash of the tail. That part of Nature cannot be harpooned, cannot be captured, still less drawn and quartered and sold. In sheer savagery—or was it perhaps in play?—the White Whale had once amputated Ahab's leg: with relentless vigilance Ahab follows the White Whale to its lair, impatient of baser catches on the way, as the great philosophers and poets have been impatient of the little harpoonings and dickerings of science and the practical life. The White Whale is not the kindly, milk-fed Absolute, in which all conflicts are reconciled and all contradictions united into a higher kind of knowledge; no, the White Whale is the sheer brute energy of the universe, which challenges and checks the spirit of man. It is only the lonely heroic spirit, who declares himself a sovereign nature, that dares follow the White Whale; and once he comes to close quarters with the creature, there is no issue but death. The White Whale is the external force of Nature and Destiny. In the end it conquers: it must conquer: until the spirit of man is itself Leviathan, and can meet its antagonist on even terms.

H. M. TOMLINSON

[The Great War and Moby Dick]‡

But who has resolved poetry into its elements? Who knows what *Christabel* means? And who knows why a book, which was

† From Lewis Mumford, *The Golden Day: A Study in American Experience and Culture* (New York: Boni and Liveright, 1926), pp. 149–50. Reprinted by permission of the author.

‡ From H. M. Tomlinson, *Gifts of Fortune* (London: William Heinemann, Ltd., 1926), pp. 108–9. Reprinted by permission of The Society of Authors, literary representative of the Estate of H. M. Tomlinson.

neglected for seventy years, should be accepted to-day as though light had only just come through it? I suppose our thoughts have veered. Certainly of late years much has happened to change them; and when our thoughts change, then the apparitions change about us. We change our thoughts and change our world. We see even in *Moby Dick* what was invisible to the people to whom the book first was given. On a winter's night, only a year or two ago, I was intrigued into a drawing-room in a London suburb to hear a group of neighbours, who were men of commerce, discuss this book of Melville's. They did so with animation and the symptoms of wonder. It could not have happened before the war. Was some unseen door now open? Were we in communication with influences that had been unknown to us? I was greatly surprised, for I knew well enough that I and they would not have been found there, ten years before, discussing such a book. The polite discussion of accepted books is all very well; but this book was dangerous. One ought not, without due consideration, to set out at night from a suburban villa to hunt a shadowy monster in the sky. Heaven alone knows where that may lead us. And my wonder was the greater when a shy stranger there, who looked more like a bank manager than a South Sea whaler, confessed during the discussion, quite casually, that Melville's book reminded him of Macbeth. Of course! Those knocks on the castle door! That was the very thought which had struck me. I looked at that man with awe, as though I was in the wake of the White Whale itself. I left that gathering much too late of a winter's night for comfort, and a blizzard struck us. But what is a blizzard at midnight to a wayfarer who has just had happy confirmation, an unexpected signal amid the bewildering chaos and disasters of his time and culture, that he is in the dawn of another age, and that other watchers of the sky know of more light.

PERCY H. BOYNTON

[The Allegory of *Moby Dick*]†

It is often said that *Moby Dick* is not an allegory. It is not merely a discoverable allegory, but in Melville's procedure it was as definitely and avowedly an allegory as *The Divine Comedy* or *Para-*

† From Percy H. Boynton, *More Contemporary Americans* (Chicago: University of Chicago Press, 1927), pp. 41–42.

dise Lost or for that matter *Pilgrim's Progress* or *Gulliver's Travels* or *The Ancient Mariner*. As Ishmael embarked "the great flood-gates of the wonder-world swung open." As the ill-fated Ahab faced his doom he cried out, "Pour ye now in, ye bold billows of my fore-gone life!" And as the ship, staved in by the charging whale, disap-peared in the waves, like Satan, "she would not sink to hell till she had dragged a living part of heaven along with her."

Moby Dick is as didactic in its sustained and applied metaphors as in its carefully documented chapters on cetology, the lore of the whale. The ocean is the boundless truth, and land is the threaten-ing reef of human error. The whiteness of the great whale figures forth the ghostly mystery of infinitude. Human life is the product of the Loom of Time, whereof the warp is necessity, the shuttle-driven thread, free-will, and chance, the stroke of the staff that drives the woof-thread to its horizontal place. The whale itself is symbol of all property and all privilege. Melville takes no chances at having these elements misunderstood or overlooked. He ex-pounds them at length and recurs to them incessantly. If it be a sin to write prose allegory, never man sinned as Melville. If it had been a sin, it would have been a sin of splendor and not of bathos; but as a matter of fact the only literary sinfulness in writing allegory consists in writing bad allegory, particularly if in so doing an other-wise good piece of narrative is spoiled—as narrative is often spoiled in purpose novels and problem novels, which are akin to allegory.

GEORGE SANTAYANA

[Melville: The Most Terrible Ranter]†

You apologize because some of your descriptions applied to the remote America of 1919: I who think of America as I knew it in the 1890's (although I vegetated there for another decade) can only accept what I hear about all these recent developments. On the other hand, when you speak of the older worthies, you seem to me to exaggerate, not so much their importance, as their distinc-tion: wasn't this Melville (I have never read him) the most terrible ranter? What you quote of him doesn't tempt me to repair the holes in my education. The paper I have most enjoyed—enjoyed

† From *The Letters of George Santayana*, ed. Daniel Cory (New York: Charles Scribner's Sons, 1955), p. 224. Copyright © 1955 Daniel M. Cory. Reprinted with the permission of Charles Scribner's Sons and Daniel Cory. George Santayana to Van Wyck Brooks from Rome (May 22, 1927) after receiving an advance copy of Brooks' *Emerson and Others* from E. P. Dutton and Company.

immensely—is the one on the old Yeats. *His* English is good: *his* mind is quick.

WILLIAM FAULKNER

["I Wish I Had Written That"]†

It is a difficult question. I can name offhand several books which I should like to have written, if only for the privilege of rewriting parts of them. But I dare say there are any number of angels in heaven today [particularly recent American arrivals] who look down upon the world and muse with a little regret on how much neater they would have done the job than the Lord, in the fine heat of His creative fury, did.

I think that the book which I put down with the unqualified thought "I wish I had written that" is Moby Dick. The Greek-like simplicity of it: a man of forceful character driven by his sombre nature and his bleak heritage, bent on his own destruction and dragging his immediate world down with him with a despotic and utter disregard of them as individuals; the fine point to which the various natures caught [and passive as though with a foreknowledge of unalterable doom] in the fatality of his blind course are swept—a sort of Golgotha of the heart become immutable as bronze in the sonority of its plunging ruin; all against the grave and tragic rhythm of the earth in its most timeless phase: the sea. And the symbol of their doom: a White Whale. There's a death for a man, now; none of your patient pasturage for little grazing beasts you can't even see with the naked eye. There's magic in the very word. A White Whale. White is a grand word, like a crash of massed trumpets; and leviathan himself has a kind of placid blundering majesty in his name. And then put them together!!! A death for Achilles, and the divine maidens of Patmos to mourn him, to harp white-handed sorrow on their golden hair.

And yet, when I remember Moll Flanders and all her teeming and rich fecundity like a market-place where all that had survived up to that time must bide and pass; or when I recall When We Were Very Young, I can wish without any effort at all that I had thought of that before Mr. Milne did.

† From The Chicago *Tribune* (July 16, 1927), 12, one of a series of letters under the general title "Confessions." Reprinted courtesy of the Chicago *Tribune*. For the column Fanny Butcher had asked William Faulkner what book he would like most to have written; this letter is his reply. Hans Burgert found the letter in the clippings made from "Confessions" by Herbert Kleist and printed it in *Studi Americani*, Vol. 9 (1963), 371–75, but with the wrong date and the inadvertent omission of twelve words. The square brackets in the letter are from the *Tribune* [*Editors' note*].

T. E. LAWRENCE

[The World's Big Books]†

I would maintain against him that these moods never produced an imaginative work the size of a mouse from any of the people sterile enough to feel certain. My notion of the world's big books are *War and Peace, The Brothers Karamazoff, Moby Dick,* Rabelais, *Don Quixote.* Of course we treat of prose. There's a fine set of cores of darkness!

GEORGE SANTAYANA

[I Have Got Stuck in the Middle]‡

I shall be curious to see your anthology and it may induce me to read Hazlitt, Halifax, and Selden, who are all unknown to me. But it is hopeless, so late in life, to fill up the lacunae in one's education. I tried the other day to read Moby Dick, but in spite of much skipping, I have got stuck in the middle. Is it such a masterpiece as they say? On the other hand, I am not too old to enjoy some novel authors: and what do you suppose was my joy at finding the theory of essence beautifully expounded in the last volume of Proust, (the second of *Le Temps Retrouvé*) and made, in a manner, the pivot of his immense work! Do read it, page 14 to 20, if you haven't yet done so.

OLIVER WENDELL HOLMES, JR.

[Rereading *Moby Dick*] §

I was talking yesterday with Morris Cohen, a most learned and able philosopher, and he said he went back and reread the classics,

† From *The Letters of T. E. Lawrence,* ed. David Garnett (New York: Doubleday & Company, Inc., and London: Jonathan Cape Ltd., 1938), p. 548. Reprinted by permission of the publishers and The Trustees of the Letters of T. E. Lawrence. T. E. Lawrence to Edward Garnett, from Karachi (December 1, 1927) on this passage from Herbert Read's review of *Seven Pillars of Wisdom* in the *Criterion: "Great books are written in moods of spiritual light and intellectual certainty."* (Lawrence's italics).

‡ From *The Letters of George Santayana,* ed. Daniel Cory (New York: Charles Scribner's Sons, 1955) p. 229. Copyright © 1955 Daniel M. Cory. Reprinted by permission of the publisher and Daniel Cory. George Santayana to Logan Pearsall Smith from Rome, December 21, 1927.

§ From *The Holmes-Pollock Letters,* ed. Mark DeWolfe Howe (Cambridge, Mass.: Harvard University Press, 1941), II, 227. Reprinted by permission of the publisher. Oliver Wendell Holmes, Jr., to Sir Frederick Pollock, from Beverly Farms, August 30, 1928.

being apt to feel his time wasted on modern books. I told him that I on the other hand always had scruples lest I was wasting time when I read the classics. I am thinking now of rereading *Moby Dick* which for several reasons would come nearer to me than to you and which seemed to me great when I half read it. I am trying to feel unscrupulous and to read it for amusement but it comes very hard.

WILLIAM S. GLEIM

[A Treasure of Hidden Meanings]†

If the reader will approach Melville's point of view with the understanding that the book is composed partly of parable and allegory, if he will read with a separate intention, he will find a treasure of hidden meanings, the existence of which the casual reader would never suspect. * * *

The allegorical expedition begins with the ship, which is itself the symbol of the *world*. This interpretation was provided by Ishmael, in his chapel meditation, when he concluded, "The world's a ship, on its passage out." Both the eastern and the western hemispheres were included in the symbolical ship, for her hull was built in America, and her masts were cut in Japan. Moreover, she was very old. "Her ancient decks were worn and wrinkled . . . . her venerable bows looked bearded, ... she was a thing of trophies—a cannibal of a craft, ... a noble craft; but somehow a most melancholy." Her name, *Pequod*, was that of a tribe of Indians, "now extinct as the ancient Medes"—which symbolized *time*. *Space* was the blank waste of water, into which Ishmael gazed at the suggestion of Captain Peleg, and into which the ship was destined to sail. *Fate* was symbolized by parts of the whale, with which the ship was abundantly furnished, for "her bulwarks were garnished like one continuous jaw, with the long, sharp teeth of the sperm whale, . . . and the tiller was in one mass, curiously carved from the lower jaw of her hereditary foe." All of which signifies that *the world is encompassed by Fate*; and that *the world is controlled by Fate*, and also that *Fate is inimical to the world*.

This symbolical ship was manned by personifications of the spiritual qualities of mankind. Captain Ahab, in his capacity of commander, personified the will, or Ego.

The *will* is suggested by the description of Ahab's determination: "The path to my fixed purpose is laid with iron rails, whereon my

† From William S. Gleim, "A Theory of *Moby Dick*," *The New England Quarterly*, Vol. 2 (July, 1929), 402–19; the quotation is from 402, 409–11. Reprinted by permission.

soul is grooved to run. Over unsounded gorges, through the rifled hearts of mountains, under torrent's beds, unerringly I rush. Naught's an obstacle, naught's an angle to the iron way." But an interesting restriction was attached to this personification, for Captain Ahab had an artificial leg, which was made of whale ivory, signifying that *the will is limited by Fate*. This interpretation is justified by the description of Ishmael's intention to go on a whaling voyage and his speculations on Fate's program, which he believed had him billed for that act:

> I think I can see a little into the springs and motives which being cunningly presented to me, under various disguises, induced me to set about performing the part I did, besides cajolling me into the delusion that it was a choice resulting from my own unbiased free will and discriminating judgment.

The characters of the three mates, Starbuck, Stubb, and Flask, are so thoroughly analysed in the chapter "Knights and Squires," that it is obvious they personify three of the Greek schools of philosophy, among which mankind is divided in a general way: *Platonism, Epicureanism, and Stoicism.* The readings of the symbols on the gold doubloon verify this identification.[1] * * *

HENRY A. MURRAY

[Melville's Exploration of the Unconscious]†

He [Melville] has not, of course, been generally admitted into academic circles. Indeed there may be a latent period of two generations before appreciative lectures are delivered upon the summit achievement of American letters; for the insensibility of the professional scholar to life forms as they emerge about him is as regular—and yet as bizarre—as a law of nature. For the learned are encased in their incapacity to experience the unusual. * * *

If I am to look very critically at the book to judge whether Melville is at all times clearly presented to my imagination, I should have to admit that there are moments when Mumford's attitude seems too rational—I might say too consciously elaborated.

Up to 1848 it is in every respect satisfactory; but at this point

1. These are among Gleim's remaining identifications: "Queequeg personified *Religion*"; "Tashtego personified *Sin*"; "Daggoo personified *Ignorance*"; Bildad "personified *Hypocrisy*"; Peleg "personified *Honesty*"; "Bulkington personified *Reason*"; "the Manx sailor personified *Prescience*"; the carpenter "personified the practical virtue, *Art*"; Pip personified "*Intuition*" [*Editors' note*].

† From Henry A. Murray, review of Lewis Mumford's *Herman Melville,* in *The New England Quarterly,* Vol. 2 (July, 1929), 524, 525–26. Reprinted by permission.

Melville discovered the Unconscious and commenced to explore it. He was aware that he was on a thrilling adventure, for he likened himself to Columbus:

> But this new world here sought, is stranger far than his, who stretched his vans from Palos. It is the world of mind; wherein in the wanderer may gaze round, with more of wonder than Balboa's band roving through the golden Aztec glades.

Melville proceeded to lose himself. This casting adrift was better, it seemed to him, than subjugating himself to a straight course in a humdrum world; "better to sink in boundless deeps than float on vulgar shoals; and give me, ye Gods, an utter wreck, if wreck I do." Mumford, in calling *Mardi* a satirical fantasy, takes little account of that initial cry of pain mounting to despair; a despair which opened the door to a torrential spiritual insurgency. "Now I am my own soul's emperor; and my first act is abdication. Hail, realm of shades!" This is the annihilation of the Ego, and to represent it we must let go the common ways and allow ourselves to be carried down in the undertow that was orchestrated into the trilogy; *Mardi, Moby Dick* and *Pierre*. This is hazardous, for at this point we are on the borderline of disintegration. But such a sojourn in darkness and chaos might lead to an awareness of Melville's dilemma which would differ somewhat from the intellectual formulations presented by Mumford. Mumford is not mysterious or ambiguous. He is supremely conscious, and his book is so lucid that the reader is never lost, but remains a willing and appreciative listener to the end.

THOMAS WOLFE

[That Magnificent Work]†

As to "Moby Dick," I read that magnificent work for the first time about six months ago in America in order to understand something about this man Melville that I had been imitating. I'm afraid these simple facts would not convince the reviewers, they would smile in a superior way and say that all this didn't matter at all, that I had soaked up "influences" from the atmosphere without knowing it, etc. God! it makes you long for the desert, Swiss cooking, lake fish—anything to bring oblivion.

† From *The Letters of Thomas Wolfe*, ed. Elizabeth Nowell (New York: Charles Schribner's Sons, 1956), p. 254. Reprinted with the permission of Charles Scribner's Sons and William Heinemann, Ltd. Copyright © 1956 Edward C. Aswell. Thomas Wolfe from Geneva to A. S. Frere-Reeves, August, 1930; a fragment of a letter, apparently never mailed [*Editors' note*].

HART CRANE

[The Value of the Details and Digressions]†

A way, way back you asked me a question about what I thought of *Moby Dick*. It has passages, I admit, of seeming innuendo that seem to block the action. But on third or fourth reading I've found that some of those very passages are much to be valued in themselves—minor and subsidiary forms that augment the final climacteric quite a bit. No work as tremendous and tragic as *Moby Dick* can be expected to build up its ultimate tension and impact without manipulating our time sense to a great extent. Even the suspense of the usual mystery story utilizes that device. In *Moby Dick* the whale is a metaphysical image of the Universe, and every detail of his habits and anatomy has its importance in swelling his proportions to the cosmic rôle he plays. You may find other objections to the book in mind, but I've assumed the above to be among them, at least, as I among others that I know, found the same fault at first.

ERNEST HEMINGWAY

[Knowledge Wrapped in Rhetoric]‡

We have had writers of rhetoric who had the good fortune to find a little, in a chronicle of another man and from voyaging, of how things, actual things, can be, whales for instance, and this knowledge is wrapped in the rhetoric like plums in a pudding. Occasionally it is there, alone, unwrapped in pudding, and it is good. This is Melville.

ARTHUR HOBSON QUINN

[Melville's Besetting Weaknesses]§

One has to wade through much that is forbidding; the confused introductory chapters and the tiresome lectures on the structure

† From *The Letters of Hart Crane, 1916–1932*, ed. Brom Weber (New York: Hermitage House, 1952), p. 404–5. Copyright © 1952 Brom Weber. Reprinted by permission of Mr. Weber. Hart Crane to Solomon Grunberg from Mixcoac, March 20, 1932.

‡ From Ernest Hemingway, *The Green Hills of Africa* (New York: Charles Scribner's Sons, 1935), p. 20. Copyright 1935 Charles Scribner's Sons; renewal copyright © 1963 Mary Hemingway. Reprinted with the permission of Charles Scribner's Sons, Jonathan Cape Ltd., and The Executors of the Ernest Hemingway Estate.

§ From Arthur Hobson Quinn, *American Fiction: An Historical and Critical Survey* (New York: D. Appleton-Century Company, 1936), p. 152. Copyright 1936; copyright renewed 1964. Reprinted by permission of Appleton-Century-Crofts, Educational Division, Meredith Corporation.

and classification of whales illustrate again Melville's besetting weaknesses, his lack of a sense of proportion and his inability to distinguish fact from fiction. But when the long journey through the Sea of Japan and the South Seas is over and the White Whale turns on its pursuers and rends them, there is painted an unforgettable scene in which the fury of man goes down, defeated by the fury of the great beast, driven to bay in its own chosen battleground.

WALTER FULLER TAYLOR

[Melville's Mythic Power]†

Intermingled with the allegory are philosophical essays brilliant in exposition and pregnant with meaning: now a dithyrambic on the dignity of human courage; now a parable on fate, necessity, free will, and chance; now an amazing take-off on the predatory cruelty of man; now a bantering chapter on Jonah; now a despairing cry that the truest of all books is Solomon's, and that *Ecclesiastes* is the fine hammered steel of woe. And wherever Melville's thought tends, whether to swift naked narrative or to the grave *obiter dicta* of philosophy, his style triumphantly envelops it, now tense with speed, now lucid in exposition, now throbbing in solemn eloquence, now rising to overwhelming power. Diverse as are the materials which Melville weaves together, they form a complete whole, even as, in the *Midsummer Night's Dream,* Shakespeare's lovers, country churls, and fairies dwell in the same romantic world, all their incongruities merely rounding out its magical completeness. In fine, Melville succeeded, like the ancient Greeks, in embodying his interpretation of life in an original, self-consistent myth, beautiful, terrible, and profoundly suggestive. Not depending, like Shelley, on the legends of a bygone age, he fashioned from his own race and time his own Prometheus—a gaunt New Bedford whaling captain who dared more terrors than the thunderbolts of Jove. * * *

Only in 1919, with the centenary of Melville's birth, did his fame begin to fulfill its early promise. A new interest in Melville's *locale* was then being created by books like Frederick O'Brien's *White Shadows in the South Seas,* and readers turned back naturally to the literary discoverer of the South Sea wonderland. Moreover, the modern mind has discovered in Melville no mere exotic romancer; it has discovered a thinker whose cynical bitterness

† From Walter Fuller Taylor, *A History of American Letters* (New York: American Book Company, 1936), pp. 137, 139–40. Reprinted by permission of the publisher.

matches its own mood of postwar disillusion. The pessimism that was so little intelligible to Melville's generation has found a response in the deepest feelings of our own. All these influences have led to an exaggerated estimate of Melville's greatness, which in all probability cannot be maintained. But no diversity of opinion, it is safe to say, will destroy his personal fascination or again deprive him of a place in our literary history. Indeed, it would be difficult to point out any author in any language, Joseph Conrad alone excepted, who can take rank with Melville as a writer of the sea.

YVOR WINTERS

[The Classification of *Moby Dick*]†

The book has more or less defied classification, yet chiefly because it fuses categories in the matter of structure, so as to produce a new structure, and because it is long and complex and has been imperfectly studied: it is beyond a cavil one of the most carefully and successfully constructed of all the major works of literature; to find it careless, redundant, or in any sense romantic, as even its professed admirers are prone to do, is merely to misread the book and to be ignorant of the history leading up to it.

R. P. BLACKMUR

[The Real Center of Interest]‡

In "Pierre" the White Whale was entirely in the protagonist's own inadequate perception of it; and the real weight of the book—what it was really about: tragedy by unconsidered virtue—was left for the author's digressions and soliloquies to carry as it could; which is to say that the book had no compositional center at all.

Something of the same sort may also be true of "Moby Dick." Is it not possible to say that Ishmael, the narrator, provides only a false center? Is it not true that a great part of the story's theme escapes him, is not recorded through his sensibility, either alone or in connection with others? Then where would the real center lie? It would lie variously, I think, in the suspense attached to the character of Ahab and in the half-imputed, half-demonstrated peril of the White Whale—the cold, live evil that is momently present. If we think of thc book in that way, we may say that its composi-

† From Yvor Winters, *Maule's Curse: Seven Studies in the History of American Obscurantism* (Norfolk, Conn.: New Directions, 1938), p. 73. Reprinted in *In Defense of Reason* (Chicago: Swallow Press, 1947), copyright 1947. Reprinted by permission of Swallow Press and Routledge & Kegan Paul, Ltd.

‡ From R. P. Blackmur, "The Craft of Herman Melville," *Virginia Quarterly Review*, Vol. 14 (Spring, 1938), 266–82; the quotation is from 272–74. Reprinted by permission.

tional form is a long, constantly interrupted but as constantly maintained suspense, using as nexuses or transitions the recurring verbal signs of Melville's allegory, Ahab's character, and the business of whaling. The business of whaling, including both the essays on anatomy and those on butchery, takes the most space and provides the most interest. All the reader has to do is to *feel* whaling as interest and he will recognize it as a compositional device mounting to the force of drama. Indeed we speak of the drama of whaling, or of cotton, or of gold, without substantial injustice to the language; and I cannot for the life of me see why the drama of whaling should not be as efficient an agent of interest, if well felt, as the drama of who fired the second shot; and with Melville there is the additional advantage that the business of whaling points to the everlasting assassin instead of the casual and no doubt remorseful murderer. Interest is the thing of prime importance, as any artist and any audience will tell you. If it takes up time and prepares for life, it does not matter how it is secured and does not fatally matter if it is overdone or vulgar in its appeal, as it is in "Moby Dick."

But is the real interest in the whaling or in the firing of the shot? Is it not always partly in the presentation, the feeling of detail and design, and partly in the image towards which the design points? Melville was lucky in "Omoo" and "Typee," to a less degree in "Mardi" and "White Jacket," and most of all in "Moby Dick"; he was lucky or it was his genius that he had material in perfect factual control with which to take up time and point towards an image—in "Moby Dick," a profound and obsessive image of life. As it happened, it was in each case the material of a special and vanishing experience, dramatic enough in its own right to require very little fictionizing—very little actualizing—to exert the invaluable hold of natural interest over the average reader. If, to interest, you add eloquence, you have all the essentials of the great novel below the first order. Many readers will be deceived and think the provision greater than it is. I have discovered a number of readers who, on being asked, reported enjoyment of a great story in a book of which Henry James would have said that it told no story to speak of; which indeed "Moby Dick" does not.

FRANK JEWETT MATHER, JR.

Reminiscences of a Melvillian†

It is an especial pleasure to an old Melvillian to follow the studies by Professor Willard Thorp and his students of our most inter-

† From Frank Jewett Mather, Jr., "Reminiscences of a Melvillian," *Princeton Alumni Weekly*, Vol. 38 (March 25, 1938), 555–56. Reprinted by permission.

esting American man of letters. It must have been sometime in 1891 when the talented but unfortunate Edward Lucas White, later author of *El Supreme* and *Andivius Hedulio,* haled me to his Baltimore lodging and in the interval of his usual, sonorous recitation of Victor Hugo's and Baudelaire's poetry read me a magnificent seagoing page from *Moby Dick*. That made me a Melvillian, and I began to hunt the first editions, but it was nearly twenty years before I had my own first of that great sea epic.

Meanwhile I read the little that had been written about Melville—an essay by Professor MacMechan buried in an academic quarterly, the prefaces of Arthur Stedman, who without success undertook an edition of a handful of Melville's books.

In the summer of 1902 I had the good luck to be a neighbor of the amiable and venerable Banker Poet, Edmund Clarence Stedman, one of the few surviving friends of the recluse custom house appraiser that Melville was in his last years. Learning of my enthusiasm for Melville, Stedman courteously gave me a letter to Miss Elizabeth Melville, who lived in one of the pioneer apartment houses of Manhattan, the Florence on Fourth Avenue. All her father's effects were there—silvery prints after Poussin and Claude on the walls. On the bookshelves I recall a manhandled edition of Beaumont and Fletcher, in folio, that would have contented Charles Lamb himself. Miss Melville granted me several interviews, talked freely of her father, and opened before my delighted eyes a japanned tin cake-box which was stuffed with Melville's archives. She let me read as I chose, save for Melville's letters to his wife. So I glanced over the unpublished manuscript of *Billy Budd,* took notes from a number of Melville's diaries—in general was in the position of a discoverer of hidden treasure. Miss Melville also gave me the incredibly rare privately printed volumes of poems, *John Marr* (1888), and *Timoleon* (1891) which Melville put together in his old age for distribution to his friends.

Since Miss Melville made me free of all this material, a book on Melville by myself seemed obvious to me. Unluckily it didn't seem obvious at all to my publisher, who felt there was no interest in Melville that justified the risking of the few hundred dollars that such a book would then have cost. Then illness, foreign travel, shifting from my old work on the *Evening Post* and *Nation* to free-lancing and teaching at Princeton, left all Melville interests in abeyance, except that by much watchful waiting I completed my first editions. Then came the centenary of Melville's birth in 1919, and, as good luck would have it, I was again in weekly journalism, on the short-lived *Review*. That meant I had an editor who almost had to print me, and I'm afraid I sorely taxed my friend Dr. Fabian Franklin's indulgence when I imposed on him two long essays on Herman Melville in successive August numbers. I may have thus hastened the demise of his excellent journal. In view of what has since been done on Melville, these essays do not now come to much, but at least they were the first serious attempt to appraise Melville on the basis of all his work. Previous criticism had pretty well confined itself to *Typee* and *Moby Dick*.

The Melville Centenary woke up literary America. Mr. Raymond Weaver rediscovered the japanned cake-box, and with more energy and better luck than mine found a publisher for the first, and in my feeling still the best, biography, *Herman Melville, Mariner and Mystic* (1921). This set the ball rolling. There has been an increasing flood of Melville literature ever since. Only the other day I received with the author's compliments an excellent German monograph bearing the imposing title *Herman Melville's Gedankengut, eine kritische untersuchung seiner weltanschaulicher Grundideen* von Dr. K. H. Sundermann. Doubtless Professor Thorp and his pupils have up their sleeves a Roland for this Oliver.

This story has a happy or an unhappy ending as you choose to look at it—happy for a Melvillian; perhaps unhappy for a mere bibliophile. The fact is the privately printed poems preyed on my mind. For my other Melville firsts I had paid coin of the realm, but *John Marr* and *Timoleon* were gifts—valueless when received, but subsequently become among the rarest of American firsts. Could I profiteer on this gracious gift of Herman Melville's daughter? Plainly I could not, but I might at least have kept quiet about it. How I came to betray my state of mind to certain colleagues in the Princeton University library I do not now recall. Suffice it to say that I found in them a sympathetic understanding of my plight, and a most friendly willingness to offer first aid to my troubled conscience. So I gave *Timoleon* and *John Marr* to the University, and then I looked at my shelf of Melvilles and realized that I no longer had and could never again hope to have all his first editions. The library was again ready to offer first aid. It agreed with me that no set would be better than a broken set for me, and generously reimbursed me for the small cost of collecting Melville firsts over twenty-five years. All this remains a little bewildering to me, but since it was to be, I am glad it was to be at Princeton. The set should be a good backlog for a future more extended Melville collection. As a bibliophile, I miss the books from my shelves; as a Melvillian, I like to think of them being read when I shall be reading no more.

As I look back over forty-five years of reading and collecting Melville, there is a pale satisfaction in recalling that I was right about Melville in 1902. But I was right at the wrong time, and if life has taught me anything, it is that to be right at the wrong time is to indulge what the schoolmen called a "morose delectation."

R. E. WATTERS

Melville's Metaphysics of Evil†

[T]he metaphysical basis of Melville's ethical cosmos may be abstracted in some such fashion as this: there is the realm of external nature, with immense latent power; this appears to man as implacable evil, lurking under a surface of placid beauty; in this world man struggles desperately to erect some purpose, to satisfy some desires, both spiritual and physical. Though chief in his own eyes, man is a relatively insignificant part of this careless universe. On the other hand, man is himself internally divided. There is a dark unknown realm of his being which he is fearful of fathoming; elements in his own nature frighten him. He struggles to integrate his energies, to bend his powers towards ends he thinks good, despite his half-conscious awareness of ambiguities in his own nature which corrupt that good; but all the while he is uncertain whether he is bound or free, agent or principal. Finally, there is a fundamental correspondence between man and the universe; man is "that inner microcosm, wherein we see the charted universe in little, as the whole horizon is mirrored in the iris of a gnat" (*Mardi*, Ch. 133).

Necessarily regarding himself as the centre of all reality, man sees the world and himself through the lenses of human values—that is, ethically. He sees a fundamental cleavage between light and dark, a polarity between good and evil forces, and these he makes concrete in symbols, both material and spiritual, the better to realize them. Then he seeks an intelligible explanation of this great dichotomy.

This, as I conceive it, was Melville's majestic theme. *Moby-Dick* is the imaginative drama of one who refused to admit anything beyond the scope of human comprehension. "No fearless fool now fronts thee," Ahab cries to the God of the corposants. "I own thy speechless, placeless power; but to the last gasp of my earthquake life will dispute its unconditional, unintegral mastery in me" (Ch. 119). Thus Ahab asserts the superiority of free intelligence to brute power, but he receives only death as the answer to his arrogant questioning.

KENNETH BURKE

[An "Efficient" Passage]‡

We should also note a "serial" quality in the "to the end of the line" mode—a kind of "withinness of withinness," as the "night"

† From R. E. Watters, "Melville's Metaphysics of Evil," *University of Toronto Quarterly*, Vol. 9 (January, 1940), 170–82; the quotation is from 178–79. Reprinted by permission of the University of Toronto Press.

‡ From Kenneth Burke, *The Philosophy of Literary Form* (Baton Rouge: Louisiana State University Press, 1941, 1967), p. 88; Vintage paperback Edition, 1957, p. 74. Reprinted by permission of the author.

company within the "day" company (paralleling the similar development, in the economic sphere, from operating companies to holding companies, controlled by "insiders"). One may get the pattern in Coleridge's line, "Snow-drop on a tuft of snow." And in *Moby Dick* there is an especially "efficient" passage of this sort, prophetically announcing the quality of Ishmael's voyage: after walking through "blocks of blackness," he enters a door where he stumbles over an ash box; going on, he finds that he is in a Negro church, and "the preacher's text was about the blackness of darkness."

HENRY ALONZO MYERS

[Ahab's Tragic Discovery]†

[E]very reader of Melville knows that the *Pequod* set out on an errand of vengeance, but few recall that to Captain Ahab the voyage was also a quest for certainty that ended in his great discovery. * * *

Had Ahab been granted opportunity to live in the light of his final insight, he would have seen the world as neither Calvinist nor romanticist sees it, for his discovery was that good and evil derive their meaning from one another. The all-destroying whale was the proof of the unconquerable Ahab, and the sorrow which gnawed at his vitals was the counterpart of the pride and resolution which carried him on. Whether in his last moment Ahab thought himself accursed or not, he accepted his fate, for he grasped the high principle of tragic morality, the principle that men pay for what they get. The price of intensity is intensity. In that one flash of insight Ahab was ready and willing to pay the price for his sky-hawk spirit. Time for further reflection would have shown him that his purpose to destroy evil was impossible, not diabolical, and that it was, after all, merely one way of coming to the destiny foreordained by his character.

WILLIAM BRASWELL

[How *Moby-Dick* is a "Wicked Book"]‡

Ahab, one might say, has taken upon himself the suffering of mankind. In a way to remind one of Jesus Christ, he is pictured as

† From Henry Alonzo Myers, "Captain Ahab's Discovery: The Tragic Meaning of *Moby Dick*," *The New England Quarterly*, Vol. 15 (March, 1942), 15–34; the quotation is from 16, 31. Reprinted by permission.

‡ From William Braswell, *Melville's Religious Thought* (Durham, N.C.: Duke University Press, 1943), pp. 66–67, 72–73. Reprinted by permission.

standing before his men "with a crucifixion in his face; in all the nameless regal overbearing dignity of some mighty woe." The "Iron Crown of Lombardy" that he wears was made, as [Stanley] Geist observes, "of the nails used in the Crucifixion." Ahab feels as though he "were Adam, staggering beneath the piled centuries since Paradise." His attack on the evil symbolized by Moby Dick, together with this arraignment of God for permitting evil, is madly enacted in behalf of mankind. At the head of thirty-six foreigners, an "embassy of the human race," Anacharsis Clootz in 1790 spoke before the French Assembly for the rights of man. Melville refers to Ahab's crew as an "Anacharsis Clootz deputation from all the isles of the sea, and all the ends of the earth, accompanying Old Ahab in the *Pequod* to lay the world's grievances before that bar from which not many of them ever come back." Most men, like Stubb, laughingly refuse to think about the problem of evil; or, if they do think about it, solve it, like Starbuck, by letting "faith oust fact." If Ahab were not intellectually honest and courageous, if he were less affected by the suffering of mankind, he would not be the tragic figure he is. As it is, too much reflection on the problem of evil brings him to madness.

The problem before the student of Melville's religious thought is how much of Melville, if any, is projected in Ahab's attitude toward the Deity. * * *

[I]n a letter to Hawthorne just after *Moby-Dick* was published, Melville says: "I have written a wicked book, and feel spotless as the lamb." He does not say a book with a wicked character in it; he says a wicked book. And of course it was a wicked book according to the Christian world in which Melville and Hawthorne lived. Melville's inability to account for evil had made him conclude that the Christian conception of a wholly benevolent Deity is wrong, and he had arrived at the point where he could give full artistic expression to his heretical view without suffering pangs of conscience.

CLIFTON FADIMAN

[Melville's Humorless Pessimism]†

A pessimism as profound as Melville's, if it is not pathological,—and his is not,—can exist only in a man who, whatever his gifts, does not possess that of humor. There is much pessimism in Shakespeare but with it goes a certain sweetness, a kind of radi-

† From Clifton Fadiman, "Herman Melville," *Atlantic Monthly*, Vol. 172 (October, 1943), 88–91; the quotation is from 89.

ance. His bad men—Macbeth, Iago—may be irretrievable, but the world itself is not irretrievable. This sense of balance comes from the fact that Shakespeare has humor, even in the plays of his later period. Melville had none. For proof, reread Chapter 100, a labored, shrill, and inept attempt at laughter. Perhaps I should qualify these strictures, for there is a kind of vast, grinning, unjolly, sardonic humor in him at times—Ishmael's first encounter with Queequeg is an example. But this humor is bilious, not sanguine, and has no power to uplift the heart.

HOWARD MUMFORD JONES

[A Minority Report]†

I hear much talk of *Moby Dick*, which was written in Lenox almost a hundred years ago, and that book is supposed to prove that the universe is evil. I had thought it had something to do with the dauntless spirit of man.

CARVEL COLLINS

[Fate and Free Will]‡

Whatever they think that *Moby-Dick* in its entirety demonstrates about free will and fate, many readers have maintained that in the first half of Chapter 47, "The Mat-Maker," Melville shows men to have freedom of will. The first half of the chapter describes both the process of weaving a rough mat and Ishmael's thoughts while passing back and forth the ball of twine which makes the woof: "here, thought I, with my own hand I ply my own shuttle and weave my own destiny into these unalterable threads." Immediately after the description of the weaving process and this report of Ishmael's thoughts about its implication, Melville divides the chapter in half by a row of asterisks at which the anthologists almost invariably and the critics all too frequently have stopped.

But the second half of the chapter seems vital to an explication of the text, for its first sentence states that "the ball of free will dropped" from Ishmael's hand at the cry of a lookout who has just sighted the first whales of the voyage, a lookout who seems to be "some prophet or seer beholding the shadows of Fate." The first half of the chapter, before the asterisk division, stresses that Ish-

† From Howard Mumford Jones, *Ideas in America* (Cambridge, Mass.: Harvard University Press, 1944), p. 219. Reprinted by permission.

‡ Carvel Collins, "Melville's *Moby Dick*," *Explicator*, Vol. 4 (February, 1946), Item 27. Reprinted by permission.

mael made his interpretation of the weaving while he was weaving; neither the author in his own person nor Ishmael in the role of narrator seems to insist that he still considers that implication valid. And surely it is Melville's irony once more at work when he harshly interrupts Ishmael's dreamily hopeful thoughts by a whaling cry which brings Ishmael back to the reality of the fated voyage so rudely that the ball—specifically said to be "of free will"—drops from his hand.

Something further in this direction could be made from the appearance in both halves of the chapter of the concept of Time, certainly additional evidence that Melville's row of asterisks is not there chiefly to end one scene and begin another but to bind the two scenes together for an ironic purpose.

This short chapter ends with the first appearance above deck of the diabolical crew of Ahab's personal whaleboat, making clear to the ship's company for the first time the true nature of the voyage. And perhaps it is here that Ishmael begins to learn that even his conservative compromise with Fate, evolved while weaving, is illusion only.

SOPHIE HOLLIS

[The Main Theme of *Moby Dick*]†

Moby Dick is more than the story of a whaling boat and its captain. It is an allegory; the green land is the oasis of faith (a bucolic, non-thinking faith); the sea is the tree of knowledge which is fraught with dangers to the peace of the soul; and the whale is the hand of God. And what is Captain Ahab, desperate man, who not only ventured on the high seas but deliberately sought that hand, not to discover its sinews and strength, but to destroy it? However, Captain Ahab could not do otherwise. Ahab was foredoomed to pursue his destiny, his damnation. This is the main theme.

JOSEPH JONES

[The Fundamental Realism of *Moby-Dick*]‡

The unevenness of Herman Melville's writing, admitted by all, seems to beget a good deal of unevenness in the criticism of it,

† From Sophie Hollis, "*Moby Dick*: A Religious Interpretation," *Catholic World*, Vol. 163 (May, 1946), 158–62; the quotation is from 158. Reprinted by permission.

‡ From Joseph Jones, "Humor in *Moby Dick*," *University of Texas Studies in English* (1945–1946), 51–71; the quotation is from 51. Reprinted by permission.

much of which naturally is directed towards *Moby Dick*. Especially unfortunate have been the attempts to attach to that novel various elaborate allegorical meanings which, when too much insisted upon, tend to give readers the idea that the book is really not about whaling at all—that the sooner they forget the unsavory business of whale-killing and mount to the crow's-nest of speculation, the better it will be for all aboard. No doubt there are important philosophical meanings in *Moby Dick* which are cloaked in mythico-mystical form; but they should not be permitted to obscure the important distinction that the book is fundamentally a realistic story which has overtones and upper levels rising naturally from it, rather than a full-feathered allegory which comes to roost on a yard-arm of the *Pequod*.

WILLARD THORP

[The Nine Chance Meetings]†

These nine chance meetings around the watery world mean more, we see, than any whaling log would have set down. They are the symbolic record of the *Pequod's* increasing isolation from all that is human, reasonable, and sane. Yet in the end, after the great shroud of the sea rolls over the *Pequod*, it is the *Rachel*, in whose search for the lost son of its captain Ahab refused to join, which rescues Ishmael.

WILLARD THORP

[The "Two *Moby-Dicks*" Hypothesis]‡

In the section of his book which follows the printing of the notes in the Chase volume, Mr. Olson offers as fact what can be received only as conjecture. Puzzled by Melville's statement to R. H. Dana, on May 1, 1850 that he was then half way in his book about a whaling voyage and by Evert Duyckinck's statement to his brother in August 1850 that the new novel was "mostly done," Mr. Olson has concluded (without an "if" or a "but") that "*Moby-Dick* was two books written between February, 1850 and August, 1851." The possibility that Moby-Dick was replanned in the course

† From Willard Thorp, "Introduction," in *Moby-Dick* (New York: Oxford University Press, 1947), pp. ix–xviii; the quotation is from xvi. Reprinted by permission.

‡ From Willard Thorp, review of Charles Olson's *Call Me Ishmael, Modern Language Notes*, Vol. 63 (February, 1948), 141–42; the quotation is from 142. Copyright © The Johns Hopkins Press. Reprinted by permission of the publishers.

of composition has already been offered as a conjecture by Leon Howard and Harrison Hayford.[1] Neither tries to turn the hypothesis into fact, as Mr. Olson does. The question cannot be gone into here, but the suggestion does not seem to me to be proved, from such evidence as we now have. It will be a pity if *Call Me Ishmael* convinces its readers that it has been proved.

RICHARD CHASE

[Three Styles in *Moby-Dick*]†

In discussing Melville's style, writers like [F. O.] Matthiessen, [William E.] Sedgwick, and [Charles] Olson have pointed out several influences: chiefly, Shakespeare, Sir Thomas Browne, and the Bible. It is clear by now that whatever may be said for or against Melville's style, he was a consciously "literary" writer, not, as used to be said, an unlettered or "natural" genius. Henry James, it could once be said, was a "literary" writer, whereas Melville was simply a great talent with no special professional sense of his medium. We can now see that Melville was fully as "literary" as James, if by "literary" we mean conscious of style (which is not to imply that Melville is the equal of James as a stylist).

Melville had other models of style besides the great English authors. One of these was the popular American rhetoric and oratory of his own time. And whereas this accounts for much of what one objects to in Melville's prose—its occasional clumsiness, its purposeless inflation, its vagueness, its jargon—it also accounts for many of his most felicitous passages. A glance at such a story as *The Obedient Wife*, written in 1840 by an anonymous author for the popular New York journal *Spirit of the Times*, will demonstrate how dependent Melville sometimes was on this sort of prose:

> There is an old story of a man who had married a young lady, and who had a friend somewhat skeptical as to the obedient tendency of the wife's disposition, much to the dissatisfaction of the Benedick, who strongly asserted, and warmly asseverated, that his will was law, and that she never by any chance disobeyed any wish or injunction of his.
>
> "Have you ever tried her in that respect?" said his friend.

1. The reference is to Howard's "Melville's Struggle with the Angel," *MLQ*, Vol. 1 (June, 1940), 195–206 (reprinted in *The Recognition of Herman Melville*, 1967) and to Hayford's Yale dissertation on Melville and Hawthorne (1945). Others to consider the hypothesis are Howard P. Vincent, *The Trying-Out of Moby-Dick* (1949) and George R. Stewart (1954, reprinted below) [*Editors' note*].

† From Richard Chase, *Herman Melville: A Critical Study* (New York: The Macmillan Company, 1949), 87–94. Copyright 1949 by Richard Chase. Reprinted by permission.

There are long passages in Melville which sound just like this. It is, of course, very consciously literary. The writer feels that he would be less literary if he wrote "who had a friend somewhat skeptical of his wife's obedience" instead of "somewhat skeptical as to the obedient tendency of his wife's disposition." It is a genuine low-Melvillian trick; and so is the delicious reference to the "Benedick," the toying with "asserted" and "asseverated," and the magniloquent humor of "Have you ever tried her *in that respect*?" The following passage, also from the *Spirit of the Times*, might easily have been written by him who tells the story of *Typee* or *Omoo* or *Mardi*.

> When we got up and rubbed our eyes, to our great disappointment we found that neither day nor wind would suit for "*Snipe Shooting*", so we sat down to our salt shad and our rye coffee, as disconsolate as Israel's maids of yore beside Babylon's waters. Looking out on the glittering expanse of Shinnecock Bay, we gazed with feelings of envy on the clam-men at anchor in their graceful whaleboats, who never knew the *ennui* arising from want of occupation, and were now engaged in destroying the happiness of many a bivalve's family circle with their merciless rakes. . . . After dinner,—a repetition of our morning's enticing fare,—we sat down to enjoy a quiet smoke. "Pooh! Pish! Psha!" muttered L——, a stately old bachelor.
>
> "Damn the day," exclaimed B——, who was an irascible ditto, not reflecting for a moment that Providence would be unwilling to increase the torrid state of the air by adding the hyper-temperature of the infernal regions. As for myself I don't exactly remember what I did, but I believe I ejected a mouthful of smoke and whistled.

Truly Ishmaelian is the philosophical humorist who here ejects his mouthful of smoke. The writer of this passage is a very literary writer, highly conscious of his allusions, careful to use a French word, proud of saying "the hyper-temperature of the infernal regions." He is jocular, reflective, acutely conscious of words. Carefully he constructs a mask of rhetoric and places it between the reader and that which is being described, hiding or merely obscuring the truth behind his featureless style. Probably he is not aware that his style *is* featureless, that what he takes to be a rich humorous-serious involution of phrase is really, much of it, blank and meaningless jargon.

There arose in this country in the 1830's and 1840's a most violent spirit of magniloquence. Oratory was one of the accomplishments of the folk hero. "I can outspeak any man," was one of Crockett's boasts. An orotund native oratory, full of bombast, humorous mythology, and rough Americanisms, emerged, as if by necessity, to express the tumultuous feelings of the people. This oratorical language, which could be heard in various forms in tall talk, in congressional addresses, in sermons and written-literature, had its effect on Melville, as did the milder humorous jargon we have glanced at above. As H. L. Mencken observes, the native rhetoric had its influence on Whitman and Mark Twain (he does not mention Melville), helping to set them apart from the conventional writers of the time, who looked back to the style of Addison and Johnson. The distinction must have been brought home to Melville in the 1850's, when he began to send short stories to literary magazines; one editor, distressed by Melville's style, suggested that he try to emulate Addison.

The following, from Mark Twain's *Life on the Mississippi*, will demonstrate the style in its more purely egomaniac mode:

> Whoo—oop: I'm the old original, iron-jawed, brass-mounted, copper-bellied corpse-maker from the wilds of Arkansas! Look at me! I'm the man they call Sudden Death and General Desolation! Sired by a hurricane, dam'd by an earthquake, half-brother to the cholera, nearly related to the small-pox on the mother's side! Look at me!

If this was an expression of the Manifest Destiny of the folk personality, its political-historical counterpart could be heard in the House of Representatives, in such speeches as the following:

> MR. SPEAKER: When I take my eyes and throw them over the vast expanse of this expansive country: when I see how the yeast of freedom has caused it to rise in the scale of civilization and extension on every side; when I see it growing, swelling, roaring, like a spring freshet—when I see all *this*, I cannot resist the idea, Sir, that the day will come when this great nation, like a young schoolboy, will burst its straps, and become entirely too big for its boots.
>
> Sir, we want *elbow-room*—the continent—the *whole* continent—and nothing *but* the continent! And we will have it! Then shall Uncle Sam, placing his hat upon the Canadas, rest his right arm on the Oregon and California coast, his left on the eastern sea-board, and whittle away the British power, while reposing his leg, like a freeman, upon Cape Horn! Sir, the day *will*—the day *must* come!

These words of "General Buncombe" have their counterparts in Melville's books, though Melville is never so vulgar a phraseologist as the General. The feeling of power, openness, space, and freedom is the central emotion in many of Melville's best passages, and as any reader of *Moby-Dick* will know, Melville purges the mood of exaltation of all vulgarities, of mere power worship, muscle-flexing, or intoxication with the *mystique* of force and space. About such a piece of oratory as the one quoted above, he would have been of two minds: he would have deplored the jingoism and the mindlessness of the sentiments; but at the same time he would have felt a deep sympathy with the speaker. In *Mardi* he had satirized just such an orator. In that book he represents his travelers as stopping off in Washington to visit the Senate. They hear a speech by a senator from the West. Roaring like a wild beast and smiting his hip with one hand and his head with the other, the speaker proceeds thus (I substitute real names for Melville's mythical ones):

> I have said it! the thunder is flashing, the lightning is crashing! already there's an earthquake in England! Full soon will the King discover that his diabolical machinations against this ineffable land must soon come to naught. Who dare not declare that we are not invincible? I repeat it, we are. Ha! ha! The audacious King must bite the dust! . . . Ha! ha! I grow hoarse; but would mine were a voice like the wild bull's . . . that I might be heard from one end of this great and gorgeous land to its farthest zenith; ay, to the uttermost diameter of its circumference.

The felicity of Melville's parody indicates clearly enough that he was aware of the false and dangerous emotions lying beneath this kind of oratory—despite the fact that he was himself not entirely proof against the oratorical mood. This kind of "screaming" caused him many doubts about the American future and convinced him that America might be throwing away all the opportunities of its wonderful youth even as it enthusiastically celebrated its own new-found confidence. He saw two aspects of the American spirit. He feared, on the one hand, that America would never be more than the "braggadocio" of the world. He hoped, on the other hand, that America was like "St. John, feeding on locusts and honey, and with prophetic voice, crying to the nations from the wilderness." Both of these possibilities he detected in the rough and fulsome cadences of American speech.

In *Moby-Dick* the language of the screamer is transmuted, when Melville is at his best, into an exalted apostrophe to power, space, and freedom. The mood is at once lyric in its poignancy and epic in the large nobility of its vision. The mood is not brutal or blind or chaotic or megalomaniac. It is serene and joyful, with the serenity and joy which follow upon the sense of great power controlled and great violence purged. It is the mood expressed by Father Mapple at the end of his sermon (which is itself perhaps the high point of American oratory):

> Delight is to him—a far, far upward and inward delight—who against the proud gods and commodores of this earth, ever stands forth his own inexorable self. Delight is to him whose

strong arms yet support him, when the ship of this base, treacherous world has gone down beneath him. Delight is to him who gives no quarter in the truth and kills, burns, and destroys all sin though he pluck it out from under the robes of Senators and Judges.

The style of *Moby-Dick* is a rhythm of three basic styles: the style of fact, the style of oratorical celebration of fact, the style of meditation moving toward mysticism. A passage from the chapter called "Nantucket" will document this:

> What wonder that these Nantucketers, born on a beach, should take to the sea for a livelihood. They first caught crabs and quohogs in the sand; grown bolder, they waded out with nets for mackerel; more experienced, they pushed off in boats and captured cod;

these are facts; but gradually the reader's attention is led away from fact toward a vision of size and power; the speech becomes metaphorical; the field of observation opens out:

> and at last, launching a navy of great ships on the sea, explored this watery world; put an incessant belt of circumnavigations around it; peeped in at Bering's Straits; and in all seasons and all oceans declared everlasting war with the mightiest animated mass that has survived the flood; most monstrous and most mountainous! That Himmalehan, salt-sea Mastodon, clothed with such portentousness of unconscious power, that his very panics are more to be dreaded than his most fearless and malicious assaults!

Note the quality of the images. The "incessant belt of circumnavigations" for size, and for the cyclical route of the voyager; "peeped in" for vision; "the flood," one of Melville's favorite symbols for the primal sense of power and space; "Himmalehan," image of the mountain; the "Mastodon" with his "portentousness of unconscious power," a phallic, imperial, and masculine image.

As the rhythm of the style turned upward and outward into space, Melville would have had the sensations he expressed in another chapter: "One often hears of writers that rise and swell with their subject, though it may seem but an ordinary one. How then with me, writing of this Leviathan? Unconsciously my chirography expands into placard capitals. Give me a condor's quill! Give me Vesuvius' crater for an inkstand! Friends, hold my arms!" And, then, Melville writing in full possession of his power, there follows the celebration of the Nantucketers:

> And thus have these naked Nantucketers, these sea hermits, issuing from their ant-hill in the sea, overrun and conquered the watery world like so many Alexanders parcelling out among them

> the Atlantic, Pacific, and Indian oceans, as the three pirate powers did Poland. Let America add Mexico to Texas, and pile Cuba upon Canada; let the English overswarm all India, and hang out their blazing banner from the sun; two thirds of this terraqueous globe are the Nantucketer's. For the sea is his; he owns it, as Emperors own empires; other seamen having but a right of way through it. . . . *There* lies his home; *there* lies his business, which a Noah's flood would not interrupt, though it overwhelmed all the millions in China. He lives on the sea as prairie cocks in the prairie; he hides among the waves, he climbs them as chamois hunters climb the Alps.

The "hermits, issuing from their ant-hill" give us an image of the "return" to the world after a "withdrawal." The "blazing banner," the sun—the sun under which the conquerors and patriarchs, the "naked Nantucketers," divide the oceans among them. The active forces here are all masculine; the feminine quantities are acted *upon*. Not far under the surface is a metaphor expressing the primeval scene of capture and division of the spoils. The whalemen are the rapers of the world. The "prairie" gives us another image of space, reminding us that the Pacific is an extension of the American land frontier. "He hides among the waves" we may read "he withdraws into the trough, the valley"; then, hunting the elusive game, he "climbs the Alps"—that is, he returns.

The style there modulates toward reflection and quiet.

> For years he knows not the land; so that when he comes to it at last, it smells like another world, more strangely than the moon would to an Earthsman.

In these words there is an abrupt sense of loss, of the need to turn back. The celestial symbol is now the moon, a feminine symbol. The faculty of sensation now invoked is smell; the inward, possessive, animal sense now replaces the projective, aspiring, and conquering one.

And then the introversion, with a reminder that a brutal power surges under the peaceful surface of meditation as it does under the delight of the oratorical mood.

> With the landless gull, that at sunset folds her wings and is rocked to sleep between the billows; so at nightfall, the Nantucketer, out of sight of land, furls his sails, and lays him to his rest, while under his very pillow rush herds of walruses and whales.

Again the idea of loss: the "land*less* gull." Notice also that the style is here recapitulating the Fall; two words help to accomplish it: "Sun*set*" and "night*fall*." The feeling of a downward motion out of space is invoked, and the sensation of inwardness: the folded wings, the furled sails, the female gull asleep in the trough of the waves. The kinaesthetic sense of horizontality and relaxation is achieved by "lays him to his rest"; and the passage leaves us with the idea of femininity, sleep, and dream; a dream, it may be, of time and the process of nature, the eternal, recapitulant rush of walruses and whales.

Melville's epic style is a rhythm which flows through a life cycle, embodying itself in the appropriate images. At the beginning of the above description of the Nantucketers, we have the style emerging from a context of fact. In the middle of the passage, the style has opened out into the full moon of light and space. The energy, the flight, of the day declines into the myth and fantasy of the afternoon, which in turn modulates into darkness, toward sleep and dream.

GEOFFREY STONE

[The Blasphemy in *Moby-Dick*]†

The blasphemy in *Moby-Dick* primarily intends no insult to other people's conception of God; it is not, like the blasphemy of Voltaire or the Victorian Samuel Butler, a mockery of beliefs assumed to be ridiculous, but an attempt on Melville's part to insult and assail the God of his own belief by confronting Him as an equal. * * *

Father Mapple's sermon, delivered early in the book, sets the tone of what might be called the book's orthodoxy, for there are at least two kinds of conflict in the story. One is Ahab's conflict with the powers and Power he is defying and the other is the conflict between Ahab's heterodox religious ideas, largely Manichaean, and the more "prudent" and submissive notions originally announced by Father Mapple and later exemplified in Starbuck, the first mate. * * *

This sermon—whose level of eloquence perhaps had not been reached since Edwards alienated his congregation at Northampton (for true eloquence does not always persuade)—preaches a stern God whose commands are hard and the reward for serving whom is not the delight offered by love but the one which a man may take in his own rectitude. There is no Christianity in the sermon and, indeed, very little concern anywhere in the book with anything that could be called specifically Christian: in neither is there a recognition of salvation as a freely bestowed gift. The orthodoxy of *Moby-Dick* is the orthodoxy of the Old Dispensation, and it is not sur-

† From Geoffrey Stone, *Melville* (New York: Sheed & Ward Inc., 1949), pp. 161, 164, 167, 186. Copyright 1949, Sheed & Ward, Inc. Reprinted by permission.

prising that 1,851 years after it had been set aside a man should find it intolerable. * * *

In Melville's world, Mr. [Charles] Olson has noted, Noah and Moses were his contemporaries, and we have seen that Christ hardly figured there at all. Melville never fully understood Christianity. "Let faith oust fact," cried Starbuck, the only Christian on the *Pequod*, though no fact of any kind is perceived except through faith.

NEWTON ARVIN

The Whale†

To speak of the structure and the texture of *Moby Dick* is to embark upon a series of paradoxes that are soberly truthful and precise. Few books of its dimensions have owed so much to books that have preceded them, and few have owed so little; not many imaginative works have so strong and strict a unity, and not many are composed of such various and even discordant materials; few great novels have been comparably concrete, factual, and prosaic, and few of course have been so large and comprehensive in their generality, so poetic both in their surface fabric and in their central nature. In form alone *Moby Dick* is unique in its period, and that too in a sense more special than the sense in which every fully achieved work of literature is unique. Such a book could only have been written by an American, and an American of Melville's generation, working as he did in a kind of isolation from the central current of European writing in his time—an isolation quite consistent with his keeping abreast of it intellectually—and, while losing something in consequence, gaining something indispensable he could not otherwise have had.

Given his kind of creative power, Melville was wholly fortunate in his literary derivations and development. As we have seen, his springboard had never been the English or European novel, not at any rate in its great characteristic mode, the mode of the social novel, the novel of manners, the novel of "real life." He belonged to a society that was in some of its aspects too archaic to find a natural place for forms so advanced as these, and his own origins, as if he belonged to the Bronze Age or at least to the Age of Migrations, were partly in oral story-telling, the story-telling of sailors and travelers, and partly in forms that were either subliterary or at the best

† From Newton Arvin, *Herman Melville* (New York: William Sloane Associates, Inc., 1950), pp. 151–93. Reprinted by permission of William Morrow and Company, Inc.

on a modestly and hesitantly literary level. He had begun as a writer of reportorial travel books, books that were simply further examples of the "journal" or "narrative," and in a certain sense he continued to be such a writer in *Moby Dick*. It is wholly natural that Owen Chase's *Narrative* should have been so vital to him, and that one pole of *Moby Dick* should be constituted by the informative chapters on whales and whaling. Melville's need as an artist was to take the small, prosy, and terribly circumscribed form he had inherited, and somehow make it a vehicle capable of bearing a great imaginative weight, of expressing a great visionary theme. His problem was to find the bridge between J. Ross Browne and Camoëns. He had quite failed to find it in *Mardi;* he had run away from his true matter in pursuit of an allegorical will-o'-the-wisp, and the result had been fiasco. A better wisdom had come to him in consequence; a better sense of his own right path. His own right path was, as Emerson would say, to "ask the fact for the form": to remain faithful to his own crass, coarse, unideal, and yet grandiose material—the life of American whalers—and to make of its unpromising images his symbols, of its hardly malleable substance his myth.

It is what he does in *Moby Dick*. There is no question here of chimerical priests and maidens, of symbolic blooms and allegorical isles and Spenserian bowers; no question of symbols wilfully imposed upon the meaning from without; no question of what Melville himself now calls "a hideous and intolerable allegory." In their stead one finds a fable almost bare in its simplicity and, on the surface, journalistic in its realism; the fable of a whaling vessel that sets out from Nantucket and, like some actual whaling vessels, comes to a disastrous end on the cruising-grounds near the Line. This tale is launched in pages so homely in their substance, despite their intensity of expression, that its earliest readers might almost have doubted whether they had to do with a "novel" or only with another and rather more dashing "narrative." It comes to a close in pages in which we are still encountering men like the bereaved Captain Gardiner and vessels like the *Rachel* of Nantucket. The skipper and the mates of the *Pequod* hail from Nantucket or the Cape or the Vineyard; all the characters, including the pagan harpooneers, and even perhaps the Parsees, are such men as might have been found, though some of them rarely, on an actual whaler of the 'forties. In their company we sail over well-known whaling routes, past familiar capes and headlands, giving chase not to fabulous monsters but to Sperm Whales and Right Whales of the sort that men had taken by the thousands, and having glimpses as we do so of other creatures—sharks, squid, swordfish, seahawks—such as Owen and Cuvier had classified. In short, with one or two great exceptions, the substance of *Moby Dick* is as faithful to sober fact as that of Owen Chase's or Ross Browne's book; if the impress on the imagination is that of a high poetic form it is not because the poetry is "allegorically" imposed on the stuff, but because the stuff is allowed to render up its own poetic essences.

It does so partly because the organizing structure of the fable—the Voyage, with its clear beginning and its predestined catastrophe—is at once so firm and simple and so large and free in its elasticity: like the structure of the *Odyssey* or the *Lusiads*, it is both strict and pliable. It is a fable, moreover, which, though it took shape in the most natural way out of a set of dense facts and tough, unromantic conditions, could nevertheless be made concrete and dramatic through a group of basic, primary symbols (the sea, the quest, the great "fish," the ship, the watery tomb) and of incidental or secondary symbols (the sword-mat, the monkey-rope, the sharks, and others) that are both immediate and primordial, both local and archetypal, both journalistic and mythopoeic. They are, moreover, at the same time wonderfully various and powerfully interrelated, so that the balance, as Coleridge would say, between "sameness" and "difference" is all but perfect. In any composition less completely integrated there might seem to be a hopeless incongruity between Ahab's pipe and the mystic Spirit-Spout, as between the jolly, unimaginative Stubb and the satanic Fedallah: in the setting of *Moby Dick* they are no more incongruous than, in the *Odyssey*, the swine of Eumaeus and the magic veil that Ino bestows on Odysseus.

Such analogies are inescapable because, after every necessary thing has been said about Melville's homely and prosaic derivations, in the bookish sense, one has to go on to say that the design and the texture of *Moby Dick*, both of them so unlike those of the classical novel of the age, abound in reminiscences of forms that are somewhat, or even very, remote from the nineteenth century. There is no doubt that this is in part the result of a conscious and artful process. There is no doubt that Melville deliberately undertook to intensify, to elevate the narration of his tale—to express the strangeness and the grandeur that were latent in it—by resorting, at one point or another, to traditional styles that had no association in anyone's mind with the Novel. The most evident examples of this, familiar to every reader of the book, are the stylistic devices that came to him from his reading of Shakespeare and other Elizabethan playwrights. Everyone is struck at once, of course, by the stage directions that accompany some of the chapters ("*Enter Ahab: Then, all*"); by the soliloquies that Ahab or Stubb or Starbuck, like Macbeth or Timon, delivers; by the chapters indeed ("Midnight, Forecastle" or "The Deck"), which are literally in theatrical form or in a form but one degree removed from it.

Some of these passages, just in themselves, are far from being very successful in execution; Melville, one feels, would have written badly for the stage, whenever he had lived. His imagination was profoundly nondramatic. Yet even so, and however oddly, the book as a whole gains something vital from these chapters, including the weaker ones, as other books have been strengthened by their imperfections. It gains as a musical composition does by shifts of rhythm and modulations of key: the total structure is by so much the more various, complex, and irregular as a result, and the threatening monotony of movement, in this as in other ways, is forestalled. Moreover, the peculiar immediacy that the dramatic style always produces is achieved, especially in such tense chapters as "Ahab and the Carpenter" and "The Deck towards the End of the First Night Watch."

This is so true, and the verbal echoes of Shakespeare are sometimes so striking, that certain writers have argued that the book has a structural rise and fall like that of Elizabethan trgedy, and a movement from scene to scene that ends by producing the five familiar "acts"; a movement that is marked thus by the great scene on the quarter-deck, by the meeting with the *Jeroboam*, the meeting with the *Samuel Enderby*, the "fourth-act" climax of "The Candles," and lastly the catastrophe itself. Scenes such as these are certainly among the moments of highest tension in *Moby Dick*, but they are dramatic only in a loose and metaphorical sense, as the scene of Dido's suicide in the *Aeneid* might be said to be dramatic; and the fact is that the structure of the book has only a superficial analogy with that of tragedy or of drama in general. The vital character of dramatic structure, as one need hardly say, is concentration; the vital character of this book's structure is expansiveness. A tragedy, in form, is ideally close, swift, and undivertible; *Moby Dick*, on the contrary, though in its own sense firm and unwasteful, is structurally open, loose, slow-paced, and ample. There are certainly tragedies that look in this direction—*Lear* and *Antony* do, and they made a great impression on Melville—but such tragedies, like some other Elizabethan plays, strain beyond the limits of that form.

If one must look for analogies that will do a little to express the effect *Moby Dick* has on us in form—and they can do no more than that at the very most—it is not to tragedy that one should turn but to heroic poetry, to the epic. And this for reasons that are not narrowly literary. The kind of life Melville was raising to the fictive level in this book was not the kind that has ever furnished, or could furnish, the stuff of plays or novels; it was a life in some of its aspects reminiscent of that led by the Achaean peoples in the days of their folk-wanderings or by the Germanic peoples in the days of theirs; the whole of American life at the time, with all its differences, was something like that. European migrants, from the sixteenth to the nineteenth century, had reverted in the Western world to a state of things that had much in common with an archaic, a "heroic" age. Here there had reappeared, as in the bronze Age and the Age of the Vikings, a population of brawlers, boasters, and bullies, as well as of proud, touchy, self-reliant, heroic individuals; and among them there had reappeared a habit of story-telling, of recitation and legendary reminiscence, shot through with a love of the grandiose and never wholly free from an under-current of superstitious fear—fear of the hostile and mysterious powers in savage nature, in forests and seas, in wild animals. The life of trappers, hunters, and frontiersmen was of that sort, and the life of whalers equally so. This is part of the complex truth to which Fedallah points when he riddlingly says that the wood of Ahab's hearse "must be grown in America."

If any aspect of this world, and specifically that of whale-hunting, was to be embodied in a mighty book that would really render its essential character, such a book would inevitably take on some of the qualities of epic poetry. And so *Moby Dick* does, both in structure and in more intangible ways. In sober fact, of course, the book is not a heroic poem but a work of its own age; yet it genuinely helps to define the formal quality of *Moby Dick* if one says that what he feels in its spacious narrative movement is not unlike what he feels in the narrative movement of the *Iliad*, of the *Odyssey*, and even of the more "literary" poems that derive from them, the *Aeneid*, the *Lusiads*. It is quite true that there is no curving back upon itself of the narrative line as there is in all but the first of these; the line in *Moby Dick* is straight ahead and undeviating, like that in the *Iliad* or in *Beowulf*. Yet the movement forward, as in all such poems, is not from climax to climax in the sharp dramatic sense, but from one wave-crest to another, from one chase or encounter to another, from cruising-ground to cruising-ground, from departure to arrival, from storm to calm. It is in short an undulant, not a peaked and valleyed line, and as a result the book has an epiclike pattern that, at least in quality, cannot be mistaken; it suggests the threefold design of the *Iliad*, or the sixfold design of the *Odyssey*, or the fivefold design of the *Lusiads*.

Exactly what the pattern is no two readers would probably agree, and in a certain sense it does not matter: what matters is the stylistic principle itself. Some readers, however, would doubtless concur in feeling that the narrative of *Moby Dick* is conducted through a series of four basic "movements," one of which is disproportionate to the others in mere bulk. All the introductory chapters, up to the sailing of the *Pequod* on that bleak Christmas day, form a clear and defined movement, like that of the first four books of the

Odyssey. A second unmistakable wave is the one that comes to its crest in the scene on the quarter-deck, when Ahab nails the doubloon to the mainmast. The whole central portion of the book, from the sunset scene in Ahab's cabin to the encounter with the bitterly misnamed craft, the *Delight*, forms a third movement; in this there are surely no breaks so marked as the first two. The fourth movement naturally begins with "The Symphony" and comes to a close with the catastrophe itself—the Epilogue forming a kind of musical coda, not wholly unlike the burning of Hector's body on the funeral pyre in the last few lines of the *Iliad*. It is certainly true that within the long third section one is conscious of other crests and troughs; the section occupies more than two-thirds of the whole book, and of course it is not written along an unvarying line. The crests are simply less high and the troughs less deep than the others; but they are there, and they are not very disproportionate among themselves. To one reader's feeling there are six of these lesser crests: the "first lowering" for a whale, the encounter with the *Jeroboam*, the passage of the *Pequod* through the Straits of Sunda and its emergence upon the Java Sea ("The Grand Armada"), the typhoon and the corposants, and finally the meeting with the *Delight*.

Meanwhile the principle of variety is observed and its effect achieved not in pitch only but in pace and key also. For surely what the descriptive and expository chapters on whales and whaling do is partly to slow down the tempo and partly to provide for a change of key. They suggest the passages of deliberate quietness and even dullness in all very large poems, and they are placed and spaced with beautiful compositional tact—the first of them ("The Advocate") appearing at the very opening of the second main movement, and the last of them ("Does the Whale Diminish?"), very near the opening of the fifth section of the third movement. The "intense *Pequod*" is now sailing northward through the China Sea; it is about to head eastward and sail through the Bashee Channel into the open Pacific; it is drawing nearer and nearer to its doom, and from this point on there can be no retardation of the narrative speed and no distraction from the spectacle of the fated cruise.

In the strictest sense Melville had no great model for the introduction of these magnificent non-narrative chapters; they sprang from his own creative feeling for composition and chiaroscuro; their only model was his own practice in his earlier books, especially *White-Jacket*. In its formal wholeness, indeed, as one has to repeat, *Moby Dick* is unprecedented and unique. No great poet has ever, before or since, brought zoology and poetry together in an even comparable way. Other great poets, however, have brought poetry together with the tangible facts of armament or equipment in a manner that *Moby Dick* does suggest, and again not for merely literary reasons. It is not Bronze Age warfare or hunting that is Melville's subject, as it was Homer's and the others', but it is an industry that had some of the aspects of warfare and certainly of the archaic hunt; and in the loving manner in which Melville lingers over his imagery of lances, harpoons, and cutting-spades, of whaleboats, whale-lines, and blubber-hooks, of cutting-in and trying-out and stowing-down, there is a shade of feeling that carries one far out of the nineteenth century and recalls again the epic minstrel and the way he lingered over his imagery of javelin and sword, shield and breastplate, chariot and ship, and such practical activities as sailing, hunting, plowing, and the performance of obligatory rites.

Of all this Melville cannot have been wholly unaware, and in the chapters in which the *Pequod* buffets its way around the Cape of Good Hope, it is hard not to feel that there is a conscious recollection of Gama and his men, in the *Lusiads*, heading eastward around the same howling Cape. From time to time, moreover, Melville launches upon the kind of sustained and formal similes that everyone recognizes as Homeric or Virgilian, and that have in *Moby Dick*, as in the *Iliad* or the *Aeneid*, an effect either of aggrandizement or of peaceful relief. The homeliest and most unexpected of these is the simile in which the whaleman's trained capacity to predict the route of the whale he is chasing is compared to the ordinary citizen's capacity to predict the arrival of a train on "the mighty iron Leviathan of the modern railway." More pastoral and more traditional than this is the familiar passage that brings together the picture of a school of Right Whales, sluggishly moving through a field of brit, and that of "morning mowers" slowly advancing their scythes through the wet grass of a marshy meadow. And the noblest, surely, of Melville's "epic" similes is that in which, in the chapter on "The Grand Armada," the great school of Sperm Whales hurrying through the Straits of Sunda is likened to an army accelerating its march through an unfriendly defile in the mountains, "all eagerness to place that perilous passage in their rear."

The imagery of armies and of warfare in fact is recurrent in *Moby Dick*, and for evident reasons. It keeps us from forgetting that butchery and carnage are close to the center of the theme, yet its lifts even them to a level on which the imagination can accept them. In general, however, the metaphors—and the allusions that have a quasi-metaphorical role—point in two opposite directions and, as a result, enhance the duality of tone that is so profound an aspect of the book's character. There are the metaphors that, like some of the similes, ennoble and aggrandize the texture of the narrative; and there are those that, like others, diminish or subdue it or even make it humorous. On the one hand, we are repeatedly put in mind of royalty or imperial dignity, of Czars and Sultans, or of the great figures of legend or history (Perseus, Alexander, the Crusaders, Tamerlane) or of Biblical story. Some of the most profound intuitions, moreover, are embodied in metaphors of architectural or monumental grandeur (the ruins of Lima, "the great dome of St. Peter's," the halls of Thermes below the Hôtel de Cluny) or in metaphors of naturalistic power and beauty ("the unabated Hudson," "one insular Tahiti," "the flame Baltic of Hell," or, perhaps most memorably of all, the meadows under the slopes of the Andes). All this is true, but it is also true that there is a constant contrapuntal play of shrunken or diminishing metaphors, and that these have a decidedly Shakespearean or at any rate Elizabethan rather than an epic quality, as when Ahab hoots at the gods as mere pugilists and cricket-players, or "Death himself" is likened to a postboy, or a Sperm Whale and his spout are compared to a portly burgher smoking his pipe of a warm afternoon. Close to these in feeling are the images that come from nineteenth-century industry or technology, the images of drilling and blasting, of mining, of cogged wheels and mechanical looms and magnetic wires, and even the "Leyden jar" of Ahab's "own magnetic life."

These latter metaphors are not without a suggestion of some of the metaphysical poets or of twentieth-century poetry; at other points in *Moby Dick* one is reminded, by the constant recurrence of imagery from animal life, of *Lear* and *Timon* on the one hand and on the other of Melville's contemporaries, the naturalistic novelists, Balzac and Zola. The Sperm Whale of course is one of the great primary symbols, and actual creatures of the sea, squid and sharks and swordfish, appear not as metaphors but as secondary symbols. In addition to these, however, which are given by the very subject, almost the whole range of animal life, wild and domestic, seems to have been scoured for images. Ahab himself is likened to a tiger, to a grizzly bear, to a wolf, a moose, a sea-lion, a walrus; and Pip even calls him "that anaconda of an old man." There is a steady, stately parade of elephants throughout the book; these greatest of land beasts are deliberately evoked as attendants, so to say, upon the greatest animal of the sea. The pagan harpooneers and the Parsees are sometimes, like Ahab, compared to tigers, and in the famous chapter on "The Whiteness of the Whale" everyone will remember the polar bear, the unspottedly white albatross, the sacred White Dog of the Iroquois, and the spectral White Steed of the Prairies. And indeed, as these allusions suggest, there is both a likeness and a difference between Melville's animal metaphors and either Shakespeare's or Balzac's. It is true that, like those writers (in their wholly dissimilar ways), he sometimes intends to suggest an analogy between the ferocity or the bestiality of men and that of beasts; but Melville's intention is more ambiguous than theirs, and it is quite as much for the sake of imparting to his theme a certain majesty, a certain grandeur, a certain strangeness of beauty, that he introduces his often splendid animals and birds.

Certainly nothing could be more eloquent of the incandescence out of which *Moby Dick* was written than the variety and the idiosyncrasy of the metaphors with which it is animated; nothing, perhaps, except the equally extraordinary resourcefulness and inventiveness of Melville's language. For this there is nothing in his earlier books to prepare us fully, though there are hints of it in the best passages of *Redburn* and *White-Jacket*. In general, however, the diction in those books is the current diction of good prose in Melville's time; it has a hardly definable personal quality. Now, in *Moby Dick*, it takes on abruptly an idiosyncrasy of the most unmistakable sort; it is a question now of Melvillean language in the same intense and special sense in which one speaks of Virgilian language, or Shakespearean, or Miltonic. It is a creation, verbally speaking; a great artifice; a particular characterizing idiom; without it the book would not exist. One of its hallmarks, as in all the other cases, is the "signature" furnished by favorite words; the favorite nouns, adjectives, and adverbs that end by coloring the fabric of the book as strongly as the use of a favorite range of hues affects the manner of a painter. Like Virgil, with his *pius*, *ingens*, and *immanis*, or Shakespeare, with his *rich*, *brave*, *sweet*, and *gentle*, Melville has his own verbal palette: it is chiefly made up of the words *wild*, *wildly*, and *wildness*, *moody* and *moodiness* ("moody Ahab," especially), *mystic* and *mystical*, *subtle*, *subtly*, and *subtlety*, *wondrous* ("most wondrous philosophies"), *nameless*, *intense*, and *malicious* ("malicious agencies"). One has only to cite these words to suggest how intimately expressive they are of *Moby Dick's* dark, violent, and enigmatic theme.

It is a matter, however, not only of characteristic words, familiar in themselves to readers of Melville's time and ours, but of characteristic *kinds* of words and of words that are again and again his own coinages or at least of a great rarity. One feels, as in all such cases, that the limits of even the English vocabulary have suddenly begun to seem too strict, too penurious, and that the difficult things Melville has to say can be adequately said only by reaching beyond those limits. He does so, perhaps most strikingly, in the constant use he makes of verbal nouns, mostly in the plural, and usually his own inventions; such nouns, for example, as *regardings*, *allurings*, *intercedings*, *wanings*, *coincidings*, and the nouns one gets in the strangely connotative phrases, "nameless invisible *domineerings*" and "such lovely *leewardings*." Almost unanalyzable is the effect these have of uniting the dynamism of the verb and the stasis of the substantive. And so of the other abstract nouns Melville loves to use in the plural—*defilements, tranquillities, unfulfilments,* "sorrow's *technicals,*" and "unshored, harborless *immensities.*" In their very unliteral pluralized form these characteristic abstractions become an elusive kind of inverted metaphor. Very different and less metaphorical, but almost as special in their effect, are the nouns Melville habitually constructs with the suffix *-ness* (*localness, landlessness, aborigalness, inter-indebtedness*) or *-ism* (*footmanism, sultanism, Titanism,* and the Carlylean *vultureism*).

Quite as abundant as the unfamiliar nouns are the unfamiliar adjectives and adverbs that do so much to give the style of *Moby Dick* its particular unconformable character. And again, just as verbal nouns are Melville's most characteristic substantives, so adjectives and adverbs based on present or past participles are his most characteristic modifiers; participial adjectives such as *officered, cymballed, omnitooled, unensanguined, uncatastrophied,* "last, *cindered* apple" and "*stumped* and *paupered* arm"; and participial adverbs such as *invokingly, intermixingly, gallopingly, suckingly, postponedly,* and *uninterpenetratingly*. These however are only the most characteristic of his modifiers; a complete list would have to include such rarities as *unsmoothable, familyless, spermy, flavorish, leviathanic,* and *unexempt* (which might have echoed in his mind from *Comus*) or (for adverbs) *diagonically, Spanishly, Venetianly,* and *sultanically*. And even beyond these one would have to glance at the sometimes odd, sometimes magnificent compounds, almost always adjectival, that give so vibrating a life to the pages of the book: "a *valor-ruined* man," "the *message-carrying* air," "the *circus-running* sun," "*teeth-tiered* sharks," and "*god-bullied* hull." There is an energy of verbal inventiveness here that it is hardly too much to call Aeschylean or Shakespearean.

It does not, curiously, express itself in the formation of unfamiliar verbs so typically as in these other ways; this is a kind of anomaly in a style of which the capacity to evoke movement, action, and all kinds of kinaesthetic sensations is so great. Melville, indeed, uses familiar or not unfamiliar verbs, again and again, with beautiful force; yet the impulsion of some of his finest passages of vehement action depends only partly on these; it depends at least as much on other parts of speech, as a characteristic paragraph such as this will suggest:

> A short rushing sound leaped out of the boat; it was the darted iron of Queequeg. Then all in one welded commotion

> came an invisible push from astern, while forward the boat seemed striking on a ledge; the sail collapsed and exploded; a gush of scalding vapor shot up near by; something rolled and tumbled like an earthquake beneath us. The whole crew were half suffocated as they were tossed helter-skelter into the white curdling cream of the squall. . . .

Nothing could be finer than a sound leaping out of a boat, or than the "something" that "rolled and tumbled beneath us," but the effect of the passage obviously depends on the vigor with which quite ordinary verbs are used, and at least as much on the vitality of the nouns and adjectives ("welded commotion," "invisible push"). Only rarely, but then sometimes with irresistible effect, does Melville create his own verbs, or virtually create them: "who didst *thunder* him higher than a throne," "he *tasks* me, he *heaps* me," "my fingers . . . began . . . to *serpentine* and *spiralize*," and "skies the most effulgent but *basket* the deadliest thunders." In all these cases, of course, he has boldly made verbs out of nouns or adjectives; and indeed, from this point of view, the manner in which the parts of speech are "intermixingly" assorted in Melville's style—so that the distinction between verbs and nouns, substantives and modifiers, becomes a half unreal one—this is the prime characteristic of his language. No feature of it could express more tellingly the awareness that lies below and behind *Moby Dick*—the awareness that action and condition, movement and stasis, object and idea, are but surface aspects of one underlying reality.

There is a passage in *Moby Dick* in which Melville deprecates the possibility that some ignorant landsmen will scout at the White Whale as "a monstrous fable, or still worse and more detestable, a hideous and intolerable allegory." It is quite plain that the remark has two edges and is meant to be ironical; it is plain, too, however, that Melville was in fact earnestly avoiding what we should now call allegory, in the sense in which we would use it of *Mardi*. The world "symbolism," in its literary bearing, had not come into use at the time *Moby Dick* was written; it was nearly twenty years before it did so, although Emerson had already dwelt with extraordinary eloquence and subtlety, in the essay on "The Poet," on the role of symbols both in experience and in art. If Melville had had the word, no doubt he would have used it in his own thinking about the book; as it was, he was limited to the older and less suitable one. As almost always happens in literary history, the *thing* had come before the term for it; and so, when Melville answered an appreciative letter of Sophia Hawthorne's, a month or two after *Moby Dick* had appeared, he expressed himself in this manner: "I had some vague idea while writing it, that the whole book was susceptible of an allegorical construction, and also that *parts* of it were—but the speciality of many of the particular subordinate allegories, were first revealed to me, after reading Mr. Hawthorne's letter which, without citing any particular examples, yet intimated the part-and-parcel allegoricalness of the whole."

There is a little touch here of the serious artist's particular sort of frivolity and disingenuousness, as one is pleased to find; it was the right tone for Melville to take, now that his book was well behind him. But of course he had had much more than a "vague idea" while writing *Moby Dick* that his fable, his images, his personages were the bearers of complex and unstatable meanings that no prosaic apprehension of them, even one that would be appropriate to other literary forms, could account for. Emerson's remarks had been highly symptomatic, as some of Carlyle's had also been, and the poetic mind in America was already symbolist in everything but the program, as Poe's and Hawthorne's work had shown and as Whitman's was soon to show. Unlike these others as he was in the special grain of his mind, Melville was at one with them in the conviction they all shared, the conviction that "objects gross" are only provisionally real, and that the eventual reality is the "unseen soul" they embody. In that familiar sense they were all "transcendentalists": their assumptions were those of romantic idealism, and their literary practice was in entire keeping with these. Ahab of course is only putting it all in his own manner when he speaks to Starbuck in a familiar passage thus: "All visible objects, man, are but as pasteboard masks. But in each event—in the living act, the undoubted deed—there, some unknown but still reasoning thing puts forth the mouldings of its features from behind the unreasoning mask." Or later, apostrophically: "O Nature, and O soul of man! how far beyond all utterance are your linked analogies! not the smallest atom stirs or lives on matter, but has its cunning duplicate in mind."

Such is Melville's personal version of the doctrine of Correspondences that lay below so much romantic and symbolist writing, as a similar doctrine of analogies lay below medieval allegory. That he entertained some such view has long been a familiar fact, and there is nothing remarkable now in saying that *Moby Dick*, in a sense that does not quite hold for any other American book, is a symbolist prose romance. Its leading images are symbols in the strict sense, not allegorical devices or emblems; symbols in the sense that their primal origins are in the unconscious, however consciously they have been organized and controlled; that on this account they transcend the personal and local and become archetypal in their range and depth; that they are inexplicit, polysemantic, and never quite exhaustible in their meanings. "The profounder emanations of the human mind," said Melville himself a little later in *Pierre*, "never unravel their own intricacies"; and he cannot have been unaware that his own book would present difficulties to the unraveler. Many of these have long since been disentangled, yet something always remains to be added, however slight, to any cluster of interpretations, however rich. It may be useful here to speak of *Moby Dick* and its meanings by adopting our own version of Dante's "fourfold interpretation" (which is of course inapplicable) and suggesting that the intricacies of the book may be reduced to four planes of significance; that these may be called the literal, the oneiric or psychological, the moral, and the mythic.

Of the first of these, the literal, not much (by definition) demands saying. What is chiefly important is not to allow ourselves to forget that it is there, just as it is in Dante's poem, and that the literary critic, like the Biblical exegete, must remember Pascal's salutary warning against two errors: "1. To take everything literally. 2. To take everything spiritually." Taking everything in *Moby Dick* "spiritually" means not taking it spiritually enough; the intangible meanings of the romance would not be so wide-reaching and deep-plunging as they are if they were not embodied in a fable of which virtually every detail has a hard, concrete, prosaic, and even naturalistic substantiality. There are some exceptions to this, as the principle of contrast demands; the Spirit-Spout is one of them, and the actual make-up of the crew is another. Miscellaneous as the real crews of the whalers were, we are not intended to suppose literal-mindedly that any one of them ever included as harpooneers a Gay-head Indian, a Negro, and Polynesian, as well as a boat's crew of Parsees, and along with them a Maltese sailor, a Tahitian sailor, an Icelandic, a Chinese, a Danish sailor, and so on. Yet all these freedoms with realism are dilatations of fact, not pure fantasies; even the Spirit-Spout doubtless had its origin in the surely quite breath-taking sight, at sea, of a Sperm Whale's jetting spout beheld at some distance on a moonlight night. The mere *scaffolding* of *Moby Dick*, as hundreds of readers have felt, would remain firm and stable if there were no question of symbols whatever.

The literalness of the book has another facet, however, to which justice has not been done. It is the facet provided largely by the factual chapters about whales and whaling. The true purpose of these chapters is to provide the book with an even intenser literalness than it otherwise has, and this on a serious intellectual level. This literalness, not of course stylistically but in substance, is that of systematic and exact knowledge; it is the literalness of the natural and especially the biological sciences. It is all, or much of it, translated into imaginative or humorous terms, and Melville insists on having his joke by arguing that the whale is not a mammal but *"a spouting fish with a horizontal tail."* Yet the motive behind these chapters remains a serious one. Transcendentalist though he was at the center of his mentality, Melville had too tough and too capacious a mind to fall willingly into mere vaporous and subjective idealism. He was a romantic idealist with a passion for actuality, for precise knowledge, for facts; he was an intuitionalist who wished, in his essential reliance on the nonrational and the superrational, not to fall a victim to mindlessness; not to forswear the sanctions of the intellect. "Undeniably," says Bardianna in *Mardi*, "reason was the first revelation; and so far as it tests all others, it has precedence over them . . . so far as it goes, for us, it is reliable."

A passage like this, one hurriedly notes, must be seen in the context of Melville's whole work; taken by itself it is misleading: the fact is of course that Melville was no simple-minded idolater of what Wordsworth had called "our meddling intellect." There was a painful division in his mind, as in the minds of many of his contemporaries, between his distrust of the discursive reason and his respect for it; he suffered deeply from the inner dissociations of his age. Yet his aspiration, like Thoreau's for example, was to triumph over them; to do justice both to "visible objects," masks as they are, and to the immaterial reality that, as he believed, lies behind them. It was an impossible task, so profoundly split, so dualized was the mind of his time, and his own as representative of it. But it was a task of which Melville intuitively felt the momentousness, and as a result *Moby Dick*, symbolist romance that it is, draws close at one pole to the bias of naturalism. The White Whale is a symbol, certainly, and even some of the details of his anatomy contribute to what he symbolizes; but their literal value is there all the while, and we must know how to give the proper, prosaic attention even to a half-humorous classification (the Folio Whale, the Octavo Whale, and so on), to the measurement of the whale's skeleton, to the facts about his blubber, his sense-organs, his spermaceti, and his flukes. We are in the company, and should recognize it, not only of Coleridge and Carlyle and Emerson but of Linnaeus and Cuvier.

We leave their company abruptly, however, when we move beyond the reading of *Moby Dick* as literal narrative and exposition, and begin to read it as what, on one plane, it is, an oneiric or dreamlike projection of Melville's unconscious wishes and obscure inward contests. *On one plane* the book is this, and on that plane only; for of course *Moby Dick* is not a dream but a work of imaginative art, and this means that it is the product of a complex creative process of which a great part has been conscious, deliberate, reflective: the formless spontaneity of an actual dream, along with much else, has been transcended. It shares with a dream, however, its sources in the unconscious, its dependence on irrational symbols, and its power to give expression to deep, instinctive, irrational fears and desires. How much of the sway it exercises over us depends on this!

When we read *Moby Dick* in this manner we are conscious of being presented at the very outset with one dominating oneiric image, the image of self-destruction; and then, as the action unrolls itself, and Ahab advances slowly to the forescene, we are given its counterpart and equivalent, the image of murderous destructiveness directed outward against the Other. From one point of view, what is dreamlike in the book may be said to move back and forth between these two poles, the suicidal wish, the longing for self-extinction, and its necessary antithesis, so deeply dependent upon it emotionally, the desire to inflict death upon what is, or what one imagines to be, the source of one's suffering. To undergo a kind of suicide is the motive that, along with the idea of the Whale (so closely bound up with it), impels Ishmael in the first place to go off to sea. Whenever, he says, he finds himself involuntarily pausing before coffin warehouses, and bringing up the rear of every funeral he meets, then he accounts it high time to get to sea as soon as he can: "With a philosophical flourish Cato throws himself upon his sword; I quietly take to the ship." There follows a series of hypnotic meditations on the allurements of the sea, of water generally, in which that element figures, though in a complex and iridescent way, as a symbol of death; of a return to the primal liquidity, oblivion, nonbeing. The sailing of the *Pequod* is to be for Ishmael a temporary passage out of existence.

Meanwhile, however, the death-wish has met with a check and a corrective; Thanatos has entered into a contest with Eros, and Ishmael, in his deathful loneliness encountering the savage Queequeg, has formed a solemn friendship with him, formed what he calls a marriage; the longing to love and to be loved has evoked its own oneiric symbol, and from this point forward Ishmael gradually ceases to be the man committed wholly to death. A dreamlike "displacement" occurs, and the accent shifts to Ahab, another embodiment of the self, and to Ahab's will to death, which expresses itself not directly as the conscious purpose of suicide, but indirectly as the purpose to wreak destruction on Moby Dick. It is true that Ishmael succumbs with part of his being to Ahab's ferocious hate: "A wild, mystical, sympathetical feeling was in me," he says; "Ahab's quenchless feud seemed mine." But the verb is "seemed" not "was," and already there is the possibility of Ishmael's recovering the will to live.

From this point on we are only intermittently and in flashes aware of him. It is Ahab in whom the most intense emotions of the dream are now concentrated. He is what our wildest, most egoistic, most purely destructive malevolence could wish to be, this old Quaker skipper from Nantucket; obsessed to the point of monomania with the will to destroy the hated thing, yet free from all mere smallnesses, "a grand, ungodly, godlike man." He is our hatred ennobled, as we would wish to have it, up to heroism. Moreover, he has in fact been terribly and vitally injured by Moby Dick. The Whale, in what looks like conscious malice, has reaped Ahab's leg away with his frightful, sickle-shaped jaw, and Ahab must now rely on a dead, artificial leg made of a Sperm Whale's jawbone. A kind of castration, in short, has been not only imagined and dreaded but inflicted, and the phallic source of vital potency has been replaced by an image of impotence and lifelessness, constructed from the skeleton of the injurer himself. Not only so, but in a kind of redoubled, repetitive, dreamlike manner, we hear that this apparently impotent limb has itself turned upon Ahab, and that before the sailing of the *Pequod* he had been found one night fallen in the streets of Nantucket with his artificial leg so twisted about that it had smitten his groin like a stake and almost pierced it.

A profound sexual injury is transparently symbolized here, and Ahab's "ivory" leg is an equivocal symbol both of his own impotence and of the independent male principle directed cripplingly against him. It had been fashioned from the polished bone of a Sperm Whale's jaw, though not of course from Moby Dick's own: what, then, does Moby Dick himself, on this deep instinctive plane, shadow forth? It would be easiest to say simply the father, the father who imposes constraint upon the most powerful instincts, both egoistic and sexual; the father also who threatens even to destroy the latter by castration and may indeed, in all but the literal sense, carry out the threat. On the deepest level, this is the oneiric truth about Moby Dick, but it is Melville with whom we have to reckon throughout, and for whom we have to remember how soon, and how overbearingly, the paternal role was played by Maria Melville. On every ground we are forced to confront a profound ambiguity in Moby Dick and to end by confessing that he embodies neither the father merely nor the mother but, by a process of condensation, the *parental* principle inclusively. Of his basic maleness there can be no question, not only because we are everywhere reminded of his preternatural power and masculine strength but because, in detail, we are required to contemplate the "battering-ram" of his head, the highly prized spermaceti with which it is so richly stored, his phallus ("The Cassock"), and his tail (with its "Titanism of power"); there is even a suggested association with the phallic serpent-god of the Ophites. Yet along with all this we cannot ignore a certain bisexuality in the image, if not literally of Moby Dick, then of the Sperm Whale generally; a bisexuality that is conveyed to us partly by the glimpses we have into his "beautiful" mouth and "the great Kentucky Mammoth Cave of his stomach"—that stomach in which, as Father Mapple's sermon reminds us, Jonah was swallowed up as in a womb—but also, and chiefly, by the obstetric imagery of the chapter (LXXVIII) in which Tashtego falls into the liquid depths of a Sperm Whale's severed head and is rescued or "delivered," like a baby, by Queequeg.

Moby Dick is thus the archetypal Parent; the father, yes, but the mother also, so far as she becomes a substitute for the father. And the emotions Moby Dick evokes in us are the violently contradictory emotions that prevail between parent and child. Too little, curiously, has been made of this; what dominates most accounts of the White Whale is the simple vindictive emotion that Ahab is alleged to feel toward him, and of course there can be no question of his Oedipal bitterness toward Moby Dick: his conviction that the Whale is the embodiment of "all the subtle demonisms of life and thought"; in short, "all evil." Yet hatred of this obsessive and even paranoid sort is but the deformation of a still more deep-seated love, and Ahab is as tightly bound to Moby Dick as an unhappy child to a parent too passionately loved. The emotion, however, that the Sperm Whale inspires is not restricted to Ahab's monomaniac vengefulness: from the very outset we are conscious also of Ishmael's feelings, and though at one pole these are identified with Ahab's, at the other they are by no means the same. They are, at any rate, more openly and obviously contradictory: the "grand hooded phantom," as it swims before Ishmael's fancy, may inspire a kind of fear but it inspires also an intensity of mystical longing that is something like love. It is a sort of love that lies behind that passionate preoccupation with every detail, however trifling, that characterizes the regarded object, and it is a sort of love, though an imperfectly fulfilled one, that brings Moby Dick before our imaginations as a creature of "majestic bulk," "pervading dignity," and "appalling beauty."

In his role of archetypal parent, in fact, Moby Dick is the object of an excessive and an eventually crippling love, as Maria Melville was for her son; and the consequence is the vital injury symbolized by the loss of Ahab's leg, an injury to the capacity for heterosexual love. Both Ahab and Ishmael suffer in this way, but Ahab far the more terribly of the two. Ishmael, by somehow preserving a complexity of feeling toward the White Whale, has preserved also his capacity for selfless love even though this is directed toward his own sex and even toward a member of his own sex, Queequeg, who embodies both the grandeur and the limitations of the primitive, the prerational, the instinctive. Nevertheless it is love that Ishmael deeply feels toward Queequeg, and it is the imagination of an even more comprehensive love that comes to him as he sits before a tub of cooling spermaceti, squeezing its congregated globules back into fragrant fluid, and washing his hands and his heart, as he does so, of "our horrible oath." The capacity to imagine an all-embracing love, which proves to be Ishmael's salvation, Ahab has fatally lost. He has lost it so far that he has succeeded in hardening his heart even toward his young wife and their child, whom he has frankly deserted; what wretched vestiges of pure human feeling are left in him go out only to the small black boy Pip, and to him reluctantly. Ahab is dedicated now to mere destruction, and he ends by attaining his suicidal wish and meeting his death by water. Ishmael, thanks to his rejection of mere hatred, survives the wreck; is picked up before he drowns by "the devious-cruising *Rachel*," the vessel that is itself a symbol of bereaved motherhood. In the end, the dream embodies a will to live triumphing over the will to die.

Meanwhile the unconscious and instinctive sources of the fable have expressed themselves in still other oneiric symbols. The very setting of the whole narrative, on board a ship from which of necessity everything female has been excluded, is itself dreamlike and wishful. Of all the countersailing vessels the *Pequod* meets, only one is an image of prosperity and jolliness, and this vessel is revealingly named the *Bachelor*—that "glad ship of good luck" which is heading back to Nantucket laden to its very bulwarks and mastheads with abounding spermaceti. The weapons with which the Sperm Whale is attacked and slaughtered are appropriately phallic symbols—harpoons, lances, cutting-spades, and the like—and if there were any uncertainty about the nature of Ahab's injury, on this instinctive plane, it would not survive a careful scrutiny of the doubloon he nails to the mainmast as a promised reward for the man who first sights Moby Dick. This golden coin from Ecuador bears on its exposed side three unmistakable symbols in the form of three Andean mountain-peaks, one of them flaming like a volcano, one bearing a tower on its top, and the third a crowing cock. Queequeg, gazing at it, as Stubb watches him from a little distance, glances from the coin to his thighbone, "comparing notes," and seems, as Stubb fancies, to find something in that vicinity: "I guess it's Sagittarius, or the Archer." The coin that is to reward the sailor who first glimpses the White Whale, and who proves to be Ahab himself, is one that symbolizes among other things, the virility that Moby Dick has destroyed.

The moral meanings of *Moby Dick*, though of course they transcend its oneiric meanings and exist in a sense on another plane, are by no means independent of them: on the contrary, the unity of the book is so masterly that only by artifice can we disentangle its various strands of significance. From the oneiric point of view Ahab is the suffering and neurotic self lamed by early experience so vitally that it can devote itself only to destructive ends and find rest only in self-annihilation. No reader of the book, to be sure, could fail to feel how imperfectly this clinical description fits the grandiose captain of the *Pequod*: he embodies a form of sickness, certainly, but in doing so he embodies also, and on a higher imaginative plane, a form of tragedy. The two, however, originate and eventuate together.

Ahab is not only the sick self; he is, for his time and place, the noblest and most complete embodiment of the tragic hero. He is modern man, and particularly American man, in his role as "free" and "independent" Individual, as self-sustaining and self-assertive Ego, of forcible will and unbending purpose all compact, inflexible, unpitying, and fell, but enlarged by both his vices and his strength to dimensions of legendary grandeur. About Ahab's moral largeness there can be no uncertainty: the cleansing effect of *Moby Dick* depends vitally upon that. He is described as not only "grand" but even "godlike," and godlike—in a sense that is at once Greek and Yankee, at once classical and contemporary—everyone feels him to be. He has such Areté, says Melville in effect, as a grim and shaggy old whale-hunter from Nantucket can have, and that is much; his very appearance suggests a demigod: "His whole high, broad form seemed made of solid bronze, and shaped in an unalterable mould, like Cellini's cast Perseus." He calls himself "proud as a Greek god," and indeed his pride is noble enough to endure the comparison. In its highest expression it is the heroic self-trust and self-regard of the modern Western man asserted in the teeth of all that would overbear and diminish him, whether natural or beyond nature. This is what Ahab affirms in the Aeschylean scene in which he defies the flaming corposants: "I own thy speechless, placeless power; but to the last gasp of my earthquake life will dispute its unconditional, unintegral mastery in me. In the midst of the personified impersonal, a personality stands here."

This is the very rapture of ideal individualism: neither Carlyle nor Emerson nor Nietzsche ever uttered it more loftily. Yet even as he pronounces his great tirade Ahab is dimly and bitterly aware that what he says is not true: what stands there is not, in the high sense, a personality, but only a proud and defiant will. Ahab has long since ceased to be a personality, if that word is to be understood as signifying a human being in all his wholeness and roundness. He has ceased to be anything but an Ego; a noble Ego, to be sure; a heroic one; but *that* rather than a Self. He is no longer a free mind: his thought has become the slave of his insane purpose. He is no longer emotionally free: his heart has become the slave of his consuming hate. Nor is he any longer morally free: his conscience too has allowed itself to be deadened and stupefied by the compulsive quest for Moby Dick. Just how empty, in this sense, is his claim to be a "queenly personality," he himself betrays when he exhibits what his monomania has done to his very conception of humanity, of "a complete man after a desirable pattern." In the scene with the old carpenter, who is making a new leg for him, Ahab, half soliloquizing, half addressing the carpenter, imagines such a man as, first, physically gigantic, and then as having "no heart at all, brass forehead, and about a quarter of an acre of fine brains."

Fine "brains," yes, as who should say "fine nerves"; not a fine and free intelligence, disinterestedly committed to the search for impersonal truth; what Ahab wants is hardly more than an anatomical organ that will act efficiently and mechanically in the service of his overbearing will. How much he cares for the intellect, in any serious sense, he demonstrates vividly enough in his destruction of the quadrant and his imprecation against science: "Science! Curse thee, thou vain toy. . . ." The capacity for pure thought had once been in him, and even in his ruin, as he leans over the bulwarks of the predestinated ship, on the day before they encounter the White Whale, Ahab has a moment of something like speculative freedom: he allows himself, in his transitory and final weakness, to wonder what unearthly thing it is that, "against all natural lovings and longings," is impelling him forward to what he knows is disaster. Even now, however, he does not sincerely wish to find the answer: what he wishes is to judge himself ultimately blameless and irresponsible, and in the next breath he gives his evasive reply: "By heaven, man, we are turned round and round in this world, like yonder windlass, and Fate is the handspike." No wonder that, a minute later, he sees the satanic Fedallah's eyes leering up at him from their watery reflection.

It is partly his momentary gleams of insight, nevertheless, that preserve Ahab's tragic stature even in his perdition. He has penetrated to one of the fatal truths about himself when he uses the phrase, "against all natural lovings and longings." His ideal man would have "no heart at all," and he himself has striven with terrible success to destroy his own great native capacity for love. To have yielded to it—to have yielded to what is clearly his ardor of affection for his wife and child, to his love for little Pip, to his spontaneous movement of compassion for the bereaved Captain Gardiner—this would have been to open a breach in the massive wall of his self-sufficiency; and so rigid is his egoistic fixity that he cannot afford or admit the slightest concession to a self-forgetful thought. The idea of pure independence has become an insanity with him: the thought of dependence in any form is a torment. It enrages him that he must be a debtor to "this blockhead" of a carpenter for a bone to stand on: "Cursed be that mortal interindebtedness which will not do away with ledgers. I would be free as air; and I'm down in the whole world's books." Again, with his wonderful, intermittent self-knowledge, Ahab is right: he is not genuinely independent, but on the contrary peculiarly dependent, and on the whole world. It is a sterile dependence, however, not a creative one, because it is imposed from without by circumstance, not accepted from within by the ethical imagination; and Ahab has his reward. He gets not independence but isolation; and, since he is after all human, it is unendurable. He has lived, as he himself says, "in a desolation of solitude," and it destroys him. He has refused to accept the interdependence that is the condition of geniunely human existence, and we can at least imagine that, like Jonah in Father Mapple's sermon, "he feels that his dreadful punishment is just." Objectively it is so.

The wild joy of self-assertion was never more contagiously rendered than in the great scene on the quarter-deck. The misery of self-assertion was never more terribly conveyed than in the stern and solemn chapters with which *Moby Dick* approaches its catastrophe. It is the succession of the one emotion by the other that imparts to the book its primordially tragic quality. In our identification with Ahab we have undergone the double movement of aggression and submission, of self-assertion and self-surrender, that is the secret of the tragic release, and we are freed by it. This is what Melville himself meant by the familiar remark in a letter to Hawthorne "I have written a wicked book, and feel spotless as the lamb." In the person of Ahab he had accepted the ultimate penalty, which he knew to be a just one, for his egoistic strivings.

The tragic error for which Ahab suffers is an archetypal one; it has both its general and its particular aspects, both its placeless and its local application. The raging egoism Ahab embodies has something in common with the Hubris of Greek tragedy, as it also has something, and still more, in common with the Christian sin of pride; but it is neither quite the one nor quite the other. There is something of Prometheus, of Agamemnon, of Oedipus in Ahab: he is guilty of an inflated arrogance similar to theirs, a similar conviction of his superiority to the mass of ordinary men. The true antithesis of Hubris, however, is moderation, and moderation is no cardinal virtue in Melville's calendar; Starbuck emobodies that, and Starbuck hovers between a golden *mediocritas* and plain mediocrity. So with the sin of pride: we are far closer to Ahab's error here, as with Melville's deep spiritual derivation from Calvinist Christianity we are bound to be. Father Mapple's sermon is intended to make us understand that Ahab, like Jonah, has in a certain sense sinned through his proud refusal to obey God's will, or its equivalent; pride and disobedience, in at any rate some dimly Christian senses, are at the root of Ahab's wickedness. The true antithesis of spiritual pride, however, is Christian humility; and this is only somewhat closer to Melville's positive thought than moderation is. A purely Christian submission and endurance, indeed, he describes in the chapter on "The Tail" as merely negative and feminine virtues, though they are, he adds, the peculiar practical virtues of Christ's teachings.

No, neither moderation nor humility is the true alternative to Ahab's error, and this because his error itself is not really Hubris and not really, in the strictest sense, spiritual pride. It is something closer to Ahab's actual world than either. Without an awareness of the gods' displeasure and jealousy in the offing, there is little intensity left in the idea of Hubris, and the conviction of the sinfulness of spiritual pride is at any rate transformed when the dogma of Original Sin is discarded. There was a level of Melville's complex mind on which the jealousy of the pagan gods could seem terribly real to him; there was certainly a level on which he was capable of darkly "believing" in Original Sin. In the fullest conscious sense, however, he believed in neither. What he felt as a menace in himself, and what he saw at work in the scene about him, was very like what Hawthorne felt and saw: a complex moral reality of which one pole was a pure and strong affirmation of the grandeur of the individual, and the other pole a wild egoism, anarchic, irresponsible, and destructive, that masqueraded in the kingly weeds of self-reliance. It is no accident that Ahab, as a whale-hunter, represents one of the great exploitative, wasteful, predatory industries of the nineteenth century; from this point of view the Whale embodies nothing so much as the normally innocent and indifferent forces of wild nature—the forests, the soil, the animal life of land and sea—that nineteenth-century man was bent on raping to his own egoistic ends. On the last day of the chase, in spite of what he has suffered at their hands, Moby Dick seems intent only on swimming as swiftly and as straight as possible away from the *Pequod*. "See!" cries the good Starbuck to Ahab. "Moby Dick seeks thee not! It is thou, thou, that madly seekest him!"

The alternative to Ahab's egoism is not, then, the ideal of "Nothing too much," nor is it a broken and a contrite heart. On one level it is an intuition that carries us beyond morality, in the usual sense, into the realm of cosmic piety; on the usual ethical level, however, it is a strong intuition of human solidarity as a priceless good. Behind Melville's expression of this, one is conscious of the gravity and the tenderness of religious feeling, if not of religious belief; it came to him in part from the Christian tradition in which he had been nurtured. The form it took in him, however, is no longer specifically Christian; as with Hawthorne and Whitman, it was the natural recoil of a sensitive imagination, enriched by the humanities of romantic idealism, against the ruinous individualism of the age. It is Melville's version of Hawthorne's "magnetic chain of humanity," of Whitman's "manly attachment": so far, it is an essentially humanistic and secular principle.

Ishmael, again, whose very name suggests a desperate estrangement, becomes nevertheless the narrative agent of these affirmations. Solitary and embittered as he first appears to us, Ishmael seems scarcely to have hardened the outermost surface of his heart: even before he has departed from New Bedford, his distrusts and his resentments have yielded to the outgoing affectionateness of "this soothing savage," Queequeg; and on the passage over to Nantucket he responds at once to the meaning of one of Queequeg's acts. A silly bumpkin, who has jeered at the outlandish appearance of Ishmael's new friend, is flung overboard by a sweep of the boom, and in spite of the fellow's behavior Queequeg risks his life in order to rescue him. When it is all over he leans back against the bulwarks of the little schooner as if to say: "It's a mutual, joint-stock world, in all meridians. We cannibals must help these Christians."

Ishmael is soon bound to Queequeg, and rejoices to be bound, in a relation of tenderest fraternity; this involves risks, appalling risks, as he learns, but these risks he is glad to take. As an oarsman under Queequeg, it becomes Ishmael's scary duty, when the body of a whale is lashed to the side of the ship, to bind himself to one end of a monkey-rope at the other end of which Queequeg is bound; secured by this, Queequeg stumbles back and forth on the whale's slippery back attempting to cut a hole in it for the insertion of the blubber-hook. As Ishmael leans over the bulwarks holding on to his end of the rope, it comes over him that he and Queequeg are now wedded indeed, and that if poor Queequeg should sink to rise no more, both honor and usage demand that Ishmael should descend with him into the depths. "My own individuality was now merged in a joint-stock company of two"—a sobering but also a softening thought. "Well, well, my dear comrade and twin-brother, thought I, as I drew in and then slacked off the rope to every swell of the sea—what matters it, after all? Are you not the precious image of each and all of us men in this whaling world?"

It is true that, in feeling this, Ishmael feels also how far he is from having a perfectly free will, how dependent he is on the mistakes and the misfortunes of other men. Yet the two kinds of dependency are here merged into one, and it is the creative dependency of fraternal emotion that prevails.

Deep as are the psychological meanings, and serious as are the moral meanings, of *Moby Dick*, they by no means exhaust between them the richness of its interest or the scope of its significance. In the end, as one reflects on the book, one is aware that one must reckon with the most comprehensive of all its qualities, the quality that can only be called mythic. Few words even in our time have been used more glibly than the word "myth"; it has ended by taking on some of the hollow sanctity of the mystic syllable Ôm in the mouths of the unenlightened. When one uses it, however, in association with *Moby Dick*, it means something precise and indispensable; and it is used here in the sense of an imagined narrative in which the leading roles are played by divine or god-like personages, engaged in symbolic actions amid symbolic objects; which embodies some form of the conflict between human wishes and nonhuman forces, and which has its roots in a philosophically serious desire to comprehend the meaning of nature and the destiny of man. The literary expression toward which myth in this sense typically moves is the epic or some closely comparable form.

If *Moby Dick* has a strongly mythic character, it is partly because the human setting out of which it emerged, as we have repeatedly seen, reproduced many of the conditions of a myth-making phase of culture. There was much in Melville's own experience too—his life among the Taipis and Tahitians, as well as much else—that, along with the bias of his own creative faculty, led straight in the mythic direction. There was a mingling in his nature, as in that of every greatly endowed poet, of the primitive and the highly civilized; of the naive and the literate, even the bookish; of the primitive capacity to "think" in symbols and the cultivated capacity to deal in abstractions. He was unique, moreover, among American writers of his time in the particular quality of his intellectual and moral seriousness; unique in his troubled preoccupation with problems that Emerson and Thoreau simply passed by, and that Hawthorne was intellectually too incurious to consider deeply. Like a truly myth-making poet's, Melville's imagination was obsessed by the spectacle of a natural and human scene in which the instinctive need for order and meaning seems mainly to be confronted by meaninglessness and disorder; in which the human will seems sometimes to be sustained but oftener to be thwarted by the forces of physical nature, and even by agencies that lie behind it; in which goodness and evil, beneficence and destructiveness, light and darkness, seem baffingly intermixed. In none of the great formulations that were available to him, neither in Calvinist Christianity nor in romantic optimism, could Melville discover a myth that for him was adequate to the lighting up of these obscurities.

Moby Dick is his endeavor to construct his own myth. The personages of the fable, ordinary as they begin by seeming, very soon take on the large outlines and the poetic typicality of figures in legend or edda. They are engaged, moreover, in an action that is profoundly archetypal—that is, in a voyage by sea that is also a hunt or a quest, and that reaches its culmination in an all but complete catastrophe. As they do so they move among primordial forces in which their destinies seem involved almost as if they were Greek or Norse or Polynesian demigods or heroes—forces such as the sea that is both the source of life and the extinction of it, the solid land that is both safety and peril, the spires of flame that must be defied but also worshipped, the wind that is sometimes "glorious and gracious" and sometimes tainted and cowardly, the sun "like a royal czar and king," and the moonlight or starlight that serves to irradiate the mystic Spirit Spout. So intense is the animation, so nearly personal is the vitality, of these elemental forces that hardly a step would be needed to transform them into actual deities. Melville himself indeed remarks that the Greeks gave the sea a deity of its own; he calls the northeast wind by its Greek name, Euroclydon, and Ahab defies the fire of the corposants in language that leaves no doubt of its mythic deification. Nowhere, however, is Melville's myth-making power at work in a more truly primordial sense than in the creation of the White Whale himself.

Here chiefly, in the aggrandizement of a huge and fearsome animal to deiform proportions, does Melville surpass all other poets of his century in the rejuvenation of myth. On this ground he is quite uncomparable; no other writer of the century can be set beside him. He himself could not wholly have realized how deep a descent he was making into the quarry of the past by penetrating so far as he did into the region of animal existence. He had some sense of this, but it was a flickering one: unavailable to him in his generation was the knowledge of primitive thought and belief that enables us now to see Moby Dick for the deeply primordial symbol he is. Only a man who had himself been a hunter of wild beasts—only a man who has been in at the kill of a tormented Sperm Whale—could have re-entered so far into the intense and complex feelings with which the primitive hunter regards the animals about him and especially his chief prey; into that lost, archaic mingling of fear and gratitude, of resentment and veneration, in which all the savage's emotions toward the animal are steeped, and which leads him again and again to endow it with an awful divinity. Of all this Melville had little or no "knowledge" but a penetrating intuition. The three pagan harpooneers on the *Pequod,* Queequeg, Tashtego, and Daggoo, have all seen Moby Dick before; when Ahab speaks for the first time of the White Whale to his crew, they and they alone are at once aware what creature it is that he means.

"Your true whale-hunter is as much a savage as an Iroquois," Melville himself says, and he adds: "I myself am a savage." Certainly in his half-fearful, half-worshipful attitude toward the Sperm Whale he was closer to the primitive than to the civilized mind; and he gives us his own clues to this when he identifies the Whale with the dragons of Perseus and St. George, or recalls that the Hindu god Vishnu was incarnate in a whale. Yet he probably did not know, literally, that for many primitive peoples—for peoples as remote from one another as the Annamese, the Tongans, and the Unalit Eskimos—the whale is, or once was, the object of a solemn cult, a sacred animal as truly as the cow or the bear was elsewhere. He probably had not heard that some of these peoples prepared themselves for a whale-hunt by fasting for days beforehand, by bathing themselves repeatedly, and by other rites; that some of them, after a whale's life had been taken, propitiated his ghost by holding a communal festival; and that others, when a dead whale was washed ashore, accorded it solemn burial and preserved its bones in a small pagoda near the sea.

Melville knew that whiteness in animals had often been a mark of special sanctity; he alludes to the sacred White Dog of the Iroquois and the White Elephant of Pegu; did he know, however, that the White Whale itself was so superstitiously regarded by the Eskimos of Bering Strait that a hunter who had helped to kill one was forbidden to do any work for four days thereafter, and that the shore where a dead White Whale had been beached was thenceforth tabu? It is of no real importance whether he knew of these things or not; in the contemplation of the great white monster and its mystic ways, he could rely upon a deeper and more primeval knowledge than any he could have acquired from Tylor or Frazer. His imagination ran before the anthropologists; he forefelt, as other poets have done, what the savants would later confirm.

He could rely, in all this, upon the aboriginal myth-making fancy, still strong in his own nature, for which birds and beasts were not simply "lower animals" but creatures somehow identifiable with the beneficent or the malignant potencies of all nature; the fancy that again and again transformed these creatures into gods—eagle-gods, bear-gods, fish-gods, and the like. Even among nineteenth-century whalers generally there may have survived, obscurely and dumbly, much more of this fearful and worshipful emotion than has ever been supposed, and Melville may be pointing to this when he makes Starbuck say of the heathen crew of the *Pequod* that the White Whale is their "demigorgon"—Demogorgon, as he should have said if he meant the mysterious infernal deity to whom Milton and Shelley allude, but he may well have been confusing Demogorgon with the creative Demiurgos of Platonic or Gnostic thought. In any case, there can be no doubt about Moby Dick's deific attributes. There is something godlike in the mere crude fact of his physical magnitude, his "majestic bulk." Physically he is the greatest of all animals that have ever existed, and in proportion to his vast magnitude is his potency, the potency that exhibits itself in his terrific speed, in the dreadful strength of his great jaw, and in the "Titanism of power" with which he wields his massive tail. He is not only physically huge and appallingly powerful, but—as one realizes when one reflects on the problem of his spout—there is in his whole being a "great inherent dignity and sublimity." Moby Dick is godlike in his beauty too, and when, after so many months of search, we at last sight him, gliding swiftly and mildly through the sea, he seems more beautiful even than Zeus himself swimming in the shape of a white bull, with Europa, toward his nuptial bower in Crete: "not Jove, not that great majesty Supreme! did surpass the glorified White Whale as he so divinely swam."

Beautiful he may be, yet to the whalemen who have encountered him, or even to those who have only heard of such encounters, there is something so terrible, so mysterious, in the ferocity and the apparently intelligent malignity with which Moby Dick has rounded upon his attackers, that they have ended by refusing to believe that such a creature is fit prey for mortal man. Some of them have persuaded themselves that he is actually ubiquitous; that he has been sighted in opposite latitudes at the same instant of time; and not only so, but that he is immortal, and that no lance forged of earthly iron can ever destroy him.

Certainly the penalty for attacking him seems always to have been death and destruction in some frightful form, yet Moby Dick appears never to have sought these encounters himself, and to have dealt out ruin only when provoked by his pursuers. Demoniac as he can be when hunted and harpooned, he himself seems rather to evade than to seek these meetings, and perhaps, as the commonsensical English ship-surgeon, Dr. Bunger, suggests, what Ahab takes for the White Whale's malice is only his awkwardness. In any case, if we regard Moby Dick not as an individual but as representative of a species, as an archetypal Sperm Whale, it is not mainly of his malice that we are reminded but of his unintentional beneficence. On occasion he may have been the apparently conscious cause of much evil and suffering, but certainly he is also the source of great and even priceless goods. For many men, both primitive and civilized, his flesh and his spermaceti have served as food. When ambergris is found in his bowels, ignoble as that derivation is, the Sperm Whale becomes the bestower upon mankind of the precious sweetness of perfume. His chief gift to them, however, has not been sweetness but light: it is of spermaceti that the best candles are made, and with sperm-oil that the best lamps are lighted. Illumination, not darkness and terror, is Moby Dick's great boon to humanity. And when we meditate on this fact, we are less sure than we would otherwise be that the mad Gabriel of the *Jeroboam* is as mad as he seems when he warns Captain Mayhew that Moby Dick is the Shaker God incarnated.

However this may be, he is certainly not the God of orthodox or even of modernist Christianity. That is the meaning of his whiteness, of that "visible absence of color" which is at the same time "the concrete of all colors," and hence is the symbol of "a colorless, all-color of atheism from which we shrink." That beautiful and frightful whiteness appeals to our souls so powerfully because it may symbolize both the most spiritual of things, even the Christian Deity, and also the things most appalling to mankind. It cannot, and in Moby Dick it does not, reassuringly and finally symbolize the Christian God, transcendent and absolute, and, however mysterious in His workings, a God of absolute love and justice and truth. A cosmic scene lorded over by the White Whale is one from which the soul-freezing possibility of an ultimate atheism is never wholly absent, and of course it was terribly present to Melville's spirit when he wrote the book. Moby Dick's whiteness, however, may and does symbolize not only negation and denial but "all colors"; all positive goods, fulfillments, benefits. It is a symbol of profound and irreducible ambiguity, but that ambiguity has a pole of lightness as well as a pole of darkness.

The White Whale is a grandiose mythic presentation of what is godlike in the cosmos as this could be intuited by a painfully meditative and passionately honest poetic mind in the heart of the American nineteenth century. Moby Dick is an Animal God such as only the imagination of that century in the Western world could have conceived and projected; a god in Nature, not beyond it; an immanent god in some sense, not a transcendent one; an emergent deity, not an Absolute; a deity that embodies the physical vastness of the cosmos in space and time as astronomy and geology have exhibited it; a deity that represents not transcendent purpose and conscious design but *mana;* energy; power—the half-conscious, half-unconscious power of blind, restless, perhaps purposeless, but always overbearing and unconquerable force. There is terror in such a conception, as indeed there is, on one side, in the Calvinist conception of a transcendently powerful and justly wrathful God; and Moby Dick owes something to the deity of Calvin and Edwards. He is not that deity, however, if only because nothing assures us that he is capable of loving man as Calvin's God loved him despite his sinfulness; we cannot imagine Moby Dick as conferring upon mankind the ultimate gift of free and unmerited grace. Yet terrible though Moby Dick is in his apparent and perhaps real indifference to men, he is also sublime, sublime as the cosmos itself is, in its unimaginable magnitude, its appalling beauty, and the demiurgic creativity of power that seems everywhere to be at work and alive within it.

This is a nature myth such as only a nineteenth-century imagination, obsessed with the spectacle of impersonal force and ceaseless physical change, could have created, though Melville had unconsciously drawn, in creating it, on a whole complex of thoughts that had come to him from reading, or reading about, Job, the Stoics, the Gnostics and Manicheans, Spinoza, and the men of science. It is a myth such as other minds of the nineteenth century were groping toward, and one can see dim analogies to Moby Dick in Schopenhauer's blind irrational Will, in Herbert Spencer's Unknowable, and still more truly in Hardy's Immanent Will or Urging Immanence. In the traditional Christian God, the omniscient and loving Father, Melville had now lost all confident belief; *that* God survived in his mind, when he wrote *Moby Dick*, only as a symbol of human fraternity and the quasi-religious sense of equality: "The great God absolute! The centre and circumference of all democracy! His omnipresence, our divine equality!" The language here seems traditional enough, but it is unsupported by anything else in the action or the imagery of the book, and the truth is that the God of Melville's fathers has yielded place, at every other point, to the godlike and portentous White Whale.

The mating of romantic idealism with the masculine sense of reality in Melville's mind has begotten here a myth that approaches, if it does not quite overtake, a naturalistic theism. The question remains: If Moby Dick embodies the deific principle in nature, what spiritual meaning can he have for mankind as an object of worship? The answer would have to be that, in the fullest sense of worship, he could have a very uncertain one, if he could have one at all. It is evident that, like Spinoza's God, Moby Dick cannot be imagined as, strictly speaking, either loving man or hating him; and, conversely, he is hardly conceived as sustainedly and satisfyingly inspiring that "intellectual love" which, according to Spinoza, the free man himself can feel toward God. A positive attitude he does nevertheless inspire, though certainly it is in the end a more austere and far less solacing attitude than that of happy and confident worship. The great clue to this, again, is the symbolism of the doubloon that Ahab nails to the mainmast. This coin was minted in the republic of Ecuador, "a country planted in the middle of the world, and beneath the great equator, and named after it; and it had been cast midway up the Andes, in the unwaning clime that knows no autumn." Arching over the mountain peaks stamped on it, one sees a segment of the zodiac and "the keystone sun entering the equinoctial point at Libra."

Obsessed with his proud and impious intrepretation of the symbols on the coin, Ahab quite fails to understand its still deeper significance, quite fails to see that the coin he himself has nailed up is an emblem, not, to be sure, of ethical moderation in the Greek sense, but of the Double Vision; the vision, so to say, of the equatorial line from which one may look out on both North and South with equal comprehensiveness; the balanced vision of the sun itself as it enters the constellation of Libra or the Scales. This is the vision, surely, with which a wise man would contemplate Moby Dick, stoically accepting the fact that the White Whale, the cosmic force, has again and again unconsciously wrought havoc and destruction, and will doubtless continue to do so; but recognizing too that Moby Dick is, or may be made to be, the source of much genuine good—of nourishment, of fragrance, of light—and that, though "I know him not, and never will," one can glory in the spectacle of his sublimity.

That is what Ishmael has revealed a capacity to do, and it is the deepest reason for his rebirth from the sea. Ahab, on the other hand, has shown no such capacity; on the contrary, he has persisted in identifying Moby Dick with "all evil," and piling upon the whale's white hump "all the general rage and hate felt by his whole race from Adam down." But this is both madness and wickedness. Evil exists, it is true; essential Evil; it is no illusion, as Emerson would have it, but a dense and unexorcisable reality. So far as the reality of Evil is that of suffering, Moby Dick is indeed the source of much of it; but that is only one aspect of his dual nature, and moreover, so far as the reality of Evil is moral, so far as Evil connotes an evil will, then Moby Dick does not embody this at all: the one who does embody it is Ahab's own harpooneer, the diabolic Fedallah, to whom Ahab has surrendered his moral freedom, and whom Stubb quite properly identifies as the devil in disguise. "One cannot sustain an indifferent air concerning Fedallah." One cannot, indeed, for he is a principle of pure negation, of hatred instead of love, vindictiveness instead of charity, destruction instead of creativeness. Ahab has sold his soul to the fire-worshipping Parsee, the Parsee who, in this case, worships fire not as a symbol of light and truth but as a symbol of raging and destructive Evil. Moby Dick, however, is indestructible, and the upshot of their impious onslaught upon him is not his but their destruction.

There would be a religious solace in this thought if one could believe that Moby Dick, with his immunity and immortality, were in conscious, benevolent collaboration with the forces of love in their struggle against the forces of hate. As it is, one must be content with the consolations of philosophy in *Moby Dick*, or rather with those of a philosophical mythology; one cannot avert one's eyes from the fact that good and innocent men—Starbuck, Queequeg, and others—are involved in Ahab's doom. One can tell oneself that mad and wicked men inevitably wreak their own destruction in attempting to thwart the workings of "nature"; one cannot tell oneself that wise and virtuous men are preserved from suffering and fatality. They only *may* be, as Ishmael is.

Something else, whoever, is suggested in the book, though only obscurely, and this is something that takes us closer, if not to religion in the fullest sense, at any rate to a certain form of natural piety. Some years after he had written *Moby Dick*, Melville was sufficiently struck by a sentence of Spinoza's, quoted by Matthew Arnold, to mark the passage in his copy of Arnold's essays. The sentence is this: "Our desire is not that nature may obey us, but, on the contrary, that we may obey nature." Already in *Moby Dick* there had been an intimation of this cosmic submissiveness. The desire to understand, to fathom, the whole truth about the White Whale—the desire that is manifest at every turn in the explanatory and meditative passages—this is at least the true beginning of wisdom. The willingness to submit, to accept, to "obey," in that sense, would naturally follow. Father Mapple, indeed, in his sermon—employing, of course, the familiar language of faith—makes provision for this when he says that "all the things that God would have us do are hard for us to do. . . . And if we obey God, we must disobey ourselves; and it is in this disobeying ourselves, wherein the hardness of obeying God consists." The "will" of nature, even if there is something godlike in it, is hardly synonymous with God's will in the Christian sense. Yet *Moby Dick* seems to say that one might arrive at a kind of peace by obeying it.

E. K. BROWN

[White Whale as "Expanding Symbol"]†

The expanding symbol is a device * * * appropriate for rendering an emotion, an idea, that by its largeness or its subtlety cannot

† From E. K. Brown, *Rhythm in the Novel* (Toronto: University of Toronto Press, 1950), pp. 56–57; 52, n.1. Reprinted by permission of the publishers.

become wholly explicit. The fixed symbol is almost entirely repetition; the expanding symbol is repetition balanced by variation, and that variation is in progressively deepening disclosure. By the slow uneven way in which it accretes meaning from the succession of contexts in which it occurs; by the mysterious life of its own it takes on and supports; by the part of its meaning that even on the last page of the novel it appears still to withhold—the expanding symbol responds to the impulses of the novelist who is aware that he cannot give us the core of his meaning, but strains to reveal now this aspect of it, now that aspect, in a sequence of sudden flashes.

The expanding symbol serves the novelist who is, to take a term from the *Aspects of the Novel*, "prophetic." A novelist of the prophetic kind differs from his brothers in that he intends not to say anything, but to "sing in the halls of fiction." * * *

The white whale is an expanding symbol, the most impressive I have found in earlier fiction. Ahab finds far more meaning in the whale than anyone else does; and Ahab's insight grows as his spirit becomes ever more preoccupied with the whale. Yet when the whale at last appears, his intelligence and malice far outrun a reader's expectations. The whale has a life of his own, and of him may also be said what Melville says of his great antagonist: "As touching all Ahab's deeper part, every revelation partook more of significant darkness than of explanatory light." But Melville's use of the white whale has an unrelenting insistence: from the early chapters to the end the whale dominates the story, with no real subsidence. Nearer to Proust's use of Vinteuil's music and Forster's use of hay is the symbol of the coffin, associated with the whale. In the second chapter Ishmael lodges in New Bedford at the Spouter Inn, kept by Peter Coffin, and reflects: "Coffin?—Spouter?—Rather ominous in that particular connexion." In the epilogue Ishmael, the sole survivor, clings to the "coffin lifebuoy," made long before to please Queequeg. The recurrence of the coffin, with deepening but never fully explicit suggestion, through the novel, is comparable in method with Forster's expanding symbols.

GORDON H. MILLS

[Fate in *Moby-Dick*]†

We have now come up squarely against the problem of fate in *Moby-Dick*. It is a complex problem that for the most part lies

† From Gordon H. Mills, "The Castaway in *Moby-Dick*," *University of Texas Studies in English*, Vol. 29 (1950), 231–48; the quotation is from 238–41. Reprinted by permission.

beyond the scope of this article, but a few things must be said about it. The issue here can be put in this way: Did Ahab deprive himself of pity by an act of will? Was he fated to die in pride, or did his will have some control?

Matthiessen's reference to *Ahab's* fatalism possibly suggests that although it is Ahab's it is not everybody's, hence perhaps that there is something like rationalization involved in it. In fact, it is obvious that if Matthiessen's statement about Ahab's fatalism is correct, Ahab was practicing free will in his assertion of it. We could not very well deny pity to one who went through what Ahab did if he could not help himself. (This is Olson's point, I take it.) Matthiessen recognized the problem in an earlier comment: "The meaning of his [Ahab's] tragedy is involved with his *conception* of the rigid Fate to which he is chained."[1] (Italics are mine.) Of course Matthiessen adds immediately that "this conception runs likewise through Ishmael's comments." But are we to understand that a belief in fate is merely an eccentric or superstitious notion of Ahab's, or is fate presented, within the framework of the novel, as a fact? If Ahab's view of fate is the same as Ishmael's, then presumably Ahab's view of fate is to be taken, within the novel, as correct. It is then not merely *Ahab's* fatalism. On the other hand, although Ishmael frequently—even in the Epilogue—refers in one way or another to the power of fate, it does not necessarily follow that Melville wished to commit Ishmael, or himself through Ishmael, to precisely the same view of fate with which he had endowed Ahab. Matthiessen does not pursue this precise problem into these latter stages.

It has been contended by G. Giovannini that Ahab was thorough-going in his fatalism, but that Ishmael himself was not,[2] and H. P. Vincent, in his recent book, indicates substantial agreement.[3] In the mat-making scene, Giovannini observes, Ishmael spoke of Ahab's "determinate, unsurrenderable wilfulness." Later Ishmael referred to Ahab's purpose as one that, "by its own sheer inveteracy of will, forced itself against gods and devils into a kind of self-assumed, independent being of its own." Giovannini concludes from this and other evidence that Ahab's pride was fatal but not fated. He is thus in accord with Matthiessen's opinion that the result of Ahab's fatalism is that there can be no unmixed pity for him.

A different avenue to approximately the same conclusion is con-

1. Charles Olson, *Call Me Ishmael* (New York, 1947), pp. 62–63; F. O. Matthiessen, *American Renaissance* (New York, 1941), 454–55.
2. G. Giovannini, "Melville and *Moby Dick*," *The Explicator*, Vol. V, no. 1 (Oct. 1946).
3. Howard P. Vincent, *The Trying-out of Moby-Dick* (Cambridge, Mass., 1949), p. 195.

tained in the interpretation of W. H. Auden. Auden feels that *Moby-Dick* is a tragedy of a type to which the reader's response is, "What a pity it was this way when it might have been otherwise," rather than the Greek, "What a pity it had to be this way."[4] Auden believes that Melville intended the reader to understand that a series of offers of divine grace was made to Ahab, partly through the medium of Pip, but that Ahab consistently refused them. Auden concludes that the last was made through the meeting with the *Rachel* and that Ahab's doom was finally certain in a psychological sense after his rejection of this offer.[5]

Thus, with the exception of Olson's, all the opinions—and evidence—that have been sketched in concerning this problem of fate lead to the conviction that at the end Melville fully intended Ahab to appear exactly as he does appear: willful, and black with hate.

The general conclusions that have so far been made possible, then, are that through the medium of Pip and Starbuck sympathy is created for Ahab, that Ahab's own sympathies were so worked upon that he felt his determination wavering, that in the end he wilfully denied whatever insight had been made available to him, and that Melville thus precluded a complete catharsis. The soundness of the last two conclusions is, of course, dependent upon the validity of the opinions cited above concerning the problem of fate.

These conclusions leave us puzzling over just what Melville intended the reader to think of the character of Ahab. Ahab was good and bad, sympathetic and unsympathetic. He did a bad thing at the end; made a bad choice. And the whole picture is complicated by the running commentary on fate offered by Ishmael, the final meaning of which can be arrived at only by laboriously disentangling a multitude of clues. *Moby-Dick* is not a neat book. (There is, indeed, an ever-present danger of supposing it a neater book than it is, and of attaching weight to trifles.) I have no wish to discuss the whole meaning of the book in this article, nor to try to explain the character of Ahab. But the evidence that has been considered leads certainly to the conclusion that Melville wished him to be a complex man, and probably to the conclusion that Melville had no neatly worked-out scheme to which Ahab's character was to be subordinate. Everyone will agree that Ahab was not simply a bad man who turned good—but was doomed; nor simply a bad man who stayed bad. Had he been either, the broad question of the meaning of the novel would have been simplified; and possibly the richness of the book would have been depleted.

4. W. H. Auden, "The Christian Tragic Hero," *New York Times Book Review*, VII (Dec. 16, 1945), 1.

5. *Ibid.*, p. 21.

MALCOLM LOWRY

[*Moby Dick* and *Under the Volcano*]†

* * * My wife says it would be more true to say that in the *Volcano* the Consul bore some relation to Moby Dick himself rather than Ahab. However it was not patterned after Moby Dick (the book) which I never studied till fairly recently (and it would seem not hard enough).

The identification, on my side, if any, was with Melville himself and his life. This was partly because I had sailed before the mast, partly because my grandfather had been a skipper of a windjammer who went down with his ship—Melville also had a son named Malcolm who simply disappeared—purely romantic reasons like that, but mostly because of his failure as a writer and his whole outlook generally. His failure for some reason absolutely fascinated me and it seems to me that from an early age I determined to emulate it, in every way possible—for which reason I have always been very fond of *Pierre* (even without having read it at all).

But to get back to the key—if any—the *Volcano* has just come out in France, where they say the key is in the Zohar. This discovery is partly due to a misleading preface by myself, written while not quite sober, but there is something in it, so I'll give you a précis of what they say for what it's worth, if I can translate it. This is in a very learned postface by one Max-Pol Fouchet and now it seems I can't translate it but I'll try to give you the gist. Now it seems I can't even give you the gist so I'll have to try instead to answer some of the points you raise in terms of what I think he says, or has some significance in terms of what I think I say—(so far as I can see, while it doesn't make you wrong, it somehow or other gives the book more thickness than even you ascribe to it, or I thought it had).

To take the points in the wrong order: first, the zodiacal significance—in my intention it had none at all, least of all in relation to Melville—I am trying to be honest, so I refer things to my wife when in doubt—the quotation you mention from *Moby Dick*, Chapter 99, I am conscious of reading now as for the first time—it never occurred to me there was any such zodiacal significance in *Moby Dick*, for that matter—and the passage now affects me

† From *Selected Letters of Malcolm Lowry*, ed. Harvey Breit and Margerie Bonner Lowry (Philadelphia: J. B. Lippincott Company, 1965), 197–99. Copyright © 1965 by Margerie Bonner Lowry. Reprinted by permission of the publisher and Harold Matson Company, Inc. Malcolm Lowry to Derek Pethick, from Dollarton, B.C., March 6, 1950. Pethick had written Lowry of his plans to talk on Lowry's *Under the Volcano* on the C.B.C. [*Editors' note.*]

supernaturally if at all, as if it meant something literal for *me*, and it was I who had been tracing the round again.

Though there is some extra evidence, if you like, in Chapter VII when the Consul is in Laruelle's tower—the Consul remembers a make of golfball called the Zodiac Zone—a lot more evidence in XI (where the intention was astronomical however). The goat means tragedy (tragedy—goat song) but goat—*cabrón*—cuckold (the horns). The scorpion is an image of suicide (scorpions sting themselves to death, so they say—Dr. Johnson called this a lie, but there is in fact some scientific evidence for it) and was no more than that—or was it? for I now see the whole book takes place "in Scorpio"—the action of the book is in one day, exactly 12 hours, seven to seven; the first chapter takes place 12 months later on the same day, so it is also in Scorpio.

Now I'll have to begin at the beginning again. The truth is, I have never certainly fully grasped the fact that *Moby Dick* was a political parable, though I can grasp the fact that Ahab (in my grandfather's eyes anyhow) is on quite an important plane a criminal. I seem to remember that Starbuck and quite a few of the crew had the same idea too, but it seemed to me that his revengeful élan was shared to the extent that one could scarcely say the whole crew were enduring toil and danger simply to gratify his desire—what about the harpooners? Yes, what about them? I don't feel on very secure ground, but I have never thought of the book before in that way.

I can see that *The Confidence Man* is a political parable; and that "The Tartarus of Maids" is a sexual one. I see the applicability of the pursuit in *Moby Dick* today all right, but it never occurred to me that it was intended in that way then, unless in the sort of jocular manner that Melville's vast appetite reaches out all over the table and couldn't help stuffing something of the sort in. Now I have written the above it seems not only illiterate, but not what I mean at all, but I'll have to let it stand. But what you say would be in line with much of Melville's later thought.

The *Volcano* is, though, and you are quite right here, quite definitely on one plan of political parable—indeed it started off as such * * *

PHILIP RAHV

Melville and his Critics†

Melville has of late nearly eclipsed Henry James as the much-favored object of critical inquiry. A few of the new studies devoted

† From Philip Rahv, "Melville and his Critics," a review of Newton Arvin's *Herman Melville*, *Partisan Review*, Vol. 17 (Sept.-Oct., 1950), 732–35. Reprinted by permission of the author.

to him are welcome contributions to scholarship; but some of the others, in which a critical approach is attempted, are of dubious value, since what is displayed in them is less insight into Melville than an addiction to the more aberrant tendencies of the contemporary literary mind. There is the new pedantry of myth, for instance, which is well on its way to converting a valid though by no means inexhaustible cultural interest into a pretentious and up-to-date version of the kind of source-and-parallel hunting now rapidly going out of fashion in the more alert academic circles. That there is a genuine mythic element in Melville is hardly open to doubt. But the myth-happy critics blow it up to vast proportions, laboring gratuitously, and in a mode of erudition peculiarly arid, to interpose between us and the reality of Melville a talmudic elaboration of mythology portentous to the point of stupefaction.

Not quite so one-sided yet unsatisfactory on the whole is the traditionalist approach to Melville. The traditionalists make what they can of him with their means, and their means are well adapted to eliminate the major contradictions in him. But these contradictions are really of an immitigable nature. At once creative and frustrating, agonisingly personal yet deeply expressive of national and universal culture, they are at the very core of Melville's modernity and the symbolic fate of his genius. Now a Melville relieved of his contradictions is, of course, a Melville removed from the shifting and perilous terrain of history and safely committed to a transcendent realm where, ceasing to be fallible and alive, no longer desperately striving for illumination in a siege of darkness, he is canonised as an exalted witness to metaphysical faith and aesthetic order.

The traditionalist aesthetic, with its profound revulsion from historicism and psychology and its inner drive toward standards of the normative-classicist type, cannot accept the real Melville or sustain him without doing violence to itself. Hence it constructs an ideal figure who is but a ghost of the man of whom Hawthorne wrote that he could neither believe nor be comfortable in his unbelief, reasoning endlessly about "everything that lies beyond human ken" even as he despaired of immortality and "pretty much made up his mind to be annihilated." Hawthorne, who was so frequently made inaccessible by the cold clarity of his nature, was moved by Melville's passion and believed in his integrity. None would now deny that integrity, but what is it, actually, if not the integrity of his riven and dissonant consciousness? This consciousness is inseparable from his art—an art which, in transforming the business of whaling into a fiery hunt ("wonder ye at the fiery hunt?") makes us see the artist in the image of those sea-captains of whom he said in *Moby Dick* that though they sailed anonymously out of Nantucket they yet became "as great and greater than your Cooke and your Krusenstern, for in their succorless empty-handedness, they, in the heathenish sharked waters, and by the beaches of unrecorded, javelin islands, battled with virgin wonders and terrors." Conrad's dictum, "In the destructive element immerse," comes to much the same thing. These "heathenish sharked waters" compose an element situated on the other side of the planet from the inland lakes of traditionalism.

Arvin, who in his present phase is perhaps freer of confining allegiances than most critics, is able to lay hold of the contradictions in Melville and to disclose their psychodynamic meaning without any squeamishness or failure in sympathy. There is no separation of man and artist in this critical portrait but an integration of the two which enforces the understanding of both in their organic unity. Eschewing all stress on biographical and historical facts for their own sake, and so controlling his account of the man Melville, of his background and character, as to enable the reader to see more clearly into his art, Arvin demonstrates anew the relevance of the biographical mode to the job of criticism when it is properly utilized and not made an end in itself. Equally credible is Arvin's use of the Freudian psychology. It is brought to bear upon Melville's experience with a maturity of judgment and power of modulation rarely found in literary contexts, where the amateurish shuffling of the formulas of neurosis is still the rule rather than the exception. In spite of long and intensive discussion, the issue of psychoanalysis in its application to literature remains unsettled, arousing hostile distrust in some quarters and excessive confidence in others. From this standpoint Arvin's book might be taken as a practical experiment, offering concrete evidence which neither the friends nor the enemies of the psychoanalytic method can afford to overlook.
* * *

The most richly assimilative of his critical tasks Arvin undertakes in his comprehensive scrutiny of that masterpiece [*Moby Dick*]. Varied resources of literary and philosophical investigation are pressed into service in an unflagging effort to grasp, to understand, to bring to light. The analysis is conducted on the four levels of the literal, the psychological, the moral, and the mythic; and it is so comprehensive an analysis that it would be impossible to do it justice in a brief résumé. Suffice it to say that it yields a reading of *Moby Dick* summing up the best that we have learned about it at the same time that it establishes some wholly new relations of meaning and a sharper perception of the coherence of its parts in the unity of imaginative possession.

The Shakespearean influence on Melville has been sufficiently charted by scholars like Olson and Matthiessen, and on that score Arvin has little to add that is newly suggestive. Of more original value is his examination of Melville's problem in seeking to discover the proper form for his narratives. Melville, as Arvin sees it, was working in isolation from the central currents of European writing, an isolation from which he both lost and gained. As *Pierre* shows, he foundered in attempting to adopt as his own the typical novelistic forms developed by his contemporaries in Europe. The passages in Arvin's study dealing with this problem and the solutions that Melville came upon, are of far more than technical importance. It is an aspect of the national literary experience that indirectly but significantly connects certain elementary considerations of manner and technique with the higher considerations of form and value.

HARRY SLOCHOWER

Freudian Motifs in *Moby Dick*†

The White Whale: The Sex-Mystery

It was suggested that Ahab's pursuit of whales is a mask for covering and relieving his private burden. However, we must ask ourselves not only what Moby Dick means to Ahab, the "old" man, but also to Ahab, as an American mythic hero.

On the level of immediate existence, the White Whale is a physical animal. But it is obvious that he means a great deal more to Melville and to Ahab. The story envelops Moby Dick with an atmosphere of strangeness and awe, with magical powers, and even with a degree of sanctity. He is pronounced a "god" and "the most devout of all beings." Here, Melville's Moby Dick assumes some of the leading characteristics which are associated with the Rhine Gold, the Golden Fleece and the Holy Grail.

Melville-criticism has popularized the notion that to Ahab the White Whale is the personification of Evil. This view is supported only by what Ahab says and consciously thinks about Moby Dick. The problem becomes more complex when we analyze Ahab's *attitude* and *behavior* towards the Whale.

Ahab fears Moby Dick, but he is also hypnotized by him. He is both repelled by the White Whale and drawn to him. The reader

† From Harry Slochower, *Complex*, No. 3 (Fall, 1950), 16–26; the quotation is from 20–24. Reprinted by permission of the author. This material forms a chapter in Dr. Slochower's book, *Mythopoesis* (Detroit: Wayne State University Press, 1970).

is expressly told that Moby Dick is a "magnet" to Ahab. If the Whale is an evil, then it is the kind of evil which Ahab does not avoid but which he seeks and *woos*. It is Ahab, not Moby Dick who is the pursuer.

The awesome, fearful and magnetic elements with which Melville surrounds Moby Dick arise in part from his embodiment of the sex-mystery. A careful reading of *Moby Dick* shows that the book is filled with genital allusions and with suggestions of the sex-act. One of the more revealing chapters is "The Gilder." Towards the close of this chapter, Melville-Ahab asks despairingly:

> Where is the foundling's father hidden? Our souls are like those orphans whose unwedded mothers die in bearing them: the secret of our paternity lies in their grave, and we must there to learn it.

This passage is preceded by references to the sea and the ship in metaphors which have sexual overtones. The sea becomes a field of "long-drawn virgin vales." The "rover" in his whale-boat has a soft "filial, confident" feeling towards the sea, as though he were passing "through the tall grass of a rolling prairie." The ship is compared to horses who show only their "erected ears, while their hidden bodies widely wade through the amazing verdure." It all seems like "some glad May-time, when the flowers of the woods are plucked." In this "mystic" mood, "fact and fancy, half-way meeting, interpenetrate, and form one seamless whole." The Symphony speaks of the sun as "a royal czar and king . . . giving this gentle air to this bold and rolling sea; even as bride and groom," and of "the loving alarms, with which the poor bride gave the bosom away." Sex-allusions are particularly crowded in the descriptions of the White Whale. They point to Moby Dick as a male-female, father-mother figure.

Male-Female Dialectic

The chapter on "The Tail" is replete with phallic and coitus imagery. It refers to the tail's "erect . . . vibrating" flukes which "shoot" out of view when the whale plunges into the deeps, his sublime "breach," discharging like "a great gun," giving forth a "light wreath of vapor" which is like "the smoke from a touch-hole," emerging out of "bottomless profundities." In the tail, the "measureless force of the whole whale seems concentrated to a point," a strength which has "much to do with magic." ("The Cassock," describing the huge male organ of the whale, would invoke an attitude of Biblical piety towards this "Grandissimus.") As Moby Dick appears, he reveals himself as "the grand god."

Moby Dick is not only a god-king-father figure. The male is joined to the female, the "foundling sire" to the "sweet mother." We have an allusion to Aphrodite, as the White Whale emerges from the waters, like "some plumed and glittering god uprising from the sea." We get a more direct indication of Moby Dick's bi-sexuality in the metaphors Melville uses to describe the whale. The head is said to be both a "battering ram" and a "dead blind wall," enveloped by a boneless toughness. It has "the rare virtue of thick walls" and "the rare virtue of interior spaciousness." The whale possesses terrifying power; yet, the immense flukes of the whale glide "with a certain slow softness" on the surface of "the masculine sea," and the tail moves with "maidenly gentleness" and "delicacy." The sight of Moby Dick, with a tall shattered pole projecting from his back, recalls to Melville the myth of Jupiter carrying Europa:

> . . . the white bull Jupiter swimming away with ravished Europa clinging to his graceful horns; his lovely leering eyes sideways intent upon the maid; with smooth bewitching fleetness, rippling straight for the nuptial bower in Crete.

The White Whale is the disguised form of the hermaphroditic mystery. Ahab invades the "man-like sea," challenging it to give up its primal secret. His attitude is a mixture of defiance and fear, of hatred and love. The White Whale is a dreaded monster and a magnetically desired object. (A similar ambiguity appears in Melville's discussion of the whale's whiteness). In "The Candles," Ahab addresses the lightning as "my fiery father." Even as he owns that the father is "omnipotent" and an "incommunicable riddle," he would dispute his "speechless placeless power." Yet, amidst his Promethean harangue, Ahab confesses that his deeper desire is to "worship," to "leap," to "burn" and to be "welded" with him. A suppliant note steals into Ahab's defiance, a womanly submissive tone, as he speaks of "the queenly personality" in himself which demands "her royal rights." He would rather not make war or hate, and he pleads: "Come in thy lowest form of love, and I will kneel and kiss thee."—A still deeper secret envelops the "foundling sire": The Mother. Ahab cries out: "My sweet mother, I know not. Oh, cruel! What hast thou done with her? There lies my puzzle."

Did Melville become aware of these elements in his work? In a letter to Hawthorne, Melville stated that he had written a "wicked book," and now felt "spotless as the lamb." *Moby Dick* is followed by *Pierre* where the theme of incest breaks out openly and where the parents are the obstacles to Pierre's becoming a man. Ludwig Lewisohn points out that the metaphors used in describing the mother's face in *Pierre* ("too familiar, yet inexplicable ... compounded so of hell and heaven ...") are similar to those employed for Moby Dick.

The Quest for Creation

The passages cited indicate that at least on one level of Melville's "associations," the White Whale stands for the feared and desired object harboring the secret of the sexes and of parental creation. It is a fearful thing, Melville tells us, "to have one's hands among the unspeakable foundations, ribs, and very pelvis of the world." Ahab's journey represents a maximum effort to face and master the riddle. But this hero is maimed, and his very efforts expose his impotence. He must depend on the crew to right his personal wrong. (For a discussion of the social myth in *Moby Dick*, see my article on "The Myth of Democratic Expectancy" in the Fall 1950 issue of THE AMERICAN QUARTERLY). By himself, crippled Ahab is inadequate to penetrate Moby Dick's "thick walls" and he fears its "interior spaciousness." The hunter is "impotent" before the prey: "The severest pointed harpoon, the sharpest lance darted by the strongest human arm, impotently rebounds from it." The wall remains "impregnable," and Ahab never reaches its "most buoyant thing within." Toil as we may, he confesses in The Symphony, "we all sleep at last on the field. Sleep? Aye, and rust amid greenness; as last year's scythes flung down, and left in the half-cut swaths." Melville draws an analogy between the fate awaiting him who would conquer Moby Dick and that which befell "the weakling youth" who desired to lift "the dread goddess' veil at Lais."

Despite these terrors, Ahab does hurl his spear at the White Whale. As Ahab sees Moby Dick successfully breaching the thick walls of the *Pequod*, he makes his final supreme effort "to give up the spear." The gesture is performed in an orgiastic frenzy and exaltation, Ahab feeling "like a billow that's all one crested comb." (The scene, with Ahab's "growing blind" again suggests the Oedipus theme). At the end, he is at last "united" to the whale by his line. The umbilical cord is retied, and Ahab sinks, like an infant, "voicelessly" into the ocean by the side of the mystery he has been unable to fathom.

The novel calls the whale "king of creation." In terms of the American myth, Ahab's voyage is the American journey to bring its birth to light. The White Whale and the sea form a composite of the bottomless depths holding the unknown and unadmitted, the hidden elements of Ahab's and of America's creative origins.

NORTHROP FRYE

[*Moby Dick*: A Romance-Anatomy]†

To sum up, then: when we examine fiction from the point of view of form, we can see four chief strands binding it together, novel, confession, anatomy, and romance. The six possible combinations of these forms all exist, and we have shown how the novel has combined with each of the other three. Exclusive concentration on one form is rare: the early novels of George Eliot, for instance, are influenced by the romance, and the later ones by the anatomy. The romance-confession hybrid is found, naturally, in the autobiography of a romantic temperament, and is represented in English by George Borrow. The romance-anatomy one we have noticed in Rabelais: a fine modern example is *Moby Dick*, where the romantic theme of the wild hunt expands into an encyclopedic anatomy of the whale. Confession and anatomy are united in *Sartor Resartus*. More comprehensive fictional schemes usually employ at least three forms: we can see strains of novel, romance, and confession in *Pamela*, of novel, romance, and anatomy in *Don Quixote*, of novel, confession, and anatomy in Proust, and of romance, confession, and anatomy in Apuleius.

I deliberately make this sound schematic in order to suggest the advantage of having a simple and logical explanation for the form of, say, *Moby Dick* or *Tristram Shandy*. The usual critical approach to the *form* of such works resembles that of the doctors in Brobdingnag, who after great wrangling finally pronounced Gulliver a *lusus naturae*. It is the anatomy in particular that has baffled critics, and there is hardly any fiction writer deeply influenced by it who has not been accused of disorderly conduct. As for the question which so many feel it necessary to ask at this point, whether Melville or Sterne "knew" that they were combining an anatomy form with a romance or a novel, the answer is, as usual, yes and no. They knew what they were doing, but they knew as creators know, not as critics explain.

ARTHUR HOBSON QUINN

[Melville's Besetting Weaknesses]‡

Indeed the early part of the book is tiresome and confused, and the lectures upon the various kinds of whales illustrate Melville's

† From Northrop Frye, "The Four Forms of Prose Fiction," *The Hudson Review*, Vol. 2 (Winter, 1950), 582–95; the quotation is from 593. Reprinted by permission from *The Hudson Review;* copyright © 1949 by The Hudson Review, Inc.

‡ From Arthur Hobson Quinn, *The Literature of the American People* (New York: Appleton-Century-Crofts, Inc., 1951), 245–246. Reprinted by permission of Appleton-Century-Crofts, Educational Division, Meredith Corporation.

besetting weaknesses, his lack of humor, and his inability to tell fact from fiction. But when the great chase nears its end and the White Whale turns on its pursuers and rends them, there is painted for us an unforgettable scene in which the fury of man goes down, defeated, by the fury of the great beast, driven to bay in its own selected battle ground.

ELMER E. STOLL

Symbolism in *Moby-Dick*†

Why, now, one wonders, all this great to-do of late years about *Moby-Dick*; Melville's name, in the process, being coupled with those of Æschylus and Sophocles, Dante, Shakespeare, and Milton; Ahab's, at the same time, with that of Prometheus? "Distinctly," says Mr. Mumford, "*Moby-Dick* belongs with the *Divine Comedy* and *Hamlet* and the *Brothers Karamazov* and *War and Peace* (p. 361). Indistinctly, I should prefer to say. That surely is not what Arnold would have called the "real estimate," the "disinterested"; and it almost seems as if there had been a conspiracy among American critics, with a few of the British complaisantly joining in. Now that we are the greatest of peoples, we must have a literature to match: by Melville's own Whitman-like Americanism, both in *Moby-Dick* and elsewhere, the critics are encouraged to think we have. But the story of a man's lifelong revenge upon a whale for thwarting him in his money-making designs upon its blubber would inadequately furnish forth a national epic, or one, as Mr. Mumford fancies, for the "ages." Grendel, in *Beowulf*, whom Mr. Van Wyck Brooks is moved to think of, *is* evil and malicious unmistakably—a "public enemy no. 1," carrying off thirty thanes at a swoop. He is quite worth the hating, the chasing and slaying.

There is probably, however, a deeper cause for the to-do—the prevalent taste for symbolism itself. Here is a conspiracy of a different sort—that of the present day tastes for symbolism, the detective story, and (in its various forms) ambiguity. On *Moby-Dick* as a "mystery story" a whole book has lately been written; but as I have said of *The Turn of the Screw* so treated,[1] in the real detective stories the mystery is, at the end, no longer "hidden," but cleared up or away. Here is none to clear up or away. Of ambiguity, to be sure, there is plenty—contradiction and paradox, dualism and antinomy. Ahab is, according to Captain Peleg "a grand ungodly, godlike man" (ch. 16); the whiteness of the whale is dubious—fair

† From Elmer E. Stoll, *Journal of the History of Ideas*, Vol. 12 (June, 1951), 440–65; the quotation is from 449–55. Reprinted by permission of the publisher and Doris P. Franklin.

1. Cf. "Symbolism in Coleridge," *PMLA* (March, 1948), 230.

or foul (ch. 42). And to the ambiguous or paradoxical the symbolist critics particularly take[2], for latitude much eases the path of interpretation. All round us today there is the Ambivalenz of the Freudians, though I have not myself seen the symbolizing mythology of the Unconscious here directly applied. That, moreover, is for the highbrows; the interest here in question is far, far older and deeper-seated than that in either Freud or Conan Doyle—is that in riddle or enigma and in poetry as the finest form of it. Even authorship, without a ghost of a reason, has become for some people a problem; and no insignificant number have thought, and think still, that Bacon, or Oxford, or Rutland penned the plays.

It is, of course, a good story, even a great one; but not, I think one of really ecumenical or perennial importance. And a story it *is*, as we have seen, not a monstrous fable or hideous and intolerable allegory; as such, moreover, it has the appropriate properties or virtues: suspense and momentum, both acceleration and also the requisite retardation, an artfully accumulated volume of interest, and a prolonged, prodigious climax. The preparations are almost without number—predictions or omens, misgivings or forebodings—some depending upon superstitition, some merely upon our common human nature. And what is more important, there are such preparations—such discreet and gradual approaches—as are calculated to make the improbable probable. Though in prose, there is, as I said, something of poetry. It is well ordered that like the other great tales of adventure and marvel, such as the *Divine Comedy*, *Robinson Crusoe*, and *Gulliver's Travels*, this one should be told in the first person, by a participant and eye-witness, who can be definite and circumstantial, yet only within the limits of his own vision or surmise. It is well ordered that we are not permitted to see or suspect what is going on under cover any more than he does; and also that he is, as we have seen, a spectator not impartial, not unadaptable. For this too we are prepared: had he not been equal, near the outset, to sleeping in the same bed with an idolatrous head-peddling cannibal, a tomahawk between his teeth? It is, moreover, at the comparatively sober New Bedford that the story starts, then moves on to Nantucket Island, then to the *Pequod*, with its crazy captain and motley, mostly half-mad crew; and somewhat as in *The Ancient Mariner* it is by stages that we leave everyday reality and enter into a world where not so unplausibly one particular whale in the wide world can be caught or sought. That chimerical project is not proposed at the outset. Captains Peleg and Bildad, part-owners, on shipboard till the pilot is dropped, know nothing of it; nor do any of the crew except the Parsee and (perhaps) the mysterious tiger-yellow set smuggled in below hatches;

2. Cf. my "Symbolism in Shakespeare," *Mod. Lang. Rev.* (Jan., 1947), 8–20.

and fully to the light it comes, though there have been glimpses of it already, not before Chapter 36, when Ahab nails the gold doubloon, the prize for him who first espies the monster, to the mainmast. That is a scène à faire, a minor climax. At the words "white whale" and "Moby-Dick," only the queerest of the crew prick up their ears. They too have seen or heard of him; for them he is not altogether a myth; and as the excitement mounts, the oath of vengeance is given and taken. *Crescit eundo*. For in Chapter 31, when Ahab had come out with the order, "If ye see a white whale split your lungs for him," Stubb exclaimed, "What do you think of that now, Flask? Aint there a small drop of something queer about that, eh? A *white* whale—did ye mark that, man?" As about the Ghost in *Hamlet* when first mentioned—the right preparation!—at first there is scepticism.

Also the characters in themselves make one another more plausible, by parallel or by contrast. The harpooners Queequeg, Tashtego, and Daggoo, as Mr. Erskine says, "follow fixed ideas"[3] somewhat like Ahab, and the Parsee is quite as fanatical as he. Starbuck on the other hand, is sensible and judicious; Stubb and Flask, sensible and humorous. By Ahab, however, the narrative interest is engrossed. In him there is dramatic development. Though with revulsions of tenderness or affection, he becomes continually more reckless and ruthless, to the growing concern and anxiety of Starbuck, Stubb, and Flask. Starbuck he threatens with a musket (ch. 109); the harpoon for the whale he tempers in the blood of the pagan Queequeg, Tashtego, and Daggoo, baptizing it in a blasphemous Latin (ch. 113); in his impatience he dashes the quadrant to the deck (ch. 118); he refuses help to the Captain of the *Rachel* (ch. 128); he will "murder" Pip the lunatic negro boy he is so fond of, should he not obey him (ch. 129); like Macbeth in his *hybris*, he trusts to the end in the Parsee's riddling prophecies. And the style? That too helps make the improbable probable—matter-of-fact or grotesque at New Bedford and Nantucket, imaginative and fantastic, high-flying and rhythmical at sea.

Still, as I read the book, it is not by any means to be accounted an immortal masterpiece; nor does it much remind me, I must confess of Æschylus, Dante, Shakespeare, or even the two Russians of our latter day. Of such a quest or mission what would Tolstoy have thought or said? And though as a whole the story is well constructed, it suffers at times from two not inconsiderable defects: padding and sensationalism. As for the latter, there is Tashtego, the Indian, desperately nailing the flag to the masthead that, true to his master, he might keep to the last the colours flying, though his master is drowning, as is he himself:

3. *The Delight of Great Books* (1928), p. 223.

> at that instant, a red arm and a hammer hovered backwardly uplifted in the open air, in the act of nailing the flag faster and yet faster to the subsiding spar. A sky-hawk that tauntingly had followed the main-truck downwards from its natural home among the stars, pecking at the flag, and incommoding Tashtego there; this bird now chanced to intercept its broad fluttering wing between the hammer and the wood; and simultaneously feeling that ethereal thrill, the submerged savage beneath, in his death-gasp, kept his hammer frozen there; and so the bird of heaven with archangelic shrieks, and his imperial beak thrust upwards, and his whole captive form folded in the flag of Ahab, went down with his ship, which, like Satan, would not sink to hell till she had dragged a living part of heaven along with her, and helmeted herself with it.

That is somewhat after the order of the stagy climax which Stevenson complains of in Hugo's *Travailleurs*, where at one and the same moment the sloop disappears over the horizon and Gilliat's suicidal head under water. A much milder but sentimental coincidence precedes this, where floating in the lovely sunset, sea and sky, sun and whale (not Moby here) "stilly died together." In either case it is of "at that instant," and in Tashtego's, of his being already submerged and "in his death-gasp," that I am complaining: the climax (of course) is waranted by the multitude of preparations and the steadily accelerated action before it as well as by the fanaticism in both Ahab's hatred and the savage's devotion. Of the climax and the battle before it even Longinus (and what more could be said?) might have approved.

This "avidity after effect," however, (as Stevenson describes it in Hugo) is by Melville outdone shortly before, as on this, the third and last day of the combat, the Parsee, killed on the second, thus reappears:

> Lashed round and round to the fish's back; pinioned in the turns upon turns in which, during the past night, the whale had reeled the involutions of the lines around him, the half torn body of the Parsee was seen; his sable raiment frayed to shreds; his distended eyes turned full upon old Ahab.

That it might be fulfilled which was spoken by Fedallah the prophet. For he was to "go before,', says Ahab, and yet reappear, to "pilot me still" (ch. 117). This prophesying itself, with its "paltering in a double sense"—"two hearses" to be seen, which turn out to be the whale's body and the sinking ship, and the fatal hemp, which turns out to be the harpoon line caught round Ahab's neck—such prophesying, I say, falls far less plausibly from the lips of a latter-day fire-worshipping whale-hunter than from those of the Weird Sisters, "goddesses of destiny," in the days of Duncan and

Edward the Confessor. No Fate has the Parsee at his beck and call. And in reading *Macbeth*, as not *Moby-Dick*, there can be a Coleridgian "willing suspension of disbelief"; but in regard to the Parsee's reappearance, after all the creature's swimming and plunging with him in the interval, his orbs turned "full upon old Ahab," that question does not even arise. The fulfilment of the prediction is in itself improbable, as not in Birnam Wood's coming to Dunsinane or in "none of woman born." And here *incredulus odi*.

As for padding or irrelevance, there is, in the middle, chapter after chapter on "cetology" (32), on whaling practices (33), on cutting-up, trying-out, and storing; single ones on ambergris, Jonah (83), and (with a ponderous humour) the cetaceans' amorous habits (88), foreign whaleships' cellars and larders (101), and a Bower in the Arsacides (102); most of which has little or no justification in narrative art. Mr. Belgion's suggestion, which Mr. Maugham reproduces, is that, "since it is a tale of pursuit, the end of the pursuit must be perpetually delayed." To be sure; but, as also Mr. Maugham seems to think, not after such a fashion as this. It is a different matter, of course, when meantime ordinary whales, with difficulty and danger, are killed, and Ishmael dwells upon the enormous size of them, by comparison measures for us the proportions of their skeletons, or reports previous cases of their prodigious destructiveness (ch. 45). Hereby he is preparing us for the entry of the portentous monster and making the subsequent catastrophe more acceptable.[4] Also by the chapter on the Whiteness of the Whale (42) he renders him not only more portentous and mysterious but (though, as we have seen, less credible) more susceptible of discovery. Likewise, by his "Chart" (ch. 44) and his "Affidavit" (45), with the account of whale haunts, feeding-grounds, and itineraries, the author endeavors to reconcile the reader to the project of finding and recognizing one particular whale, encountered years before, and obviously at liberty meanwhile (if not killed and boiled already) to swim far and wide, up and down, within as well as over, the limitless waters of the earth. But argument, with documentary evidence, however convincing; an affidavit as in Chapter 45 or a "So help me Heaven" as at the close of the Town Ho's story (ch. 54);—these all are not imaginative, artistic methods of reconcilement. Not demonstration or adjuration, but suggestion and contrast are the way. So it is with Dante, Shakespeare, or Coleridge himself, who really produce the "willing suspension of disbelief," as I have shown elsewhere[5], while they deal with still greater marvels. By the example in *Hamlet* Melville does not sufficiently profit. "Tush, tush," Horatio protests, "'twill not appear."

4. *Cf. Erskine, op. cit.*, p. 230.

5. *Shakespeare Studies* (1927), pp. 206–10.

> Most like; it harrows me with fear and wonder.
>
> How now, Horatio! you tremble and look pale.
> Is not this something more than fantasy?
>
> Before my God. I might not this believe
> Without the sensible and true avouch
> Of mine own eyes.

And Dante? As I have said before, when, at the outset, in the "selva oscura," the poet meets the being who later turns out to be the shade of Virgil:

> "Have pity on me," I cried to him, "what so' thou art, or shade or real man." Like the ghosts of folklore and of Shakespeare, only then does he speak when "spoke to." But then
>
> Risposemi: "Non uomo, uomo gia fui."
>
> It is all done indirectly, dramatically, by silence and speech and the effect of both together. There is no attempt to picture his shadowy, transparent form. Dante thought him a spirit, possibly a man.—"No man, a man I was," is (in the original) the eerie and penetrating reply. But the most convincing thing is the question "or shade or real man"—*od ombra od uomo certo*. The order is unusual, upsetting—his first thought is of a shade, he is in the land of shades already. (*Poets and Playwrights*, p. 283)

HENRY NASH SMITH

[An Exegesis of Chapter 102]†

There are a number of difficulties in the passage. The role of the sun, for example, is confusing. As weaver-god the sun tends to be personified, and he is anthropomorphic enough to be deafened; but the sun is also a flying shuttle, and the act of weaving seems sometimes that of a person tending a loom, sometimes the action of the loom itself. The skeleton of the whale is inactive yet also seems engaged in weaving; it is Death yet also a god capable of begetting offspring. Chapter 47 ("The Mat-Maker") has prepared us to see in the process of weaving a complex analogical statement concerning fate, free will, and chance; this implication is present here also, and the skeleton-loom takes on some of the character of fate. But at the end of the chapter, in the position where Melville ordinarily

† From Henry Nash Smith, "The Image of Society in *Moby-Dick*," in MOBY DICK *Centennial Essays* (Dallas: Southern Methodist University Press, 1953), pp. 59–75; the quotation is from pp. 61–63. The essay was read at the *Moby-Dick* centennial celebration at Williams College on September 2–4, 1951.

develops his important symbolic inferences, the warning that our thoughts may be overheard seems odd and trivial after the grave suggestions that have been thrown out immediately before, and it is not congruous with the remarks concerning Death and Life that immediately follow. The vital activity of the plants merges indistinguishably with the mechanical activity of the loom, so that the machine does not seem here to be an inorganic menace to life. And since the tone of the chapter is playful on the whole, we are restrained from giving to these cosmic materials the weight they might have in a different setting.

The difficulties presented by "A Bower in the Arsacides" are highly suggestive. The chapter provides abundant evidence that industrialism and technology had made a deep impression on Melville: he associates images drawn from this source with ideas of the greatest moment. But the material is not fully worked out; its meaning seems to be urgent, yet is not brought to formal clarity. The industrial imagery associated with Ahab is more consistent. It is always malign in implication, and its cumulative effect lends to him an impressive strength. This imagery has seemed to support the interpretation of Ahab as an embodiment of the inhuman will-to-power which Melville discerned in developing American capitalism. Yet I do not think that the industrial imagery, taken as a whole, provides, or was meant to provide, a coherent image of American society. I should like to inquire whether *Moby-Dick* contains such an image. To some extent this is to ask whether the subject matter of the science of sociology was present as an identifiable concept to Melville's mind. Such an inquiry might seem trivial, but it is not necessarily so; for it is the basis for raising the further question of whether society functions as an entity in the action of the book. And in a work of art, *Esse est percipi.*

LAWRANCE THOMPSON

[The Underlying Theme in *Moby-Dick*] †

He [Melville] was temperamentally and artistically inclined to strike the Byronic pose and rebaptize himself, not in the name of the Father, but in the name of Satan. Even if we are forced to see in Melville's sophomoric attitude a certain indication of arrested development, it is better to recognize him for what he was than to inflate his attitude into something which it was not.

† From Lawrance Thompson, *Melville's Quarrel with God* (Princeton: Princeton University Press, 1952), pp. 242–43. Copyright 1952, Princeton University Press; Princeton Paperback, 1966. Reprinted by permission of Princeton University Press.

Baldly stated, then, Melville's underlying theme in *Moby-Dick* correlates the notions that the world was put together wrong and that God is to blame; that God in his infinite malice asserts a sovereign tyranny over man and that most men are seduced into the mistaken view that his divine tyranny is benevolent and therefore acceptable; but that the freethinking and enlightened and heroic man will assert the rights of man and will rebel against God's tyranny by defying God in thought, word, deed, even in the face of God's ultimate indignity, death.

FATHER FRANCIS X. CANFIELD

[The Lesson of *Moby-Dick*]†

Both authors [the authors of the Book of Job and of *Moby-Dick*] have the same lesson to teach: man is powerless to know the Almighty. His ways are not ours. God directs the events of day-to-day living and even draws good out of evil. Our attitude should be one of humble submission.

ROBERT FROST

[Does Wisdom Matter?]‡

That's an awful story really.[1] I think it the worst outrage ever written. The purpose couldnt be anything but to discredit God. But I am glad you take the position that Melville's wrongness, unsoundness or whatever we call it matters next to nothing at all in our judgement of him as a great story teller, one of America's splendors in art. Does wisdom matter, I once asked in public. My answer was then and is now and as yours is, not at all or at least hardly at all. I must confess you do take away from Melville's stature a little in making him bother to believe in a God he hates. How could he have failed to see he had got round by a series of insensible cog-slips to where he should have changed God's name to Devil. He seems rather weak on the brain side. But as you say never mind. We may admire him more wrong than almost anybody

† From Father Francis X. Canfield, "Moby-Dick and the Book of Job," *Catholic World*, Vol. 174 (January, 1952), 254–60; the quotation is from 260. Reprinted by permission.

‡ From *Selected Letters of Robert Frost*, edited by Lawrance Thompson (New York: Holt, Rinehart and Winston, 1964), pp. 553–54. Portion of a letter from Robert Frost to Lawrance Thompson, from Amherst, around May 1, 1952.

1. The "awful story" is *Billy Budd* [*Editors' note*].

but Hawthorne right. It should be a lesson to undergraduates not to pay too much attention to the disproportionately long hours their lecturers spend on a good poet's good or bad philosophy so called. What an inducement to endless discourses a poet offers who begins as a bad thinker and ends up another kind of thinker. In his last state he may be too easily mistaken for a good thinker. He's a godsend to the critics just the same. Graham Greene's formula for an entertaining salvation is to have sinned deeply and repented greatly. Always lots of nonsense abroad. He must be thinking of St. Augustine more than St. Thomas Acquinas. Thomas was a good boy from first to last. I believe he weighed too much, but the Church will have it his weight was glandular.

Did it ever occur to you there was a certain air of nouveau richeness to Herman's style as if he wasnt quite a Bostonian but it couldnt be helped. He had (or may be suspected of having) the embarrassment of a parvenu with his hands and feet (metrical feet) in Mass society. I began to notice it years ago when I read Typee aloud at home. He tried to be elegant without having first got sophisticated. In another way Marquand has suffered more than necessary from the ineffability of Boston. The editor of the Boston Globe said to me once if he and I weren't perturbed in our Harvard days by the Porcillian Club it was because we didn't know of its existance.

CHARLES OLSON

[The Most Prevalent Error of Melville Criticism]†

[*Melville's Use of the Bible,* by Nathalia Wright,] goes a very great way to help to right perhaps the most prevalent error of contemporary Melville critique—the tendency of it to exaggerate the New Testament and Christ as against the less conscious attention Melville gave the Old Testament as a source * * *

ALBERT CAMUS

[Melville: Un Créateur de Mythes]‡

Il est à peine moins commode de parler en quelques pages d'une oeuvre qui a la dimension tumultueuse des océans où elle est née

† From Charles Olson, "Materials and Weights of Herman Melville," *The New Republic,* Vol. 127 (September 8, 1952), pp. 20–21; the quotation is from 20. Reprinted by permission of *The New Republic,* © 1952, Harrison-Blaine of New Jersey, Inc.

‡ Albert Camus, "Herman Melville," *Les Ecrivains Célèbres,* Vol. 3 (Paris, Lucien Mazenod, 1953), pp. 128–29. Reprinted by permission of Editions d'Art Lucien Mazenod.

que de résumer la Bible ou de condenser Shakespeare. Mais pour juger au moins du génie de Melville, il est indispensable d'admettre que ses ouvrages retracent une expérience spirituelle d'une intensité sans égale et qu'ils sont en partie symboliques. Certains critiques ont discuté cette évidence qui ne paraît plus guère discutable. Ces livres admirables sont de ceux, exceptionnels, qu'on peut lire de façons différentes, à la fois évidents et mystérieux, obscurs comme le plein soleil et pourtant limpides comme une eau profonde. L'enfant et le sage y trouvent également nourriture. L'histoire du capitaine Achab, par exemple, lancé de la mer australe au Septentrion à la poursuite de Moby Dick, la baleine blanche qui lui a coupé la jambe, peut sans doute se lire comme la passion funeste d'un personnage fou de douleur et de solitude. Mais elle peut aussi se méditer comme l'un des mythes les plus bouleversants qu'on ait imaginés sur le combat de l'homme contre le mal et sur l'irrésistible logique qui finit par dresser l'homme juste contre la création et le créateur d'abord, puis contre ses semblables et contre lui-même. N'en doutons pas, s'il est vrai que le talent recrée la vie, alors que le génie, de surcroît, la couronne de mythes, Melville est d'abord un créateur de mythes.

J'ajouterai que ces mythes, contrairement à ce qu'on en a dit, sont clairs. Ils ne sont obscurs que dans le mesure où la racine de toute douleur et de toute grandeur est enfouie dans la nuit de la terre. Ils ne le sont pas plus que les cris de Phèdre, ou les silences de Hamlet, ou les chants de triomphe de Don Giovanni. Il me semble pouvoir dire au contraire (et ceci mériterait un grand développement) que Melville n'a jamais écrit que le même livre indéfiniment recommencé. Ce livre unique est celui d'un voyage, d'abord animé de la seule et joyeuse curiosité de la jeunesse (*Typee*, *Omoo*, etc.), ensuite habité par une angoisse de plus en plus brûlante et égarée. *Mardi* est le premier, et magnifique, récit où Melville déclare ouverte cette quête que rien n'apaisera et au bout de laquelle, pour finir, "poursuivants et poursuivis fuient sur un océan sans bords". C'est dans cet ouvrage que Melville prend conscience du fascinant appel qui, sans cesse, retentit en lui. "J'ai entrepris un voyage sans carte." Et encore: "Je suis le chasseur sans repos, celui qui n'a pas de foyer." *Moby Dick* ne fera que pousser à la perfection les grands thèmes de *Mardi*. Mais la perfection artistique ne suffisant pas non plus à étancher la sorte de soif dont il est question ici, Melville recommencera dans *Pierre ou les Ambiguïtés*, chef-d'oeuvre manqué, à peindre la quête de génie et du malheur dont il consacrera l'échec ricanant au cours du long voyage sur le Mississipi qui fait le sujet de *l'Homme de confiance*. * * *

Mais ceci, qui devait être indiqué, ne doit égarer personne sur le vrai génie de Melville et sur la souveraineté de son art. La santé, la force, un humour jaillissant, le rire de l'homme y éclatent. Il n'a pas ouvert la boutique de sombres allégories qui enchantent aujourd'hui la triste Europe. En tant que créateur, il est par exemple aux antipodes de Kafka dont il fait sentir les limites artistiques. Chez Kafka, l'expérience spirituelle, pourtant irremplaçable, déborde l'expression et l'invention qui restent monotones. Chez Melville, elle s'équilibre à elles et y trouve constamment son sang et sa chair. Comme les plus grands artistes, Melville a construit ses symboles sur le concret, non dans le matériau du rêve. Le créateur de mythes ne participe au génie que dans la mesure où il les inscrit dans l'épaisseur de la réalité et non dans les nuées fugitives de l'imagination. Chez Kafka, la réalité qu'il décrit est suscitée par le symbole, le fait découle de l'image, chez Melville le symbole sort de la réalité, l'image naît de la perception. C'est pourquoi Melville ne s'est jamais séparé de la chair ni de la nature, obscurcies dans l'oeuvre kafkéenne. Le lyrisme de Melville, qui fait penser à celui de Shakespeare, se sert au contraire des quatre éléments. Il mêle la Bible et la mer, la musique des flots et des sphères, la poésie des jours et une grandeur atlantique. Il est inépuisable comme ces vents qui courent les océans déserts pendant des milliers de kilomètres et, arrivés à la côte, trouvent encore la force de raser des villages entiers. Il souffle, comme la démence de Lear, au-dessus des mers sauvages où se tapit Moby Dick et l'esprit du mal. Quand la tempête est passée, et la destruction totale, voici l'etrange apaisement qui monte des eaux primitives, la pitié silencieuse qui transfigure les tragédies. Au-dessus de l'équipage muet, le corps parfait de Billy Budd tourne alors doucement au bout de sa corde dans la lumière grise et rose du jour qui grandit.

T. E. Lawrence plaçait *Moby Dick* à côté des *Possédés* ou de *Guerre et Paix*. On peut y joindre sans hésiter *Billy Budd, Mardi, Benito Cereno* et quelques autres. Ces livres déchirants, où la créature est accablée mais où la vie, à toutes les pages, est exaltée, sont des sources inépuisables de force et de pitié. On y trouve la révolte et le consentement, l'amour indomptable et sans terme, la passion et la beauté, le langage le plus haut, le génie enfin. "Pour perpétuer son nom, disait Melville, il faut le sculpter sur une lourde pierre et le couler au fond de la mer: les abîmes durent plus que les sommets." Les abîmes ont en effet leur vertu douloureuse, comme eut la sienne l'injuste silence où vécut et mourut Melville, et le vieil océan qu'il laboura sans relâche. De ces ténèbres incessantes, il tira au jour ses oeuvres, visages d'écume et de nuit, sculptés par les eaux, et dont la royauté mystérieuse commence à peine de rayonner sur nous qu'elle nous aide déjà à sortir sans effort de notre continent d'ombres, pour aller enfin vers la mer, la lumière et son secret.

JAMES D. KOERNER

[The Scholarly Junkyard of *Moby-Dick* Criticism]†

One scarcely knows, in fact, where to begin in surveying such a scholarly junkyard where the weary and unsuspecting White Whale becomes all things to all men. * * *

It is no easy task * * * to come at *Moby-Dick* anew, sloughing off all of the nonsense that has been written about it. * * * *Moby-Dick* is the relatively simple and very ancient story of man's search for the meaning of life. * * * Although Captain Ahab is obviously not Everyman, so maddened is his desire to grapple with the Problem of Evil, and thereby the explanation, of the universe, yet he is surely symbolic of the universal fear and hatred that man has felt since the dawn of reason toward the apparent malevolence and inscrutability of that universe. * * *

[Of the "complex ambiguities" and "prolific symbology":] Because one doesn't understand these things, one need not assume that they are profundities; they may be mere obscurities.

GEORGE R. STEWART

The Two *Moby-Dicks*‡

V

Of special importance for the theory being developed is the section consisting of Chapters 16–22, which I have here termed the

† From James D. Koerner, "The Wake of the White Whale," *Kansas Magazine* (1954), 42–50; the quotation is from 43, 46, 49. Reprinted by permission.

‡ From George R. Stewart, *American Literature*, Vol. 25 (January, 1954), 417–48; the quotation is from 433–48. Reprinted by permission of the author and Duke University Press. The whole of Stewart's very long article is of interest. It is the fullest elaboration of the theory, also considered by Leon Howard, Harrison Hayford, Howard P. Vincent, and Charles Olson, that Melville began *Moby-Dick* as something nearer a simple whaling adventure story than what it finally became. The theory often involves consideration of some event—such as Melville's meeting with Hawthorne and his reading of Hawthorne's *Mosses from an Old Manse* in August, 1850—which precipitated a significant spiritual or intellectual development and led to a more or less extensive recasting of the manuscript. Stewart takes the view that there was an "original story" (which he calls Ur-Moby-Dick or UMD) surviving in "very slightly revised" form in Chapters 1–15; that there is an important group of chapters (16–22, the "Transition") which "represent the original story with a certain amount of highly important revision"); and that Chapters 23 through the "Epilogue" were written after Melville "reconceived" the story, although they may preserve certain passages of UMD, "doubtless somewhat revised." Stewart argues for this theory not only with the already assembled external evidence but also from largely fresh in-

Transition. In order to make clearer the significance of this section, I now present, tentatively, some ideas as to the actual procedure in the writing of *Moby-Dick*.

In accordance with evidence now only partially presented, I believe that Melville wrote a large part of UMD subsequent to Chapter 15, and that that book was in Duyckinck's words "mostly done." Melville, however, developed other ideas, which were eventually to take shape in MD. He therefore went back over his manuscript, like any professional author trying to save as much as he could of what he had written. He decided that the first fifteen chapters could be allowed to stand about as they were. He then undertook to splice (we may use a seaman's term) his new story on. The Transition represents this splicing. Here he retained his original manuscript, but revised it, probably by the procedure of cutting out certain passages and inserting new ones. Thus he presumably had some description of the original *Pequod*, which had a wheel, doubtless lacked the sea-ivory fittings, and was in general a more usual ship. We can hardly think that he closed his description of his original *Pequod* with the philosophical commentary so unlike UMD: "A noble craft, but somehow a most melancholy! All noble things are touched with that."

This splicing process was apparently brought to an end with Chapter 22, and from that point on, I believe that Melville wrote essentially a new book, only here and there making use of what he had already written.

The Transition is therefore of especial importance and must be examined carefully. As I have already stated, it seems to be connected more closely with UMD than with MD. Of the seven chapters, four can be considered unrevised and therefore wholly UMD, viz., 17, 18, 20, and 22. The other three seem to show some important revisions.

The first of these is Chapter 16. In spite of revision this chapter still suggests UMD in several details. For instance, Cape Horn is three times mentioned in connection with the route of the ship.

---

ternal evidence. These are his main groups of internal evidence: contradictory statements in the book, such as an unexplained shift in Ishmael's intention to sail around Cape Horn, not the Cape of Good Hope; "shifts in conception and function of characters," among them Ishmael, Queequeg, Ahab, Moby Dick, Bulkington, Stubb, and Flask; shifts in style ("UMD is plain, even prosy and colloquial" and "differs from MD by lacking almost entirely the elements of the conventional poetic style of the nineteenth century"); a shift in the number of Shakespearean echoes (from few in UMD to many in MD); a shift in atmosphere ("UMD is realistic, homey, and even folksy" while "MD is notable for its lack of shabbiness and for its approach to both epic and tragic grandeur"); and a discrepancy between the symbolic names ("canting names") in *Moby-Dick* and those which seem to have no symbolic significance (Stewart notes that when a "name seems to have significance and yet that significance is not displayed in the character, as with Stubb and Flask" the "anomaly may indicate that these names were first used in UMD and lost their appropriateness when the book was rewritten") [*Editors' note*].

When Captain Peleg speaks of the loss of Ahab's leg, he says merely that it was bitten off by "the monstrousest parmacetty." He does not say that this was the White Whale, that it was Moby Dick, or that it was a whale which had an allegorical or otherworldly qualities. It is merely a very large whale. We should expect that Captain Peleg would have known "the whiteness of the whale," if it had been established at that time in Melville's mind. While for the sake of suspense Melville might not have wished to reveal it at this point, we would expect at least that Peleg would have made some reference to indicate that there was something more than merely a large whale involved in this case. It should also be noted that Ishmael is here still definitely a character and not a mere mouthpiece for the author and that the general style of writing characteristic of UD is maintained.

On the other hand, this chapter is notable for several new suggestions that come into the story. The style changes somewhat. Just at the end of Chapter 15 we have an occurrence of the highly colloquial "says I." In Chapter 16 the more formal "said I" is used. The chapter also contains some philosophical passages, thus becoming suggestive of the latter part of the book. It also introduces the character of Ahab, who dominates all of MD, although the Ahab here introduced is not altogether the same character as the Ahab of MD.

Of most importance of all in Chapter 16, particularly in connection with Ahab's character, is one paragraph that I shall label the "insight passage." It occurs near the middle of the chapter, after the three captains have been introduced; and must be quoted in full:

> So that there are instances among them of men, who, named with Scripture names—a singularly common fashion on the island—and in childhood naturally imbibing the stately dramatic thee and thou of the Quaker idiom; still, from the audacious, daring, and boundless adventure of their subsequent lives, strangely blend with these unoutgrown peculiarities, a thousand bold dashes of character, not unworthy a Scandinavian sea-king, or a poetical Pagan Roman. And when these things unite in a man of greatly superior natural force, with a globular brain and a ponderous heart; who has also by the stillness and seclusion of many long night-watches in the remotest waters, and beneath constellations never seen here at the north, been led to think untraditionally and independently; receiving all nature's sweet or savage impressions fresh from her own virgin voluntary and confiding breast, and thereby chiefly, but with some help from accidental advantages, to learn a bold and nervous lofty language—that man makes one in a whole nation's census—a mighty pageant creature, formed for noble tragedies. Nor will it at all

detract from him, dramatically regarded, if either by birth or other circumstances, he have what seems a half wilful over-ruling morbidness at the bottom of his nature. For all men tragically great are made so through a certain morbidness.

This passage is extremely important in that it brings in for the first time almost all the ideas which are seen in the character of Ahab later in the story and from which develop the special qualities of *Moby-Dick*. Melville seems suddenly to have realized that by having his chief character a Quaker he could justify the use of the so-called poetic language which was considered necessary for poetry in the mid-nineteenth century, that is, particularly the use of *thou* and *thee*. Along with this he justifies in this passage the use of "a bold and nervous lofty language" such as would be "formed for noble tragedies." He goes on to say that this character would be equally good if he should have "a half wilful over-ruling morbidness." In other words, Melville here seems suddenly to take fire, to see his way toward the device of poetic language, to catch the conception of a great tragic character, to see a kind of tragic flaw that at the same time can exist in that character and produce the tragedy.

This passage is the first in which we feel the Shakespearean influence begin to take over. Not only does Melville mention "tragedies," but he also makes a comparison with "a Scandinavian sea-king, or a poetical Pagan Roman." The most natural assumption is that he was thinking of Hamlet in the former instance. Certainly the only probable nominees for his Roman would be Brutus or some other character from Shakespeare's Roman plays.

I cannot allow my discussion of the Insight Passage to rest even at this point. It should be noted that the paragraph really has no connection with what precedes or follows. It even begins with what is grammatically an incomplete sentence. Moreover, this sentence fragment is introduced with the words *so that*, but it would be difficult to determine just in what way the passage that follows can be considered the result of what has just gone before. The introductory *so that* seems a kind of makeshift device. Closely considered, the passage is thus remarkably isolated and unconnected.

I shall here permit myself what may be considered a flight of fancy. What I should like to point out is that the passage sounds a great deal like a kind of memorandum that an author writes to himself. The few really important ideas about which any serious novel shapes itself are likely to come to an author suddenly. During weeks or months he has been turning the subject over in his mind. Then, in an instant, *he sees!* At such moments he is very likely to get the idea down on paper as rapidly as possible, in a kind of panic that he will forget something. (I am not now writing in theory or at second hand; I have done it myself.)

This paragraph sounds to me like such a memorandum. There is no reason to suppose that it was written originally to stand at this place. It was much more likely written when Melville was still considering how to finish UMD, and this may represent the immediate result of that moment of insight which made him finally decide to abandon UMD, and sent him back to splice MD to UMD and go ahead to finish *Moby-Dick*.

Chapters 17 and 18 revert to UMD. Queequeg is again the hero, Ishmael is the ordinary character, the language is commonplace, philosophy is lacking, and so is Ahab.

Ahab reappears as a character in Chapter 19 and the shadowy figure of Elijah also suggests MD. In general, however, the chapter seems a part of UMD. For instance, Ahab is called Old Thunder. On the whole, also, the characterization of Ahab here presented is more in common with that of an ordinary brutal, even murderous, mad sea captain, than with the tragic hero with which Ahab is later absorbed. The previous details of Ahab's life, moreover, though twice mentioned in this chapter, are never afterwards explained to us. It seems unusual that our imaginations should thus be stimulated twice, and never satisfied later. Like Ishmael and Queequeg at the time, we know, even at the end of the book, nothing about Ahab when he lay dead for three days and nights, nothing about the deadly scrimmage with the Spaniard, nothing about the silver calabash that he spit into. We do, to be sure, learn a great deal about his losing of the leg, but not of these other matters. All these suggest, once again, that the story was pointed for another course.

Chapter 20 seems to be wholly UMD.

Chapter 21 has some foreshadowings of Ahab's unusual boat crew and with its reintroduction of Elijah also suggests the atmosphere of MD. But Elijah's suggestion of seeing Ishmael again before the grand jury is something else that never occurs later in the book, although actually I should take this as a mere amphiboly of the half-crazy Elijah, for I can scarcely see how UMD could ever have got around to a grand jury. Finally, the poor comedy of Queequeg's sitting on the rump of the sleeping sailor is definitely in the atmosphere of UMD.

The last chapter of the Transition is Chapter 22. Even to the use of the colloquial tag "thinks I," it seems to be wholly UMD. . . .

The Transition therefore serves as a kind of introduction to MD. In particular, it describes Ahab, partly in terms reminiscent of UMD, but partly in terms of his actual career in *Moby-Dick*. Moreover, the *Pequod* has been introduced as a strange craft, and a "plant" has been made for the sudden appearance of Fedallah and his men. By means of Elijah an atmosphere of mystery has been foreshadowed.

Nevertheless four of the seven chapters of the Transition seem to be just as straight UMD as anything that has gone before. The shift to MD comes sharply after Chapter 22.

VI

From Chapter 23 onward we are in the full course of MD—suddenly and surely.

Chapter 23 itself is as typical an example as can be found of the fully developed manner of MD. It is allegorical, philosophical, and poetic. It lacks the homey, realistic, and humorous qualities of UMD, and may be called a fine example of "high seriousness." Here, for the first time except for a few in Father Mapple's sermon, appear poetic forms and words: *wonderfullest, unrestingly, fain, succor, landlessness, ocean-perishing, mortalities, 'gainst*. As poetic devices we have pathetic fallacy, apostrophe, and such a striking simile as "indefinite as God."

As previously noted, Bulkington's voyage has here become one of four years, thus suggesting the generally heightened effect of MD.

Chapters 24 and 25 introduce the first cetology. Obviously the cetology fits in with the atmosphere of MD and not with that of UMD. In Chapter 1 Ishmael has spoken of the "shabby business" of whaling. This will never do for an epic and tragic story. So whaling has to be built up into something magnificent and even royal. This is accomplished largely by the cetological chapters, and it is doubtless significant that two of these occur close to the opening of MD.

Chapters 26 and 27 bear the same title and can be considered together. Doubtless some similar chapter or chapters existed in UMD, since it would have been necessary to introduce the characters. But I fail to see any trace of such earlier work, and would suppose a complete rewriting. The mates indeed have already appeared in passages which we have reason to think are UMD, but in Chapters 26 and 27 they are presented in the manner of MD and for its purposes. In correspondence with the cosmic spirit of MD the three mates are represented as from three different parts of the country, and the three harpooners as of three different races, to whom Fedallah is soon to be added as a fourth.

A new technique of MD also appears in Chapter 26 with the words "thought Starbuck." From this point on, Ishmael is generally able to reproduce what people are thinking, and he has thus ceased to be a mere character in the book and has become a spokesman of the all-knowing author.

Chapter 27 introduces the philosophical idea of the Isolatoes, which has scarcely appeared in UMD. By indicating the foreign nature of the crew the chapter still further emphasizes the cosmic nature of MD.

Chapter 28 is Ahab's both in title and content, thus pointing clearly ahead to MD. His character in this chapter, although fully in accord with the implications of the Insight Passage, is vastly removed from that of the boorishly tyrannical and bloodily named captain who has been foreshadowed in the Transition by Elijah and Peleg. We can note especially: ". . . moody stricken Ahab stood before them with a crucifixion in his face; in all the nameless regal overbearing dignity of some mighty woe."

This chapter, just at its end, also contains the first of the Homeric similes that are so characteristic of MD.

Chapter 29 brings in the dramatic method almost fully. Its very title is a stage direction: "*Enter Ahab: to him, Stubb.*" This chapter shows Ishmael continuing to reproduce material which as an actual character he could not have known; thus he says of Ahab ". . . he would mutter to himself." The chapter also contains a long soliloquy, and much language that is obviously reminiscent of Shakespeare.

There is no need to go any further, chapter by chapter, for by this point, after the sharp break between Chapters 22 and 23, we are fully launched in MD.

VII

We may also consider whether in MD have been preserved any sections of a previously written UMD. If UMD was "mostly written" before Melville began with MD, we should suspect that as a professional writer he would have tried to salvage something of what he had done, merely for economy's sake.

I think that there are some such passages, although the evidence, by its very nature, can scarcely be conclusive and we are here likely to fall into the fallacy of trusting to a subjective judgment, that is, of merely thinking that a certain passage represents UMD when it is actually the result of the author's temporary reversion to his original style. To escape this subjectivism I have applied two tests. (1) The passage shall in its general atmosphere, style, etc. resemble UMD. (2) The passage shall show certain peculiarities or anomalies which can be objectively described and which can be explained as more suitable to UMD than to the present *Moby-Dick*.

One such passage comprises the first part of Chapter 96, "The

Try-works" (the first five paragraphs and possibly the sixth). In atmosphere this section is very realistic, and in style and atmosphere resembles UMD. It also contains some features worthy of special note. One is the long sentence in the first person which seems to indicate not merely Ishmael as a real character, but even some memory of Melville's from the *Acushnet*. The sentence reads:

> It was in the left hand try-pot of the Pequod, with the soapstone diligently circling round me, that I was first indirectly struck by the remarkable fact, that in geometry all bodies gliding along the cycloid, my soapstone for example, will descend from any point in precisely the same time.

Also of interest is the fact that Stubb is mentioned as the one to "oversee the business" of lighting the try-works. There is no reason in the present *Moby-Dick* why he should be so designated, and so we may suspect that his presence indicates UMD, in which we have shown reason to believe he was more prominent. Most important, however, is the sentence: "It was about nine o'clock at night that the Pequod's try-works were first started on this present voyage." Why, we have a right to ask, in Chapter 96 after the *Pequod* has been killing whales for months, comes now this sudden reference to the *first* starting of the try-works? Obviously this passage should have come after the killing of the first whale. The only explanation I can offer is that this section, which runs on without break into the latter part of the chapter, must be a remnant of UMD. Probably it stood originally much closer to the beginning of the book. In writing MD Melville apparently came to see rather gradually the possibilities of fire as a symbol. Thus, in mid course, he changed the Mohammedan-named Fedallah into a Parsee. He also wrote the magnificent latter part of Chapter 96, and to save himself time and creative strain he quite naturally used a page or two of his original UMD manuscript to introduce the chapter. His failure to harmonize it with its new position can be attributed to the high pressure under which he was working. Doubtless he always intended to work through the whole book more carefully at some time, but he was actually working under pressure clear to the end.

As another section possibly based largely on UMD I would include much of Chapter 48, "The First Lowering," and all of the following chapter, "The Hyena." Again the atmosphere suggests UMD. Ishmael is a very real person, who gets wet and complains about it, and who is not able to read other people's minds. The whales also are real, with no touch of allegory. The language is colloquial, rather than poetic. Chapter 48 may indeed have been largely rewritten—for one reason, to make use of Fedallah's crew, unless indeed these were also in UMD, of which we have no proof to the contrary and only the general feeling that they are more suitable to MD. But several special features may be noted as anomalous in these chapters. (1) As a title "The Hyena" seems to me to make no sense. There is indeed a reference to a joke, but to tie this to the idea of a laughing hyena is a slender bond. Of course I cannot say but that Melville may have had some association with hyenas that I lack, but the simplest explanation to me is that the chapter, a very short one, was originally longer, and that the significance of its title was destroyed when the chapter was cut. (2) In Chapter 48 Stubb is called "the third mate." He is also characterized (in bad grammar) rather curiously in words that are scarcely borne out elsewhere: "Stubb was one of those odd sort of humorists, whose jollity is sometimes so curiously ambiguous, as to put all inferiors on their guard in the matter of obeying them." (3) The point of view in the earlier part of Chapter 48 is curious. We should remember that point of view is a curiously stable literary quality; once established, it can be shifted only by very careful work, and Melville had previously written little except a kind of semi-fiction and was not skilled at such a delicate technique. In this case the question is: "In which boat is Ishmael?" He is certainly not in Ahab's or in Flask's. In the latter part of the chapter he is certainly in Starbuck's. But in the earlier part he seems to be in Stubb's. Note that when Stubb's and Starbuck's boats diverge, Starbuck goes out of the picture, and we are given the words of Stubb. Later we have mention of Tashtego, Stubb's harpooner, "whose eyes had been setting to windward like two fixed stars." This is surely too intimate a detail to be observed from another boat, and in any case the discovery of the whale might just as well have been made from Starbuck's boat. Only later is Ishmael surely in Starbuck's boat. Then Melville definitely establishes the point of view by writing "our sail," and after that Stubb is absent.

A possible UMD legacy is Chapter 61, "Stubb kills a Whale." We note again the realistic atmosphere and style. At the risk of having it thought that I have developed a fixation, I point once more to the prominence of Stubb. But again the question must be: "Why Stubb?" If Ishmael was in Starbuck's boat, we should expect "Starbuck kills a Whale." In this chapter, as in Chapter 48, the point of view is Stubb's boat. To be sure the pronoun used is "they," not "we," but such a change would have been easy in revision. There are other points in this chapter also. Ahab acts like the real captain of a whaling ship, in a rather un-Ahab-like fashion. Moreover, the *Pequod* is steered by a wheel! Finally, although this may be a mere slip, Daggoo is mentioned where Tashtego is obviously meant (just at the end of the chapter.)

As another example I mention Chapter 67, "Cutting In." Besides the realistic atmosphere, it twice in one paragraph contains the words: "Starbuck and Stubb, the mates." We may surely think this very strange. When whole long sections have already been devoted to describing the mates and when they have several times appeared in action, why should the author think it necessary thus to specify—and twice! A suggestion is that this chapter once stood closer to the beginning and that there had not yet been any fixation of these two characters.

Another chapter definitely to be suspected of having been part of UMD is Chapter 72, "The Monkey-Rope." Its atmosphere suggests UMD. The significance of its footnote in connection with the character of Stubb has been discussed in Section III.

Other passages show the atmosphere and style of UMD, but fail to provide good objective evidence. Among these are parts of Chapter 78, "Cistern and Buckets," and Chapter 81 "The Pequod meets the Virgin." If, however, it can be considered that a few passages have been definitely shown to represent UMD, then the assumption must be that a considerable number do. Naturally Melville would have revised most of the passages so that inconsistencies were eliminated.[1]

VIII

A natural inquiry is: "What was the story of UMD?" Howard, who does not hold definitely to anything more than a severe revision, seems to commit himself no further than that Melville originally planned a much more straightforward story of the whaling industry than he finally wrote. Vincent believes that it was "a whaling voyage pure and simple," and goes on to postulate that the original novel was "quite possibly" an expansion of what is now Chapter 54, "The Town-Ho's Story."

Probably most people who believe in UMD at all would agree with the general position taken by both Howard and Vincent. As for Vincent's special hypothesis, I cannot see that he has enough evidence to make it tenable, except in the very tentative way that he presents it. His chief argument is that the brutality of ships' officers toward seamen was a favorite theme of Melville's that he

1. *Pierre* was written immediately after *Moby-Dick*, and autobiographical details have been noticed in it. Of particular interest in the present connection, the manner in which Pierre writes his book suggests in some respects the manner in which *Moby-Dick* was written. Certain support for the present theory can be drawn from *Pierre*. For instance, from the letter received by Pierre from his publishers (Book 26, Part 4) it can be argued that Melville's publishers had reason to expect UMD, not *Moby-Dick*. On the whole, however, *Pierre* lends only general, not specific support to the theory. In addition, it is always hazardous to argue biographical data from a novel. I therefore carry the matter no farther.

had recently used in both *Redburn* and *White-Jacket.* But this argument, as long as it is based on external evidence only, cuts both ways. The fact that Melville had just dealt with this topic in two novels would argue against his taking up the same subject in a third. On the other hand, certain support can be derived from internal evidence.

The internal evidence to be drawn from *Moby-Dick* as to the plot of UMD consists of the various foreshadowings (see Sections II, III, and V) and the sections of UMD that seem to be incorporated in *Moby-Dick* in more or less unrevised form (see Section VII). Unfortunately, there is a good deal of speculation involved in all these matters, and to speculate on the basis of speculation is hazardous in the second degree.

We may first approach the problem negatively, that is, attempt to determine whether certain features now present in *Moby-Dick* were or were not present in UMD. In this connection, two interesting questions are: (1) Did UMD have a white whale? (2) Was the ship sunk by a whale? The existence of Fedallah and his men I consider secondary to these two primary matters.

Although the two ideas had already been linked in *Mocha Dick,* and although Moby Dick obviously derived from that name, there is no necessity of assuming that the two were always linked in Melville's mind. The *Essex* was sunk by a whale of ordinary color, and that story seems to have had a strong effect upon Melville. I shall therefore discuss the two matters separately.

1) Was Moby Dick, or a white whale, part of UMD? The evidence is contradictory and inconclusive. Melville's letter to Dana with its "blubber is blubber" passage and also the "shabby part" passage of Chapter 1 seem to indicate that nothing so unusual as a white whale was included. On the other hand, his reference in his letter of June 27 to certain "wild legends" definitely suggests something out of the ordinary. The mention of the "snow hill" in Chapter 1 would be conclusive, if it were not for the ease with which such a slight revision could have been later inserted at the end of the chapter.

2) Was the ship sunk by a whale? Again we may quote "blubber is blubber," "shabby part," and "wild legends," and end in general inconclusiveness. Probability is perhaps more on the side of the sinking by a whale than of the white whale, since Melville is known to have been interested in the story of the *Essex.*

Nevertheless, as opposing the sinking of the ship by any means, I wish to cite three of the small matters already mentioned in Section II, viz., that Queequeg is to take "his last long dive," that Ishmael likes to "land on barbarous coasts," and that on leaving Nantucket he seems to see ahead "meads and glades so eternally vernal." The suggestion that the voyage was to end on such a coast and amid such greenery recalls the actual ending of Melville's voyage on the *Acushnet*. And what more likely than that he should again be thinking in terms of his own autobiography? He had certainly done so in all his novels so far, with the partial exception of *Mardi*.

To pass thus from the negative to the positive approach, I would make the suggestion, though it can scarcely be more than a suggestion—that UMD was intended to end where Typee began.

If forced to construct my idea of the whole story I would put it about as follows:

> Sailing to the Pacific by way of Cape Horn, Ishmael and Queequeg experienced many adventures of whaling. Their ship, the *Pequod*, was a conventional whaling ship, steered by a wheel and carrying a normal crew of about thirty officers and men. One of the seamen was named Bulkington; he figured in various incidents and was remarkable for his physical strength. The one-legged captain was nicknamed "Old Thunder," and his word was "growl and go." From him Ishmael, a green-horn at whaling, received many kicks, but Ishmael respected and got along well with the somewhat eccentric third mate, named Stubb, in whose boat he served for a time at least. Meanwhile Queequeg was the hero. Unfortunately, in the pursuit of a large and vicious whale (which may have been a white one) Queequeg was entangled with the line and jerked out of the boat headforemost in "his last long dive." Shortly afterward, the objectionable features of the ship overbalanced the agreeable ones for Ishmael, and he deserted at a tropical island.

The above summary, although I do not wish to express much confidence in it, is not imaginary. Every statement is based upon evidence which has already been presented in this study. The question is whether the evidence is sufficiently strong.

IX

Thus far, this study has proceeded on the assumption that, having nearly completed UMD, Melville conceived the present *Moby-Dick* and thereupon revised Chapters 16–22 and went on to write the rest of the book. This is undoubtedly an oversimplification, and we should now consider a little more carefully what must have been the process of remaking UMD into *Moby-Dick*.

If we assume UMD to have been a mere whaling voyage, lacking even the white whale and the sinking of the ship, an extraordinary number of new ideas are necessary to transform this into the present novel. I shall list the chief ones, trying to work from simplicity to complexity and therefore follow what is a logical and quite possibly a chronological order.

1) First of all may have come the idea of the sinking of the ship by a whale, as in the case of the *Essex*.

2) Next may have followed the idea of having the whale a particular whale, which (like Mocha Dick) would be white and bear a name.

3) By this point the story was obviously ceasing to be that of a simple whaling voyage; in addition, the author felt the necessity of establishing in the reader's mind such facts as that a whale could be white, could bear a name, and could sink a ship. Hence sprang the cetology.

4) The next step was probably the reconception of "Old Thunder" as Captain Ahab, that "grand, ungodly, gold-like man," one of those who are "formed for noble tragedies." Probably this and the next two ideas arose in Melville's mind as different aspects of the same general idea or at least in such rapid succession as to be undistinguishable. All three are included in the Insight Passage.

5) At this same point, then, Melville conceived the idea of using a poetic style, justifying his decision partly upon the realization that a Quaker sea captain as described in the Insight Passage would use "a bold and nervous lofty language."

6) At this same point also, Melville apparently began to think in terms of a Shakespearean—that is, a dramatic—presentation.

7) As a corollary to the introduction of the white whale and the reconception of Ahab, Fedallah and his crew now entered the story.

8) Having gone thus far with allowing poetic and Shakespearean techniques to take over, Melville began to allow play to his never well-controlled love of philosophizing.

9) Finally—never completely and perhaps never altogether consciously—Melville introduced the allegorical elements.

Thus considered, *Moby-Dick* may well be the final result not merely of one false start but of several. Perhaps we should not merely think of UMD, but of UMD-1, UMD-2, etc. Actually some such hypothesis seems, if not absolutely necessary, at least very useful, to epxlain the extraordinary length of time and expenditure of energy that went into the book after August, 1850.

If there is one thing that seems certain about Melville as a writer, it is that he did not plan a book carefully to begin with or even think it through in his mind. In addition to *Moby-Dick*, others of his books start in one direction and then shift, so that the reader who likes the first part of the book is likely to be disappointed in the last part, and vice versa.

If a writer is unable to think his book through at first trial, he may also be unable to think it through at second trial or at third.

Thus we may conceive of Melville—his creative imagination always outrunning his critical judgment and his technical skill—having first one idea and writing rapidly and viogrously a book of that sort. But a new idea comes and takes possession of him. He decides to discard much that he has already written, revise the rest, and write much anew. But when he is well started again, a third idea comes and takes possession, etc., etc.

As any novelist can tell you, this is the most laborious of all methods. It is the method of a man building a house from mere preliminary plans and then forced to tear down what he has already built when he wishes to make changes, instead of merely changing the plans on paper. The novelist is certain to find such a method not only consuming in time and physical energy, but also extremely consuming in creative energy and even frustrating. In Melville's case we know that in writing *Moby-Dick* he not only expended many months even after August, 1850, but also wore himself out and brought himself close to frustration.

Whether, almost wholly lacking external evidence, any scholar can ever work out these details of the writing of *Moby-Dick*, I am uncertain. The purpose of this study has been only to consider the primary shift from the original UMD to something less simple, which afterwards became—doubtless after several more shifts—our present complex and ever-challenging *Moby-Dick*.

EDMUND BERGLER

[Moby Dick as Cruel Pre-Oedipal Mother]†

More than a hypothesis cannot be offered. Moby-Dick, living in the ocean (of which Melville said: "the sea is life whose waters of deep woe are brackish with the salt of human tears"), symbolizes the infant's fantasy of the cruel, pre-Oedipal mother of earliest infancy. (One is reminded of Hart Crane's death: he committed suicide by leaping from a liner in mid-Atlantic. Crane had written, "The bottom of the sea is cruel." One is reminded, too, of Joseph Conrad's equation of "the cruel sea" with the home of the sailor.) The child becomes masochistically attached to the pre-Oedipal mother; when the attachment is attacked and vetoed by the superego, a pseudo-aggressive defense is instituted. Melville quite obviously sympathizes with Ahab's hatred. This first defense, too, is

† From Edmund Bergler, "A Note on Herman Melville," *American Imago*, Vol. 2 (Winter, 1954), 385–97; the quotation is from 387. Reprinted by permission of the Wayne State University Press.

vetoed, and guilt for the pseudo-aggression is either counterposed, rationalized, or fully negated. Thus Melville must present both the query of the reasonable Starbuck: "Vengeance on a dumb brute?" and the sense of impending doom which surrounds Ahab from his first entrance on the scene, to his final destruction.

Melville's formulation—"sea . . . salt of human *tears*"—is especially revealing. projecting upon the infant's situation, it means that fluid is not given by another, but *autarchically* produced by the infant, who lives on his own woes and "tears" (fluid!). This formulation reminds me of something a blocked poet once told me in analysis (after coming to an understanding of oral mechanisms): tears are a "magic gesture" with which mortals prove to themselves their "fluid woe-autarchy." The theory sounded fantastic to me at the time, but I am no longer certain that the poet was not—at least partly—on the right track.

HARRY LEVIN

[A Fourfold Scheme of Interpretation]†

[T]he fourfold scheme of interpretation that Dante invited his readers to follow, which extends the meaning beyond the literal to the three figurative levels—allegorical, moral, and anagogical. * * * [T]he literal tells us what happens, the allegorical what to believe, the moral what to do, and the anagogical whither to strive. Thus, literally *Moby Dick* is concerned with the voyage of the Pequod, the subject of whaling, the science of cetology; allegorically with society on shipboard, the parable of Ahab's "irresistible dictatorship;" morally with a series of object-lessons, such examples as the monkey-rope, the ligature of brotherhood that binds Ishmael to Queequeg; and anagogically . . . "*Quo tendas*? whither art thou striving?"

That is the question, and Melville offers no categorical answer. * * *

[T]he anagoge, which for Dante is the fulfilment of providential design, for Melville remains an ultimate question-mark. His overwhelming whale has been identified with—among other concepts—nature, fate, sex, property, the father-image, God Himself. It has meant various things to varying critics because it is Melville's enigma, like the doubloon nailed by Ahab to the mast, which signifies dollars to the Second Mate, the Zodiac to the First Mate,

† From Harry Levin, *Learners and Discerners*, ed. Robert Scholes (Charlottesville: University Press of Virginia, 1964). First published in *Symbolism and Fiction* by Harry Levin (Charlottesville: University Press of Virginia, 1956), pp. 33, 34, 35–36. Reprinted by permission of the publisher.

and the universe to the Captain. Shall we ever identify Moby Dick? Yes, when we have sprinkled salt on the tail of the Absolute; but not before.

VAN WYCK BROOKS

[Melville's Use of Literary Bitumen]†

In one of his letters, Melville praised what he called "oldageifying youth in books," as one of the two great arts that were yet to be discovered, and he tried in *Redburn* to extract and reproduce the antiquated style of an obsolete Liverpool guide-book. The seventeenth-century flavour of many a page of *Moby Dick* was the fruit of a taste as consciously cherished and developed as the taste of certain American painters from William Page to Duveneck for the so-called "brown sauce" of the school of Munich. These painters also wished to achieve the amber patina of age, the sombre harmonious richness of so many old masters, attempting to reach this normal effect of the gradual oxidation of the oil by constantly using bitumen as an undertone and glaze. Melville used literary bitumen in a similar fashion.

GRANVILLE HICKS

[The Meaning of Ishmael's Survival]‡

There is a word to be said about the epilogue. Are we to assume that, as Ahab deserves his death, Ishmael has earned his survival? Up to a point this is a fair interpretation: Ishmael, unlike Starbuck, can recognize the evil in the universe, and yet he does not give way to Ahab's obsession; moreover, he has learned to appreciate "the very milk and sperm of kindness," whereas Ahab has sealed himself off from other men in proud and contemptuous loneliness. Yet I think that Melville had no intention of weighing Ishmael against Ahab, and that may be one reason why Ishmael virtually vanishes from the book in the last forty chapters. His survival is an accident—"It so chanced. . . . I was he whom the Fates ordained

† From Van Wyck Brooks, *From A Writer's Notebook* (New York: E. P. Dutton & Company, 1958), p. 101. Copyright © 1958 by Van Wyck Brooks. Reprinted by permission of E. P. Dutton & Co., Inc., and J. M. Dent & Sons Ltd.

‡ From Granville Hicks, "A Re-Reading of *Moby Dick*," in *Twelve Original Essays on Great American Novels*, ed. Charles Shapiro (Detroit: Wayne State University Press, 1958), pp. 44–68; the quotation is from 67–68. Reprinted by permission of the Wayne State University Press and Mr. Hicks.

. . ."—but not, of course, in terms of Melville's literary design. The impact of the novel would be different if there were no one to say in effect what Ishmael says specifically at the end of the *Town-ho*'s story. "So help me Heaven, and on my honor the story I have told ye, gentlemen, is in substance and in its great items, true. I know it to be true; it happened on this ball; I trod the ship; I knew the crew. . . ."

One might also say in deliberate paradox that Ishmael survives in order to remind us that he has existed. So far have we come, so completely has Ahab taken over the novel, that Ishmael has slipped away from us without our noticing it. This is part of the grand strategy of the novel. It rises to tremendous heights, and we are so awed by them that we forget the massive foundations by which they are supported. Ishmael has done his work well, domesticating us on the *Pequod*, lecturing us indefatigably on his great subject, letting us see for ourselves Ahab and his mighty antagonist not only in their grandeur but also in all their complexity. He does his work and then makes himself invisible until suddenly he rises from the sea to speak the words of the servant in Job: "And I only am escaped alone to tell thee." We see him then revolving like another Ixion in the "slowly wheeling circle," the "closing vortex" caused by the *Pequod's* sinking, until he reaches the "vital centre" that provides the means of salvation. And now we realize that Ishmael has a story too, but it is chiefly left to our imaginations.

HARRY LEVIN

[The *Moby-Dick* Industry]†

[I]f you look up Melville in the four-volume *Cambridge History of American Literature* (1917–21), you will find that he occupies less than four pages. Graduate schools have recently been doing their utmost to compensate for previous neglect; and the investigation of *Moby-Dick* might almost be said to have taken the place of whaling among the industries of New England.

ROBERT L. PETERS

[The Significance of Bulkington]‡

Characteristic of *Moby Dick* is Melville's use of seemingly transient, insignificant persons and episodes to illuminate and vivify

† From Harry Levin, *The Power of Blackness* (New York: Alfred A. Knopf, 1958), p. vi. Reprinted by permission of the publisher.

‡ Robert L. Peters, "Melville's *Moby Dick*," *Explicator*, Vol. 16 (April, 1958), Item 44. Reprinted by permission.

major characters and themes. One such person is Bulkington, the self-isolated sailor, who first appears in Chapter 3, and who is interpreted generally as a figure antithetical to Ahab. To William Ellery Sedgwick (*Herman Melville: The Tragedy of Mind*, pp. 125f.), for example, Bulkington, like Ishmael, is characterized by his faith; Ahab by his lack of it. To Lawrance Thompson (*Melville's Quarrel with God*, pp. 169-171), Bulkington forms one pole of "the fundamental conceptual antithesis" in *Moby Dick*, "the clash between the concept of freedom and the concept of tyrannous and brutal enslavement." And to Richard Chase (*Herman Melville: A Critical Study*, p. 41), Bulkington is "the Democratic hero" worthy of admiration, while Ahab is "the exploiter whose exploitation is all of himself and his fellows." I wish to demonstrate that Bulkington should rightly be compared with, not contrasted to, Ahab; for no other character, with the possible exception of Father Mapple, better prepares us for the meaning of Ahab's tragic struggle with the whale.

Bulkington's first appearance is brief. He is one of the whalers who have just debarked and who enter the Spouter Inn where Ishmael sits waiting for the evening to pass. When the men begin to roister, the observant Ishmael notices that one of the group holds himself "somewhat aloof," as though he does not wish "to spoil the hilarity of his shipmates by his own sober face." This man "at once" interests Ishmael. Presently, however, the sailor disappears; and when his comrades run shouting after him, Ishmael assumes that he must be a "huge favorite."

Clearly present in Melville's brief paragraph is the germ of a potentially profound character: Bulkington is "sober," introspective; he stands separate from, yet has a distinct power over, his human group; and for some reason he is impelled to withdraw physically from that group.

Chapter 23, "The Lee Shore," is a short chapter devoted entirely to Bulkington, or rather to Ishmael's impassioned analysis of his character. On that frigid winter night Ishmael views Bulkington standing at the helm. Then Ishmael, when he considers that the sailor has just returned from a dangerous four years' voyage and that he is again ready to brave the perilous mid-winter sea, feels a "sympathetic awe and fearfulness" which leads him to create a "six-inch chapter," a commemoration, a kind of miniature requiem, a "stoneless grave" for Bulkington.

What is the nature of this commemoration? It is a spun song of varied rhythm and intensity. It commences in slow tempo: the sentences are long, qualified, multi-claused. Ishmael has been discoursing to the reader. But in the second paragraph the point of view shifts and Bulkington himself is addressed; the tempo quickens; the tenuosity and marvelous alliteration of the early paragraph are even more emphatic. In the final section short ejaculatory exclamations work to a rolling majestic close:

> But as in landlessness alone resides the highest truth, shoreless, indefinite as God—so, better it is to perish in that howling infinite, than be ingloriously dashed upon the lee, even if that were safety! For worm-like, then, oh! who would craven crawl to land! Terrors of the terrible! is all this agony so vain? Take heart, take heart, O Bulkington! Bear thee grimly, demigod! Up from the spray of thy ocean-perishing—straight up, leaps thy apotheosis!

More significantly, this commemoration is a panegyric upon those men who brave the fanged, untraveled sea; by extension Melville praises those Bulkingtons and Ahabs who with a consuming, Thoreau-like mental self-reliance, unhampered by any religious-ethical dogmas, strive to chart and to pursue "mortally intolerable truth," even though they are aware, as Ahab is, that to be within striking range of that truth, to see it floundering clear and menacing in the broad ocean of the mind can lead to nothing but self-destruction. I must emphasize here that the nature of this truth as symbolized by the whale is compounded good and evil. The mysterious universal forces acting on man, at times nourishing him (spring showers, bountiful seas, lucrative orchards), at times maiming him (cyclones, earthquakes, avalanches), find ample thriving in Leviathan's hulk. But the torturing search, the attack, the self-sacrifice, so Melville clamorously declares, raises man to god-head. Bulkington is a "demi-god." This chapter is the record of his "apotheosis." And, on an important level of meaning, Ahab's struggle has the grandeur of a god's. In Chapter 37, "Sunset," a soliloquy more revealing than any other of Ahab's true nature, this is clear. And there is further evidence at the close of Chapter 44, "The Chart," where Ahab is seen as a Prometheus figure.

Bulkington in his relation to other men also foreshadows Ahab. Both are brooding isolated thinkers; both have a certain, though different, power over other human beings. And in yet another sense they are alike: Melville in apotheosizing Bulkington is actually paying tribute to all courageous men who have perished in the fastness of the sea—Bulkington, because of his introspection and power to stimulate the author's imagination, stands as an idealized summation of such men; and Ahab, burning Ahab, is the archetype of all the prophets of the Everlasting Nay who have striven to tear the mind and soul clear of their black seas.

These then are the specific connections. What do they contribute to the novel's structure? Melville's analysis of Bulkington is like the early introduction of a major symphonic theme, or a leitmotiv: surrounded as it is in introductory material we hear it briefly and move on. But the pattern is sure, so that when our theme reappears it is more credible and absorbing, and the artist is free to move more directly to the intricate heart of his form. And since Melville inbues Ahab with both purity and sin, and since the nature of Ahab's excess so dominates the final chapters, Bulkington is ballast for the good in Ahab, a good Melville does not intend that we forget.

C. HUGH HOLMAN

[The Major Weakness of *Moby-Dick*]†

[The "major difficulty in interpreting *Moby-Dick*" is] the difficulty of properly evaluating the meaning and understanding the structure of a work of art which contains a peculiarly fascinating character who so absorbs our imagination (and, perhaps, that of the author on occasion) that the work begins to appear to be that character's, regardless of who is the intended hero. Such a difficulty in regard to *Paradise Lost* has led some critics to read the poem as the tragedy of Satan. In *Moby-Dick* that "grand, ungodly, godlike man," Captain Ahab, becomes another such figure. Like Milton's Satan, and perhaps for many of the same reasons, he fires our imagination and enlists our reluctant sympathy as no other character in the novel does. Here the error is not only that we read the novel as the tragedy of Ahab rather than the "divine comedy" of Ishmael, but that we tend to lose sight of Ishmael, who is, at best, a passive hero. Perhaps it was in such terms as these that Sedgwick [1944] was thinking when he said that Ahab's story was Shakespearean and Ishmael's Dantesque. Here the major weakness of the novel is to be found. Thematically the story is that of the passive Ishmael; in terms of plot and action, which bolster and explain the Ishmael story, Ahab is the center. Such an imperfect fusion of two elements results from Melville's having written the book on two different levels at two different times. It results, too, from Melville's ignorance of the importance of precisely defining the relation of the narrator to the story he narrates.

LESLIE A. FIEDLER

[*Moby Dick* as a Love Story]‡

This [foregoing summary] is the book's essential plot, its "novelistic" rather than poetic center, but alone it tells scarcely anything

† From C. Hugh Holman, "The Reconciliation of Ishmael: *Moby-Dick* and the Book of Job," *South Atlantic Quarterly*, Vol. 57 (Autumn, 1958), 477–90; the quotation is from 482–83. Reprinted by permission of the Duke University Press.

‡ From Leslie A. Fiedler, *Love and Death in the American Novel* (New York: Criterion Books, 1960), pp. 530–31.

about the book's essential themes. Those themes are projected by two dark-skinned characters, supernumeraries in the action, who represent the polar aspects of the id, beneficent and destructive. The first is the Polynesian harpooner, Queequeg, whose relationship to Ishmael threatens to take over the entire book in its first portion; and the second is the Parsee, Fedallah, who is yoked to Ahab by a link as passionate, though quite different from that which joins the first two. The Parsee and the Polynesian are associated with two other representatives of the primitive, also harpooners, the Indian, Tashtego, and the African, Dagoo. Yellow, brown, red, and black, they seem, considered together, rather emblems than characters, signifying the four quarters of the globe and the four elements as well, for Dagoo is carefully identified with the earth, Tashtego with the air, the Parsee with fire, and Queequeg with water. Only Queequeg and Fedallah *thematically* matter, however, since they alone are used to represent the basic conflict which lies at the heart of the book, the struggle between love and death. Queequeg stands for the redemptive baptism of water (or sperm), and around him the "Western" or sentimental story which is one half of *Moby Dick* develops; while Fedallah stands for the destructive baptism of fire (or blood), and around him the gothic or Faustian romance which is its other half unfolds. But it is Queequeg who wins, though the two never meet face to face, Eros which triumphs over Thanatos.

Moby Dick must be read not only as an account of a whale-hunt, but also as a love story, perhaps the greatest love story in our fiction. In light of the development of the highbrow Western from Cooper to Hemingway, it is clear that the absence of women in *Moby Dick* indicates not the absence of love from the novel, but its presence in the peculiar American form of innocent homosexuality.

MURRAY KRIEGER

[The Meaning of Ishmael's Survival]†

Some literal-minded commentators, and some merely disdainful ones, have suggested that Ishmael was saved from the catastrophe because there had to be someone left to relate the tale. They have to support them the words from *Job* that head the Epilogue ("And I only am escaped alone to tell thee"). Normally one does not want to take such a suggestion seriously enough to bother noting

† From Murray Krieger, *The Tragic Vision* (Chicago: University of Chicago Press, 1960), pp. 254–55, 257–58.

that with another point of view Melville could dispense with a narrator. But in a more profound sense this suggestion cannot be so lightly dismissed. We have seen that there is in *Moby Dick* an unending tension between the ethical and the tragic, what in the terms of the novel Percival has called the humanities and the inhumanities. Ishmael, as pseudo author on both sides of the oppositions, claims a fully human order in which they melt. But we discover that he is indeed the pseudo author and not a character; that, having assimilated his characters, he must create an orderly object out of them and must move beyond the tensions if he is to manage to control them and to avoid their divisive, Manichaean tendencies that threaten to rend the aesthetic quality of his story. * * * In considering Ishmael's role as the comprehensive narrator, we might say that he is fundamentally without a commitment. If we wished to play down the significance of his relations with Queequeg and of other suggestions of a transcendent grace which moves within him, we could travel even further from the direction of affirmation than I did earlier. We could argue that he is saved at the end, not through a grace that his faithfulness has earned, but through the insistence of a demanding God that the *Pequod*'s story be told. And Ishmael is chosen as the one to escape alone to tell us not because of his final affirmative commitment but because of his unique noncommitment, his powers of universal assimilation.

J. B. PRIESTLEY

[*Moby Dick*: Not Allegorical but Symbolical]†

He is a morbid, ambiguous, unfinished character; one half of him a belated Elizabethan genius, the other half an untalented, cranky, pseudo-philosophic, mock-profound type, familiar enough in or near New York throughout this age. Though we include him here among the novelists, simply because he is generally accepted as one, he is not really a novelist. Not even his sea stories, including the posthumous, powerful but over-praised *Billy Budd*, are those of a novelist; *Typee* and *Omoo* are romanticised travel books; *Mardi*, though some of its writing has a new power, is an unsuccessful attempt to turn the travelogue into philosophical fiction; *The Confidence Man* is a good idea bungled through inadequate technique; and *Pierre*, though it anticipates some of our newest fiction by rebellious inverts, reads as if a Jacobean tragedian, a Ford or a Tourneur, had tried to collaborate with the young editor of a

† From J. B. Priestley, *Literature and Western Man* (New York: Harper & Row, 1960), pp. 237, 238. Reprinted by permission of A. D. Peters & Co., London.

mid-nineteenth-century college magazine. What remains, like a whale among halibut and turbot, is *Moby Dick*. And where *Moby Dick* is weak, it is worse than the average goodish novel. We do not always know who is telling the story; there is too much information, breaking the narrative, about whales and whaling (probably because Melville originally intended it to be a semi-documentary book); the best characters are not kept steadily in our sight; there is too much eloquence for its own sake, too many salutations "to the possibilities of the immense Remote, the Wild, the Watery, the Unshored". But where it is strong, it is better than a good novel. It moves into another dimension. It takes on the quality of dramatic and epic poetry. * * *

In spite of Hawthorne's influence, to which we probably owe Melville's more ambitious re-drafting of the book, *Moby Dick* is not allegorical, in Hawthorne's familiar manner, but truly symbolical, which means that a single inner meaning cannot be attributed to it. The whale itself is entirely evil only in the mind of Captain Ahab, the figure on humanity's quarter-deck, the will that drives the ship on its tragic quest, the mind in its complete self-dependence, in its ruthless opposition to the whale as a force of Nature, in its appalling *hubris*. The whale is neither good nor evil. It is the mighty Other or Opposite, what we leave when we split totality and claim half as our own before demanding the whole again, Nature as against Man, the unconscious as against consciousness, the feminine as against the masculine principle; and the more we separate ourselves from it, challenge it, hunt it and hope to destroy it, the more powerful, menacing, and finally destructive it becomes. In the rich but unbalanced and neurotic nature of Melville, like the age to which he belongs, there is no reconciling element, no principle of integration; he cannot help seeing life in terms of the opposites, of a Manichean conflict; and his tragic story of Captain Ahab and the *Pequod* and the White Whale (all colours except black are contained in white), with its epic grandeur and flashing poetry of phrase, is his deepest and truest account of himself and his time.

WILLIE T. WEATHERS

Moby Dick and the Nineteenth-Century Scene†

The fictional events of *Moby Dick* and the actual events of the period present a striking parallelism of fact and fiction. This rela-

† From Willie T. Weathers, *University of Texas Studies in Literature and Language*, Vol. 1 (Winter, 1960), 477–501; the quotation is from 477, 484, 486–87, 498, 499–500, 501. Reprinted by permission. The article suggests more parallels of Jefferson with Bulkington and Garrison with Ahab than these excerpts indicate [*Editors' note*].

tionship perhaps sheds light on why the realistic adventure tale which Melville had begun early in 1850 and promised to his publisher by autumn of the same year evolved into the philosophical and allegorical novel which was completed with difficulty by the autumn of 1851. For the parallelism indicates that this is not merely a twofold but a threefold story, which interweaves a political "allegory," a narrative history, and a metaphysical anagoge; the metaphysical question was made doubly acute for Melville by the national crisis of 1850. The political venture called in Jefferson's First Inaugural Address the "world's best hope" was now threatened by a dissension which could be safely reconciled only if the democratic faith in natural man's benevolence and reasonableness was based on a sound metaphysical premise. In picturing the catastrophe wrought by a captain who aspired to godhood, Melville indicates a deep concern with the problem of political leadership, but fear of the romantic concept of the 'hero," the god-man guided by his divine intuition. The historical evidence supports belief that Bulkington, the *Pequod*'s pilot as she leaves harbor, is meant for commentary on the tragic flaw in Ahab's leadership by recalling the rational idealist Thomas Jefferson; and that the characterization of the *Pequod*'s irrational captain is indebted not only to the Promethean rebels and reformers of myth and literature, but more immediately to the radical abolitionist and moral perfectionist, William Lloyd Garrison. * * *

When, on February 1, 1850, he [Melville] landed in New York from a four-month absence in Europe, he found the nation violently torn over the abolition issue precipitated by its expansionist policy and engaged in agitation over the Compromise Bill. Soon after his arrival, he began *Moby Dick*.

It is easy to see why, despite his determination to make this novel what the buying public wanted, he could not so deflect the tenor of his thoughts; and there is good reason to believe that the "germinous seeds" dropped by Hawthorne's *Mosses* in July were preceded by a spring sowing while Melville was still resident in New York City. On May 7–8 the American Anti-Slavery Society held there a spectacular convention which must have made him acutely aware that not only the fate of the Union but the fundamental rights of free men rested in the hands of a body politic dangerously irrational. The future of the promised land was being jeopardized by uncompromising idealists as well as by materialists. As Jefferson had warned, "if on a temporary superiority of the one party, the other is to resort to a scission of the Union, no federal government can ever exist.[1]

Presiding at the convention meetings was Garrison, the most uncompromising of the abolition leaders. This radical New Eng-

1. James Truslow Adams, *The Living Jefferson* (New York, 1936), pp. 282–83.

land moralist and autocratic editor of the *Liberator* had, by 1850, repudiated both Church and Constitution as hypocritical protectors of slavery, and was advocating disunion. The chief item on his agenda was condemnation of the Compromise Bill. For a week, the New York yellow press had been fomenting public opposition to the convention, and a mob organized by Tammany Hall and led by a heckler named Rynders broke it up at its third session. The last two meetings were held in the New York Society Library, of which Melville was a member, and it seems likely that he witnessed at least some of the stormy events. Certainly he would have read full accounts of them; and even the papers opposed to Garrison agreed that the mob's real victory was not over abolition but freedom of speech.[2]

Once one has the key, the incidents of the first twenty-eight chapters of Ishmael's adventures seem to be Melville's personal narrative of the events and thoughts which led him to turn his whaling tale into a philosophical quest and a national warning. In Ishmael's New Bedford experiences, which begin on a stormy night, the expensive inns of the Crossed Harpoons and the Sword-Fish that he passes by, and the Negro church that he stumbles into and dubs the "Trap," are reminders of the materialistically inspired Mexican War and the slavery dilemma it created. The ancient Spouter-Inn suggests the orthodox Christian abolitionism in which Melville first sought an answer: a dubious yet hopeful refuge, for despite the inn's right-whale bar,[3] and its walls hung with rusty harpoons and the picture of a foundering Trinitarian ship, it nevertheless receives the poor and encourages brotherhood. Thereafter follow in succession Ishmael's uneasy rest at the inn until he has brought himself to sleep with Queequeg, his natural brother; the sailors' chapel with its tablet-reminders of other courageous whalers and its sermon on individual moral obligation to service and sacrifice; Ishmael's choice of ship and shipmates, after some hesitation at the Try-Pots, in the coalition of independents and idealists federated along the keel of the *Pequod;* and finally, his first sight of the *Pequod*'s captain. This meeting brings the account to May of 1850, when Melville seems to have found his initial inspiration for the story of Ahab.

As one studies the life and character of William Lloyd Garrison and the history of abolitionism from 1830 to 1850, the parallels between Garrison's story and Ahab's become so striking as to compel the conclusion that Melville's Promethean hero is indebted

2. Russell B. Nye, *William Lloyd Garrison and the Humanitarian Reformers* (Boston, 1955), pp. 153–56; Lindsay Swift, *William Lloyd Garrison* (Philadelphia, 1911), pp. 278–85.

3. In Melville's "Cetology" the right whale seems to symbolize the earlier and more conservative post-Reformation Christian-democratic principles.

not merely to the generic humanitarian reformer of mid-nineteenth-century America but to this particular New England abolition crusader. * * *

There are miscellaneous minor incidents in Garrison's life which are paralleled in the narrative incidents of *Moby Dick,* such as Garrison's calling himself "stormproof" and Ahab's dubbing himself "Old Thunder" and refusing in the storm to use the lightning rods; or Ahab's throwing his lighted pipe into the sea as Garrison's friend Rogers had thrown his cigar into the river, when on a trip with Garrison he was reproved for thus desecrating "his anti-slavery mouth." The injury to the ivory leg when Ahab visits the English ship recalls the rebuff to Garrison's moralistic methods suffered on visits to England and Scotland.[4] Of particular significance to Melville's political Jeremiad is his inversion of the Tarquin legend in the episode when Ahab's hat is snatched and carried far aloft by a sea-hawk and then dropped into the sea, an incident possibly reminiscent of Garrison's loss of a never-recovered hat when, in 1835, a mob dragged him rope-bound through the streets of Boston. At any rate, the warning in the Tarquin allusion is clear: the American eagle should not place the badge of leadership on the head of a Christian anarchist. The warning is repeated at the conclusion of the novel, when the red flag of anarchy catches the sea-hawk in its folds and carries him to destruction along with the ship of freedom. * * *

Through seven of the nine ships met, Melville points out the defects which he sees in the romantic individualism of the day. Three of these whalers are European, the rest American. The whaleless German *Jungfrau,* without oil even for her own lamps, suggests that Neoplatonic mysticism is inadequate support for practical democracy, as witnessed by Germany's abortive revolution of 1848. The French *Rosebud*'s loss of profit from the dead leviathan she has picked up—an allusion to the demise of the first republic and the increasingly obvious instability of the two-year-old second—is ascribed to the uncooperativeness of her captain and crew. The practical materialism of the *Samuel Enderby*'s one-armed captain reflects laissez-faire economic individualism which had replaced the idealism of England's abolition movement of the 1830's and dulled the active interest in American abolition which had prevailed during that period.

The defect common to four of the six American ships is detachment from the nation's political problems. The results of this detachment in organized religion are reflected in the bleached wreck of the *Albatross,* symbol of the orthodox Church's failure to implement by action its teachings of brotherly love; and in the

4. Swift, pp. 109, 126; Nye, pp. 127–28, 138–39.

quarantine of the Shaker ship *Jeroboam* (named for the first king of Israel after the division of the tribes), representative of the current epidemic of isolated and self-sufficient religious communities. Among individuals it is seen in the transcendental optimism of the *Bachelor* (American twin of the melancholy German *Virgin*), who in ignoring the White Whale's existence seems to follow the Emersonian injunction to leave government "to clerks and desks": and in the theism of the "miserably misnamed" *Delight*, ironic refutation of Father Mapple's doctrine that "top-gallant delight is to him, who acknowledges no law or lord, but the Lord his God, and is only a patriot to heaven."[5] The similar condition of the *Albatross* and the *Delight* indicates Melville's combination of sympathy for Garrison's arraignment of orthodox Christianity and condemnation of his Christian anarchy.

Against the negative warnings of these four ships are set the positive messages of the *Town-Ho* and the *Rachel*. The former, whose name is the cry announcing sight of a whale, is encountered near the Cape of Good Hope. In vouching for the truth of her story of the White Whale's act of moral justice, Ishmael seems to be assuring the doubting Spaniards to whom he repeats it that, despite the violation of American Democracy's ideals in the Mexican War, history justifies a continuation of faith in the Constitution's promise of impartial justice. Although the same White Whale has carried off the *Rachel's* sons, Jeremiah's promise to the biblical Rachel that her children (for whom she weeps as they pass her tomb on their way into captivity) will eventually be freed, implies Melville's prophecy of the ultimate triumph of democratic idealism over the injustice of the Fugitive Slave Law. It is the *Rachel* who rescues Ishmael, afloat on the buoy of Queequeg's coffin. Melville's salvation from the fears expressed in his apostrophe to Bulkington is his faith in the moral sense as defined by Jefferson: a combination of altruistic emotions with rational judgment. His warning is against altruism divorced from reason; and his promise in their union, ultimate triumph for America's constitutional guarantees of liberty and justice, and thereby safety for the hope of a free world. * * *

Recognition of the political allegory in *Moby Dick* reveals more fully the novel's artistry as well as its thought. In the clearer illumination of the thought one sees that the earlier chapters are not an imperfectly integrated "first" *Moby Dick*, but an essential prologue to the drama; and that the chapters of choral comment never digress from the drama's central theme. One sees too the artistic justification for Melville's shift from the first-person viewpoint in

5. Father Taylor of Boston, considered the original of Father Mapple, and Garrison were both conspicuous speakers at the 1840 Chardon Street Convention of the Friends of Universal Reform. (Swift, pp. 202–04)

prologue, epilogue, and choral comment to the omniscient treatment of Ahab's tragedy. The narrative of Ishmael's thoughts and feelings is the personal story of a man who cherishes democratic freedom; the tragedy of the *Pequod* and her Captain is an epic story of the democratic nation which bears "the ark of the liberties of the world."

CHARLES H. FOSTER

[*Moby-Dick* as Antislavery Allegory]†

Primarily, Melville expressed the democratic revolt agitating him in the spring and summer of 1851 through radical passages and sometimes chapters inserted into the previously written portions of *Moby-Dick*. These interpolations occur too infrequently to color very seriously our reading of the semi-realistic, semi-comic chapters introducing Ishmael and Queequeg or the subsequent chapters giving substance to the drama of Man versus the Whale. The insertions were, however, clearly part of the author's ultimate meaning and they deserve an attention they have not been given. Furthermore, the obvious passion with which they were written makes it probable that toward the close of *Moby-Dick* Melville adapted the tragedy of Ahab and the Whale to a more radical meaning than has been suspected. The insertions are important not only in themselves but important for what they may tell us concerning the meaning in the final, crucial, intensely symbolic third of Melville's masterpiece.

To judge from its rhetoric, so very different from the pedestrian prose he employs in the early chapters describing Ishmael and Queequeg, one of Melville's late insertions was the sermon preached by Father Mapple. The reference to a clergyman's speaking the dangerous truth in the letter to Hawthorne in early June, 1851 suggests approximately when the sermon was written; and when we open it up there is much in it which looks clearly like Melville's response to the Sims case of a few months earlier. This we see when the minister makes his second point, the application of the text from *Job* to himself "as an anointed pilot-prophet, or speaker of true things." Father Mapple sees nothing but woe in store for the clergyman "who seeks to please rather than to appal . . . whose good name is more to him than goodness . . .

† From Charles H. Foster, "Something in Emblems: A Reinterpretation of *Moby-Dick*," *The New England Quarterly*, Vol. 34 (March, 1961), 3–35; the quotation is from 16–18, 20–21, 22–26, 27–29. Reprinted by permission of the publisher and the author.

who, in this world, courts not dishonor!" The "delight and deliciousness" of rôle truly fulfilled is his "who against the proud gods and commodores of this earth, ever stands forth his own inexorable self . . . who gives no quarter in the truth, and kills, burns, and destroys all sin though he pluck it out from under the robes of Senators and Judges . . . who acknowledges no law or lord, but the Lord his God, and is only a patriot to heaven."

In his own lofty rhetoric Melville here expressed an anti-slavery doctrine extremely well known in 1850–1851, the doctrine of the "higher law," which William H. Seward in opposing the extension of slavery stated in this sober fashion in March, 1850: "We hold no arbitrary authority over anything, whether acquired lawfully or seized by usurpation. The Constitution regulates our stewardship. . . . But there is a higher law than the Constitution, which regulates our authority over the domain. . . . The territory is a part, no inconsiderable part, of the common heritage of mankind, bestowed upon them by the Creator of the universe. We are his stewards, and must so discharge our trust as to secure in the highest attainable degree their happiness."[1] * * *

We are here once more confronted with Chief Justice Shaw bowing under the Court House chain at the time of the Sims case,[2] and it seems likely that Melville also remembered Shaw in his miniscular denunciation. Certainly if we had asked Melville in some game of rapid-fire identification to furnish specific names for the members of various professions, he would have said "Shaw" when we called out "judge," and it is difficult to imagine that he could have written the word without also recalling his father-in-law, particularly when we note the context of implied judicial decisions concerning slavery.

In any case when we understand that Father Mapple's sermon preaches extreme abolition doctrine without naming slavery, we have no trouble with "Senators." Melville may have recalled Senator John C. Calhoun, whom he had attacked as Nulli, that is the Nullifier, in *Mardi*, but after 1850 the evil senator undoubtedly meant for him as for other opponents of slavery primarily Daniel Webster of Massachusetts. In the spring of 1851 Webster was, to be sure, no longer a senator; in the summer of 1850 he had been

1. William H. Seward, "Freedom in the New Territories," speech in the Senate, March 11, 1850, in George E. Baker, editor, *The Works of William H. Seward* (New York, 1853), 1, 74.
2. In an earlier section of his article (not reprinted here) Foster reviews the celebrated Sims case of April, 1851, in which Melville's father-in-law, Lemuel Shaw, Chief Justice of the Massachusetts Supreme Court, remanded a fugitive slave named Thomas Sims to the custody of his owner in Chatham County, Georgia. The aged Shaw had (in Wendell Phillips's words) "bowed his burly person" to crawl under the chain the City Marshal had used to encircle the Court House. See Leonard W. Levy, *The Law of the Commonwealth and Chief Justice Shaw* (Cambridge, 1957), pp. 91–104 [*Editors' note*].

appointed Secretary of State. So far as the liberals were concerned, however, the memorable act of his career was his speech, "The Constitution and the Union," delivered in the Senate on March 7, 1850, advocating passage of the Fugitive Slave Act, the cessation of antislavery agitation, and recognition of the South as the injured party in its conflict with the North.

A pessimistically shaped American scholar, a transcendentalist-reformer like Ishmael does not necessarily step out of character in reporting Father Mapple's passionate convictions, but Ishmael is still a problem. Mr. C. L. R. James finds Melville's narrator "a completely modern young intellectual who has broken with society and wavers constantly between totalitarianism and the crew" and he traces Ishmael's pessimism to "an unbearable sense of social crisis" in "a special class," "chiefly intellectuals and the idle rich who cannot decide what attitude they should take toward a changing society."[3] Such a reading fits nicely with the interpretation I am making of *Moby-Dick* but I fear it is more complimentary to Melville than true. The speculative, Narcissistic Ishmael of the opening chapter is not quite the same person as the sea-going innocent who is kidded by the landlord of the Spouter Inn and whom we later see in comic encounters with Mrs. Hussey and Captains Peleg and Bildad; and it is difficult to reconcile the comic-realistic Ishmael with the reporter of the sermon or the disenchanted Ishmael of "The Whiteness of the Whale." Ishmael is not a well defined "central intelligence"; rather he is a composite resulting from Melville's changing intentions: comic from the first intention to write a picaresque novel; pessimistic from the second intention to write a Shakespearean tragedy of Man versus the Whale; radical from the final intention to make *Moby-Dick* a democratic, an antislavery fable.

In my reading, Melville's sense of social crisis consequent upon the remanding of Thomas Sims led him not into pessimism but into revolt against Judge Shaw. Consider the close of the first chapter, "Knights and Squires," from which Mr. James takes the title of his Melville book. * * *

This prayer was, indeed, defiance of Judge Shaw. The remarks about our "divine equality" and about God as "The centre and circumference of all democracy" coupled with the conviction that God had lifted Andrew Jackson to power constituted precisely the complex of sentiments against which Shaw had ranged himself in one of his most famous decisions, that concerning Abner Kneeland, whose conviction on a charge of blasphemy he had sustained in

3. C. L. R. James, *Mariners, Renegades and Castaways: The Story of Herman Melville and the World We Live In* (New York, 1953), pp. 44, 107.

1838. As rationalist-pantheist, Kneeland had offended in 1833, much as Emerson was later to do, by finding the individual so deeply rooted in deity that private judgment, private religious experiences and insights could be elevated to an authority superior to the dictates of the Bible and clergy; and, again like Emerson, Kneeland had obviously looked forward to a revolution in the economic and political as well as the religious spheres. But Kneeland was committed to more than Emerson's "one-man revolution." He was a Jacksonian Democrat and ultimately a socialist.[4]

As a defender of the standing order, Shaw had made short, abrupt work of Kneeland. He had given no reasoned consideration of the evidence against him and he had acted with such clearly political prejudice and such faint regard for democratic principles, that over one hundred and sixty-seven liberals, beginning with William Ellery Channing and including Parker, Emerson, Ripley, Garrison, and Alcott, had signed a petition to the Governor of Massachusetts for Kneeland's unconditional pardon.[5] Governor Edward Everett, a conservative Unitarian-Whig like Shaw, had done nothing about Kneeland's case, but the petition must inevitably have rankled Shaw.[6] We can imagine his irritation on finding Melville, as he might have phrased matters, spouting Kneeland's doctrine and aligning himself with those irresponsible radicals, those Free Thinkers and Transcendentalists, those New England Robespierres, who had dared to sign the petition to Governor Everett.

Melville himself may well have felt that in his prayer he had given all too obvious an expression of his radicalism. In any case, we do not find another passage of this kind for twenty-six chapters and when we come to "The Town-Ho's Story," celebrating Steelkilt's democratic revolt against Radney, there are no statements as explicit as those in the prayer. It is also notable that Melville placed "The Town-Ho's Story" among chapters dealing with cetology and they inevitably encourage us to read that fable of revolt more as an incident of life on a whaler than as an illustration of the punishment overtaking the man who dares injustice and indignity toward his fellow man. If we have not attended carefully to Melville's radical insertions, we may not see that Steelkilt is one of the meanest mariners named in the prayer and we may overlook Moby Dick as divine agent destroying the personification of authoritarianism and injustice.

4. Levy, *The Law of the Commonwealth and Chief Justice Shaw*, pp. 45–46, 58.
5. *The Law of the Commonwealth and Chief Justice Shaw*, pp. 51–58.
6. The petition began: "Because the punishment proposed to be inflicted is believed to be at variance with the soundest expositions of those civil and religious rights which are at once founded in our nature, and guaranteed by the constitutions of the United States and this Commonwealth. . . ." W. H. Channing, *The Life of William Ellery Channing, D.D.* (Boston, 1880), p. 505.

"The Town-Ho's Story" is apparently the last of the important radically democratic insertions but it is not the last evidence we have in *Moby-Dick* of Melville's private war on *status quo*. There is good ground for supposing that the democratic prayer in Chapter 16 was written after he had invented the Negro boy, Pip, in Chapter 93. The title of this chapter, "The Castaway," certainly fits well with the term "castaways" in the prayer. Pip's first appearance in Chapter 40, "Forecastle, Midnight," in any case seems a matter about which we should be suspicious. The general sentiment among the sailors in this chapter has been that Ahab is "a grand old cove" and "We are the lads to hunt him up whales." Melville has done the chapter in the form of a poetic drama, and it may be that Pip's appearance here and the language he uses are appropriate; but I sense a new departure, a sterner rhetoric when he shrinks under the windlass and prays: "Oh, thou big white God aloft there somewhere in yon darkness, have mercy on this small black boy down here; preserve him from all men who have no bowels to feel fear." Melville may, of course, have invented Pip at precisely this point, but it is from the adventure alone in the immensity of ocean and sky, when he leaps the second time from a whale boat in Chapter 93, that Pip becomes divinely mad, wise and eloquent. It seems likely, therefore, that Melville invented Pip in Chapter 93 and then went back inserting the prayer about "castaways" in Chapter 16 and Pip's own prayer to "the big white God" in Chapter 40.

All this argues, of course, that there is an antislavery meaning symbolized in the relationship of Ahab with Pip. That Ahab, who will soon baptize his harpoon in the name of the devil, should cry "Hands off from that holiness" when he discovers that the Manxman has seized Pip because of his mad talk, and that he should tell him "Thou touchest my inmost centre, boy; thou art tied to me by cords woven of my heartstrings," and name him henceforth the sharer of his cabin, is strange and unexpected. Possibly we should account for Pip, as F. O. Matthiessen does, in terms of the relationship of King Lear with the Fool.[7] I suspect, however, that there is more here than adaptation of Shakespeare. On his very first appearance Pip is the Negro, calling on the "big white God" to have mercy on "this small black boy," and it is as Negro as well as Fool that I think we should see him.

In the days immediately preceding the fatal chase of Moby Dick, Ahab is being humanized so that we may feel pity as well as fear in experiencing the tragedy. As Ahab will soon show humanity in thinking of home and family with Starbuck, so now he shows true human rightness in his attitude toward the Negro. The Stubbs of

7. *American Renaissance*, pp. 449–451.

this world may desert poor black boys with the argument: "We can't afford to lose whales by the likes of you; a whale would sell for thirty times what you would, Pip, in Alabama. Bear that in mind, and don't jump any more." The tragic hero must possess a grand humanity which can be touched by the humanity and divinity of the Negro and which inevitably leads him to say, "If thou speakest thus to me much more, Ahab's purpose keels up in him." Ahab's purpose does not, of course, keel up in him. Ultimately he despises our human inter-indebtedness and he soon yields again to Fedallah, the devil or his representative, and concentrates once more on the impious pursuit of Moby Dick.

In Ahab's turning his back on Pip in Act V of the tragedy, Melville may have symbolized Judge Shaw's repudiation of the Negro in the Sims case; but in Ahab Melville symbolized primarily the same person implied in Father Mapple's "Senators," Daniel Webster. There are a number of grounds for this identification. In his funeral address on Webster in 1852. Theodore Parker said: "Surely he was immensely great. When he spoke, he was a grand spectacle. His noble form, so dignified and masculine; his massive head; the mighty brow, Olympian in its majesty; the great, deep, dark eye, which, like a lion's, seemed fixed on objects afar off. . . . He magnetized men by his presence; he subdued them by his will more than by his argument."[8] Here is suggestion of Ahab as we first see him in what I suspect is another late insertion: "His whole high, broad form, seemed made of solid bronze, and shaped in an unalterable mould, like Cellini's cast Perseus. . . . Captain Ahab stood erect, looking straight out beyond the ship's ever-pitching prow. There was an infinity of firmest fortitude, a determinate, unsurrenderable wilfulness, in the fixed and fearless, forward dedication of that glance. Not a word he spoke; nor did his officers say aught to him; though by all their minutest gestures and expressions, they plainly showed the uneasy, if not painful, consciousness of being under a troubled master-eye."

Nor is this all. Parker saw in Webster's face not only nobility and indomitable power but also tragedy: "What a sad face he wore,—furrowed by passion, by ambition, that noble brow scarred all over with the records of a hard, sad life. . . . It is a face of sorrows,—private, public, secret woes. . . . In that ambition-stricken face his mother would not have known her child!"[9] Melville painted essentially the same portrait in Ahab: "And not only that, but moody stricken Ahab stood before them with a crucifixion in

8. Theodore Parker, "Discourse Occasioned by the Death of Daniel Webster," preached in Boston, October 31, 1852, in *Additional Speeches, Addresses, and Occasional Sermons* (Boston, 1855), 1, 262.

9. Parker, "Discourse," p. 288.

his face; in all the nameless regal overbearing dignity of some mighty woe!"

We also seem close to Webster in Ahab's manipulation and magnetizing of his crew through demagogic oratory; and we may find Webster symbolized in his relation with a political associate in Ahab's conflict with Starbuck. * * *

In his momentary opposition and ultimate submission to Ahab, Starbuck bears considerable resemblance to Robert C. Winthrop of Boston. In the light of conscience, Winthrop, who had studied law with Webster and who was in a sense his first mate, had risked political disfavor by refusing to endorse Webster's March 7 speech, and after he had been appointed Senator from Massachusetts as Webster's successor, he opposed passage of the Fugitive Slave Act. Theodore Parker wrote him: "I can only ascribe your conduct to such motives as ought to animate a manly man,—*a desire to do what is absolutely right*."[10] But there was weakness as well as strength in Winthrop. Horace Mann noted this weakness: "I do not think Mr. Winthrop has sustained himself very well. He ought to have carried the war into Africa, or, at least, to have repelled the intruders from his own territory."[11] Winthrop's ineffectiveness came apparently from the same source as Starbuck's capitulation to Ahab: he could not face down the "concentrating brow" of his captain. When President Fillmore sought Winthrop's advice as to whether he or Webster should be appointed Secretary of State, Winthrop told him "no one was better aware than myself of the awful character of Webster's frowns. . . ."[12]

Ahab's baptism of his harpoon in the name of the devil is also, I believe, a veiled comment on Daniel Webster. There are good reasons, to be sure, for agreeing with Charles Olson that Ahab is "Conjur Man" using "black magic" to achieve his "vengeful ends." Olson's discovery of the blasphemous baptism in a fuller form on the fly-leaf of a volume of Shakespeare also justifies his view that Melville planned to use the baptism in some allegory or fable or poetic drama contrasting black and white magic, "madness" and "right reason," as two extreme ways of invoking the power of the universe. Ahab and Pip, admittedly, illustrate such a contrast, while Fedallah's rôle in deceiving Ahab with false prophecy is, as Mr. Olson suggests, parallel to the rôle of the Weird Sisters in *Macbeth*.[13] But it is a mistake to suppose that Melville was developing the theme of black magic in and for itself. This may have

10. Robert C. Winthrop, Jr., *A Memoir of Robert C. Winthrop* (Boston, 1897) p. 142.
11. *A Memoir of Robert C. Winthrop*, p. 139.
12. *A Memoir of Robert C. Winthrop*, p. 131.
13. Charles Olson, *Call Me Ishmael* (New York, 1947), pp. 53–58.

been his intention when he began the revision of *Moby-Dick*, but it is only very late in the book, less than a hundred pages from the close, that Ahab "deliriously" howls, "Ego non baptizo te in nomine patris, sed in nomine diaboli" as he tempers the harpoon in the blood of the pagan harpooners. The baptism occurs in the complex of symbols and incidents through which Melville is expressing response to the slavery crisis and in their momentousness Ahab's words obviously symbolize some major act of evil in that crisis.

There can be, given all we now see concerning Melville's ultimate meaning, only one act he could have had in mind: Webster's March 7, 1850, speech, the sign, so far as the liberals were concerned, that the senior senator from Massachusetts had sold his soul to the devil. The supposition that in his advocacy of the Fugitive Slave Act and in other matters in his speech Webster was consciously committing wrong, bargaining his soul, as it were, for proslavery support in his consuming ambition to be President, is, of course, an over-simplification. But it was an over-simplification widely entertained in 1850–1851, and Melville was no lonely critic in supposing that Webster, like Ahab in his pursuit of Moby Dick, was interested only in a personal triumph and would do anything to achieve it. In fact Melville may have been helped to his invention of Ahab's blasphemous baptism by the imagery concerning Webster in a poem tolling dismally in everyone's mind in 1850–1851, Whittier's "Ichabod":

> Revile him not, the Tempter hath
> A snare for all . . .
>
> Scorn! would the angels laugh, to mark
> A bright soul driven,
> Fiend-goaded, down the endless dark,
> From hope and heaven!

In any case, if we understand the baptism as a symbol for Webster's apostacy in defending slavery, we see easily why Melville should tell Hawthorne it was the "secret motto" of the book. The baptism is Melville's unmistakable verdict that however grand and godlike Ahab may be, however much he is the master of men and of language, however much we may find our own account in his war with the gods and fate, we are finally to view him as the "ungodly man," the denier of God, the partner of the devil. Here, of course, Melville made symbolically his most violent attack on political and social conservatism, and it was quite appropriate that he should call Hawthorne's attention to the baptism as the master-key unlocking the ultimate meaning of *Moby-Dick*. * * *

ROBERT SHULMAN

[The Whale's Deliberate Malice]†

Much recent criticism tries to minimize the Whale's deliberate malice. One should note that the concluding view of Moby Dick is unqualified, and that it is Ishmael's, not Ahab's. Those ultimately mysterious natural and supernatural forces symbolized by the whale are, it seems, neither blindly neutral or indifferent to man but rather actively hostile to his purposes and desires. Some readers choose to meld that hostile, defiant, destructive power into a tranquil, deep vision of an ultimate, all-encompassing, mystically accepted God within Whom the conflict of good and evil becomes supremely unimportant. Such readers might pay more careful attention to the imagery and emphasis which Melville seems quite deliberately to have intended.

GLAUCO CAMBON

Ishmael and the Problem of Formal Discontinuities in *Moby-Dick*‡

Ishmael is the artist in the act of telling us, and struggling to understand, his crucial experience. When his autobiography becomes the history of the *Pequod* and Ahab, he is liberated from his "hypos" for the second time, and in a deeper sense: he attains the liberation of imaginative objectivity. Thus his vanishing from the stage after a certain point does not constitute a breach of poetical continuity, but a dialectical movement that reproduces and expands the repeated transition from narrative to drama, from memory to visionary actuality, from conjuring subjectivity to conjured objectivity. It will help to recall that Chapter 32 ("Cetology") humorously describes the sizes of the various species of whales in terms of book-formats, an obvious literary metaphor, and

† From Robert Shulman, "The Serious Function of Melville's Phallic Jokes," *American Literature,* Vol. 33 (May, 1961), 179–94; the quotation is from 192, n. 19. Reprinted by permission of Duke University Press.

‡ From Glauco Cambon, "Ishmael and the Problem of Formal Discontinuities in *Moby-Dick,*" *Modern Language Notes*, Vol. 76 (June, 1961), 516–23; the quotation is from 523.

that the allusions to the story as a book in the making (often attuned to self-mockery) abound significantly.[1]

If so, it should be possible to accept Ishmael as a *persona* of Melville, invisibly present *through* his narration when he ceases to be directly present *in* it; and that this persona, even as he ceases to have objective existence, has dramatic existence as actor-spectator of a half-remembered, half-conjured action. Ishmael is the self-ironizing writer seeking, and finally achieving, realization through self-effacement in the work of art; following him in the process, we see the poetry arise from its (cetological) materials, and the discontinuities acquire the meaning of imaginative gestures within the context of a work in progress. They are indeed the structural equivalents of the copious hyperboles which animate Melville's baroque prose.

WARNER BERTHOFF

[The Four "Worlds" of *Moby-Dick*]†

Of all Melville's work it was *Moby-Dick* which, in its magnitude and boldness of design, laid the heaviest tribute upon his descriptive powers, and most strenuously tested his ambition to seek out the deeper logic of fact and appearance. It is of course his masterpiece. And one great factor in his accomplishment in *Moby-Dick* is the grandeur and animation of the settings, which in turn do not merely illustrate the book's action and themes but actively create them. The larger part of the narrative is simply the patiently detailed yet consistently high-spirited setting out of a scene sufficiently vast and prodigious to contain the central drama and justify its intensity. Melville's job is to create for us the huge "world" he means dramatically to exploit. This must be done, we are told at the end of Chapter 69, for perfectly practical reasons: a mass of particular facts must be faithfully explained so that when the climax comes we can follow its concentrated moments of action at their proper pace. But what is actually amassed in the long, richly digressive descriptive chronicle spun out by Ishmael is something more than we need for keeping track of the material events of the story. It is its own end and justification. The narrative, in

1. See the end of chapter 32 ("Cetology"), the beginning of chapter 63 ("The Crotch"), the end of chaper 102 ("A Bower in the Arsacides"), and the passage in chapter 104 ("The Fossil Whale") that begins: "One often hears of writers that rise and swell with their subject, though it may seem but an ordinary one. How, then, with me, writing of this Leviathan? . . ."

† From Warner Berthoff, *The Example of Melville* (Princeton: Princeton University Press, 1962), pp. 78–89.

the large, is nothing less than a confession *à fond* of the several "worlds" human existence marvelously moves through—and in this multiform context Ahab himself is in some danger of becoming only an incidental marvel, one among many, and a rather mechanical one at that. At a certain date in our acquaintance with the book *Moby-Dick* we are no longer in doubt about the outcome; nor can we still be entirely surprised or astounded by the more highly wrought individual passages, of meditation, description, comedy, bravura declamation, analogy-running, or whatever, though we continue to be charmed by them. What does still lay claim on us then, and perhaps more powerfully than ever, is the imaginative coherence and embrace of the whole. The correspondences, the insistent illusion of a universe brimful of consenting and conspiring phenomena ceaselessly interacting, prove to be not forced but in the nature of the revealed materials. "Nothing exists in itself," Ishmael casually announces—a declaration which could seem rankest undergraduate sophistry, if it was not delivered, without emphasis, by someone who (starting in the first sentence of the first chapter with his own simple name) has proved himself able to call up and exactly identify so great a host of particular phenomena, of things as (to our eyes and in our hands) they actually are.

It should be evident that by "setting" I mean something more than the environment or material occasion within which the drama is played out. I mean rather that whole context, as the narrative establishes it, out of which the action rises—a context of idea and feeling as well as of observation and description; I mean all that in the convenient language of recent criticism may be called the "world" of behavior peculiar to an author's vision of existence. In *Moby-Dick* four distinct "worlds" may be defined, and all are fundamental to the import of the novel as Melville built it up.

(1) With the narrative beginning ashore and staying ashore for twenty-odd chapters, the first "world" put before us is that of the dry land, or at least the thronged edges of it: New York, New Bedford, Nantucket, and the streets, chapels, inns, and offices to be met on the way to the sea. It has its own solid attractions. There are chowder shops and good fellowship, there is the chance of fresh adventure, there is easy access to the earth's far corners and wildest wonders, and there is no shortage of incidental curiosities close at hand. In contrast to the Liverpool of *Redburn* or the New York of *Pierre* and "Bartleby," the cities and harbors of *Moby-Dick* seem hospitable places on the whole, and are presented with a good deal of homely charm and idealizing humor. But the land-world of this part of the book also supplies just as much motive as is needed for heading us willingly out into the "open independence of the sea." It is, successively, a dream-tormented world of unsatisfied yearnings,

a "stepmother" world, a "wolfish" world, a world which "pays dividends" to sharp practice, a finished and unameliorable world of frost, death, teeth-chattering, and the sorrows of the orphaned, and of poverty and hard bargaining; a world finally (as even in the intensifying rush of the book's closing movement the figures of the carpenter and blacksmith do not let us forget) which is continually casting away the human wrecks and derelicts it has stripped and ruined.

(2) It is, in short, the world of men, whose "permanent constitutional condition," we are told, is "sordidness." The next broad context which the narrative begins to build up is also a world of men, but here Melville develops a different emphasis. For this is the self-sufficient world of the quaint, rare, old, noble, trophy-garnished, battle-worn, cannibalistic, melancholy *Pequod;* and Melville's purpose in describing it is to show it as a fit instrument for Ahab and his purpose and for all the "high and mighty business of whaling." The ship takes the center of the stage in Chapter 16, and continues to make a vividly heraldic presence throughout the rest of the book. Primarily a maneuverable slaughterhouse, as the narrative troubles to make spectacularly clear, she is at the same time, in the nature of her business of manufacturing oil, "among the cleanliest things of this tidy earth." Her high qualities are displayed in a series of brilliant and precise physical images: rushing after her boats in the first lowering, beating her way into the sleet and swell of the Cape storms, gliding through yellow meadows of brit, pressing up the Sunda Strait in chase of an armada of whales and being chased in turn by armed pirates, and so on. As the concentrated foreground of the book's developing action, she has her own great part to play in it, and a series of descriptive epithets is used, in the manner of epic formulae, to point this up: so we hear of "the tranced ship," the "intense Pequod," "the fated Pequod," "the madly merry and predestinated craft," and—perhaps most beautiful and foreboding of all—"the ivory Pequod."

Coincidentally the ship is shown to be a virtual city of the races and talents of men. From the first we are encouraged to think of her as a paradigm of the marvelous hive of corporate human life (though Melville does not impose that symbolism on the whole novel)—she is at once a parliament, guildhall, factory, and fortress, and goes "ballasted with utilities" like the world-renewing Ark itself. Different phases of the work that goes on aboard her and in her boats furnish metaphors for the different ways of "this world," as in chapters like "The Line" or "Fast Fish and Loose Fish." Mostly, however, the skills and practices of whaling are described for their own sake and in their own full detail, so that the fanciful analogies which are Melville's trademark in chapter-endings are usually erected on an already solid ground of factual interest. Indeed the long succession of passages describing the crew at its jobs makes up a "song for occupations" as comprehensive and ecstatic as Whitman's. Conversely we find Melville turning back to the general routine of common earthly labor for descriptive metaphors, invoking the whole range of its trades, tools, and artifacts in aid of his exposition. Such effects, we must agree, are wonderfully natural in *Moby-Dick*. For merely to describe one feature of the whale's anatomy or of the practical business of stripping it down is to give an impression of surveying no small part of the fantastic material apparatus by which ordinary civilized life is maintained. Consider the following:

> Let us now with whatever *levers* and *steam-engines* we have at hand, *cant over* the sperm whale's head, so that it may lie bottom up; then, ascending by a *ladder* to the summit, have a peep down the mouth; and were it not that the body is now completely separated from it, with a *lantern* we might descend into the great Kentucky Mammoth Cave of his stomach. But let us hold on here by this tooth, and look about us where we are. What a really beautiful and chaste-looking mouth! from *floor* to *ceiling*, lined, or rather *papered* with a glistening white membrane, glossy as *bridal satins*.
>
> But come out now, and look at this portentous lower jaw, which seems like the long narrow *lid* of an immense *snuff-box*, with the *hinge* at one end, instead of one side. If you *pry it up*, so as to get it overhead, and expose its rows of teeth, it seems a terrific *portcullis*; and such, alas! it proves to many a poor wight in the fishery, upon whom these *spikes* fall with *impaling* force. But far more terrible is it to behold, when fathoms down in the sea, you see some sulky whale, floating there suspended with his prodigious jaw, some fifteen feet long hanging straight down at right-angles with his body, for all the world like a *ship's jib-boom*. . . .
>
> In most cases this lower jaw—being easily *unhinged* by a practised artist—is disengaged and *hoisted* on deck for the purpose of extracting the ivory teeth, and furnishing a supply of that hard white whalebone with which the fishermen fashion *all sorts of curious articles, including canes, umbrella-stocks, and handles to riding-whips*.
>
> With a long, weary *hoist* the jaw is dragged on board, as if it were an *anchor*; and when the proper time comes—some few days after the other work—Queequeg, Daggoo, and Tashtego, being all *accomplished dentists*, are set to drawing teeth. With a keen *cutting-spade*, Queequeg *lances* the gums; then the jaw is *lashed down to ringbolts*, and *a tackle being rigged* from aloft, they drag out these teeth, *as Michigan oxen drag stumps of old oaks out of wild wood-lands*. There are generally forty-two teeth in all; in old whales, much worn down, but undecayed; *nor filled*

after our artificial fashion. The jaw is afterwards *sawn into slabs,* and *piled away like joists for building houses.* (End of Chapter 74; italics mine, of course.)

This is not the sort of passage usually brought forward to make claims for *Moby-Dick*; yet only a writer of extraordinary attentiveness, and compassion, toward the common "works and days" of human life would ever have thought to compose it, or have managed it so cleanly. In the same vein is this single throwaway sentence in the chapter on the *Pequod*'s carpenter: "Like all sea-going ship carpenters, and more especially those belonging to whaling vessels, he was, to a certain off-handed, practical extent, alike experienced in numerous trades and callings collateral to his own; the carpenter's pursuit being the ancient and outbranching trunk of all those numerous handicrafts which more or less have to do with wood as an auxiliary material." I cite it here simply for the way in which, in the casual closing phrases, an altogether incidental piece of information has opened out into something larger and curiously moving—into an acknowledgment of that whole humble order of practical arts which lies at the very root of civilization; arts springing from the support given human life by the simplest commodities of nature, and developed in this case by certain aboriginal chippers and carvers from whom we all must acknowledge descent. Though quite unidealizingly, the sentence serves once more to remind us how *Moby-Dick* is not only a melodrama of the catastrophe of one crazed man's overweening defiance and pride, but an unflaggingly heroic celebration of all mankind's laborious tenure of the physical earth.

No account of the setting of *Moby-Dick* in this common world of human labor and effort would be complete without reference to the accompanying conception, periodically renewed and developed with a great variety of illustration, of "man in the ideal"—which is to say, in the large, in history, in legend, in the depths of his natural being, in all the contributing circumstance of his astonishing characters and enterprise. In both the inventoried descriptions of whaling and the bouts of violent action, our attention is constantly drawn back to the men of the *Pequod* and those capacities and virtues we are to know them by. During the long middle stretches of the book, Stubb and Queequeg in particular hold the foreground, observed at this or that office of their trade. They are, in a sense, their trade's representative heroes. Yet the coolness under pressure, the flamboyant nonchalance, the unconscious courage and power to learn to associate with them are simply the practical virtues a fortiori of the whole race of seagoing men. (An early précis of these virtues stands out: the high-flown chapter in praise of those "naked Nantucketers" who "live on the sea, as prairie cocks in the prairie," and have marked out two-thirds of the "terraqueous globe" as their empire.) Melville's democratic idealism and glorification of the "kingly commons" are shown as rooted in fact, in the conduct of ordinary men at their ordinary tasks. But as we gradually learn the force and extent of these virtues, we also gradually get a sense of their limits, and an intimation of other and stranger human attributes less readily described though not a bit less real. On the fringes of the main action hover other, weird, unknown races of man—Lascars, Manillas, Parsees—such as "civilized, domesticated people in the temperate zone only see in their dreams, and that but dimly," races full of the "ghostly aboriginalness of earth's primal generations" and testifying to who knows what further depths in the strange creature, man; and these, too, contribute something to the whole context of the developing narrative.

(3) The men of the *Pequod* and their exploits are the practical measure also of the next "world" we can discern in *Moby-Dick*, the non-human world of the sea and the indifferent elements. At the climax of the first lowering after whales, we get a concentrated image of this confrontation of powers, men against nature (it concludes a passage cited by D. H. Lawrence to show Melville's mastery of "violent, chaotic physical motion"). A whale escapes Ishmael's boat; then a squall blows up: "The wind increased to a howl; the waves dashed their bucklers together; the whole squall roared, forked, and crackled around us like a white fire upon the prairie, in which, unconsumed, we were burning; immortal in the jaws of death." Against the exactly realized violence of the scene, this spectacular assertion of heroism does not seem exorbitant. We note, though, that it is an anonymous, corporate heroism. Man alone, acting individually, comes off less well in this awesome setting, or so chapters like "The Mast-Head" and "The Try-Works" powerfully suggest. A different kind of encounter with the "heartless immensity" of the sea drives the cabin-boy Pip out of his mind, adrift among "strange shapes of the unwarped primal world." And though for Ahab, studying his charts and plotting a course, the sea and its mysteries are (at first) only so many instruments for "the more certain accomplishment of that monomaniac thought of his soul," that seems more and more one further proof of madness in him.

For the great expanse of the sea remains, and dwarfs the most extravagant human pretensions; "two thirds of the fair world it yet covers." Its vastness corresponds ambiguously to the grandeur of Ahab's design—corresponds ironically, of course, insofar as it is literally immeasurable, and wholly indifferent to the character and purposes of men. Its very mildness is tormenting; the haunting descriptions of its moments of sun-burnished serenity, prairie-meadow loveliness, or moonlit quietness are invariably shaded by undertones of another sort, so that the stillness is "preternatural," the beauties are "appalling" and "unearthly," "all space" is felt to be "vacating itself of life," and the mild billows support only such a "formless, chance-like apparition of life" as the giant squid. Prolonged exposure to these weird, uncivil spheres of being, in "exile from Christendom and civilization," reduces men (rather, "restores" them, Melville pointedly writes) to a condition of "savagery." And Ishmael apart, the virtues-in-trade of the men of the *Pequod* are chiefly savage virtues. Their splendor is a primitive splendor that suits their character as great warriors, hunters, migratory navigators, efficient agents all of the hive-disciplined assault on nature; we see that they thrive as creatures in a world of creatures, and that none are better adapted to this world than those ghostly aboriginals (Fedallah is one) from "unchanging Asiatic communities" where the "memory of the first man [is] a distinct recollection."

(4) In the nature of their trade's incessant conflict with the non-human elements, the whalemen are also described as peculiarly subject to superstition and legend-making; the book comes naturally by its solid foothold in folklore. This is not just a consequence of the ignorance, the "savagery," of those sailing before the mast. Starbuck, too, is presented as equally superstitious, though by way of "intelligence" rather than "ignorance," and Ishmael himself is distinguished by a fine readiness of sympathy for everything phantomlike and enigmatical. And it is particularly through Ishmael's thoughtful and excited narrative witness that the free passage of our attention is secured into the final, furthest "world" set out in *Moby-Dick*—the world of "inscrutable" things, unknown depths, unanswerable questions, "ungraspable phantoms," "pyramidical silences," hieroglyphic riddles, "celestial thoughts" which are "to reason absurd and frantic," "bodiless" agents, "sourceless primogenitures" and fatherless specters; a world that communicates to men only in signs, portents, and equivocal omens, and seems intelligible only to madmen like Ahab or Pip, yet is felt at times to control human destinies to the last detail.[1]

Inevitably, in evoking this spectral outer sphere of things, certain

1. It is this fourth world in particular which is spoken for by the special vocabulary of pluralized participles and noun-abstractions which characterizes Melville's rhetoric at the time of the writing of *Moby-Dick*, just as the book's rich vocabulary of objects and names speaks for the solid environment of "this world." In effect a whole new lexicon of description is created, and it seems to indicate corresponding new doctrines and systems of reality. In *Pierre* this lexicon is entrusted, for long passages, with the whole job of statement, becoming a kind of substitute for concrete observation, and the effect is ruinous—in a weirdly original way.

words, terms, and concepts are used which, though drawn from commonest usage, may reasonably suggest that Melville had some single interpretive scheme for the book as a whole, which it is the job of criticism to identify. Religious allusions are a critical instance of this, and have been a great source of concern to systematizing commentators and exegetes.[2] But when the narrative speaks, in context, of "the interlinked terrors and wonders of God," or relates its heroes' doings to the "mighty, earthly marchings" of the "great democratic God," it does so, I think, without commitment to any identifiable creed or any consistent and paraphrasable "philosophy." Melville's imagination remains, even at these extremities, man-centered and pragmatical. The farthest mysteries of existence remain "those . . . we dream of," and are matched always by the palpable mysteries of human behavior. Consider, for example, the idea of "fate," one of the major terms for the forces conceived to be in play in *Moby-Dick*. By itself, as an independent force, it would be mechanical as a component in the story—and we may well feel that the narrative is least convincing when, in the closing stages, it halfway adopts certain allegoristic conventions of the so-called "fate-tragedy."[3] Only as "fate" is made in one way or another a function of mankind's ordinary and characteristic existence does it take on imaginative validity—when presented, for instance, as a conceit of Ishmael's personal bravado, or, more profoundly, in the haunting evocation of the "weaver-god" (Chapter 102), through the deafening humming of whose ceaseless work the world's "thousand voices" may nevertheless be heard to speak.

So even this final "world" of the unknown and inscrutable is rejoined in *Moby-Dick* to a conception of the life of human-kind in time and space. The joining is effected not alone by transcendental correspondences and "linked analogies" (though these are regularly appealed to). The reference is unfailingly to the mortal presence of the species, man. Thus, the thing that is held to be most horror-striking about the sea and its creatures is the knowledge that they preceeded man and will survive him. The whale's terrors are "antemosaic" and "unsourced," and they will exist the same "after all human ages are over"; correspondingly, as the book ends, the indifferent sea rolls on again as it did long before men ever went down to it in ships. Still, these "pre-adamite" and post-human ages are

2. On the other hand the standard work on this subject, Nathalia Wright's monograph, *Melville's Use of the Bible* (Durham, 1949), is admirably free of interpretive racking.

3. The serious claim that an inhuman Fate rules the acts of men comes to us, however, largely through Ahab's late soliloquies and can be understood as a delusion of his monomania. In order to maintain itself, the enormity of pride in him would require the supposition of some worthy supernatural antagonist. Ahab of course is a powerful pleader and will always persuade some readers to see things as he sees them. It is interesting how many interpretations of Melville's masterpieces are written from the point of view of his villains * * *

not divisible from the span of human history. In passages that tell how the miseries of mortal men descend straight from the aboriginal gods, and how the pre-historic angels "consorted with the daughters of men," Melville appeals in his rough and ready fashion to a myth that a whole succession of hetero-Christian poets and visionaries (consider Blake, Whitman, Yeats, D. H. Lawrence) has found wonderfully seductive—a myth of pre-adamite personages who led a life not unlike ours yet with certain radical exemptions from what we most fear in it: from death, from carnality, from familial combat and dislocation, from the indifferent plenitude of nature, from the blindness of history. Like the conception of fate this myth is ultimately one more way of measuring human experience and feeling. For Melville, it is one means among several of expressing perhaps the furthest intuition in *Moby-Dick*, the intuition of an *anima mundi*, or (to use his words) of a "deep, blue, bottomless soul, pervading mankind and nature," of which the mysterious sea is the prime symbol. All this is most beautifully expressed, I think, in the much remarked chapter in praise of the "mysterious, divine Pacific," as the *Pequod* at last enters its ominous waters—and we may note how the imaginative figure is rendered in terms of the particular souls of individual men:

> There is, one knows not what sweet mystery about this sea, whose gently awful stirrings seem to speak of some hidden soul beneath; like those fabled undulations of the Ephesian sod over the buried Evangelist St. John. And meet it is, that over these sea-pastures, wide-rolling watery prairies and Potters' Fields of all four continents, the waves should rise and fall, and ebb and flow unceasingly; for here, millions of mixed shades and shadows, drowned dreams, somnambulisms, reveries; all that we call lives and souls, lie dreaming, dreaming, still; tossing like slumberers in their beds; the ever-rolling waves but made so by their restlessness.

Set against this image, the career of an Ahab cannot make any finally pre-emptive claim on our concern; and we might well say that in such a passage *Moby-Dick* turns away from the design of tragedy even while dramatically the action is preparing to simulate a tragic denouement. The story of Ahab, we feel, does not quite measure up to its own richest imaginative setting.

A last point. In *Moby-Dick* the various "worlds" which compose the book's setting (and so much of its substance) are not made to cohere philosophically, or allegorically. They need every lodgment in common fact that Melville can manage to give them. They satisfy us as they satisfy our sense of reality. Yet in the descriptive mass of the narrative, subtlety does appeal to subtlety, and Melville, as he builds up and inquires into the contexts that activate his impressive story, and in the process enlarges that very sense of reality, magnificently justifies the challenge he throws out to his reader: that "without imagination no man can follow another into these halls."

KEN KESEY

[McMurphy Prepares for Bed]†

He goes to getting ready for bed, pulling off his clothes. The shorts under his work pants are coal black satin covered with big white whales with red eyes. He grins when he sees I'm looking at the shorts. "From a co-ed at Oregon State, Chief, a Literary major." He snaps the elastic with his thumb. "She gave them to me because she said I was a symbol."

LOWRY NELSON, JR.

[Ahab as Gothic Hero]‡

It would be too simple to say that the "mystery tale" or the gothic novel arose in reaction to rationalism or empiricism or "science." In fact, it could be urged that it could arise only under their influence, since they create the right atmosphere for willing though temporary suspension of disbelief. *The Castle of Otranto* and *Vathek* are mainly titillations of sensuality, whether simple shudder or sadomasochism. They seem, strangely enough, still within the imaginative and moral scope of Voltaire and Dr. Johnson. With *The Monk* and with *Frankenstein* we enter upon new possibilities. *The Monk* is transitional, in that some attempt is made, despite the mere sensationalism, to delineate the complex psychological reactions to abnormal situations. But it is in *Frankenstein* that the mythic possibilities of the genre begin to emerge. Instead of a parade of horrors and marvels, the gothic novel has begun to suggest a mythology of the mind. Fantasy and exoticism, employed before as mere claptrap, become elemental and symbolic; decorative oddity becomes new myth. If these seem claims too large to be sus-

† From Ken Kesey, *One Flew Over the Cuckoo's Nest* (New York: The Viking Press, Inc., and London: Methuen & Co. Ltd., 1962), p. 81. Reprinted by permission of The Viking Press, Inc., and Laurence Pollinger, Ltd.

‡ From Lowry Nelson, Jr., "Night Thoughts on the Gothic Novel," *The Yale Review*, Vol. 52 (December, 1962), 236–57; the quotation is from 250–51; 253–56. The section on *Moby-Dick* quoted here does not indicate the full scope of the essay.

tained so narrowly, the examples given may be urged as symptomatic of larger changes. We must at least allow that "realism" in the nineteenth century was "realistic" in plumbing mythic or symbolic depths, that such writers as Dickens and Browning were caught betwixt and between (between, for instance, merry old England and the gloomy old jungles of the mind), and that the continuity from *The Scarlet Letter* to *The Rose Tattoo* is fairly obvious.

The gothic hero's most successful immediate heirs are Heathcliff and Ahab. If one were to rehearse briefly the similarities between *Wuthering Heights* and *Moby Dick* one might catalogue the following: they are both set in remote or isolated surroundings; both novels are narrated by quite ordinary people; good impulses in the heroes have been thwarted or affronted and both are bent on massive and calculating revenge; both heroes bear marks of difference (Heathcliff's darkness suggesting the cursed race of Ham, and Ahab's scar the mark of Cain): the origins of both heroes are relatively vague; both are guilt-haunted wanderers whose skills for good (their omnicompetence in practical matters) are diverted to the service of "evil." Besides, both novels are quite unchristian, perhaps for the time daringly so: the pagan Queequeg comes off much better than the Quakers and the "grand, ungodly, godlike" Ahab pursues his quest under a ceremonial covenant with the crew of his own diabolistic invention; in *Wuthering Heights* religion is almost savagely parodied in the figure of the bigoted Joseph and supernatural reality in the novel is quite unsanctioned by conventional Christianity. * * *

Ahab too is a distant cousin of Werther, the Ancient Mariner, and the Byronic figures. His neo-Faustian or neo-Promethean traits are clear enough. He belongs also in the company of guilt-haunted wanderers or reluctant scapegoats, bent on revenge or escape or expiation or simply knowledge. But he is neither reconciled, like Faust, nor confined by God, like Prometheus. The universe of *Moby Dick,* like that of *Wuthering Heights* and *Frankenstein,* is almost frighteningly without either God or devil; the God of conventional fiction, even a tyrant God, has effectually disappeared, just as the devil of earlier gothic diabolism has disappeared as the archfiend. In a universe without the presence of divine justice or retribution, notions of good and evil lose their simple polarity and generate shadowy and unexpected complexities. William Blake, to put it starkly, had called conventional good evil and conventional (in his sense of energetic, inventive, liberating) evil good. Again starkly, *Moby Dick* seems to ask what is good and what is evil, and to assert that the struggle is not between any external forces but rather within the turbulence of the mind. The solipsism or even narcissism of Ahab is quite evident: his wife and children receive only passing or even careless mention; he masterfully preserves his solitude though he is, to begin with, relatively isolated on the open seas; his monomaniacal interest is to pursue his savage and mysterious alter ego which, in costing him his leg, has consumed a part of him. Ocean, isolation, pursuit, monster: no wonder *Moby Dick* seems open to infinite exegesis.

It is at least arguable that the basic traits that make the novel so symbolically suggestive are those deriving eventually from the gothic novel: its simple unsocial setting, its omnicompetent hero, its embodiment of nether forces of the mind, and its "confusion" of conventional good and evil. Even of the claptrap of gothic fiction we discern significant though somewhat reinterpreted remnants. Ahab's single name seems to suggest, like Heathcliff's or Ambrosio's or, for that matter, like Frankenstein's monster's namelessness, a lonely and perhaps sinister independence from social ties. Ahab too is emblematically "stricken" and "blasted" in the scar described as "a slender rod-like mark, lividly white," which may well be the birthmark of a son of Cain. His gaze is withering and imperious, like Vathek's and Melmoth's, when he first confronts his crew. "And not only that, but moody stricken Ahab stood before them with a crucifixion in his face; in all the nameless regal overbearing dignity of some mighty woe." When his black entourage mysteriously appear from below deck, they seem mute supers from an old gothic drama, indeed, from *Vathek*. His mysterious communion with Fedallah, their leader, is a strangely tantalizing version of overt communion with the devil. But since the forces of good and evil must remain complexly intertwined for the success of Melville's sophisticated design, any silly diabolism would destroy the balance. In preserving such balance as he does, Melville interiorizes the struggle and makes it personal, not theological or social. Further gothic traits, such as the prophecies of "the old squaw Tistig" and "Elijah," add minor and less successful touches of the eerie.

Most important is Ahab's pursuit of the whale. It is both a search for significant evil and for his own identity. Only by knowing and conquering the whale can Ahab find peace with himself. It is supremely ironic and instructive that Ahab should perish at the moment of knowledge or, better, self-knowledge. That knowledge, as in the garden of Eden, was the knowledge of evil and good, since not to know evil is, in this world, not to know good. At the very end Ahab seems to pour forth his essence. He urges the billows to carry him on to Moby Dick, and cries out: "Towards thee I roll, thou all-destroying but unconquering whale." He commands Tashtego to nail his banner higher as the ship sinks. Ishmael, the only survivor, sees a "red arm and a hammer" above the waves in their hopeless office. At that moment a sky-hawk plummets down and is caught between the hammer and the spar: "so the bird of heaven, with archangelic shrieks, and his imperial beak thrust upwards, and his whole captive form folded in the flag of Ahab, went down with his ship, which, like Satan, would not sink to hell till she had dragged a living part of heaven with her, and helmeted herself with it." Though the resonances are almost too deafening, we may remember that Ahab's Biblical prototype was indeed regal or imperial Ahab of cursed memory. We also realize that the emblematic bird is an image of falling Lucifer which, in being bound up in the flag of the Pequod, is also richly symbolic of Ahab. Another great hero of defiance, beyond good and evil, has challenged supreme mystery to the death. But is the whale evil and God or Ahab good? That dilemma for exegetes is a heritage of the gothic novel.

In *Frankenstein, Moby Dick,* and *Wuthering Heights* there occurs a final moment of intimate confrontation. After Frankenstein lingeringly dies on Walton's ship, the mysteriously clairvoyant monster appears for the last time in a kind of anguish to know the end of his despairing hope. Walton enters the cabin where his dead friend lies. "Over him hung a form which I cannot find words to describe; gigantic in stature, yet uncouth and distorted in appearance. . . . When he heard the sound of my approach he ceased to utter exclamations of grief and horror and sprung towards the window." "That is also my victim!" the monster exclaims. "In his murder my crimes are consummated; the miserable series of my being is wound to its close! Oh, Frankenstein! generous and self-devoted [i.e., self-doomed] being! what does it avail that I now ask thee to pardon me? I, who irretrievably destroyed thee by destroying all thou lovedst. Alas! he is cold, he cannot answer me." As in the other two novels, the conclusion is a complex tangle of identities and motives of love and hate, of good and evil. In the last moments of *Moby Dick* Ahab is forcibly caught up by the line that suddenly coils round his neck, rips him from the boat, and binds him forever to the harpoon-studded whale. Whether Moby Dick is fatally "stricken" or simply struck remains an ambiguity of Melville's archaizing diction. At the end of *Wuthering Heights* we see, through the eyes of Lockwood, the final "union" of Cathy and Heathcliff: on his last visit Lockwood lingered around their graves "and wondered how anyone could ever imagine unquiet slumbers, for the sleepers in that quiet earth." But we know enough about the protagonists and their interpreter to take Emily Brontë's masterful conclusion at its fullest ironic ambiguity. The struggle is inconclusive and the suggestion that, despite Lockwood, it continues beyond the grave invokes the timelessness and the implacability of its mental model in the subconscious where there is no time or respite. In all three novels good and evil become in the end emblematically inseparable: there is great good and great evil, but which is really which?

EDWIN S. SHNEIDMAN

[An Example of an Equivocal Death]†

* * *

It might be most appropriate to conclude this chapter by presenting, by way of example, some excerpts from a singularly interesting case.[1] The study I have chosen is taken from a uniquely comprehensive study of death and lives by Herman Melville. It is the case of the equivocal death—was it accident, suicide, or what?—of Melville's tortured, obsessively possessed, fury-driven, cetusized man: Captain Ahab of the "Pequod."[2]

The procedure called the "psychological autopsy" (used at the Suicide Prevention Center) involves obtaining psychological data about the behaviors and statements of the deceased in the days before his death, from which information an extrapolation of intention is made over the moments of, and the moments directly preceding, his cessation. In the case of Captain Ahab, I shall proceed as though I were preparing a report for an imaginary Nantucket coroner, including some sort of recommendation as to what labelings would be the most appropriate on his imaginary death certificate. The focus will be an attempt to come to some kind of reso-

† From Edwin S. Shneidman, "Orientations toward Death," in *The Study of Lives*, ed. Robert W. White (New York: Atherton Press, 1963), pp. 221–27. Reprinted by permission of the publisher, Atherton Press, Inc.

1. In a new appendix to a reprinting of this essay in the *International Journal of Psychiatry*, Vol. 2 (March, 1966), 167–220, Shneidman says of its composition: "it was written in 1961–1962, the year of the greatest intellectual excitement of my life, when I was privileged to be a U. S. Public Health Service Special Research Fellow at Harvard University, studying with that incomparable man, Professor Henry A. Murray" [*Editors' note*].

2. The reader is referred to Henry A. Murray's masterful psychological studies of Melville: "In Nomine Diaboli," in *Moby-Dick Centennial Essays* (Dallas: Southern Methodist University Press, (1953), pp. 3–29, originally published in *New England Quarterly*, XXIV (1951), 435–452; Milton R. Stern, ed., *Discussions of Moby Dick* (Boston: D. C. Heath and Company, 1960), pp. 25–34; and Richard Chase, ed., *Melville:* "A Collection of Critical Essays" (Englewood Cliffs, N.J.: Prentice-Hall, Inc., 1962), pp. 62–74; and his "introduction" to Melville's *Pierre, or The Ambiguities* (New York: Hendricks House, 1949), pp. xiii–ciii.

lution concerning Ahab's intention types and Psyde categories. But first, some facts: specifically how did the end of his life occur?

Facts

For Ahab's death, we have the following account (from Chapter 135) of his last actions: "The harpoon was darted; the stricken whale flew forward; with igniting velocity the line ran through the groove;—ran foul. Ahab stooped to clear it; he did clear it; but the flying turn caught him round the neck, and noiselessly as Turkish mutes bowstring their victim, he was shot out of the boat, ere the crew knew he was gone. . . ." On first thought, it might sound as though Ahab's death were pure accident, an unintentioned death, the cessation of a Psydepostponer; but let us see where our second thoughts lead us. Perhaps there is more.

Background

It is possible to view *Moby Dick* as a great, sonorous Mahlerlike symphony— *Das Lied von der See*—not primarily about the joy of life nor the pessimism engendered by a crushing fate, but rather as a dramatic and poetic explication of the psychodynamics of death. And, within the context of this thought, is it not possible that Moby Dick, the great *white* whale, represents the punishment of death itself? In Chapter 28, when Ahab makes his first appearance on the "Pequod" at sea, the word "white" is used three times in one paragraph to describe Ahab: a head-to-toe scar on Ahab's body, "lividly whitish"; an allusion to a "white sailor," in the context of Captain Ahab's being laid out for burial; and "the barbaric white leg upon which he partly stood." Everywhere, reference to the pallor of death; and if there is still any question, the case of "white death" is made explicit in the discussion of the whiteness of the whale (Chapter 42), in which we are told: "It cannot well be doubted, that the one visible quality in the aspect of the dead which most appals the gazer, is the marble pallor lingering there; as if indeed that pallor were as much the badge of consternation in the other world, as of mortal trepidation here. And from that pallor of the dead, we borrow the expressive hue of the shroud in which we wrap them. Nor even in our superstitions do we fail to throw the same snowy mantle round our phantoms; all ghosts rising in a milk-white fog—Yea, while these terrors seize us, let us add that even the king of terrors, when personified by the evangelist, rides on his pallid horse."

And if the great white whale is death, then is not the sea itself the vessel of death? Melville sets this tone for his entire heroic narrative in his stunning opening passage:

> Call me Ishmael. Some years ago—never mind how long precisely—having little or no money in my purse, and nothing particular to interest me on shore, I thought I would sail about a little and see the watery part of the world. It is a way I have of driving off the spleen, and regulating the circulation. Whenever I find myself growing grim about the mouth; whenever it is a damp, drizzly November in my soul; whenever I find myself involuntarily pausing before coffin warehouses, and bringing up the rear of every funeral I meet; and especially whenever my hypos get such an upper hand of me, that it requires a strong moral principle to prevent me from deliberately stepping into the street, and methodically knocking people's hats off—then, I account it high time to get to sea as soon as I can. This is my substitute for pistol and ball. With a philosophical flourish Cato throws himself upon his sword; I quietly take to the ship. . . .

And again, much later, in the description of the blacksmith (Chapter 112), we read:

> Death seems the only desirable sequel for a career like this; but Death is only a launching into the region of the strange Untried; it is but the first salutation to the possibilities of the immense Remote, the Wild, the Watery, the Unshored; therefore, to the death-longing eyes of such men, who still have left in them some interior compunctions against suicide, does the all-contributed and all-receptive ocean alluringly spread forth his whole plain of unimaginable, taking terrors, and wonderful, new-life adventures; and from the hearts of infinite Pacifics, the thousand mermaids sing to them—"Come hither, broken-hearted; here is another life without the guilt of intermediate death; here are wonders supernatural, without dying for them. Come hither! bury thyself in a life which, to your now equally abhorred and abhorring, landed world, is more oblivious than death. Come hither! put up *thy* grave-stone, too, within the churchyard, and come hither, till we marry thee!"

If any case is to be made for subintention—Psyde-chancing, Psyde-hastening, Psyde-capitulating, Psyde-experimenting behavior patterns—then, at the least, two further background issues need to be involved: the concept of unconscious motivation and the concept of ambivalence. Ahab's chronicler would not have, in principle, resisted the concept of subintention, on the grounds of its involving unconscious motivation, for (in Chapter 41) he says:

> Such a crew, so officered, seemed specially picked and packed by some infernal fatality to help him to his monomaniac

> revenge. How it was that they so aboundingly responded to the old man's ire—by what evil magic their souls were possessed, that at times his hate seemed almost theirs; the White Whale as much their insufferable foe as his; how all this came to be—what the White Whale was to them, or how to their unconscious understandings, also, in some dim, unsuspected way, he might have seemed the gliding great demon of the seas of life—all this to explain, would be to dive deeper than Ishmael can go. The subterranean miner that works in us all, how can one tell whither leads his shaft by the ever shifting, muffled sound of his pick?

That which is most sharply and most accurately characteristic of the subintentioned person—namely, the ubiquitous ambivalence, the pervasive psychological coexistence of logical incompatibles—is seen vividly in the following internal dialogue of life and death, of flesh and fixture, (as reported in Chapter 51) within Ahab:

> Walking the deck with quick, side-lunging strides, Ahab commanded the t'gallant sails and royals to be set, and every stunsail spread. The best man in the ship must take the helm. Then, with every mast-head manned, the piled-up craft rolled down before the wind. The strange, upheaving, lifting tendency of the taff-rail breeze filling the hollows of so many sails, made the buoyant, hovering deck to feel like air beneath the feet; while still she rushed along, as it two antagonistic influences were struggling in her—one to mount directly to heaven, the other to drive yawingly to some horizontal goal. And had you watched Ahab's face that night, you would have thought that in him also two different things were warring. While his one live leg made lively echoes along the deck, every stroke of his dead limb sounded like a coffin-tap. On life and death this old man walked.

And within Ahab, toward Moby Dick, there were deep ambiguities.

Method

In any psychological autopsy it is important to examine the method or the instrument of death and, especially, the victim's understandings and subjective estimations of its lethal works. Ahab was garroted by a free-swinging whale-line. We are warned in Chapter 60) that "... the least tangle or kink in the coiling would, in running out, infallibly take somebody's arm, leg, or entire body off ..."; we are forewarned "... of this man or that man being taken out of the boat by the line, and lost"; and we are warned again, "All men live enveloped in whale-lines. All are born with halters round their necks; but it is only when caught in the swift, sudden turn of death, that mortals realize the silent, subtle, ever-present perils of life." Ahab knew all this; nor was he a careless, accident-prone man. The apothecary knows his deadly drugs; the sportsman knows the danger of his weapons; the whaler captain—that very whaler captain who, instead of remaining on his quarter-deck, jumped to "the active perils of the chase" in a whale-boat manned by his "smuggled on board" crew—ought to know his whale-lines.

Questions

Having described the precise circumstances of Ahab's death, and having mentioned some background issues deemed to be relevant, I would now pose some questions concerning his demise: Was Ahab's death more than simple accident? Was there more intention than un-intention? Was Ahab's orientation in relation to death entirely that of Psyde-postponing? Are there discernible subsurface psychological currents that can be fathomed and charted, and is there related information that can be dredged and brought to the surface? Specifically, can Ahab's death be described as victim-precipitated homicide; that is, is this an instance in which the victim stands up to subjectively calculated overwhelming odds, inviting destruction by the other? Let us see.

Extracts

Ahab led a fairly well-documented existence, especially insofar as the dark side of his life was concerned. *Moby Dick* abounds with references to various funereal topics: sleep, coffins, burials, soul, life-after-death, suicide, cemeteries, death, and rebirth.

But—as in a psychological autopsy—we are primarily interested in interview data from everyone who had known the deceased, especially in what our informants can tell us about Ahab's personality, insofar as his orientations toward death are known. It should be recognized that in some important ways Captain Ahab's psychological autopsy will be a truncated and atypical one, especially with respect to the range of informants; there is no information from spouse, parents, progeny, siblings, collaterals, neighbors; there are only mates, some of the more articulate shipboard subordinates, captains of ships met at sea, and, with terrifying biblical certitude, Elijah.

As we know, all the possible informants, listed below, save Ishmael, perished with Captain Ahab and are technically not available for interview. Only Ishmael's observations are direct; all else is secondhand through Ishmael, colored by Ishmael, and perhaps with no more veridicality than Plato's reports of Socrates. We shall have to trust Ishmael to be an accurate and perceptive reporter.

Our primary informant, Ishmael, reflected about Captain Ahab in twenty-five separate chapters (specifically chapters 16, 22, 27, 28, 30, 33, 34, 36, 41, 44, 46, 50, 51, 52, 73, 100, 106, 115, 116, 123, 126, 128, 130, 132, and 133). Starbuck, the chief mate of the "Pequod," is next: there are nine separate encounters with, or reports about, his captain (in chapters 36, 38, 51, 118, 119, 123, 132, 134, and 135). Next is Stubb, the second mate, with seven separate anecdotes (to be found in chapters 28, 31, 36, 73, 121, 134, and 135). All the others are represented by one or two bits of information apiece: Elijah (in chapters 19 and 21); Gabriel of the "Jeroboam" (Chapter 71); Bunger, the ship's surgeon of the "Samuel Enderby" (100); the blacksmith (113); the Captain of the "Bachelor" (115); Flask, the third mate (121); the Manxman (125); and the carpenter (127).

Knowing that the limitations of space simply do not permit me to document the essence of each informant's remarks, either with appropriate quotations or abbreviated résumés, how can I summarize all the data? Perhaps my best course would be to concentrate on the general features that one would look for in any psychological autopsy. Thus, the information distilled from interviews with Ishmael, Starbuck, Stubb, and all the others, might, in a dialogue of questions and answers, take the following form.

(1) Hidden psychosis? Not at the beginning of the voyage, but certainly at the end (and indeed from Chapter 36 on—"the chick that's in him picks the shell. 'Twill soon be out."), the madness in Ahab was blatant, open, known. His monomania was the official creed of his ship. Along with his other symptoms, his psychiatric syndrome was crowned with a paranoid fixation. But what matters in Ahab is not so much the bizarrely shaped psychological iceberg which many saw above the surface, but rather the hugeness of the gyroscopically immovable subsurface mass of other-destruction and self-destruction. We know the poems about fire and ice. Ahab is a torrid, burning, fiery iceberg. (2) Disguised depression? Ahab was openly morbid and downcast. His was not exactly psychotic depression, nor can we call it reactive depression for it transcended the bounds of that definition. Perhaps best it might be called a "character depression," in that it infused his brain like the let-go blood from a series of small strokes in the hemisphere. (3) Talk of death? The morbid talk of death and killing runs through reports about Ahab like an *idée fixe*. (4) Previous suicide attempts? None is reported. (5) Disposition of belongings. Ahab, after forty solitary years at sea, had little in the way of self-possessions or interpersonal belongings. His wife, he said, was already a widow; his interest in the possible profits from the voyage was nil; his withdrawal from meaningful material possessions (and his loss of joy with

them) is perhaps best indicated by his flinging his "still lighted pipe into the sea" and dashing his quadrant to the deck—both rash acts for a sailor-captain.

In Ahab's conscious mind, he wanted to kill—but have we not said that self-destruction can be other-destruction in the 180th degree? Figuratively speaking, the barb of the harpoon was pointed toward him; his brain thought a thrust, but his arm executed a retroflex. Was his death "accident"? If he had survived his psychodynamically freighted voyage and had returned unharmed to Nantucket's pier, *that* would have been true accident. Men can die for nothing—most men do; but some few big-jointed men can give their lives for an internalized something: Ahab would not have missed this opportunity for the world.

What further evidence can be cited bearing on the issue of subintentioned cessation? With his three harpooners before him, with their harpoons turned up like goblets, Ahab (in Chapter 36) commands them, in this maritime immolation scene, as follows: " 'Drink, ye harpooneers! drink and swear, ye men that man the deathful whaleboat's bow—Death to Moby Dick! God hunt us all, if we do not hunt Moby Dick to his death!' " Kill or be killed; punish or be retributed; murder or suicide—how the two are intertwined.

In Ahab's case, we have no suicide note or other holograph of death, but, *mirabile dictu,* we do have (in Chapter 135) Ahab's last thoughts:

> I turn my body from the sun. . . . Oh, lonely death on lonely life! Oh, now I feel my topmost grief. Ho, ho! from all your furthest bounds, pour ye now in, ye bold billows of my whole foregone life, and top this one piled comber of my death! Towards thee I roll, thou all-destroying but unconquering whale; to the last I grapple with thee; from hell's heart I stab at thee; for hate's sake I spit my last breath at thee. Sink all coffins and all hearses to one common pool! and since neither can be mine, let me now tow to pieces, while still chasing thee, though tied to thee, thou damned whale! *Thus,* I give up my spear!

What is to be particularly noted in this is the prescience of Ahab. "I spit my last breath at thee," he says. How does he know that it is to be his *last* breath? Where are the sources of his premonitions? What are the contents of his subintentions? Does this not remind us of Radney, the chief mate of the "Town-Ho" (Chapter 54) who behaved as if he "sought to run more than half way to meet his doom"? Is this not exactly what the tantalizer says to his "all-destroying but unconquering" executioner in cases of victim-precipitated homicide?

Recommendation

It is suggested that Captain Ahab's demise was goal-seeking behavior that made obsessed life *or* subintentioned death relatively unimportant to him, compared with the great press for the discharge of his monomania of hate. He dared, and made, that murderous death-white whale kill him. He could not rest until he was so taken. (Did Satan *provoke* God into banishing him?) Ahab invited cessation by the risks that he ran; he was a Psyde-chancer. He permitted suicide. Consider Ahab's psychological position: what could he have done, to what purpose would any further voyages have been, if he *had* killed the symbol of his search? It was, from Ahab's point of view, the time; and in his unconscious wish, it was the "appropriate death." *In nomine ceti albini!*

ALAN HEIMERT

Moby-Dick and American Political Symbolism†

In the process of canonizing Herman Melville as a major American writer, critics have generally failed to touch on the specific political context of his works. Yet *Moby-Dick* was produced in the very months of one of America's profoundest political crises: the controversy surrounding the "Compromise of 1850." Recently Charles H. Foster re-examined *Moby-Dick* in terms of one aspect of this crisis. To Foster, Melville's recorded responses to the Fugitive Slave Law suggest that *Moby-Dick* unfolded, and may be read on one level, as "a fable of democratic protest."[1] But horror over slavery was but one ingredient—albeit the most familiar to students of literature—in an excitement which, in 1850, comprehended the nation's entire political life. * * *

In the *Pequod* Melville created a ship strikingly similar to the vessels which rode the oratorical seas of 1850. It sails under a red flag, and its crew—in all its "democratic dignity"—comprises a "deputation from all the isles of the earth." But the *Pequod* is clearly reminiscent of Longfellow's *Union;* it is put together of "all contrasting things" from the three sections of the United States: "oak and maple, and pine wood; iron, and pitch, and hemp." And the *Pequod* is manned (as we are reminded at each crucial moment

† From Alan Heimert, "*Moby-Dick* and American Political Symbolism," *American Quarterly,* Vol. 15 (Winter, 1963), 498–534; the quotation is from 498, 501–2, 506, 508–10, 513, 517–19, 522, 526–27, 528–29, 529–31, 532–34. Reprinted by permission of the author and the publisher, the University of Pennsylvania.

1. Charles H. Foster, "Something in Emblems: A Reinterpretation of *Moby-Dick,*" *New England Quarterly,* XXXIV (March 1961), 35.

in its career) by *thirty* isolatoes—all, Melville remarks, "federated along one keel."

The *Pequod*'s mates, moreover, are "every one of them Americans; a Nantucketer, a Vineyarder, a Cape man." But of the three only one seems truly a New Englander or even a Northerner in terms either of the sectional iconography of the day or of Melville's own. Starbuck, who hails from the "prudent isle" of Nantucket and is ever-loyal to the commercial code of that island's "calculating people," is recognizably a Yankee. But good-humored Stubb seems a representative of that "essentially Western" spirit which Melville would attribute to the "convivial" frontiersman, Ethan Allen. Stubb's speech is not in the Cape Cod idiom; it is studded with references to "broad-footed farmers" and images and chickens and milldams. For Stubb, harpooning a whale is "July's immortal Fourth," on which he yearns for "old Orleans whiskey, or old Ohio, or unspeakable Monongahela"—not the rum associated with the genuine Yankee. The "Vineyarder," the "very pugnacious" Flask, seems likewise closely related to that "fiery and intractable race" which Melville discovered in the south of Vivenza. Flask, who speaks of his "Martha's Vineyard plantation," reacts to whales in terms of the southern *code duello:*

> He seemed to think that the great Leviathans had personally and hereditarily affronted him; and therefore it was a sort of point of honor with him, to destroy them whenever encountered.

The harpooneers, finally, who are so "generously" supply "the muscles" for the "native American" mates, are representatives of the three races on which each of the American sections, it might be said, had built its prosperity in the early nineteenth century. Stubb's squire is an Indian; Starbuck's comes from the Pacific islands. And Flask, perched precariously on Daggoo's shoulders, seems, like the southern economy itself, sustained only by the strength of the "imperial negro." * * *

That Melville associated the quest of the "sublime" White Whale with imperial aspirations is most strongly suggested by the central three "gams" of *Moby-Dick*. The German captain of the *Jungfrau* "evinced his complete ignorance of the White Whale," and that of the *Bouton-de-Rose* claims never to have heard of Moby-Dick. (But the Frenchman is gulled of one "Fast-Fish," as his nation of Louisiana, by the fast-talking Stubb.) The commander of the *Samuel Enderby* has met the White Whale, but once bested, will not make another effort to capture him. The American Whigs' contentment in the secure course of non-empire, moreover, is reflected in the gam with the *Bachelor*, whose captain simply refuses to allow that Moby-Dick exists. He stuffs his hands into his pockets "in self-complacent testimony to his entire satisfaction," and he and his crew enjoy a surfeit of plenty. Aboard the *Pequod,* the prudent Starbuck, drearily lecturing Ahab of the "owners," would chart a similarly politic course. But here, of course, the White Whale—his "quietude but the vesture of tornadoes"—works his infallible and fatal fascination. * * *

Echoes not only of Parker, but of Phillips, Garrison, and other opponents of the Fugitive Slave Law, in the "lofty rhetoric" of Father Mapple have suggested to Charles H. Foster that *Moby-Dick* carries a brief in behalf of the "higher law." Foster reads Mapple's sermon as Melville's judgment on his father-in-law, Judge Shaw, who delivered the first opinion returning a fugitive from the free soil of Massachusetts, and inevitably, as a condemnation of Webster.[2] It may well be that *Moby-Dick* does reflect Melville's "sense of social crisis consequent upon the remanding of Thomas Sims." But it is difficult to follow Foster in his arguments that Ahab is a caricature of Webster and Mapple's sermon a judgment on Ahab.[3]

True it is that Webster did feel something of the woe promised by Father Mapple to "him who seeks to pour oil upon the waters when God has brewed them into a gale." (And Parker, we may surmise, experienced that "inward delight," which comes, in Mapple's words, to him "who gives no quarter in the truth, and kills, burns, and destroys all sin though he pluck it out from under the robes of Senators and Judges.") Yet it is far from easy to see the historical Webster shadowed forth in the pridefully rebellious Ahab of Melville's romance. Webster—at least in the decades after his participation in the secession-prone Rockingham Convention—had said or done little to challenge an establishment for which, in 1850, he stood as advocate. Seen in the light of political fact and iconography, the career of Ahab would seem to parallel, not the compromising tolerance of Daniel Webster, but a defiance attributed, in the year Melville wrote *Moby-Dick,* only to the outright advocates of slavery. Expansionism itself had been viewed as a launching of the national ship without "anchor, compass or chart," but it was the proslavery argument, as developed in the 1840s by an unyielding Calhoun, that struck Northerners as the ultimate dashing of the nation's heavenly quadrant—a substitution of prideful man's personal "compass" for the "unerring guide" given him by God.[4] The neutral, even devious Webster who inspired Whittier's "Ichabod"

2. Foster, pp. 17–18.
3. *Ibid.,* pp. 21, 25–26.
4. *Congressional Globe, Appendix,* 29th Congress, 2nd Session, 242 (hereafter the form *CG–A,* 29–2, 242 will be used—or *CG* if the citation is not to the *Appendix*); William H. Marsh, *God's Law Supreme. A Sermon . . . Delivered at Village Corners, Woodstock, Conn., . . . Nov. 28, 1850* (Worcester, 1850), p. 21.

seems an unlikely model for an Ahab who in "fatal pride" blasphemously *inverts* the *Pequod*'s compass.

Much of Mapple's rhetoric, moreover, seems inapplicable to Ahab, who is prepared to breast the elements and even defy them; he is not disposed to calm the elements but like Lear bids the hurricanoes crack. That Mapple seems to echo Parker does not make of Ahab's career "an antislavery fable,"[5] for Mapple does not speak of the *Pequod*'s captain: surely Melville's Ahab is no cowardly, slouching Jonah. He does not ignore his God but quarrels with Him; in action, Ahab gives no more quarter than Mapple's estimable Hebrew prophets. The sermon, if it have any clear object whatever, seems rather addressed to prudent men like Starbuck—and, presumably, to such souls as Ishmael, so sensitive to the ironies and ambiguities of human conduct as to question any easy moral absolute. * * *

Another of the *Pequod's* passengers is Pip, the "Alabama Boy" whose plight is made more pathetic by his being somehow originally from Connecticut. His presence mocks the *Pequod*'s entire venture, for Pip's words are a tragic parody of a fugitive-slave handbill. "One hundred pounds of clay reward for Pip; five feet high—looks cowardly—quickest known by that." He is told by the unconcerned Stubb never to jump again, since "A whale would sell for thirty times what you would, Pip, in Alabama." To which remark Melville appends a general observation: "though man loved his fellow, yet man is a money-making animal." In 1850 not only the Kentuckian Henry Clay, but many "money-making" Northerners were ready to blink the immorality of slavery and deny freedom to the fugitive. Quite rightly, therefore, Foster likens the abandonment of Pip to the Sims decision. But again he does not show how such an interpretation can be made consistent with his thesis that Ahab is Shaw-Webster. For in *Moby-Dick*, Pip is succored by Ahab, who far from agreeing with those "oblivious of suffering man," issues a ringing indictment of northern hypocrisy and indifference to the Negro's welfare: "Ye did beget this luckless child, and have abandoned him, ye creative libertines!" Ahab's cry—"There can be no hearts above the snow-line"—introduces no Websterian apologia, surely, but rather an elevated version of the defense of southern charity that Melville in *Mardi* had put in the mouth of Calhoun. * * *

Of all Americans, Calhoun impressed his contemporaries as being the most "pained with fearful apprehension, doubt, distrust, dismay." His anxieties, Calhoun insisted, were not irrational, but the result of "scientific" study. In the "anonymous" campaign biography of 1843 he praised himself for possessing "the highest and rarest faculty of a statesman," an analytical method that gave

5. Foster, p. 21.

him "an insight into futurity far beyond the usual range of human vision." This, Calhoun explained, "is the faculty of considering circumstances in their combinations, and of determining their relative power in propelling events." In the late 1840s Calhoun methodically studied—like Melville's Ahab tracing the courses of sperm whales—the combinations of political events,—or "junctures," as Calhoun preferred to style them. In 1850 he decided that the crucial "juncture" had been reached; believing that "to temporize, is but to increase the evil," Calhoun issued a final defiant challenge to the Union.[6]

It is of course impossible to know precisely how the Union's outrageous strength presented itself to Calhoun's mind as he prepared his last address. Just as Ahab, as the end of his quest neared, took "speechless refuge, as it were, among the marble senate of the dead," so too did Calhoun, consumed with fatal illness, compose in solitude the speech he would be too weak to read on the fourth of March. But by directing his most savage rhetorical lances against sentimentalized versions of the Constitution, the Union and the Founding Fathers, Calhoun gives the impression that he took the agent, at least, of the North's power to be no abolitionist, but rather Daniel Webster. When, on the third day, Webster rose to answer him, Calhoun knew he had rightly gauged his nemesis.

For two decades, and certainly since his first brow-to-brow confrontation with Calhoun during the Nullification Crisis, Webster had been celebrated as the nonpareil embodiment of the "national idea." He was never to write the volume of Constitutional commentary that Unionists eagerly awaited. Nevertheless, Webster's reputation as Defender of the Union was secure—sustained as it was by historical orations that made Webster seem as American as "the rocks of our hills," the very "impersonation" of the strength and unity of the Republic. Emerson believed the American people looked on Webster "as the representative of the American Continent." On the seventh of March, 1850, Webster strove to live up to his public image by posing, in his exordium, as one whose comprehension was "as broad as the country for which we act." He closed his appeal by explicating the figure on the buckler of Achilles as foretelling a United States washed by the "two great seas of the world." To many this peroration seemed the epitome and culmination of Webster's career.[7] Yet ironically, Webster in

6. *CG*, 31–1, 542; James E. Cabot, *A Memoir of Ralph Waldo Emerson* (2 vols.; Cambridge, 1887), Appendix F, II, 751; *CG-A*, 29–2, 211; *CG-A*, 29–1, 430; [John C. Calhoun], *Life of John C. Calhoun* . . . (New York, 1843), pp. 69–70; *CG*, 31–1, 622.

7. Rufus W. Griswold, *The Prose Writers of America* . . . (Philadelphia, 1847), p. 21; Rufus Choate, in *The Law Reporter*, XV (December 1852), pp. 465–66; Emerson, "The Fugitive Slave Law," in *Miscellanies (The Complete Works of Ralph Waldo Emerson*, Centenary Ed., Boston [1832], XI, 221; Bowen, "The Action of Congress," *North American Review*, LXXI, 265–66; *CG*, 31–1, 476, 483; "John Randolph," *New York Quarterly*, II (July 1853), 221.

1850 stood before the world the personification of a continental empire that a venturesome Democracy had captured for America.

In the complex contemporary image of Webster, two qualities dominated: "colossal power" and equally massive intellect. It was said of him, as "of the Pyramids, that one can only appreciate their full size, when standing at the base." Webster was likened, in his monumental majesty, to the rock cliffs of the New England shore and to his own "granite hills of New Hampshire," especially Monadnock. Unassailable though Webster seemed, it was the actual exercise of his "vast strength" that inspired in Frances Bowen a "feeling of sublimity." Webster's strength seemed to E. P. Whipple "half-leaning on his own right arm," and Horace Binney Wallace (in an essay which was at once a Unionist document and a Whig literary manifesto) declared that Webster's mind, even when "enraged, is never disturbed." Though his gnarled muscles "attest the utmost strain, his countenance remains placid, serene, and undisturbed." As an orator Webster employed few rhetorical flourishes; his most remarkable effects were achieved wordlessly—as when, in 1843, saluting the Bunker Hill Monument, rising above him in "silent, but awful utterance," Webster paused, stood himself in stony silence, and drew "long and loud applause." Nor did he engage in "violent contortions, or unnatural efforts"; in debate Webster seemed always "collected, calm and perfectly at ease." Unless, that is, he felt personally challenged, in which case his words poured forth in a thunderous torrent, his gestures became "perpetual and violent," and his whole manner "that of a different man," oppressive and overpowering. His latent capacities known, Webster moved through the Senate with "the stately air of irresistible power." His repose—not "of inanition or irresolution," but "of magnificent energy"—was an emblem of the Republic itself, its power seldom used but ever in reserve.[8] * * *

The Ishmael of *Moby-Dick*, it should be noted, was appalled by the Whale's "spiritual whiteness"—not by the malignant power that aroused "Ahab's quenchless feud." Possibly Webster himself called up a similar "peculiar apparition" to Melville's soul, but it was not the Senator's moral ambivalence, we may be sure, that

8. "Daniel Webster's Real Glory," in *The Life and Writings of George Washington Doane* (4 vols.; New York, 1861), IV, 464; Edward Everett, "The Death of Daniel Webster," *Orations and Speeches on Various Occasions*, (4 vols.; Boston, 1889), III, 159; Bowen, "The Works of Daniel Webster," *North American Review*, LXXV (July 1852), 92; Whipple, "Daniel Webster as an Author," *North American Review*, LIX (July 1844), 58; Wallace, "The Prose Writers of America," *Southern Literary Messenger*, XVI (April 1850), 235; Samuel M. Smucker, *The Life, Speeches, and Memorials of Daniel Webster* . . . (Boston, 1859), p. 472; "The Works of Daniel Webster," *Brownson's Quarterly Review*, VI (July 1852), 368; "The Completion of the Bunker Hill Monument," *The Works of Daniel Webster* (4th ed., 6 vols., Boston, 1853), I, 86; Edward Everett, in *Works of Webster*, I, 82; E. L. Magoon, *Living Orators in America* (New York, 1849), p. 57. John Ware, *Memoir of the Life of Henry Ware Jr.* (2 vols., Boston, 1846), I, 144.

troubled John C. Calhoun when he in 1850 confronted the Union's "Great Embodiment." For Calhoun, though not such a genius as Webster, was nevertheless also a genius according to the definitions of his age. To many Americans, then as now, Calhoun's careful analyses seemed, by comparison to Webster's ponderous arguments, "the purer thought." On the floor of the Senate Webster appeared to "crush" most opponents under a massive fist, but Calhoun's incisive mind worked as a "very Damascus blade," keen and finely tempered. While Webster overwhelmed like "serried infantry," an embattled Calhoun hurled "darts." Calhoun's thoughts, observed his fellow-Senator from South Carolina, "leaped from his mind, like arrows from a well-drawn bow."[9]

However commentators might metaphorically arm Calhoun, his mind was never fully understood in his day, and especially not by Northerners. Yankees admired Calhoun's "Spartan model" and his "severe regime," but they could not understand why a Southerner, of all people, should be so "rigidly intellectual" and show so little "imagination or fancy." Like Melville's Ahab, Calhoun seemed to lack the "low, enjoying power" and to experience "moments of softness" only when with or thinking of his family. Such an emotionless "intellectual constitution" could be explained, it appeared, only by Calhoun's education at Yale. (Calhoun too, had "been in colleges, as well as 'mong the cannibals.") Well might Calhoun's mind be blamed on Timothy Dwight, or compared to that of Jonathan Edwards; for Calhoun seemed in his time the last avatar of numbing eighteenth-century "Calvinistic logic." Like Ahab—whose ideal man had "no heart at all" and "about a quarter of an acre of fine brains"—Calhoun was dedicated to the proposition that "invincible mind" made "man the lord of the world."[10] * * *

Of the *Pequod*'s crew, but one member is sufficiently detached to perceive the ambiguities inherent in the "ungodly, godlike" Ahab's feud with a Whale of "ghastly whiteness." Though Ishmael is temporarily deprived of his free will, he is permitted (in part by his ability to sense the comic overtones in the high tragedy of Ahab's career) to resume his role as observer of events. He eventually escapes the *Pequod's* destruction and alone lives to tell its story. From Ishmael's position on the "margin of the scene" may

9. Smucker, *Life of Webster*, pp. 86, 472; Judge Hathaway, "*Proceedings in the Court of Common Pleas on the Death of Daniel Webster,*" *The Law Reporter*, XV (December 1852), 531; John S. Jenkins, *The Life of John Caldwell Calhoun* (Auburn, New York, 1850), p. 378; Senator Butler, quoted in Thomas Hart Benton, *Thirty Years' View* ... (2 vols.; New York, 1856), II, 748.

10. "Works of American Statesmen," *Putnam's*, I, 648; Griswold, *Prose Writers*, p. 173; Magoon, *Living Orators*, p. 227; James Parton, "John C. Calhoun," *North American Review*, CI (October 1865), 386; "Speech ... delivered in the House of Representatives, June 24th, 1812," *The Works of John C. Calhoun* (6 vols.; New York, 1854–57), II, 30.

be gathered hints of Melville's own perspective on the political struggles of 1850. Ishmael's rescue was itself clearly previsioned in the oratorical themes of the Compromise year. "I am looking out for no fragment upon which to float away from the wreck," intoned Webster in his exordium on March 7, "but for the good of the whole." In this image, endlessly repeated and imaginatively embroidered by speakers of many persuasions, were embodied the nation's fears of beholding the broken and dishonored fragments of a once glorious Union.[11] But the shipwreck in *Moby-Dick*, followed as it is by Ishmael's salvation, emerges as a symbol of hope to the faithful disciples of democracy. * * *

Ishmael, who, buoyed by the coffin, floats away from the wreck, had seen Queequeg as "George Washington cannibalistically developed." Such a Washington expressed the convictions of the Democracy, who had long struggled to divest the Revolutionary general of the civilized veneer laid on him by Whig eulogists. Robert Rantoul, for one, insisted that a realistic portrait of Washington would repeat "the character of Jackson."[12] In *Israel Potter*, where Melville desecrated the Bunker Hill Monument in order to protest the Whigs' sentimental and genteel perversions of the American past, he also cast his admiring gaze, not on the diplomatic and polished Franklin, but on that "barbarian in broadcloth," John Paul Jones. And thus in *Moby-Dick* Ishmael, by attaching himself to an uncivilized Queequeg, proclaims his ties to the primitive and "natural" democracy which Melville celebrates in his rousing hymn to the "great democratic God" who raised Andrew Jackson higher than a kingly throne.

Party lines are drawn in the very first chapter of *Moby-Dick*, where the "Whaling Voyage of One Ishmael" is juxtaposed with a "Grand Contested Election for the Presidency of the United States." The conjecture quickly takes on added significance as Ishmael steps up, aboard the *Pequod*, to a "strange sort of tent, or rather wigwam," tufted like the head of a sachem. This peculiar structure resembles nothing so much as the famous symbol of Tammany, and Ishmael is quickly located within the Democratic Party by his derisive reference to Bildad as "an incorrigible old hunks." The term could have meant in 1850—particularly to one of Melville's background—only the conservative Democrats, the "Hunkers" to whom profit was more important than principle.[13] If this episode is, as one suspects, Melville's invitation to approach *Moby-Dick* as something of a political "fable," then Ishmael's point of view has been clearly identified with the "Barnburners," or "Free-

11. *CG*, 31–1, 476; *CG-A*, 31–1, 382.
12. Robert Rantoul Jr., "Oration at Scituate" (July 4, 1838), in *Memoirs, Speeches and Writings* . . . (Boston, 1854), p. 274.
13. *A Dictionary of Americanisms on Historical Principles*, ed. Mitford M. Mathews (Chicago, 1956), p. 850.

Soilers," as their opposition to the extension of slavery eventually led them to be called. * * *

Free-Soil Democracy had its origin in the Baltimore Convention of 1844, where the South, rejecting Van Buren, strove to tighten its grip on the Party by adopting the two-thirds rule. The consequent Barnburner revolt seemed—especially as the insurgency presented itself as a movement by younger Democrats against their experienced elders—as a "mutiny" by "fresh water lads."[14] This crisis is strikingly parallelled in the *Town-Ho* section of *Moby-Dick*. The abortive mutiny of ten crewmen out of thirty, the early defection of seven of Steelkilt's associates, the ultimate capitulation of the others and the successful commandeering of another ship, follow closely the sequence of historical events from 1844, through the state-by-state bolts from the Party, to the Utica Convention of 1848 and the formation of the Free-Soil Party at Buffalo. Moreover, the geographical center of the new party was the very canal and lake region from which Steelkilt and his supporters came. The radical Free-Soil sentiment of New York and upper Ohio seems echoed in the "agrarian freebooting impressions" ascribed to the *Town-Ho's* mutinous mate. The tyrannical Radney, finally, has southern characteristics. Introduced as a "Vineyarder," he is "quite as vengeful and full of social quarrel as the backwoods seaman, fresh from the latitudes of buck-horn handled Bowie-knives." The account of Steelkilt's long being "retained harmless and docile" by the "inflexible firmness" of Radney, "only tempered by that common decency of human recognition which is the meanest slave's right," could well stand as a paraphrase of the grievances with which David Wilmot introduced his Proviso. The Free-Soil revolt flourished on the refusal of northern Democrats like Wilmot to remain the "white slaves" of the South.[15]

Such a history makes all the more fascinating the suggestion of various critics that Melville intended the *Town-Ho's* story to convey an alternative policy to that of the *Pequod*. Of course the exemplary mutiny in no way alters the fated course of the *Pequod*, but it is possible that the *Town-Ho's* tale was conceived originally by Melville as something other than a mere interlude. Perhaps he did not always imagine the *Pequod's* voyage as ending in disaster. It may be that in the hypothesized version of *Moby-Dick* the ultimate control of events was assigned to Bulkington. And this charismatic person, even as briefly glimpsed, strikingly resembles Thomas Hart Benton, the idol of radical Democrats and, in early 1850, the hope of those who would preserve the Union without sacrifice of Jacksonian principle.

14. "Remarks by Ogden Hoffman," in *The Proceedings of the Union Meeting, Held at Castle Garden, October 30, 1850* (New York, 1850), p. 33; *Speech of John Minor Botts, at a Dinner at Powhatan Court-House, Va., June 15, 1850* (n.p., n.d.), pp. 14–15.

15. *CG-A*, 29–2, 316.

Like Bulkington's, Benton's "neck and chest were of very large proportions," and his "powerful frame" seemed "capable of enduring fatigue, both mental and physical, under which few other men could bear up." It was said that when in debate Benton set his "dazzling" white teeth and undertook to "play Indian, no savage that ever infested the wilderness could cope with" the stolid and fearless Missouri Senator. The dark-complexioned, southern-accented Benton hailed from—not the "Alleganian Ridge in Virginia"—but the nearby Carolina mountains. Exactly like Bulkington, however, Benton had "reminiscences that did not seem to give him much joy." (Throughout life he professed to be pained by his early duel with Andrew Jackson.) In *Moby-Dick* a brawny, fearless Bulkington is seen getting the *Pequod* underway as "solitary and alone" as Benton had been when he first set the Democracy "in motion" behind the expunging resolution. Just as Bulkington disappears from the helm, so too was Benton, the "Palinarus of the Democracy," unexpectedly dropped as the Party's pilot. Loyal to Van Buren in the Convention of 1844, Benton in 1848 became himself a man without a party. Hailed by the *Democratic Review* as a "fearless thinker," he persisted in his intellectual and political independence. Benton refused to bow before a pro-slavery Missouri electorate and, in late 1850, lost the Senate seat he had held through five tempestuous terms.[16]

In Melville's apotheosis, Bulkington is conjured to "take heart," knowing that his soul, too, had grimly and intrepidly resisted the winds conspiring to cast it "on the treacherous, slavish shore." But however spiritually triumphant, the "demigod" Bulkington is denied by Melville—for reasons we may only surmise—the authority that perhaps was once to be his in the critical moments of the *Pequod's* voyage. By Bulkington's departure Melville seems to imply that by the end of 1850 the alternatives of the Democracy were severely, even fatefully, limited. Though Steelkilt is reported still alive after Radney's death (as Van Buren survived Polk), the *Town-Ho's* tale ends on a note of elegy, not of prophecy. The *Pequod's* doom is foreshadowed by the sad burial aboard the *Delight*. (A sardonic echo of Father Mapple's fanatic pleasure in the "higher law"?) Aboard the *Delight* is seen a shroud similar in import to the "winding sheet" of the Republic invoked in 1850 by those who despaired for the Union.

Such foreboding was also voiced in the Compromise debates by references to the Biblical Rachel. To nineteenth-century Americans, Rachel was more than a sentimental mother; she epitomized

16. *Democratic Review*, I (October 1837), 86–89; S. M. Maury, *The Statesmen of America in 1846* (Philadelphia, 1847), pp. 59–60; Magoon, *Living Orators*, p. 337; Dyer, *Famous Senators*, pp. 196–97; Henry S. Foote, *Casket of Reminiscences* (Washington, 1874), pp. 332–335; Schlesinger, *Age of Jackson*, p. 487.

the patriarchs of Israel who mourned for the downfall of their nation. As one Unionist cried in 1850, were Washington "permitted to speak, would he not, like the good old prophet, have cried out, 'O that my head were waters, and my eyes a fountain of tears, that I might weep day and night for my people'?" So often were tears shed in anticipation of the "sad and heart-rending spectacle" of the "dissolution of Union," that when in August the Compromise seemed all but buried, Jefferson Davis could taunt its friends for their "eternal wailing . . . , like Rachel weeping for her children, and would not be comforted because they were not."[17] * * *

Even the passage of the Fugitive Bill did not represent an ultimate crisis for those true believers who held, with George Bancroft, "that submission is due to the popular will, in the confidence that the people, when in error, will amend their doings." This faith, vouchsafed neither to Calhoun nor Webster, nor even to the impatient Garrison and Parker, but delivered in 1850 only to hearty Jacksonians, Melville seems to have embodied in the *Rachel* of *Moby-Dick*. Deviously cruising, still searching after her children, the *Rachel* becomes, in the end, an emblem of Bancroft's confident appeal "to the more enlightened collective reason of tomorrow."[18] The *Rachel*—as necessary to Ishmael's salvation as Queequeg's coffin—comes before us, finally, an avatar of the same undying democratic faith that Melville glorified in the apotheoses of Jackson, of Steelkilt and of Bulkington. The world into which Ishmael survives is not, to be sure, so carefree and joyful as that of the Whiggish *Bachelor*; life aboard the *Rachel* is perforce "without comfort." But whatever its "constitutional" peculiarities, the *Rachel* points to a future that is not without charity and not, perhaps most importantly, without hope.

Whatever the ultimate meanings of *Moby-Dick*, its themes are not unrelated to the American political situation in the stormy Compromise year of 1850. Its narrative sequences, at least, follow closely a pattern comformable to the reigning symbolism of politics. This is not to say that *Moby-Dick* is decipherable as the very allegory that Melville carefully warns readers against attributing to his romance. It of course became much more as Melville's Ishmael departed from his role of narrator to press inquiries into metaphysical realms only glimpsed by Melville's contemporaries. A final determination of the relationship of Melville's completed product to the politics of the era is impossible—if only because for Melville himself there was no precise distinction between the "types" that shadowed forth the meaning of the universe and the images by which such a meaning could be communicated.

17. *CG-A*, 31–1, 127, 715, 1551.

18. Bancroft, "Oration, Delivered at the Commemoration, in Washington, of the Death of Andrew Jackson, *Literary and Historical Miscellanies* (New York, 1857), p. 470.

But our appreciation of *Moby-Dick* is considerably enhanced by the realization that, during its trying-out as well as during its composition, Melville was profoundly stirred by political developments. If remoter influences—Melville's literary sources, for instance—also had a share in his creative process, it is well to remember that, as Emerson knew, "the artist must employ the symbols in use in his day and nation to convey his enlarged sense to his fellow men." Such familiar symbols were provided only by the political drama that engrossed Americans in the mid-nineteenth century. Melville seized them, and of course reworked and amplified them, and in doing so seated much of Romanticism in judgment, not merely on Calhoun and Webster, but on all that these statesmen represented in and to the American mind. This Melville accomplished without doing violence to a symbolic universe he shared with his countrymen. Though his Ahab, for instance, was not simply an allegorized Calhoun, the central character of *Moby-Dick* did think, act and even look like the demonic, yet admirable, Senator who to many Americans seemed a reincarnation of the Ahab of old. The entire narrative structure of *Moby-Dick,* indeed, stands as testimony to the internal consistency of a political symbolism that for no American was devoid of some significance.

One need not deny Melville's genius in order to conclude that the greatness of *Moby-Dick* derived at least in part from Melville's personal and intellectual engagement in the fortunes of the Democracy. Had he not been involved, and had he not been so sensitive to the hidden, even ultimate, meanings of the political drama, Melville would not have been able to perceive and predict with such uncanny accuracy the true political dynamic of his age. While some Americans spoke of Ships of State hovering over dreadful vortices, while others brandished hickory poles and still others stood enthralled by the dark sublimity of Calhoun or the moral grandeur of Webster, Melville managed to codify, as it were, the nation's political rhetoric. By doing so he created in *Moby-Dick* a masterpiece that in its coherence, as in its universality, outranks not only as literature, but as political insight, the utterances that served Melville as his raw material.

Melville was not alone in his visceral democracy, nor was he in 1850 the only patriot who loved the Union. But few of his contemporaries—participants in the political wars or commentators—realized that the Compromise of 1850 represented, in essence, a victory for an economic entente, an outgrowth of the Industrial Revolution, which needed peace in order to preserve and enhance its status. Not that evidence for such a conclusion was lacking in 1850; for through the din of debate over slavery could be heard the insistent partisans of American manufactures, neglecting no opportunity to promote such favorite programs as a protective tariff:

> Mr. Speaker, I desire a change in the conduct of this Government. I would have everything about an American ship of American growth. . . . The naval architect should fashion his keel, and hull and spars, from American wood. . . . Her cordage and sheeting should be of American hemp. [19]

Calhoun was defeated in 1850, and the South brought to heel after 1860, by an industrial and financial complex which, in the act of destroying the slave-power, also nearly interred Jacksonian Democracy. And Ahab too was taken to his doom, not by the Whale alone, nor even by the sea that engulfed the *Pequod*, but—in fulfillment of the Parsee's enigmatic prophecies—by two symbols of the American System: a ship whose visible wood was American, and a bow-line of Kentucky hemp.

PAUL BRODTKORB, JR.

Others: The Basic Relation†

We can get closer[1] to men like Ishmael, who are less forbiddingly of a piece, who show signs of occasional indecision, and seem rather like ourselves at times. Thus the last major way of encountering the other is also embodied in a fictional technique that reflects a mode of perception. As the book proceeds, the purely comic portraiture loses priority, and the narrator begins to let us overhear private soliloquies, interior conversations less spoken than thought. The other seems much less of an external object to us; it is almost as if we, together with Ishmael (who simply disappears at such points), *become* the other.

But we do so by virtue of a literary convention. And partly because the convention here is noticeably archaic (soliloquies are

19. *CG-A*, 31–1, 195.

† From Chapter 4 of Paul Brodtkorb, Jr., *Ishmael's White World: A Phenomenological Reading of Moby Dick* (New Haven: Yale University Press, (1965), pp. 61–82.

1. Closer than to men like Queequeg and Fedallah. At the beginning of this chapter, Brodtkorb advances the argument that the "separation between narrator and reader" suggested by the "slight retreat" Ishmael makes in the second sentence of Ch. 1 "goes on to become the fundamental relation between the narrator and the other characters, even between the narrator and himself as character." Brodtkorb adds (p. 51): "An edgy alternation of emotional advance and retreat, this dance of estrangement requires that the perceiving self be always *outside*, a spectator, a voyeur, however much the self might wish to become more completely engaged with those separated from it" [*Editors' note*].

not "realistic" even in the nineteenth-century romance terms that Melville employs) it calls attention to itself as theatrical; we notice it as a convention—one that forcibly simplifies the complexities of private mental experience. When we "become" the other by means of a soliloquy, we are not in the presence of an unmediated encounter; instead, we remain within the consciousness of a storyteller who *imagines* the other. Thus we break out of solipsism into an inter-subjective world by a technique which maintains the problematic boundaries of selfhood: overtly, the gap between self and other has been bridged, but covertly its eternal existence is acknowledged.

What is revealed of the other by this last method is therefore not inmost, essential selfhood. What is revealed is something like the little lower layer, a stylized, ordered substratum, the revelation of which makes us aware of Ishmael's awareness that an exterior role—Ahab, say, the inflexibly fixed captain bent on revenge—has interior components; and, most typically, that what comprises the interior is self-divided, in process, debating with itself even as it creates masks and roles to conceal its tenuous balances. Thus Starbuck's role of "staid, steadfast man, whose life for the most part was a telling pantomime of action" (Ch. 26) is revealed in soliloquy to be capable of harboring a consciousness whose "miserable office" is "to obey, rebelling; and worse yet, to hate with touch of pity!" (Ch. 38).

Sometimes Ishmael is willing to go beyond the more presentation of self-division in order to find abstract, conventional terms for the components of this divided self:

> Starbuck's body and Starbuck's coerced will were Ahab's, so long as Ahab kept his magnet at Starbuck's brain; still he knew that for all this the chief mate, in his soul, abhorred his captain's quest, and could he, would joyfully disintegrate himself from it, or even frustrate it. [Ch. 46]

Spirit or soul ("the eternal, living principle" [Ch. 44] in a man) is here at war with mind or will (the "life-spot" [Ch. 44] of a man where the spirit resides "leagued with" the mind), which in turn controls body, the outer vessel of the self—these three elements, which may operate together harmoniously as well as discordantly, constitute one schema of total identity for Ishmael.

Of the inwardly discordant characters, Ahab, who outwardly "did long dissemble" (Ch. 41), is of course the major example. When Ishmael analyzes him, he uses terms similar to those he uses to explain Starbuck. An important occasion for analysis is provided by Ahab's behavior during his frequent nightmares, when "a wild cry would be heard through the ship; and with glaring eyes Ahab would burst from his state room" (Ch. 44). Outwardly the "unappeasedly steadfast hunter of the white whale," inwardly Ahab is torn apart, so that at night

> this Ahab that had gone to his hammock, was not the agent that so caused him to burst from it in horror again. The latter was the eternal, living principle or soul in him; and in sleep, being for the time dissociated from the characterizing mind, which at other times employed it for its outer vehicle or agent, it spontaneously sought escape from the scorching contiguity of the frantic thing, of which, for the time, it was no longer an integral. But as the mind does not exist unless leagued with the soul, therefore it must have been that, in Ahab's case, yielding up all his thoughts and fancies to his one supreme purpose; that purpose, by its own sheer inveteracy of will, forced itself against gods and devils into a kind of self-assumed, independent being of its own. Nay, could grimly live and burn, while the common vitality to which it was conjoined, fled horror-stricken from the unbidden and unfathered birth. Therefore, the tormented spirit that glared out of bodily eyes, when what seemed Ahab rushed from his room, was for the time but a vacated thing, a formless somnambulistic being, a ray of living light, to be sure, but without an object to color, and therefore a blankness in itself. God help thee, old man, thy thoughts have created a creature in thee; and he whose intense thinking thus makes him a Prometheus; a vulture feeds upon that heart for ever; that vulture the very creature he creates. [Ch. 44]

The conceptual gist of this difficult passage would seem to be that, when asleep, Ahab's soul, temporarily dissociated from what has insanely used it, rebels. Yet the judiciously analytic Ishmael faced with Ahab's psychic profundities does not simplify his analysis to any such "gist." The passage is full of complex abstractions, qualifications, extensions, synonyms with subtle distinctions implied between them, and second thoughts. Ishmael's first hypothesis is that soul, the eternal, living principle, is dissociated in sleep from Ahab's dominant mind, a mind which in the daytime uses soul for its "outer vehicle or agent." But here Ishmael corrects himself: since mind does not exist apart from soul even in sleep, the first analysis must be wrong. Ishmael tries again: Ahab's mind has created a purpose which at first reflexively characterizes that mind, then itself grows into a discrete entity of monstrous proportions (a vulture feeding upon the heart of its Prometheus-creator) from which flees the "common vitality"—soul plus mind[2]—now animat-

2. "Common vitality" I construe to mean in context that vitality or animating principle which is both soul and mind ("the mind does not exist unless leagued with the soul") rather than a vague ordinary vitality which would be out of keeping with Ishmael's labored attempt at precision here.

ing Ahab's body. The second try, however, is not wholly successful either: it leaves Ahab's "independent purpose" spatially unaccounted for (perhaps a literal-minded quibble, yet the passage does have the air of analytic interpretation as well as of poetry) and it blurs the relation between "common vitality" and "tormented spirit"—presumably one of identity, but we can't be sure—because unstated distinctions seem to be implied. In short, there are loose ends to the precision of Ishmael's analysis; he makes too many abstract synonyms. Indeed, the whole passage, in addition to being susceptible of that kind of exegetical attention it has often received, also shows Ishmael unable to create and revise sufficiently quickly enough static abstractions to keep up with the shifting complexity that is his experience of Ahab. The initially statue-like Ahab of the quarter-deck, "shaped in an unalterable mould, like Cellini's cast Perseus" (Ch. 28), his bone leg steadied in an auger hole as if he were a component part of the ship, has here become fragmented almost into incoherence.

Part of what this suggests is that "becoming" the other—becoming, for example, Ahab—by means of soliloquy is more of a deception than my first account of it (on pages 61–62 [318–19]) suggested, for it seems we have become the other only to be able to explain him less convincingly than when he appeared to us as a distanced, animate object, wholly exterior, but at the same time possibly more favorable to the categorial manipulations of the mind—more accessible to thinking about *because* we experienced him as an object. The Ahab of the soliloquies and Ishmael's analyses exists in the duration of time, changing from moment to moment in his secret proportions, and in this moment of nightmare has become "a blankness in itself," a formula which, perversely, seems more adequately descriptive of him even when he is awake than "crazy Ahab" does. The latter is touched with hypocrisy: it pretends to explain Ahab by labeling him, but the label is simply the name that we gave to others with whom we can make little or no contact, and therefore can have no real sense of; while the former at least focuses unequivocally on the mystery of Ahab's being. Ahab is a blankness, a whiteness (Ishmael is aware that "blank" means "white" in his usage of it in chapter 42), with all the ambiguity of that color; but he is also a strange kind of emptiness, a lack, and perhaps a lack in Ishmael's and our rationalizing understanding of him as well as a lack in himself. But how, from our point of view, can a blankness be understood; a being so tormented, so at war with himself; so often at interior variance with his exterior, however much the latter signals the division within; a man, as Ishmael admits near the end (and the sense of which admission has been repeated throughout like a refrain), "every revelation" of whose "deeper part" partakes "more of significant darkness than of explanatory light" (Ch. 106)?

The way in which Ishmael tends to understand Ahab is suggested by the phrase (already cited in context near the end of the quotation on page 63 [320]), "without an object to color." Because these words occur soon after the scientific theory (quoted on page 33, above) that earthly colors are not inherent in substances, but are illusions bestowed upon substances by the whiteness of light which itself contains all other colors, what is meant by the phrase is something like this: the mysterious self of Ahab, the mind-soul, is a "ray of living light" which requires for its normal daytime existence an "object to color." Like light, the self contains all possibilities of color, but color other than white can be selectively drawn out of the self's blankness only by its having an object—that is, a goal. The self is here conceived of as a kind of closed circuit between itself and some purpose within itself that can give it normal human character. Since to the Starbuckian triad mind-soul-body must be added object or purpose, and since it is in fact Ahab's willful purpose that characterizes him in his inflexible moods when he is "for ever Ahab," it is Ahab's purpose which is the focus of most of Ishmael's major analyses of him.[3] If Ahab differs from the common run of men chiefly in his sheer *quantity*, in his "greatly superior natural force, with a globular brain and a ponderous heart," all of which adds up to "one in a whole nation's census—a mighty pageant creature, formed for noble tragedies" (Ch. 16); if, as Peleg says, "There's a good deal more of him" (Ch. 16); or, as Elijah says, "*He's* got enough . . . [soul] to make up for all deficiencies of that sort in other chaps" (Ch. 19); then all these quantitative differences come together and achieve definition in the strength of his characterizing purpose. When he is the self-divided Ahab, his purpose momentarily waning, he more obviously "has his humanities" (Ch. 16); he seems more anonymous, more an ordinary fellow creature; it is easier, then, to feel that "all of us are Ahabs" (Ch. 23)—but even then, the force of his self-divisions is greater than most men ever experience, and this force points right back to the singular purpose that sets him apart from all men: as Ishmael says, the "symptoms" of his nightmare ambivalence are "but the plainest tokens of . . . [the] intensity" of "his own resolve" (Ch. 44).

Ahab as the Problematic Other

Ahab's purpose, selectively absorbing a characterizing tonality from the "ray of living light" that is his mind-soul, in turn colors

3. For example, those in chapters 41, 44, and 46.

the total Ahab, as well as everything that comes within his view. His major moods are the moods of his purpose, not the passive vagaries of most other men whose mood patterns are less clearly defined. The restful light of early evening is rejected—"This lovely light," he says, "it lights not me" (Ch. 37)—because it is out of harmony with his mood-world, a darker, tenser world than Ishmael's. Light for Ahab is restricted to those flames that can match his inner fires: the flaring, ghostly corpusants, the sharp clear blaze of lightning, both leaping momentarily out of darkness.

The effect of his purpose on Ahab's identity can perhaps best be understood against the context of experienced time, which is implied in Ishmael's first sight of him. Ishmael notes the statue-like determination of the body itself, then the whitish rodlike mark that runs down the side of his face and neck and signals the inner self-division, then the posture, "erect, looking straight out beyond the ship's ever-pitching prow" (Ch. 28). Captain Ahab's glance, here, is one of total "forward dedication"; for to have such an intense purpose as he has is to live always projected ahead of oneself into the future.

If one has such a purpose, the present does not count at all except as one must live through it in order to allow the future to approach. When the present intrudes to put off the future, it is impatiently brushed aside:

> Up Burtons and break out? Now that we are nearing Japan; heave-to here for a week to tinker a parcel of old hoops? . . . Begone! Let it leak! [Ch. 109]

To live in the future is to live in the mind, and actuality is displaced to that realm: "What things real are there," asks Ahab, "but imponderable thoughts?" (Ch. 127). The merely substantial is despised as mechanical ('D'ye feel brave men, brave?" asks Ahab, and when Stubb responds puppet-like on cue with "As fearless fire," Ahab mutters, "And as mechanical" [Ch. 134]. Yet living with the mind focused on the future nevertheless requires enduring the present, and because the present *is* full of things, like Burtons, and men, like Starbuck, that often seem to impede the future's approach, present substances must be worked upon, molded, coerced, "for be a man's intellectual superiority what it will, it can never assume the practical, available supremacy over other men, without the aid of some sort of external acts and entrenchments, always, in themselves, more or less paltry and base" (Ch. 33). The future-living mind is well aware of the baseness of what must be done, but because the future goal is everything, its anticipation colors the present activities so that even tricks like magnetizing a new compass needle with bogus cabalism can give pleasure to one whose quality of mind they would ordinarily be below. Anything in the present that can serve becomes a lever with which to move the future closer. Men are not men, but tools to be manipulated for the sake of the future; carefully, to be sure, because "of all tools used in the shadow of the moon, men are most apt to get out of order" (Ch. 46). In such enterprises, Ahab is successful: "I thought," he says, "to find one stubborn, at the least; but my one cogged circle fits into all their various wheels, and they revolve" (Ch. 36); and he is not wrong in his appraisal of their actions, for they respond to his view of them. "Like machines, they dumbly moved about the decks, ever conscious that the old man's despot eye was on them" (Ch. 130).

In all such instances, the future, as purpose, has determined the present; and because Ahab's purpose is difficult, if not impossible, to achieve, the present takes on the character of that kind of purpose-future. Substances are hard and sharp, splintered bones and iron lances. Action is sudden, angular, and shot through with the destructively fortuitous. Forces are antagonisms: Zoroastrian dark struggles with light, good with evil, in a power-world in which "the real owner of anything is its commander" (Ch. 109). It is a stern, withholding, father-world rather than a yielding and loving mother-world ("My sweet mother I know not," says Ahab in the fire speech in chapter 119); and women have no place in it except to be yearned for in moments when purpose wanes, nor has feminine pity—its purposive emotions are hate, despair, anxiety, and fear.

The Ahab created by Ahab's purpose lives in a world that reflects him. "The firm tower, that is Ahab; the volcano, that is Ahab; the courageous, the undaunted, and virtuous fowl, that, too, is Ahab; all are Ahab; and this round globe is but the image of the rounder globe, which, like a magician's glass, to each and every man in turn but mirrors back his own mysterious self" (Ch. 94)—here, confronting the doubloon, Ahab speaks for himself and his world; what he says may be true in a subtler, more qualified way for each and every man, but it requires no subtilization to apply to him. He spreads his psyche over all, making the world into *a* world, his world, a coherent universe of certain, dominant physiognomic tone. Others become aspects of him, as well as his tools. In Starbuck he sees, at the end, that part of him which tries to pull him back to home, his memories of wife and child:

> I see my wife and child in thine eye. No, no; stay on board, on board!—lower not when I do; when branded Ahab gives chase to Moby Dick. That hazard shall not be thine. No, no! not with the far away home I see in that eye! [Ch. 132]

Fedallah embodies Ahab's willful purpose in its aspects of self-betrayer, the Narcissus image that stares out of the water-world at him:[4]

> Ahab crossed the deck to gaze over on the other side; but started at two reflected, fixed eyes in the water there. Fedallah was motionlessly leaning over the same rail. [Ch. 132]

(Two chapters earlier, Ahab and Fedallah "stood far parted in the starlight; Ahab in his scuttle, the Parsee by the main-mast; but still fixedly gazing upon each other; as if in the Parsee Ahab saw his fore-thrown shadow, in Ahab the Parsee his abandoned substance" [Ch. 130]; earlier yet, "Ahab chanced so to stand, that the Parsee occupied his shadow; while, if the Parsee's shadow was there at all it seemed only to blend with, and lengthen Ahab's" [Ch. 73].) Pip, like Ahab, is mad, and his madness flees from the same sort of existence that Ahab madly fights. As Ahab is secretly self-divided, other selves within his range of power are divided, even as they carry out his purpose to the point of becoming "one man, not thirty" (Ch. 134), and that man, Ahab.

Material substance often takes on the image of Ahab's purpose in peculiar ways. The Pequod, embarking from Nantucket, "thrusts her vindictive bows into the cold, malicious waves" (Ch. 23), looking like a whale because she wears "the chased bones of her enemies" (Ch. 16). So much is she a whale, that, "while one sperm whale only fights another sperm whale with his head and jaw . . . he chiefly and contemptuously uses his tail" (Ch. 86) in fights with men and boats; but when Moby Dick sinks the Pequod, he does it the honor of ramming it with "the solid white buttress of his forehead" (Ch. 135). Ahab, too, has been made over by his object, as Lewis Mumford first noted, into a queer kind of image of the thing he hunts: Moby Dick has his terrifying white buttress of a forehead—Ahab's brow is so prominent it scares Stubb ("I was so taken all aback with his brow, somehow. It flashed like a bleached bone" (Ch. 29); Ahab's leg is cut off—Moby Dick has "three holes punctured in his starboard fluke" (Ch. 36); both Ahab and the whale are old. As Ahab and the Pequod both resemble whales, so does Ahab in his thoughts become his boat: "I leave a white and turbid wake," he says, "pale waters, paler cheeks, where'er I sail" (Ch. 37); and as the mates issue "from the cabin with orders so sudden and peremptory . . . it was plain that they but commanded vicariously" (Ch. 38), as if Ahab were the Pequod's vitalizing principle.

4. M. O. Percival in *A Reading of Moby Dick* (Chicago, 1950) was the first of many to suggest that the Parsee could be understood as "the subtly maddened part of Ahab's mind" (p. 41).

He did not always have this purpose that can so coerce the matter of his world, but it is not totally alien to what he once was; rather, it is a monstrous outgrowth of the early Ahab. The purpose is constantly linked to his willful mind, a mind that, however humanly insane its premises and conclusions, is nevertheless calculatingly logical. Even in his

> broad madness, not one jot of his great natural intellect had perished. That before living agent, now became the living instrument. If such a furious trope may stand, his special lunacy stormed his general sanity, and carried it, and turned all its concentered cannon upon its own mad mark; so that far from having lost his strength, Ahab, to that one end, did now possess a thousand fold more potency than ever he had sanely brought to bear upon any one reasonable object. [Ch. 41]

His madness has increased his intellectual powers, and does nothing to prevent his thinking in the terminology of categories and syllogisms ("Look ye, pudding-heads should never grant premises" [Ch. 108], he advises the carpenter, after having led him to an abstruse and, from his point of view, absurd conclusion). Typically, his mind reaches conclusions rigorously based on the premises he is willing to grant, which are mad ones by ordinary standards. But even the young Ahab was an intellectual of sorts: "Ahab's been in colleges, as well as 'mong the cannibals; been used to deeper wonders than the waves . . ." (Ch. 16), says Peleg; and when Ahab originally went to sea, his "globular brain . . . [had] by the stillness and seclusion of many long night-watches in the remotest waters, and beneath constellations never seen here at the north, been led to think untraditionally and independently; receiving all nature's sweet or savage impressions fresh from her own virgin voluntary and confiding breast . . ." (Ch. 16). Ahab, like Ishmael, has learned about the world from his life at sea, and intellectualized it.

His mad purpose, then, can be seen as the absurd but nevertheless logical outcome of an argument based upon what his life on the sea has taught him. Like most men, he has generalized his personal experience beyond his special predicament; but unlike most men, he has been willing to draw the most far-reaching conclusions from it, and totally commit himself to them. His madness is in part his intellectual rigor and his insistence on the signification of all things. The argument that supports his insane purpose is most effectively suggested by him in his speech to the corpusants in chapter 119. There he acknowledges that the fire-gods are full of "speechless, placeless power," but he asserts that they are not ethical: "To neither love nor reverence wilt thou be kind; and e'en for hate thou canst but kill; and all are killed." Like the God of the

Book of Job, they torment good men for their own secret purposes; unlike the Jobean God, they do not cease tormenting until death. "Come in thy lowest form of love," Ahab says, "and I will kneel and kiss thee"; but because Ahab has never had intimations of the gods in this form, he asserts: "Oh, thou clear spirit, of thy fire thou madest me, and like a true child of fire, I breathe it back to thee." Ahab's hate is expressed in irony, here: on the one hand, he suggests that the defiance he proposes reflects the nature of the gods, therefore honors them; on the other hand, he means that the only way a man of integrity can relate to malicious or irresponsible deity is to defy it. The white whale, to Ahab the Leviathan emblem of all gods like these and identified with "all his intellectual and spiritual exasperations" (Ch. 41), must be killed in order to get back at his ultimate tormentors; their "right worship" must be "defiance" to a good man who has seen the dim light. The "darker half" of nature sustains Ahab "with a prouder, if a darker faith" (Ch. 116).

At this point I should like to digress to the problem of the evaluation of Ahab, who has been weighed by criticism in many different scales. During the 1920s the dominant tendency was to identify Ahab's viewpoint with Melville's (more recent critics—Thompson, for one—sometimes still do this); later, the pendulum swung to relatively simple condemnation of Ahab; while since the '30s most critics, perhaps, have paid at least lip service to some kind of balance of attitudes, usually, however, shifting over to condemnation in the end. Ahab's fire speech illustrates much of the difficulty in evaluating him: the argument implied in it will seem, to a Christian, insane, but to those less committed it can suggest a view of the human condition that has claims of its own to at least metaphorical validity. Everything depends upon whether one is willing to grant Ahab's assumptions, or their emotional bases. *Are* the gods as Ahab describes them, or will there be a reconciliation after death that will reveal the unethical character of much of human experience—that the bad often prosper and the good often fail; that all die, and many innocents die in horrible ways—to have been beside the point? Are human ethics irrelevant to a divine ethic, which supersedes them, and which fallen man can no longer even begin to comprehend? Or, to put the case negatively, do the gods even take notice of man? *Are* there any gods? Ahab has no evidence that any of this is so, and, perhaps hastily (he has after all had fleeting intimations of chaos and atheism: "Sometimes I think there's naught beyond" [Ch. 36], he says to Starbuck), Ahab concludes that there *is* no evidence other than what is available to him. On that basis he constructs his insane purpose, and on that basis his ethically monstrous act of sacrificing the Pequod's crew has its own higher ethos.

How can one judge such a man objectively? Starbuck, the law-abiding nominal Christian, finds Ahab "blasphemous" (Ch. 36). Stubb, further removed from Christianity, grudgingly approves:

> Well, well; I heard Ahab mutter, "Here some one thrusts these cards into these old hands of mine; swears that I must play them, and no others." And damn me, Ahab, but thou actest right; live in the game, and die it! [Ch. 118]

Ishmael, formerly a Presbyterian but now more liberal in his persuasion, calls Ahab insane; as, ethically, most readers of his book would. Thus the book itself contains a spectrum of judgments, and Ishmael reports them all.

In fact, he incorporates their range. Even as he condemns Ahab, there is something in Ishmael that shares Stubb's reaction. Ishmael calls Ahab mad, yet he says "all mortal greatness is but disease" (Ch. 16), which allows for Ahab's being great. He calls Ahab mad, yet in his account of Pip's madness he suggests that man's insanity may be heaven's sense, which allows, on some unearthly scale of values, for Ahab's being right. This isolates the problem. Father Mapple's sermon, dropping the most discordant elements of its colloquial style, concludes with a peroration that defines the religious hero.

> Delight is to him . . . who against the proud gods and commodores of this earth, ever stands forth his own inexorable self. . . . Delight is to him, who gives no quarter in the truth, and kills, burns, and destroys all sin though he pluck it out from under the robes of Senators and Judges. [Ch. 9]

Though, like Ahab's, Father Mapple's God is known to him chiefly by His rod, He is clearly a different God from Ahab's; *or*, so Ahab might argue, He is the same God, but Mapple has failed to draw the correct conclusions about His nature from what Mapple has himself experienced of that God, as distinct from the stories of Him Mapple has read. To grant the Ahabian argument at least hypothetical status is illuminating, for then the behavior in relation to God that Mapple advocates is (granting Ahab his kind of God) seen to be Ahab's behavior; and it is the behavior of a saint.[5]

It is true that Father Mapple's sermon defines the religious hero

5. W. H. Auden, with Percival a Kierkegaardian reader of *Moby Dick*, sees Ahab as a religious hero, negatively manifested, in his book *The Enchafèd Flood* (London, 1951). I am indebted to both Auden and Percival in this analysis of Ahab, though more for attitudes than specific arguments.

in a way which some have held to be inconsistent, but his definition may alternatively be understood as figuring an existential paradox: the story of Jonah demonstrates that religious man must subordinate his own desires to God's will—"if we obey God, we must disobey ourselves"; yet the religious man also, somehow, "stands forth his own inexorable self." The apparent contradiction is perhaps chiefly one of viewpoint: from the outside and from the normal, ethical viewpoint, a saint may look like a self-willed madman; while, subjectively, he may be obeying God. His intensity of insane selfhood may be the sign of God-possession.[6] The dividing line between saint and madman is often so unclear that it is the long, careful, posthumous process of canonization, not the popular judgment of the moment, that must confer official sanctity. Something of what is implied by the existence of this process far antedates the Catholic Church in the religious category of *trial*, exemplified by the Judaic stories of Abraham and Job.

Within the category of *trial*, as Kierkegaard has explicated it in *Fear and Trembling* and elsewhere, ethical considerations do not obtain because God has teleologically suspended them. If Abraham had followed his ethical promptings and behaved so as prematurely to spare the life of his son Isaac, he would have disobeyed God—his temptation *away* from religious heroism was precisely the normal, humanely *ethical;* Job's ethical justifications before God prove to be beside the point, finally, when God's nonethical "answer" comes. Each religious hero is in a divine trial of the steadfastness of his faith; moreover, it is a trial the very existence of which he cannot be aware of (otherwise not his faith but his prudence would be tested); and within the conditions of which normally ethical behavior could as easily be against the will of God as not. All of which is why, although the ethical and religious spheres may overlap in human existence, they are by no means congruent;[7] and why any contemporary who did not happen to hear the voice of God commanding Abraham must until the last moment of reversal have judged Abraham ethically, and condemned him; and why, even if Ahab were a saint on trial, he must be condemned by Starbuck, Ishmael, and us—for we do not hear the voices.

6. Auden's definition in Kierkegaardian terms of the religious hero is similar: "Religious authority . . . arises . . . from a relation to truth. But the religious definition of truth is . . . that it is absolute. The religious hero is one who is committed to anything with absolute passion, i.e., to him it is the absolute truth, his god. The stress is so strongly on the absolute that though he may be passionately related to what, ethically . . . is false, he is a religious hero and has religious authority over the one who is lukewarmly or dispassionately related to what is true." [p. 86]

7. If God's actions in the Old Testament are any evidence, human ethics do not exist within God's realm. God is absolute; for Him there can be no *necessary* consequences no matter what He chooses to do. Existentially, ethics are pragmatic means for accomplishing ends; divinely, ethics would be superfluous because God accomplishes His will without any such means: He says, "Let there be light," and there is.

Precisely this inability to hear seems to be a major point of the fire scene. (Earlier, of course, it is not outside voices that Ahab hears but the ethically perverse voice of his own conscience; yet God may speak in the voice of conscience, too, at least according to the Quakers, and Ahab is a Quaker.) In his dialogue with the fire, Ahab acts out hearing supernatural voices; or, to put it minimally, understanding the message of the flames' vibrations. We do not hear the voices or know what the flames convey; we hear only Ahab's response to the fire, and must infer for ourselves what the fire says. It is possible that Ahab's performance may be merely opportune showmanship to impress the crew when a fortuitous display of St. Elmo's fire occurs (he has "acted" often enough before for such reasons); or the fire may be god-directed at him, and his responses accurate. We cannot know because, beyond the eeriness of the light of the corpusants, and the appropriateness of its purity to the gods, Ishmael, rather uncharacteristically, gives us no statement or even opinion on the matter. Evidently he does not know. Therefore we are in the exact position of having to judge if a man of obviously great spiritual presence is a heroic madman—here, a fraud in the service of his real madness—or a heroic saint.

And potentially a saint, even though he disobeys the fire-gods; because to their all but overwhelming power he gives "no quarter in the truth." Despite his inner division, like a saint he wills one thing; like Father Mapple's religious hero, Ahab "stands forth his own inexorable self" in that he is willing to kill, burn, and destroy in the name of that possessing vision of truth which he has become, a vision which nevertheless dimly seems to see "some unsuffusing thing beyond" (Ch. 119) the fire-gods[8] to which all their "eternity is but time" and all their creativeness mechanical—some unsuffusing thing, it should be added, which might be placing Ahab on trial, a trial of the existence of which neither Ishmael nor we nor even Ahab could yet be aware. Like Abraham's, Ahab's temptation away from heroism is the ethical, as Pip and Starbuck embody it.

To sum up the argument thus far, we cannot know that Ahab is religiously wrong. We can simply note that his behavior seems cruel, as when in the name of his total commitment he rejects the plea of the Rachel's captain to help find his son; that such behavior destroys society; and that from the humanly ethical standpoint (the only one which most humans, after all, can take) this must seem wrong, however repeatedly individuals and societies are expendable in a religious context, as evidenced by many Bible stories.

But that the ethical context is not the only one in the book against which to set Ahab is suggested, first, by Ishmael's writing this kind of book about Ahab at all. If Ahab were clearly and only a

8. Ahab's fire speech is also discussed on page 91 below.

madman, there would be no point in presenting him as a kind of hero, metaphorically as well as literally *above* other men on his quarter-deck, a man who *does* more and *says* more, "a Khan of the plank, and a king of the sea, and a great lord of Leviathans" (Ch. 30),[9] a "mighty pageant creature, formed for noble tragedies" (Ch. 16). In fact, this inflated perspective exists in the book more directly presented to us than the one out of which Ishmael says he created his Ahab, that of the "poor old whale-hunter" in "all his Nantucket grimness and shagginess" (Ch. 33), which would be all the Ahab the book needed were he merely to be experienced by us as "crazy Ahab." As it is, when Ahab speaks with the full force of Melville's power of words, there is no judging him; his madness becomes like Lear's, transcending itself along with situation and personality. Why give Ahab such power? Why let him speak "a bold and nervous lofty language" (Ch. 16) that creates a Shakespearean atmosphere around him which provides its own implicit moral perspective on him?[10] Why define madness as heaven's sense; say that Ahab has "a crucifixion in his face" (Ch. 28); note that in his titanic nightmares "he sleeps with clenched hands; and wakes with his own bloody nails in his palms" (Ch. 44)? Ahab even "in all his fatal pride" (Ch. 124) does not think of himself in quite these terms; the terms, and the evaluations implied, belong to Ishmael, who, whether he fully means it or not, does present Ahab as a kind of religious hero. And because he does, against this implied religious context there can be no question whether Ahab's passion is true or false; the religion it is in service of may be true or false, but not the passionate heroism, nor its religious character. Nor does insanity taint the heroism, for if all mortal greatness is no more than disease, Ahab's insanity, to normally ethical judgment, is

9. These formulas may well be ironic, but this seems to be a case of that sort of Ishmaelean irony (discussed below, pages 135–37) about which one cannot be *sure*. Out of context, the words seem to imply their opposite in order to mock Ahab's pride; but in context, Ahab has by no means yet demonstrated hybris worthy of Ishmael's scorn: they merely serve to indicate Ishmael's recollection (occasioned by the sight of Ahab seated on a whalebone tripod stool) of "old Norse times" and "the thrones of the sea-loving Danish kings." Perhaps the hyperbole is self-directed irony as much as directed against Ahab: perhaps the irony undercuts that part of Ishmael which must see Ahab in so exalted a way—undercuts, that is, that part of himself which admires Ahab's self-willed certainty enough to make of it an heroic attribute even though he suspects a fatal error in that certainty. The direction of the irony, in any case, does not seem univocal.

10. Some philosophers, most notably perhaps Martin Heidegger, suggest that people who speak different languages experience different worlds. (The idea is part of the common ground between European phenomenology and the philosophy of the British analytic school; I might add that many American academicians will be familiar with the issue of language's radical participation in fact from the poetry and poetics of Wallace Stevens, or from the writings in linguistics of Benjamin Lee Whorf.) Such a formulation is at best controversial, and will not be insisted upon here. But it may be safe to assert that in *Moby Dick* the Shakespearean aura around Ahab's speech is of a piece with the kind of world he experiences, and that that world is of a greater range and depth than, say, Flask's. For a discussion of the formulation cited at the beginning of this note see Richard Schmitt, "In Search of Phenomenology," *Review of Metaphysics, 15,* No. 3 (1962).

the necessary disease of his greatness of passion. Nor does that insanity disqualify the potential accuracy of Ahab's vision of evil even to the "reasonable" Ishmael: in a world which at any or all levels may be divinely or ethically chaotic, ethical madness, religiously manifested, may have its own validity. What, in short, is in question for Ishmael is never the actuality, but the moral value and final cosmic context, of Ahab's heroism.[11]

To all such presentational evidence may be added the many well-known passages that in relative degrees of directness tend to justify Ahab. There is the passage that advocates the value of glorious death in the service of high and dangerous truths:

> Know ye, now, Bulkington? Glimpses do ye seem to see of that mortally intolerable truth; that all deep, earnest thinking is but the intrepid effort of the soul to keep the open independence of her sea; while the wildest winds of heaven and earth conspire to cast her on the treacherous, slavish shore?
>
> But as in landlessness alone resides the highest truth, shoreless, indefinite as God—so, better is it to perish in that howling infinite, than be ingloriously dashed upon the lee, even if that were safety! . . . Terrors of the terrible! is all this agony so vain? . . . Up from the spray of thy ocean-perishing—straight up, leaps thy apotheosis! [Ch. 23]

(In Ishmael's re-presentation of him, Ahab, too, has been apotheosized.) There is Ishmael's remark on sharks fighting over a dead whale: "If you have never seen that sight, then suspend your decision about the propriety of devil-worship" (Ch. 64); and Queequeg's summary comment: "Queequeg no care what god make him shark . . . wedder Fejee god or Nantucket god; but de god wat made shark must be one dam Ingin" (Ch. 66). There are, in fact, many more often-quoted passages that could be construed in Ahab's defense; but it seems pointless to rehearse them here.

It is, then, contrary to all such signs of a hidden sympathy for Ahab's outrageous purpose that Ishmael, as narrator, usually main-

11. The tendency of much otherwise excellent Melville criticism finally to condemn Ahab often involves a prior reduction of the sort of stature granted Ahab by Ishmael's presentation of him. But surely problematic heroes who escape clear ethical evaluation are not that unprecedented in literature even before the romantic movement. Consider all the literary figures who embody great force of spirit instead of unambiguous virtue; whose abnormally passionate aspirations are defeated by the gods, or merely by the cyclical everydayness of the world; whose violations of common decency are somehow part of their heroism, which is finally an affront to common decency. If Ahab evokes from Stubb, and from some readers, an un-Christian respect for his inviolable integrity of purpose, Ahab's admirers are part of a tradition that goes back at least as far as the stoics, who also valued individual honor even when it went against the good of the community. (That part of Ishmael which is constrained to present Ahab as a hero, despite what his ethical knowledge tells him, *is* stoic; a reason for the affinity is suggested on page 125, below.)

tains an open and direct negative moral estimate of Ahab. Yet, this does not really seem to be a question of a horizontal split between narrator and character, a narrator who admits that the character Ishmael against part of his will got caught up in Ahab's purpose, and who from time to time must reestablish his presence in order to note that fact, and ethically disapprove; but rather a question of a vertical split between aspects of the narrator, who, in retelling, partly relives his life as character, and cannot disavow what he once was. To some extent he still is what he once was in his attitudes, and does not *want* to disavow these parts of the past and present Ishmael. Because both positive and negative attitudes remain, each must be given weight: on the question of Ahab's final mortal status, Ishmael is, though in a more diffuse and hidden sense, as self-divided as Ahab is, and as divided as critics ever since have been.

Ahab's more clearly delineated self-division becomes sharpest near the end of the book. Defined *as* Ahab by his purpose, in chapter 132 he becomes momentarily detached from it, and in this lucid interval the gap between his purpose and him is enormous:

> Forty years of continual whaling . . . for forty years to make war on the horrors of the deep! Aye and yes, Starbuck, out of those forty years I have not spent three ashore. When I think of this life I have led; the desolation of solitude it has been . . . away whole oceans away, from that young girl-wife I wedded past fifty, and sailed for Cape Horn the next day . . .

The speech in context is a long one, an emotional counterpoise to the passion of his goal in that what it says is deeply, agonizingly felt. Then, the "natural," self-regarding part of himself goes on to question why he acts as he does:

> What is it, what nameless, inscrutable, unearthly thing is it; what cozzening, hidden lord and master, and cruel, remorseless emperor commands me; that against all natural lovings and longings, I so keep pushing, and crowding, and jamming myself on all the time; recklessly making me ready to do what in my own proper, natural heart, I durst not so much as dare? Is Ahab, Ahab? Is it I, God, or who, that lifts this arm?

He does not question where his coercive purpose came from in the first place, merely what keeps it so insistently before him. Yet he might have asked that question, too. Originally, his purpose grew within him over a long period:

> It is not probable that this monomania in him took its instant rise at the precise time of his bodily dismemberment. Then, in

> darting at the monster, knife in hand, he had but given loose to a sudden, passionate, corporal animosity; and when he received the stroke that tore him, he probably but felt the agonizing bodily laceration, but nothing more. Yet, when by this collision forced to turn towards home, and for long months of days and weeks, Ahab and anguish lay stretched together in one hammock, rounding in mid winter that dreary, howling Patagonian Cape; then it was, that his torn body and gashed soul bled into one another; and so interfusing, made him mad. That it was only then, on the homeward voyage, after the encounter, that the final monomania seized him, seems all but certain . . . [Ch. 41]

Forced against his will to return home, bedded and at one with his anguish, enduring the warring elements of the Patagonian Cape, Ahab rebels against this absolute interruption of his freedom. His body and soul bleed into one another to form a unitary maimed being which Ahab, refusing to acknowledge it as himself, passionately disavows. After long weeks of brooding over his condition, he intellectualizes all the elements of the accident, as well as his own present suffering, and the weather, into an emblem of "all his intellectual and spiritual exasperations." It is then that he becomes coldly rational about his purpose; at first, merely reacting against his antagonist in "sudden, passionate, corporal animosity," he has now chosen to become that animosity, and he thereby orders an impulse into a reason for his continued existence. If his exterior fate has required his inmost character for its working out, that character was, originally, no more than a strong tendency to intellectualize into coherent patterns. Beyond this, it was open; yet this was enough to prevent him from experiencing what happened to him as Captain Boomer, for example, of the Samuel Enderby saw *his* encounter with the white whale: the result of awkwardness rather than malice. Ahab's characterizing mind sees malice, which is patterned and purposive though its purposes may be obscure, rather than awkwardness, which is mere meaningless chance. After his accident, in choosing to live only in relation to it, Ahab has changed its character from that of a meaningless blow from elemental forces into a chosen fate. He makes the accident into the central event and meaning of his life, and thereby retroactively makes himself responsible for what has happened to him even though he was not at first responsible. It is as if, in Maurice Blanchot's fine summary phrase, "freedom and personal impulses much more than the movement of an irresistible mechanism were the true paths of fatality."[12]

Originally Ahab's purpose came upon him as a choice con-

12. ". . . comme si la liberté et les impulsions personnelles, beaucoup plus que le mouvement d'un mécanisme inéluctable, étaient les vraies voies de la fatalité." See "Le Secret de Melville," *Faux-Pas* (10th ed. Paris, 1943), p. 285.

structed out of an impulse and an accident. Now, at the end of the book, he asks how his purpose can be so irrevocably fixed. He decides in favor of an exterior fatality, concluding that he is driven by God, by forces analogous to those of the wind against which he can do nothing. His decision expresses an emotional paradox: Ahab feels his original choice was not free, even as he rebels in favor of freedom.

After the moment of tormented self-regard, Ahab's purpose again takes over, and as it does, his eyes meet Fedallah's reflected in the water. A short while later his purpose has once more fully become him and is experienced as "immutably decreed": "Ahab is for ever Ahab, man. ... 'Twas rehearsed ... a billion years before this ocean rolled" (Ch. 134).

The claims of home upon his "natural" self are put and felt at their strongest just before their final and total rejection, and Ahab's death. The gap between self and purpose is made, here, momentarily, to seem absolute; then, the futurity of purpose suddenly flows into the present to fill it, and go back "a billion years" besides; it fills all of time. But this purpose is to become death, and as "all collapsed, and the great shroud of the sea rolled on as it rolled five thousand years ago" (Ch. 135), the filling of time seems like an emptiness.

Ahab has made his future determine his present, even as he has made his past (*his* past, chosen by him to be seen in a certain way out of many potential ways during those weeks of anguished retrospection when it flowed through his characterizing mind) determine his future. Because it is his kind of past that always comes to meet him from his future, he has always lived ahead of himself, *having* no other present but the empty one his future gives him. Even in conversation, he is normally ahead of those with whom he talks, those whose concerns are in the present.[13] The gap, the emptiness, of the end has been there from the moment in which his choice came alive within him. It is as if Ahab's final extreme individualism has been an attempt to put boundaries to the inner lack from which he suffers, even as his individualism creates that lack: in this sense it is that he is at all times "a ray of living light," but

13. Two examples of dialogue will serve to illustrate the simple point meant here:

"The oil in the hold is leaking, sir. We must up Burtons and break out." [Ahab is incredulous.] "Either do that, sir, or waste in one day more oil than we may make good in a year. What we come twenty thousand miles to get is worth saving, sir."

"So it is, so it is; if we get it."

"I was speaking of the oil in the hold, sir."

"And I was not speaking or thinking of that at all. Begone!"

[Ahab:] "How the soot flies! This must be the remainder the Greek [Prometheus] made the Africans of. Carpenter, when [the blacksmith] is through with that buckle, tell him to forge a pair of steel shoulder-blades; there's a pedlar aboard with a crushing pack."

"Sir?"

"Hold; while Prometheus is about it, I'll order a complete man . . ." etc. [108]

also a "blankness." Thus, we, along with Ishmael, encounter Ahab in the book's present, but he "is" always in the future, eluding us. Having the most character of all, Ahab is yet a kind of vacuum, an emptiness, a nothingness; as such we cannot really understand him humanly, and because we cannot, he must seem to us "crazy."

Ishmael's finally inconclusive moral evaluation of Ahab is not separable from his finally inconclusive effort to understand Ahab. With the two exceptions of the comic perspective, which accepts otherness rather than investigate it, and of the vision of love, which is excluded from Ahab's world, Ishmael has tried to understand Ahab by all the means remaining at his disposal: he first saw Ahab as an animate object, then "became" Ahab in soliloquy, then analyzed what he had seen from without and experienced from within. What his extended consideration of Ahab reveals about the Other is at least this: even those who at first seem of a piece—that is, are "characters"—cannot be adequately known; and, partly because they cannot, they cannot be morally judged, even when their behavior seems most strongly to call for such judgment. It is not that to understand is to forgive, but that understanding, condemnation, and forgiveness are all equally impossible without intentionally or unintentionally blinding oneself to part of the evidence.

Ahab has hunted the white whale, and the hunt has been like a hunt for himself, because he *is* the hunt and the purpose of the hunt; and the end of the hunt is death. As Ahab has hunted the whale, so Ishmael has hunted them both. When Ahab and Moby Dick disappear under the great shroud of the sea, tied to each other in eternal opposition, distorted, Narcissistic mirror images of each other, Ishmael is left behind to ponder his failure to reach the depths with them, and doubtless to give thanks that he has not. But something in him is compelled, like the ancient mariner, to tell the whole long story over and over again, to those who will listen.[14] Each telling is a new attempt to fill the emptiness left by his experience of Ahab and the whale, to fill it with meaning.

MARTIN GREEN

[The Insignificance of Ishmael]†

What is quite unambiguous is that Ishmael is *not* a point of view on the problems that concern Melville through Ahab. He is

14. The comparison of Ishmael with the ancient mariner is no more than a tentative suggestion here; it will be developed further near the end of Chapter 6, below.

† From Martin Green, *Re-Appraisals: Some Commonsense Readings in American Literature* (New York: W. W. Norton, 1965), 96–97.

not (as both Richard Chase [1949] and Marius Bewley [1959] say) an alternative to Ahab in his response to Moby Dick, or to the doubloon, or to the quest. He has nothing to say on such subjects; 'The Whiteness of the Whale' is not written in Ishmael's voice, but Melville's; he does not exist in relation to them. Indeed, after the first few chapters, Ishmael does not exist at all. His name alone survives (recurs), as a narrative device of the crudest kind. The attempt to make him into an alternative—Melville's preferred and proffered alternative—to Ahab, is a fine example of the critic's need to mythify the book he is discussing. If there *were* any unity between the epic and the romance parts of *Moby Dick*, it would no doubt *be* by means of Ishmael. But in point of fact there is no such unity; magnificent as some parts are, the book does not exist as a whole; the two genres [epic and romance] function on different levels of the imagination, and also in different directions. Ishmael's disintegration and disappearance is one of the marks of this.

WALTER E. BEZANSON

[Dahlberg and Melville]†

It makes one sad that the longest and most ambitious essay among these bitter alms should be a virulent attack on Melville. Sad, not for Melville, but because *Moby-Dick* has so obviously permeated Dahlberg's imagination that his rancorous attack is virtually a public self-castigation. If he has finally put himself on the scaffold, he mounts it in darkness, like Dimmesdale. His own writing reflects Melville's reaching for epic themes, his strained poetic-pedantic style, his debt to the ancients and Elizabethans, his demonism and antiquarianism, his word lust, his sometimes hapless struggles with form. As willful pariah he has long called himself Ishmael, meaning both the Hagar's son of Genesis and the castaway of *Moby-Dick*. And now Ishmael is suddenly the scorned Hamitic one. Dahlberg's earlier attack, in *Can These Bones Live*, also exploited Melville's sexual and religious trials, following lines set in Lawrence's *Studies;* but there an avid relish for the books justified writing about them. This time there is little pleasure and no comedy.

"I have changed my mind about Herman Melville," Dahlberg solemnly announces, "for I once loved this Cyclops whose father is Oceanus." The attack begins and ends with a single theme: that

† From Walter E. Bezanson, "The Critical Furies of Edward Dahlberg," a review of Dahlberg's *Alms for Oblivion*, in *Criticism*, Vol. 8 (Winter, 1966), 97–101; the quotation is from 99–101. Reprinted by permission of the Wayne State University Press.

Melville was a misogynist, that his imagination was homosexual, and therefore that *Moby-Dick* is perverted and false. Because of "scorifying deprivations" Melville lusted after men and beasts, but not women. It was Melville's affliction that "his vitals froze in all latitudes," and this is why *Moby-Dick* is a congealed and frigid tale. "After the blubber pots and the love scenes of these corrugated, mammoth Don Juans of the sea, what virile male reader does not yearn for the witty bouts between a smell-smock and a flirt, or a sweet bosom that would set Ilium on fire?" We need "the thighs of Aspasia or the rump of Lais of Corinth," but not whales. Melville "should have been an amorist," and he wasn't.

Sir Herbert's notion in the foreword that "this indignation is fundamentally moral" is almost as funny-sad as the indignation itself, which is clearly psychological. As for Dahlberg, what book was he reading before he fell out with it? The triumphant announcement that *Moby-Dick* is a book without women, that the whale is phallic, that Ishmael takes Queequeg as a wife, that the chapter "A Squeeze of the Hand" is sexual, and so on—these things he has noticed now for the first time, at the age of sixty-two? They are all in Lawrence, some even in Dahlberg's own writings. All that is new here is Dahlberg's reaction; holy whiteness is suddenly a terror. One might hope for more from the author of *The Sorrow of Priapus* (1957), that bizarre, brilliant compendium of fables on the concupiscence and malice of men and beasts, for which Ben Shahn did such superb drawings. But Dahlberg may not be as interested in sex as he keeps saying he is. In any case he is in no mood in this essay to cope with the complexities of Melville's sexuality, either in his life or works. He can now see only a sodomite imagination in Ishmael, and a vast "Hamitic" (by which he means homosexual) dream in his narrative. Even then what fascinates him is not the dream but his own nausea before it.

In a kind of classic demonstration of how rage can choke insight Dahlberg keeps pointing at some of the flaws of *Moby-Dick* without being able to articulate his findings. The novel is without motion. Ahab's monomania is merely "picturesque" and static (the beginning of a good insight). Ishmael's narrative is dour and humorless (perhaps so, to a humorless reader). The characters are flat and the cetology is a bore because Melville "had almost no knowledge of people" and knew little about whaling. The book is "shabbily written"; Melville dashed it off in a year, "made no corrections, and never rewrote any moiety of it." So it goes, insights, half truths, and misinformation tumbling over each other. What a shock, then, to note Read's abject capitulation in the foreword:

> I confess I had always shared the common admiration for Melville's allegorical epic, but never was an illusion of mine so

> immediately shattered. . . . Mr. Dahlberg takes his stand on what is most central to literature, the language, and he has no difficulty in showing that *Moby-Dick* is "shabbily written."

More accurately, Dahlberg has no difficulty in dealing with Melville's language because he acknowledges none. What kind of discrimination underlies a list of thirteen examples of "mock fury" (a good hard problem) that includes: "the last gasp of his earthquake life" (a fair instance); "the whale's head" (a simple naming, and all that he quotes); and "the delta of his forehead's veins" (an effective trope, unless he can show otherwise)? What are we to make of twelve other passages dumped out with absolutely no comment other than "Is this the 'honest manna of literature'?"—when to one innocent reader, at least, five of the twelve are perfectly straightforward English prose? Or six passages merely dubbed "canorous lines," in some kind of presumed contrast? Right or wrong he leaves everything undone. Having neither the head nor the patience for rational criticism, he should stick to his feral outbursts and disjointed grotesqueries, which now and then enliven the mind. In this essay, however, one is not given much choice. Either we read how Cotton Mather, "the father of the Christian homosexual," made women-haters of Melville, Poe, Whitman, and Thoreau, and so threatens us with perversion, "the black angel of our century." Or we watch exercises, described above, in what has to be called Gnu Criticism.

At one point in *Truth Is More Sacred,* during an exchange of letters on James, Read got up his courage:

> You are absolute for truth, and like a Grand Inquisitor, would send to the stake any author who in any respect offends your dogma. . . . I could not live so intolerantly. I am a relativist, grateful for any glance of beauty that I encounter as I read, and not anxious to erect monuments of granite on Parnassus. I am always for discrimination, which I would oppose to judgment.

No doubt Dahlberg is a difficult friend to have and for whom to write prefaces. Yet one wonders how Sir Herbert could forget himself so quickly as to draw the lance in benighted defense of this essay, and even go on to offer Dahlberg as one who above all applies "the test of style, and by always returning to this test, by insisting on very little else, . . . becomes a critic of a most salutary kind." To the contrary. Dahlberg prolongs into the twentieth century an eccentric remnant of what he himself calls "American radicalism, which is half Bible socialism, half sex cult." He is himself one of the "malcontents," one of the "truth-and-vision-cranks," whose loss he moans. Whatever may still be salutory for criticism in that tradition Dahlberg has twisted by his Ishmael-anguish. He refuses to study style. He insists only on himself.

Most of the virtue of *Alms for Oblivion* lies in the intensity of Dahlberg's reminiscences about writers he knew. The uses of the "criticism" are essentially autobiographical, as documents for the inner history of a tormented man. Seen from outside, Dahlberg belongs to the karate school of criticism. No matter if the heart is troubled; when the hand has been sufficiently hardened, one chop does it.

THOMAS WOODSON

Ahab's Greatness: Prometheus as Narcissus†

In the popular mind *Moby-Dick* has always been Ahab's book. A spectacular, melodramatic old sea captain, a literary cousin of Long John Silver and Captain Hook, embarks on an excitingly fateful voyage of revenge. Of course he is thwarted, but after all he is not likeable enough to succeed. The reader's vicarious daring is satisfied and his awe of the white whale lingers on.

Literary critics, more concerned with the intellectual issues raised by Melville's art than with the adventurous plot, have turned their attention from Ahab to Ishmael, the author's narrator and spokesman. Ahab, who at first seemed an arch-romantic self-projection, we now tend to see as a case-study of Romantic "madness," an American counterpart of the Victorian monstrous egotist typified by Emily Bronte's Heathcliff. He is also seen as an incarnation of the Romantic "dark" hero, rebellious towards the bourgeois world, alienated from the comforts of traditional faith, pitting himself against all obstacles to reach and rifle the secrets of the Infinite and Absolute. He is most frequently compared to Milton's Satan, Byron's Manfred and Goethe's Faust. Such a figure calls forth ethical judgments, most often unfavorable ones. The archaic Elizabethan rhetoric Melville has put in Ahab's mouth brings to mind such morally excessive hero-villains as Macbeth and Richard III, Tamerlane and Faustus. Various writers have accused Ahab of embodying the dark Puritan hatred of nature, the nineteenth-century capitalist greed for forceful acquisition, and even the insane persuasiveness of a twentieth-century dictator.

All these characterizations are certainly just in some measure; Ishmael's more prudential and speculative approach to the voyage allows us to accept the horrible truths of the story with a greater

† Thomas Woodson, "Ahab's Greatness: Prometheus as Narcissus," *ELH, A Journal of English Literary History*, Vol. 33 (September, 1966), 351–69.

hopefulness and self-respect than if Ahab completely dominated our perception of it. But we still have to come to terms with Ahab. To dismiss him as a madman, a Satan or a Byronic egotist is too simple. For instance, much has been made of his Biblical name; "Ahab of old," says Peleg to Ishmael, "was a crowned King!" and Ishmael answers: "And a very vile one. When that wicked King was slain, the dogs, did they not lick his blood?"[1] But in many ways our Ahab is no more comparable with the Old Testament schemer and murderer than is Ishmael with his primal namesake, whose hand was to be against every man, and who signaled his bitterness by mocking God. Ishmael insists that Ahab is a great man, a tragic hero; it seems appropriate here to reexamine his character with sympathy towards this judgment, leaving the ethical atmosphere in the background, and concentrating on what actually is said about him in Ishmael's narrative and in his own words.

The most fruitful starting-point for study of Ahab's personality is not, perhaps, Captain Peleg's description of him to Ishmael, but Ishmael's later meditation on the hierarchy of rank on a whaler (Ch. 33, "The Specksynder"). Ishmael observes that Ahab "sometimes masked himself" behind the "forms and usages" of rank, the "external arts" of practical power, but that these are not the true index of his greatness. Ishmael speaks here in his role as "tragic dramatist" rather than as plebeian observer of his dictatorial captain. As a dramatist he struggles to put into words what haunts him still about Ahab: "But Ahab, my Captain, still moves before me in all his Nantucket grimness and shagginess; . . . I must not conceal that I have only to do with a poor old whale-hunter like him; and, therefore, all outward majestical trappings and housings are denied me. Oh, Ahab! what shall be grand in thee, it must needs be plucked at from the skies, and dived for in the deep, and featured in the unbodied air!" (p. 130.) It would be possible to take the last phrases of this statement ironically, were it not for Ishmael's obvious preference for democratic "shagginess" over "majestical trappings." Ahab's true greatness will not be contained or exposed in forms, trappings, housings. It is harder to find, but (Ishmael's urgent tone insists) it must be found.

The angle of approach to Ahab I am proposing depends upon the ramifications of these phrases: "plucked at from the skies, and dived for in the deep, and featured in the unbodied air!" What is really vital is Ahab's relationship to the great forces of nature; Ishmael can only know Ahab through the "bold and nervous lofty language" which, he has already told us, Ahab himself learned by "receiving all nature's sweet or savage impressions fresh from her

1. *Moby-Dick*, Ch. 16, p. 77. Page references are to the Norton Critical Edition of *Moby-Dick*.

own virgin voluntary and confiding breast," thereby becoming "a mighty pageant creature, formed for noble tragedies" (Ch. 16, "The Ship," p. 71). Ahab was "formed" by the language of nature, but this is a different kind of "form" than that given by human culture. Paradoxically, nature's language seems not available to man, since Ishmael finds no "voluntary and confiding breast" from which to learn it, but only the empty immensities of sea and sky. He must "pluck" and "dive" for knowledge which he mistakenly presumes Ahab to possess already.

Above, all, Ishmael must "feature" Ahab's greatness "in the unbodied air." He must create verbally a face for Ahab in the unsubstantial, phantasmal world of the air. Much later Ahab announces defiantly that he *does* in fact exist in the mode Ishmael here prescribes for him. "In the midst of the personified impersonal, a personality stands here" (Ch. 119, "The Candles," p. 417). Man must affirm his own uniqueness in order to exist as man. The affirmation is of itself heroic and tragic, both for character and dramatist.

Thus Ishmael links himself to Ahab in an underlying way. Ahab's self-assertion, however excessive and immoral in social terms, is necessary to the imaginative logic of the novel. Ishmael's plucking and diving to feature him are verbal counterparts of Ahab's destructive quest for Moby-Dick. In this sense Melville, standing behind Ishmael directly and Ahab obliquely, has "written a wicked book."[2] And Ishmael's desperate search for words is really parallel to Ahab's "bold and nervous lofty language" which, as we soon learn, has *not* brought him definite knowledge of nature's secrets: the virgin teases and deludes; she "absolutely paints like the harlot, whose allurements cover nothing but the charnel-house within" (Ch. 42, "The Whiteness of the Whale," p. 170). Ahab, addressing the captured whale's head, senses the inadequacy of all human language to the problem he insists on solving: "O Nature, and O soul of man! how far beyond all utterance are your linked analogies!" (Ch. 70, "The Sphynx," p. 264). Similarly, Ishmael, after an extended essay on the featureless face of the whale, gives up in despair: ". . . how may unlettered Ishmael hope to read the awful Chaldee of the Sperm Whale's brow? I but put that brow before you. Read it if you can." (Ch. 79, "The Prairie," p. 293.)[3]

2. There are, of course, many passages in *Moby-Dick* which will not support the intensity of tone I evoke here. Ishmael plays other roles, and other characters occasionally divert us from Ahab's moral centrality. But Melville's famous remarks to Hawthorne about his "secret motto" and "wicked book" indicate Ahab's importance to him. My emphasis here on the common problems of Ahab, Ishmael and Melville is anticipated (as are other aspects of my argument) by Charles Feidelson, *Symbolism and American Literature* (Chicago, 1953), pp. 27–35. I am further indebted for comments and suggestions to my colleagues William Charvat, Julian Markels and Joan Webber.

3. Ishmael also comments on the formlessness of the whale's appearance and the consequent impossibility of understanding it in Ch. 55, "Of the Monstrous Pictures of Whales," p. 228; and Ch. 86, "The Tail," p. 317–18.

Ahab's most extended statement of his problem, it is universally recognized, comes in the "Quarter-deck" chapter. Insisting to Starbuck that he is intent on more than "vengeance on a dumb brute," Ahab reveals his belief that "in each event—in the living act, the undoubted deed—there, some unknown but still reasoning thing puts forth the mouldings of its features from behind the unreasoning mask" (p. 144). He goes on to characterize Moby-Dick as "the unreasoning mask," the white wall which Nature has "shoved near" to him. Nature's intelligent creativity, then, is not the body of the whale but the essential "features" of itself which it seems to reveal in a mysterious way "from behind." If we can trust Melville's use of "features" here to correspond to "featured" in the passage about Ahab's greatness, both whale and whale-hunter possess a hidden and ultimately dynamic existence; Ahab in chasing Moby-Dick feels himself to be "thrusting through the wall," the "pasteboard mask" of mere external form. Ishmael in writing about Ahab, feels he must "pluck" and "dive" in the sky and sea to understand the real Ahab behind the mask of "forms and usages."

Ahab talks of the "mouldings" of Nature's essential features. This curious word seems to mean the forming power, that which creates patterns and forms in matter. The word is typical of the stylistic idiosyncracy of *Moby-Dick* Thornton Wilder has pointed to, Melville's coinage of plural gerunds.[4] I would guess that Melville's choice of "mouldings" in this context stems from his reading of *King Lear*, and particulary from Lear's magnificent apostrophe to the elements during the storm on the heath in Act III, scene 2:

> You sulph'rous and thought-executing fires,
> Vaunt-couriers of oak-cleaving thunderbolts,
> Singe my white head! And thou, all-shaking thunder,
> Strike flat the thick rotundity o' the world!
> Crack Nature's moulds, all germens spill at once
> That makes ingrateful man!

While Lear's speech is tonally closer to Ahab's address to the fire in the "Candles" chapter much later, Ahab here implies a similar "thought-executing" violence: "the living act, the undoubted deed" he soon explains as "the unrecking and unworshipping things that live; and seek, and give no reasons for the torrid life they feel!"

According to this evidence Ahab, no less than Ishmael, is a Romantic naturalist believer in an interflow of spiritual and mental energy between the human mind as perceiver and the phenomena of nature as the objects of perception. While nature may appear as an impenetrable mystery (epitomized by the "unbodied air"), unsubstantial and "impersonal," it is also the mask-like creation of "some unknown but still reasoning thing," which "moulds" and

4. Thornton Wilder, "Towards an American Language," *Atlantic Monthly*, CXC July, 1952), 36.

gives body and form to it. The "impersonal" is "personified," Ahab puts it in the "Candles" chapter. Hence Ahab's quest for Moby-Dick, in whom he has found that "all the subtle demonisms of life and thought . . . were visibly personified, and made practicably assailable" (Ch. 41, "Moby-Dick," p. 160). Ahab's "mad" purpose is to destroy that which he seeks. In this he responds to the power of nature as he understands it. To live, to create a substantial body for oneself, is to destroy the *other*: man finds behind nature a competing mind and creative force; in order to become himself, man must destroy this competing other. To repeat and complete a quotation from Ahab I gave earlier: "O Nature, and O soul of man! how far beyond all utterance are your linked analogies! not the smallest atom stirs or lives on matter, but has its cunning duplicate in mind" (p. 264). Although Ahab seems here only to endorse an orthodox Romantic faith in the interinanimation of mind and nature (for example, Emerson's "Me" and "Not-Me"), by avoiding the syntactic parallel of "matter" to "mind," by claiming that each atom "lives *on* matter," he announces his belief that to live (to "stir") is to destroy, to feed on that which is outside the self. Ishmael comes to understand this outlook in a much more general way when he speaks of the "universal cannibalism of the sea; all whose creatures prey upon each other, carrying eternal war since the world began" (Ch. 58, "Brit," pp. 235–36). But for Ahab the mind is a cannibal as well as the body. And perhaps the greatest of Melville's achievements in writing *Moby-Dick* is to make us see in Ahab the naked dramatic identity of creative and destuctive impulses within the human soul.

The notion that nature can be treacherously destructive is certainly not Ahab's secret—all the characters, even Starbuck, earnestly subscribe to it—but only Ahab sees it as a challenge to the essence of his being. It would be possible to show how each of the other voyagers refuses to see what Ahab sees, but it seems best to let one extreme case illustrate Melville's thinking about the opposite alternative to the personality of Ahab: the carpenter, whose breadth of experience leads Ishmael to wonder if he possesses "some uncommon vivacity of intelligence. But not precisely so. For nothing was this man more remarkable, than for a certain impersonal stolidity as it were; impersonal, I say; for it so shaded off into the surrounding infinite of things, that it seemed one with the general stolidity discernible in the whole visible world; which while pauselessly active in uncounted modes, still eternally holds its peace, and ignores you, though you dig foundations for cathedrals. Yet was this half-horrible stolidity in him, involving, too, as it appeared, an all-ramifying heartlessness" (Ch. 107. "The Carpenter," p. 388).

The carpenter's stolidity is a kind of muteness, an inability to express himself (evidenced in the next chapter by his soliloquy, which says nothing). The carpenter is "the personified impersonal" in human form. Ahab addresses him half-mockingly as "man-maker" and "Prometheus," requesting him to construct a heartless mechanical man with "about a quarter acre of fine brains": a creation which, because of its inhumanity, could withstand the malicious power of nature.[5] Similarly, as the chase nears its end Ahab sees the entire crew, and particularly his direct subordinates Starbuck and Stubb as "mechanical" men, mere metallic instruments of his own will encountering the opposing will embodied in Moby-Dick.[6]

One phrase in Melville's description of the carpenter is particularly interesting: "the surrounding infinite of things." Whereas Ahab's greatness was to be "featured in the unbodied air," the carpenter's "impersonality" shades off into a world of bodies without sensible life. While Ahab is to become more human, more tragic, as he emerges from the infinite dead world of matter, the carpenter fades out of view back into this world, into the meaninglessness Ishmael contemplated in 'The Whiteness of the Whale" as the "colorless, all-color of atheism from which we shrink" (Ch. 42, p. 169).

In making this distinction between Ahab and the carpenter I have assumed an opposition in meaning between "personality" and "things."[7] It would follow from the whole pressure of Western intellectual history—from Descartes and Locke to Hume and Kant to Coleridge and Emerson—that Melville would accept the assumption of a cleavage between mind and matter. The "Descartian vortices" Ishmael discovers in the sea from "The Masthead,"

5. For a different view of this passage, see Richard Chase, *Herman Melville* (New York, 1949), pp. 47–48. According to Chase, Ahab willingly transforms himself into a mechanical monster. But Ahab's heavy, mockingly ironic tone indicates to me that he rejects the mechanical man as a grim joke.

6. See pp. 438, 452, 459.

7. It is true that the English language did not demand in Melville's day, any more than it does now, such an opposition. While the OED gives a definition of "thing" as "a being without life or consciousness, an inanimate object, as distinguished from a person or living creature," it also gives much more general definitions, e.g.. "That which exists individually (in the most general sense, in fact or in idea); that which may be in any way an object of perception . . .; a being, an entity (including persons, when personality is not considered)."

A concordance to *Moby-Dick* would probably reveal that in a majority of instances Melville uses "thing" in a general, innocuous way. But even in casual usage "thing" seems naturally human, as in Emerson's dictum: "The one thing in the world, of value, is the active soul." The tone here is not far from that of another Emersonian phrase: "the ghastly reality of things." An interesting case where the casual meaning becomes suddenly serious is this moment in Emerson's "Ode: Inscribed to W. H. Channing":

> Boston Bay and Bunker Hill
> Would serve things still;
> Things are of the snake.

All the major American Romantic writers seem to have been aware of this potential explosiveness in style.

as well as Ahab's comments on "linked analogies," support this conclusion. But a close reading of *Moby-Dick* brings out interesting information about Melville's use of the word "thing," and particularly about that word when it is put in Ahab's mouth. For example, to go back to the "Quarter-deck" passage, he there describes his cosmic opponent as "some unknown but still reasoning thing," repeating the word a few sentences later: "That inscrutable thing is chiefly what I hate; and be the white whale agent, or be the white whale principal, I will wreak that hate upon him" (p. 144). In terms of my distinction, a "reasoning thing" is a contradiction. But again, a bit later in the same speech he speaks of the pagan sailors as "unrecking and unworshipping things, that live; and seek, and give no reasons for the torrid life they feel!" (p. 144). Once more, in the same chapter, Ahab overcomes the objecting minds of Starbuck, Stubb and Flask: "It seemed as though, by some nameless, interior volition, he would fain have shocked into them the same fiery emotion accumulated within the Leyden jar of his own magnetic life. The three mates quailed before his strong, sustained, and mystic aspect. . . . 'In vain!' cried Ahab; 'but, maybe, 'tis well. For did ye three but once take the full-forced shock, then mine own electric thing, *that* had perhaps expired from out me' " (pp. 145–46). The last of these instances seems to obliterate any clear separation between Ahab ("I," "a personality") and his enemy world ("the unbodied air," "the surrounding infinite of things"). The word "thing" connotes a vagueness which defies my effort to catch and define it, unless Ahab himself contains the malicious, inscrutable force he opposes. The power within him is described as vaguely as the power of nature ("some nameless, interior volition"), and the imagery pictures his mind as a mechanical force, a magnet, an "electric thing" which shocks in a thoroughly physical manner.

Is Ahab a "thing?" Is he simply a source of physical energy, a spark of voltage opposing a similar electrical charge housed in Moby-Dick? If so, my previous defense of Ahab's humanity is invalid. The various metaphors and similes Melville uses in describing Ahab give abundant support to our seeing a consistently "mechanical" Ahab. Early in the book he is compared to a cannonball, a pyramid, a hurricane, a railway train, a mortar, and a tornado. Later we see him as a javelin, a mechanical vice, a seam of iron, an anvil, a splintered helmet, a scythe, a piece of steel.[8] At a crucial point in the final chase of Moby-Dick he sees himself as "a braver thing—a nobler thing" than the wind (p. 461).

8. Pp. 112, 115, 144, 147, 160, 193, 358, 400, 403, 435, 442, 445, 463.

Nevertheless, Ahab's greatness consists in his selfhood, his humanity. He fascinates us as a character partially because his literary integrity, his identity as a personality, is so consistently in danger of destroying itself. Aware that he destroys the spiritual independence of Starbuck and Stubb, he further recognizes the inhumanly destructive "thing" within himself. He contains within himself the fierce, wild energy of nature. It is no sterile convention of epic style which leads Melville to compare Ahab to a giant tree, to a mountain, a river, a volcanic crater and, finally to the sea itself.[9] All these are substantial bodies which can "feature" the book's hero "in the unbodied air," though none of them can exhaust his meaning or reach to his essence.

Ishmael confessed to looking forward with dismay to his task of characterizing and explaining Ahab. After the crucial "Quarter-deck" scene he devotes several chapters to an analysis of Ahab's purpose and of what can be said about his opponent, the White Whale. This analysis concludes with "The Chart," a chapter which relates Ahab's private goals to those of the crew, and which ends by characterizing him as "a Prometheus." Since so many interpretations (including this one) of *Moby-Dick* rely so heavily on that mythological identification, it should be worthwhile to quote and examine the entire paragraph carefully:

> Often, when forced from his hammock by exhausting and intolerably vivid dreams of the night, which, resuming his own intense thoughts through the day, carried them on amid a clashing of phrensies, and whirled them round and round in his blazing brain, till the very throbbing of his life-spot became insufferable anguish; and when, as was sometimes the case, these spiritual throes in him heaved his being up from its base, and a chasm seemed opening in him, from which forked flames and lightnings shot up, and accursed fiends beckoned him to leap down among them; when this hell in himself yawned beneath him, a wild cry would be heard through the ship; and with glaring eyes Ahab would burst from his state room, as though escaping from a bed that was on fire. Yet these, perhaps, instead of being the unsuppressable symptoms of some latent weakness, or fright at his own resolve, were but the plainest tokens of its intensity. For, at such times, crazy Ahab, the scheming, unappeasedly steadfast hunter of the white whale; this Ahab that had gone to his hammock, was not the agent that so caused him to burst from it in horror again. The latter was the eternal, living principle or soul in him; and in sleep, being for the time dissociated from the characterizing mind, which at other times employed it for its outer vehicle or agent, it spontaneously

9. E.g., pp. 110, 111, 418, 438; 111; 161, 400; 443; 462.

> sought escape from the scorching contiguity of the frantic thing, of which, for the time, it was no longer an integral. But as the mind does not exist unless leagued with the soul, therefore it must have been that, in Ahab's case, yielding up all his thoughts and fancies to his one supreme purpose; that purpose, by its own sheer inveteracy of will, forced itself against gods and devils into a kind of self-assumed, independent being of its own. Nay, could grimly live and burn, while the common vitality to which it was conjoined, fled horror-stricken from the unbidden and unfathered birth. Therefore, the tormented spirit that glared out of bodily eyes, when what seemed Ahab rushed from his room, was for the time but a vacated thing, a formless somnambulistic being, a ray of living light, to be sure, but without an object to color, and therefore a blankness in itself. God help thee, old man, thy thoughts have created a creature in thee; and he whose intense thinking thus makes him a Prometheus; a vulture feeds upon that heart for ever; that vulture the very creature he creates.

This is a difficult passage to follow, primarily because of the clumsiness of the grammatical references and the abstractness of Melville's distinction between "characterizing mind" and "eternal living principle or soul."[10] Behind the passage seems to be a distinction between thinking and feeling, some such psychological insight as Hawthorne's famous (and sometimes confusing) separation of "head" and "heart." But this rhetorical overflow of qualifications blunts the clarity of the distinction; the repeated "which's," "this's," "these's" and "the latter" make the passage difficult reading; it is hard to tell which idea is subject of a given clause, and which is object. To make matters worse, the soul is first an "agent," then a "principle"; Ahab's "tormented spirit" (presumably the soul) glares from his "bodily eyes," but his body (or is it his soul?) is at the same moment "a vacated thing."

Even so, the general sense of the characterization is clear. Ahab's "one supreme purpose" (destroying Moby-Dick) attains "a kind of self-assured, independent being" which takes control of his "characterizing mind." This mind is a fire, imaged as the chasm of hell "from which forked flames and lightning shot up"; this mind can "grimly live and burn"—its life is its self-consuming burning, while the soul, "the eternal living principle," "the common vitality," escapes as the body of Ahab escapes from the confinement of the cabin and the bed "that was on fire."

The passage does not make clear whether the mind or the soul is the *real* Ahab. Is the soul "a vacated thing," and the mind a

10. For an analysis of this paragraph which focuses on Ishmael's epistemological problems, see Paul Brodtkorb, Jr., *Ishmael's White World: A Phenomenological Reading of Moby Dick* (New Haven, 1965), pp. 62–81. [Reprinted above—*Editors' note.*]

"frantic thing?" Has his mind driven his soul out of his being in a Faustian bargain for power and intellectual strength? Then the mind is "vacated" by the soul, and is a "blankness in itself" because it cannot "color" the moral life of conscience. As his thoughts become dreams, they are no longer controlled by his "characterizing mind," and flood over his reasoning, "charting" abilities; he becomes "a formless somnambulistic being," a subject parallel in meaning to the object Ishmael originally despaired of "featuring."

If my speculations here seem as tortured as Melville's prose, it is to contend that Ahab as Prometheus is not simply a devil who has lost what Captain Peleg called "his humanities." Ahab is a divided man, self-alienated and confused by the very uncertainty of his relation to his world. Just as Ahab here (or an aspect of him) is "a ray of living light, to be sure, but without an object to color," so the verbal process which gradually forms the book *Moby-Dick* is a ray of living light searching frantically to make language *form* something out of itself.

Ahab is Prometheus, not stealing fire from the gods, but suffering the agony of an internal vulture. In fact, Melville's version of the myth is peculiarly Romantic and modern in that all the action is internalized—the fire and the vulture both exist within the hero's mind. The vulture is Ahab's purpose, which destroys him; but the object of the quest, the humanizing fire, is synonymous with the vulture. It is the essence of Ahab's experience that man is frustrated by an inadequacy within himself; either he fails utterly to join himself to an external significance, to a "reasoning thing" which "features" itself, and his "ray of living light" becomes "a blankness in itself"; or life allows an easy, sliding, deceptive identification and fusing of mind and thing, as self becomes "thing," and the light becomes the fire and the vulture both, collapsing all life-giving distinctiveness in a suicidal cannibalism.

It is on these terms, it seems to me, that Ahab becomes one of the most interesting of Romantic intellectual heroes. Nineteenth-century man, so earnestly obsessed with extending his mental and physical control over all the vast deserts and oceans of the planet, confronts more starkly than his predecessors the *otherness* of nature, and part of him recoils in terror. At the same time he exuberantly revives his faith in irrational knowledge, in the mysterious correspondence of mind and matter; he absorbs nature into himself, coloring it with his own spirit: the result is solipsism. Ahab is peculiar in that he carries on both of these processes with full awareness of the dangers of both. He is a Prometheus whose fire consumes him; carrying out Ishmael's prophecy from the first chapter, he is also a Narcissus, "who because he could not grasp the tormenting, mild image he saw in the fountain, plunged into it and was drowned" (p. 14).

An important imaginative tendency in *Moby-Dick* is, then, the tormenting identification and fusion of Ahab with Moby-Dick. Out of his "tormented sleep" Ahab once imagines himself as successfully completing his purpose: "Oh Moby Dick, I clutch thy heart at last!" (Ch. 123, "The Musket," p. 423). To "clutch" the whale's heart is like (too much like) "grasping" the self-image in the fountain, just as Melville must have felt it to be agonizingly like "plucking" Ahab's greatness from the skies. Life, Ishmael tells us, is an "ungraspable phantom"; Ahab knows this; he admires the carpenter's vice, pinching his hand in it, because "I like a good grip; I like to feel something in this slippery world that can hold, man" (Ch. 108, "Ahab and the Carpenter," p. 390). But later he laments in soliloquy: "Oh! how immaterial are all materials! What things real are there, but imponderable thoughts?" (Ch. 127, "The Deck," pp. 432–33). Hence his obsession with "things" though they be "inscrutable" or "unknown but still reasoning," as in the "Quarter-deck" chapter. If "thoughts" and "things" can connect and unite, without denying the separateness of each other, then Ahab is himself substantially real. But Ahab is haunted by the unknowability of "things," and turns desperately to solipsism. He asks the carpenter: "How dost thou know that some entire, living, thinking thing may not be invisibly and uninterpenetratingly standing precisely where thou now standest; aye, and standing there in thy spite?" (Ch. 108, "Ahab and the Carpenter," p. 391). Here the "vacated thing," the "blankness" of a self-consuming Prometheus, and the haunting phantom of a tormented Narcissus become one.

Ahab's desperate defiance, I have implied, is really an intimate part of Melville's own urge to write *Moby-Dick*. It is understandable that a writer grappling with such a problem should resort to a turbulent, sometimes logically incoherent style. Alfred Kazin, in a brilliant "introduction" to the book's meaning, has noted in the style a "peculiarly loping quality, as if it were constantly looking for connectives, since on the subject of the whale no single word or statement is enough."[11] Thornton Wilder's observation about Melville's coinage of verbal nouns and adjectival adverbs (" . . . the whale shed off *enticings*," ". . . the last *whelmings intermixingly* poured themselves over the sunken head of the Indian at the mainmast," pp. 447, 469, italics mine), points to a similar purpose: the style converts naming words (nouns, adjectives) into actions

11. Alfred Kazin, "Introduction" to the Riverside Edition of *Moby-Dick* (Boston, 1956); reprinted in *Contemporaries* (Boston, 1962) and in *Melville: A Collection of Critical Essays*, ed. Richard Chase (Englewood Cliffs, N. J., 1962), p. 47.

(verbs, adverbs), trying to bring every object to life, desperately projecting animation into "things" and fighting the "blankness" it senses within itself.

It is in the characterization of Ahab that we notice the mocking trickiness of language as it strives to thwart the style's affirmative urge. Peleg's description of him as a "grand, ungodly, god-like man" (p. 76) begins this pattern by both affirming and denying Ahab's grasping of the divine. He is "god-like" (and Promethean) in that he *creates* his own image of the world, but is "ungodly" in that he rebels against his existence as a *creature* of forces beyond his control. The same sort of word-play mocks him in the final sentence of the passage on his "intolerably vivid dreams of the night": "thy thoughts have *created* a *creature* in thee; . . . that vulture the very *creature* he *creates*." Stylistically Ahab's tragedy consists in his failure to keep saying "I" meaningfully; striving to remain the grammatical subject of his world, who acts upon objects or "things" and creates or destroys them, he constantly lapses into the passivity of an object, acted upon, created or destroyed. Early in the book he defines his identity by playing with the word which tells what Moby-Dick has done to him: "I now prophesy that I will dismember my dismemberer" (Ch. 37, "Sunset," p. 147). A moment earlier in the same soliloquy, he attempts to convert the creaturely connotations of "madness" into independent creative action: "They think me mad—Starbuck does; but I'm demoniac, I am madness maddened. That wild madness that's only calm to comprehend itself." In these moments of bravado he thinks he understands himself by enlisting language against the "personified impersonal" opposing him. But actually he is continually in doubt of his identity. His own name mocks and haunts him, as he gradually comes to give it a talismanic significance. Observing the symbols on the doubloon, he confidently announces to himself: "all are Ahab," but later he is jolted by Starbuck's warning: "let Ahab beware of Ahab." In his most profound moment of self-doubt in "The Symphony," he asks "Is Ahab, Ahab? Is it I, God, or who, that lifts this arm?" Finally after the second day of the chase, he reasserts his name, but now in the context of a world empty of personality, able only to *be* by repeating his name: "Starbuck, of late I've felt strangely moved to thee; ever since that hour we both saw—thou know'st what, in one another's eyes. But in this matter of the whale, be the front of thy face to me as the palm of this hand—a lipless, unfeatured blank. Ahab is for ever Ahab, man. This whole act's immutably decreed" (pp. 359, 394, 445, 459). This spectrum of statements reveals the word "Ahab" to mean "everything" (absorbing all significance into itself) or "nothing" (drained of any intrinsic meaning by the pull of extrinsic forces). Ahab is never sure whether he is everything or nothing. Narcissistically he says of the doubloon, "this round gold is but the image of the rounder globe, which, like a magician's glass, to each and every man in turn but mirrors back his own mysterious self. Great pains, small gains for those who ask the world to solve them; it cannot solve itself." (Ch. 99, p. 359) The world cannot "solve" or understand itself, but Ahab is willing to try. The mystery of things and the mystery of self become the same problem to him.

The mocking ambiguity of language is present even in the naming of Ahab's ship, the *Pequod*. The fierce and warlike New England Indian tribe for which the ship is named was called by its neighboring tribes the "Pequots," or "destroyers." As Ishmael notes, the Pequots are now "as extinct as the ancient Medes": the "destroyers" were destroyed, and the same fate awaits Ahab and his crew. The ship itself, "a thing of trophies," a "cannibal of a craft," decked out to resemble the whale it pursues, is simultaneously a symbol of Moby-Dick and of Ahab, of the ambiguity of "destroyer" and "destroyed." There is a similar grim joke in Ishmael's characterization of the Nantucket whale-hunters as "fighting Quakers . . . Quakers with a vengeance" (Ch. 16, "The Ship," pp. 67, 71) As a "Quaker," Ahab is supposed to tremble before the power of God, but as a whaler he causes the whales to tremble. But finally, of course, his destroying power is itself destroyed; asserting his divinity as the active subject of his world, he is driven back to becoming its suffering object.

Ahab finally comes to understand what is happening to him. In a conversation about "The Log and Line" with the Manxman, he says: "'Twill hold, old gentleman. Long heat and wet, have they spoiled thee? Thou seem'st to hold. Or, truer perhaps, life holds thee, not thou it." As usual, Ahab thinks as a symbolist, linking the old sailor by analogy to the rope. But this very imaginative process turns the sailor into a "thing," a creature of "life" and a grammatical object. Learning that the sailor was born "in the little rocky Isle of Man," Ahab continues his symbolic speculations, unable to resist the pun which makes them universal and personal: "Here's a man from Man; a man born in once independent Man, and now unmanned of Man; which is sucked in—by what? Up with the reel! The dead, blind wall butts all inquiring heads at last." (Ch. 125, p. 427). It is interesting that the "dead, blind wall" (identified in "The Quarter-deck" with Moby-Dick) is now actively "butting," no longer merely an obstacle to be thrust through to reach the "unknown but still reasoning thing." Later, at the conclusion of the chase, "the solid white buttress" of Moby-Dick's forehead (another "lipless, unfeatured blank") smites the ship's bow, and destroys it (Ch. 36, p. 144; Ch. 135, p. 468).

It is apparent that in the later chapters of the book Ahab becomes both more and more fiercely assertive and more and more fatalistic. Critics have attacked him for inconsistency, but it seems more accurate to see him as more clearly understanding the division in himself between the humanity which wants to say "I" and the hard truth that the mirroring world makes him into a "thing." His address to the fire in "the Candles" reveals his narcissistic Prometheanism. He tells the crew: "the white flame but lights the way to the white whale," identifying fire with whale. But he needs a closer identification, out of which he can free himself from his oppressive creatureliness: "I would fain feel this pulse, and let mine beat against it; blood against fire!" As he "fronts" the "personified impersonal," he hopes to "stand" more distinctly as a human personality, defined by his "blood" against the fire. He touches the flames: "I own thy speechless, placeless power; said I not so? Nor was it wrung from me; nor do I now drop these links. Thou canst blind; but I can then grope. Thou canst consume; but I can then be ashes." Ahab recognizes the insignificance of man's self-making—he can only "grope," can only "be ashes"; these are minimal assertions. He goes on to turn language against itself: "Light though thou be, thou leapest out of darkness; but I am darkness leaping out of light, leaping out of thee!" According to all traditional symbolism darkness is formless and empty; Ahab in his despair seeks to invert this meaning, but he cannot. His dilemma is complete: to be someone, he must be nothing.

But he is heartened by his human power of speech, the power by which he has asserted the "speechless, placeless power" of the fire. He presses this advantage: "I know that of me, which thou knowest not of thyself, oh, thou omnipotent. There is some unsuffusing thing beyond thee, thou clear spirit, to whom all thy eternity is but time, all thy creativeness mechanical. Through thee, thy flaming self, my scorched eyes do dimly see it." In characterizing the opposing power of nature as "unsuffusing," Ahab achieves a small victory. To suffuse is to spread, to cover, to fill the formless with substance. This the human imagination can do, but the essential force of nature cannot. Ahab accordingly concludes his speech by verbally *becoming* the fire, the repellant otherness he defies: "Leap! leap up, and lick the sky! I leap with thee; I burn with thee; would fain be welded with thee; defyingly I worship thee!" (Ch. 119, pp. 416-17). In this peculiar way he does "feature" himself in the "unbodied air."

Alfred Kazin has defined the unique literary effect of *Moby-Dick* as Melville's ability to "make you feel that he knows, as a writer, what it is like to be the eyes of the rock, the magnitude of the whale, the scalding sea, the dreams that lie buried in the Pacific. It is all, of course, seen through human eyes—yet there is in Melville a cold, final, ferocious hopelessness, a kind of ecstatic masochism, that delights in punishing man, in heaping coals on his head, in drowning him."[12] Ahab's eyes and voice are the most eloquent vehicles of this "ecstatic masochism." Melville establishes this effect through Ahab's imagery. A particularly striking pattern is one probably derived from the rural New England setting in which Melville wrote the book. Describing Moby-Dick's spout to the harpooneers, Ahab compares it to "a whole shock of wheat" (p. 143). Later Ishmael says of Ahab's mutiliaton: "Moby Dick had reaped away Ahab's leg, as a mower a blade of grass in the field" (p. 160). Through these comparisons the man and the whale change places; they are alternately the mower (the destroyer of life) and the thing mowed. This ambiguity returns at the end of Ahab's poignant speech to Starbuck in "The Symphony": "But it is a mild, mild wind, and a mild looking sky; and the air smells now, as if it blew from a far-away meadow; they have been making hay somewhere under the slopes of the Andes, Starbuck, and the mowers are sleeping among the new-mown hay. Sleeping? Aye, toil we how we may, we all sleep at last on the field. Sleep? Aye, and rust amid greenness, as last year's scythes flung down, and left in the half-cut swaths" (p. 445). Gradually, as Ahab feels his nostalgic mood dissipate into the brutal present reality of the chase, he changes from the sentient human mower into the rusting scythe, becoming only a used-up "thing" in a world of cold wintry desolation.

His despair at becoming a scythe, the instrument of the implacable anti-human life-force, is matched and extended by the imagery of the "Chase" chapters. There, finally, Ahab identifies with the air and the sea, with the restless, aimless, eternal motions of wind and waves. Whereas earlier he thought analogically, following the traditional religious identification of wind with the human breath of inspiration ("Would now St. Paul would come along that way, and to my breezelessness bring his breeze!" Ch. 70, p. 264), now he faces the wind with primitive directness as an equal force in a world of forces: "Were I the wind, I'd blow no more on such a wicked, miserable world. I'd crawl somewhere to a cave, and slink there. And yet, 'tis a noble and heroic thing, the wind! who ever conquered it?" (Ch. 135, p. 460). This Lear-like "madness" reveals the elemental nakedness of man's place in nature. On the last day Ahab tells Starbuck: "Some men die at ebb tide; some at low water; some at the full of the flood;—and I feel now like a billow that's all one crested comb" (p. 462). A conventional metaphor suddenly becomes a statement of identity. Ahab's human energy, he now realizes hopelessly but defiantly, has no more force upon the impenetrable rock-like nature of things than that of a momen-

12. Kazin, *Melville: A Collection of Critical Essays*, p. 46.

tary wall of water. He repeats the image in his final speech: "Oh, lonely death on lonely life! Oh, now I feel my topmost greatness lies in my topmost grief. Ho, ho! from all your furthest bounds, pour ye now in, ye bold billows of my whole foregone life, and top this one piled comber of my death!" (p. 468). This "one piled comber" breaks upon the whale, as the whale's "predestinating head" breaks upon the ship; "then all collapsed, and the great shroud of the sea rolled on as it rolled five thousand years ago." Like the ship, like the wave, Ahab's personality collapses, slipping back into the undifferentiated oneness of the empty sea. His vulture-like mind consumes itself; the "tormenting, mild" image of himself he saw in the water fades as the ripples left by a dropping pebble fade into ever-widening circles. But the mighty voice remains; Ishmael still plucks at the sky and dives into the deep to make it heard.

Ahab's character is a unique feature of American Romanticism; not one or all of Poe's and Hawthorne's dark Gothic isolatoes can match him. Melville has taken the imagination far down an endless corridor with Ahab (though he evidently intended to lead Pierre Glendinning even farther). The Ahab who stands facing the fiery corpusants is really a "representative man" (to appropriate Emerson's phrase), as representative of the American Romantic imagination as Henry Thoreau standing on the shores of Walden, announcing: "I went to the woods because I wished to live deliberately, to front only the essential facts of life . . . I wanted to live deep and suck out all the marrow of life, to live so sturdily and Spartan-like as to put to rout all that was not life, to cut a broad swath and shave close, to drive life into a corner, and reduce it to its lowest terms. . . ." Thoreau's stubborn recognition of the reality of "things" combines with his insatiable appetite for experience: "If you stand right fronting and face to face to a fact, you will see the sun glimmer on both its surfaces, as if it were a cimeter, and feel its sweet edge dividing you through the heart and marrow. . . . Be it life or death, we crave only reality."[13] Ahab's career stems from the same faith, the same craving, but as he knows it the dividing edge is not sweet. To stare with Ahab into the heart of the fire is to see life reduced to its lowest terms with an impact Thoreau could barely imagine.

Walt Whitman sometimes felt the force of an Ahab-like narcissism, as in "As I Ebb'd with the Ocean of Life":

> I too Paumanok,
> I too have bubbled up, floated the measureless float,
> and been washed on your shores,
> I too am but a trail of drift and debris,

13. Henry David Thoreau, "Where I Lived and What I Lived For," in *Walden*; *Writings* (Boston, 1906), II. 100–1, 109.

I too leave little wrecks upon you, you fish-shaped
island.

Whitman's imagination of disaster is like Thoreau's, particular and fully naturalistic. Thoreau knows what it feels like to be an animal, or a fish, or a bird; Whitman knows the pull of the infinite ocean, its power to turn a healthy body into "sea-drift," atomized "little wrecks." But only Ahab knows the ultimate emptiness on the other side of the mirror; at the end he sees himself reduced to a billow, to a brief disturbance on the blank surfacc of 'things." Like the wake of the unconquered whale, he is "a thing writ on water" (Ch. 134, p. 453). It is through Melville's awareness of such a potential evanescence in human speech itself that we should see his featuring of Ahab.

BRIGID BROPHY, MICHAEL LEVEY, AND CHARLES OSBORNE

[The Great White Elephant]†

So they constructed a synthetic one for the film? But only by a grievous misjudgment did the one in the book ever pass for genuine. Even on the level of natural-historical observation Moby Dick isn't a true whale. 'Be it known,' writes the narrator, 'that, waiving all argument, I take the good old-fashioned ground that the whale is a fish'—a wrong guess which he can't even square with his own apprehension of the facts, since he later writes of 'nursing mothers' among whales. Still less is Moby Dick the organic product of a true imagination. He's a mere inflated pretend-whale, inflated by the sheer wish that American literature should run to profundity.

The humblest claim made for Melville by his idolators is that he spins a good yarn: and he belies even that. Three-quarters of *Moby Dick* is a monument to Melville's inability to get down to telling his story at all. A hundred or so chapters elapse in dissertations, digressions, moralizings, symbolizings and chunks quoted from dictionaries and encyclopaedias before the narrative proper starts; and when it does, it turns out to be a slight little anecdote which comes too quickly and goes for almost nothing. Conrad, with all his technical cunning, would have been hard put to it to elaborate a short

† Brigid Brophy, Michael Levey, and Charles Osborne, "Moby Dick or The White Whale," *Fifty Works of English (and American) Literature We Could Do Without* (New York: Stein and Day Publishers, 1967), pp. 73–75.

story out of the captain who, having lost a leg to the unique albino whale, seeks vengeance so monomaniacally and so recklessly as to lose his own life, his crew's and his ship. Melville is simply not up to the swift graphic narrative required by the externals of the tale. He muddies the action alternately with bathos and with would-be poeticisms and inversions: 'as if sucked into a morass, Moby Dick sideways writhed'; 'three of the oarsmen—who foreknew not the precise instant of the dart, and were therefore unprepared for its effects—these were flung out'. The internals, the psychology, Melville cannot even make a put at, since he cannot create Captain Ahab's obsession but can only refer to it. Indeed, the whole of *Moby Dick* is a gigantic memorandum, to the effect 'What a story this would make, if told by someone who knew how to tell stories'. Even that is a mis-estimate: it wouldn't.

Melville is not a novelist: he is an annotator and labeller. Throughout the superfluous hundred chapters before he appears, the white whale's shadow is cast at the reader in advance; and Melville, who is basically a lantern-lecturer (of the kind whose own chiaroscuro mannerisms provoke audiences to say 'What an actor he'd make'—again a mis-estimate: he wouldn't), constantly labels—but never *makes*—the shadow 'portentous'. Ishmael (that most confusing of narrators, since he narrates information he can't, within the terms of his own narrative, have possessed) hasn't so much as set foot on a whaler when he first calls a whale 'a portentous and mysterious monster'. In a sailors' lodging house he sees a painting of a whale which he twice in a paragraph describes as 'portentous'. By the time he's on board, even the appetites of the ship's company strike him as 'portentous'. The only item in the book that might be truly labelled portentous is Ishmael's own narrative manner. 'All these things are not without their meanings', he portentously says—without, however, saying what the meanings are, unless they lurk in the intellectual pretentiousness whereby he speaks of two dead whales' heads as 'Locke's head' and 'Kant's'. Sharks eating whales' corpses are pronounced by Ishmael 'a part of the universal problem of all things'. What, however, isn't?

Many novelists have tried to anticipate the critic's task by writing both narrative and a commentary alongside it pointing out the deeper beauties, profundities and significances of the narrative. Melville alone has supplied the commentary without supplying the narrative.

Moby Dick is shadow play by a Victorian-Gothic whale of papier-mâché. When he spouts, up comes a cacophonous false rhetoric ('meads and glades so eternally vernal that . . .'). When he sports, he is grotesque in his whimsy ('as when the red-cheeked, dancing girls, April and May, trip home'), obese in his facetiousness ('he was stopped on the way by a portly Sperm Whale, that begged a few moments' confidential business with him') and ungainly in his sprightliness ('The act of paying is perhaps the most uncomfortable infliction that the two orchard thieves entailed upon us'). He's worst of all when he fumbles for a metaphysical conceit in which to embody an emotional moment: 'Their hands met; their eyes fastened; Starbuck's tears the glue.'

Distended with hot air himself, Melville's whale can beget no progeny except wind eggs. One of them contained just life enough to hatch into the crocodile in *Peter Pan*. Otherwise, the whale is father to nothing but the dozens of novels which, with only the proper name altered, have repeated his burly opening sentence, 'Call me Ishmael', and the misconceptions that (a) the Great American Novel can be written by thinking about writing it instead of thinking about whatever it is about, (b) that it must be about brutality to animals, and (c) that brutality to animals, if pursued by men whose tears are the glue which fasten their eyes to the eyes of their fellow men, is manly and portentous. (Where did all the great white whales go? They went Hemingway.) *Moby Dick* is American literature's pseudo-founding-father, its false prophet in fake biblical prose, its Reproduction Antique ancient monument. American literature is now old enough and good enough to sell off the great white elephant.

HEINZ KOSOK

Ishmael's Audience in "The *Town-Ho*'s Story"†

Nobody seems to have given much thought to the question why in "The *Town-Ho*'s Story" Ishmael deviates from the normal narrative manner of *Moby-Dick*. It will be remembered that Ishmael learns the story (which concerns certain events on an earlier voyage of the *Town-Ho*) from Tashtego to whom it has been communicated "with Romish injunctions of secresy" by one of "three confederate white seamen" during a gam with the *Town-Ho*, "but the following night Tashtego rambled in his sleep, and revealed so much of it in that way, that when he was wakened he could not well withhold the rest". Ishmael, however, does not present the story as he heard it then from Tashtego but as he told it, on another voyage, to a group of listeners entirely different in type from the *Pequod*'s crew; and his evasive explanation for this choice

† From Heinz Kosok, "Ishmael's Audience in 'The *Town Ho*'s Story,'" *Notes and Queries*, Vol. 14, n.s. (February, 1967), 54–56. Reprinted by permission of the publisher, Oxford University Press, London.

is calculated to arouse the reader's suspicions: "For my humor's sake, I shall preserve the style in which I once narrated it at Lima, to a lounging circle of my Spanish friends. . . ."

This procedure is unusual in two respects: first, Ishmael here leaves his rather rigid time scheme. All the other parts of *Moby-Dick* are told either as they occurred at the time of the Pequod's voyage, or as they are recalled and commented upon by the narrator, whose own position in the present is indicated several times, even to the point of ironic exaggeration ("fifteen and a quarter minutes past one o'clock P.M. of this sixteenth day of December, A.D. 1851."). "The *Town-Ho*'s Story" on the other hand is told at some point in time *between* the events on the *Pequod* and the narrator's present. Second, and more important, "The *Town-Ho*'s Story" is the only part of *Moby-Dick* in which it becomes clear not only *when*, but also *to whom* Ishmael tells his story.

The chief discussions of "The *Town-Ho*'s Story" have in various ways tried to account for this most unusual procedure. For Sherman Paul, the "scene of the telling of the story in 'corrupt' Lima, to men conditioned by Catholic mysteries and yet unbelieving, forms a contrast to the heightened all-pervading religious content of the tale and reaffirms Ishmael's devotion to the mysterious fatalities of life".[1] Don Geiger thinks that Ishmael describes "to these orthodox Catholic landsmen an even more marvelous divinity than the miraculous one to which they pay their skeptical and gentlemanly respects".[2] James Dean Young treats "The *Town-Ho*'s Story on the same level as the other eight gams of the Pequod and does not comment on the peculiarity of its presentation.[3] Warner Berthoff sees a double purpose in the frame action of the story: on the one hand, "Melville brings Ishmael's audience of cavaliers back into view, using their gravely attentive reactions to support the tone and point up certain colorful details, and to ratify the strangeness and excitement of the story's wilder passages". On the other hand, the frame serves as a "formal gathering of these events and characters into recollection and some order of imaginative understanding".[4] While Paul's, Geiger's and Berthoff's observations are useful, none of their suggestions are entirely satisfactory. Paul, perhaps, inadvertently comes nearest to an explanation when he notices that the "audience of entertainment-expecting Dons . . . are driven to outbursts of incredulity *much as the reader* who at

1. Sherman Paul, "Melville's 'The *Town-Ho*'s Story,'" *American Literature*, xxi (1949/50), 212–22, p. 212.
2. Don Geiger, "Melville's Black God: Contrary Evidence in 'The *Town-Ho*'s Story,'" *American Literature*, xxv (1953/54), 464–71, p. 465.
3. James Dean Young, "The Nine Gams of the *Pequod*," *American Literature*, xxv (1953/54), pp. 449-63.
4. Warner Berthoff, *The Example of Melville* (Princeton, 1962), p. 135. Berthoff (pp. 133–38) has the most extensive discussion of Melville's narrative, technique in "The *Town-Ho*'s Story".

this point in *Moby-Dick* first encounters the whale . . .",[5] but he does not follow up this observation.

It is the purpose of this note to suggest that in "The *Town-Ho*'s Story" Melville's choice of the audience has a very definite aim: he here presents a deliberate dramatization of his own reading public. The reactions of Ishmael's listeners are very much the same as the reactions of Melville's audience, as he had experienced them after the publication of his earlier novels and as he expected them to be after that of *Moby-Dick*. This theory can be substantiated by a closer investigation of the story.

It has frequently been noted that, on a superficial level, there are many parallels between "The *Town-Ho*'s Story" and the general outline of *Moby-Dick*. Both stories are told by the same narrator, they both deal with certain unusual events on a whaling ship, in both cases the same white whale brings destruction to one of the chief characters, and there are several close resemblances between these characters.[6] Therefore, in spite of certain important differences between the two works (which have been discussed at length by Geiger and Paul), for the purpose of the present study "The *Town-Ho*'s Story" can be considered as an epitome of *Moby-Dick*, or at least as an abbreviated and simplified version similar enough to the novel to evoke analogous emotions in the reader. It is possible, then, that there are parallels between Ishmael's attitude to his story and Melville's attitude to his novel as a whole.

Ishmael gives the place where he originally told the story as Lima, a city curiously associated in Melville's imagination with evil and corruption. This is confirmed in the story where one of Ishmael's listeners quotes the proverbial saying "Corrupt as Lima". It soon becomes evident that Lima is a symbol of the world in general, and Don Pedro, another member of the audience, stresses this by stating explicitly "The world's one Lima". The scene of the telling of the story is therefore a corrupt world, dominated by evil.

The first characteristic Ishmael observes in his listeners is the easy and leisurely manner in which they receive the story of the tragic events on the *Town-Ho*. They are a "lounging circle" of gentlemen, "smoking upon the thick-gilt tiled piazza of the Golden

5. Paul, op. cit., p. 212.

6. If one accepts the theory that Melville re-wrote *Moby-Dick* to a large extent, it may be suggested that the first version of the novel possibly had an even closer resemblance to "The *Town-Ho*'s Story" for the character in *Moby-Dick* whom Steelkilt resembles more than any other is Bulkington, who, according to the *Ur-Moby-Dick* theory, was destined for an important rôle in the novel and was only at a later stage rejected by the author. If originally Bulkington was designed as the opponent of Captain Ahab, "The *Town-Ho*'s Story" may very well represent a simplified and abbreviated version of the *Ur-Moby-Dick*, with the central conflict between a brutal and overbearing sea-captain and a passionate but noble sailor. For the most extensive discussion of the *Ur-Moby-Dick* theory see George R. Stewart, "The Two *Moby-Dicks*," *American Literature*, xxv (1953/54), 417–48.

Inn", and instead of breathless fascination they show merely a polite interest in their guest's "amusing" story. Melville here comments on the contrast between his own creative agony while writing *Moby-Dick*, and the material and intellectual comfort of his readers, which was hardly conducive to a proper understanding of the meaning of the novel. This lack of understanding, which Melville had experienced after the publication of *Mardi* and which he again expected for *Moby-Dick*, is evinced by the Peruvian Dons at the Golden Inn. Whenever they interrupt Ishmael's narrative, they prove their insufficient concentration, their interest in superficial and irrelevant detail, and their inability to grasp the central problem of the story.

The first two of these interruptions occur when Ishmael mentions Lake Erie and Buffalo and the Erie Canal. In both cases the dramatic tension of the story is diminished because Ishmael, with obvious unwillingness, has to answer these irrelevant questions. The first time he replies as briefly as possible; the second time, however, he begins to realize that his story may gain added significance from a description of Steelkilt's and Radney's homes: "... ere proceeding further I will tell ye what our Canallers are; for such information may throw side-light upon my story". In other places, too, Ishmael comments on the value of factual information. After discussing the respective duties of boys and able seamen, he remarks: "I mention all these particulars so that you may understand exactly how this affair stood between the two men". This sounds very much like a justification for the inclusion of the bulk of factual detail in *Moby-Dick*. Melville knew from his first two novels how much his readers were interested in factual information. In *Moby-Dick*, especially in the cetological chapters, he included more information than in any other of his works, but he integrated it into the plot and not only made it "throw side-light" upon his story, but employed it so that the reader could "understand exactly how this affair stood" between Captain Ahab and the White Whale. In one place of "The *Town-Ho*'s Story", however, Ishmael refuses to be side-tracked from the straight course of his narrative: he has reached the dramatic moment when Moby Dick is sighted from the *Town-Ho*.

> 'Moby Dick!' cried Don Sebastian; 'St. Dominic! Sir sailor, but do whales have christenings? Whom call you Moby Dick?'
>
> 'A very white, and famous, and most deadly immortal monster, Don;—but that would be too long a story'.

Unlike Ishmael, Melville in his novel anticipated his readers' curiosity on this point, and to satisfy it wrote chapter 41, "Moby Dick".

Curiosity about irrelevant detail, which Ishmael turns into relevant subject matter, is one of the dominant traits of Ishmael's audience. The second, and equally important, characteristic is conformity to religious conventions. They are not at all sincere believers, genuinely upset by certain unorthodox aspects of Ishmael's story. When the narrator mentions that sinners "most abound in holiest vicinities," Don Pedro, "with humorous concern," asks "Is that a friar passing?". In other words, it does not matter whether Ishmael has uttered an irreverency but whether a friar has heard it: the audience is not concerned about the truth or falsity of such a statement but about its propriety. This attitude becomes even clearer at the end, where Ishmael, with deep seriousness, confirms the truth of his story and is ready to swear on it before a priest: " 'Though there are no Auto-da-Fés in Lima now,' said one of the company to another: 'I fear our sailor friend runs risk of the archiepiscopacy. Let us withdraw more out of the moon-light. I see no need for this' ". Melville, of course, was aware of the probability that *Moby-Dick,* even more so than his earlier novels, would be criticized for its apparent irreverence (it is hardly necessary to quote his famous statement "I have written a wicked book, and feel spotless as the lamb" in support of this). He knew that many of his readers would rather reject the "truth" he felt he had written, than allow him to violate the teachings of their churches, however little they might believe in them. They would be afraid that, in the words of Don Sebastian, "this may grow too serious". Several early reviews of *Moby-Dick* show that Melville was not far off the mark when he predicted such a reception for his novel.

One more common trait of Melville's readers can be discovered in Ishmael's audience: they are far less concerned about the tale's spiritual meaning than its surface authenticity.

> 'Are you through?' said Don Sebastian, quietly.
>
> 'I am, Don.'
>
> 'Then I entreat you, tell me if to the best of your own convictions, this your story is in substance really true? It is so passing wonderful! Did you get it from an unquestionable source? Bear with me if I seem to press.'
>
> 'Also bear with all of us, sir sailor; for we all join in Don Sebastian's suit,' cried the company, with exceeding interest.

Melville had repeatedly experienced such an attitude after the publication of *Typee* and *Omoo*. But while his readers were only interested to know whether he had really seen the things he described, Melville himself, in *Moby-Dick,* was convinced that he had spoken a higher truth, because he had emotionally lived through Ahab's quest; therefore Ishmael can confirm with complete assurance: "So help me Heaven, and on my honor the story I have told ye, gentlemen, is in substance and its great items, true".

In "The *Town-Ho*'s Story", then, the reader is placed on the same level as Ishmael's audience, who thus becomes an image of Melville's reading public. To judge from this story, Melville's opinion of his readers was certainly not favourable; and the reaction to his works in the nineteenth century proved its justification.

BERNARD MOSHER AND DOUGLASS WIGMORE

The Mobled Dick†

"But who, O who, had seen the mobled Queen—"

Hamlet

Ch. 1: The opening scene of *Moby-Dick* is laid at Nantucket. [Ishmael says] "This is my substitute for pistol and balls." Ch. 2: As Ishmael is about to enter the Spouter-Inn in New Bedford, he comes upon a simple scene that embodies in miniature all the evil which the world's mask of innocence blandly hides. A beggar lies shivering in the streets. Ch. 3: His sketch of the Spouter-Inn, its hoarse, salt landlord, its delicious clam chowder, the frightful Mowrèe harpooner whose bed the hero has to share, enchant the imagination and chisel the memory. [Ishmael's] soul, like Bulkington's, his sleeping partner, keeps "the open independence of the sea." Here are two orphans . . . Queequeg the South Sea Island heathen and Ishmael the Massachusetts inlander. Ch. 4: But though he [Ishmael] is in bed . . . he is not this time trying to crawl up his mother's chimney. He embraces no woman, only another male. Ch. 9: In Father Mapple's sermon . . . the fundamental proposition is asserted: "But what then? Methinks that what we call my shadow here on earth is my true substance." [T]he minister makes his second point, the application of the text from *Job* to himself "as an anointed pilot-prophet or speaker of true things." As Father Mapple sinks in exhaustion to the floor of his pulpit, he breathes —"O Father!—chiefly known to me by Thy rod." In this acknowledgment lies the essence of the inhumanity of his sermon. Ch. 10: They divide between them Ishmael's wordly goods (Melville, who cannot resist overdetermining everything, makes it thirty pieces of silver), and discuss the counter-claims of their rival religions. Ish-

† From "The Mobled Dick: An Imperfect Summary of *Moby-Dick* Maliciously Compiled from Sundry Authentic Accounts Published by the Best Contradictory Authorities," with the kind permission of the compilers, Bernard Mosher and Douglass Wigmore.

mael is not merely an orphan; he is an exile, searching alone in the wilderness, with a black man for his only friend. Ch. 16: Ahab . . . [is] a godlike ungodly old man. Ch. 17: But his [Queequeg's] significance as ethos, after we leave him awaking at the Spouter-Inn from his Ramadan, appears only once more. Ch. 18: Mrs. Hussey and Ishmael . . . decide Queequeg has killed himself despite the sign at the desk demanding "No suicides." Ch. 23: Next Bulkington, the unaffiliated man of pure, unquestioning spirituality, is swept overboard at the start of the voyage (how isolated he would have been among the *Pequod*'s crew!). Once aboard the *Pequod* Ishmael seems almost to cease breathing. Rather than regret his "disappearance," many critics admire his new role as an epic poet or dramatist or choric embodiment of the consciousness of the crew. But Ishmael does not disappear as suddenly as Bulkington, washed overboard in the "Lee Shore" chapter. (Some critics even suggest that as an ideal norm Bulkington never really disappears!) Ch. 26: Ahab is, of course, the atheistical captain of the tormented soul; and his crew, so Melville says, is "chiefly made of mongrel renegades, and cast-aways and cannibals." Ch. 27: Queequeg and his fellow-harpooners, both savages, one of them a Red Indian from the lakes, the other a coal-black man from Africa, are the happiest, because the most fanciful of the minor sketches. Ch. 28: When Ahab finally steps forth on the quarter-deck, he lives up in appearance to the image created in fancy. . . . Two physical features command the attention of the gaping sailors. As Ishmael stares at him he notices first a huge white scar running down the side of his face—a face wreathed in wretched long strands of gray hair. Ch. 29: At night Ahab paces the deck and his wooden leg pounding on the deck creates such a noise some of crew are kept awake. Ch. 36: Captain Ahab has the Steward bring out wine, twice, and the flagon is passed around in a ceremony dedicated to the destruction of Moby Dick. Ch. 40: The wine casks are opened and the crew lives it up through the night, drinking and shouting and singing. Ch. 48: The skipper and the mates of the *Pequod* hail from Nantucket or the Cape or the Vineyard; all the characters, including the pagan harpooneers, and even perhaps the Parsees, are such men as might have been found, though some of them rarely, on an actual whaler of the 'forties. Ch. 54: Shortly after we pull alongside the *Town-Ho* for a Gam, or social meeting between two crews. We learn—and keep secret from Ahab—that they have lost a man to the jaws of Moby Dick. "Just between daybreak and sunrise," the topwatch spied out Moby-Dick and involuntarily cried, " 'Jesu, what a whale,' " calling out Christ's name instinctively at the critical moment when the whale had come to take from Steelkilt his revenge. Forced labor at the pumps . . . created a mutiny which was interrupted by the appearance of Moby Dick. The boats were lowered but the harpooner on the boat nearest him was devoured by the Great White Whale. The ship made harbor and most of the crew deserted for fear of encountering Moby Dick. Ch. 59: The crew of the *Pequod* one day beholds a monstrous white squid, so large that it seems to fill the whole horizon and to loom far above the sea into the heavens. Ch. 66: Sharks will consume a whale in six hours, Ishmael tells us. But in the Indian Ocean (where the *Pequod* is at anchor) the sharks are fewer and less voracious. Ch. 70: Ahab . . . muses what sights and sounds the creature has seen in the great sea depths. Ch. 93: In a chapter titled "The Castaway" we learn how little Pip on his first whale chase had leapt in terror into the sea and was abandoned as Stubb pursued the whale. . . . When saved by the ship, "the little negro went about the deck an idiot." Ch. 95: The Cassock itself turns out to be the foreskin of the whale. . . . Ishmael has described how a section of the whale's foreskin is made into a garment for the "mincer." Dressed in a coverall made of dried whaleskin turned inside out, the "mincer" cuts the blubber into "Bible leaves" (slices). Ch. 96: Ishmael falls asleep at the tiller one midnight, as the "Pequod" is passing through the Java seas heading northwest toward the haunts of the great sperm whales. Waking up, but not yet aware that he has been asleep, Ishmael finds himself staring into the mouth of hell: "a jet gloom, now and then made ghastly by flashes of redness," an infernal scene through which giant shadow-shapes like devils are moving about some dreadful work. He is "horribly conscious of something fatally wrong"; "a stark bewildered feeling as of death" comes over him. Then he realizes—just in time to swing about, grasp the tiller, and save the ship from capsizing—that he has turned in his sleep and is facing the two furnaces, "try-pots," amidships, and the three black harpooners stoking the masses of whale blubber from which the oil is extracted ("tryed-out"). Ch. 99: Melville directs our attention to the shining gold-piece which he has nailed to the mainmast as a reward for him who first sighted the White Whale. Ch. 107: As Fedallah is drowning, Ahab, for no overt cause, moans for the "unforgiven ghosts of Gomorrah." The Words in the soul rise to the lips on a sudden, because no lust can sink them. Ch. 110: Queequeg . . . is shown at one point as simply refusing to die . . . but not before he has made his own coffin. . . . for a while . . . this wondrously engraved coffin serves as his seabag. There is, at least once, a noble pathos in the description of Queequeg's death: "An awe that cannot be named would steal over you as you sat by the side of this waning savage, and saw as strange things in his face, as any beheld who were bystanders when Zoroaster died." Ch. 118: Ahab . . .

even throws the quadrant overboard. Ch. 132: [E]ven "the lovely aromas in that enchanted air" were unable, for more than a moment, to "dispel . . . the cantankerous thing" in Ahab's soul. Ch. 135 [Then comes] Ahab's last sight of the Parsee tangled in the harpoons on Moby Dick's back. When the third day of the chase began, Moby Dick seemed tired, and the *Pequod's* boats soon overtook him. . . . [Moby Dick] ran a muck, Tartar fashion, right at the persecuting whaler, and seizing the vessel in his mouth, as a schoolboy of tender years would a cherry, smashed her to pieces with a single bite. . . . All except Ishmael perished. He was rescued by a passing ship after clinging for hours to Queequeg's canoe-coffin, which had bobbed to the surface as the *Pequod* sank. Although the savage harpooneers get nearest the whale, the savage universe, it is Ahab and the Parsee, the European and the Asiatic, who carry the pursuit to its ultimate end—while a single American survives to tell the tale! "Epilogue": [Ishmael] ends the book as a baby reborn from the sea in Queequeg's coffin.

An Annotated Bibliography

Since *MOBY-DICK as Doubloon* contains the basic evidence for the study of the reception and early critical history of *Moby-Dick*, reviews and later comments through 1920 are not listed here. More recent selections in *Doubloon* are not normally included except to show other reprintings. To make the bibliography most useful to readers interested in tendencies in Melville scholarship, we have made the arrangement chronological, like the arrangement of the table of contents, and have provided cross-references for certain articles which deal with common critical problems. Annotations are phrased to give the authors' opinions, not necessarily ours (e.g., "Ahab, not Ishmael, is the real center of meaning"), yet we have ventured judgments when it seemed appropriate. When titles are self-explanatory we have not provided annotations. Our principle throughout has been to make the bibliography complementary to the selections in *Doubloon*.

Anyone specially interested in the Melville revival will find two other annotated bibliographies helpful. The first is Willard Thorp, *Herman Melville: Representative Selections* (New York: American Book Company, 1938), pp. cxxxiii–clxi, including items from the 1850's essays through the late 1930's. The second is Michael Zimmerman, "Herman Melville in the 1920's: An Annotated Bibliography," *Bulletin of Bibliography*, Vol. 24 (Sept.–Dec., 1964) 117–120, 106 [*sic*]; (Jan.–April, 1965), 139–144. Maurice Beebe, Harrison Hayford, and Gordon Roper prepared an unannotated bibliography of Melville criticism for *Modern Fiction Studies*, Vol. 8 (Autumn, 1962), 312–346; the *Moby-Dick* section, arranged alphabetically by author, is 333–342. The best survey of Melville scholarship through the mid-1950's is that by Stanley T. Williams in *Eight American Authors* (New York: *MLA*, 1956; New York: Harcourt Brace, 1963). For each year since 1963 James Woodress has edited an annual volume called *American Literary Scholarship*, published by Duke University Press, each with a chapter surveying and evaluating the most recent work on Melville. Willard Thorp wrote the first four essays; Merton M. Sealts, Jr., succeeded Thorp for the 1967 volume. For items appearing after the publication of *MOBY-DICK as Doubloon*, one may consult the monthly *Abstracts of English Studies*, the bibliography in each issue of *American Literature*, and the annual bibliography of the *Publications of the Modern Language Association*, as well as *American Literary Scholarship*.

A few names of journals have been abbreviated:
AL: American Literature
AQ: American Quarterly
ELH: English Literary History
ELN: English Language Notes
ESQ: Emerson Society Quarterly
MLN: Modern Language Notes
MLQ: Modern Language Quarterly
NCF: Nineteenth-Century Fiction
NEQ: New England Quarterly
PMLA: Publications of the Modern Language Association
SSF: Studies in Short Fiction
TSLL: Texas Studies in Literature and Language

For most years there appear two subheadings: *Books*, which includes books, pamphlets, annuals—anything dated merely by the year—and *Articles*, which includes anything dated more specifically as to season, month, or day of month. We use a simplified version of the *MLA* form, reducing the number of commas and omitting "Vol." and "Pp." Volume numbers are given arabic rather than roman numerals. Both in the text of *Doubloon* and in the bibliography we list the publishers of all books, since the interest and lack of interest of various publishers in Melville is part of the history of his reputation.

1921
BOOK

Weaver, Raymond M. *Herman Melville: Mariner and Mystic* (New York: Doran, 1921); reprinted New York: Pageant Books, 1960. The pioneer biography. Its successors have corrected errors of fact and interpretation. Contains background information on whaling.

1922
BOOK

Canby, H. S. "Conrad and Melville," in *Definitions, First Series* (New York: Harcourt, Brace, 1922) 257-268. Melville a greater artist but lesser craftsman than Conrad.

ARTICLES

Colum, Padraic. "*MD* as an Epic: A Note," *Measure,* 13 (March 1922) 16–18; reprinted as "Epic of the Sea" in *A Half-Day's Ride* (New York: Macmillan, 1932) 175–179. Theme, characters, and style of *MD* are epical, not novelistic. Colum arranges passages as verse.

Colcord, Lincoln. "Notes on *MD,*" *Freeman* 5 (Aug. 23, 1922) 559–562; (Aug. 30, 1922) 585–587. An "appreciation" with unusual stress on technique; criticism of Melville for not exploiting seamanship and for allowing Hawthorne's influence to mar the ending of *MD.* Reprinted in Parker (1967) and Vincent (1969).

1923
BOOKS

Lawrence, D. H. "Herman Melville's *MD,*" in Studies in *Classic American Literature* (New York: Seltzer, 1923) 214–240; reprinted New York: Doubleday Anchor, 1953. The chapter is reprinted in Stern (1960) and Vincent (1969). An earlier, fuller version is in *The Symbolic Meaning,* ed. Armin Arnold (London: Centaur, 1962) 217–250; (New York: Viking, 1964) 211–228. Ancestor of much mytho-psychoanalytic criticism. The white whale is the deepest blood-being of the white race.

Van Doren, Carl. "Mocha Dick," in *Roving Critic* (New York: Knopf, 1923) 97–99. Story about "Mocha Dick" by J. N. Reynolds is called a source of *MD.*

ARTICLES

Wells, W. H. "*MD* and Rabelais," *MLN* 38 (Feb. 1923) 123. Cites Rabelais parallels for "The Whiteness of the Whale." See Quinn (1952).

Sullivan, J. W. N. "Herman Melville," *Times Literary Supplement* (July 26, 1923) 493–494; reprinted in *Aspects of Science, Second Series* (New York: Knopf, 1926) 190–205.

Woolf, Leonard. "Herman Melville," *Nation and Athenæum* 33 (Sept. 1, 1923) 688. Melville wrote the most execrable English, yet *MD* is a great book. Excerpted in the Norton Critical Edition of *MD* (1967).

1924

Van Doren, Carl. "Mr. Melville's *MD,*" *Bookman* (New York) 59 (April 1924) 154–157. Variety of possible interpretations a mark of *MD*'s greatness. Ahab a Faust and a Lucifer. Length and blank verse objectionable but there is powerful control and superb language.

1925
BOOK

Mumford, Lewis. *Aesthetics, a Dialogue* (New York: Troutbeck, 1925). Quoted in Freeman (1926) 120–121. The "irrelevancies" of *MD* are essential to its form.

ARTICLE

Van Doren, Carl. "Lucifer from Nantucket. An Introduction to *MD,*" *Century* 110 (Aug. 1925) 494–501; reprinted in *American Criticism, 1926* (New York:

Harcourt Brace, 1926) 308–325 and *Century Readings in the English Essay*, ed. Louis Wann, revised edition (New York: Appleton-Century, 1939) 541–547. Ahab as Yankee Faust and Lucifer whom Melville might have become.

1926
BOOKS

Ashley, Clifford W. *The Yankee Whaler* (Boston: Houghton Mifflin, 1926). Excellent account of whaling, with illustrations. References to *MD passim.*

Freeman, John. *Herman Melville* (London: Macmillan, 1926). A biography (dependent upon Weaver, 1921) and a critical study.

1927
BOOKS

Brooks, Van Wyck. *Emerson and Others* (New York: Dutton, 1927) 195–205. *MD* is carefully constructed as an epic. Reprinted from *Freeman* 7 (May 16, 1923); the text in *Doubloon* is from the *Freeman.*

Forster, E. M. "Prophecy," in *Aspects of the Novel* (New York: Harcourt, Brace, 1927); reprinted New York: Harcourt, Brace, 1950 (181–212). Warns against codifying meanings of *MD*, whose essence is "prophecy."

Parrington, V. L. "Herman Melville," in *Main Currents in American Thought*, (New York: Harcourt, Brace, 1927) II, 258–267; reprinted New York: Harvest, n.d. (II, 249–259). Based on Weaver (1921); discusses Melville and democracy.

ARTICLE

Pattee, F. L. "Herman Melville," *American Mercury* 10 (Jan. 1927) 33–43.

1928
BOOKS

Clark, Harry Hayden. "American Literary History and American Literature," in *The Re-Interpretation of American Literature, ed.* Norman Foerster (New York: Harcourt, Brace, 1928). *MD* as a protesting recoil from the extravagances of Romantic thought.

Erskine, John. "*MD*," in *The Delight of Great Books* (Indianapolis: Bobbs-Merrill, 1928) 223–240. *MD* a poetic prose tragedy.

Hohman, Elmo Paul. *The American Whaleman* (New York: Longmans, Green, 1928). Best book on practical and economic side of whaling.

1929
BOOK

Mumford, Lewis. *Herman Melville* (New York: Harcourt, Brace, 1929 and New York: Literary Guild, 1929). New edition, slightly revised and corrected, New York: Harcourt, Brace, 1963. Superseded in details of biography (and in criticism based on biographical errors) but still valuable for main biographical and critical conception. Excerpted in Parker (1967) 188–193.

ARTICLE

Gleim, W. S. "A Theory of *MD*," *NEQ* 2 (July 1929) 402–419. An allegorical, Swedenborgian interpretation, giving fixed meanings to characters and major materials. See Gleim (1938).

1931

Rourke, Constance M. *American Humor* (New York: Harcourt, Brace, 1931) 191–200; reprinted New York: Doubleday Anchor, 1953, 154–160. Discusses folklore elements; Melville moved with the American temper in *MD.*

1932
BOOKS

Calverton, V. F. *The Liberation of American Literature* (New York: Scribner's, 1932) 271–273. A sociological interpretation; *MD* indicts U.S. capitalist society.

DeVoto, Bernard. *Mark Twain's America* (Boston: Little, Brown, 1932) 312–313. Unfavorable comparisons of *MD* with *Huckleberry Finn*. Reprinted in the Norton Critical Edition of *MD* (1967).

Lewisohn, Ludwig, *Expression in America* (New York: Harper, 1932) 186–193. Reprinted as *The Story of American Literature* (New York: Modern Library, 1939) 153–193. Very unfavorable judgment of Melville and his works. Briefly excerpted in the Norton Critical Edition of *MD* (1967).

ARTICLES

Ament, William S. "Bowdler and the Whale: Some Notes on the First English and American Editions of *MD*," *AL* (March 1932) 39–46. Textual comparisons: the English edition was expurgated. Does not recognize that it was also corrected by Melville. Superseded by the section "Textual Problems of *Moby-Dick*" in the Norton Critical Edition (1967) 471–477.

Hughes, Raymond G. "Melville and Shakespeare," *Shakespeare Association Bulletin* 7 (July 1932) 103–112. Lists parallel passages of borrowings in *MD*.

Homans, George C. "The Dark Angel: The Tragedy of Herman Melville," *NEQ* 5 (Oct. 1932) 699–730. *Mardi*, *MD*, and *Pierre* a tragedy in three acts. Action is intellectual, not physical.

1933
BOOKS

Brooks, Van Wyck. "Herman Melville," in *Dictionary of American Biography* (New York: Heath, 1933) 522–526.

Edgar, Pelham. "Herman Melville and *MD*," in *The Art of the Novel* (New York: Macmillan, 1933) 130–135. General interpretation.

ARTICLE

Couch, H. N. "*MD* and the Phaedo," *Classical Journal* 28 (Feb. 1933) 367–368. Last paragraph of Ch. 7 is from Plato.

1934

Howard, Leon. "A Predecessor of *MD*," *MLN* 49 (May 1934) 310–311. A possible source is Hart's *Miriam Coffin*, a whaling novel.

1935

MacDonald, Allan. "A Sailor among the Transcendentalists," *NEQ* 8 (Sept. 1935) 307–319. On the original of Father Mapple.

1936
BOOKS

Quinn, Arthur H. "Herman Melville and the Exotic Romance," in *American Fiction* (New York: Appleton-Century, 1936) 149–157. Dissent on Melville's stature.

Taylor, Walter F. "Herman Melville," in *A History of American Letters* (New York: American Book, 1936) 131–140. Revised as *The Story of American Letters* (Chicago: Regnery, 1956). The earlier book contains a bibliography, 506–509. Survey approach.

ARTICLE

Adams, Frederick B., Jr. "The Crow's Nest," *Colophon* n.s. 2 (Autumn 1936) 148–154. Melville in Ch. 35 satirized his source, Scoresby.

1937

Sundermann, Karl. *Herman Melvilles Gedankengut* (Berlin: Collignon, 1937). Catalogues Melville's ideas.

1938
BOOKS

Gleim, W. S. *The Meaning of MD* (New York: Brick Row Bookshop, 1938). Highly detailed allegorical reading. Contains useful survey of previous interpretations. Reprinted New York: Russell & Russell, 1962.

Olson, Charles. "Lear and *MD*," *Twice a Year* 1 (1938) 165–189. Included in revised, condensed form in Olson (1947). Shakespeare precipitated *MD*.

Thorp, Willard. "Introduction," in *Herman Melville: Representative Selections* (New York: American Book, 1938) xi–cxxix. Still an excellent introduction to Melville and *MD*. See esp. lxv–lxxiv, reprinted in Parker (1967).

Winters, Yvor. "Herman Melville and the Problems of Moral Navigation," in *Maule's Curse* (Norfolk, Conn.: New Directions, 1938) 53–89. Reprinted in his *In Defense of Reason* (New York: Swallow, 1947) 200–233.

ARTICLES

Blackmur, R. P. "The Art of Herman Melville," *Virginia Quarterly Review* 14 (Spring 1938) 266–282. An expanded version titled "The Craft of Herman Melville: A Putative Statement" is in *The Expense of Greatness* (New York: Arrow, 1940) 139–166 and is reprinted in Chase (1962) and elsewhere. Melville is not a master of fictional technique; he exploits other forms—e.g., the sermon.

Berkelman, Robert G. "*MD*: Curiosity or Classic?" *English Journal, College Edition* 27 (Nov. 1938) 742–755. Poses and mediates extreme views of form of *MD* and of central problem of Melville's identification with Ahab.

1939
BOOKS

Anderson, Charles R. *Melville in the South Seas* (New York: Columbia University Press. 1939); reprinted New York: Dover, 1966. Fullest account of Melville's Pacific years and use of sources in his sea narratives.

Geist, Stanley. *Herman Melville: The Tragic Vision and the Heroic Ideal* (Cambridge, Mass.: Harvard University Press, 1939). Harvard Honors Theses in English, No. 12. A brilliant reading, but confined to *MD* and *Pierre*. Reprinted New York: Octagon, 1966.

Simon, Jean. *Herman Melville: Marin, Métaphysicien, et Poète* (Paris: Boivin, 1939). Most copies of this suggestive critical biography were destroyed during the war. The Library of Congress has one of the few copies in the U. S. Simon's book was based on a closer study of the manuscript collections than any American study published before 1951.

ARTICLES

Parks, Aileen Wells. "Leviathan: An Essay in Interpretation," *Sewanee Review* 47 (Jan.-March 1939) 130–132. An amusing parody which has been taken at face value.

Forsythe, Robert S. Review of Gleim's *The Meaning of MD*, *AL* 11 (Nov. 1939) 308–309. Agrees that *MD* has allegorical meanings but rejects attempt to give every action and person an allegorical equivalent.

Forsythe, Robert S. "Emerson and *MD*," *Notes & Queries* 177 (December 23, 1939) 457–458. Emerson in 1834 heard of a ferocious white whale, Old Tom. See the Norton Critical Edition of *MD* (1967) 571.

1940
BOOK

Gabriel, Ralph H. "Melville: Critic of Mid-Nineteenth Century Beliefs," in *The Course of American Democratic Thought* (New York: Ronald, 1940) 67–77. See revised second edition (New York: Ronald, 1956) 70–79. Melville opposed the dominant ideas of his age.

ARTICLES

Kellogg, Remington, "Whales, Giants of the Sea," *National Geographic* 67 (Jan. 1940) 35–90. Well illustrated.

Randall, D. A., and J. T. Winterich. "One Hundred Good Novels. Melville, Herman: *MD*," *Publishers Weekly* 136 (Jan. 24, 1940) 255–257. Brief collation and notes.

Scott, S. W. D. "Some Implications of the Typhoon Scenes in *MD*," *AL* 12 (March 1940) 91–98.

Howard, Leon. "Melville's Struggle with the Angel," *MLQ* 1 (June 1940) 195–206. Major discussion of Melville's "artistry"; holds that Melville never developed "a permanent, dependable craftsmanship." Advances what became known as the theory that there were "two *Moby-Dicks*," an original more literal one and the version that was completed and published. Reprinted in Parker (1967).

1941
BOOK

Matthiessen, F. O. *American Renaissance* (New York: Oxford University Press, 1941) 396–466 and *passim*. Valuable discussion of such aspects as Melville's language, his debt to Shakespeare, and his relation to Transcendentalism. Reprinted New York: Oxford University Press, 1968. A section on the Shakespearean language in *MD*, 421–431, is reprinted in Parker (1967).

1942
ARTICLE

Myers, Henry A. "Captain Ahab's Discovery: The Tragic Meaning of *MD*," *NEQ* 15 (March 1942) 15–34. Reprinted in *Tragedy: A View of Life* (Ithaca: Cornell University Press, 1956). See also his *Are Men Equal* (New York: Putnam's, 1945) 46–56.

1943
BOOKS

Braswell, William. *Melville's Religious Thought* (Durham: Duke University Press, 1943); reprinted New York: Pageant, 1959.

Stovall, Floyd. *American Idealism* (Norman: University of Oklahoma Press, 1943) 67–73. Melville's relation to Transcendentalism.

ARTICLE

Fadiman, Clifton. "Herman Melville," *Atlantic Monthly* 172 (Oct. 1943) 88–91. Reprinted as "Introduction" in the Harper's Modern Classics edition of *MD* (1950) and elsewhere. For the general reader; notorious for charges that Melville lacked humor.

1944
BOOK

Sedgwick, William E. *Herman Melville: The Tragedy of Mind* (Cambridge, Mass.: Harvard University Press, 1944) 82–136. Detailed interpretation of Melville's major works as revealing the development of his mind. The Norton Critical Edition of *MD* (1967) reprints 84–88 and 119–126.

ARTICLE

Walcutt, Charles C. "The Fire Symbolism in *MD*," *MLN* 59 (May 1944) 304–310. Relates fire symbolism to central meaning. See Myers (1942).

1945
BOOK

Brooks, Van Wyck. *The World of Washington Irving* (New York: Dutton, 1945) *passim*. Detailed and evocative recreation of the literary milieu.

ARTICLES

Watters, R. E. "Melville's Sociality," *AL* 17 (March 1945) 33–49. Melville stressed the value of social group and showed evils of "insulated" individualism such as Ahab's.

Watters, R. E. "Melville's Isolatoes," *PMLA* 60 (Dec. 1945) 1138–1148; reprinted with slight alterations in Stern (1960). On Melville's "Ishmael" characters; not limited to *MD*.

Auden, W. H. "The Christian Tragic Hero," *New York Times Book Review* 50 (December 16, 1945) 1, 21; reprinted in *Tragedy: Modern Essays in Criticism*, Englewood Cliffs: Prentice-Hall, 1963) 234–238. Ahab contrasted to Greek tragic hero.

1946
BOOK

Jones, Joseph. "Humor in *MD*," *University of Texas Studies in English* (1945–46) [1946] 51–71. Refutation of Fadiman (1943); Stubb as a comic character.

ARTICLES

McCloskey, John C. "*MD* and the Reviewers," *Philological Quarterly* 25 (Jan. 1946) 20–31. Hetherington rejects this article in his "Early Reviews of *MD*" in Hillway-Mansfield (1953) and Stern (1960) as well as Hetherington (1961). Superseded by the publication of the original reviews in *Doubloon*.

Jones, Joseph. "Ahab's 'Blood-Quench': Theatre or Metallurgy?" *AL* 18 (March 1946) 35–37. On Ch. 113, "The Forge."

Giovannini, G. "Melville's *MD*," *Explicator* 5 (Oct. 1946) Item 7. A reply to Collins (1946), which is reprinted in *Doubloon*.

1947
BOOKS

Brooks, Van Wyck. *The Times of Melville and Whitman* (New York: Dutton, 1947) *passim*. See Brooks (1945).

Levin, Harry. "Don Quixote and *MD*," in *Cervantes Across the Centuries*, ed. Angel Flores and M. J. Bernardete (New York: Dryden, 1947) 217–226. Reprinted in Harry Levin, *Contexts of Criticism* (Cambridge, Mass.: Harvard University Press, 1957) 97–109. *Don Quixote* a complementary and not major influence.

Olson, Charles. *Call Me Ishmael* (New York: Reynall & Hitchcock, 1947); reprinted New York: Grove, 1958. See Olson (1938). The chapter "Ahab and His Fool" is reprinted in the Norton Critical Edition of *MD* (1967).

ARTICLES

Arms, George. "*MD* and 'The Village Blacksmith,'" *Notes & Queries* 192 (May 3, 1947) 187–188. Suggests story of Perth is satiric counterpoise to Longfellow's poem.

Baker, Carlos. "Of Arts and Artifacts." *New York Times Book Review* 52 (Aug. 10, 1947) 2. On the "substance of things and the substance of thought" in great novels; *MD* vitalizes the facts and artifacts of whaling.

Hull, William. "*MD*: An Interpretation," *Etc.* 5 (Autumn 1947) 8–21. Sees *MD* in terms of General Semantics.

Belgion, Montgomery. "Heterodoxy on *MD*?" *Sewanee Review* 55 (Winter 1947) 108–125; reprinted as "Introduction," in *MD* (London: Cresset, 1947).

1948
BOOKS

Arvin, Newton. "Introduction," in *MD* (New York: Rinehart, 1948) v–x.

Bowers, David. "Democratic Vistas," in *Literary History of the United States*, ed.

Robert E. Spiller *et al.* (New York: Macmillan, 1948) 345–357. Melville in relation to Transcendentalism.
Cowie, Alexander. "Herman Melville," in *The Rise of the American Novel* (New York: American Book, 1948) 363–411. General survey.
Thorp, Willard. "Herman Melville," in *Literary History of the United States,* ed. Robert E. Spiller *et al.* (New York: Macmillan, 1948) 441–471.

ARTICLES

Fiedler, Leslie. "Come Back to the Raft Ag'in, Huck Honey!" *Partisan Review* 15 (June 1948) 664–671, reprinted in *An End to Innocence* (Boston: Beacon, 1955). An American myth of love—white youth in an innocent homoerotic friendship with a man of a colored race. See Fiedler (1960).
Maugham, Somerset. "*MD*," *Atlantic Monthly* 181 (June 1948) 98–104; reprinted in *Great Novelists and Their Novels* (Philadelphia: Winston, 1948) 211–232 and as "Introduction," in *MD* (Philadelphia: Winston, 1949). Terse strictures on the form of *MD*.
Short, R. W. "Melville as Symbolist," *University of Kansas City Review* 15 (Autumn 1948) 38–46.
Heflin, Wilson L. "The Source of Ahab's Lordship over the Level Lodestone," *AL* 20 (Nov. 1948) 323–327. Source of Ch. 124.
Pommer, Henry F. "Herman Melville and the Wake of the *Essex*," *AL* 20 (Nov. 1948) 290–304. Melville's use of the *Essex* (which was sunk by a Whale) as a source for *MD*.
Cook, Reginald L. "Big Medicine in *MD*," *Accent* 8 (Winter 1948) 102–109; reprinted in Stern (1960). Magic in *MD* heightens the drama.

1949
BOOKS

Chase, Richard. *Herman Melville: A Critical Study* (New York: Macmillan, 1949) 43–102. Stresses folklore in *MD*. Ahab as a "false Prometheus."
Geismar, Maxwell. "Introduction," in *MD* (New York: Pocket Books, 1949) v–x. comments on myth and imagery.
Stone, Geoffrey. *Herman Melville* (New York: Sheed & Ward, 1949). Interprets *MD* from Catholic vantage-point, emphasizing irreligious aspects.
Vincent, Howard P. *The Trying-Out of Moby-Dick* (Boston: Houghton Mifflin, 1949); reprinted Carbondale: Southern Illinois University Press, 1965. Detailed study of use of whaling sources, with running interpretation. Excerpted briefly in the Norton Critical Edition of *MD* (1967).
Wright, Nathalia. *Melville's Use of the Bible* (Durham: Duke University Press, 1949). Valuable comments on style, imagery, character types, etc. The chapter on Melville's imagery (20–45) is reprinted in Parker (1967).

ARTICLES

Cowie, Alexander. "Symbols Ahoy," *CEA Critic* 11 (Jan. 1949) 7–8. Advice on teaching *MD*.
Parks, Henry B. "Poe, Hawthorne, Melville: An Essay in Sociological Criticism," *Partisan Review* 16 (Feb. 1949) 157–165. On the authors' treatments of such themes as isolation, abnormal sexuality, self reliance, and idealism.
Paul, Sherman. "Melville's 'The *Town Ho*'s Story,'" *AL* 21 (May 1949) 212–221; reprinted in Stern (1960).
Paul, Sherman. "Morgan Neville, Melville, and the Folk Hero," *Notes & Queries* 194 (June 25, 1949) 278. Bulkington and Steelkilt are in Western tall tale tradition; comparisons to Mike Fink, the last of the boatmen.
Hubben, William. "Ahab, the Whaling Quaker," *Religion in Life* 18 (Summer 1949) 363–373. *MD* in light of 1940's religious confrontation of evil.
Leyda, Jay. "Ishmael Melville: Remarks on Board Ship Amazon," *Boston Public Library Quarterly* 1 (October 1949) 119-134. Suggests Melville's cousin Thomas as a model for Ishmael.
Weber, Walter. "Some Characteristic Symbols in Herman Melville's Works," *English Studies (Luedeke Anniversary Number)* 30 (Oct. 1949) 217–224.
Lash, Kenneth. "Captain Ahab and King Lear," *New Mexico Quarterly Review* 19 (Winter 1949) 438–445. Analysis of both as truly original characters.

1950
BOOKS

Arvin, Newton. *Herman Melville* (New York: Sloane, 1950) 143–193; reprinted New York: Viking Compass Books, 1957. Probably the best single long critical essay on *MD*.
Auden, W. H. *The Enchafèd Flood: or, The Romantic Iconography of the Sea* (New York: Random House, 1950). Many interpretative suggestions in terms of Romantic images and symbols; 115–124 are reprinted in Vincent (1969).
Howard, Leon. "Introduction,' in *MD* (New York: Modern Library, 1950) v–xvi. Includes the best very brief summary of Melville's life.
Paul, Sherman. "Introduction," in *MD* (New York: Dutton [Everyman's Library], 1950) vii–xvi. Contrasts Ishmael and Ahab; Melville in *MD* tried to give his turmoils cosmic validity.
Percival, M. O. *A Reading of MD* (Chicago: University of Chicago Press, 1950). A Kierkegaardian reading; 14–23 are reprinted in Vincent (1969).
Pommer, Henry F. *Milton and Melville* (Pittsburgh: University of Pittsburgh Press, 1950). Milton's influence on language, themes, and characters in Melville; comparisons of Ahab and Milton's Satan.
Sealts, Merton M. Jr. "Melville and the Shakers," *Studies in Bibliography* 2 (1949–1950 [1950]) 105–114.
Tomlinson, H. M. *The Face of the Earth* (Indianapolis: Bobbs-Merrill, 1950). Personal appreciation.

ARTICLES

Hall, James B. "*MD*: Parable of a Dying System," *Western Review* 14 (Spring 1950) 223–226. *MD* embodies a commentary on capitalism.
Lewis, R. W. B. "Melville on Homer," *AL* 22 (May 1950) 116–176. Melville as a reader of Homer. See Lewis's *The American Adam* (1955) 139–145; reprinted in Vincent (1969).
Spangler, Eugene R. "Harvest in a Barren Field: A Counterpoint," *Western Review* 14 (Summer 1950) 305-307. Argues great need for better criticism of Melville's works.
Weeks, Donald. "Two Uses of *MD*," *American Quarterly* 2 (Summer 1950) 155–164. The uses are (1) to enlarge our idea of form and structure in the novel and (2) to enlarge our conception of responsibility.
Slochower, Harry. "*MD*: The Myth of Democratic Expectancy," *American Quarterly* 2 (Fall 1950) 259–269; reprinted in Stern (1960). *MD* sounds the motifs of creation and quest; Melville stands ambivalently between individualism and coordination.
Frye, Northrop. "The Four Forces of Prose Fiction," *Hudson Review* 2 (Winter 1950) 582–595; reprinted in his *Anatomy of Criticism* (Princeton: Princeton University Press, 1957) 303–314. Form of *MD* is "romance-anatomy."
Murray, Henry A. Review of Vincent's *The Trying-Out of MD*, *NEQ* 23 (Dec. 1950) 527–530. Praise, with important qualifications.

1951
BOOKS

Gilman, William H. "Jackson and Ahab," in *Melville's Early Life and Redburn* (New York: New York University Press, 1951) 272–273. Characteristics of Jackson in *Redburn* anticipate those of Ahab.
Quinn, Arthur H. "The Romance of the Frontier," in *The Literature of the American People* (New York: Appleton-Century 1951) 243–247. Unappreciative. Retains perspective of literary historians of 1900's and 1910's.
Howard, Leon. *Herman Melville: A Biography* (Berkeley: University of California Press, 1951; reprinted 1958. The standard biography, basic to any serious study of Melville.
Leyda, Jay. *The Melville Log: A Documentary Life of Herman Melville*, 2 vols. (New York, Harcourt, Brace, 1951). Monumental and perceptive documentary biography, containing excerpts of letters and reviews, naval documents, Melville's marginalia, etc. The most important work of Melville scholarship. Reprinted with a new supplement, New York: Gordian Press, 1969.

ARTICLES

Watters, R. E. "The Meanings of the White Whale," *University of Toronto Quarterly* 20 (Jan. 1951) 155–168; reprinted in Stern (1960).

Babcock, C. Merton. "Melville's Backwoods Seamen," *Western Folklore* 10 (April 1951) 126–133. New England whaling as an American frontier movement; Melville's use of folklore.

Paul, Sherman. "Hawthorne's Ahab," *Notes & Queries* 196 (June 9, 1951) 255–257. Ethan Brand and Ahab.

Bell, Millicent. "Pierre Bayle and *MD*," *PMLA* 66 (Sept. 1951) 626–648. Bayle's *Dictionary* a major source for *MD*; 626–636 are reprinted in Parker (1967). See Sherbo (1955).

Stafford, John. "Henry Norman Hudson and the Whig use of Shakespeare," *PMLA* 66 (Sept. 1951) 649-661. Extremely valuable background for Melville's use of Shakespeare in his essay on Hawthorne and in *MD*. A contextual study rare in Melville criticism.

Gross, John J. "The Rehearsal of Ishmael: Melville's 'Redburn,'" *Virginia Quarterly Review* 27 (Autumn 1951) 581–600.

Roper, Gordon. "Melville's *MD*, 1851–1951," *Dalhousie Review* 31 (Autumn 1951) 167–179. Brief survey of the changing reputation of *MD*.

Babcock, C. Merton. "The Language of Melville's 'Isolatoes,'" *Western Folklore* 10 (Oct. 1951) 285–289.

Murray, Henry A. "In Nomine Diaboli," *NEQ* 24 (Dec. 1951) 435–452; reprinted in Hillway-Mansfield (1953); Stern (1960); Chase (1962); Vincent (1969). Major psychological interpretation and charming personal reminiscence of Murray's first reading of *MD*.

1952
BOOKS

Davis, Merrell R. *Melville's Mardi: A Chartless Voyage* (New Haven: Yale University Press, 1952); relevant for full treatment of Melville's reading in 1847–1848. Reprinted Hamden, Conn.: Shoe String Press, 1967.

Mansfield, Luther S. and Howard P. Vincent, eds. *Moby-Dick; or, The Whale* (New York: Hendricks House, 1952). Superseded as a text by the Norton Critical Edition (1967) but still valuable for its 250 pages of explanatory notes, which include quotations from many of the sources of *MD*.

Reed, Herbert. *English Prose Style, Revised Edition* (London: Bell, 1952); reprinted Boston: Beacon, 1955 (164–165, 198–200). Uses passages from *MD* and *Billy Budd* for stylistic analysis; not in 1928 edition.

Stafford, John. *The Literary Criticism of "Young America"* (Berkeley: University of California Press, 1952). Valuable background for American literary nationalism of Melville's essay on Hawthorne and *MD*. Miller (1956) draws on this book and does not supersede it.

Thompson, Lawrance. *Melville's Quarrel with God* (Princeton: Princeton University Press, 1952) 3–17, 147–246.

ARTICLES

Adams, R. P. "Romanticism and the American Renaissance," *AL* 23 (Jan. 1952) 419–432. *MD* as an example of "negative Romanticism."

Babcock, C. Merton. "The Vocabulary of *MD*," *American Speech* 28 (May 1952) 91–101.

Wright, Nathalia. "*Mosses From an Old Manse* and *MD*: The Shock of Discovery," *MLN* 67 (June 1952) 387–392. Hawthorne as an influence on fire imagery in *MD*; reprinted in Vincent (1969).

Wilder, Thornton. "Toward an American Language," *Atlantic Monthly* 180 (July 1952) 31–42. Discusses modern characteristics of *MD*.

Babcock, C. Merton. "Melville's World's-Language," *Southern Folklore Quarterly* 16 (Sept. 1952) 177–182.

Paul, Sherman. Review of Mansfield-Vincent edition of *MD*, *NEQ* 25 (Sept. 1952) 423–424. Criticizes mixture of notes and criticism. Sees a general recent retreat from interpretation to the fortress of external facts.

Olson, Charles. "Materials and Weights of Herman Melville," *New Republic* 127 (Sept. 8, 1952) 20–21; (Sept. 15, 1952) 17–18, 21. An attack on the Mansfield-Vincent edition and other recent Melville criticism for not dealing with the totality of Melville's effort.

Quinn, Patrick H. Poe's "Imaginary Voyage," *Hudson Review* 4 (Winter 1952) 562–585. Argues (579–585) that *Arthur Gordon Pym* influenced *MD*, especially in use of whiteness. See Wells (1923).

1953
BOOKS

Brooks, Van Wyck. *Writer in America* (New York: Dutton, 1953) 20. Melville defective in structure.

Feidelson, Charles. *Symbolism and American Literature* (Chicago: University of Chicago Press, 1953) *passim*. The Norton Critical Edition of *MD* (1967) reprints 28–35 and 240–246.

Hillway, Tyrus, and Luther S. Mansfield, eds. *MD Centennial Essays* (Dallas: Southern Methodist University Press, 1953).

Henry A. Murray. "In Nomine Diaboli"	3–21
Tyrus Hillway. "A Preface to *MD*"	22–29
Walter E. Bezanson. "*MD*: Work of Art"	30–58
Henry Nash Smith. "The Image of Society in *MD*"	59–75
Ernest E. Leisy. "Fatalism in *MD*"	76–88
Hugh W. Hetherington. "Early Reviews of *MD*"	89–122
Perry Miller. "Melville and Transcendentalism"	123–152
Randall Stewart. "Melville and Hawthorne"	153–164
Wilson L. Heflin. "Melville and Nantucket"	165–179

A valuable collection. Some of the essays are not available elsewhere. See Murray (1951) and Hetherington (1961). Bezanson is reprinted in the Norton Critical Edition of *MD* (1967) and excerpted in Vincent (1969).

James, Cyril Lionel Robert, *Mariners, Renegades, and Castaways: The Story of Herman Melville and the World We Live In* (New York: C. L. R. James, 1953). A personal interpretation; Ahab as capitalist.

Metcalf, Eleanor Melville. *Herman Melville: Cycle and Epicycle* (Cambridge: Harvard University Press, 1953). Includes previously unpublished family letters and legends.

ARTICLES

Howard, Leon. Review of the Mansfield-Vincent edition of *MD*, *NCF* 7 (March 1953) 303–304; finds it a copious, valuable, and puzzling book.

Kligerman, Charles. "The Psychology of Herman Melville," *Psychoanalytic Review* 40 (April 1953) 125–143. General psychoanalytic formulation.

Granger, Bruce Ingham. "The Gams in *MD*," *Western Humanities Review* 8 (Winter 1953–54) 41–47.

1954
BOOKS

Brown, Clarence A. "The Aesthetics of Romanticism," in *The Achievement of American Criticism* (New York: Ronald, 1954) 149–182. General essay on American Romantic critics, with a summary of Melville's views (166–170).

Cunliffe, Marcus. "Melville and Whitman," in *The Literature of the United States* (Harmondsworth, Middlesex: Penguin, 1954) 105–119. A critical survey. Ahab is both villain and hero; Melville felt that both virtues and vices depend on a certain excess.

Koerner, James D. "The Wake of the White Whale," *Kansas Magazine* (1954) 42–50. Surveys recent scholarship and interprets *MD*.

ARTICLES

Geiger, Don. "Melville's Black God: Contrary Evidence in 'The *Town-Ho*'s Story,'" *AL* 25 (Jan. 1954) 464–471; reprinted in Stern (1960).

Gilman, William H. Review of the Mansfield-Vincent edition of *MD*, *MLN* 69 (Jan. 1954) 63–65. A thoughtful appraisal, pointing out editorial lapses and the mixture of factual and interpretative notes, but praising the assembling of a "vast amount of information, most of it available nowhere else."

Hutchinson, William H. "A Definitive Edition of *MD*," *AL* 25 (Jan. 1954) 472–478. Collation shows Mansfield-Vincent edition to be a somewhat imperfect reprint of the first American edition. Like Ament (1932) this note is superseded by the discussion in the Norton Critical Edition of *MD* (1967) 471–498.

Stewart, George R. "The Two *Moby-Dicks*," *AL* 25 (Jan. 1954) 417–448. See Howard (1940 and 1951); Olson (1947); Vincent (1949); and Stone (1956). The currency given the theory by Stewart is obvious in much later criticism, where the theory tends to be stated as fact. See Weathers (1960) and Foster (1961).

Young, James Dean. "The Nine Gams of the *Pequod*," *AL* 25 (Jan. 1954 449–463; reprinted in Stern (1960).

Babcock, C. Merton. "Melville's Whaling Vocabulary," *American Speech* 29 (Oct. 1954) 161–174.

Rockwell, Frederick S. "DeQuincey and the Ending of *MD*," *NCF* 9 (Dec. 1954) 161–168.

Bergler, Edmund. "A Note on Herman Melville," *American Imago* 11 (Winter 1954) 385–397. Melville a masochist in his whole life, personal and literary. The white whale is the bad pre-Oedipal mother.

1955
BOOKS

Fogle, Richard H. "Organic Form in American Criticism: 1840–1870," in *The Development of American Literary Criticism*, ed. Floyd Stovall (Chapel Hill: University of North Carolina Press, 1955) 75–111, esp. 102–106. Discusses Melville's acceptance of the doctrine of organic form.

Lewis, R. W. B. *The American Adam: Innocence, Tragedy, and Tradition in the Nineteenth Century* (Chicago: University of Chicago Press, 1955). Study of a major literary-cultural myth of America.

Rosenberry, Edward. *Melville and the Comic Spirit* (Cambridge, Mass.: Harvard University Press, 1955) 108–138; 105–115 are reprinted in the Norton Critical Edition of *MD* (1967).

Spiller, Robert E. *The Cycle of American Literature* (New York: Macmillan, 1955) 89–99, reprinted New York: Mentor Books, 1957, 77–83. General survey.

Tindall, William York. *The Literary Symbol* (New York: Columbia University Press, 1955); reprinted Bloomington: Indiana University Press, 1959. Examines some critical approaches to the symbolism of the white whale.

ARTICLES

Sherbo, Arthur. "Melville's Portuguese Catholic Priest," *AL* 26 (Jan. 1955) 563–564. Explains a point about Ch. 83 that had puzzled Bell (1951).

Miller, James E. "Hawthorne and Melville: The Unpardonable Sin," *PMLA* 70 (March 1955) 91–114.

Willson, Lawrence. "Yet Another Note on *MD*," *Dalhousie Review* 35 (Spring 1955) 5–15. A moralist approach; *MD* is Melville's *Paradise Lost*.

Cook, Charles H., Jr. "Ahab's 'Intolerable Allegory,'" *Boston University Studies in English* 1 (Spring-Summer 1955) 45–52; reprinted in Stern (1960).

Millhauser, M. "The Form of *MD*," *Journal of Aesthetics and Art Criticism* 13 (June 1955) 527–532. Argues the form is tragic.

Parke, John. "Seven *Moby-Dicks*," *NEQ* 28 (Sept. 1955) 319–338; reprinted in Stern (1960). Seven "layers" on which *MD* can be read.

Battenfeld, David H. "The Source of the Hymn in *MD*," *AL* (Nov. 1955) 393–396; reprinted in the Norton Critical Edition of *MD* (1967). Father Mapple's hymn adapted from Psalm 18 in hymnbook of Dutch Reformed Church.

Grdseloff, Dorothee. "A Note on the Origin of Fedallah in *MD*," *AL* 27 (Nov. 1955) 396–403. See her *Melville's Orienda* (1961), under the name Finkelstein.

1956
BOOKS

Baird, James. *Ishmael* (Baltimore: Johns Hopkins University Press, 1956); reprinted New York: Harper Torchbook, 1960. Extended discussion of Queequeg, whale, whiteness, Parsee, vortex, etc.

Kazin, Alfred. "Introduction," in *MD* (Boston: Houghton Mifflin, 1956) v-xiv; reprinted under various titles in *Atlantic Monthly* 198 (Nov. 1956) 81–85; in Stern (1960); in Kazin's *Contemporaries* (Boston: Little, Brown, 1962) 29–46; and in Chase (1962). For the general reader.

Levin, Harry. *Symbolism and Fiction* (Charlottesville: University of Virginia Press, 1956); reprinted in *Contexts of Criticism* (Cambridge: Harvard University Press, 1957) 190–207. Includes discussion of the relation between literal and symbolic meanings of a work, with *MD* used for examples.

Miller, Perry. *The Raven and the Whale: The War of Words and Wits in the Era of Poe and Melville* (New York: Harcourt, Brace, 1956); reprinted New York: Harcourt, Brace [Harvest Books], n.d.). Vivid but somewhat unreliable recreation of Melville's New York literary milieu. See Stafford (1952).

ARTICLES

Weidman, Jerome. "*MD*: An Appreciation," *Holiday* 19 (Feb. 1956) 50–55.

Marx, Leo. "The Machine in the Garden," *NEQ* 29 (March 1956) 27–42. Compares industrial and fire imagery in Hawthorne's "Ethan Brand" and in "The Try-Works." See Marx (1964).

Beach, Joseph Warren. "Hart Crane and *MD*," *Western Review* 20 (Spring 1956) 183–196. Influence of *MD* on Crane's "Voyages." Incidental strictures on Melville's prose in *MD*.

Osbourne, R. V. "The White Whale and the Absolute," *Essays in Criticism* 6 (April 1956) 160–170.

Beach, Joseph Warren. Review of Franz Stanzel's *Die Typischen Erzahlsituationen im Roman*, *AL* 28 (May 1956) 250–252. Comments on two causes of the general bagginess of form in *MD*.

Stern, Milton R. "The Whale and the Minnow: *MD* and the Movie," *College English* 17 (May 1956) 470–473. Suggests usefulness of comparison for teaching *MD*.

Ward, J. A. "The Function of the Cetological Chapters in *MD*," *AL* 28 (May 1956) 164–183.

Jeffrey, Lloyd N. "A Concordance to the Biblical Allusions in *MD*," *Bulletin of Bibliography* 21 (May-Aug. 1956) 223–229.

Stone, Edward. "*MD* and Shakespeare," *Shakespeare Quarterly* 7 (Autumn 1956) 445–448. See Stewart (1954); Melville did use Shakespeare in earlier pages of *MD*.

1957
BOOKS

Chase, Richard. *The American Novel and Its Tradition* (Garden City: Doubleday, 1957) 89–113. Attempts to define what is specifically American in American novels, including *MD*. Excerpted in *Critical Approaches to American Literature*, eds. Ray B. Browne and Martin Light (New York: Crowell, 1965) I, 260–272.

Stewart, Randall. "The Vision of Evil in Hawthorne and Melville," in *The Tragic Vision and the Christian Faith* (New York: Association Press, 1957) 238–263; reprinted, substantially, in his *American Literature and Christian Doctrine* (Baton Rouge: Louisiana State University Press, 1958) 73–102.

Stern, Milton R. *The Fine Hammered Steel of Herman Melville* (Urbana: University of Illinois Press, 1957). Melville as a naturalist; not mainly on *MD*.

ARTICLES

Dale, T. R. "Melville and Aristotle: The Conclusion of *MD* as a Classical Tragedy," *Boston University Studies in English* 3 (Spring 1957) 45–50.

Wheeler, Otis. "Humor in *MD*: Two Problems," *AL* 29 (May 1957) 203–206.

Jaffé, David. "Some Origins of *MD*: New Finds in an Old Source," *AL* 29 (Nov. 1957) 263–277. The "old source" is Wilkes's *Narrative of the U.S. Exploring Expedition* (1845).

Kennedy, Richard S. "The Theme of the Quest," *English Record* 8 (Winter 1957) 2–17. Discusses Ahab's quest for and conflict with the powers of the universe, and Ishmael's quest for self-knowledge.

1958
BOOKS

Friedrich, Gerhard. *In Pursuit of MD* (Wallingford, Pa.: Pendle Hill, 1958). A Quaker reading.

Hicks, Granville. "A Re-Reading of *MD*," in *Twelve Original Essays on Great American Novels*, ed. Charles Shapiro (Detroit: Wayne State University Press, 1958) 44–68.

Levin, Harry. *The Power of Blackness* (New York: Knopf, 1958) *passim*.

Kirsch, James. "The Enigma of *MD*," *Journal of Analytical Psychology* (London) 3 (1958) 131–148.

ARTICLES

Lowry, Thomas C. F. "Melville's *MD*, XXXI," *Explicator* 16 (Jan. 1958) Item 22.
Peters, Robert L. "Melville's *MD*," *Explicator* 16 (April 1958) Item 44. Argues that Bulkington resembles Ahab.
Stern, Milton R. "Some Techniques of Melville's Perception," *PMLA* 73 (June 1958) 251–259: reprinted in Stern (1960).
Miller, Paul W. "Sun and Fire in Melville's *MD*," *NCF* 13 (Sept. 1958) 139–144.
O'Daniel, Therman B. "An Interpretation of the Relation of the Chapter Entitled 'The Symphony' to *MD* as a Whole," *CLA Journal* 2 (Sept. 1958) 55–57.
Holman, C. Hugh. "The Reconciliation of Ishmael: *MD* and the Book of Job," *South Atlantic Quarterly* 57 (Autumn 1958) 477–490.
Phelps, Leland R. "*MD* in Germany," *Comparative Literature* 10 (Fall 1958) 349–355.
Welsh, Alexander. "A Melville Debt to Carlyle," *MLN* 73 (Nov. 1958) 489–491.
Leiter, Louis. "Queequeg's Coffin," *NCF* 13 (Dec. 1958) 249–254.
Vogel, Dan. "The Dramatic Chapters in *MD*," *NCF* 13 (Dec. 1958) 239–247.

1959
BOOKS

Betts, William W., Jr. "*MD*: Melville's Faust," *Lock Haven Bulletin* 1 (1959) 31–44. Goethe's *Faust* influenced character of Ahab; the Parsee is Ahab's Mephistopheles.
Bewley, Marius. *The Eccentric Design* (New York: Columbia University Press, 1959) 187–219. Discusses form and politics of novel. Excerpted in *Critical Approaches to American Literature*, eds. Ray B. Browne and Martin Light (New York: Crowell, 1965) I, 273–290.
Charvat, William. "Melville and the Common Reader," *Studies in Bibliography* 12 (1959) 41–57. Melville's career in fiction as it reflects tensions between Melville and his society.
Mayoux, Jean Jacques. *Melville* (Paris: Editions du Seuil, 1959); English translation New York: Grove, 1960. Brief survey with many pictures.
Sewall, Richard B. "*MD*," in *The Vision of Tragedy* (New Haven: Yale University Press, 1959) 92–105; reprinted as a Yale Paperbound, 1962.
Ziegler, Arthur, "*MD*," in *From Homer to Joyce: A Study Guide to Thirty-Six Great Books*, ed. J. Sherwood Weber, *et al.* (New York: Holt, 1959) 210–217. Includes bibliography and list of editions.

ARTICLES

Rosenberry, Edward H. "Queequeg's Coffin-Canoe: Made in *Typee*," *AL* 30 (Jan. 1959) 529–530.
Satterfield, John. "Perth: An Organic Digression in *MD*," *MLN* 74 (Feb. 1959) 106–107. Perth modeled on Hephaestus. Enforces epic interpretations of *MD*.
Dahl, Curtis, "MD's Cousin Behemoth," *AL* 31 (March 1959) 21–29. Comparison of *MD* to Cornelius Mathew's *Behemoth* (1839).
Miller, James E., Jr. "Melville's Search for Form," *Bucknell Review* 8 (Dec. 1959) 260–276. Consideration of elements that Melville synthesized into the form of *MD*.

1960
BOOKS

Bowen, Merlin. *The Long Encounter: Self and Experience in the Writings of Herman Melville* (Chicago: University of Chicago Press, 1960).
Creeger, George R. "The Symbolism of Whiteness in Melville's Prose Fiction," *Jahrbuch für Amerikastudien* 5 (1960) 147–163.
Fiedler, Leslie. *Love and Death in the American Novel* (New York: Criterion, 1960) 523–552; reprinted Cleveland: Meridian Books, 1962. Interpretation of *MD* in terms of myth, symbol, psychoanalysis.
Howard, Leon. *Literature and the American Tradition* (New York: Doubleday, 1960) 169–186. General survey.
Krieger, Murray. *The Tragic Vision* (New York: Holt, Rinehart and Winston, 1960) 249–260. Speculates on possible thematic significance of Ishmael's survival in context of theoretical problems of the New Criticism.

Stern, Milton R., ed. *Discussions of MD* (Boston: Heath, 1960). Stern provides an introduction and reprints 15 essays, 14 of them on MD: Hetherington (1953), Cook (1948), Murray (1951), Lawrence (1923), Slochower (1950), Kazin (1956), Cook (1955), Parke (1955), Watters (1951), Paul "Melville's 'The *Town-Ho*'s Story.'" (1949), Geiger (1954), Young (1954), Watters ("Melville's Isolatoes," 1945), and Stern (1958). The final essay is R. P. Warren's "Melville the Poet."

ARTICLES

Seelye, John D. "The Golden Navel: The Cabalism of Ahab's Doubloon," *NCF* 14 (March 1960) 350–355.

Cameron, Kenneth W. "A Note on the Corposants in *MD*," *ESQ* 19 (Second Quarter 1960) 22–24.

Jaffé, David. "The Captain Who Sat for the Portrait of Ahab," *Boston University Studies in English* 4 (Spring 1960) 1–22. Suggests Captain Charles Wilkes was Melville's model for Ahab.

Violette, W. L. "*MD*: A Study in Symphonic Prose," *Literary Criterion* (Mysore, India) 4 (Summer 1960) 19–23.

Dahlberg, Edward. "*MD*—An Hamitic Dream," *Literary Review* 4 (Autumn 1960) 87–118; reprinted in *Varieties of Literary Experience*, ed. Stanley Burnshaw (New York: New York University Press, 1962) 183–213, and in *Alms for Oblivion* (Minneapolis: University of Minnesota Press, 1964). Former admirer now rejects Melville at length as unhealthful.

Kaplan, Charles. "Jack Burden: Modern Ishmael," *College English* 22 (Oct. 1960) 19–24. Both Ishmael and Warren's character in *All the King's Men* move from ignorance and isolation to knowledge and identity with humanity.

Clubb, Merrel D. "The Second Personal Pronoun in *MD*," *American Speech* 35 (December 1960) 252–260.

Rosenberry, Edward H. "Awash in Melvilliana," *NEQ* 33 (Dec. 1960) 525–528. Essay-review of recent publications.

1961
BOOKS

Borton, John. *Herman Melville: The Philosophical Implications of Literary Technique in MD* (Amherst: Amherst College Press, 1961). Amherst College Honors Thesis Number 6. Melville's techniques of presenting Ahab, Ishmael, and Captain Vere and their views, in relation to his philosophy in *MD* and *Billy Budd*; treats "The Whiteness of the Whale" chapter as crucial.

Finkelstein, Dorothee Metlitsky. *Melville's Orienda* (New Haven: Yale University Press, 1961). Melville's knowledge and use of Near East; discusses Zoroastrian element in *MD* and possible sources for Fedallah.

Geiger, Don. "Demonism in *MD*," in *The Age of the Splendid Machine* (Tokyo: Hukuseido Press, 1961) 75–102. Analyzes techniques by which Chapters 55–66 develop theme of the monstrous, savage quality of reality.

Hetherington, Hugh W. "*MD*," in *Melville's Reviewers* (Chapel Hill: University of North Carolina Press, 1961) 189–226 and *passim*. Pioneer work on the subject, but quotations are often unrepresentative and inaccurate.

Hoffman, Daniel G. *Form and Fable in American Fiction* (New York: Oxford University Press, 1961) 221–278. A major interpretative essay.

Howard, Leon. *Herman Melville* (Minneapolis: University of Minnesota Press, 1961) 19–27. University of Minnesota Pamphlets on American Writers, No. 13. Brief survey of Melville's life and works; 18–25 are in Vincent (1969).

ARTICLES

Ward, Robert S. "Longfellow and Melville: The Ship and the Whale," *ESQ* 22 (First Quarter 1961) 57–63.

Heller, Louis G. "Two Pequot Names in American Literature," *American Speech* 36 (Feb. 1961) 54–57. Name in *MD* and *The Last of the Mohicans*.

Goldfarb, Russell, and Clare Goldfarb. "The Doubloon in *MD*," *Midwest Quarterly* 2 (Spring 1961) 251–258.

Roudiez, Leon S. "Camus and *MD*," *Symposium* 15 (Spring 1961) 30–40. See his "Strangers in Melville and Camus," *French Review* 31 (Jan. 1958) 217–226.

Hoffman, Daniel G. "*MD*: Jonah's Whale or Job's?" *Sewanee Review* 69 (April-June 1961) 205–224. See sections 1, 5, and 7 of Chapter 13 in Hoffman (1961) above.

Schless, Howard H. "*MD* and Dante: A Critique and a Time Scheme," *Bulletin of the New York Public Library* 65 (May 1961) 289–312. Ishmael is a reflective onlooker like Dante in the *Inferno*. Time of *MD* is from Christmas to Easter. However, see time scheme set out in Ch. 44.

Shulman, Robert. "The Serious Functions of Melville's Phallic Jokes," *AL* 33 (May 1961) 179–194.

Cambon, Glauco. "Ishmael and the Problem of Formal Discontinuities in *MD*," *MLN* 76 (June 1961) 516–523. Justifies the insertion of the dramatic chapters by appeals to classical precedents.

Humphreys, A. R. "Herman Melville," *John O'London's* 4 (July 6, 1961) 18–19. Comments on *MD* and *Billy Budd*. See Humphreys (1962).

Stavrou, C. N. "Ahab and Dick Again," *TSLL* 3 (Autumn 1961) 309–320.

1962
BOOKS

Anderson, Quentin. "Introduction," in *MD* (New York: Collier Books, 1962).

Berthoff, Warner. *The Example of Melville* (Princeton: Princeton University Press, 1962) *passim*. A general account of Melville as a literary craftsman; probably the best introductory critical book on Melville's work as a whole.

Chase, Richard, ed. *Melville: A Collection of Critical Essays* (Englewood Cliffs: Prentice-Hall, 1962). Chase provides an introduction and reprints eleven essays, of which five are on *MD*: Kazin (1956), Chase (1957), Murray (1951), Blackmur (1938), and Bewley (1959).

Humphreys, A. R. *Herman Melville* (Edinburgh: Oliver and Boyd, 1962); reprinted New York: Grove, 1962, 41–82.

Jacque, Valentina. "*MD* in Russian," *Soviet Literature* No. 6 (1962) 185–187. On the 1961 Russian translation.

McEniry, W. Hugh. "Some Contrapuntal Themes in Herman Melville," in *Essays in Modern American Literature*, Number 31, 14–25.

Miller, James E., Jr. *Reader's Guide to Herman Melville* (New York: Farrar, Straus [Noonday], 1962) 75–117. Despite the title, not a guide to the general reader but a personal interpretation in terms of a comprehensive mythic pattern of Ishmael as an example of the "Young Seeker."

Stanonik, Janez. *MD: The Myth and the Symbol, A Study in Folklore and Literature* (Ljubljana, Yugoslavia: Ljubljana University Press, 1962). Collects materials about white whales in folklore and interprets *MD* in their light. Contains some relevant quotations from the Pittsfield *Sun* not reprinted elsewhere.

ARTICLES

Brashers, H. C. "Ishmael's Tattoos," *Sewanee Review* 70 (Jan.-March 1962) 137–154. Ishmael learns the mystic-religious lesson of Queequeg's tattoos.

Farnsworth, Robert M. "Ishmael to the Royal Masthead," *University of Kansas City Review* 28 (March 1962) 183–190. Ishmael as narrator and character; Ahab, not Ishmael, is the real center of meaning.

McAleer, John J. "Poe and Gothic Elements in *MD*," *ESQ* 27 (Second Quarter 1962) 34.

Lutwak, Leonard. "Melville's Struggle with Style," *Forum* (Houston) 3 (Spring-Summer 1962) 11–17.

Booth, Thornton Y. "*MD*: Standing Up to God," *NCF* 17 (June 1962) 33–43. Treats relationship to Book of Job.

McClary, Ben Harris. "Melville's *MD*," *Explicator* 21 (Sept. 1962) Item 9. Ishmael's "Save me!" to landlord Coffin foreshadows his being saved by Queequeg's coffin.

Cameron, Kenneth Walter. "Etymological Significance of Melville's *Pequod*," *ESQ* 29 (Fourth Quarter 1962) 3–4.

The *Melville Supplement* of *Emerson Society Quarterly* 29 (Fourth Quarter 1962) contains seven articles on MD:

Gordon Roper. "On Teaching *MD*," 2–4.

Millicent Bell. "The Irreducible *MD*," 4–6.

Walter E. Bezanson. "The Context of Melville's Fiction," 9–12. *MD* in relation to Melville's other fiction, his life, and the orbit of culture.

Merton M. Sealts, Jr. "Approaching Melville Through 'Hawthorne and his Mosses,'" 12–15.

William Braswell. "The Main Theme of *MD*," 15–17. Stresses Ahab's importance and the "wickedness" of *MD*.

Robert M. Farnsworth. "From Voyage to Quest in Melville," 17–20. Advance of Ishmael as narrator over Redburn as narrator.

Luther S. Mansfield. "Symbolism and Biblical Allusion in *MD*," 20–23.

The *Herman Melville Special Number* of *Modern Fiction Studies* 8 (Autumn 1962) contains two articles on *MD*:
Horsford, Howard C. "The Design of the Argument in *MD*," 233–251. *MD* as Melville's response to the intellectual disintegration of faith.
Sister Mary Ellen, I. H. M. "Duplicate Imagery in *MD*," 252–264. Ahab and Moby Dick are described in similar imagery, notably the image of the "wrinkled brow."
In addition the issue contains a Melville bibliography:
Maurice Beebe, Harrison Hayford, and Gordon Roper. "Criticism of Herman Melville: A Selected Checklist," 312–346. The General Criticism section is 313–325; the *MD* section is 333–342.
Braude, William G. "Melville's *MD*," *Explicator* 21 (Nov. 1962) Item 23. A note on the word "Pequod."
Eby, Cecil D., Jr. "William Starbuck Mayo and Herman Melville," *NEQ* 35 (Dec. 1962) 515-520. A possible influence on whaling chapters.
Shulman, Robert. "Melville's Thomas Fuller: An Outline for Starbuck and an Instance of the Creator as Critic," *MLQ* 23 (Dec. 1962) 332–353.
Thompson, Lawrance. "*MD*: One Way to Cut In," *Carrell* 3 (Dec. 1962) 1–12. The way is to see that there are two interwoven plots, the plot concerning what happened to Ahab and Moby Dick and the plot concerning what happened to Ishmael.

1963
BOOKS

Franklin, H. Bruce. "*MD*: An Egyptian Myth Incarnate," in *The Wake of the Gods: Melville's Mythology* (Stanford: Stanford University Press, 1963) 53–98. A rigorous mythic interpretation in which the particular myth which orders and defines the action in *MD* is that of the struggle between Osiris (Ahab) and Typhon (Moby Dick). Vincent (1969) reprints 54–61.
Hillway, Tyrus. *Herman Melville* (New York: Twayne, 1963) 83–106. A general account. Does not replace previous biographies.
Kaul, A. N. *The American Vision: Actual and Ideal Society in Nineteenth-Century Fiction* (New Haven: Yale University Press, 1963) 258–275. Sees the glory and tragedy of Ahab's egotism counterposed against Ishmael's recognition of sociality.
Maxwell, D. E. S. *American Fiction: The Intellectual Background* (New York: Columbia University Press, 1963) 162–165 and *passim*. Stresses the mixed good and evil in both Ahab and Moby Dick. Ishmael emerges with new insight, but Ahab is a tragic hero who attains no self-enlightenment.

ARTICLES

Engstrom, Alfred G. "The Single Tear: A Stereotype of Literary Sensibility," *Philological Quarterly* 42 (Jan. 1963) 106–109. Places Ahab's tear within a long and curious literary tradition.
Weissbuch, Ted N., and Bruce Stillians. "Ishmael the Ironist: The Anti-Salvation Theme in *MD*," *ESQ* 31 (Second Quarter 1963) 71–75. Ishmael is physically but not otherwise saved.
Boies, J. J. " 'The Whale' Without Epilogue," *MLQ* 24 (June 1963) 172–176 Omission of "Epilogue" from first English edition negates interpretation of ending as Ishmael's "rebirth"; *MD* is nihilistic, begins and ends with death. This treatment of "Epilogue" as a late addition to the Harper edition is not supported by an examination of the facts of publication.
Rose, E. J. "Melville, Emerson, and the Sphinx," *NEQ* 36 (1963) 249–258.
Hirsch, David H. "The Dilemma of the Liberal Intellectual: Melville's Ishmael," *TSLL* 5 (Summer 1963) 169–188. *MD* as a biblical, not classical, epic.
Guttman, Allen. "From *Typee* to *MD*: Melville's Allusive Art," *MLQ* 24 (Sept. 1963) 237–244. Allusions in *MD*, unlike those in Melville's earlier works, are fully woven into the fabric of the book.
McClary, Ben Harris. "Melville, Twain, and the Legendary 'Tennessee Poet,' " *Tennessee Folklore Society Bulletin* 29 (Sept. 1963) 63–64. Melville and Twain both refer to a notable Tennessee poet on whom nothing else has been found. Twain calls his poet Edward J. Billings.
Boies, J. J. "Melville's Quarrel with Anglicanism," *ESQ* 33 (Fourth Quarter 1963) 75–79.
Gleason, Philip. "*MD*: Meditation for Democracy," *Personalist* 44 (Autumn 1963) 499–517.

Halverson, John. "The Shadow in *MD*," *AQ* 15 (Fall 1963) 436–446. A Jungian interpretation.
Rust, R. Dilworth. "Vision in *MD*," *ESQ* 33 (Fourth Quarter 1963) 73–75. Eye imagery in *MD*.
Lockerbie, D. Bruce. "The Greatest Sermon in Fiction," *Christianity Today* 8 (Nov. 8, 1963) 9–12.

1964
BOOKS

Clough, Wilson O. *The Necessary Earth: Nature and Solitude in American Literature* (Austin: University of Texas Press, 1964) 125–131. Sees Ahab as "within the American pattern of the student of nature and solitude."
Heffernan, William A. "M's Primitives: Queequeg and Fedallah," *Lock Haven Review* 6 (1964) 45–52. Takes conflict of values represented by Queequeg and Fedallah as "the core of *MD*."
Mansfield, Luther S. "Some Patterns from M's 'Loom of Time,'" in *Essays on Determinism in American Literature*, ed. Sydney J. Krause (Kent, Ohio: Kent State University Press, 1964) 19–35.
Marx, Leo. *The Machine in the Garden: Technology and the Pastoral Ideal in America* (New York: Oxford University Press, 1964) 277–319. Compares "Ethan Brand" and "The Try-Works" (Ch. 96).

ARTICLES

Cannon, Agnes Dicken. "Melville's Use of Sea Ballads and Songs," *Western Folklore* 23 (Jan. 1964) 1–16. Melville uses sea songs for realistic descriptions, for indicating emotional moods of his characters, for recasting into his own symbolic works.
Gale, R. L. "Melville's *MD*: Chapters 91–93," *Explicator* 22 (Jan. 1964) Item 32. On Chs. 91–93 as a unit, in which ambergris and Pip are juxtaposed symbolically.
Ingalls, Jeremy. "The Epic Tradition: A Commentary," *East-West Review* 1 (Spring 1964) 42–69. Distinction between saga and epic; sees the classic tragedy of Ahab enclosed within the epic of Ishmael.
McCarthy, Paul. "A Note on Teaching *MD*," *ESQ* 35 (Second Quarter 1964) 73–79.
Strauch, Carl F. "The Problem of Time and the Romantic Mode in Hawthorne, Melville, and Emerson," *ESQ* 35 (Second Quarter 1964) 50–60. Sees Queequeg and Ishmael as paired for survival against Ahab.
Donow, Herbert S. "Herman Melville and the Craft of Fiction," *MLQ* 25 (June 1964) 181–186. Melville as a novelist "only in the vaguest sense of that word," unable to dramatize the action in *MD*.
Moore, Jack B. "Ahab and Bartleby: Energy and Indolence," *SSF* 1 (Summer 1964) 291–294. Melville's use of Gnosticism.
Hultin, Neil C. "Melville's Search for Meaning," *Discourse* 7 (Autumn 1964) 454–461. The ultimate failure of the search for meaning is foreshadowed by the "Etymology" and "Extracts."
Strandberg, Victor H. "God and the Critics of Melville," *TSLL* 6 (Autumn 1964) 322–333. Mainly a reply to Thompson (1952).
Watts, Robert Alan. "The 'Seaward Peep': Ahab's Transgression," *University Review* (formerly the *University of Kansas City Review*) 31 (Dec. 1964) 133–138. The sea as Oversoul which whalers (deep thinkers) strive for: Ahab transgresses against his own sanity, his fellow men, and union with God.

1965
BOOKS

Brodtkorb, Paul Jr. *Ishmael's White World: A Phenomenological Reading of MD* (New Haven: Yale University Press, 1965). Brilliantly attentive to the patterns of ideas in *MD*, marred only by slighting of external evidence, by rhetorical excesses (such as persistently calling Ishmael a liar), and by anachronistic treatment of Ishmael as an Existentialist hero full of boredom, dread, and despair. The best critical book devoted only to *MD*.
Fussell, Edwin. *Frontier: American Literature and the American West* (Princeton: Princeton University Press, 1965) 256–280.
Green, Martin. *Re-Appraisals: Some Commonsense Readings in American Literature* (N Y: W. W. Norton, 1965) 87–107. Challenges the Chase-Bewley formu-

lation of the romance as the characteristic American genre; finds epic parts of MD more successful than romance parts.

Howard, Leon. "Herman Melville, *Moby Dick*" in *The American Novel from Cooper to Faulkner*, ed. Wallace Stegner (New York: Basic Books, 1965), 25–34.

Howard, Leon. "Herman Melville's *MD*," The Voice of America Forum Lectures, The American Novel Series, No. 3 (Washington: The Voice of America, [1965]), 1–7. A condensed, basic, provocative introductory pamphlet.

Lunt, Dudley C. *The Road to the Law* (New York: Norton, 1965) 14–15. An expert legal comment on M's use of law in Ch. 89, "Fast-Fish and Loose-Fish."

Martin, Terence. *Teaching a Novel: MD in the Classroom* (New York: College Entrance Examination Board, 1965) 3–14. Pamphlet containing script of a kinescope of the Commission on English of the CEEB.

ARTICLES

Mengeling, Marvin E. "*MD*: The Fundamental Principles," *ESQ* No. 38 (First Quarter 1965) 74–87. Polarities (optimism vs. pessimism, head vs. heart, etc.) are keys to *MD*.

Austin, Allen. "The Three-Stranded Allegory of *MD*," *College English* 26 (Feb. 1965) 344–349. The 3 strands are its pessimistic naturalism, its satire of transcendentalism, and its satire of Christianity.

Yu, Beongcheon. "Ishmael's Equal Eye: The Source of Balance in *MD*," *ELH* 32 (March 1965) 110–125. *MD* is Ishmael's "cultural autobiography" with "the Ahab tragedy" added onto this matrix.

Beum, Robert. "Melville's Course," *Dalhousie Review* 45 (Spring 1965) 17–33. Examination of M's failure in *Mardi* and success in *MD*; for success images and structures had to fit both his emblematic and his narrative purposes.

Ellen, Sister Mary. "Parallels in Contrast: A Study of M's Imagery in *MD* and *Billy Budd*," *SSF* 2 (Spring 1965) 284–290. Sight imagery of *MD* split in *BB* into images dealing with heroism, foreboding, and authority.

Wright, Nathalia. "MD: Jonah's or Job's Whale?" *AL* 37 (May 1965) 190–195. Taking MD as Jonah's whale, Mapple sees it as good, Ahab as Evil; Ishmael sees it as a Job's whale, without moral significance. The moral world described in some 42 cetological chapters is a world neither good nor evil but "sheerly marvelous," like the natural world in *Job*.

Sister Cleopatra. "*MD*: An Interpretation," *Literary Half-Yearly* 6 (July 1965) 49–54. The whale symbolizes God in punishing Ahab.

Sullivan, Sister Mary Petrus. "*MD*: Chapter 129, 'The Cabin,'" *NCF* 20 (Sept. 1965) 188–190. Ahab lost his chance for salvation by not responding to Pip's need for love.

Ross, Morton L. "Captain Truck and Captain Boomer," *AL* 37 (Nov. 1965) 316. Boomer's "mania for introduction" may be drawn from a character in Cooper's *Homeward Bound*.

1966
BOOKS

Browne, Ray B. "Popular Theatre in *MD*," in *New Voices in American Studies*, Ed. Ray B. Browne, Donald M. Winkelman, and Allen Hayman (Purdue: Purdue University Press, 1966), 89–101.

Buckley, Vincent. "The White Whale as Hero." *Critical Review* (formerly the *Melbourne Critical Review*) 9 (1966) 1–21. In so tirelessly scrutinizing the white whale's power and mystery, Melville is by analogy scrutinizing God and man and the natural world; "if Ahab's emotions are endorsed (and I think that they are endorsed only momentarily, if at all) what is endorsed is an assault upon the metaphysical order composed of those three."

Adams, Robert Martin. *Nil: Episodes in the Literary Conquest of Void During the Nineteenth Century* (New York: Oxford University Press, 1966) 131–148. Ch. 6, "Masks, Screens, Guises: M and Other" deals with nothingness in *MD*.

Bridgman, Richard. *The Colloquial Style in America* (New York: Oxford University Press, 1966) 69–72. Colloquial dialogue in Ch. 43.

ARTICLES

Woodruff, Stuart C. "Stubb's Supper," *ESQ* 43 (Second Quarter 1966) 46–48. Implications of the sharks' supper and Stubb's treatment of Fleece.

Fiess, Edward. "Byron's Dark Blue Ocean and M's Rolling Sea," *ELN* 3 (June 1966) 274–278.

Vargish, Thomas. "Gnostic *Mythos* in *MD*," *PMLA* 81 (June 1966) 272–277. Melville's use of such gnostic ideas as that of an imperfect Creator and creation. Important suggestions about some of Ahab's late speeches.
Schroeder, Fred E. H. "Enter Ahab, Then All: Theatrical Elements in Melville's Fiction." *Dalhousie Review* 46 (Summer 1966) 223–232.
Rosenfeld, William. "Uncertain Faith: Queequeg's Coffin and M's Use of the Bible." *TSLL* 7 (Winter 1966) 317–327. On Ishmael's "sad" salvation; parallels John: 3 and Chs. 126–127 of *MD*.

1967
BOOKS

Guetti, James. *The Limits of Metaphor: A Study of Melville, Conrad, and Faulkner* (Ithaca: Cornell University Press, 1967).
Hayford, Harrison, and Hershel Parker, eds. *Moby-Dick* (New York: Norton, 1967). This Norton Critical Edition is the first edition of *Moby-Dick* based upon the knowledge that Melville made corrections, revisions, and additions in the English edition and the first based upon the recognition that many textual corruptions persisted in both early editions. See "The Text: History, Variants, and Emendations, 471–498," especially the discussion of "Textual Problems of *Moby-Dick*," 471–477; the list of "Substantive Variants Between *Moby-Dick* and *The Whale*," 477-486; and "English Readings Adopted," 486–490. The Norton Critical Edition also contains maps, a section on "Whaling and Whalecraft," a section of "Reviews and Letters by Melville," a section of "Analogues and Sources," and a section of "Criticism." Under "Criticism" are the following subsections: "Contemporary Reviews: 1851–1853, five items; "Interim Appraisals: 1893–1913, four items; "Revival and Reaction: 1917–1936," eight items; "Academic Criticism: 1932–1962, ten items; and "Biography," one item. The one biographical essay is Leon Howard's "The Composition of *Moby-Dick*" (1951); the ten items under "Academic Criticsm" are from Thorp (1938), Geist (1938), Sedgwick (1944), Olson (1944), Bezanson (1953), Feidelson (1953), Lewis (1955), Rosenberry (1955), Sewall (1959), and Berthoff (1962).
Parker, Hershel, ed. *The Recognition of Herman Melville* (Ann Arbor: University of Michigan Press, 1967). This book (on all of Melville's works, not just *Moby-Dick*) contains the reviews in the London *Spectator*, the New York *Daily Tribune*, the New York *Literary World*, the New York *Harper's New Monthly Magazine*, and the New York *Spirit of the Times*. In addition to some pieces also reprinted in *Doubloon*, it contains later nineteenth-century comments on *Moby-Dick* by Robert Buchanan (1885); Julian Hawthorne and Leonard Lemmon (1892); by an anonymous reviewer of the Stedman edition in the New York *Critic* (1893); and by J. St. Loe Strachey (1893). Among the early twentieth-century selections are essays on *Moby-Dick* by Carl Van Doren, Frank Jewett Mather, Jr., Lincoln Colcord, Cesare Pavese, and sections on *Moby-Dick* from Raymond Weaver's and Lewis Mumford's biographies. The last section of the book, "Academic Recognition: 1938–1967," contains essays on *Moby-Dick* by Thorp (1938), Howard (1940), Matthiessen (1941), Bell (1951), and Berthoff (1962). First published in this anthology is an essay by John D. Seelye on Melville's structural relativism, with comments on *Moby-Dick*: "The Ironic Diagram," 347–364. Less relevant to *Moby-Dick* but of general interest is another essay first published in *The Recognition of Herman Melville*, Walker Cowen's "Melville's 'Discoveries': A Dialogue of the Mind with Itself," 333–346, on Melville's marginalia.

ARTICLES

Cowan, S. A. "In Praise of Self-Reliance: The Role of Bulkington in *Moby-Dick*," *AL* 38 (Jan. 1967) 547–556. Questions the notion that Melville was satirizing Transcendentalism in *MD*.
Maxwell, J. C. "Three Notes on *MD*," *Notes & Queries* 14 (Feb. 1967) 53; on allusions to Addison's *Cato* in Ch. 2 and Ch. 78; and use of "Ancient Mariner" in Ch. 87.
Ellison, Jerome. "How to Catch a Whale: Evil, Melville, and the Evolution of Consciousness," *Michigan Quarterly Review* 6 (Spring 1967) 85–89. Advises building a stable intellectual platform on Jung's theories.
Lefcowitz, Allan and Barbara. "Ahab's Other Leg: Notes on Melville's Symbolic Method," ESQ 47 (Second Quarter 1967) 23–28. Treats leg as example of the working of Ishmael's symbolic consciousness, involving gradual transition of fact into symbol.

Travis, Mildred K. "Melville's Furies: Technique in *Mardi* and *MD*," *ESQ* 47 (Second Quarter 1967) 71–73. Takes the ships the *Pequod* meets as the Greek Furies, warning against the chase.

Hirsch, David H. "Melville's Ishmaelite," *American Notes & Queries* 5 (April 1967) 115–116. The Ishmael whose hand is set against every man's is Ishmael (and Melville) as writer, not Ishmael as sailor.

Eldridge, Herbert G. "'Careful Disorder': The Structure of *MD*," *AL* 39 (May 1967) 145–162. Not a satisfactory treatment. See Bezanson (1953) and Brodtkorb (1965) for contrasting approaches.

Senescu, Betty Cobey. "Melville's *MD*," *Explicator* 25 (May 1967) Item. 78. Ahab dies an accidental, unheroic death.

Eby, Cecil D., Jr. "Another Breaching of 'Mocha Dick,'" *ELN* 4 (June 1967) 277–279.

Fiedler, Leslie, "Ishmael's Trip," *Listener* (London) 78 (August 3, 1967) 134–136. Ishmael's mythic voyage.

Sewall, Richard B. "Ahab's Quenchless Feud: The Tragic Vision in Shakespeare and Melville," *Comparative Drama* 1 (Fall 1967) 207–218. Ahab's feud mirrors Melville's own tragic awareness of the human condition.

Blanch, Robert J. "Captain Ahab, the Outsider," *English Record* 18 (Oct. 1967) 10–14.

Josephs, Lois. "Teaching *MD*: A Method and an Approach," *English Journal* 55 (Nov. 1967) 1115–1119.

1968
BOOKS

Dryden, Edgar A. *Melville's Thematics of Form* (Baltimore: Johns Hopkins, 1968) 83–113. A chapter on "Ishmael as Teller: Self-Conscious Form in *MD*." Compare with Bezanson (1953) and Brodtkorb (1965).

Vincent, Howard P., ed. *Melville and Hawthorne in the Berkshires: A Symposium* (Kent, Ohio: Kent State University Press, 1968). This Melville Society Annual for 1966 (consisting mainly of talks delivered at the Melville-Hawthorne Conference held at Williamstown and Pittsfield in September, 1966) contains six essays dealing in part or in whole with *Moby-Dick*:

Morse Peckham. "Hawthorne and Melville as European Authors" 42–62.

John D. Seelye. "The Structure of Encounter: Melville's Review of Hawthorne's *Mosses*" 63–69.

Maurita Willett. "The Letter A, Gules, and the Black Bubble" 70–78.

Albert McLean. "Spouter Inn and Whaleman's Chapel: The Cultural Matrices of *MD*" 98–108.

F. De Wolfe Miller. "Another Chapter in the History of the Great White Whale" (A new analogue of *MD*: William Comstock's account of an attempt to take a white whale, purportedly from *Whaling in the Pacific*, a chapter of which was published in the Nantucket *Telegraph* for August 7, 1843:"Whaling in the South Pacific. Encounter with a White Whale.") 109–117.

Shneidman, Edwin S. "The Deaths of Herman Melville" 118–143.

ARTICLES

Liebman, Sheldon W. "The 'Body and Soul' Metaphor in *MD*," *ESQ* No. 50 (First Quarter 1968) Supplement, 29–34.

Dillingham, William B. "The Narrator of *MD*." *English Studies* 49 (Feb. 1968) 20–29.

Aspiz, Harold. "Phrenologizing the Whale." *NCF* 23 (June 1968) 18–27.

Powers, William. "Bulkington as Henry Chatillon," *Western American Literature* 3 (Summer 1968) 153–155. Unconvincing suggestion that Bulkington is modeled on character in *The Oregon Trail*.

Walcutt, Charles C. "The Soundings of *MD*," *Arizona Review* 24 (Summer 1968) 101–116. General, derivative survey of composition of *MD*.

Isani, Mukhtar Ali. "The Naming of Fedallah in *MD*," *American Literature* 40 (Nov. 1968) 380–385. In Moore's *Lalla Rookh* two characters are named Fadladeen and Abdalla.

Markels, Julian. "*King Lear and MD*: The Cultural Connection," *Massachusetts Review* 9 (Winter 1968) 169–176.

1969
BOOKS

Vincent, Howard P., ed. *Charles E. Merrill Studies in Moby-Dick* (Columbus, Ohio: Charles E. Merrill, 1969). This anthology includes five reviews (the same five as in *The Recognition of Herman Melville*, 1967); Archibald MacMechan's 1899 essay (which is also excerpted in *Recognition* and *Doubloon*); Lincoln Colcord's 1922 essay, "Notes on *Moby-Dick*" (also reprinted in *Recognition*); D. H. Lawrence's "Herman Melville's *Moby Dick*," in *Studies in Classic American Literature* (1922); Henry A. Murray's "In Nomine Diaboli" (1951); Howard C. Horsford's "The Design of the Argument in *Moby Dick*" (1962); an excerpt from Walter E. Bezanson's *Moby-Dick*: Work of Art" (1953; reprinted in full—except for introductory remarks—in the Norton Critical Edition of *Moby-Dick*); Leon Howard's "The Creation of *Moby-Dick*" (1961); Nathalia Wright's "*Mosses from an Old Manse* and *Moby Dick*: The Shock of Discovery" (1952); M. O. Percival's "Captain Ahab and Moby Dick" (1950); R. W. B. Lewis's "*Moby-Dick* and Homer" (1955); H. Bruce Franklin's "*Moby-Dick* as Myth" (1963); Cesare Pavese's "The Literary Whaler" (also reprinted in *Recognition*); Marius Bewley's "*Moby-Dick* and Creative Force" (1959); W. H. Auden's "Ishmael-Melville" (1950); Conrad Aiken's "*Moby Dick* and the Puritan Dream" (1958); William Faulkner's letter to Fanny Butcher, July 16, 1927; and Hart Crane's poem, "At Melville's Tomb" (1926).

ARTICLES

Simpson, Eleanor E. "Melville and the Negro: From *Typee* to 'Benito Cereno,'" *American Literature* 41 (March 1969) 19–38. Section on *MD* (25–32) summarizes Foster (1961) but fails to test his theory of the composition of *MD* against known facts.

Hoffman, Michael J. "The Anti-Transcendentalism of *MD*," *Georgia Review* 23 (Spring 1969) 3–16.

Spofford, William K. "Melville's Ambiguities: A Re-evaluation of 'The *Town-Ho*'s Story,'" *American Literature* 41 (May 1969) 264–270. Mainly a review of interpretations.

Glasser, William, "*MD*," *The Sewanee Review* 77 (Summer 1969) 463–486. An examination of "the distinguishing features of the world within the novel," focusing on the differences between the way Ahab reacts to this world and the way other characters react to it.

The special Melville number of *Studies in the Novel* 1 (Winter 1969) contains three articles on *MD*:

Hennig Cohen. "Melville's Tomahawk Pipe: Artifact and Symbol," 397–400.
Carl F. Strauch. "Ishmael: Time and Personality in *MD*," 468–483.
Thomas Werge. "*MD* and the Calvinist Tradition," 484–506.

The issue also contains "A Checklist of Melville Criticism, 1958–1968," compiled by J. Don Vann.

SOME FORTHCOMING STUDIES

For the Northwestern-Newberry Edition of *Moby-Dick* Harrison Hayford and Hershel Parker have a "Historical Note" on the composition, publication, critical reception and later critical history of *Moby-Dick*. The text of the Norton Critical Edition of *Moby-Dick* is being very slightly altered to conform with that of the Northwestern-Newberry Edition, which is intended to be standard. Reviews of *Moby-Dick* and *The Whale* discovered too late for inclusion here, such as one found by Mrs. David Bennett in the London *News of the World* (Nov. 2, 1815), and one found by Gordon Roper in the Toronto *Globe* (Nov. 29, 1851), will be published in journals like *American Literature*.